Lecture Notes in Computer Science 4949

Commenced Publication in 1973
Founding and Former Series Editors:
Gerhard Goos, Juris Hartmanis, and Jan van Leeuwen

Robert M. Hierons   Jonathan P. Bowen
Mark Harman (Eds.)

Formal Methods and Testing

An Outcome of the FORTEST Network
Revised Selected Papers

 Springer

Volume Editors

Robert M. Hierons
Brunel University
School of Information Systems, Computing and Mathematics
Uxbridge, Middlesex UB8 3PH, UK
E-mail: rob.hierons@brunel.ac.uk

Jonathan P. Bowen
Mark Harman
King's College London, Department of Computer Science
Strand, London WC2R 2LS, UK
E-mail: jpbowen@gmail.com, mark.harman@kcl.ac.uk

Library of Congress Control Number: 2008923977

CR Subject Classification (1998): D.2, D.3, F.3, K.6

LNCS Sublibrary: SL 2 – Programming and Software Engineering

ISSN   0302-9743
ISBN-10   3-540-78916-2 Springer Berlin Heidelberg New York
ISBN-13   978-3-540-78916-1 Springer Berlin Heidelberg New York

Springer is a part of Springer Science+Business Media

springer.com

© Springer-Verlag Berlin Heidelberg 2008

Typesetting: Camera-ready by author, data conversion by Scientific Publishing Services, Chennai, India
Printed on acid-free paper   SPIN: 12249992   06/3180   5 4 3 2 1 0

Preface

With the growing significance of computer systems within industry and wider society, techniques that assist in the production of reliable software are becoming increasingly important. The complexity of many computer systems requires the application of a battery of such techniques. Two of the most promising approaches are formal methods and software testing. Traditionally, formal methods and software testing have been seen as rivals. Thus, they largely failed to inform one another and there was very little interaction between the two communities. In recent years, however, a new consensus has developed. Under this consensus, these approaches are seen as complementary. This has introduced the prospect of collaboration between individuals and groups in these fields and work such as that contained in this book.

This book, which came out of the Formal Methods and Testing (FORTEST) network [3], includes 12 peer-reviewed chapters on ways in which formal methods and software testing complement each other. FORTEST was formed as a network established under UK EPSRC funding that investigated the relationships between formal (and semi-formal) methods and software testing. In particular, it was concerned with ways in which these areas complement each other. This is an exciting area of research that has led to a number of significant results produced in both industry and academia. While the EPSRC funding for FORTEST was for a fixed period only, FORTEST is now a subject group of two BCS Special Interest Groups: Formal Aspects of Computing Science (BCS FACS) and Special Interest Group in Software Testing (BCS SIGIST).

FORTEST has considered a wide range of testing activities, including static testing techniques (such as model-checking and theorem proving) as well as dynamic testing. Its members have investigated a wide range of problems of interest to the testing and formal methods communities. Examples include: automating (black-box) test generation; producing tests likely (or guaranteed) to detect certain types of fault; using static analysis to support software testing; methods for reasoning about test effectiveness; producing tests that are likely to find faults in systems formally refined from specifications; and using tests to explore assumptions underlying proofs. While much of the work in this area has concerned the problem of generating tests from formal specifications and models, there is a much wider range of ways in which these fields might interact. In particular, there is the interesting question of the relationships between static testing and dynamic testing.

The relationship between formal methods and software testing has received significant attention since the late 1980s. Seminal work during this period includes the paper by Dick and Faivre on testing from a VDM specification [4] and work on testing from algebraic specifications (see, for example, [2, 6]), the latter introducing a framework. More recently, the term *model-based testing* has been introduced in order to describe an important aspect of this area (see, for example, [1, 5, 7, 11]). However, there is much earlier research on this topic. For example, in 1956 Moore used the term Gedanken-Experiments to describe testing and provided a conceptual framework in which to discuss testing from a finite state machine [10]. Later Hennie showed how test sequences can be produced from finite state machines [8].

In several important ways, software testing is unlike any other form of engineering testing process. Though it bears some similarities with other engineering testing activities, software testing differs because of the discrete behavior of the artifacts under test and the enormous variety of different scenarios for which testing must cater.

It is often said, quoting Dijkstra's famous aphorism, that testing can only reveal the presence of bugs, but not their absence. This has led some to conclude that testing is nothing more than an admission of defeat; why should energy be poured into such a doomed endeavor? This view misses two crucial points. Firstly, there is work that shows that formalized testing can indeed establish correctness, albeit with respect to a set of well-defined assumptions. Such testing can also be automated. Secondly, in many real-world situations, there is no viable alternative to testing. Therefore, there is a pressing need for research that addresses familiar engineering concerns; how can software testing become better, faster and cheaper? In this respect, testing is very much like other testing activities in any other engineering discipline.

Software testing reaches beyond software engineering and computer science, drawing in other disciplines that cover a very broad spectrum of activity. It involves such disparate elements as psychology, traditional engineering and even philosophy. This astonishing breadth has made the problems of software testing appealing to academics for several decades. However, this broadness has also, until recently, tended to dissuade researchers from more theoretical computer science research communities. Hitherto, there has been in these communities something of a perception of testing as an inherently informal, ad hoc activity that will not submit to any reasonable formal analysis.

This book aims to challenge this misconception, thereby stimulating wider interest in software testing problems within theoretical computer science research communities. The book consists of 12 chapters by leading researchers and groups in software testing and, in particular, in the problems of formalizing software testing techniques. This work shows how testing raises new questions for theoreticians: testing throws up new forms of interesting non-standard semantics, requires complexity analysis, builds on and uses formal specification notations, and can be combined with existing static analysis techniques. The book also shows how testing activities can be formalized so that it is possible to reason formally about the outcomes of a testing activity.

Testing is an activity designed to reveal bugs. As might be expected, there is plenty of challenging and exciting research in this volume on this aspect of software testing. However, the reader will also find examples of formalisms within which it is possible to prove correctness up to certain well-defined levels of abstraction, purely using testing. There is also much work on hybrid techniques that combine pure testing with other strands of computer science research. The crucial issue of automation is a recurrent theme. It is the key to meeting the engineering imperatives for testing in the real world. Such automation brings with it important formal proof obligations at the meta-level. That is, can we establish the correctness of the systems that will automate testing – *Quis custodiet ipsos custodes?*

Having finished the book, the reader will hopefully conclude that there is much about software testing that can be submitted to a formal analysis and that there is a great deal to be gained from such a formalization. It is also hoped that readers from the formal methods community will be motivated to consider software testing as a possible application for their work: there remain plenty of interesting, important unsolved problems in formal aspects of software testing.

Each of the 12 chapters in this book describes a way in which the study of formal methods and software testing can be combined in a manner that brings the benefits of formal methods (e.g., precision, clarity, provability) with the advantages of testing (e.g., scalability, generality, applicability).

Tretmans provides an overview of labelled transition systems (LTS), input output transition systems (IOTS) and the "ioco" input/output conformance relation. He also describes how test cases can be generated from an IOTS using ioco. Process algebras such as CCS, CSP, and LOTOS have been developed in order to specify or model systems in which there is a significant amount of concurrency. Since their semantics can be described in terms of LTSs there has been a significant amount of interest in testing using an LTS. Different notions of observations that can be made by the tester lead to a rich set of implementation relations and the test generation process depends upon the implementation relation used. The observation that there is an asymmetry between input and output led to the introduction of IOTs, which are essentially LTSs in which the labels/events are partitioned into inputs and outputs. The system under test (SUT) cannot block input and the environment cannot block output from the SUT: these observations place constraints which have an impact on testing and are encapsulated in the ioco implementation relation.

The chapter by Campbell et al. covers the Spec Explorer tool, developed and in use at Microsoft, which enables model-based testing of reactive systems in an object-oriented style. Testing is often undertaken in a haphazard manner and model-based testing allows a more rigorous and systematic approach to be taken. The development of the Spec Explorer tool has been demand-driven by users and it has been used for testing parts of operating systems, .NET components, etc. The chapter presents the concepts and foundational aspects of the tool in a formal manner. In conclusion, issues of importance for the development of the next generation of testing tools are considered.

Many systems have timing constraints and this has led to interest in specifying real-time systems and testing against such specifications. Hessel et al. describe approaches for testing against a timed input/output transition system (TIOTS). A TIOTS is essentially an LTS in which input and output are differentiated and time is included. The authors define an implementation relation rtioco that is similar to ioco, with real-time. They then show how tests can be developed offline (produced prior to test execution) or online (produced during test execution) and describe how these have been implemented in a tool based on the UPPAAL model-checker.

The chapters by Chen, Hierons and Ural and by Ammann, Offutt and Xu both concern testing based on finite state machines (FSMs). The chapter by Chen, Hierons and Ural concerns the problems of observability and controllability in testing state-based models using a distributed test environment. In such an environment, there are many coordination problems that present themselves. How do the separate testers know what input/output sequences are being observed by the other testers? This chapter shows how these problems can be overcome. The work is important because of the large number of systems that can be modelled using a state-based formulation and because of the increasing incidence of geographic separation, which increases the difficulty of testing such distributed state-based systems.

The chapter by Ammann, Offutt and Xu considers the problems of representation and achievement of coverage for systems modelled by state-based formulations and by graphical structures. The chapter considers the underlying graphical representation of the state-based models and addresses the question of what form of predicates should be extracted from these graphical representations. The paper draws together two strands of research on software testing: testing from FSM models and testing based on coverage of graphical representations of source code.

The chapter by Bogdanov provides a summary of the literature on testing from X-machines. X-machines are extended versions of FSMs. The extensions for X-machines are specifically tailored to testing and aim to make them inherently easy to test. Bogdanov provides a valuable introduction to this topic for the non-specialist. He is careful to avoid the detailed and somewhat dense formal notation that is often required in papers presenting specific contributions on X-machines, making this an excellent starting point for the interested outsider. This treatment makes the chapter ideal for the reader who wishes to discover more about this important and powerful approach to testing for state-based models.

The chapter by Gaudel and Le Gall presents an approach to the testing of data type implementations using an algebraic specification approach. Conformance may then be checked formally against the satisfaction of axioms. The approach can be generalized to specification methods that include data types in a variety of formalisms. The approach has been applied in both academic and industrial studies, typically for existing systems. The approach has been successful in identifying missing test cases that could have caused serious problems later if they had remained undiscovered until after deployment of the software.

The chapter by Vilkomir and Bowen describes testing criteria using the Z formal specification notation. It covers both the existing MC/DC (modified condition/decision coverage) criterion and also a new and stronger RC/DC (reinforced condition/decision coverage) criterion. The latter may be useful for critical software where an extra level of confidence is required. The formalization in Z revealed deficiencies and ambiguities in the informal description of MC/DC, allowing these to be given a specific meaning. A pleasing aspect of the specification of RC/DC is that the specification of MC/DC can be reused and augmented with an additional predicate to specify the stricter criterion. The chapter includes an example to demonstrate use of the criteria and an illustration of why RC/DC could be beneficial in a system where the highest level of assurance is required.

There are many different test criteria and test generation techniques and this naturally leads to the question of which is best. While "best" depends on a number of factors and can refer to issues of cost as well as effectiveness, the focus to date has been on effectiveness. Weyuker describes the attempts that have been made to theoretically compare test criteria and points to the deficiencies in these approaches. One problem identified with all of these approaches is that they refer to idealized versions of test criteria and techniques rather than how testers actually use them. Weyuker argues that the only way of overcoming this is through empirical evaluation using case studies and experiments, but also points to the problems of carrying out experiments in software engineering (e.g., what are typical programs, specifications, faults, etc?). She concludes by suggesting that real progress is only likely to be made through a combination of empirical evaluation through case studies and advances in the theory.

The chapter by Schieferdecker et al. covers the TTCN-3 testing technology, which is used widely in the telecommunications sector. TTCN-3 is a new textual and graphical notation with a precise syntax, based on the earlier TTCN (tree and tabular combined notation). The language was developed by industry and academia to allow black-box and gray-box testing. It enables both test specification and execution. TTCN-3 has an intuitive operational semantics and is typically used for testing conformance and interoperability of protocols. However, it is also applicable to functionality testing of systems based on software. It is often used in safety-critical domains. The chapter gives an overview of the TTCN-3 language and some examples of use.

The chapter by Harman et al. concerns the transformation of programs to improve testability. Perhaps counter-intuitively, the approach does not maintain the original traditional semantics of the program under test; rather, it suggests the existence of interesting non-standard semantics. The transformations seek to improve the performance of testing for a particular test data generation technique, using a combination of standard and novel transformation rules. The chapter provides both an introduction to the area and also a set of open problems still to be solved. Thus it is suitable for both those requiring an introduction to the approach and also those wishing to develop the area further as part of their own research.

The chapter by Littlewood, Popov, Strigini and Shryane is concerned with techniques for locating faults in software. There are many such fault-finding techniques in the literature and a test manager would be forgiven for deciding that they should simply use several of these to achieve a "belt and braces approach" to their test effort. This chapter reveals that there are subtle dependencies between the different fault-finding techniques that mean one cannot necessarily make straightforward judgments as to the overall effectiveness of the combined techniques. To avoid this problem, the authors show how the concept of diversity of techniques can be defined formally and used to ensure that the power of the combined techniques more closely approaches the sum of the power of the separate parts, as the test manager might have hoped.

We would like to thank the authors for their contributions, without which this book would not have been possible. Thanks are also due to the reviewers for their detailed, constructive reviews of each chapter and to the staff of Springer for their assistance and guidance in seeing this volume through to publication. This work grew out of the editors' involvement in and management of the United Kingdom EPSRC-funded FORTEST project. FORTEST, the FORmal Methods and TESTing Network, drew together the testing and formal methods communities in a network of research meetings, workshops and other events from 2001 to 2005. For further information, see *www.fmnet.info/fortest*.

We hope that you will find this volume stimulating reading and that the contributions herein might raise awareness in the testing community of the potential applications for formal methods and also that it may raise interest in testing as an application area for the formal methods community. There is much that these two, largely disjoint, research communities have to gain. The FORTEST network and other related activities have gone some way to bringing the two together. This book is one fruit of that union. We sincerely hope that there will be many more to come.

February 2008

Robert M. Hierons
Jonathan P. Bowen
Mark Harman

Acknowledgements. Selected authors of papers reviewed the chapters for this collected volume. These included: Paul Ammann, David Binkley, Jessica Chen, Marie-Claude Gaudel, Anders Hessel, Pascale La Gall, Jens Grabowski, Wolfgang Grieskamp, Bogdan Korel, Kim Larsen, Bev Littlewood, Brian Nielsen, Jeff Offutt, Paul Pettersson, Nikolai Tillmann, Jan Tretman, Hasan Ural, Margus Veanes, Sergiv Vilkomir. The FORTEST Network on formal methods and testing [3], of which all the editors were members, was funded by the UK Engineering and Physical Sciences Research Council (EPSRC) under grant number GR/R43150 from 2001 to 2005. Chapter 12 originally appeared in the *IEEE Transactions on Software Engineering* journal [9] and is reproduced here with permission.

References

1. Barnett, M., Grieskamp, W., Nachmanson, L., Schulte, W., Tillmann, N., Veanes, M.: Towards a tool environment for model-based testing with AsmL. In: Petrenko, A., Ulrich, A. (eds.) FATES 2003. LNCS, vol. 2931, pp. 252–266. Springer, Heidelberg (2004)

2. Bouge, L., Choquet, N., Fibourg, L., Gaudel, M.-C.: Test sets generation from algebraic specifications using logic programming. Journal of Systems and Software 6(4), 343–360 (1986)

3. Bowen, J.P., Bogdanov, K., Clark, J., Harman, M., Hierons, R., Krause, P.: FORTEST: Formal methods and testing. In: Proc. 26th Annual International Computer Software and Applications Conference (COMPSAC 2002), Oxford, UK, August 26–29, 2002, pp. 91–101. IEEE Computer Society Press, Los Alamitos (2002)

4. Dick, J., Faivre, A.: Automating the generation and sequencing of test cases from model-based specifications. In: Larsen, P.G., Woodcock, J.C.P. (eds.) FME 1993. LNCS, vol. 670, pp. 268–284. Springer, Heidelberg (1993)

5. Farchi, E., Hartman, A., Pinter, S.: Using a model-based test generator to test for standard conformance. IBM Systems Journal 41(1), 89–110 (2002)

6. Gaudel, M.-C.: Testing can be formal too. LNCS, vol. 915, pp. 82–96. Springer, Heidelberg (1995)

7. Grieskamp, W.: Multi-paradigmatic model-based testing. In: Havelund, K., Núñez, M., Roşu, G., Wolff, B. (eds.) FATES 2006 and RV 2006. LNCS, vol. 4262, pp. 1–19. Springer, Heidelberg (2006)

8. Hennie, F.C.: Fault-detecting experiments for sequential circuits. In: Proceedings of Fifth Annual Symposium on Switching Circuit Theory and Logical Design, Princeton, New Jersey, pp. 95–110 (November 1964)

9. Littlewood, B., Popov, P.T., Strigini, L., Shryane, N.: Modeling the effects of combining diverse software fault detection technique. IEEE Transactions on Software Engineering 26(12), 1157–1167 (2000)

10. Moore, E.P.: Gedanken-experiments. In: Shannon, C., McCarthy, J. (eds.) Automata Studies, Princeton University Press, Princeton (1956)

11. Utting, M., Legeard, B.: Practical Model-Based Testing: A Tools Approach. Morgan Kaufmann Publishers (2007)

Table of Contents

Model Based Testing
with Labelled Transition Systems

Jan Tretmans

Embedded Systems Institute, Eindhoven,
and Radboud University, Nijmegen,
The Netherlands
jan.tretmans@esi.nl

Abstract. Model based testing is one of the promising technologies to meet the challenges imposed on software testing. In model based testing an implementation under test is tested for compliance with a model that describes the required behaviour of the implementation. This tutorial chapter describes a model based testing theory where models are expressed as labelled transition systems, and compliance is defined with the 'ioco' implementation relation. The ioco-testing theory, on the one hand, provides a sound and well-defined foundation for labelled transition system testing, having its roots in the theoretical area of testing equivalences and refusal testing. On the other hand, it has proved to be a practical basis for several model based test generation tools and applications. Definitions, underlying assumptions, an algorithm, properties, and several examples of the ioco-testing theory are discussed, involving specifications, implementations, tests, the ioco implementation relation and some of its variants, a test generation algorithm, and the soundness and exhaustiveness of this algorithm.

1   Introduction

Software testing. Systematic testing is one of the most important and widely used techniques to check the quality of software. Testing, however, is often a manual and laborious process without effective automation, which makes it error-prone, time consuming, and very costly. Estimates are that testing consumes 30–50% of the total software development costs. The tendency is that the effort spent on testing is still increasing due to the continuing quest for better software quality, and the ever growing size and complexity of systems. The situation is aggravated by the fact that the complexity of testing tends to grow faster than the complexity of the systems being tested, in the worst case even exponentially. Whereas development and construction methods for software allow the building of ever larger and more complex systems, there is a real danger that testing methods cannot keep pace with construction. This may seriously hamper the development of future generations of software systems.

Model based testing. One of the new technologies to meet the challenges imposed on software testing is *model based testing*. In model based testing a *model* of

R.M. Hierons et al. (Eds.): Formal Methods and Testing, LNCS 4949, pp. 1–38, 2008.

the desired behaviour of the *implementation under test* (IUT) is the starting point for testing. Model based testing has recently gained attention with the popularization of modelling itself both in academia and in industry. The main virtue of model based testing is that it allows test automation that goes well beyond the mere automatic execution of manually crafted test cases. It allows for the algorithmic generation of large amounts of test cases, including test oracles, completely automatically from the model of required behaviour. If this model is valid, i.e., expresses precisely what the system under test should do, all these tests are also provably valid.

From an industrial perspective, model based testing is a promising technique to improve the quality and effectiveness of testing, and to reduce its cost. The current state of practice is that test automation mainly concentrates on the automatic execution of tests, but that the problem of test generation is not addressed. Model based testing aims at automatically generating high-quality test suites from models, thus complementing automatic test execution.

From an academic perspective, model based testing is a natural extension of formal methods and verification techniques, where many of the formal techniques can be reused. Formal verification and model based testing serve complementary goals. Formal verification intends to show that a system has some desired properties by proving that a model of that system satisfies these properties. Thus, any verification is only as good as the validity of the model on which it is based. Model based testing starts with a (verified) model, and then intends to show that the real, physical implementation of the system behaves in compliance with this model. Due to the inherent limitations of testing, such as the limited number of tests that can be performed, testing can never be complete: testing can only show the presence of errors, not their absence.

Sorts of model based testing. There are different kinds of model based testing depending on the kind of models being used, the quality aspects being tested, the level of formality involved, and the degree of accessibility and observability of the system being tested. In this contribution we consider model based testing as *formal, specification based, active, black-box, functionality testing.*

It is *testing*, because it involves checking some properties of the IUT by systematically performing experiments on the real, executing IUT, as opposed to, e.g., formal verification, where properties are checked on the level of formal descriptions of the system. The kind of properties being checked are concerned with *functionality*, i.e., testing whether the system correctly does what it should do in terms of correct responses to given stimuli, as opposed to, e.g., performance, usability, reliability, or maintainability properties. Such classes of properties are also referred to as quality characteristics. The testing is *active*, in the sense that the tester controls and observes the IUT in an active way by giving stimuli and triggers to the IUT, and observing its responses, as opposed to passive testing, or monitoring.

The basis and starting point for testing is the *specification*, which prescribes what the IUT should, and should not do. The specification is given in the form of some model of behaviour to which the behaviour of the IUT must conform. This model is assumed to be correct and valid: it is not itself the subject of testing or validation. Moreover, the testing is *black-box*. The IUT is seen as a black box without internal detail, which can only be accessed and observed through its external interfaces, as opposed to white-box testing, where the internal structure of the IUT, i.e., the code, is the basis for testing.

Finally, we deal with *formal testing*: the model, or specification, prescribing the desired behaviour is given in some formal language with precisely defined syntax and semantics. But formal testing involves more than just a formal specification. It also involves a formal definition of what a conforming IUT is, a well-defined algorithm for the generation of tests, and a correctness proof that the generated tests are sound and exhaustive, i.e., that they exactly test what they should test.

Goal. The aim of this contribution is to be a tutorial for a particular model based testing theory, viz. the **ioco**-testing theory for labelled transition systems. This theory uses labelled transition systems as models for specifications, implementations, and tests, and a formal implementation relation called **ioco** defines conformance between implementations (IUTs) and specifications. Moreover, there is an algorithm to generate test cases, for which there is a completeness theorem (soundness and exhaustiveness) expressing that the algorithmically generated test cases exactly test for **ioco**-conformance. All of these aspects are elaborated in the following sections.

There are a couple of test generation tools, which implement, more or less directly, the **ioco**-testing theory, e.g., TVEDA [1], TGV [2], the AGEDIS TOOL SET [3], TESTGEN [4], and TORX [5]. As such, this contribution also aims at giving the theory behind these tools.

The main source for this contribution is [6]. The most important technical change with respect to [6] is the input enabledness of test cases, which was inspired by [7]; see Section 3.5.

Overview. Section 2 starts with a framework for formal, model based testing introducing the required concepts, artefacts, and relations between them. This formalism independent framework should provide a structure for discussing formal testing, and it should allow classification and comparison of different formal testing approaches. Section 3 describes the models and languages used in this contribution: labelled transition systems, and some variants of them to model specifications, implementations, and test cases. Moreover, a process language for representing them is introduced. Section 4 discusses, and formally defines the implementation relation **ioco**, which expresses what a correct implementation of a given specification should, and should not do. The algorithm for the generation of test cases from a specification is presented in Section 5. That section also considers test execution, and the correctness of the test generation algorithm. Finally, in Section 6 a few concluding remarks are given.

This contribution intends to be a tutorial accessible for anyone with some basic formal, mathematical knowledge. This implies that some readers may want to skip some of the introductory sections, in particular, the basic definitions about transition systems in Sections 3.1 and 3.2. Also Section 4.2 can be skipped; it only contains variations on the main theme which are not strictly necessary for understanding the subsequent sections.

2   Formal Testing

When performing formal, specification based testing there are different concepts and objects that we need. This section presents these concepts and objects, and the relations between them. This constitutes a kind of framework for formal testing of an implementation with respect to a formal specification of its functional behaviour. This framework, which is at a high level of abstraction, and which does not make any reference to a specific specification formalism, is depicted in Figure 1, and is explained in this section. In Sections 3, 4, and 5 these concepts will then be concretized and instantiated with the testing theory of labelled transition systems.

Implementation. The first thing needed for testing is the *Implementation Under Test* IUT. The IUT is the system being tested. An implementation can be a real, physical object, such as a piece of hardware, a computer program with all its libraries running on a particular processor, an embedded system consisting of software embedded in some physical device, or a process control system with sensors and actuators. Since we deal with black-box testing, an implementation is treated as a black-box exhibiting behaviour and interacting with its environment, but without knowledge about its internal structure. The only way a tester can control and observe an implementation is via its interfaces. The aim of testing is to check the correctness of the behaviour of the IUT on its interfaces.

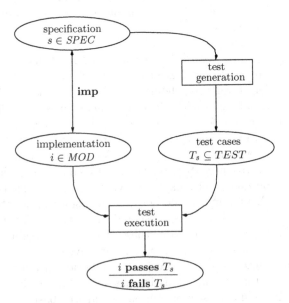

Fig. 1. The formal, specification based testing process

Specification. Correctness of an IUT is expressed as conformance to a *specification*. The specification prescribes what the implementation should do, and what it should not do. In formal testing the specification is expressed in some formal language, i.e., a language with a formal syntax and semantics. Let this language, i.e., the set of all valid expressions in this language, be denoted by $SPEC$, then a specification s is an element of this language: $s \in SPEC$. By means of testing we want to check whether the behaviour of the IUT conforms to s.

Conformance. To check whether the IUT conforms to a specification s we need to know precisely what it means for an IUT to conform to s, i.e., a formal definition of conformance is required. Such a definition should relate implementations to specifications. But, if we want to define such a relation between implementations and specifications, we encounter a problem. Whereas a specification s is a formal object taken from a formal domain $SPEC$, an implementation under test is not amenable to formal reasoning. An IUT is not a formal object: it is a real, physical thing, which consists of software, hardware, physical components, or a combination of these, on which only experiments and tests can be performed.

In order to formally reason about implementations we do a little trick: we make the assumption that any real implementation under test IUT can be modelled by some formal object i_{IUT} in a set of models MOD. The domain MOD is a-priori chosen, and is referred to as the universe of implementation models. This assumption is commonly referred to as the *test assumption*. Note that the test assumption presupposes a particular domain of models MOD, and that it is only assumed that a valid model i_{IUT} of the IUT exists in this domain, but not that this model i_{IUT} is a-priori known.

Thus, the test assumption allows reasoning about implementations under test as if they were formal implementations in MOD. This is what we will do from now on. Consequently, conformance can be expressed by a formal relation between models of implementations and specifications. Such a relation is called an *implementation relation* $\mathbf{imp} \subseteq MOD \times SPEC$. An implementation model i is said to be correct with respect to $s \in SPEC$ if $i \ \mathbf{imp} \ s$.

Testing. The behaviour of an implementation is investigated by performing experiments on it. An experiment consists of supplying stimuli to the implementation and observing its responses. The specification of such an experiment, including both the stimuli and the expected responses, is called a *test case*, and it is formally expressed as an element of some domain of test cases $TEST$. The process of applying a test to an implementation is called *test execution*. Test execution may be successful, meaning that the observed responses correspond to the expected responses, or it may be unsuccessful. The successful execution of a test t to an implementation i is expressed as i **passes** t; unsuccessful execution is denoted as i **fails** $t \Leftrightarrow i$ **passes** t. This is easily extended to a *test suite* $T \subseteq TEST$: i **passes** $T \Leftrightarrow \forall t \in T : i$ **passes** t.

Conformance testing. Conformance testing involves assessing, by means of testing, whether an implementation conforms, with respect to implementation relation **imp**, to its specification. Hence, the notions of conformance, expressed by **imp**, and of test execution, expressed by **passes**, have to be linked in such a way that from test execution an indication about conformance can be obtained. So, for conformance testing we are looking for a test suite T_s such that

$$\forall i \in MOD : \quad i \text{ \textbf{imp} } s \iff i \text{ \textbf{passes} } T_s \tag{1}$$

A test suite with this property is said to be *complete*; it can distinguish exactly between all conforming and non-conforming implementations, i.e., testing is a complete decision procedure for **imp**-conformance to s. For practical testing this is a very strong requirement: complete test suites are infinite, and consequently not practically executable. Hence, usually a weaker requirement on test suites is posed: they should be *sound*, which means that all correct implementations, and possibly some incorrect implementations, will pass them; or, in other words, any failing implementation is indeed non-conforming, but not the other way around. Soundness corresponds to the left-to-right implication in (1). The right-to-left implication is referred to as *exhaustiveness*; it means that all non-conforming implementations are detected.

It may seem that the meaning of these concepts is reversed with respect to their usual meaning, where soundness means that no false deductions can be made, and completeness means that all correct deductions can be made. Testing, however, is about detecting errors, so that a deduction corresponds to the detection of an error. Consequently, soundness in testing means that no false deductions, i.e., no false detections of errors, can be made. Analogously, exhaustiveness (completeness) in testing means that all correct deductions can be made, i.e., that all errors can be detected.

Test generation. The systematic, algorithmic generation of test suites from a specification for a given implementation relation is called *test generation*: $gen_{\text{imp}} : SPEC \to \mathcal{P}(TEST)$, (where $\mathcal{P}(TEST)$ denotes the power set of $TEST$, i.e., the set of all subsets of $TEST$). Such an algorithm is complete (sound, exhaustive) if the generated test suites are complete (sound, exhaustive) for all specifications.

Test generation is the most beneficial and visible aspect of model based testing: it allows the automatic production of large and provably sound test suites.

Conclusion. For model based testing we need a formal specification language $SPEC$, a domain of models of implementations MOD, an implementation relation **imp** $\subseteq MOD \times SPEC$ expressing correctness, a test execution procedure **passes** $\subseteq MOD \times TEST$ expressing when a model of an implementation passes a test case, a test generation algorithm $gen_{\text{imp}} : SPEC \to \mathcal{P}(TEST)$, and a proof that a model of an implementation passes a generated test suite if and only if it is **imp**-correct. The process of formal, specification based testing is schematically depicted in Figure 1.

The next sections will elaborate these concepts for the formalism of labelled transition systems. This means that we will use (variants of) labelled transition systems

for *SPEC* (Section 3.3), *MOD* (Section 3.4), and *TEST* (Section 3.5), that conformance is expressed as a relation on labelled transition systems (Section 4), that
test execution of a labelled transition system test with an implementation is defined (Section 5.1), and that a test generation algorithm is presented (Section 5.2),
which is proved to generate sound and exhaustive labelled transition system test
suites from a labelled transition system specification (Section 5.3).

Bibliographic notes. This framework for model based testing comes from [8,9],
with inspiration concerning test assumptions and test hypotheses from [10,11].
There are also international standardization efforts in this direction [12]. The
next sections will consider this framework instantiated with labelled transition
systems, but also other formalisms may be used, e.g., Finite State Machines
(FSM, Mealy Machines) [13], Abstract Data Types [11], object oriented formalisms [14], or (mathematical) functions [15].

3   Models

Model based testing uses formal specifications, models of implementations, and
test case descriptions; see Figure 1. This section presents the modelling formalisms on which these specifications, models, and descriptions are built. The
basic model that we use in our formal testing theory is that of a *labelled transition
system*, which is defined in Section 3.1. Section 3.2 considers the representation
of labelled transition systems by a formal language. Subsequently, three variants
of labelled transition systems are presented: labelled transition systems with inputs and outputs (Section 3.3), input-output transition systems (Section 3.4),
and test transition systems (Section 3.5), which are used to model specifications,
implementations, and test cases, respectively.

3.1   Labelled Transition Systems

A labelled transition system is a structure consisting of states with transitions,
labelled with actions, between them. The states model the system states; the
labelled transitions model the actions that a system can perform.

Definition 1. *A labelled transition system is a 4-tuple $\langle Q, L, T, q_0 \rangle$ where*

- *Q is a countable, non-empty set of states;*
- *L is a countable set of labels;*
- *$T \subseteq Q \times (L \cup \{\tau\}) \times Q$, with $\tau \notin L$, is the transition relation;*
- *$q_0 \in Q$ is the initial state.*

We write $q \xrightarrow{\mu} q'$ if there is a transition labelled μ from state q to state q', i.e.,
$(q, \mu, q') \in T$. The informal idea of such a transition is that when the system
is in state q it may perform action μ, and go to state q' . Suppose that in
state q' the system can perform action μ', i.e., $q' \xrightarrow{\mu'} q''$, then these transitions
can be composed: $q \xrightarrow{\mu} q' \xrightarrow{\mu'} q''$, which is written as $q \xrightarrow{\mu \cdot \mu'} q''$. In general, the

composition of transitions $q_1 \xrightarrow{\mu_1 \cdot \mu_2 \cdot \ldots \cdot \mu_n} q_2$ expresses that the system, when in state q_1, can perform the sequence of actions $\mu_1 \cdot \mu_2 \cdot \ldots \cdot \mu_n$, and may end in state q_2. The use of *may* is important here: because of non-determinism, it may be the case that the system can also perform the same sequence of actions, but end in another state: $q_1 \xrightarrow{\mu_1 \cdot \mu_2 \cdot \ldots \cdot \mu_n} q_3$ with $q_2 \neq q_3$.

Definition 2. *Let A be a set. Then A^* is the set of all finite sequences over A, with ϵ denoting the empty sequence. If $\sigma_1, \sigma_2 \in A^*$ are finite sequences, then $\sigma_1 \cdot \sigma_2$ is the concatenation of σ_1 and σ_2.*

Definition 3. *Let $p = \langle Q, L, T, q_0 \rangle$ be a labelled transition system with $q, q' \in Q$, and let $\mu, \mu_i \in L \cup \{\tau\}$.*

$$
\begin{array}{lll}
q \xrightarrow{\mu} q' & \Leftrightarrow_{\mathrm{def}} & (q, \mu, q') \in T \\
q \xrightarrow{\mu_1 \cdots \mu_n} q' & \Leftrightarrow_{\mathrm{def}} & \exists q_0, \ldots, q_n : q = q_0 \xrightarrow{\mu_1} q_1 \xrightarrow{\mu_2} \ldots \xrightarrow{\mu_n} q_n = q' \\
q \xrightarrow{\mu_1 \cdots \mu_n} & \Leftrightarrow_{\mathrm{def}} & \exists q' : q \xrightarrow{\mu_1 \cdots \mu_n} q' \\
q \xrightarrow{\mu_1 \cdots \mu_n} \!\!\!\!/ & \Leftrightarrow_{\mathrm{def}} & not \; \exists q' : q \xrightarrow{\mu_1 \cdots \mu_n} q'
\end{array}
$$

Example 1. Figure 2 presents five examples of labelled transition systems representing candy machines. There is a button interaction *but*, and labels for chocolate *choc* and liquorice *liq*. The transition systems are represented as graphs, where nodes represent states and labelled edges represent transitions. The dangling arrow points to the initial state.

The tree q represents the labelled transition system

$\langle \{q_0, q_1, q_2, q_3\}, \{but, liq, choc\}, \{ \langle q_0, but, q_1 \rangle, \langle q_1, liq, q_2 \rangle, \langle q_1, choc, q_3 \rangle \}, q_0 \rangle$.
For r we have that $r_0 \xrightarrow{but} r_1$, and also $r_0 \xrightarrow{but} r_2$. Moreover, $r_0 \xrightarrow{but \cdot liq} r_3$, so also $r_0 \xrightarrow{but \cdot liq}$, but $r_0 \xrightarrow{but \cdot choc} \!\!\!\!/$.

The labels in L represent the observable actions of a system; they model the system's interactions with its environment. Internal actions are denoted by the special label τ ($\tau \notin L$), which is assumed to be unobservable for the system's environment. Also states are assumed to be unobservable for the environment. Consequently, the observable behaviour of a system is captured by the system's

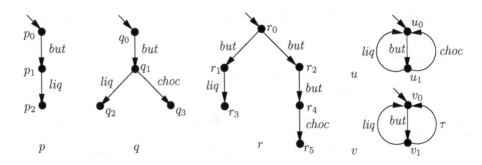

Fig. 2. Labelled transition systems

ability to perform sequences of observable actions. Such a sequence of observable actions is obtained from a sequence of actions under abstraction from the internal action τ. If q can perform the sequence of actions $a \cdot \tau \cdot \tau \cdot b \cdot c \cdot \tau$ $(a, b, c \in L)$, i.e., $q \xrightarrow{a \cdot \tau \cdot \tau \cdot b \cdot c \cdot \tau} q'$, then we write $q \overset{a \cdot b \cdot c}{\Longrightarrow} q'$ for the τ-abstracted sequence of observable actions. We say that q is able to perform the *trace* $a \cdot b \cdot c \in L^*$. These, and some other notations and properties are formally given in Definition 4.

Definition 4. *Let* $p = \langle Q, L, T, q_0 \rangle$ *be a labelled transition system with* $q, q' \in Q$, $a, a_i \in L$, *and* $\sigma \in L^*$.

$$
\begin{aligned}
q &\overset{\epsilon}{\Longrightarrow} q' &&\Leftrightarrow_{\text{def}} & q &= q' \text{ or } q \xrightarrow{\tau \cdot \ldots \cdot \tau} q' \\
q &\overset{a}{\Longrightarrow} q' &&\Leftrightarrow_{\text{def}} & \exists q_1, q_2 &: q \overset{\epsilon}{\Longrightarrow} q_1 \overset{a}{\longrightarrow} q_2 \overset{\epsilon}{\Longrightarrow} q' \\
q &\overset{a_1 \cdots a_n}{\Longrightarrow} q' &&\Leftrightarrow_{\text{def}} & \exists q_0 \ldots q_n &: q = q_0 \overset{a_1}{\Longrightarrow} q_1 \overset{a_2}{\Longrightarrow} \ldots \overset{a_n}{\Longrightarrow} q_n = q' \\
q &\overset{\sigma}{\Longrightarrow} &&\Leftrightarrow_{\text{def}} & \exists q' &: q \overset{\sigma}{\Longrightarrow} q' \\
q &\overset{\sigma}{\nRightarrow} &&\Leftrightarrow_{\text{def}} & \text{not } \exists q' &: q \overset{\sigma}{\Longrightarrow} q'
\end{aligned}
$$

Example 2. In Figure 2:

$u_0 \overset{but \cdot liq \cdot but \cdot choc}{\Longrightarrow} u_0$, $v_0 \overset{but \cdot but \cdot but \cdot liq}{\Longrightarrow} v_0$, and $u_0 \overset{but \cdot but}{\nRightarrow}$.

In our reasoning about labelled transition systems we will not always distinguish between a transition system and its initial state. If $p = \langle Q, L, T, q_0 \rangle$, we will identify the process p with its initial state q_0, and, e.g., we write $p \overset{\sigma}{\Longrightarrow}$ instead of $q_0 \overset{\sigma}{\Longrightarrow}$. With this in mind, we give some additional definitions and notations in Definition 5, which are exemplified in Example 3.

Definition 5. *Let* p *be a (state of a) labelled transition system, and* $\sigma \in L^*$.

1. $init(p) =_{\text{def}} \{ \mu \in L \cup \{\tau\} \mid p \overset{\mu}{\longrightarrow} \}$
2. $traces(p) =_{\text{def}} \{ \sigma \in L^* \mid p \overset{\sigma}{\Longrightarrow} \}$
3. p **after** $\sigma =_{\text{def}} \{ p' \mid p \overset{\sigma}{\Longrightarrow} p' \}$
4. P **after** $\sigma =_{\text{def}} \bigcup \{ p$ **after** $\sigma \mid p \in P \}$, *where* P *is a set of states.*
5. P **refuses** $A =_{\text{def}} \exists p \in P, \forall \mu \in A \cup \{\tau\}: p \overset{\mu}{\nrightarrow}$, *where* P *and* A *are sets of states and labels, respectively.*
6. $der(p) =_{\text{def}} \{ p' \mid \exists \sigma \in L^*: p \overset{\sigma}{\Longrightarrow} p' \}$
7. p *has* finite behaviour *if there is a natural number* n *such that all traces in* $traces(p)$ *have length smaller than* n.
8. p *is* finite state *if the number of reachable states* $der(p)$ *is finite.*
9. p *is* deterministic *if, for all* $\sigma \in L^*$, p **after** σ *has at most one element. If* $\sigma \in traces(p)$, *then* p **after** σ *may be overloaded to denote this element.*
10. p *is* image finite *if, for all* $\sigma \in L^*$, p **after** σ *is finite.*
11. p *is* strongly converging *if there is no state of* p *that can perform an infinite sequence of internal transitions.*
12. $\mathcal{LTS}(L)$ *is the class of all image finite and strongly converging labelled transition systems with labels in* L.

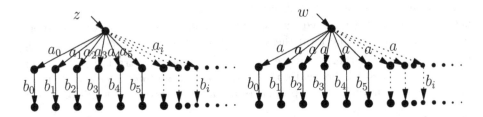

Fig. 3. An image-finite and an image-infinite transition system

In the sequel $\mathcal{LTS}(L)$ will be our basic class of models. We restrict this class to *strongly converging* and *image finite* transition systems to make it possible to algorithmically compute an **after**-set. It will turn out that the computation of these sets is crucial for the test generation algorithm; see Section 5.2. Most of the results presented in the next sections are also valid without these restrictions, but at the expense of some extra complexity.

Example 3. All possible execution sequences of process r in Figure 2 are given by $traces(r) = \{\epsilon,\ but,\ but{\cdot}liq,\ but{\cdot}but,\ but{\cdot}but{\cdot}choc\}$. Process u has infinitely many traces: $traces(u) = \{\epsilon,\ but,\ but{\cdot}liq,\ but{\cdot}choc,\ but{\cdot}liq{\cdot}but,\ \dots\ \}$, but although the set of traces has infinitely many elements, each trace, by definition, has finite length.

Some states in which a system can be **after** a trace are: r **after** $\epsilon = \{r_0\}$; r **after** $but = \{r_1, r_2\}$; r **after** $but{\cdot}choc = \emptyset$; v **after** $but{\cdot}liq{\cdot}but = \{v_0, v_1\}$.

We have that q **after** but **refuses** $\{but\}$, but not q **after** but **refuses** $\{liq\}$, and not q **after** but **refuses** $\{but, liq\}$. Moreover, r **after** but **refuses** $\{but\}$ and r **after** but **refuses** $\{liq\}$, but not r **after** but **refuses** $\{but, liq\}$. For v we have that $v \overset{but{\cdot}liq}{\Longrightarrow}$, but also v **after** but **refuses** $\{liq\}$.

The three processes p, q and r have finite behaviour and are finite state; u and v are finite state, but have infinite behaviour. Transition systems p, q, and u are deterministic, whereas r and v are non-deterministic. All five processes are image finite.

The transition system z in Figure 3 is deterministic, has infinitely many states, but has finite behaviour, and is image finite: for each $i \in \mathbb{N}$, z **after** a_i is a singleton. The system w in Figure 3 is not deterministic and not image finite: w **after** a has infinitely many states.

3.2   Representing Labelled Transition Systems

Labelled transition systems constitute a powerful semantic model to reason about processes, such as specifications, implementations, and tests. However, except for the most trivial processes, like the ones in Figure 2, an explicit representation as 4-tuple, or a representation by means of a tree or a graph is usually not feasible. Realistic systems easily have billions of states, so that drawing or enumerating them is not an option. We need another way of representing a transition system, and the usual way is to define a language with labelled transition systems as its operational semantics. Each expression in such a language defines, through its semantics, a labelled transition system. Expressions can be combined with language operators, so that complex transition systems can be composed from simpler ones. We call such a language a *process language*.

There exist many process languages. We use a variant of the language LOTOS, for which we introduce some of the constructs that are used in the sequel to define test cases, test execution, and the composition of systems. Since this text is not intended as a tutorial in such languages, we refer to the standard literature for a more detailed treatment.

The language expressions defining labelled transition systems are called *behaviour expressions*. We have the following syntax for behaviour expressions, where $a \in L$ is a label, B is a behaviour expression, $\mathcal{B}$ is a countable set of behaviour expressions, $G \subseteq L$ is a set of labels, and P is a *process name*.

$$B \ ::= \ a \ ; \ B \ \mid \ \mathbf{i} \ ; \ B \ \mid \ \Sigma \, \mathcal{B} \ \mid \ B \, \| [\, G \,] \| \, B \ \mid \ \mathbf{hide} \ G \ \mathbf{in} \ B \ \mid \ P$$

The *action prefix expression* $a \, ; \, B$ defines the behaviour, which can perform the action a and then behaves as B, i.e., $a \, ; \, B$ defines the labelled transition system which makes a transition labelled a to the transition system defined by B. The expression $\mathbf{i} \, ; \, B$ is analogous to $a \, ; \, B$, the difference being that $\mathbf{i}$ denotes the internal action τ in the transition system.

The *choice expression* $\Sigma \, \mathcal{B}$ denotes a choice of behaviour. It behaves as one of the processes in the set $\mathcal{B}$. This choice is determined by the first transition which is made. We use $B_1 \,\square\, B_2$ as an abbreviation for $\Sigma \{B_1, B_2\}$, i.e., $B_1 \,\square\, B_2$ behaves either as B_1 or as B_2. The expression $\mathbf{stop}$ is an abbreviation for $\Sigma \, \emptyset$, i.e., it is the behaviour which cannot perform any action, so it is the deadlocked process.

The *parallel expression* $B_1 \, \| [\, G \,] \| \, B_2$ denotes the parallel execution of B_1 and B_2. In this parallel execution all actions in G must synchronize, whereas all actions not in G (including τ) can occur independently in both processes, i.e., *interleaved*. We use $\|$ as an abbreviation for $\| [\, L \,] \|$, i.e., sychronization on all observable actions, and $\| \| \|$ as an abbreviation for $\| [\, \emptyset \,] \|$, i.e., full interleaving and no synchronization.

The *hiding expression* $\mathbf{hide} \ G \ \mathbf{in} \ B$ denotes the transition system of B where all labels in G have been hidden, i.e., replaced by the internal action τ.

The last language constructs are *process definitions* and *process instantiations*. A *process definition* links a process name to a behaviour expression: $P \, := \, B$. The name P can then be used as a process instantiation in behaviour expressions to stand for the behaviour contained in its corresponding process definition.

As usual, parentheses are used to disambiguate expressions. If no parentheses are used ';' binds stronger than '$\square$', which binds stronger than '$\| [\, G \,] \|$', which in turn binds stronger than $\mathbf{hide}$. The parallel operators are read from left to right, but note that they are not associative for different synchronization sets. So, $\mathbf{hide} \ a, c \ \mathbf{in} \ a; B_1 \, \| \, b \, ; B_2 \,\square\, c; B_3 \, \| \| \| \, d; B_4$ is read as

$$(\mathbf{hide} \ a, c \ \mathbf{in} \ (((a; B_1) \, \| \, ((b \, ; B_2) \,\square\, (c; B_3))) \, \| \| \| \, (d; B_4)))$$

Table 1. Structural operational semantics

$$\frac{}{a\,;B \xrightarrow{a} B} \qquad \frac{}{i\,;B \xrightarrow{\tau} B} \qquad \frac{B \xrightarrow{\mu} B'}{\Sigma\,B \xrightarrow{\mu} B'}\; B \in \mathcal{B},\ \mu \in L \cup \{\tau\}$$

$$\frac{B_1 \xrightarrow{\mu} B_1'}{B_1\,||[G]||\,B_2 \xrightarrow{\mu} B_1'\,||[G]||\,B_2} \qquad \frac{B_2 \xrightarrow{\mu} B_2'}{B_1\,||[G]||\,B_2 \xrightarrow{\mu} B_1\,||[G]||\,B_2'}\; \mu \in (L \cup \{\tau\})\backslash G$$

$$\frac{B_1 \xrightarrow{a} B_1',\ B_2 \xrightarrow{a} B_2'}{B_1\,||[G]||\,B_2 \xrightarrow{a} B_1'\,||[G]||\,B_2'}\; a \in G \qquad \frac{B_P \xrightarrow{\mu} B'}{P \xrightarrow{\mu} B'}\; P := B_P,\ \mu \in L \cup \{\tau\}$$

$$\frac{B \xrightarrow{a} B'}{\textbf{hide } G \textbf{ in } B \xrightarrow{\tau} \textbf{hide } G \textbf{ in } B'}\; a \in G \qquad \frac{B \xrightarrow{\mu} B'}{\textbf{hide } G \textbf{ in } B \xrightarrow{\mu} \textbf{hide } G \textbf{ in } B'}\; \mu \notin G$$

The formal semantics of a process language is usually formally defined in the form of structural operational semantics. Such a semantic definition consists of axioms and inference rules which define for each behaviour expression the corresponding labelled transition system; see Table 1. Consider as an example the axiom for $a\,;B$. This axiom is to be read as: an expression of the form $a\,;B$ can always make a transition $\xrightarrow{a}$ to a state from where it behaves as B. Consider as another example the inference rule for $\Sigma\,B$. Suppose that we can satisfy the premiss, i.e., B can make a transition labelled μ to B', and $B \in \mathcal{B}$, and μ is an observable or internal action, then we can conclude that $\Sigma\,B$ can make a transition labelled μ to B'. We give the remaining axioms and rules for our language in Table 1 without further comments.

Example 4. Behaviour expressions representing the processes of Figure 2 are:

$$
\begin{aligned}
p\ &:\ but;\ liq;\ \textbf{stop} \\
q\ &:\ but;\ (\ liq;\ \textbf{stop} \ \square\ choc;\ \textbf{stop}\ ) \\
r\ &:\ but;\ liq;\ \textbf{stop} \ \square\ but;\ but;\ choc;\ \textbf{stop} \\
u\ &:\ U\ \text{where}\ U\ :=\ but;\ (\ liq;\ U \ \square\ choc;\ U\ ) \\
v\ &:\ V\ \text{where}\ V\ :=\ but;\ (\ liq;\ V \ \square\ \textbf{i};\ V\ )
\end{aligned}
$$

These behaviour expressions are not unique, e.g., we could also choose

$$
\begin{aligned}
p\ &:\ but;\ liq;\ liq;\ \textbf{stop}\ ||\ but;\ liq;\ choc;\ \textbf{stop} \\
q\ &:\ but;\ \Sigma\{liq;\ \textbf{stop},\ choc;\ \textbf{stop}\}
\end{aligned}
$$

The parallel operator in particular can be used to efficiently represent large transition systems. Consider the process p of Figure 2 which has 3 states. The interleaving of p with itself, $p\,|||\,p$, has $3 \times 3 = 9$ states; and $p\,|||\,p\,|||\,p$ has 27 states, and so forth.

Also infinite-state processes can be represented with finite expressions, e.g., Y with $Y := a\,;\ (\ b\,;\ \textbf{stop}\ |||\ Y\ )$ has infinitely many states; it can perform actions a and b but it can never do more b's than a's. The infinite-state transition system z in Figure 3 can be written as $\Sigma\{\,a_i\,;\,b_i\,;\,\textbf{stop}\mid i\in\mathbb{N}\,\}$.

Finally, note that not every behaviour expression represents a transition system in $\mathcal{LTS}(L)$, e.g., the image-infinite transition system w of Figure 3 can be expressed in our language: $\Sigma\{\,a\,;\,b_i\,;\,\textbf{stop}\mid i\in\mathbb{N}\,\}$. Also the transition system defined by $\textbf{hide}\ a\ \textbf{in}\ P_0$, where $P_i\ :=\ a\,;\,P_{i+1}\ \Box\ b_i\,;\,\textbf{stop}$ with $i\in\mathbb{N}$, is not in $\mathcal{LTS}(L)$; it is neither image finite, nor strongly converging. In the rest of this paper we will not bother about the semantics being only partially defined.

3.3 Inputs and Outputs

A labelled transition system defines the possible sequences of interactions that a system may have with its environment. These interactions are abstract, in the sense that they are only identified by a label; there is no notion of initiative or direction of the interaction, nor of input or output. An interaction can occur if both the process and its environment are able to perform that interaction, implying that they can also both block the occurrence of the interaction. The communication between a system and its environment is symmetric. When the environment is also a labelled transition system this communication can be expressed in our language by the parallel synchronization operator $|[\,G\,]|$, where the labels in G model the possible interactions.

Although this paradigm of abstract interaction is sufficient for analysing and reasoning about many applications, there are also systems which communicate in a different way, in particular those systems that we will consider for testing. Those systems do not abstract from initiative and direction; they do distinguish between actions initiated by the environment, and actions initiated by themselves. They communicate via *inputs* and *outputs*: outputs are actions initiated by the system, and inputs are actions initiated by the environment.

We define *labelled transition system with inputs and outputs* to model systems for which the set of actions is partitioned into input actions contained in an input label set L_I, and output actions in an output label set L_U. (The 'U' refers to 'uitvoer', the Dutch word for 'output', which is preferred to avoid confusion between L_O (letter 'O') and L_0 (digit zero)).

Definition 6. *A labelled transition system with inputs and outputs is a 5-tuple* $\langle Q, L_I, L_U, T, q_0\rangle$ *where*

- $\langle Q, L_I\cup L_U, T, q_0\rangle$ *is a labelled transition system in* $\mathcal{LTS}(L_I\cup L_U)$;
- L_I *and* L_U *are countable sets of* input labels *and* output labels, *respectively, which are disjoint:* $L_I\cap L_U=\emptyset$.

The class of labelled transition systems with inputs in L_I *and outputs in* L_U *is denoted by* $\mathcal{LTS}(L_I, L_U)$.

Inputs are usually decorated with '?' and outputs with '!'. Labelled transition systems with inputs and outputs are used as formal specifications in our testing theory, i.e., $\mathcal{LTS}(L_I, L_U)$ instantiates the class of specifications *SPEC*; see

Section 2. Of course, this does not mean that specifications have to be written explicitly as labelled transition systems: any language with labelled transition system semantics suffices, for example, the process language defined in Section 3.2.

3.4 Input-Output Transition Systems

Labelled transition systems with inputs and outputs do not really differ from normal labelled transition systems. We define *input-output transition systems* to model systems with inputs and outputs, in which outputs are initiated by the system and never refused by the environment, and inputs are initiated by the system's environment and never refused by the system. This means that the system is always prepared to perform any input action, i.e., all inputs are enabled in all states.

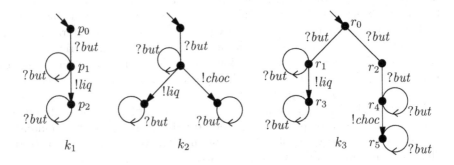

Fig. 4. Input-output transition systems

Definition 7. *An* input-output transition system *is a labelled transition system with inputs and outputs* $\langle Q, L_I, L_U, T, q_0 \rangle$ *where all input actions are enabled in any reachable state:*

$$\forall q \in der(q_0), \ \forall a \in L_I : \ q \xrightarrow{a} $$

The class of input-output transition systems with inputs in L_I and outputs in L_U is denoted by $\mathcal{IOTS}(L_I, L_U) \subseteq \mathcal{LTS}(L_I, L_U)$.

Example 5. In Figure 2 only v is an input-output transition system, when $L_I = \{?but\}$ and $L_U \supseteq \{!liq\}$. Some other input-output transition systems are given in Figure 4. In k_1 we can push the button $?but$, which is an input for the candy machine, and then the machine outputs liquorice $!liq$. After $?but$ has been pushed once, and also after the machine has released $!liq$, any more pushing of $?but$ has no effect: k_1 makes a self-loop and does not change state. In fact, k_1, k_2, and k_3 are almost the same transition systems as p, q, and r in Figure 2, interpreting $L_I = \{?but\}$ as inputs and $L_U = \{!liq, !choc\}$ as outputs, and the difference being that self-loop transition have been added to make them input enabled; this adding of input self-loops is sometimes referred to as *angelic completion*.

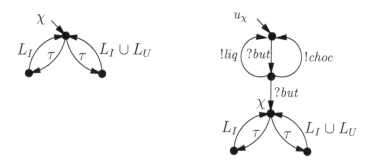

Fig. 5. Demonic completion

Another way of making systems input-enabled is to add a special error state, and to add transitions to this error state for all non-specified inputs. In Figure 5 yet another completion method, viz. *demonic completion*, is used to make u in Figure 2 input enabled: all non-specified inputs lead to the *chaos* process χ. Once in χ any behaviour is possible.

Since input-output transition systems are just a special kind of labelled transition systems, all definitions for them apply. In particular, the parallel synchronization operator $\parallel$ is used to model the communication between a system s and its environment e. Naturally, the set L_I of inputs of s should correspond to the outputs of e, and the set L_U of outputs of s are the inputs of e: $e \in \mathcal{IOTS}(L_U, L_I)$. Since the inputs of s are always enabled, e can autonomously determine whether an action in L_I will occur, or not. Conversely, since all actions in L_U are always enabled in e, it is up to s to determine whether an action in L_U occurs, or not. If s cannot perform an output action, it can only wait until e performs one of e's outputs. Such a state without output actions, where s cannot autonomously proceed, is called *suspended*, or *quiescent*. A quiescent state q is denoted as $\delta(q)$. If, and only if, both s and e are quiescent then there is no way to proceed: they are in *deadlock*.

A system s with environment e is in deadlock after trace σ if there is no possible action to proceed: $(s \parallel e)$ **after** σ **refuses** L. For non-input-enabled transition systems this means

$$\exists A_s, A_e \subseteq L : A_s \cup A_e = L$$
$$\text{and } s \textbf{ after } \sigma \textbf{ refuses } A_s \text{ and } e \textbf{ after } \sigma \textbf{ refuses } A_e \tag{2}$$

For input-output transition systems this is simplified, since s can never refuse actions in L_I: if s **after** σ **refuses** A_s then $A_s \subseteq L_U$. Analogously, if e refuses something it must be a subset of L_I. Since $L_I \cap L_U = \emptyset$, the only sets satisfying (2) are $A_s = L_U$ and $A_e = L_I$, i.e., when both s and e are quiescent: $\delta(s)$ and $\delta(e)$.

Although this rationale for introducing quiescence is based on input-output transition systems, the definition applies equally well to non-input-output transition systems, and since in subsequent sections we will indeed consider quiescence also for non-input-enabled transition systems, it is generally defined in Definitions 8 and 9 for labelled transitions with inputs and outputs.

Definition 8. *Let $p \in \mathcal{LTS}(L_I, L_U)$.*

1. *A state q of p is* quiescent, *denoted by $\delta(q)$, if $\forall \mu \in L_U \cup \{\tau\}: q \xrightarrow{\mu} \!\!\!\!\!\not\;$*
2. *The* quiescent traces *of p are those traces that may lead to a quiescent state:*
   $$Qtraces(p) =_{\text{def}} \{ \sigma \in L^* \mid \exists p' \in (p \text{ after } \sigma): \delta(p') \}$$

An observer looking at a quiescent system does not see any outputs. This particular observation of seeing nothing can itself be considered as an event. It turns out to be convenient to express this 'seeing nothing', i.e., quiescence, as a special 'output action'; it is denoted by δ ($\delta \notin L \cup \{\tau\}$). Once we have this special action we can also consider transitions with δ. Such a transition $p \xrightarrow{\delta}$ expresses that p allows the observation of quiescence, i.e., p cannot perform any output action. In this way the absence of outputs is made into an explicitly observable event. Since quiescence implies that no real transition is performed, the goal state after a δ-transition is always the same as the start state, so $p \xrightarrow{\delta} p$ if $\delta(p)$.

With δ-transitions it is also possible to extend traces with δ. For example, $p \xRightarrow{\delta \cdot ?a \cdot \delta \cdot ?b \cdot !x}$ expresses that initially p is quiescent, i.e., does not produce outputs, but p does accept input action $?a$, after which there are again no outputs; when then input $?b$ is performed, the output $!x$ is produced. Traces that may contain the quiescence action δ, are called *suspension traces*.

Definition 9. *Let $p = \langle Q, L_I, L_U, T, q_0 \rangle \in \mathcal{LTS}(L_I, L_U)$.*

1. $L_\delta =_{\text{def}} L \cup \{\delta\}$
2. $p_\delta =_{\text{def}} \langle Q, L_I, L_U \cup \{\delta\}, T \cup T_\delta, q_0 \rangle$,
   with $T_\delta =_{\text{def}} \{ q \xrightarrow{\delta} q \mid q \in Q, \delta(q) \}$
3. *The* suspension traces *of p are* $Straces(p) =_{\text{def}} \{ \sigma \in L_\delta^* \mid p_\delta \xRightarrow{\sigma} \}$

From now on we will usually include δ-transitions in the transition relations, i.e., we consider p_δ instead of p, unless otherwise indicated. Definitions 3, 4, and 5 also apply to transition systems with label set L_δ.

In our testing theory it will be assumed that an implementation under test can be modelled as an input-output transition system, i.e., $\mathcal{IOTS}(L_I, L_U)$ instantiates the class of models of implementations MOD, where L_I and L_U are assumed to be the same as given for the specification; see Section 2. Since models of implementations are only assumed to exist, the language representation issue does not play a role for implementations. Whereas implementations are input-enabled, specifications are not necessarily input-enabled. This difference allows having partial specifications; this will be elaborated in Section 4, in particular in Examples 9 and 10.

Example 6. For k_1 in Figure 4 we have that $\delta(p_0)$, $\delta(p_2)$, but not $\delta(p_1)$ because state p_1 can perform output $!liq$.

As explained above, the definition of quiescence is not restricted to input-enabled systems. It can be applied to any transition system with inputs and

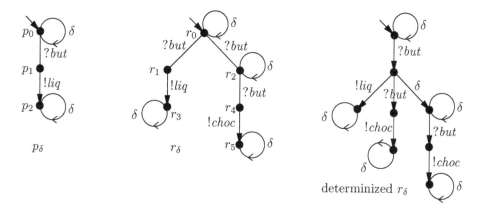

Fig. 6. Quiescence

outputs. If in Figure 2 we take $L_I = \{?but\}$ and $L_U = \{!liq, !choc\}$, then for process p we have: $\delta(p_0)$, $\delta(p_2)$, but not $\delta(p_1)$.

In Figure 6, quiescence has been made explicit by adding the δ-transitions for p and r of Figure 2. So, we have, for example, $p_\delta \xRightarrow{\delta \cdot ?but \cdot !liq \cdot \delta \cdot \delta}$, and the suspension trace $?but \cdot \delta \cdot ?but \cdot !choc \in Straces(r)$, but $?but \cdot \delta \cdot ?but \cdot !liq \notin Straces(r)$. Since $\delta(r_2)$ but not $\delta(r_1)$ we know that we are in the right branch after having observed $?but \cdot \delta$. In the determinization of r_δ this is even more explicit: after the sequence $?but \cdot \delta$ the continuation is $?but \cdot !choc$. This determinization of r_δ, which may serve as a kind of canonical representation of transition systems modulo equality of suspension traces, is sometimes referred to as the *suspension automaton* of r. In such a determinization a δ-transition is not necessarily a loop anymore, and an output- and δ-transition may be enabled in one state. Determinizing a transition system to which δ-transitions have been added is not the same as adding δ-transitions to a determinized transition system. Moreover, there are deterministic transition systems over $L_I \cup L_U \cup \{\delta\}$ for which there is no labelled transition system for which it is the suspension automaton.

3.5 Test Cases

A test case is a specification of the behaviour of a tester in an experiment carried out on an implementation under test. In this experiment the tester serves as a kind of artificial environment of the implementation. Following the discussion in Section 3.4 about the communication between an implementation and its environment, an implementation can do three different things: it can accept any input in L_I, it can produce an output in L_U, or it can remain quiescent. This implies that the tester, being this environment, must provide these inputs, must be able to observe these outputs, and must be able to observe quiescence if there is no output. Moreover, the tester should be input-enabled for all actions in L_U. The behaviour of such a tester is also modelled as an input-output transition system, but, naturally, with inputs and outputs exchanged. For observing quiescence, we add a special label θ to the transition systems modelling tests ($\theta \notin L_I \cup L_U \cup \{\tau, \delta\}$). The occurrence of θ in a test indicates the detection of quiescence δ; i.e., the observation that no output is produced by the implementation. Theoretically, this means that the tester has to wait for an infinite amount of time in order to conclude that implementation does not, and will never produce any output. More practically, one could think of θ as being implemented as the expiration of a time-out. Of course, care should be taken when choosing such a (finite) time-out value in order to have confidence that after an output-less time-out period the system indeed is quiescent.

Combining the above, we have that test cases are in the first place processes in $\mathcal{IOTS}(L_U, L_I \cup \{\theta\})$. But, based on the observation that the execution of a test case is an experiment under control of the tester, a few restrictions are added. First, there must be a mechanism in test cases to assign verdicts. This is accomplished by having two special verdict states called **pass** and **fail**, which are sink states, i.e., once in **pass** (**fail**) the test case cannot leave that state anymore. Second, in order to make it possible to assign a verdict within finite time, test cases should always allow reaching a **pass** or **fail** state within finitely many transitions. Third, in order to keep the tester in control, unnecessary non-determinism should be avoided. In the first place, this implies that the test case itself is deterministic. In the second place, this means that a tester should never offer more than one input action (from the perspective of the implementation) at a time. Since the implementation is able to accept any input action, offering more inputs would always lead to an unnecessarily non-deterministic continuation of the test run. Having a deterministic test case does not imply that a test run has a unique result: due to non-determinism in the implementation under test, and due to non-determinism in the test run itself, the repetition of a test run may lead to a different result; see also Section 5.1. Altogether, we come to the following definition of the class of test transition systems $\mathcal{TTS}$, which instantiates the domain of test cases $TEST$; see Section 2.

Since the use of 'input' and 'output' in a test case is always confusing (and it will be even more confusing once we start the discussion on test execution, where implementations and tests come together), we try to use the convention that 'input' and 'output' always refer to the inputs and outputs of the specification and implementation under test. Consequently, input-enabledness of a test case means that all actions in L_U are enabled. Also the decorations '?' and '!' refer to the use of actions in the specification (or implementation). The special action θ is indeed special: it is considered neither input, nor output.

Definition 10

1. *A test case t for an implementation with inputs in L_I and outputs in L_U is an input-output transition system $\langle Q, L_U, L_I \cup \{\theta\}, T, q_0 \rangle \in \mathcal{IOTS}(L_U, L_I \cup \{\theta\})$ such that*
   - *t is finite state and deterministic;*
   - *Q contains two special states **pass** and **fail**, **pass** $\neq$ **fail**, with*
     pass $:= \Sigma \{ x ; \textbf{pass} \mid x \in L_U \cup \{\theta\} \}$
     fail $:= \Sigma \{ x ; \textbf{fail} \mid x \in L_U \cup \{\theta\} \}$

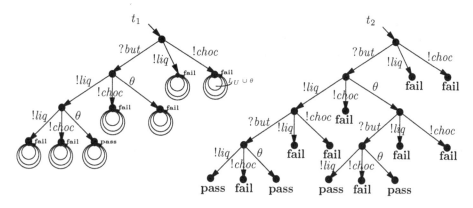

Fig. 7. Test cases

- t has no cycles except those in states **pass** and **fail**
  (formally: for $\sigma \in (L \cup \{\theta\})^* \setminus \{\epsilon\}$: $q \overset{\sigma}{\Longrightarrow} q$ implies $q = $ **pass** or $q = $ **fail**)
- for any state $q \in Q$ of the test case
  either $init(q) = \{a\} \cup L_U$ for some $a \in L_I$
  or $init(q) = L_U \cup \{\theta\}$.
2. The class of test cases for implementations with inputs L_I and outputs L_U
   is denoted as $\mathcal{TTS}(L_U, L_I)$.
3. A test suite T is a set of test cases: $T \subseteq \mathcal{TTS}(L_U, L_I)$.

Example 7. Figure 7 gives two example test cases with $L_I = \{?but\}$ and $L_U = \{!liq, !choc\}$. Test case t_1 provides input $?but$ to an implementation. If this is successful t_1 expects to receive $!liq$ from the implementation followed by nothing, i.e., quiescence. Any other reaction is considered erroneous and leads to **fail**.

In test case t_2 the loops in the states **pass** and **fail** have been omitted. Since they are only there to make the test case input enabled, we will omit them from now on.

3.6 Some Bibliographic Notes

Labelled transition systems are a basic model in formal theories. Many languages for processes, in particular process algebras, use transition systems for their operational semantics, which is usually defined through structured operational semantics; [16] may serve as a literature entry. The language presented here is mainly inspired by LOTOS [17,18].

Input-output transition systems are analogous to Input/Output Automata (IOA) [19], and to Input-Output State Machines [1], but they differ from classical Finite State Machines or Mealy Machines. Input-output transition systems differ marginally from Input/Output Automata in input enabling: instead of requiring *strong input enabling* as in [19] ($\forall a \in L_I : p' \overset{a}{\longrightarrow}$), input-output transition systems allow input enabling via internal transitions (*weak input enabling*, $\forall a \in L_I : p' \overset{a}{\Longrightarrow}$). Moreover, as is usual for labelled transition systems, all internal actions are denoted by the same label τ, which is possible, since we do not consider fairness explicitly, so we do not need to express a partitioning of output and internal actions to pose fairness requirements as in Input/Output Automata. Testing is only about finite behaviours.

4   The Implementation Relation

The purpose of this section is to define precisely when an implementation in $\mathcal{IOTS}(L_I, L_U)$ is correct with respect to a specification in $\mathcal{LTS}(L_I, L_U)$, i.e., to define an implementation relation; see Section 2. There are many ways of defining an implementation relation. In principle, any relation between $\mathcal{IOTS}(L_I, L_U)$ and $\mathcal{LTS}(L_I, L_U)$ could serve as an implementation relation, but, of course, some relations appear more natural and intuitive than others. The main relation that we consider is called **ioco**, and it is defined in Section 4.1. Subsequently, Section 4.2 discusses some variants and properties of **ioco**.

4.1   The Implementation Relation *ioco*

The implementation relation on which we build our test theory is **ioco**, which is abbreviated from input-output conformance. Informally, an implementation $i \in \mathcal{IOTS}(L_I, L_U)$ is **ioco**-conforming to specification $s \in \mathcal{LTS}(L_I, L_U)$ if any experiment derived from s and executed on i leads to an output from i that is foreseen by s. A special output of i is the absence of outputs as modelled by quiescence δ; see Section 3.4. This means that if i is quiescent then s should have the possibility to be quiescent, too. A formal definition of **ioco** starts with defining the set *out* of possible outputs. This set can contain the special label δ. It is defined for a single state, and then generalized to a set of states. The latter is used in combination with **after** (Definition 5.3): $out(\, p\ \textbf{after}\ \sigma\,)$ gives all possible outputs occurring after having performed the trace $\sigma \in L_\delta^*$.

Definition 11. *Let q be a state in a transition system, and let Q be a set of states, then*

1. $out(q) =_{\text{def}} \{\, x \in L_U \mid q \xrightarrow{x} \,\} \cup \{\, \delta \mid \delta(q)\,\}$
2. $out(Q) =_{\text{def}} \bigcup \{\, out(q) \mid q \in Q\,\}$

Example 8. Some examples for k_3 in Figure 4:

$$
\begin{array}{lll}
out(\,k_3\ \textbf{after}\ \epsilon\,) & = out(r_0) & = \{\delta\} \\
out(\,k_3\ \textbf{after}\ \delta\,) & = out(r_0) & = \{\delta\} \\
out(\,k_3\ \textbf{after}\ !liq\,) & = out(\emptyset) & = \emptyset \\
out(\,k_3\ \textbf{after}\ ?but\,) & = out(r_1) \cup out(r_2) = \{!liq, \delta\} \\
out(\,k_3\ \textbf{after}\ ?but{\cdot}?but\,) & = out(r_1) \cup out(r_4) = \{!liq, !choc\} \\
out(\,k_3\ \textbf{after}\ ?but{\cdot}\delta{\cdot}?but\,) & = out(r_4) & = \{!choc\} \\
out(\,k_3\ \textbf{after}\ ?but{\cdot}?but{\cdot}!liq\,) & = out(r_3) & = \{\delta\} \\
out(\,k_3\ \textbf{after}\ ?but{\cdot}\delta{\cdot}?but{\cdot}!liq\,) = out(\emptyset) & = \emptyset
\end{array}
$$

The informal idea that 'any output produced by i has been foreseen in s' is formally expressed by requiring that the out-set of the implementation is a subset of the out-set of the specification. This should hold for any state, but due to non-determinism we do not exactly know in which state we are during testing. What can be observed is the suspension trace $\sigma \in L_\delta^*$ executed so far, which may lead to different states. The set p **after** σ collects all these possible current states, so $out(p\ \textbf{after}\ \sigma)$ contains all possible outputs, possibly including δ, after σ. This set, when obtained from the implementation, must be included in the analogous set obtained from the specification, but only if σ is a suspension trace of the specification. Altogether, these considerations lead to Definition 12.

Definition 12. *Given a set of input labels L_I and a set of output labels L_U, the relation* **ioco** $\subseteq \mathcal{IOTS}(L_I, L_U) \times \mathcal{LTS}(L_I, L_U)$ *is defined as follows:*

$$i\ \textbf{ioco}\ s \quad \Leftrightarrow_{\text{def}} \quad \forall \sigma \in Straces(s): \quad out(i\ \textbf{after}\ \sigma) \subseteq out(s\ \textbf{after}\ \sigma)$$

The fact that **ioco** only requires inclusion of out-sets for the suspension traces of the specification, together with the fact that specifications can be non-input enabled, makes it possible to have *partial* specifications. For suspension traces which are not in $Straces(s)$ there is no requirement whatsoever on the implementation, which implies that an implementation is free to implement anything it likes after such a trace. Such a trace is said to be *underspecified*. In many situations it can be beneficial to a have a partial specification, whereas in other situations a *complete* specification is preferred: a complete specification specifies after every trace what should happen. Completeness can always be achieved with **ioco** by having an input enabled specification: if $s \in \mathcal{IOTS}(L_I, L_U)$ then there are no underspecified traces.

Example 9. Figure 8 gives some implementations and specifications with $L_I = \{?a, ?b\}$ and $L_U = \{!x, !y\}$:

i_m **ioco** s_n	s_1	s_2	s_3	s_4
i_1	ioco	ioco	io¢o	ioco
i_2	io¢o	ioco	io¢o	io¢o
i_3	ioco	ioco	ioco	ioco
i_4	io¢o	io¢o	io¢o	ioco

Specification s_1 specifies that after input $?a$ output $!x$ must occur, which is expressed as: $out(s_1\ \textbf{after}\ ?a) = \{x\}$. Implementation i_1 satisfies this requirement, but i_2 and i_4 do not: $out(i_2\ \textbf{after}\ ?a) = \{x, y\} \not\subseteq \{x\}$, $out(i_4\ \textbf{after}\ ?a) = \{x, \delta\} \not\subseteq \{x\}$. For i_3, $out(i_3\ \textbf{after}\ ?a) = \{x\} \subseteq out(s_1\ \textbf{after}\ ?a)$. Moreover, $out(i_3\ \textbf{after}\ ?b) = \{y\} \not\subseteq out(s_1\ \textbf{after}\ ?b) = \emptyset$, but since $?b \notin Straces(s_1)$ this does not matter, and hence i_3 **ioco** s_1.

We see from i_2 **io¢o** s_1 that an implementation should not produce more outputs than allowed by the specification, and from i_4 **io¢o** s_1 that the implementation should not be quiescent, when the specification expects an output. But from i_3 **ioco** s_1 we see that an implementation may have additional features, in

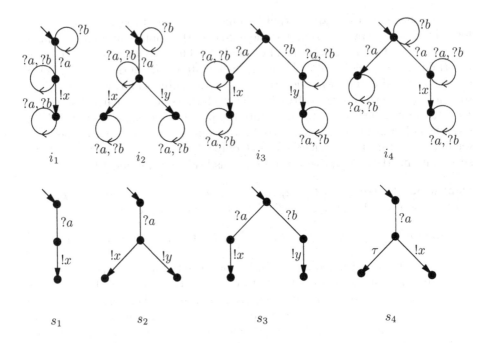

Fig. 8. Implementations and specifications with **ioco**

this case the behaviour $?b \cdot !y$; the specification is *partial*, or *underspecified* for $?b$: s_1 does not prescribe any requirements for behaviour that follows $?b$, and an implementation is completely free to do anything it likes after $?b$.

Specification s_2 requires that after input $?a$ either output $!x$ or $!y$ is performed. This means that i_1, i_2, i_3 **ioco** s_2, but not i_4 **ioco** s_2, since i_4 may not produce any output at all: $out(i_4 \textbf{ after } ?a) = \{x, \delta\} \nsubseteq \{x, y\}$.

We see from i_1 **ioco** s_2 that an implementation may have less outputs than the specification allows, but having no output at all is not allowed.

Specification s_3 specifies that output $!x$ must be performed after $?a$, and $!y$ after $?b$. Implementations i_1, i_2, and i_4 are quiescent after $?b$, so they are not **ioco**-correct; i_3 does satisfy this requirement.

Specification s_4 specifies that after $?a$ either output $!x$ should be produced, or the implementation may be quiescent: $out(s_4 \textbf{ after } ?a) = \{x, \delta\}$. Only i_2 may produce output $!y$ and is not **ioco**-correct.

The implementations can also be mutually compared. Of course, i_k **ioco** i_k for $k = 1, 2, 3, 4$, since **ioco** is reflexive on $\mathcal{IOTS}(L_I, L_U)$. Furthermore, only i_1 **ioco** i_2, i_4. Mutually comparing the specifications does not make sense, since the specifications are not input enabled, so **ioco** is not defined.

Example 10. Consider Figure 4. We have that k_1 **ioco** k_2: an implementation capable of only producing $!liq$ conforms to a specification that prescribes to produce either $!liq$ or $!choc$. Although k_2 is deterministic according to Definition 5.9, in fact, it specifies in an input-output context that after $?but$ there is a non-deterministic choice between supplying $!liq$ or $!choc$.

If we want to specify a machine that produces both *liquorice* and *chocolate*, then two buttons are needed to select the respective candies, cf. s_3 in Example 9:

$$?liq\text{-}button \; ; \; !liq \; ; \; \textbf{stop} \quad \square \quad ?choc\text{-}button \; ; \; !choc \; ; \; \textbf{stop}$$

On the other hand, $k_2 \text{ ioƈo } k_1$ and $k_2 \text{ ioƈo } k_3$: if the specification prescribes to produce only $!liq$ then an implementation shall not have the possibility to produce $!choc$.

We have $k_1 \text{ ioco } k_3$, but $k_3 \text{ ioƈo } k_1$ and $k_3 \text{ ioƈo } k_2$, since k_3 may refuse to produce anything after the *button* has been pushed once, whereas both k_1 and k_2 will always output something; formally: $\delta \in out(\, k_3 \textbf{ after } ?but\,)$, whereas $\delta \notin out(\, k_1 \textbf{ after } ?but\,)$ and $\delta \notin out(\, k_2 \textbf{ after } ?but\,)$.

Figure 2 contains three non-input-enabled transition systems, which may serve as specifications. We have $k_1 \text{ ioco } p$, and $k_2 \text{ ioƈo } p$. Also p is underspecified: p does not specify what should happen after the *button* has been pushed twice, since $?but\cdot?but \notin Straces(p)$.

Moreover, $k_1 \text{ ioco } q$ and $k_2 \text{ ioco } q$, but $k_3 \text{ ioƈo } p$ and $k_3 \text{ ioƈo } q$. As before, this is the case because $\delta \in out(\, k_3 \textbf{ after } ?but\,)$, whereas $\delta \notin out(\, p \textbf{ after } ?but\,)$ and $\delta \notin out(\, q \textbf{ after } ?but\,)$.

4.2 Some Variations and Properties of *ioco*

Generalization. The implementation relation **ioco** (Definition 12) requires that the *out*-set of the implementation be a subset of the specification's *out*-set for all traces in the set of suspension traces of the specification. By making this set of suspension traces a parameter of the relation a family of implementation relations is defined.

Definition 13. *Let* $\mathcal{F} \subseteq (L_I \cup L_U \cup \{\delta\})^*$ *be a set of suspension traces,* $i \in \mathcal{IOTS}(L_I, L_U)$, *and* $s \in LTS(L_I, L_U)$.

$$i \text{ ioco}_\mathcal{F} \; s \quad \Leftrightarrow_{\text{def}} \quad \forall \sigma \in \mathcal{F}: \quad out(\, i \textbf{ after } \sigma\,) \; \subseteq \; out(\, s \textbf{ after } \sigma\,)$$

Typically, the set $\mathcal{F} \subseteq L_\delta^*$ depends on the specification s. Clearly, $i \text{ ioco } s$ iff $i \text{ ioco}_{Straces(s)} \; s$, but also some other relations for specific $\mathcal{F}$ have been given names, and, based on sub-setting of the respective sets $\mathcal{F}$ these relations can be easily compared.

Definition 14. *Let* $i \in \mathcal{IOTS}(L_I, L_U)$, $s \in LTS(L_I, L_U)$.

1. $i \leq_{ior} s \;\; =_{\text{def}} \;\; i \text{ ioco}_{L_\delta^*} s$
   iff $\quad \forall \sigma \in L_\delta^*: \; out(\, i \textbf{ after } \sigma\,) \; \subseteq \; out(\, s \textbf{ after } \sigma\,)$
2. $i \text{ ioconf } s \;\; =_{\text{def}} \;\; i \text{ ioco}_{traces(s)} s$
   iff $\quad \forall \sigma \in traces(s): \; out(\, i \textbf{ after } \sigma\,) \; \subseteq \; out(\, s \textbf{ after } \sigma\,)$
3. $i \leq_{iot} s \;\; =_{\text{def}} \;\; i \text{ ioco}_{L^*} s$
   iff $\quad \forall \sigma \in L^*: \; out(\, i \textbf{ after } \sigma\,) \; \subseteq \; out(\, s \textbf{ after } \sigma\,)$

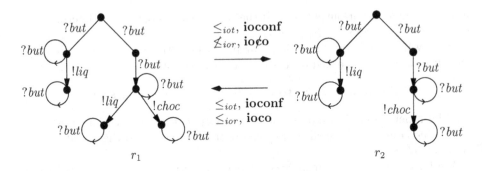

Fig. 9. The difference between $\leq_{iot}$ and $\leq_{ior}$

Proposition 1

1. $\leq_{ior}$ and $\leq_{iot}$ are preorders on $\mathcal{IOTS}(L_I, L_U)$, i.e., they are reflexive and transitive when restricted to input-enabled transition systems.

2. $\mathcal{F}_1 \subseteq \mathcal{F}_2$ implies $\mathbf{ioco}_{\mathcal{F}_1} \supseteq \mathbf{ioco}_{\mathcal{F}_2}$

3. $\leq_{ior} \subset \left\{ \begin{array}{c} \leq_{iot} \\ \mathbf{ioco} \end{array} \right\} \subset \mathbf{ioconf}$

4. $i \leq_{ior} s$ iff $Straces(i) \subseteq Straces(s)$.

5. $i \leq_{iot} s$ iff $traces(i) \subseteq traces(s)$ and $Qtraces(i) \subseteq Qtraces(s)$

Example 11. The difference between $\leq_{iot}$ and $\leq_{ior}$, and between **ioconf** and **ioco** is illustrated with the processes r_1 and r_2 in Figure 9: r_1 **ioconf** r_2, but r_1 **io$\not{c}$o** r_2; in terms of *out*-sets: $out(r_1 \text{ after } ?but \cdot \delta \cdot ?but) = \{!liq, !choc\}$ and $out(r_2 \text{ after } ?but \cdot \delta \cdot ?but) = \{!choc\}$.

Intuitively, after pushing the *button*, we observe that nothing is produced by the machine, so we push the *button* again. Machine r_1 may then produce either *liquorice* or *chocolate*, while machine r_2 will always produce *chocolate*. When we use the relation **ioconf**, the observation always terminates after observing that nothing is produced; quiescence can only be an element of the *out*-set, but it cannot occur in the trace leading to the state where the *out*-set is calculated. Hence, there is no way to distinguish between entering the left or the right branch of r_1 or r_2; after the *button* is pushed twice, both machines may produce either *liquorice* or *chocolate*: $out(r_{1,2} \text{ after } ?but \cdot ?but) = \{!liq, !choc\}$.

Partial specifications. In Section 4.1 it was mentioned that two conditions make it possible to have *partial* specifications, viz. first, that **ioco** only requires inclusion of *out*-sets for the suspension traces of the specification, and, second, that specifications are non-input enabled.

If the first condition is changed to inclusion of *out*-sets for all possible suspension traces in L_δ^*, the relation $\leq_{ior}$ is obtained; see Definition 14.1. From Proposition 1.4 it follows that $\leq_{ior}$ indeed does not allow partiality: all behaviours of a $\leq_{ior}$-correct implementation, as expressed by its suspension traces, are contained in those of the specification. This is also valid for underspecified specifications in $\mathcal{LTS}(L_I, L_U) \backslash \mathcal{IOTS}(L_I, L_U)$, which implies that it does not make sense to have an underspecified specification in combination with $\leq_{ior}$.

With respect to the second condition, if specifications are input enabled, i.e., **ioco** is restricted to a relation *on* $\mathcal{IOTS}(L_I, L_U)$, and there are no underspecified traces anymore, then what remains turns out to be exactly the relation $\leq_{ior}$.

Proposition 2

1. $\sigma \in Straces(p)$ iff $out(p \text{ after } \sigma) \neq \emptyset$
2. If $i, s \in \mathcal{IOTS}(L_I, L_U)$ then i **ioco** s iff $i \leq_{ior} s$
3. If $p, q \in \mathcal{IOTS}(L_I, L_U)$, and $s \in \mathcal{LTS}(L_I, L_U)$ then
   p **ioco** q and q **ioco** s imply p **ioco** s.
4. **ioco** is a preorder on $\mathcal{IOTS}(L_I, L_U)$.

Underspecified traces and uioco. Another relation in the family **ioco**$_\mathcal{F}$ is **uioco**. For the rationale for **uioco** consider r in Figure 2 as a specification with $L_I = \{?but\}$ and $L_U = \{!liq, !choc\}$. Since r is not input enabled, it is a partial specification. For example, $?but \cdot ?but \cdot ?but$ is an underspecified trace, and any behaviour is allowed after it. On the other hand, $?but$ is clearly specified; the allowed outputs after it are $!liq$ and δ. For the trace $?but \cdot ?but$ the situation is less clear. According to **ioco** the expected output after $?but \cdot ?but$ is $out(r \text{ after } ?but \cdot ?but) = \{!choc\}$. But suppose that in the first $?but$-transition r moves non-deterministically to state r_1 (the left branch) then one might argue that the second $?but$-transition is underspecified, and that, consequently, any possible behaviour is allowed in an implementation. This is exactly where **ioco** and **uioco** differ: **ioco** postulates that $?but \cdot ?but$ is not an underspecified trace, because there exists a state where it is specified, whereas **uioco** states that $?but \cdot ?but$ is underspecified, because there exists a state where it is underspecified.

Formally, **ioco** quantifies over $\mathcal{F} = Straces(s)$, which are all possible suspension traces of the specification s. The relation **uioco** quantifies over $\mathcal{F} = Utraces(s) \subseteq Straces(s)$, which are the suspension traces without the possibly underspecified traces, i.e., see Definition 15.1, all suspension traces σ of s for which it is *not* possible that a prefix σ_1 of σ ($\sigma = \sigma_1 \cdot a \cdot \sigma_2$) leads to a state of s where the remainder $a \cdot \sigma_2$ of σ is underspecified, that is, a is refused.

An alternative characterization of **uioco** can be given by transforming a partial specification into an input enabled one with demonic completion using the chaos process χ, as explained in Example 5. In this way the specification makes explicit that after an underspecified trace anything is allowed.

Definition 15. *Let* $i \in \mathcal{IOTS}(L_I, L_U)$, *and* $s \in \mathcal{LTS}(L_I, L_U)$.

1. $Utraces(s) =_{\text{def}} \{ \sigma \in Straces(s) \mid \forall \sigma_1, \sigma_2 \in L_\delta^*, a \in L_I :$
$$\sigma = \sigma_1 \cdot a \cdot \sigma_2 \text{ implies not } s \text{ after } \sigma_1 \text{ refuses } \{a\} \}$$
2. i **uioco** s $\Leftrightarrow_{\text{def}}$ i **ioco**$_{Utraces(s)}$ s

Example 12. Because $Utraces(s) \subseteq Straces(s)$ it is clear (proposition 1.2) that **uioco** is not stronger than **ioco**. That it is strictly weaker follows from the following example. Take r in Figure 2 as (partial) specification, and consider

r_1 and r_2 from Figure 9 as potential implementations. Then r_2 **iođo** r because $!liq \in out(r_2$ **after** $?but\cdot?but)$ and $!liq \notin out(r$ **after** $?but\cdot?but)$, but r_2 **uioco** r because $?but\cdot?but \notin Utraces(r)$. Also r_1 **iođo** r, but in this case also r_1 **uiođco** r because $?but\cdot\delta\cdot?but \in Utraces(r)$, $!liq \in out(r_1$ **after** $?but\cdot\delta\cdot?but)$ and $!liq \notin out(r$ **after** $?but\cdot\delta\cdot?but)$.

Variants. A couple of other variations on **ioco** have been defined:

TGV-ioco. TGV is a tool for the automatic synthesis of test cases for non-deterministic systems [2]. Its underlying theory is analogous to the **ioco** theory with a small extension. TGV deals with divergences or livelocks consisting of τ-loops. Such a livelock is given an *unfair* semantics, which means that the system can loop for ever. This implies that an external observer will not see any progress in the system, i.e., the observer will see quiescence.

mioco. The relation multi-**ioco** extends **ioco** with multiple channels [20]. Each action belongs to exactly one input channel or output channel. Each output channel can be quiescent, and moreover each input channel can be blocked meaning that the channel (temporarily) does not accept any inputs. Analogous to **ioco**, **mioco** requires that the outputs, output quiescences, and input blockings occurring in an implementation, are included in those of the specification.

(r)tioco. Different(real)-timed-**ioco** relations have been defined: [21,22,23]. The difficulty, and the difference between the different versions of timed-**ioco** is the treatment of quiescence. Quiescence in **ioco** means that no outputs are produced, not now and not in the future. If time is an explicit parameter in the models, it is also possible to require and observe that no outputs are produced for a specified period of time, whereas 'in the future' should be defined more precisely with explicit mentioning of time.

ioco$_r$. Sometimes, the level of granularity of the actions in the implementation is different from that of the specification, i.e., the label sets L_I and L_U of specification and implementation cannot be assumed to be the same. Usually, this means that one abstract action of the specification is implemented by a sequence of actions in the implementation. This is called action refinement, and leads to a relation **ioco$_r$** [24].

sioco. Actions are sometimes parameterized with data. In order to avoid state explosion during test generation, this data is treated in a symbolic way, leading to a symbolic-**ioco** [25]. Whereas the other variants above exend or alter **ioco**, **sioco** does not change it; it only gives another representation of the relation in case data variables and parameters are involved.

hioco. Hybrid systems are systems in which discrete actions and continuous variables play a role. Ongoing research aims at defining a relation hybrid-**ioco** to formalize the relation between a hybrid transition system implementation and its specification.

Compositional testing. With the popularization of component based development it is desirable that also testing and integration can be based on components, i.e., that successfully tested components can be integrated into correctly functioning systems. Unfortunately, this is not directly the case for **ioco**-correctness: the composition of two **ioco**-correct implementations i_1 and i_2, communicating through actions in V, and modelled as **hide** V **in** $i_1 \| [V] \| i_2$, is not necessarily **ioco**-correct to the composition of their specifications; see Proposition 3.1. Technically, this means that **ioco** is not a precongruence for the hiding and parallel operators. Intuitively, it can be understood by seeing that a component's specification may have underspecified traces after which the component's implementation may show any possible behaviour. In a composition with another component this behaviour may lead to undesired behaviour which is not allowed by the composition of the specifications. This problem can be avoided by having no underspecified traces: the precongruence property does hold for input enabled specifications; see Proposition 3.2.

Proposition 3. Let $i_k \in \mathcal{IOTS}(L_{Ik}, L_{Uk})$ and $s_k \in \mathcal{LTS}(L_{Ik}, L_{Uk})$ for $k = 1, 2$, be two components, such that they have disjoint inputs and disjoint outputs: $L_{I1} \cap L_{I2} = L_{U1} \cap L_{U2} = \emptyset$. Let $V = (L_{I1} \cap L_{U2}) \cup (L_{U1} \cap L_{I2})$ be the set of their common interactions.

1. i_1 **ioco** s_1 and i_2 **ioco** s_2 does not *imply*
   (**hide** V **in** $i_1 \| [V] \| i_2$) **ioco** (**hide** V **in** $s_1 \| [V] \| s_2$)

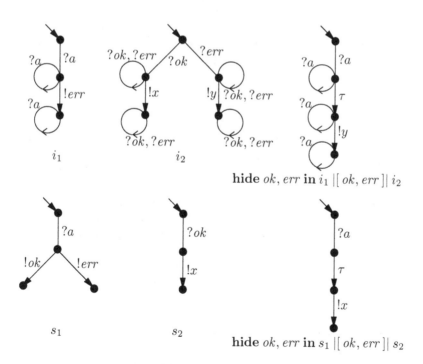

Fig. 10. Compositional testing

2. If s_1, s_2 are input-enabled, i.e., $s_k \in \mathcal{IOTS}(L_{Ik}, L_{Uk})$ for $k = 1, 2$; then
i_1 **ioco** s_1 and i_2 **ioco** s_2 implies that
(**hide** V **in** $i_1 \| [V] \| i_2$) **ioco** (**hide** V **in** $s_1 \| [V] \| s_2$)

Example 13. Consider specifications s_1 and s_2 and implementations i_1 and i_2 in Figure 10. The input set for s_1 and i_1 is $L_{I1} = \{a\}$; the outputs of s_1 and i_1 are equal to the inputs of s_2 and i_2: $L_{U1} = L_{I2} = \{ok, err\}$; the outputs of s_2 and i_2 are $L_{U2} = \{x, y\}$.

Specification s_1 specifies that upon input $?a$ an output $!ok$ or $!err$ shall be produced, which is **ioco**-correctly implemented in i_1. The partial specification s_2 specifies that on input $?ok$ the output $!x$ shall be provided, which i_2 correctly implements; hence, i_1 **ioco** s_1 and i_2 **ioco** s_2. But upon composing i_1 and i_2 the additional behaviour of i_2, viz. providing output $!y$ for input $?err$ that is underspecified in s_2, causes incorrect behaviour with respect to the composition of the specifications: (**hide** ok, err **in** $i_1 \| [ok, err] \| i_2$) **iocо** (**hide** ok, err **in** $s_1 \| [ok, err] \| s_2$).

4.3   Some Bibliographic Notes

The relation **ioco** inherits many ideas from other relations on transition systems defined in the literature. Its roots are in the theory of testing equivalence and preorders [26,27], where the relation testing preorder on transitions systems is defined by explicitly introducing the environment, or tester, and the observations that a tester can make of a system. Some developments, which build on these testing preorders, are of importance for **ioco**. In the first place, there was the introduction of more powerful testers, which can detect not only the occurrence of actions but also the absence of actions, i.e., refusals, in [28], and the addition of a special label θ to observe refusals in [29]. A second development was a testing theory based on testing preorders, where a conformance relation **conf**, and test generation algorithms were defined by restricting all observations of testing preorder testers to those traces that are explicitly contained in the specification [30]. A third development was the application of the principles of testing preorder to Input/Output Automata (IOA) in [31], where it was shown that testing preorder coincides with quiescent trace preorder [32] when requiring that inputs are always enabled. The relation **ioco** inherits from all these developments. The definition of **ioco** follows the principles of testing preorder with tests that can also detect the refusal of actions. Outputs and always enabled inputs are distinguished analogous to IOA, and, moreover, a restriction is made to only the traces of the specification as in **conf**.

Whereas this section first presented **ioco** and then introduced **ioco**$_{\mathcal{F}}$, $\leq_{ior}$, $\leq_{iot}$, and **ioconf** as variants, the historical development, and the way they were presented in [6], were the other way around: it started with $\leq_{iot}$, and then **ioconf**, $\leq_{ior}$, **ioco**, and **ioco**$_{\mathcal{F}}$ followed. Moreover, the original definitions are given as testing relations as in [26,27], and the definitions in this text were propositions in [6].

Another interesting historical event was the development of the testing theory for the tool TVEDA [1], which occurred independently and without reference to an underlying theory of testing equivalence or refusal testing, but only based on intuition and formalization of existing protocol testing practice and experience. This resulted in a relation called R_1 which strongly resembles **ioco**. This may be another indication, apart from all case studies done since then, of the practical relevance of **ioco**.

The relation **uioco**, also called **ioco**$_U$, was the result of studying congruence and compositionality properties for **ioco** in [33]. The anomaly of non-deterministic underspecified traces was also remarked in [7,34].

Most of the complete proofs for **ioco** can be found in [6, technical report version].

5   Testing with Labelled Transition Systems

Now that we have formal specifications, implementations, test cases, and the implementation relation **ioco** expressing correctness, we can start the discussion on testing. We are looking for a test generation algorithm that derives a set of tests from a specification, so that by executing these tests we know, or at least can get an indication, whether an implementation **ioco**-conforms to that specification. For that, we first have to discuss what test execution is, and what it means to pass a test. This is done in Section 5.1. Then the test generation algorithm is given in Section 5.2. Subsequently, Section 5.3 shows that this algorithm has the required correctness properties, that is, the generated test suites detect all and only non-conforming implementations. This means that such a generated test suite can serve as a decision procedure for **ioco**-conformance.

5.1   Test Execution

A test run of a test case $t \in \mathcal{TTS}(L_U, L_I)$ with an implementation under test $i \in \mathcal{IOTS}(L_I, L_U)$ is an experiment where the test case supplies inputs to the implementation, while observing the outputs, and the absence of outputs (quiescence) of the implementation. This might be described as the parallel synchronization $t \parallel i$ (Section 3.2), but this does not take into account the peculiarities of the special labels δ and θ. Hence, we extend $\parallel$ to $\rceil\parallel$ to take into account that θ is used to observe quiescence δ; see Definition 16.1.

A test run $t \rceil\parallel i$ can always continue, i.e., it has no deadlocks. This follows from the construction of a test case; see Definition 10.1: for each state t' of a test case either $init(t') = \{a\} \cup \{L_U\}$ for some $a \in L_I$, or $init(t') = L_U \cup \{\theta\}$. In the former case the action a can always be performed on the implementation since i is input enabled. In the latter case either i produces some output $x \in L_U$, or i is quiescent. In both cases the test run can continue, be it with an infinite sequence of θ actions. Since **pass** and **fail** are sink states a test run can be stopped if one of these is reached. The trace of $t \rceil\parallel i$ to that point identifies the test run; it can be seen as the test log of the test run.

Since an implementation can behave non-deterministically, different test runs of the same test case with the same implementation may lead to different terminal states, and hence to different verdicts. An implementation passes a test case if and only if all possible test runs lead to the verdict **pass**. This means that each test case must be executed several times in order to explore all possible non-deterministic behaviours of the implementation, and, moreover, that a particular fairness must be assumed on implementations, i.e., it is assumed that an implementation by re-execution of a test case shows all its possible non-deterministic behaviours with that test case.

Definition 16. Let $t \in \mathcal{TTS}(L_U, L_I)$ and $i \in \mathcal{IOTS}(L_I, L_U)$.

1. Running a test case t with an implementation i is expressed by the parallel operator $\| : \mathcal{TTS}(L_U, L_I) \times \mathcal{IOTS}(L_I, L_U) \to \mathcal{LTS}(L_I \cup L_U \cup \{\theta\})$ which is defined by the following inference rules:

$$\frac{i \xrightarrow{\tau} i'}{t \| i \xrightarrow{\tau} t \| i'} \qquad \frac{t \xrightarrow{a} t', \ i \xrightarrow{a} i'}{t \| i \xrightarrow{a} t' \| i'} \ a \in L_I \cup L_U \qquad \frac{t \xrightarrow{\theta} t', \ i \xrightarrow{\delta}}{t \| i \xrightarrow{\theta} t' \| i}$$

2. A test run of t with i is a trace of $t \| i$ leading to one of the states **pass** or **fail** of t:

$$\sigma \text{ is a test run of } t \text{ and } i \ \Leftrightarrow_{\text{def}} \ \exists i' : t \| i \xrightarrow{\sigma} \textbf{pass} \| i' \text{ or } t \| i \xrightarrow{\sigma} \textbf{fail} \| i'$$

3. Implementation i passes test case t if all test runs go to the **pass**-state of t:

$$i \textbf{ passes } t \ \Leftrightarrow_{\text{def}} \ \forall \sigma \in L_\theta^*, \ \forall i' : t \| i \xrightarrow{\sigma}\!\!\!\!\!\not\to \textbf{fail} \| i'$$

4. An implementation i passes a test suite T if it passes all test cases in T:

$$i \textbf{ passes } T \ \Leftrightarrow_{\text{def}} \ \forall t \in T : i \textbf{ passes } t$$

If i does not pass the test suite, it fails: $i \textbf{ fails } T \ \Leftrightarrow_{\text{def}} \ \exists t \in T : i \textbf{ passes } t.$

Example 14. Consider the test cases in Figure 7 and the implementations in Figure 4. The only test run of t_1 with k_1 is $t_1 \| k_1 \xrightarrow{?but \cdot !liq \cdot \theta} \textbf{pass} \| k_1'$, so k_1 **passes** t_1.
For t_1 with k_2 there are two test runs:
$t_1 \| k_2 \xrightarrow{?but \cdot !liq \cdot \theta} \textbf{pass} \| k_2'$, and $t_1 \| k_2 \xrightarrow{?but \cdot !choc} \textbf{fail} \| k_2''$, so k_2 **fails** t_1.
Also k_3 **fails** t_1: $t_1 \| k_3 \xrightarrow{?but \cdot !liq \cdot \theta} \textbf{pass} \| k_3'$, but also $t_1 \| k_3 \xrightarrow{?but \cdot \theta} \textbf{fail} \| k_3''$.
When t_2 is applied to k_3 we get:
$t_2 \| k_3 \xrightarrow{?but \cdot !liq \cdot ?but \cdot \theta} \textbf{pass} \| k_3'$, $t_2 \| k_3 \xrightarrow{?but \cdot \theta \cdot ?but \cdot !choc} \textbf{fail} \| k_3''$, so k_3 **fails** t_2.

5.2 Test Generation

Now all ingredients are there to present an algorithm to generate test cases from a labelled transition system specification, which test implementations for **ioco**-correctness. To see how such test cases may be constructed, we consider the definition of **ioco**; see Definition 12. We see that to test for **ioco** we have to check whether $out(\,i \textbf{ after } \sigma\,) \subseteq out(\,s \textbf{ after } \sigma\,)$ for each $\sigma \in traces(s)$. Basically, this can be done by having a test case t that executes σ: $t \| i \xRightarrow{\sigma} t' \| i'$. After this the test case should check whether the produced outputs by i' are allowed by s. This can be done by having transitions from t' to **pass**-states for all allowed outputs – those in $out(\,s \textbf{ after } \sigma\,)$ – and transitions to **fail**-states for all erroneous outputs – those not in $out(\,s \textbf{ after } \sigma\,)$. Special care should be taken for the special output δ: δ models the absence of any output, which matches with the θ-transition in the test case. Consequently, the θ-transition will go the **pass**-state if quiescence is allowed – $\delta \in out(\,s \textbf{ after } \sigma\,)$ – and to the **fail**-state if the specification does not allow quiescence at that point.

All this is reflected in the following test generation algorithm. The algorithm is recursive: the first transition of the test case is derived from the states in which the specification can initially be, after which the remaining part of test case is recursively derived from the specification states reachable from the inital states via this first test case transition. The algorithm is non-deterministic in the sense that in each recursive step it can be continued in many different ways: the test case can be terminated with the test case **pass** (choice 1); the test case can continue with any input allowed by the specification, which can be interrupted by an arriving output (choice 2); or the test case can wait for an output and check it, or conclude that the implementation is quiescent (choice 3). Each choice for continuation results in another, valid test case. Also here the set L_U, i.e., the specification's outputs, contains the inputs of the generated test case, and L_I its outputs.

Algorithm 1. *Let $s \in \mathcal{LTS}(L_I, L_U)$ be a specification, and let S initially be $S = s \textbf{ after } \epsilon$.*

A test case $t \in \mathcal{TTS}(L_U, L_I)$ is obtained from a non-empty set of states S by a finite number of recursive applications of one of the following three non-deterministic choices:

1.

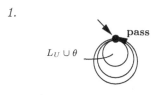

$t := \textbf{pass}$

2.

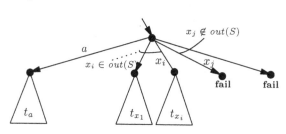

$$t := \quad a \ ; \ t_a$$
$$\Box \ \Sigma \ \{ \ x_j \ ; \ \textbf{fail} \mid x_j \in L_U, \ x_j \notin out(S) \ \}$$
$$\Box \ \Sigma \ \{ \ x_i \ ; \ t_{x_i} \mid x_i \in L_U, \ x_i \in out(S) \ \}$$

where $a \in L_I$ *such that* S **after** $a \neq \emptyset$, t_a *is obtained by recursively applying the algorithm for the set of states* S **after** a, *and for each* $x_i \in out(S)$, t_{x_i} *is obtained by recursively applying the algorithm for the set of states* S **after** x_i.

3.

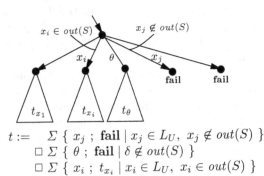

$$t := \quad \Sigma \ \{ \ x_j \ ; \ \textbf{fail} \mid x_j \in L_U, \ x_j \notin out(S) \ \}$$
$$\Box \ \Sigma \ \{ \ \theta \ ; \ \textbf{fail} \mid \delta \notin out(S) \ \}$$
$$\Box \ \Sigma \ \{ \ x_i \ ; \ t_{x_i} \mid x_i \in L_U, \ x_i \in out(S) \ \}$$
$$\Box \ \Sigma \ \{ \ \theta \ ; \ t_\theta \mid \delta \in out(S) \ \}$$

where for each $x_i \in out(S)$, t_{x_i} *is obtained by recursively applying the algorithm for the set of states* S **after** x_i, *and* t_θ *is obtained by recursively applying the algorithm for the set of states* S **after** δ.

Algorithm 1 generates a test case from a set of states S. This set represents the set of all possible states in which the specification can be at the given stage of the test case generation. Initially, this is the set s **after** $\epsilon = q_0$ **after** ϵ, where q_0 is the initial state of s. Then the test case is built step by step. In each step there are three ways to make a test case:

1. The first choice is the single-state test case **pass**, which is always a sound test case. It stops the recursion in the algorithm, and thus terminates the test case.
2. In the second choice test case t attempts to supply input a to the implementation, and subsequently behaves as test case t_a. Test case t_a is obtained by recursive application of the algorithm with the set S **after** a, which is the set of specification states that can be reached via an a-transition from some current state in S. Moreover, t is prepared to accept any output of the implementation (not quiescence) that might occur before a is supplied. Analogous to t_a, each t_{x_i} is obtained from S **after** x_i.
3. The third choice consists of checking the next output of the implementation. In this case the test case does not attempt to supply an input; it waits until an output arrives, and if no output arrives it observes quiescence. If the response, whether a real output or quiescence, is not allowed, i.e., $x_j \notin out(S)$, the test case terminates with **fail**. If the response is allowed the algorithm continues with recursively generating a test case from the set of states S **after** x_i.

Example 15. Test case t_1 of Figure 7 can be obtained from specification p in Figure 2 using Algorithm 1:

1. Initially, $S = p$ **after** $\epsilon = \{p_0\}$.
2. Choice 2 is made, i.e., we try to give an input to the implementation. The only input with S **after** $a \neq \emptyset$ is $?but$, so $t_1 := ?but; t_1^2 \ \square \ !liq; \textbf{fail} \ \square \ !choc; \textbf{fail}$.
3. To obtain t_1^2, the next output of the implementation is checked (choice 3): $t_1^2 := !liq; t_1^3 \ \square \ !choc; \textbf{fail} \ \square \ \theta; \textbf{fail}$.
4. For t_1^3 the output is checked again (choice 3), where now the only allowed response is quiescence: $t_1^3 := !liq; \textbf{fail} \ \square \ !choc; \textbf{fail} \ \square \ \theta; t_1^4$.
5. For t_1^4 we stop (choice 1): $t_1^4 := \textbf{pass}$.

After putting all pieces together, we obtain t_1 of Figure 7 as a test case for p.

Example 16. Test case t_2 of Figure 7 can be generated from v in Figure 2:

1. Initially, $S = v$ **after** $\epsilon = \{v_0\}$.
2. In the first step input $?but$ is tried: $t_2 := ?but; t_2^2 \ \square \ !liq; \textbf{fail} \ \square \ !choc; \textbf{fail}$, after which $S = \{v_0\}$ **after** $?but = \{v_0, v_1\}$.
3. The allowed outputs are checked: $out(S) = out(\{v_0, v_1\}) = \{!liq, \delta\}$. This leads to the test case $t_2^2 := !liq; t_2^3 \ \square \ !choc; \textbf{fail} \ \square \ \theta; t_2^4$.
4. For t_2^3 we continue with $S = \{v_0, v_1\}$ **after** $!liq = \{v_0\}$. Another input $?but$ is tried: $t_2^3 := ?but; t_2^5 \ \square \ !liq; \textbf{fail} \ \square \ !choc; \textbf{fail}$.
5. Then the output is checked again, which may be $!liq$ or δ: $t_2^5 := !liq; t_2^6 \ \square \ !choc; \textbf{fail} \ \square \ \theta; t_2^7$.
6. The test case is stopped: $t_2^6 := \textbf{pass}$ and $t_2^7 := \textbf{pass}$.
7. Further with t_2^4: this is the test case after quiescence has been observed; t_2^4 is generated from $S = \{v_0, v_1\}$ **after** $\delta = \{v_0\}$. From $\{v_0\}$ another input $?but$ can be supplied: $t_2^4 := ?but; t_2^8 \ \square \ !liq; \textbf{fail} \ \square \ !choc; \textbf{fail}$.
8. Analogous to t_2^5 the output is checked: $t_2^8 := !liq; t_2^9 \ \square \ !choc; \textbf{fail} \ \square \ \theta; t_2^{10}$.
9. After this the test case is stopped: $t_2^9 := \textbf{pass}$ and $t_2^{10} := \textbf{pass}$.

When concatenating these pieces the test case t_2 of Figure 7 is obtained. It is clear that this is only one test case which can be generated. Infinitely many different test cases can be generated from specification v by considering longer and longer test cases.

5.3   Completeness of Test Generation

Now all ingredients are there to present the main result of the **ioco** test theory, viz. that the test cases generated with Algorithm 1 can detect all, and only all, non-**ioco** correct implementations. Before giving this completeness result we first formally define what completeness is in the context of **ioco** testing. Moreover, a complete test suite is usually infinitely large, and not executable in a practical situation, as is shown, for instance, for the system v in Example 16. Consequently, a distinction is made between test suites which detect only errors – but possibly not all of them – and test suites which detect all errors – and possibly more. The former are called sound, and the latter exhaustive; see also Section 2.

Definition 17. *Let s be a specification and T a test suite; then for* **ioco***:*

$$T \text{ is complete } \Leftrightarrow_{\text{def}} \forall i \in \mathcal{IOTS}(L_I, L_U): \quad i \text{ ioco } s \qquad \text{iff} \qquad i \text{ passes } T$$
$$T \text{ is sound } \Leftrightarrow_{\text{def}} \forall i \in \mathcal{IOTS}(L_I, L_U): \quad i \text{ ioco } s \text{ implies } i \text{ passes } T$$
$$T \text{ is exhaustive } \Leftrightarrow_{\text{def}} \forall i \in \mathcal{IOTS}(L_I, L_U): \quad i \text{ ioco } s \qquad \text{if} \qquad i \text{ passes } T$$

Theorem 2.1 expresses that all tests generated with the algorithm are sound, i.e., give the result **fail** only if the implementation is not **ioco**-correct. Theorem 2.2 states that all possible test cases together form an exhaustive (and thus complete) test suite, which means that for any **ioco**-incorrect implementation there is, in principle, a test case generated with Algorithm 1, that can detect that incorrect implementation.

Theorem 2. *Let $s \in \mathcal{LTS}(L_I, L_U)$ be a specification, and let T_s be the set of all test cases that can be generated from s with algorithm 1; let gen $: \mathcal{LTS}(L_I, L_U) \to \mathcal{P}(\mathcal{TTS}(L_U, L_I))$ be a test derivation function satisfying $gen(s) \subseteq T_s$; then:*

1. *$gen(s)$ is sound for s with respect to* **ioco***;*
2. *T_s is exhaustive for s with respect to* **ioco***.*

Exhaustiveness is more a theoretical result than a practical one. Theoretically, it implies that any non-conforming implementation can be detected, i.e., that there are no errors that can never be detected. From a practical perspective, an exhaustive test suite, except for the most trivial systems such as p in Figure 2, will contain infinitely many test cases, and thus can never be executed in finite time. The question of which test cases to generate and execute from the infinitely large exhaustive test suite is referred to as *test selection*. Such a selection of test cases should minimize the test costs, e.g., in terms of the necessary test execution time, while maximizing the probability of detecting errors. Test selection is an important yet difficult topic, but it is not further discussed here.

Example 17. In Example 15 test case t_1 of Figure 7 was generated from specification p in Figure 2. Indeed, we had in Example 10: k_1 **ioco** p, k_2 **io̸co** p, and k_3 **io̸co** p, which is consistent with the test execution results from Example 14: k_1 **passes** t_1, k_2 **fails** t_1, and k_3 **fails** t_1.

5.4   Bibliographic Notes

In the original definition of test cases, and in the original test generation algorithm, test cases were not input enabled [6]. This resulted in a paradox where environments are assumed to be input enabled for the outputs of the system, but test cases, being particular environments, are not. It also meant that test cases could prevent the system from performing an output. Inspired by timed test generation algorithms [23], and by [7], test cases were redefined to be input enabled.

The issue of test selection is studied in many papers, e.g., by using test purposes [2,35], by using metrics [36,37], by defining an integral over the space of implementations [38], by approximate analysis [39], by coverage analysis [40], and many others.

An annotated bibliography of testing transition systems can be found in [41].

6   Concluding Remarks

This contribution has presented a model based testing theory for labelled transition systems. Labelled transition systems were introduced as models for specifications, implementations, and tests, and a process language for representing complex transition systems was given. An important point of the theory is the definition of formal correctness between a specification and an implementation. This was done with the implementation relation **ioco**. Some variants of **ioco** were briefly discussed, and in particular the notion of partial specification has been elaborated. A test generation algorithm was given, and it was proved to be complete, i.e., to generate test suites which can exactly test for **ioco** conformance.

Although the emphasis in this contribution was on the theory of model based testing, such theory is only useful if it is supported by model based test tools, in particular test generation tools. Although the principles of the test generation algorithm are not very complex, the application to any realistically sized transition system specification is far beyond what is manually feasible. And, of course, by trying to do it manually, one of the great benefits of model based testing, viz. the automatic generation of large quantities of large tests, would be lost. Prototype tools implementing this test theory exist, e.g., TVEDA [1], TGV [2], THE AGEDIS TOOL SET [3], TESTGEN [4], and TORX [5], and also quite a number of case studies have been performed with these tools, see, e.g., [42,43,44,45].

One of the most important open issues in this model based testing theory is the question of test selection. Since exhaustive testing of any realistic system is not an option, an important question is which test cases should be generated and executed, and why one test suite is better than another one. The tools mentioned above use different approaches, from completely random as in TORX, to a manual approach where a user has to provide *test purposes* to steer the selection process. Other approaches are defining some measures of coverage, e.g., using heuristics for coverage of transition systems such as traversing every state at least once, heuristic measures from classical software testing such as equivalence partitioning or boundary value analysis, explicitly defining fault models, or assuming some test hypothesis for the implementation under test. Related to the question of test selection is the issue of how the completeness, coverage, or quality of an automatically generated test suite can be expressed, measured, and, ultimately, controlled. Even more intriguing is the question how a measure of test suite quality can be related to a measure of product quality. After all, product quality is the ultimate reason to make efforts to do testing.

References

1. Phalippou, M.: Relations d'Implantation et Hypothèses de Test sur des Automates à Entrées et Sorties. PhD thesis, L'Université de Bordeaux I, France (1994)
2. Jard, C., Jéron, T.: TGV: Theory, Principles and Algorithms: A Tool for the Automatic Synthesis of Conformance Test Cases for Non-Deterministic Reactive Systems. Software Tools for Technology Transfer 7(4), 297–315 (2005)

36   J. Tretmans

3. Hartman, A., Nagin, K.: The AGEDIS Tools for Model Based Testing. In: Int. Symposium on Software Testing and Analysis – ISSTA 2004, pp. 129–132. ACM Press, New York (2004)
4. He, J., Turner, K.: Protocol-Inspired Hardware Testing. In: Csopaki, G., Dibuz, S., Tarnay, K. (eds.) Int. Workshop on Testing of Communicating Systems 12, pp. 131–147. Kluwer Academic Publishers, Dordrecht (1999)
5. Tretmans, J., Brinksma, E.: TorX: Automated Model Based Testing. In: Hartman, A., Dussa-Zieger, K. (eds.) First European Conference on Model-Driven Software Engineering, Imbuss, Möhrendorf, Germany, p. 13 (2003)
6. Tretmans, J.: Test generation with inputs, outputs and repetitive quiescence. Software—Concepts and Tools 17(3), 103–120 Also: Technical Report No. 96-26, Centre for Telematics and Information Technology, University of Twente, The Netherlands (1996)
7. Petrenko, A., Yevtushenko, N., Huo, J.L.: Testing Transition Systems with Input and Output Testers. In: Hogrefe, D., Wiles, A. (eds.) TestCom 2003. LNCS, vol. 2644, Springer, Heidelberg (2003)
8. Brinksma, E., Alderden, R., Langerak, R., Lagemaat, J.v.d., Tretmans, J.: A formal approach to conformance testing. In: de Meer, J., Mackert, L., Effelsberg, W. (eds.) Second Int.Workshop on Protocol Test Systems, pp. 349–363. North-Holland, Amsterdam (1990)
9. Tretmans, J.: Testing Concurrent Systems: A Formal Approach. In: Baeten, J.C.M., Mauw, S. (eds.) CONCUR 1999. LNCS, vol. 1664, pp. 46–65. Springer, Heidelberg (1999)
10. Bernot, G., Gaudel, M.G., Marre, B.: Software testing based on formal specifications: a theory and a tool. Software Engineering Journal, 387–405 (November 1991)
11. Gaudel, M.C.: Testing can be formal, too. In: Mosses, P.D., Schwartzbach, M.I., Nielsen, M. (eds.) CAAP 1995, FASE 1995, and TAPSOFT 1995. LNCS, vol. 915, pp. 82–96. Springer, Heidelberg (1995)
12. ISO/IEC JTC1/SC21 WG7, ITU-T SG 10/Q.8: Information Retrieval, Transfer and Management for OSI – Framework: Formal Methods in Conformance Testing. Committee Draft CD 13245-1, Proposed ITU-T Recommendation Z.500. ISO – ITU-T, Geneve (1997)
13. Petrenko, A.: Fault Model-Driven Test Derivation from Finite State Models: Annotated Bibliography. In: Cassez, F., Jard, C., Rozoy, B., Dermot, M. (eds.) MOVEP 2000. LNCS, vol. 2067, pp. 196–205. Springer, Heidelberg (2001)
14. Campbell, C., W., G., Nachmanson, L., Schulte, W., Tillmann, N., Veanes, M.: Model-Based Testing of Object-Oriented Reactive Systems with Spec Explorer. Technical Report MSR-TR-2005-59, Microsoft Research, Redmond, USA (2005)
15. Koopman, P., Alimarine, A., Tretmans, J., Plasmeijer, R.: Gast: Generic Automated Software Testing. In: Peña, R., Arts, T. (eds.) IFL 2002. LNCS, vol. 2670, pp. 84–100. Springer, Heidelberg (2003)
16. Milner, R.: Communication and Concurrency. Prentice-Hall, Englewood Cliffs (1989)
17. Bolognesi, T., Brinksma, E.: Introduction to the ISO specification language LOTOS. Computer Networks and ISDN Systems 14, 25–59 (1987)
18. ISO: Information Processing Systems, Open Systems Interconnection, LOTOS - A Formal Description Technique Based on the Temporal Ordering of Observational Behaviour. International Standard IS-8807. ISO, Geneve (1989)

19. Lynch, N., Tuttle, M.: An introduction to Input/Output Automata. CWI Quarterly 2(3) (1989) 219–246 Also: Technical Report MIT/LCS/TM-373 (TM-351 revised), Massachusetts Institute of Technology, Cambridge, U.S.A. (1988)
20. Heerink, L.: Ins and Outs in Refusal Testing. PhD thesis, University of Twente, Enschede, The Netherlands (1998)
21. Krichen, M., Tripakis, S.: Black-Box Conformance Testing for Real-Time Systems. In: Graf, S., Mounier, L. (eds.) SPIN 2004. LNCS, vol. 2989, Springer, Heidelberg (2004)
22. Larsen, K., Mikucionis, M., Nielsen, B.: Online Testing of Real-Time Systems using Uppaal. In: Grabowski, J., Nielsen, B. (eds.) FATES 2004. LNCS, vol. 3395, pp. 79–94. Springer, Heidelberg (2005)
23. Brandán Briones, L., Brinksma, E.: A Test Generation Framework for quiescent Real-Time Systems. In: Grabowski, J., Nielsen, B. (eds.) FATES 2004. LNCS, vol. 3395, pp. 64–78. Springer, Heidelberg (2005)
24. Bijl, M.v.d., Rensink, A., Tretmans, J.: Action Refinement in Conformance Testing. In: Khendek, F., Dssouli, R. (eds.) TestCom 2005. LNCS, vol. 3502, pp. 81–96. Springer, Heidelberg (2005)
25. Frantzen, L., Tretmans, J., Willemse, T.: Test Generation Based on Symbolic Specifications. In: Grabowski, J., Nielsen, B. (eds.) FATES 2004. LNCS, vol. 3395, pp. 1–15. Springer, Heidelberg (2005)
26. De Nicola, R., Hennessy, M.: Testing Equivalences for Processes. Theoretical Computer Science 34, 83–133 (1984)
27. De Nicola, R.: Extensional Equivalences for Transition Systems. Acta Informatica 24, 211–237 (1987)
28. Phillips, I.: Refusal testing. Theoretical Computer Science 50(2), 241–284 (1987)
29. Langerak, R.: A testing theory for LOTOS using deadlock detection. In: Brinksma, E., Scollo, G., Vissers, C.A. (eds.) Protocol Specification, Testing, and Verification IX, pp. 87–98. North-Holland, Amsterdam (1990)
30. Brinksma, E., Scollo, G., Steenbergen, C.: LOTOS specifications, their implementations and their tests. In: Bochmann, G.v., Sarikaya, B. (eds.) Protocol Specification, Testing, and Verification VI, pp. 349–360. North-Holland, Amsterdam (1987)
31. Segala, R.: Quiescence, fairness, testing, and the notion of implementation. In: Best, E. (ed.) CONCUR 1993. LNCS, vol. 715, pp. 324–338. Springer, Heidelberg (1993)
32. Vaandrager, F.: On the relationship between process algebra and Input/Output Automata. In: Logic in Computer Science, Sixth Annual IEEE Symposium, pp. 387–398. IEEE Computer Society Press, Los Alamitos (1991)
33. Bijl, M.v.d., Rensink, A., Tretmans, J.: Compositional Testing with IOCO. In: Petrenko, A., Ulrich, A. (eds.) FATES 2003. LNCS, vol. 2931, pp. 86–100. Springer, Heidelberg (2004)
34. Huo, J.L., Petrenko, A.: On Testing Partially Specified IOTS through Lossless Queues. In: Groz, R., Hierons, R.M. (eds.) TestCom 2004. LNCS, vol. 2978, pp. 2004–2016. Springer, Heidelberg (2004)
35. Vries, R.d., Tretmans, J.: Towards Formal Test Purposes. In: Brinksma, E., Tretmans, J., eds.: Formal Approaches to Testing of Software – FATES, Number NS-01-4 in BRICS Notes Series, University of Aarhus, Denmark, BRICS, pp. 61–76 (2001)
36. Curgus, J., Vuong, S.: Sensitivity analysis of the metric based test selection. In: Kim, M., Kang, S., Hong, K. (eds.) Int.Workshop on Testing of Communicating Systems 10, pp. 200–219. Chapman & Hall, Boca Raton (1997)

37. Feijs, L., Goga, N., Mauw, S., Tretmans, J.: Test Selection, Trace Distance and Heuristics. In: Schieferdecker, I., König, H., Wolisz, A. (eds.) Testing of Communicating Systems XIV, pp. 267–282. Kluwer Academic Publishers, Dordrecht (2002)

38. Brinksma, E.: On the coverage of partial validations. In: Nivat, M., Rattray, C., Rus, T., Scollo, G. (eds.) AMAST 1993. BCS-FACS Workshops in Computing Series, pp. 247–254. Springer, Heidelberg (1993)

39. Jeannet, B., Jéron, T., Rusu, V., Zinovieva, E.: Symbolic Test Selection based on Approximate Analysis. In: Halbwachs, N., Zuck, L.D. (eds.) TACAS 2005. LNCS, vol. 3440, Springer, Heidelberg (2005)

40. Groz, R., Charles, O., Renévot, J.: Relating Conformance Test Coverage to Formal Specifications. In: Gotzhein, R. (ed.) FORTE 1996, Chapman & Hall, Boca Raton (1996)

41. Brinksma, E., Tretmans, J.: Testing Transition Systems: An Annotated Bibliography. In: Cassez, F., Jard, C., Rozoy, B., Dermot, M. (eds.) MOVEP 2000. LNCS, vol. 2067, pp. 187–195. Springer, Heidelberg (2001)

42. Groz, R., Risser, N.: Eight Years of Experience in Test Generation from FDTs using TVEDA. In: Mizuno, T., Shiratori, N., Higashino, T., Togashi, A. (eds.) Formal Desciption Techniques and Protocol Specification, Testing and Verification FORTE X /PSTV XVII 1997, Chapman & Hall, Boca Raton (1997)

43. Clarke, D., Jéron, T., Rusu, V., Zinovieva, E.: Automated Test and Oracle Generation for Smart-Card Applications. In: Attali, S., Jensen, T. (eds.) E-smart 2001. LNCS, vol. 2140, pp. 58–70. Springer, Heidelberg (2001)

44. Sardis, I.C., Heuillard, M.,, T.: AGEDIS Case Studies: Model-Based Testing in Industry. In: Hartman, A., Dussa-Zieger, K. (eds.) First European Conference on Model-Driven Software Engineering, Imbuss, Möhrendorf, Germany (2003)

45. Vries, R.d., Belinfante, A., Feenstra, J.: Automated Testing in Practice: The Highway Tolling System. In: Schieferdecker, I., König, H., Wolisz, A. (eds.) Testing of Communicating Systems XIV, pp. 219–234. Kluwer Academic Publishers, Dordrecht (2002)

Model-Based Testing of Object-Oriented Reactive Systems with Spec Explorer

Margus Veanes, Colin Campbell, Wolfgang Grieskamp, Wolfram Schulte,
Nikolai Tillmann, and Lev Nachmanson

Microsoft Research, Redmond, WA, USA
{margus,wrwg,schulte,nikolait,levnach}@microsoft.com,
colin@modeled-computation.com

Abstract. Testing is one of the costliest aspects of commercial software development. Model-based testing is a promising approach addressing these deficits. At Microsoft, model-based testing technology developed by the Foundations of Software Engineering group in Microsoft Research has been used since 2003. The second generation of this tool set, Spec Explorer, deployed in 2004, is now used on a daily basis by Microsoft product groups for testing operating system components, .NET framework components and other areas. This chapter provides a comprehensive survey of the concepts of the tool and their foundations.

1 Introduction

Testing is one of the costliest aspects of commercial software development. Not only laborious and expensive, it also often lacks systematic engineering methodology, clear semantics and adequate tool support.

Model-based testing is one of the most promising approaches for addressing these deficits. At Microsoft, model-based testing technology developed by the Foundations of Software Engineering group in Microsoft Research has been used internally since 2003 [19,6]. The second generation of this tool set, Spec Explorer [1], deployed in 2004, is now used on a daily basis by Microsoft product groups for testing operating system components, .NET framework components and other areas. While we can refer the reader to papers [21,30,13,12,36] that describe some aspects of Spec Explorer, this chapter provides a comprehensive survey of the tool and its foundations.

Spec Explorer is a tool for testing reactive, object-oriented software systems. The inputs and outputs of such systems can be abstractly viewed as parameterized action labels, that is, as invocations of methods with dynamically created object instances and other complex data structures as parameters and return values. Thus, inputs and outputs are more than just atomic data-type values, like integers. From the tester's perspective, the system under test is controlled by invoking methods on objects and other runtime values and monitored by observing invocations of other methods. This is similar to the "invocation and call back" and "event processing" metaphors familiar to most programmers. The outputs of reactive systems may be unsolicited, for example, as in the case of event notifications.

Reactive systems are inherently nondeterministic. No single agent (component, thread, network node, etc.) controls all state transitions. Network delay, thread scheduling

R.M. Hierons et al. (Eds.): Formal Methods and Testing, LNCS 4949, pp. 39–76, 2008.
© Springer-Verlag Berlin Heidelberg 2008

and other external factors can influence the system's behaviour. In addition, a system's specification may leave some choices open for the implementer. In these cases, the freedom given to the implementer may be interpreted as nondeterminism, even if a given version of the system does not exploit the full range of permitted behaviour. Spec Explorer handles nondeterminism by distinguishing between *controllable* actions invoked by the tester and *observable* actions that are outside of the tester's control.

Reactive systems may be "large" in terms of the number of possible actions they support and the number of runtime states they entail. They can even have an unbounded number of states, for example, when dynamically instantiated objects are involved. Spec Explorer handles infinite states spaces by separating the description of the *model* state space which may be infinite and finitizations provided by *user scenarios* and *test cases*.

The following sections provide a detailed overview of Spec Explorer foundations.

Section 2 introduces the methodology used by Spec Explorer with a small example, a distributed chat server. The system's behaviour is described by a *model program* written in the language Spec# [2], an extension of C#. A model program defines the state variables and update rules of an *abstract state machine* [23]. The states of the machine are first-order structures that capture a snapshot of variable values in each step. The machine's steps (i.e., the transitions between states) are invocations of the model program's methods that satisfy the given state-based *preconditions*. The tool *explores* the machine's states and transitions with techniques similar to those of explicit state model checkers. This process results in a finite graph that is a representative subset of model states and transitions. Spec Explorer provides powerful means for visualizing the results of exploration. Finally, Spec Explorer produces test cases for the explored behaviour that may be run against the system under test to check the consistency of actual and predicted behaviour.

Subsequent sections give a more in-depth look at the semantic foundations of Spec Explorer. In Section 3, we introduce *model automata*, an extension of interface automata over states that are first-order structures. The basic conformance notion, *alternating simulation* [4,15], is derived from interface automata. Model automata also include the concept of *accepting states* familiar in formal languages, which characterize those states in which a test run is conclusive. Model automata include states and transitions, but they extend traditional model-based testing by admitting open systems whose transitions are not just a subset of the specification's transitions and by treating states as first-order structures of mathematical logic.

Section 4 gives techniques for *scenario control*, in cases where the model describes a larger state space than the tester wants to cover. Scenario control is achieved by *method restriction*, *state filtering*, *state grouping* and *directed search*. This section also introduces the exploration algorithm.

Section 5 describes our techniques for test generation. Traditionally, test generation and test execution are seen as two independent phases, where the first generates an artefact, called the *test suite*, that is then interpreted by the second phase, test execution. We call this traditional case *offline testing*. However, test generation and test execution can be also folded in one process, where the immediate result of test execution is used to prune the generation process. This we call *online testing* (also called "on-the-fly" testing in the literature). Online testing is particularly useful for reactive systems with large state spaces where deriving an exhaustive test suite is not feasible. In the testing framework presented here, both the online case and the offline case are viewed as special cases of the same general testing process. In the offline case the input to the test execution engine (discussed in Section 6) is a test suite in form of a model automaton of a particular form. In the online case the input to the test execution engine is a dynamic unfolding of the model program itself, i.e. the test suite has not been explicitly precomputed.

Section 6 discusses the conformance relation (alternating refinement) that is used during both online and offline testing. We address the problem of harnessing a distributed system with an observationally complete "wrapper" and of creating bindings between abstract entities (such as object identities) found in the model and the system under test.

The chapter closes with a survey of related work in Section 7 and a discussion of open problems in Section 8.

Users perspective. The focus of this chapter is on the foundations of the tool. The main functionality of Spec Explorer from *users perspective* is to provide an integrated tool environment to develop models, to explore and validate models, to generate tests from models, and to execute tests against an implementation under test. The authoring of models can be done in MS Word that is integrated into Spec Explorer, or in a plain text editor. Spec Explorer supports both AsmL and Spec# as modelling languages. Several examples of how modelling can be done in either of those languages is provided in the installation kit [1]. A central part of the functionality of Spec Explorer is to visualize finite state machines generated from models as graphs. This is a very effective way to validate models and to understand their behaviour, prior to test case generation. Generated test cases can either be saved as programs in C# or VB (Visual Basic), and executed later, or generated tests can also be directly executed against an implementation under test. The tool provides a way to bind actions in the model to methods in the implementation. A project file is used where most of the settings that the user chooses during a session of the tool are saved. Internally, the tool has a service oriented architecture that allows more sophisticated users to extend the tool in various ways. Most of the services provide a programmatic access to the data structures used internally and the various algorithms used for test case generation. The best way to get a more comprehensive user experience for what Spec Explorer is all about, is to install it and to try it out.

2   A Sample: Chat

To illustrate the basic concepts and the methodology of Spec Explorer, we look at a simple example: a distributed chat system. We will also refer back to this sample to illustrate points made in later sections.

The chat system is a distributed, reactive system with an arbitrary number of clients. Each client may post text messages that will be delivered by the system to all other clients that have entered the chat session. The system delivers pending messages in FIFO order with local consistency. In other words, a client always receives messages from any given sender in the order sent. However, if there are multiple senders, the messages may be interleaved arbitrarily.

```
class Client {
  bool entered;
  Map<Client,Seq<string>> unreceivedMsgs;

  [Action] Client() {
    this.unreceivedMsgs = Map;
    foreach (Client c in enumof(Client), c != this){
      c.unreceivedMsgs[this] = Seq{};
      this.unreceivedMsgs[c] = Seq{};
    }
    entered = false;
  }

  [Action] void Enter()
    requires !entered; {
    entered = true;
  }

  [Action] void Send(string message)
    requires entered; {
    foreach (Client c in enumof(Client), c != this, c.entered)
      c.unreceivedMsgs[this] += Seq{message};
  }

  [Action(Kind=ActionAttributeKind.Observable)]
  void Receive(Client sender, string message)
    requires sender != this &&
             unreceivedMsgs[sender].Length > 0 &&
             unreceivedMsgs[sender].Head == message; {
    unreceivedMsgs[sender] = unreceivedMsgs[sender].Tail;
  }
}
```

Fig. 1. Model program written in Spec# specifying the possible behavior of a chat system. The Map and Seq data types are special high-level value types of Spec# that provide convenient notations like display and comprehensions (Seq{} denotes the empty sequence). The Action attribute indicates that a method is an action of the abstract state machine given by the model program. The **enumof**(T) form denotes the set of instances of type T that exist in the current state. The **requires** keyword introduces a method precondition.

Figure 1 shows the Spec# model of the chat system. The model consists of a class that represents the abstract state and operations of a client of a chat session. Each instance of the class will contain two variables. The variable entered records whether the client instance has entered the session. A mapping unreceivedMsgs maintains separate queues for messages that have been sent by other clients but not yet received by this client. Messages in the queues are "in flight". Note that the model program is not an example implementation. No client instance of an implementation could be expected to maintain queues of messages it has not yet received! Not surprisingly, modelling the expected behaviour of a distributed system is easier than implementing it.

We model four actions:

- The Client constructor creates an instance of a new client. The state of the system after the constructor has been invoked will include empty message queues between the new client and all previously created client instances. These queues can be thought of as virtual one-way "channels" between each pair of client instances. There will $n(n-1)$ queues in the system overall if there are n clients.
- The Enter action advances the client into a state where it has entered the chat session. A Boolean-valued flag is enough to record this change of state.
- The Send action appends a new message to the queues of unreceived messages in all other clients which have entered the session.
- The Receive method extracts a message sent from a given sender from the sender's queue in the client.

Typically the terms "input" and "output" are used either relative to the model or relative to the system. To avoid possible confusion, we use the following terminology: The Send *action* is said to be *controllable* because it can be invoked by a user to provide system input. The Receive action is *observable*; it is an output message from the system.

For a model like in Figure 1, Spec Explorer extracts a representative behaviour according to user-defined parameters for scenario control. To do this Spec Explorer uses a state exploration algorithm that informally works as follows:

1. in a given model state (starting with the initial state) determine those invocations — action/parameter combinations — which are *enabled* by their preconditions in that state;
2. compute successor states for each invocation;
3. repeat until there are no more states and invocations to explore.

The parameters used for the invocations are provided by parameter generators which are state dependent; if in a given state the parameter set is empty, the action will not be considered. Default generators are selected automatically (for example, for objects the default parameter generator delivers the **enumof**(T) collection). Enabledness is determined by the precondition of the method. Besides of the choice of parameters, the exploration can be pruned by various other scenario control techniques (see Section 4).

Figure 2 shows a scenario extracted from the chat model as a model automaton (cf. Section 3). State filters restrict the number of clients and avoid the case where the same message is sent twice by a client. The message parameter of the Send method is restricted to the value "hi". Additional method restrictions avoid sending any messages before both the two clients have been created and entered the session (cf. Section 4 for a discussion of scenario control).

The nodes of the graph in Figure 2 represent distinct states of the system as a whole. The arcs are transitions that change the system state. Each state in the graph is either *passive* or *active*. Ovals represent active states where a client may give the system new work to do. Diamonds represent passive states where the client may wait for an action from the system or transition into an active state after a state-dependent timeout occurs.

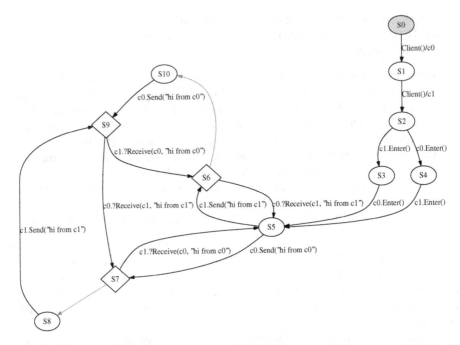

Fig. 2. A model automaton of a scenario, extracted from the chat model program and visualized by Spec Explorer, with two clients (c0 and c1) and a fixed message send by each client ("hi from ..."). The initial state is shown in grey. Actions labels prefixed by "?" indicate observable actions. Labels without prefix indicate controllable actions. Active states (where no observable actions are expected) are shown as ovals. Passive states (where the tester may observe system actions) are shown as diamonds. The unlabeled transitions represent an internal transition ("timeout") from passive to active.

We say that a model and an implementation under test (IUT) *conform* if the following conditions are met: The IUT must be able to perform all transitions outgoing from an active state. The IUT must produce no transitions other than those outgoing from a passive state. Every test must terminate in an accepting state. In other words, these conditions mean that the system being tested must accept all inputs provided by the tester and only produce outputs that are expected by the tester. Further, to prevent unresponsive systems from passing the test, tests must end in an expected final state.

Note that in some passive states there is a race between what the tester may do and what the system may do. The timeout transition, here represented by a transition with no label, indicates that an internal transition from a passive state to an active state occurred without observing output from the system. In other words, nothing was observed in the time the tester was willing to wait (cf. Section 5).

The scenario shown in Figure 2 does not yet reveal the chat system's desired property of local consistency, i.e., preserving the ordering of messages from one client. For that scenario we need at least three clients, where one of them posts at least two messages. In this case we should observe that the ordering of the two messages is preserved from the receiver's point of view, regardless of any interleaving with other messages. Figure 3

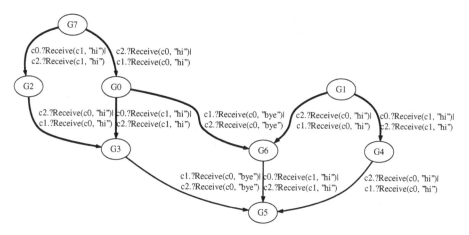

Fig. 3. A *projection* on a model automaton extracted and visualized by Spec Explorer for a scenario with three clients, where client c0 sends two messages ("hi" and "bye") in order, client c1 sends one message ("hi"), and client c2 does not send any message. The projection groups states equivalent under a user defined grouping function into one node, and in the visualization merges arcs between these nodes. In this case, the range of the grouping function is a mapping of clients to the sequences of messages which have been sent by that client but not yet received by *all* the other clients. This visualization also hides all transitions with actions different from Receive, and hides loops on grouped states.

illustrates local consistency. The full model automaton underlying this view has too many transitions to be amenable for depiction in this context. However, the projected view (where some states are grouped together) shows that there is no path where the "bye" message of client c0 is received before the "hi" message of the same client.

The actual conformance testing of an implementation based on model automata as described above happens either *offline* or *online* ("on-the-fly") in Spec Explorer. For offline testing, the model automaton is reduced to an automaton that represents a test suite and can then be compiled to a stand-alone program. The resulting program encodes the complete oracle as provided by the model. For online testing, model exploration and conformance testing are merged into one algorithm. If the system-under-test is a non-distributed .NET program, then all test harnessing will be provided automatically by the tool. In other cases, the user has to write a wrapper in a .NET language which encapsulates the actual implementation, using .NET's interoperability features. This technique has been used to test a very wide variety of systems, including distributed systems and components that run in the operating system kernel.

We describe the foundations of modelling and testing techniques that have been developed at Microsoft Research specifically for dealing with large, reactive and distributed systems. We place these techniques in the context of *Spec Explorer* , a model-based testing tool we have developed that is in daily use in the production cycle at Microsoft Corporation.

We start by giving an overview in this section of the basic approach, and then provide complete definitions in individual sections.

Transition systems formalize conformance testing. The term *model-based testing* refers to any kind of testing based on transition systems. However, this encompasses a broad category of techniques.

Labeled Transition Systems (LTSs) are a practical and theoretically sound way to test the evolution of semi-independent state spaces. There is a well developed body of testing literature (called *"ioco"* theory – input-output conformance) [35,11,33] based on LTSs. This approach checks for *conformance* by checking that traces of observed system transitions are included in the set of all possible traces of a *specification*.

Interface automata [16] are an extension to LTSs that addresses the issue of open systems. They do this by making a distinction between input transitions and output transitions (a distinction not seen in LTSs). Although interface automata were developed for hardware verification applications, we have found that they are a useful abstraction for testing as well [38]. In some states, input is enabled, and the tester can drive the system forward by giving it new things to do; at other times the system and its environment choose what happens next. This is like a game where players take turns. Sometimes it is the tester's turn to make a move; sometimes it is the systems.

Conformance for interface automata is defined in terms of *alternating simulation*. Unlike conformance based on trace inclusion, alternating simulation allows us to define conformance for an open system that may accept more kinds of input than our specification describes. However, for any specified input, a complete description of output behaviours is defined.

Let's start with an example of a network-based chat system to illustrate the basic concepts.

Example 1. The Chat system is a distributed, reactive system that permits an arbitrary number of clients. Each client may post text messages that will be delivered by the system to all other clients that have entered the chat session. The system delivers pending, unreceived messages in FIFO order with local consistency. In other words, a given client always receives messages from any given sender in the order sent. However, if there are multiple senders, the messages may be interleaved arbitrarily. Figure 4 shows a typical scenario of the chat system's behaviour as an interface automaton.

The nodes of the graph represent distinct states of the system. The arcs represent transitions that change the system state. Each state in the graph is either *passive* or *active*. Ovals represent active states where a client may give the system new work to do. Diamonds represent passive states where the client waits for an action from the system or transitions into an active state after a state-dependent timeout occurs.

First-order structures define system state. *Abstract State Machines* (ASMs) [10,23,24] are a branch of mathematical logic and model theory that extends the semantic foundations by Turing machines. We find them useful for testing because they provide powerful and convenient ways to construct the kinds of automata needed for testing. ASM states are first-order structures. Guarded update rules (a "program") define possible transitions between states. Our experience shows that this form is more practical for reactive systems than using a graphical input language for individual transitions.

We introduce *model automata*, a conservative extension of interface automata over states that are first-order structures. Model automata also include the concept of *accepting*

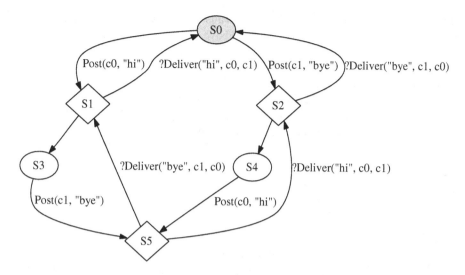

Fig. 4. Exploration of the Chat model with two clients (c0 and c1), a fixed message ("hi" sent by c0 and "bye" sent by c1) and the restriction that the number of pending deliveries for each client is at most 1. The initial state is shown in grey. Action labels prefixed by "?" indicate observable actions. Labels without prefix indicate controllable actions. Active states are shown as ovals. Passive states are shown as diamonds. The unlabeled transitions represent an internal transition ("timeout") from passive to active.

states familiar in formal languages. As in the LTS-based approach, model automata depend on states and transitions, but they extend traditional model-based testing by admitting open systems whose transitions are not a subset of the specification's transitions and by treating states as first-order structures of mathematical logic.

The states we consider are full first-order structures of mathematical logic. First-order structures include a vocabulary of named values and functions that can express queries.

Example 2. The states of the chat example can be seen as states with variables, as shown in Figure 1. Actions labels are also structured as *action methods* with parameters and return values.

Table 1. States of the Chat example, corresponding to Figure 4, showing the queues of pending messages between each client. If there are n clients, then there are $n(n-1)$ such queues.

State	Msgs from c0 to c1	Msgs from c1 to c0	Mode
S0	Seq{ }	Seq{ }	Active
S1	Seq{"hi"}	Seq{ }	Passive
S2	Seq{ }	Seq{"bye"}	Passive
S3	Seq{"hi"}	Seq{ }	Active
S4	Seq{ }	Seq{"bye"}	Active
S5	Seq{"hi"}	Seq{"bye"}	Passive

Model programs compactly encode large transition systems. Here is a *model program* that describes the chat system shown above, written in the Spec# language. We extend the description with some additional functionality beyond what was shown in Figure 4. The state of the system consists of instances of the class `Client` that have been created so far, and a map `Members` that for each client specifies the messages that have been sent but not yet delivered to that client as sender queues. Each sender queue is identified by the client that sent the messages in the queue. In the initial state of the system there are no clients and and `Members` is an empty map.

```
class Client
type Message = string;
type SendersQueue = Map<Client,Seq<Message>>;
type MemberState = Map<Client,SendersQueue>;

MemberState Members = new Map();
```

Next we describe the actions methods of the system. These are methods with preconditions that say in which state of the system they may occur and for which input parameters. There are four action methods for the chat system: the *controllable* action methods `Create`, `Enter`, `Send`, and the *observable* action method `Deliver`. An action is *enabled* if the Boolean expressions given by the `requires` clauses are true with respect to the actual parameters of the method call and the values of the state variables in the current state.

The `Create` action method creates a new instance of the `Client` class, as a result of this action the **enumof**(`Client`) set is extended with the new client.

```
Client! Create()
{ return new Client(); }
```

A client that is not already a member of the chat session may join the session. A client `c` becomes a member of the chat session when the action `Enter(c)` is called. When a client joins the session, the related message queues are initialized appropriately.

```
void Enter(Client! c)
  requires c notin Members;
{ foreach (Client d in Members) Members[d][c] = Seq{};
  Members[c] = Map{d in Members; <d,Seq{}>}};
```

A member of the chat session may post a message for all members except himself to receive. When a sender posts a message, the message is appended at the end of the corresponding sender queue of each of the other members of the session.

```
void Post(Client! sndr, Message msg)
  requires sndr in Members && Members.Size > 1;
{ foreach (rcvr in Members)
    if (rcvr != sndr) Members[rcvr][sndr] += Seq{msg}; }
```

A message being delivered from a sender to a receiver is an observable action or a notification call-back that occurs whenever the chat system forwards a particular message to a particular client. When a delivery is observed, the corresponding sender queue of the receiver has to be nonempty, and the message must match the first message in that queue or else local consistency is violated. If the preconditions of the delivery are satisfied then the delivered message is simply removed from the corresponding sender queue of the recipient.

```
void Deliver(Message msg, Client! sndr, Client! rcvr)
  requires rcvr in Members && sndr in Members[rcvr];
  requires Members[rcvr][sndr].Length > 0 &&
           Members[rcvr][sndr].Head == msg;
{ Members[rcvr][sndr] = Members[rcvr][sndr].Tail; }
```

Encoding a specification of the system's intended behavior in an abstractly executable form is not the same as writing a second implementation. The model program does less than the implementation. Its purpose is to capture the states of the system that affect the observable behaviour of interest.

Exploration produces a model automaton. The model program can be unwound into a model automaton. Unwinding The model automaton defined by a model program is a complete unwinding or expansion of the program. An *explicit state model checking algorithm* is used to compute the (possibly infinite) space of all possible sequences of method invocations that 1) do not violate the pre- and postconditions and invariant of the system's contracts and 2) are relevant to a user-specified set of test properties [19].

If the model is infinite state, unwinding does not terminate. Spec Explorer thus includes practical features that control how the state space is explored. We mention two of these: *State groupings* allow the exploration to prune away states that are distinct but indistinguishable under a user-provided equivalence relation [12]. Avoiding isomorphic cases that differ in the choice of input but have identical runs results in a body of tests with a better chance of detecting a conformance discrepancy. *State-dependent parameter generation* allows the computation of the parameter domains of each action with respect to the current state. This can make exploration more efficient by reducing the search for input parameters to feasible cases.

Traversal of automata underlies automatic test generation. Test cases can be automatically generated by *traversing the graph* of the model automaton. The graph also serves as a *test oracle*: a test fails if observed transitions of the implementation under test do not match transitions in the graph. Additionally, successful test runs must begin in the *initial state* and terminate in an accepting state. *Accepting states* are states that satisfy a user-specified logical condition that says whether the system is in a final, de-initialized state. In this example, the accepting state occurs whenever the message queues are empty.

Although any traversal of the graph is a possible trace of the system, we can only choose moves in the active states (i.e., those drawn as ovals in the graph). A state where the system can choose from among more than one move represents nondeterminism from the observers point of view. This means a test case is not a just sequence of actions but a tree of actions and possible system responses. Executing a test is like a so-called *game against nature* where a players opponent chooses moves randomly. Spec

Explorer implements game strategies using Markov decision processes as a technique for intelligently choosing input actions that broaden the coverage of nondeterministic tests [30].

When dealing with model programs that have very large state spaces, we can combine the state exploration and test case generation into an online algorithm called *on-the-fly testing* [36].

When testing in its on-the-fly mode, Spec Explorer exploration engine makes moves based on the observed history of the test run. This allows it to omit exploration of nondeterministic branches that were not taken by the implementation during the test run. It can also be run in a way that attempts to match the distribution of actions exercised during testing to an application profile (i.e. a histogram of action frequencies) given as input.

Spec Explorer users rely on both pre-generated, offline tests with complete behavioural coverage over a restricted domain of system inputs and online tests generated on the fly which randomly sample a larger number of system inputs.

Conformance can be formally defined as alternating simulation. Differences between the predicted and actual system behaviour are called conformance failures. What constitutes a difference is mathematically defined in terms of alternating refinement of interface automata. *Alternating refinement* means that the system under test must accept at least as many inputs as the interface automaton defines (it may accept more inputs) and that, conversely, the test harness must accept at least as many outputs as the system may produce (it may accept more outputs than the system is capable of producing) [15].

Test execution implements the conformance relation. Our test graphs are also used to *automatically harness* the implementation for conformance testing. Spec Explorer can instrument a .NET assembly, that is a managed code library of the common language runtime of Microsoft, and cause implementation methods corresponding to model actions to be invoked as needed.

Running a test results in a trace log that shows a comparison of expected versus actual behaviour. A failing test run is shown in Table 2. This test run observed that the particular chat system implementation being tested did not deliver messages in the order posted, as required by the specification. The server delivered in LIFO order instead of FIFO.

Table 2. A failing test run of the chat implementation

Step	Invocation	From State	To State	Status
1	Post(c0, "hi")	S0	S1	Succeeded
2	?Timeout	S1	S1'	Succeeded
3	Post(c0, "bye")	S1'	S7	Succeeded
4	?Deliver("bye", c0, c1)	S7	S2	FAILED: observed Deliver("bye", c0, c1), expected Deliver("hi", c0, c1)

3 Model Programs and Model Automata

In this section we describe the semantic framework on which Spec Explorer is built upon. We introduce the notion of *model automata* as an extension of interface automata [16,15] over first-order structures. Instead of the terms "input" and "output" that are used in [15] we use the terms "controllable" and "observable" here. This choice of terminology is motivated by our problem domain of testing, where certain operations are under the control of a tester, and certain operations are only observable by a tester.

3.1 States

A *state* is a first-order structure over a vocabulary Σ; its universe of values is denoted by $\mathcal{U}$ and is assumed to be fixed for all states. The vocabulary symbols are *function symbols*; each function symbol has a fixed arity and is given an interpretation or meaning in s. The interpretation of some function symbols in Σ may change from state to state. The function symbols whose interpretation may change are called *state variables* or dynamic functions [23]. The set of state variables is denoted by $\mathcal{V}$. Any ground term over $\Sigma - \mathcal{V}$ has the same interpretation in all states. As far as this paper is concerned, all state variables are either nullary or unary. A *dynamic universe* C is a dynamic unary Boolean function; we say that o *is in* C if $C(o) = true$.

We assume that $\mathcal{U}$ contains a distinguished element for representing undefinedness, denoted by undef. All functions in Σ have total interpretations in $\mathcal{U}$, mapping to the undef value as required. Note that we do not assume that undef can be denoted by a symbol in Σ.

Given a first-order structure s over Σ and a vocabulary $V \subseteq \Sigma$, we use the notation $s{\restriction}V$ for the reduct of s to the vocabulary V. We write $S{\restriction}V$ for $\{s{\restriction}V : s \in S\}$.

By a *state based expression* E we mean a term over Σ that may contain (logical) variables, i.e. placeholders for values. If E contains no (logical) variables, E is said to be *ground* or *closed*. If E contains variables all of which are among $\mathbf{x} = x_1, \ldots, x_n$ we indicate this by $E[\mathbf{x}]$, and given closed terms $\mathbf{v} = v_1, \ldots, v_n$ over $\mathcal{F} \cup \mathcal{V}$ we write $E[\mathbf{v}]$ for the closed expression after substituting or replacing each x_i in E by v_i for $1 \leq i \leq n$. The value of a closed state based expression E in a state s is denoted by $E(s)$. We write $E(S)$ for $\{E(s) : s \in S\}$, where s is a set of states.

3.2 Model Automata

Definition 1. An *model automaton* M has the following components:

- A set S of *states* over a *vocabulary* Σ, where Σ contains a finite sub-vocabulary $\mathcal{V}$ of *state variables* or *dynamic functions*.
- A nonempty subset S^{init} of S called *initial states*.
- A subset S^{acc} of S called *accepting states*.
- A set *Acts* of *actions* that are (ground) terms over $\Sigma - \mathcal{V}$. *Acts* is a disjoint union of *controllable actions Ctrl* and *observable actions Obs*.
- A *transition relation* $\delta \subseteq S \times Acts \times S$

M is *deterministic* if for any state s and action a there is at most one state t such that $(s, a, t) \in \delta$, in which case we write $\delta(s, a) = t$. *In this paper we consider only deterministic model automata.*

When it is clear from the context, we often say automata for model automata. Notice that actions have the same interpretation in all states, this will allow us later to relate actions in different states in a uniform way. Intuitively, a state is uniquely defined by an interpretation of the symbols in V.

For a given state $s \in S$, we let $Acts(s)$ denote the set of all actions $a \in Acts$ such that $(s, a, t) \in \delta$ for some t; we say that a is *enabled* in state s. We let $Ctrl(s) = Acts(s) \cap Ctrl$ and $Obs(s) = Acts(s) \cap Obs$.

In order to identify a component of a model automaton M, we sometimes index that component by M, unless M is clear from the context. When convenient, we denote M by the tuple

$$(S^{\text{init}}, S, S^{\text{acc}}, Obs, Ctrl, \delta).$$

We will use the notion of a sub-automaton and a reduct when we define tests in Section 5.1. Tests are special automata that have been expanded with new state variables and actions but that preserve the transitions when the additional state variables and actions are ignored.

Definition 2. A model automaton M is a *sub-automaton* of a model automaton N, in symbols $M \subseteq N$, if $S_M \subseteq S_N$, $S_M^{\text{init}} \subseteq S_N^{\text{init}}$, $S_M^{\text{acc}} \subseteq S_N^{\text{acc}}$, $Ctrl_M \subseteq Ctrl_N$, $Obs_M \subseteq Obs_N$, and $\delta_M \subseteq \delta_N$.

We lift reduction on vocabularies, $S{\restriction}V$, to automatons:

Definition 3. Given an automaton M and a vocabulary $V \subseteq \Sigma_M$, we write $T{\restriction}V$ for the following automaton N, called the *reduct* of M to V:

- $S_N = S_M{\restriction}V$, $S_N^{\text{init}} = S_M^{\text{init}}{\restriction}V$, $S_N^{\text{acc}} = S_M^{\text{acc}}{\restriction}V$,
- $Acts_N$ is the set of all a in $Acts_M$ such that a is a term over V,
- $\delta_N = \{(s{\restriction}V, a, t{\restriction}V) : (s, a, t) \in \delta_M, a \in Acts_N\}$.

M is called an *expansion* of N.

A reduct of an automaton to a subset of the state variables may collapse several states into a single state, which is illustrated later. Therefore, projection does not always preserve determinism. In this paper, projections are used in a limited way so that the resulting automaton is always deterministic.

3.3   Model Programs

A model program P declares a finite set $\mathcal{M}$ of action methods and a set of state variables V. A state of P is given by the values (or interpretations) of the state vocabulary symbols Σ that occur in the model program. The value of a state variable in $V \subseteq \Sigma$ may change as a result of program execution. Examples of function symbols whose interpretation does *not* change are built-in operators, data constructors, etc. A nullary state variable is a normal (static) program variable that may be updated. A unary state variable represents either an instance field of a class (by mapping from object identities to the value of that field) or a dynamic universe of objects that have been created during program execution.

Each action method m, with variables $\mathbf{x}$ as its formal input parameters, is associated with a state based Boolean expression $Pre_m[\mathbf{x}]$ called the *precondition* of m. The execution of m in a given state s and with given actual parameters $\mathbf{v}$, produces a sequel state where some of the state variables have changed. In general the execution of m may also do other things, such as write to an external file, or prompt up a dialog box to a user, but abstractly we consider m as an *update rule* that is a function that given a state and actual parameters for m that satisfy the precondition of m, produces a new state t where some state variables in $\mathcal{V}$ have been updated.

A model program can be written in a high level specification language such as AsmL [25] or Spec# [7], or in a programming language such as C# or Visual Basic. A guarded update rule in P is defined as a parameterized method, similar to the way methods are written in a normal program. A guarded update rule defined by a method is called an *action method*.

The model automaton M_P defined by a model program P is a complete unwinding of P as defined below. We omit the subscript P from M_P when it is clear from the context. Since model programs deal with rich data structures, states are not just abstract entities without internal structure, but full first-order structures. We define actions and the state to state transition function δ_M that represents execution of actions. Unlike an explicit transition system with given sets of nodes and arcs, the states and transitions of a model program must be *deduced* by executing sequences of atomic actions starting in the initial state. For this reason, we use the term *exploration* to refer to the process of producing δ_M.

The set of initial states S^{init} is the singleton set containing the state with the initial values of state variables as declared in P. The set of all states S is the least set that contains S_M^{init} and is closed under the transition relation δ_M defined below.

Example 3. Consider the Chat example. The set $\mathcal{V}$ contains the dynamic universe `Client` for the instances to that type (denoted as **enumof**`(Client)` in Spec#), and a unary dynamic function for the `entered` and `unreceivedMsgs` instance fields. In the initial state of the model, say s_0, there are no elements in `Client`, and the unary functions that represent the instance fields map to undef. In addition, Σ contains other function symbols such as the empty sequence, `Seq{}`, the binary Boolean function `in` that in this context checks if a given element is in the domain of a map, etc. All the symbols in $\Sigma - \mathcal{V}$ have the same interpretation or meaning in all states in S_M, whereas the interpretation of symbols in $\mathcal{V}$ may change from state to state.

3.4 State Exploration

Actions are not considered as abstract labels but have internal structure. The vocabulary of non-variable symbols $\Sigma - \mathcal{V}$ is divided into the following disjoint sub-vocabularies: a set $\mathcal{F}$ of function symbols for operators and constructors on data, and a set $\mathcal{M}$ of function symbols for methods.

An *action* over $(\mathcal{M}, \mathcal{F})$ is a term $m(v_1, \ldots, v_k)$ where $m \in \mathcal{M}$, $k \geq 0$ is the arity of m, and each v_i is a term over $\mathcal{F}$. Each parameter of m is either an input parameter or an output parameter. We assume that all the input parameters precede all the output parameters in the parameter list of m. When the distinction between input parameters and output parameters is relevant we denote $m(v_1, \ldots, v_k)$ by $m(v_1, \ldots, v_l)/v_{l+1}, \ldots, v_k$, where $v_1, \ldots, v_l$, $l \le k$, are input parameters. The set of all actions over $(\mathcal{M}, \mathcal{F})$ is denoted by $Acts_{\mathcal{M}, \mathcal{F}}$, or simply $Acts$, when $\mathcal{F}$ and $\mathcal{M}$ are clear from the context. Any two terms over $\mathcal{F}$ are equal if and only if they denote the same value in $\mathcal{U}$, and the value of a term over $\mathcal{F}$ is the same for all states in $S_{\mathcal{M}}$. The symbols in $\mathcal{M}$ have the term interpretation, i.e. $m(\mathbf{v})$ and $m'(\mathbf{v})$ are equal if and only if m and m' are the same symbol and $\mathbf{v}$ and $\mathbf{w}$ are equal.

Given an action $a = m(\mathbf{v})/\mathbf{w}$ and a state s, a is enabled in s (i.e., $a \in Acts_M(s)$) if the following conditions hold:

- $Pre_m[\mathbf{v}]$ is true in s;
- The invocation of $m(\mathbf{v})$ in s yields the output parameters $\mathbf{w}$.

Let $Acts_m(s)$ denote the set of all enabled actions with method m in state s. The set of all enabled actions $Acts_M(s)$ in a state s is the union of all $Acts_m(s)$ for all action methods m; s is called *terminal* if $Acts_M(s)$ is empty. Notice that $Acts_m(s)$ may be infinite if there are infinitely many possible parameters for m. The set $Acts_M$ is the union of all $Acts_M(s)$ for all s in S_M.

Given $a = m(\mathbf{v})/\mathbf{w} \in Acts_M(s)$, we let $\delta_M(s, a)$ be the target state of the invocation $m(\mathbf{v})$. The invocation of $m(\mathbf{v})$ in a state s can be formalized using ASM theory [23]. Formally, a method invocation produces a set of *updates* that assign new values to some state variables that are then applied to s to produce the target state with the updated values. The interested reader should consult [25] for a detailed exposition of the update semantics of AsmL programs, or [18] that includes the update semantics for the core language constructs.

Example 4. To illustrate how exploration works, let us continue from Example 3. We can invoke the `Client` constructor method in state s_0, since the precondition is *true*. This invocation produces an update that adds a new object, say `c0`, to the dynamic universe `Client`. Let s_1 be the resulting state. We have explored the following transition: $\delta(s_0, \mathtt{Client()}/\mathtt{c0}) = s_1$.

From state s_1 we can continue exploration by invoking `c0.Enter()`.[1] The precondition $Pre_{\mathtt{Enter}}[\mathtt{c0}]$ requires that `c0` is a member of `Client` (due to the type declaration) and that `c0.entered` is false. Thus `c0.Enter()` is enabled in s_1. The invocation produces updates on the dynamic unary function for `entered`. Let the new target state be s_2. We have thus explored the transition $\delta(s_1, \mathtt{c0.Enter()}) = s_2$.

3.5   Controllable and Observable Actions

In order to distinguish behaviour that can be controlled from behaviour that can only be observed, the methods in $\mathcal{M}$ are split into *controllable* and *observable* ones. This induces, for each state s, a corresponding partitioning of $Acts_M(s)$ into controllable actions $Ctrl_M(s)$ and observable actions $Obs_M(s)$ which are enabled in s. The action set $Acts_M$ is partitioned accordingly into Obs_M and $Ctrl_M$.

---

[1] The notation $o.f(\ldots)$ is the same as $f(o, \ldots)$ but provides a more intuitive object-oriented view when o is an object and f a field or a method of o.

Example 5. In the Chat server model there are three action methods `Client`, `Enter`, and `Send` that are controllable, and a single observable action method `Receive`. The reason why `Receive` is observable is that it corresponds to a reaction of the system under test that cannot be controlled by the tester.

In Spec Explorer, observable and controllable actions can either be indicated by attaching corresponding .NET attributes to the methods in the source text of the model program, or by using the actions settings part of the project configuration for the model.

3.6 Accepting States

The model program has an *accepting state condition* that is a closed Boolean state based expression. A state s is an *accepting state* if the accepting state condition is true in s. The notion of accepting states is motivated by the requirement to identify model states where tests are allowed to terminate. This is particularly important when testing distributed or multi-threaded systems, where it is not always feasible to stop the testing process in an arbitrary state, i.e., prior tests must first be finished before new tests can be started. For example, as a result of a controllable action that starts a thread in the IUT, the thread may acquire shared resources that are later released. A successful test should not be finished before the resources have been released.

Formally, there is an implicit controllable *succeed* action and a special terminal *goal* state g in S_M, s.t. for all accepting states s, $\delta_M(s, succeed) = g$. It is assumed that in the IUT the corresponding method call takes the system into a state where no observable actions are enabled. Thus, ending the test in an accepting state, corresponds to choosing the *succeed* action.

In every terminal non-accepting state s there is an implicit controllable *fail* action such that $\delta_M(s, fail) = s$. It is assumed that the corresponding action in the implementation is not enabled in any state. In other words, as will become apparent from the specification relation described below, if a terminal non-accepting model state is reached, the test case fails.

Example 6. A natural accepting state condition in the Chat example is to exclude the initial state and states where pending messages have not yet been received. In such a state there are no observable actions enabled:

```
enumof(Client).Size > 0 &&
Forall{ c in enumof(Client), s in c.unreceivedMsgs.Keys;
        c.unreceivedMsgs[s].Length == 0}
```

3.7 State Invariants

The model program may also have *state invariants* associated with it. A state invariant is a closed Boolean state based expression that must hold in all states. The model program *violates* a state invariant φ if φ is false in some state of the model, in which case the model program is not valid. A state invariant is thus a safety condition on the transition function or an axiom on the reachable state space that must always hold.

Example 7. We could add the following state invariant to the Chat example:

```
Forall{ c in enumof(Client); c notin c.unreceivedMsgs.Keys }
```

It says that no client should be considered as a possible recipient of his own messages. This state invariant would be violated, if we had by mistake forgotten the c != **this** condition in the **foreach**-loop in the body of the `Client` method in Figure 1.

Execution of an action is considered to be an atomic step. In Example 7 there are "internal states" that exists during execution of the `Client` action; however, these internal states are not visible in the transition relation and will not be considered for invariant checking by the Spec Explorer tool.

4   Techniques for Scenario Control

We saw in Section 3 how the methods of a model program can be unwound into a model automaton with controllable and observable actions. In typical practice, the model program defines the *operational contract* of the system under test without regard for any particular test purpose. Hence, it is not unusual that a model program may correspond to an automaton with a large or even infinite number of transitions. When this happens we may want to apply techniques for selectively exploring the transitions of the model program. These techniques are ways of limiting the scenarios that will be considered. They allow us to produce automata that are specialized for various *test purposes* or goals that the tester wishes to achieve. This is also a useful technique for analyzing properties of the model, regardless of whether an implementation is available for testing.

In the remainder of this section, we introduce techniques for scenario control used by Spec Explorer. We define each technique as a function that maps a model automaton M into a new automaton M' with the property described. These techniques take advantage of the fact that states are first-order structures that may be queried and classified. The techniques also rely on the fact that the transition labels are structured into action names with parameter lists (terms and symbolic identifiers).

We will describe the following techniques:

- *Parameter selection* limits exploration to a finite but representative set of parameters for the action methods.
- *Method restriction* removes some transitions based on user-provided criteria.
- *State filtering* prunes away states that fail to satisfy a given state-based predicate.
- *Directed search* performs a finite-length walk of transitions with respect to user-provided priorities. States and transitions that are not visited are pruned away. There are several ways that the search may be limited and directed.
- *State grouping* selects representative examples of states from user-provided equivalence classes [12,19].

4.1   Parameter Selection

Using the action signatures of Section 3, we define parameter selection in terms of a relation, D, with $(s, m, \mathbf{v}) \in D$ where $s \in S$, $m \in Acts$, and $\mathbf{v}$ are tuples of elements in $\mathcal{F}$ with as many entries as m has input parameters.

The result of applying parameter selection D to M is an automaton M' whose transition relation is a subset of the transition relation of M. A transition $\delta_M(s, m(\mathbf{v})/\mathbf{w}) = t$

of M is included as a transition of M' if $(s, m, \mathbf{v})$ is in D. The initial states of M' are the initial states of M. The states of M' consist of all states that are reachable from an initial state using the transition rules of M'.

Note that if there is no $\mathbf{v}$ such that $(s, m, \mathbf{v}) \in D$, no transition for m will be available in the state s: parameter selection can also prune away actions, and overlaps to that end with method restriction.

Implementation. The Spec Explorer tool provides a user interface for parameter selection with four levels of control. Rather than populate the relation D in advance, the tool uses expressions that encode the choice of parameters and evaluates these expressions on demand.

Defaults. Spec Explorer uses the type system of the modeling language as a way to organize default domains for parameter selection. The user may rely upon built-in defaults provided by the tool for each type. For example, all action input parameters of type **bool** will be restricted in all states to the values **true** and **false** by default. Moreover, all input parameters which represent object instances will default to all available instances of the object type in the given state.

Per Type. If the tool's built-in parameter domain for a given data type is insufficient, the user may override it. This is done by giving an expression whose evaluation in a each state provides defaults for parameters of the given type.

Per Parameter. The user may specify the domain of individual parameters by a state-based expression, overriding defaults associated with the parameter's type. If not otherwise specified, the tool will combine the domains associated with individual parameters of a method (either defined directly with the parameter or with the parameter's type) to build a Cartesian product or a pairwise combination of the parameter domains.

Per Method. The user can also define parameter tuples for a given method explicitly by providing a state based expression which delivers a set of tuples. This allows one to express full control over parameter selection, expressing dependencies between individual parameter selections.

Example 8. For the Chat example given in Section 2, the `Send` action has an implicit parameter **this** and an explicit parameter `message`. By default, the parameter domain of parameter `this` ranges over all client instances, while `message` ranges over some predefined strings. These domains come from the defaults associated with the types of the parameters, `Client` and **string** respectively. We can change the default by associating the domain `Set{"hi"}` with the parameter `message`. Combined with the default for type `Client`, this would be equivalent to providing explicit parameter tuples with the expression `Set{c in enumof(Client); <c, "hi">}`.

4.2 Method Restriction

An action m is said to be *enabled* in state s if the preconditions of m are satisfied. We can limit the scenarios included in our transition system by strengthening the preconditions of m. We call this *method restriction*.

To do this the user may supply a parameterized, state-based expression e as an additional precondition of m. The action's parameters will be substituted in e prior to evaluation.

The result of applying method restriction e to M is an automaton M' whose transition relation is a subset of the transition relation of M. A transition $\delta_M(s, m(\mathbf{v})/\mathbf{w}) = t$ of M is included as a transition of M' if $e[\mathbf{v}](s)$ is true. The initial states of M' are the initial states of M. The states of M' consist of all states that are reachable from an initial state using the transition rules of M'.

Example 9. In the Chat sample, we used method restriction to avoid that clients send messages before all configured clients are created and entered the session. To that end, we used an auxiliary type representing the *mode* of the system, which is defined as follows:

```
enum Mode { Creating, Entering, Sending };

Mode CurrentMode {
  get {
    if (enumof(Client).Size < 2)
      return Mode.Creating;
    if (Set{c in enumof(Client), !c.entered;c}.Size < 2)
      return Mode.Entering;
    return Mode.Sending;
  }
}
```

Now we can use expressions like `CurrentMode == Mode.Creating` to restrict the enabling of the actions `Client`, `Enter` and `Send` to those states where we want to see them.

Note that in this sample we are only restricting controllable actions. It is usually safe to restrict controllable actions since it is the tester's choice what scenarios should be tested. Restricting observable actions should be avoided, since their occurrence is not under the control of the tester and may result in inconclusive tests.

4.3   State Filtering

A state filter is a set S_f of states where $S^{init} \subseteq S_f$. Applying state filter S_f to automaton M yields M'. A transition $\delta_M(s, m(\mathbf{v})/\mathbf{w}) = t$ of M is included as a transition of M' if $t \in S_f$. The initial states of M' are the initial states of M. The states of M' consist of all states that are reachable from an initial state of M' using the transition rules of M'.

Implementation. Spec Explorer allows the user to specify the set S_f in terms of a state-based expression. A state s is considered to be in S_f if $e(s)$ is true.

Example 10. In the Chat sample, we used a state filter to avoid states in which the same message is posted more than once by a given client before it has been received. The filter is given by the expression:

```
Forall{c in enumof(Client), s in c.unreceivedMsgs.Keys,
   m1 in c.unreceivedMsgs[s], m2 in c.unreceivedMsgs[s]; m1!= m2}
```

This has the effect of pruning away all transitions that result in a state which does not satisfy this expression. Note that in the case of the Chat sample, this filter in combination with the finite parameter selection and finite restriction on the number of created clients makes the extracted scenario finite, since we can only have distinct messages not yet received by clients, and the number of those messages is finite.

4.4 Directed Search

When the number of states of M is large, it is sometimes useful to produce M' using a stochastic process that traverses (or explores) M incrementally. Bounded, nondeterministic search is a convenient approach. The version used in Spec Explorer allows the user to influence the choice of scenarios by fixing the probability space of the random variables used for selection. Transitions and states are explored until user-provided bound conditions are met, for example, when the maximum number of explored transitions exceeds a fixed limit. Suitably weighted selection criteria influence the kinds of scenarios that will be covered by M'.

For the purposes of exposition, we can assume that the directed search algorithm operates on a model automaton that has already been restricted using the methods described in sections 4.1 to 4.3 above.

The general exploration algorithm is given in Figure 5. It assumes two auxiliary predicates:

- *InBounds* is true if user-given bounds on the number of transitions, the number of states, etc., are satisfied.
- *IncludeTarget*(s, a, t) is true for those transitions (s, a, t) that lead to a desired target state. By default, *IncludeTarget* returns true. (We will see in Section 4.5 an alternative definition.)

In the algorithm the variable *frontier* represents the transitions to be explored and is initially set to all those transitions which start in an initial state. The variable *included* represents those states of M' whose outgoing transitions have been already added to the

var *frontier* $= \{(s, a, t) \mid s \in S^{\text{init}}, (s, a, t) \in \delta\}$
var *included* $= S^{\text{init}}$
var $\delta' = \varnothing$
while *frontier* $\neq \varnothing \wedge$ *InBounds*
    choose $(s, a, t) \in$ *frontier*
    frontier $:=$ *frontier* $\setminus \{(s, a, t)\}$
    if $t \in$ *included* $\vee$ *IncludeTarget*(s, a, t)
        $\delta' := \delta' \cup \{(s, a, t)\}$
        if $t \notin$ *included*
            frontier $:=$ *frontier* $\cup \{(t, a', t') \mid (t, a', t') \in \delta\}$
            included $:=$ *included* $\cup \{t\}$

Fig. 5. Directed search in Spec Explorer

frontier, and is initially set to the initial states of M. The variable δ' represents the computed transition relation of the sub-automaton M'. The algorithm continues exploring as long as the frontier is not empty and the bounds are satisfied. In each iteration step, it selects some transition from the frontier, and updates δ', *included* and *frontier*.

Upon completion of the algorithm, the transitions of M' are the final value of δ'. The initial states of M' are the initial states of M. The states of M' consist of all states that are reachable from an initial state of M' using the transitions of M'. (This will be the same as the final value of *included*.)

The freedom for directing search of this algorithm appears in the **choose** operation. We can affect the outcome by controlling the way in which choice occurs. We consider two mechanisms: *per-state weights* and *action weights*.

Per-state weights prioritize user-specified target states for transitions of controllable actions. The weight of state s is denoted by ω_s. At each step of exploration the probability of choosing a transition whose target state is t is

$$prob(t) = \begin{cases} 0, & \text{if } t \notin T; \\ \omega_t / \sum_{s \in T} \omega_s, & t \in T. \end{cases}$$

where $T = \{t \mid (s, a, t) \in frontier, a \in Ctrl\}$.

As an alternative to per-state weights, we can introduce action weights that prioritize individual transitions.

Let $\omega(s, m, \delta')$ denote the weight of action method m in state s with respect to the current step of the exploration algorithm and the transitions found so far in δ'. If $m_1, \ldots, m_k$ are all the controllable action methods enabled in s, then the probability of an action method m_i being chosen is

$$prob(s, m_i, \delta') = \begin{cases} 0, & \text{if } \omega(s, m_i, \delta') = 0; \\ \omega(s, m_i) / \sum_{j=1}^{k} \omega(s, m_j, \delta'), & \text{otherwise} \end{cases}$$

The state of the exploration algorithm, namely, the set of transitions already selected for inclusion (δ'), may affect an action method's weight. This occurs in the case of *decrementing action weights* where the likelihood of selection decreases with the number of times a method has previously included in δ'. A more detailed exposition of action weights is given in [36].

Implementation. Weights are given in Spec Explorer as state-based expressions that return non-negative integers.

4.5 State Grouping

State grouping is a technique for controlling scenarios by selecting representative states with respect to an equivalence class. We use a state-based grouping expression G to express the equivalence relation. If $G(s) = G(t)$ for states s and t, then s and t are of member of the same group under grouping function G. The G-group represented by a state s is the evaluation of G with respect to state s, namely $G(s)$. $S_{/G}$ denotes the set of all G-groups represented by the elements of set S.

State groupings are useful for visualization and analysis (as we saw in Section 2), but they can also be used as a practical way to prune exploration to distinct cases of interest for testing, in particular to avoid exploring symmetric configurations.

For a given model automaton M and a state $s \in S_M$, let $[s]_{G_i}$ denote the set of states which are equivalent under one grouping G_i, i.e., the set $\{s' \mid s' \in S_M, G_i(s') = G_i(s)\}$.

We can limit exploration with respect to state groupings $G_1, \ldots, G_n$ by using state-based expressions the yield the desired number of representatives of each group. Let $B_1, \ldots, B_i$ be state-based *bound* expressions which evaluate to a non-negative integer for each i, $1 \leq i \leq n$.

Pruning based on state-grouping bounds can be interpreted in the context of the bounded search algorithm shown in Figure 5, if the *IncludeTarget*(s, a, t) predicate is defined as $\exists (i \in \{1 \ldots k\}) \# ([t]_{G_i} \cap included) < B_i(t)$. In other words, a newly visited target state is included if there exists at least one state grouping of the target state whose bound has not yet been reached. Note that the effect of pruning with state grouping depends on the strategy used by the exploration algorithm, i.e., the order in which states and transitions are explored.

Implementation. Spec Explorer visualizes a state grouping G of model automaton M as a graph. The nodes of the graph are elements of $S_{/G}$. Arc a is shown between $G(s)$ and $G(t)$ if $(s, a, t) \in \delta_M$.

Figure 3 is a drawing produced by Spec Explorer using this technique.

Example 11. Recall the model automaton for the Chat sample in Figure 2. Here, after two clients have been constructed, two different orders in which the clients enter the session, as well as two different orders in which clients send the message "hi" are represented. We might want to abstract from these symmetries for the testing problem at hand. This can be achieved by providing a state grouping expression which *abstracts* from the object identities of the clients:

```
Bag{c in enumof(Client);
       <c.entered,Bag{<s,m> in c.unreceivedMsgs; m}>}
```

In the resulting model automaton, the scenarios where clients enter in different order and send messages in different order are not distinguished. Note that with n clients there would be $n!$ many orders that are avoided with the grouping. The use of groupings has sometimes an effect similar to partial order reduction in model-checking.

5   Test Generation

Model based test generation and test execution are two closely related processes. In one extreme case, which is also the traditional view on test generation, tests are generated in advance from a given specification or model where the purpose of the generated tests is either to provide some kind of coverage of the state space, to reach a state satisfying some particular property, or to generate random walks in the state space. We call this *offline testing* since test execution is a secondary process that takes the pre-generated tests and runs them against an implementation under test to find discrepancies between the behaviour of the system under test and the predicted behaviour. Tests may include aspects of expected behaviour such as expected results, or may be intended just to drive the system under test, with the validation part done separately during test execution. In another extreme, both processes are intertwined into a single process where tests are generated on-the-fly as testing progresses. We call this mode of testing *online testing*, or *on-the-fly testing*.

In the testing framework presented here, both the online case and the offline case are viewed as special cases of a general testing process in the following sense. In the offline case the input to the test execution engine (discussed in Section 6) is a test suite in form of a model automaton that is pre-generated from the model program. In the online case the input to the test execution engine is a dynamic unfolding of the model program itself, i.e., the test suite has not been explicitly pre-computed.

5.1 Test Suites and Test Cases

Let M be a finitization of the automaton M_P of the model program P; M has been computed using techniques described in Section 4. Recall that M is a finite sub-automaton of M_P. A test suite is just another automaton T of a particular kind that has been produced by a traversal of M as discussed in Section 5.2. A *path of T from s_1 to s_n* is a sequence of states $(s_1, s_2, \ldots, s_n)$ in T such that there is a transition from s_i to s_{i+1} in T.

Definition 4. A *test suite* generated from an automaton M is an automaton T such that:

1. The states in T may use new state variables called *test variables*, i.e. $\mathcal{V}_M \subseteq \mathcal{V}_T$.
2. The set of action methods $\mathcal{M}_T$ of T contains a new controllable action (method) *Observe* of arity 0 and a new observable action (method) *Timeout* of arity 0 that are not in Σ_M. *Observe* and *Timeout* are called *test actions* and corresponding transitions in T are called *test transitions*. For any test transition $\delta_T(s, a) = t$, $s \restriction \Sigma_M = t \restriction \Sigma_M$.
3. The reduction of T to Σ_M is a sub-automaton of M, i.e. $T \restriction \Sigma_M \subseteq M$.
4. An accepting state is reachable from every state in S_T.
5. For all non-terminal states $s \in S_T$, either
    (a) s is *active*: $Ctrl_T(s) \neq \varnothing$ and $Obs_T(s) = \varnothing$, or
    (b) s is *passive*: $Obs_T(s) \neq \varnothing$ and $Ctrl_T(s) = \varnothing$.
    The target state of a transition is passive if and only if it is an *Observe*-transition.
6. For all transitions $\delta_T(a, s) = t$, there is no path in T from t to s.

By a *test case* in T we mean the sub-automaton of T that includes a single initial state of T and is closed under δ_T. Given a state $s \in S_T$, $s \restriction \Sigma_M$ is called the *corresponding state* of M.

Here is an intuitive explanation for each of the conditions: 1) The use of test variables makes it possible to represent traversals of M, i.e. to record history that distinguishes different occurrences of corresponding states in M. 2) The *Observe* action encodes the decision to wait for an observable action. The *Timeout* action encodes that no other observable action happened. Test actions are not allowed to alter the corresponding state of M. 3) For all states $s \in S_T$, all properties of the corresponding state of M carry over to s. Typically, there may be several initial states in T; all test cases start in the corresponding initial state of M. Moreover, each transition in T, other than a test transition, must correspond to a transition in M. Note that the source and the target of any test transition must correspond to the same state in S_M. 4) It must be possible to end each test case in an accepting state. In particular, each terminal state must correspond to accepting state of M. 5) The strategy of a test, whether to be passive and expect an observable action or to be active and invoke a controllable action is made explicit by the *Observe* action. If several controllable actions are possible in a given active state, one is chosen randomly. 6) The test suite does not loop, i.e., T is a directed asyclic graph (dag). This guarantees termination of a test, either due to a conformance failure or due to reaching a terminal accepting state.

The distinction between a test suite and a single test case will only be relevant during test execution, when the distinction is irrelevant we say that T is a *test*. Note that if M itself satisfies all these properties, M can be considered as a test (that is a single test case because M has a single initial state). A test T is *control deterministic* if for all active states $s \in S_T$, $Ctrl_T(s)$ is a singleton set. A test T is *observationally deterministic* if for all passive states $s \in S_T$, $Obs_T(s)$ is a singleton set. A test is *deterministic* if it is both control deterministic and observationally deterministic.

Given a test T and an active state $s \in S_T$, we write $T(s)$ for a choice of an action $a \in Ctrl_T(s)$.

Implementation. In Spec Explorer tests are represented explicitly in the offline case as sets of action sequences called test segments. Test segments are linked together to en-code branching with respect to observable actions. In a deterministic test, the segments correspond to test sequences in the traditional sense. Some segments may be used mul-tiple times, there is an additional test variable that records the number of times each segment has been used to guarantee termination of test execution.

Example 12. Consider the following model program P with $M = \{F, G, H\}$ where all action methods are controllable and have arity 0, and $V = \{mode\}$.

```
enum Mode = {A,B,C}
Mode mode = A;
void F() requires mode == A {mode = B;}
void G() requires mode == B {mode = C;}
void H() requires mode == B {mode = C;}
```

Suppose that the accepting state condition is that mode is C. Consider also a model program P' that is P extended with an action I that takes the model back to its initial state:

```
void I() requires mode == C {mode = A;}
```

The full exploration of P (P') yields a finite automaton $M = M_P$ ($M' = P_{P'}$) shown in Figure 6.

States of M are denoted by the value of mode. A deterministic test T for M, as illustrated in Figure 6, uses an additional state variable, say n, that represents the "test case number" (similarly for T'). Each state of T is labelled by the pair $(n, mode)$. In Spec Explorer the test T is represented by the action sequences (F, G) and (F, H). Note that M itself is a test for M, where $M(B)$ is a random choice of G or H.

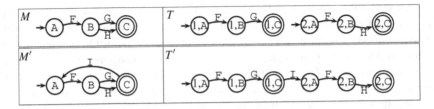

Fig. 6. Automaton M (M') for the model program P (P') in Example 12; T is a test for M and M'; T' is a test for M'

Each $m \in \mathcal{M}$ with formal input parameters $\mathbf{x}$ is associated in Spec Explorer with a positive real valued state based expression $Weight_m[\mathbf{x}]$ whose value by default is 1. The weight of an action $a = m(\mathbf{v})/\mathbf{w}$ in a state s is given by $Weight_m[\mathbf{v}]$. A random choice of an action $a \in Ctrl_T(s)$ in an active state s has probability

$$\frac{Weight_T^s(a)}{\sum_{b \in Ctrl_T(s)} Weight_T^s(b)}.$$

5.2 Traversal Algorithms

Given M, a traversal algorithm produces a test suite T for M, for a particular test purpose. A test purpose might be to reach some state satisfying a particular condition, to generate a transition coverage of M, or to just produce a set of random walks. There is extensive literature on different traversal algorithms from deterministic finite state machines [29], that produce test suites in form of test sequences. When dealing with non-deterministic systems, the game view of testing was initially proposed in [3] and is discussed at length in [39].

In the following we discuss the main definitions of test purposes used in our framework. The definitions can be analyzed separately for control deterministic and control non-deterministic (stochastic) tests. For ease of presentation, we limit the discussion to control deterministic tests. We introduce first the following notion.

Definition 5. An *alternating path P of T starting from s* is a tree with *root s*:

- P has no sub-trees and is called a *leaf*, or
- P has, for each state $t \in \{\delta_T(s, a) \mid a \in Acts_T(s)\}$ an immediate sub-tree that is an alternating path of T starting from t.

In the case when T is deterministic, any alternating path is also a path and vice versa. The difference arises in the presence of observational non-determinism. Intuitively, an alternating path takes into account *all* the possible observable actions in a passive state, whereas a path is just a branch of some alternating path. We say that an alternating path P *reaches* a set S of states if each leaf of P is in S.

Definition 6. Let T be a test for M.

1. Given a subset $S \subseteq S_M$, T *covers* S if $S \subseteq S_T \upharpoonright \Sigma_M$.
2. T *covers all transitions* of M if $T \upharpoonright \Sigma_M = M$.

3. Given a subset $S \subseteq S_M$, T *can reach* S if there is a path from some initial state of T to a state t such that $t \upharpoonright \Sigma_M \in S$.
4. Given a subset $S \subseteq S_M$, T *is guaranteed to reach* S if, for some initial state s of T, there is an alternating path of T from s to a state t such that $t \upharpoonright \Sigma_M \in S$.
5. Given a grouping G for M, T *covers* G, if $G(S_M) = G(S_T \upharpoonright \Sigma_M)$.

For active tests, the definitions are more or less standard, and execution of a test case produces the given coverage. In the case of reactive systems with observable actions, assumptions have to be made about fairness and the probabilities of the observable actions. In the general case, we have extended the Chinese postman tour algorithm to non-deterministic systems. For alternating reachability a version of Dijkstra's shortest path can be extended to alternating paths, that is used, if possible, to generate tests that are guaranteed to reach a a set of states. Both algorithms are discussed in [30]. For computing test cases that optimize the expected cost, where the system under test is viewed as nature, algorithms from Markov decision process theory can be adapted [9].

Implementation. In Spec Explorer, the algorithms discussed in [30] have been implemented for the purposes of reaching a set of states and for state and transition coverage. Also in Spec Explorer, the desired set of states is always specified by a state based expression. Each action is associated with a cost and a weight using a state based expression as well. Weights are used to calculate action probabilities. Spec explorer uses the value iteration algorithm for negative Markov decision problems, that is discussed in [9], to generate tests that optimize the expected cost where the observable actions are given probabilities.

For certain traversal algorithms in Spec Explorer, such as a random walks, the tests are limited to a maximum number of steps. Once the maximum number has been reached the test continues with a shortest path to an accepting state. For other test purposes, such as transition coverage, one may need to re-execute some of the test segments in order to observe different observable actions from the same underlying state. In such cases, there is a limit on the number of tries related to each segment that always limits each test to a finite number of steps. In those cases, the tests are not explicitly represented as automata, but implicitly by a program that produces the tests dynamically (during test execution) from the segments generated from M.

Example 13. Consider M in Example 12. The test T for M that is illustrated in Figure 6 covers all transitions of M.

5.3   Online Test Generation

Rather than using pre-generated tests, in *online* testing or *on-the-fly* testing, test cases are created dynamically as testing proceeds. Online testing uses to the model program "as is". The online technique was motivated by problems that we observed while testing large-scale commercial systems; it has been used in an industrial setting to test operating system components and Web service infrastructure.

We provide here a high level description of the basic OTF (on-the-fly) algorithm [38] as a transformation of M. Given a model program P, let $M = M_P$. OTF is a transformation of M that given a desired number of test cases n and a desired number of steps k in each test case, produces a test suite T for M. The OTF transformation is done lazily during test execution. We present here the mathematical definition of T as a non-deterministic unfolding of M, where the choices of observable actions reflect the observable actions that take place during test execution. The choices of controllable actions are random selections of actions made by the OTF algorithm. It is assumed that an accepting state is reachable from every state of M.

T has the test variables *TestCaseNr*, *StepNr* that hold integer values, and a Boolean test variable *active*. OTF produces test cases T_i with *TestCaseNr* $= i$ for $1 \leq i \leq n$.

Each T_i is an unfolding of M produced by the following non-deterministic algorithm. Consider a fixed T_i. Let s_0 be the initial state of M. We let s denote the current state of M. Initially $s = s_0$, *StepNr* $= 0$, and *active* $= true$.

The following steps are repeated first until *StepNr* $= k$, or s is a terminal state, and after that until s is an accepting state.

1. Assume *active* $= true$. If $Ctrl_M(s) \neq \varnothing$ and $Obs_M(s) \neq \varnothing$ choose randomly to do either either (1a) or (1b), else if $Ctrl_M(s) \neq \varnothing$ do (1a), otherwise do (1b).
   (a) Choose randomly a controllable action $a \in Ctrl_M(s)$, let $t = \delta_M(a, s)$, and let a be the only action enabled in the current state and let *StepNr* $:=$ *StepNr* $+ 1$, *active* $:= true$, $s := t$.
   (b) Let *Observe* be the only action enabled in the current state and switch to passive mode *active* $:= false$.
2. Assume *active* $= false$. All actions in $Obs_M(s)$ and *Timeout* are enabled in the current state, no controllable actions are enabled. Choose non-deterministically an action $a \in Obs_M(s) \cup \{Timeout\}$, let *StepNr* $:=$ *StepNr* $+ 1$, *active* $:= true$, and if $a \neq Timeout$ let $s := \delta_M(a, s)$.

A single test case in T formally an unfolding of M from the initial state in form of an alternating path from the initial state, all of whose leaves are accepting states and either the length of each branch is at least k, and ends in a first encounter of an accepting state, or the length of the branch is less than k and ends in a terminal accepting state. Since T is created during execution, only a single path is created for each test case that includes the actual observable actions that happened.

Implementation. The implementation of OTF in Spec Explorer uses the model program P. Action weights are used in the manner explained in Example 12, to select controllable actions from among a set of actions for which parameters have been generated from state based parameter generators. Besides state based weights one can also associate *decrementing weights* with action methods. Then the likelihood of selection decreases with the number of times a method has previously been used, i.e. the weight expression depends on the test variables. The OTF algorithm is discussed in more detail in [36,38].

6   Test Execution

We discuss here the conformance relation that is used during testing. The testing process assumes that the implementation under test is encapsulated in an observationally complete "wrapper", that is discussed first. This is needed in order to be able to guarantee termination of test execution. We then discuss how object bindings between the implementation and the model world are maintained and how these bindings affect the conformance relation. Next, the conformance relation is defined formally as an extension of alternating simulation. Finally, we discuss how action bindings are checked and how the conformance engine works.

6.1 Observational Completeness of Implementation under Test

The actual implementation under test may be a distributed system consisting of subsystems, a (multithreaded) API (application programmers interface), a GUI (graphical user interface), etc. We think of the behaviour of the IUT (implementation under test) as an automaton I that provides an interleaved view of the behaviour of the subsystems if there are several of them. The implementation uses the same set of function symbols $\mathcal{F}$ and action methods $\mathcal{M}$ as the model. Values are interpreted in the same universe $\mathcal{U}$. For testability, the IUT is assumed to have a wrapper N that provides an *observationally complete* view of the actual behaviour in the following sense:

1. The action method vocabulary $\mathcal{M}_N$ of N is $\mathcal{M}$ extended with the test actions *Observe* and *Timeout* used in tests.
2. The reduct of N to $\Sigma_{M_{\text{IUT}}}$ is M_{IUT}.
3. For each state $s \in S_N$, *Observe* $\in Ctrl_N(s)$ and, given $t = \delta_N(s, Observe)$, $Obs_N(t) \neq \varnothing$, and $Obs_I(t) \subseteq Obs_N(t) \subseteq Obs_I(t) \cup \{Timeout\}$.
4. Only *Observe* transitions to a state of N where observable actions are enabled.

Implementation. The timeout action is approximated by using a state based expression that determines the amount of time to wait for observable actions from I to occur. In general, the timeout may not necessarily indicate absence of other actions, e.g., if the waiting time is too short.

6.2 Object Bindings

The universe $\mathcal{U}$ includes an infinite sub-universe $\mathcal{O}$ of *objects*. Each object $o \in \mathcal{O}$ has a name and any two distinct object names in a given automaton denote distinct objects in $\mathcal{O}$. An automaton M and an automaton N may use distinct objects in their actions. We want to compare the executions of M and N modulo a partial isomorphism from the set of objects used in M to the set of objects used in N. The isomorphism is partial in the sense that it only relates objects that have been encountered in actions. The isomorphism between objects extends naturally to arbitrary values in the so called background universe that includes maps, sets, sequences, etc. The theory of background is worked out in detail in [8], where objects are called reserve elements.

By an *object binding function* σ from M to N, we mean a partial injective (one-to-one) function over $\mathcal{O}$ that induces a partial isomorphism, also denoted by σ, from actions in M to actions in N. Given an action a of M, we write $\sigma(a)$ or $a\sigma$ for the corresponding action in N. Given that $\sigma(o) = o'$, we say that o *is bound to* o' *in* σ and denote it by $o \mapsto_\sigma o'$; we omit σ and write $o \mapsto o'$ when σ is clear from the context.

6.3 Refinement of Model Automata

The refinement relation from a model P_1 to an implementation P_2 is formalized as the refinement relation between the underlying automata

$$M_i = (S_i^{\text{init}}, S_i, S_i^{\text{acc}}, Obs_i, Ctrl_i, \delta_i), \quad \text{for } i \in \{1, 2\}.$$

The following definitions of alternating simulation and refinement for model automata extend the corresponding notions of interface automata as defined in [15]. We denote the universe of finite object binding functions by *Bind*.

Definition 7. An *alternating simulation* from M_1 to M_2 is a relation $\rho \subset S_1 \times Bind \times S_2$ such that, for all $(s, \sigma, t) \in \rho$,

1. For each action $a \in Ctrl_1(s)$, there is a smallest extension θ of σ such that $a\theta \in Ctrl_2(t)$ and $(\delta_1(s, a), \theta, \delta_2(t, a\theta)) \in \rho$;
2. For each action $a \in Obs_2(t)$, there is a smallest extension θ of σ such that $a\theta^{-1} \in Obs_1(s)$ and $(\delta_1(s, a\theta^{-1}), \theta, \delta_2(t, a)) \in \rho$.

The intuition behind alternating simulation is as follows. Consider fixed model and implementation states. The first condition ensures that every controllable action enabled in the model must also be enabled in the implementation modulo object bindings, and that the alternating simulation relation must hold again after transitioning to the target states, where the set of object bindings may have been extended for objects that have not been encountered before. The second condition is symmetrical for observable actions, going in the opposite direction. The role of object bindings is important; if a model object is bound to an implementation object then the same model object cannot subsequently be bound to a different implementation object and vice versa, since that would violate injectivity of an object binding function.

In the special case when no objects are used, it is easy to see that the projection of ρ to states is an alternating simulation from M_1 to M_2 viewed as interface automata, provided that controllable actions are considered as input actions and observable actions are considered as output actions [15]. In general though, alternating simulation with object bindings cannot be reduced to alternating simulation because object bindings are not known in advance and may be different along different paths of execution; this is illustrated with the following example.

Example 14. Consider the chat example. Let $M_1 = M_{\text{chat}}$ and let M_2 be the automaton of a chat system implementation. Consider the following sequence of transitions in M_1:

$$(s_0, \texttt{Create()}/\texttt{c1}, s_1), \quad (s_1, \texttt{Create()}/\texttt{c2}, s_2)$$

In other words, two clients are created one after another. Assume these are the only controllable actions enabled in s_0 and s_1. The same method call in the initial state of the implementation, say t_0 would result in different objects being created each time Create is invoked. For example, the following transitions could be possible in the implementation:

$$(t_0, \texttt{Create()}/\texttt{d1}, t_1), \quad (t_1, \texttt{Create()}/\texttt{d2}, t_2),$$
$$(t_0, \texttt{Create()}/\texttt{e1}, t_3), \quad (t_3, \texttt{Create()}/\texttt{e2}, t_4), \dots$$

There is an alternating simulation from M_1 to M_2 where c1 is bound to d1 and c2 is bound to d2 along one possible path, or where c1 is bound to e1 and c2 is bound to e2 along another path.

Definition 8. A *refinement* from M_1 to M_2 is an alternating simulation from M_1 to M_2 such that $S_1^{init} \times \{\varnothing\} \times S_2^{init} \subset \rho$.

A refinement relation is essentially an alternating simulation relation that must hold from all initial states (with no initial object bindings). We say that M_1 *specifies* M_2, or M_2 *conforms to* or *is specified by* M_1, if there exists a refinement from M_1 to M_2. Again, it is easy to see that when there are no objects then the refinement relation reduces essentially to refinement of interface automata as defined in [15]. The following example shows a case when refinement does not hold due to a conflict with object bindings.

Example 15. Let M_1 be as in Example 14, and let M_3 be the automaton of a buggy implementation that in successive calls of Create returns the same object that is created initially after the first call. For example the transitions of M_3, where t_0 is the initial state, could be:

$$(t_0, \texttt{Create()}/\texttt{d1}, t_1), \quad (t_1, \texttt{Create()}/\texttt{d1}, t_2)$$

Let us try to build up a refinement relation ρ iteratively following definitions 7 and 8. Initially $(s_0, \varnothing, t_0) \in \rho$. After the first iteration,

$$(s_0, \varnothing, t_0), (s_1, \{\texttt{c1} \mapsto \texttt{d1}\}, t_1) \in \rho.$$

After another invocation of Create from s_1 there are two distinct objects c1 and c2 in s_2. It is not possible to further extend ρ, since one would need to extend $\{\texttt{c1} \mapsto \texttt{d1}\}$ with the binding c2 $\mapsto$ d1 that would identify two distinct model objects with the same implementation object.

6.4   Checking Enabledness of Actions

We describe in more detail, given a model automaton $M = M_P$ and an implementation automaton N, a procedure for deciding if an action a of M and an action b of M can be bound by extending a given set of object bindings σ. It is assumed here that the signatures of M and N are such that $\mathcal{F} = \mathcal{F}_M = \mathcal{F}_N$ and $\mathcal{M} = \mathcal{M}_M = \mathcal{M}_N$.

Implementation. Spec Explorer provides a mechanism for the user to bind the action methods in the model to methods with matching signatures in the IUT. Abstractly, two methods that are bound correspond to the same element in $\mathcal{M}$.

In the following we describe how, in a given model state s with a given set σ of object bindings, a controllable action $a = m(\mathbf{v})/\mathbf{w}$ is chosen in M and how its enabledness in N is validated.

1. Input parameters $\mathbf{v}$ for m are generated in such a way that the precondition $Pre_m[\mathbf{v}]$ holds in s. All object symbols in $\mathbf{v}$ must already be bound to corresponding implementation objects, otherwise a can not be bound to any implementation action.

2. The method call $m(\mathbf{v})$ is executed in the model and the method call $m(\mathbf{v}\sigma^{-1})$ is executed in the implementation.
3. The method call in the model produces output parameters $\mathbf{w}$ and the method call in the implementation produces output parameters $\mathbf{w}'$. Values in $\mathbf{w}$ and $\mathbf{w}'$ are compared for equality and σ is extended with new bindings, if an extension is possible without violating injectivity, otherwise the actions cannot be bound.

Conversely, in order to check enabledness of an observable implementation action $a = m(\mathbf{v})/\mathbf{w}$ in the model the following steps are taken.

1. A binding error occurs if there is an implementation object in $\mathbf{v}$ that is not in σ and a corresponding model object cannot be created. If σ can be extended to σ', $Pre_m[\mathbf{v}\sigma']$ is checked in s. If the precondition does not hold, a is not enabled in the model.
2. The method call $m(\mathbf{v}\sigma')$ is executed in the model yielding output parameters $\mathbf{w}'$.
3. This may yield a conformance failure if either σ' cannot be extended or if the values do not match.

Example 16. Calling a controllable action a in the model may return the value 1, but IUT throws an exception, resulting in a conformance failure. A binding violation occurs if for example the implementation returns an object that is already bound to a model object, but the model returns a new object or an object that is bound to a different implementation object.

6.5   Conformance Automaton

The conformance automaton is a machine that takes a model M, a test T and an observationally complete implementation wrapper N. It executes each test in T against N. The conformance automaton keeps track of the set of object bindings. The following variables are used:

- A variable *verdict*, that may take one of the values *Undecided, Succeeded, Failed, TimedOut*, or *Inconclusive*.
- A set of object bindings β that is initially empty.
- The current state of T, s_T.
- The current state of N, s_N.

For each initial state s_0 of T, the following is done. Let $s_T = s_0$. Let s_N be the initial state of N. The following steps are repeated while *verdict* = *Undecided*.

Observe: Assume s_T is passive. Observe an action $b \in Obs_N(s_N)$ and let $s_N :=$ $\delta_N(b, s_N)$. There are two cases:
    1. If β can be extended to β' such that $a = b\beta'^{-1} \in Obs_M(s_T)$ then $\beta := \beta'$.
        (a) If $a \in Obs_T(s_T)$ then $s_T := \delta_T(a, s_T)$.
        (b) Otherwise *verdict* := *Inconclusive*.
    2. Otherwise, if $a = $ *Timeout* then *verdict* := *TimedOut* else *verdict* := *Failed*.
Control: Assume s_T is active. Let $a = T(s_T)$ and let $s_T := \delta_T(a, s_T)$. There are two cases:

1. If β can be extended to β' such that $b = a\beta' \in Ctrl_N(s_N)$ then $\beta := \beta'$ and $s_N := \delta_N(b, s_N)$.
2. Otherwise $verdict := Failed$.

Finish: Assume s_T is terminal. Let $verdict := Succeeded$.

An inconclusive verdict corresponds to the case when the test case has eliminated some possible observable actions, i.e., an observable action happens but the test case does not know how to proceed, although the observable action is enabled in the model. One may consider a class of *complete* tests T such that for each passive state s, $Obs_T(s_T) \supseteq Obs_M(s_T)$, to avoid inconclusive verdicts. The test produced by the OTF transformation is complete in this sense. The *TimedOut* verdict is a violation of the specification from T to N but not a violation of the specification from M to I. However, if the verdict is *Failed* then I does not conform to M, which follows from the assumption that the reduct of T to Σ_M is a sub-automaton of M and that the reduct of N to Σ_I is I.

Implementation. The inconclusive verdict is currently not implemented in Spec Explorer; it is the testers responsibility to guarantee that the test is complete or to tolerate a failure verdict also for inconclusive tests.

The implementation of the conformance automaton does not know the full state of N. The description given above is an abstract view of the behaviour. In particular, the choice of an observable action a in $Obs_N(s_N)$ corresponds to the implementation wrapper producing an action a, which is guaranteed by observational completeness of N.

7   Related Work

Extension of the FSM-based testing theory to nondeterministic and probabilistic FSMs received attention some time ago [22,31,40]. The use of games for testing is pioneered in [3]. A recent overview of using games in testing is given in [39]. Games have been studied extensively during the past years to solve various control and verification problems for open systems. A comprehensive overview on this subject is given in [15], where the game approach is proposed as a general framework for dealing with system refinement and composition. The paper [15] was influential in our work for formulating the testing problem by using alternating simulation of automata. The notion of alternating simulation was first introduced in [4].

Model-based testing allows one to test a software system using a specification (a.k.a. a model) of the system under test [6]. There are other model-based testing tools [5,26,27,28,34]. To the best of our knowledge, Spec Explorer is the first tool to support the game approach to testing. Our models are Abstract State Machines [10,23,24]. In Spec Explorer, the user writes models in AsmL [25] or in Spec# [7].

The basic idea of online or on-the-fly testing is not new. It has been introduced in the context of labelled transition systems using "*ioco*" (input-output conformance) theory [35,11,33] and has been implemented in the TorX tool [34]. Ioco theory is a formal testing approach based on labelled transition systems (that are sometimes also called I/O automata). An extension of ioco theory to symbolic transition systems has recently been proposed in [17].

The main difference between alternating simulation and ioco is that the system under test is required to be input-enabled in ioco (inputs are controllable actions), whereas alternating simulation does not require this since enabledness of actions is determined dynamically and is symmetric in both ways. In our context it is often unnatural to assume input completeness of the system under test, e.g., when dealing with objects that have not yet been created. An action on an object can only be enabled when the object actually exists in a given state. Refinement of model automata also allows the view of testing as a game, and one can separate the concerns of the conformance relation from how you test through different test strategies that are encoded in test suites.

There are other important differences between ioco and our approach. In ioco theory, tests can in general terminate in arbitrary states, and accepting states are not used to terminate tests. In ioco, quiescence is used to represent the absence of observable actions in a given state, and quiescence is itself considered as an action. Timeouts in Spec Explorer are essentially used to model special observable actions that switch the tester from passive to active mode and in that sense influence the action selection strategies in tests. Typically a timeout is enabled in a passive state where also other observable actions are enabled; thus timeouts do not, in general, represent absence of other observable actions. In our approach, states are full first-order structures from mathematical logic. The update semantics of an action method is given by an abstract state machine (ASM) [23]. The ASM framework provides a solid mathematical foundation to deal with arbitrarily complex states. In particular, we can use state-based expressions to specify action weights, action parameters, and other configurations for test generation. We can also reason about dynamically created object instances, which is essential in testing object-oriented systems. Support for dynamic object graphs is also present in the Agedis tools [26].

Generating test cases from finite model automata is studied in [9,30]. Some of the algorithms reduce to solving negative Markov decision problems with the total reward criterion, in particular using value iteration [32], and the result that linear programming yields a unique optimal solution for negative Markov decision problems after eliminating vertices from which the target state is not reachable [14, Theorem 9].

The predecessor of Spec Explorer was the AsmLT tool [6]. In AsmLT accepting states and timeouts were not used. The use of state groupings was first studied in [19] and extended in [12] to multiple groupings.

8   Conclusion

We have presented the concepts and foundations of Spec Explorer, a model-based testing tool that provides a comprehensive solution for the testing of reactive object-oriented software system. Based on an accessible and powerful modeling notation, Spec#, Spec Explorer covers a broad range of problems and solutions in the domain, including dynamic object creation, non-determinism and reactive behaviour, model analysis, offline and online testing and automatic harnessing.

Being used on a daily basis internally at Microsoft, user feedback indicates that improvements to the approach are necessary. We identify various areas below, some of which we are tackling in the design and implementation of the next generation of the tool.

Scenario control. Scenario control is the major issue where improvements are needed. Currently, scenario control is realized by parameter generators, state filters, method restriction, state grouping, and so on. For some occasions, describing scenario control can be more challenging than describing the functionality of the test oracle. This is partly because of the lack of adequate notations for scenario control, and also because fragments of the scenario control are spread over various places in the model and configuration dialog settings, making it hard to understand which scenarios are captured.

It would be desirable to centralize all scenario control related information as one "aspect" in a single document, which can be reviewed in isolation. Moreover, scenario-oriented notations like use cases would simplify formulating certain kind of scenarios.

We are currently working on an extension of our approach that allows the user to write scenarios in an arbitrary modelling style, such as Abstract State Machines or Use Cases. The scenario control can be seen as an independent model, which can be reviewed and explored on its own. *Model composition* combines the scenario control model with the functional model.

Model Composition. Another important issue identified by our users is model composition. At Microsoft, as is typical in the industry as a whole, product groups are usually organized in small feature teams, where one developer and one tester are responsible for a particular feature (part of the full functionality of a product). In this environment it must be possible to model, explore and test features independently. However, for integration testing, the features also need to be tested together. To that end, Spec Explorer users would like to be able to compose compound models from existing models. For the next generation of the tool, we view the scenario control problem as a special instance of the model composition problem.

Symbolic exploration. The current Spec Explorer tool requires the use of ground data in parameters provided for actions. This restriction is sometimes artificial and required only by underlying technical constraints of the tool. Consider the Chat example from earlier in the chapter: it does not really matter which data is send by a client, but only that this same data eventually arrives at the other clients. For the next generation of the tool, we are therefore generalizing exploration to the symbolic case [20]. We will use an exploration infrastructure that connects to an underlying constraint solver.

Measuring coverage and testing success. One major problem of model-based testing is developing adequate coverage and test sufficiency metrics. Coverage becomes particularly difficult in the case of internal non-determinism in the implementation: how can behavioural coverage be achieved for observable actions of the implementation? Testing success is often measured in industry by rates of bug detection; however, model-based testing might show lower bug counts since bugs can be discovered during modelling and resolved before any test is ever run.

Failure analysis and reproduction cases. Understanding the cause of a failure after a long test run is related to a similar problem in the context of model-checking. There might be a shorter run that also leads to the error and which should be used as the reproduction case passed to the developer. Moreover, in the case of non-deterministic systems, it is desirable to have a reproduction sample that discovers the error reliably with every run. Generating reproduction cases is actually closely related to the problem of online testing, but here we want to drive the IUT into a certain state where a particular error can be discovered. Some of these problems can be recast as problems of test strategy generation in the game-based sense. We are currently extending the work started in [9] to online testing, using Markov decision theory for optimal strategy generation from finite approximations of model automata. For online testing, we are also investigating the use of model-based learning algorithms [37].

Continuing testing after failures. If a failure is detected by model-based testing – offline or online – testing can usually not be continued from the failing state, since the model's behavior is not defined for that case. In practice, however, the time from when a bug is discovered and when it is fixed might be rather long, and it should be possible to continue testing even in the presence of bugs. Current practice is to modify scenarios to deal with this problem, but there could be more systematic support for dealing with this standard situation.

In this chapter we have provided a detailed description of the foundations of the model-based testing tool Spec Explorer. The tool is publicly available from [1]. The development of the features in the tool have in many respects been driven by demands of users within Microsoft. Model-based testing is gaining importance in the software industry as systems are becoming more complex and distributed, and require formal specifications for interoperability. Spec Explorer has shown that model-based testing can be very useful and can be integrated into the software development process. There are several interesting directions for further research in which the technology can be improved. Some of the main directions are compositional modelling, improved online algorithms, and symbolic execution.

References

1. Spec Explorer tool. public release January 2005, updated release October 2006,
   http://research.microsoft.com/specexplorer
2. Spec# tool (public release, March 2005)
   http://research.microsoft.com/specsharp
3. Alur, R., Courcoubetis, C., Yannakakis, M.: Distinguishing tests for nondeterministic and probabilistic machines. In: Proc. 27th Ann. ACM Symp. Theory of Computing, pp. 363–372 (1995)
4. Alur, R., Henzinger, T., Kupferman, O., Vardi, M.: Alternating refinement relations. In: Sangiorgi, D., de Simone, R. (eds.) CONCUR 1998. LNCS, vol. 1466, pp. 163–178. Springer, Heidelberg (1998)
5. Artho, C., Drusinsky, D., Goldberg, A., Havelund, K., Lowry, M., Pasareanu, C., Rosu, G., Visser, W.: Experiments with test case generation and runtime analysis. In: Börger, E., Gargantini, A., Riccobene, E. (eds.) ASM 2003. LNCS, vol. 2589, pp. 87–107. Springer, Heidelberg (2003)
6. Barnett, M., Grieskamp, W., Nachmanson, L., Schulte, W., Tillmann, N., Veanes, M.: Towards a tool environment for model-based testing with AsmL. In: Petrenko, A., Ulrich, A. (eds.) FATES 2003. LNCS, vol. 2931, pp. 264–280. Springer, Heidelberg (2004)

7. Barnett, M., Leino, R., Schulte, W.: The Spec# programming system: An overview. In: Barthe, G., Burdy, L., Huisman, M., Lanet, J.-L., Muntean, T. (eds.) CASSIS 2004. LNCS, vol. 3362, pp. 49–69. Springer, Heidelberg (2005)

8. Blass, A., Gurevich, Y.: Background, reserve, and Gandy machines. In: Clote, P.G., Schwichtenberg, H. (eds.) CSL 2000. LNCS, vol. 1862, pp. 1–17. Springer, Heidelberg (2000)

9. Blass, A., Gurevich, Y., Nachmanson, L., Veanes, M.: Play to test. In: Grieskamp, W., Weise, C. (eds.) FATES 2005. LNCS, vol. 3997, pp. 32–46. Springer, Heidelberg (2006)

10. Börger, E., Stärk, R.: Abstract State Machines: A Method for High-Level System Design and Analysis. Springer, Heidelberg (2003)

11. Brinksma, E., Tretmans, J.: Testing Transition Systems: An Annotated Bibliography. In: Cassez, F., Jard, C., Rozoy, B., Dermot, M. (eds.) MOVEP 2000. LNCS, vol. 2067, pp. 187–193. Springer, Heidelberg (2001)

12. Campbell, C., Veanes, M.: State exploration with multiple state groupings. In: Beauquier, D., Börger, E., Slissenko, A. (eds.) 12th International Workshop on Abstract State Machines, ASM 2005, March 8–11, 2005, Laboratory of Algorithms, Complexity and Logic, University Paris 12 – Val de Marne, Créteil, France, pp. 119–130 (2005)

13. Campbell, C., Veanes, M., Huo, J., Petrenko, A.: Multiplexing of partially ordered events. In: Khendek, F., Dssouli, R. (eds.) TestCom 2005. LNCS, vol. 3502, pp. 97–110. Springer, Heidelberg (2005)

14. de Alfaro, L.: Computing minimum and maximum reachability times in probabilistic systems. In: Baeten, J.C.M., Mauw, S. (eds.) CONCUR 1999. LNCS, vol. 1664, pp. 66–81. Springer, Heidelberg (1999)

15. de Alfaro, L.: Game models for open systems. In: Dershowitz, N. (ed.) Verification: Theory and Practice. LNCS, vol. 2772, pp. 269–289. Springer, Heidelberg (2004)

16. de Alfaro, L., Henzinger, T.A.: Interface automata. In: Proceedings of the 8th European Software Engineering Conference and the 9th ACM SIGSOFT Symposium on the Foundations of Software Engineering (ESEC/FSE), pp. 109–120. ACM, New York (2001)

17. Franzen, L., Tretmans, J., Willemse, T.A.C.: Test generation based on symbolic specifications. In: Grabowski, J., Nielsen, B. (eds.) FATES 2004. LNCS, vol. 3395, pp. 1–15. Springer, Heidelberg (2005)

18. Glässer, U., Gurevich, Y., Veanes, M.: Abstract communication model for distributed systems. IEEE Transactions on Software Engineering 30(7), 458–472 (2004)

19. Grieskamp, W., Gurevich, Y., Schulte, W., Veanes, M.: Generating finite state machines from abstract state machines. In: ISSTA 2002. Software Engineering Notes, vol. 27, pp. 112–122. ACM, New York (2002)

20. Grieskamp, W., Kicillof, N., Tillmann, N.: Action machines: a framework for encoding and composing partial behaviors. International Journal of Software Engineering and Knowledge Engineering 16(5), 705–726 (2006)

21. Grieskamp, W., Tillmann, N., Veanes, M.: Instrumenting scenarios in a model-driven development environment. Information and Software Technology 46(15), 1027–1036 (2004)

22. Gujiwara, S., Bochman, G.V.: Testing non-deterministic state machines with fault-coverage. In: Kroon, J., Heijunk, R.J., Brinksma, E. (eds.) Protocol Test Systems, pp. 267–280 (1992)

23. Gurevich, Y.: Evolving Algebras 1993: Lipari Guide. In: Börger, E. (ed.) Specification and Validation Methods, pp. 9–36. Oxford University Press, Oxford (1995)

24. Gurevich, Y., Kutter, P.W., Odersky, M., Thiele, L. (eds.): ASM 2000. LNCS, vol. 1912. Springer, Heidelberg (2000)

25. Gurevich, Y., Rossman, B., Schulte, W.: Semantic essence of AsmL. Theoretical Computer Science 343(3), 370–412 (2005)

26. Hartman, A., Nagin, K.: Model driven testing - AGEDIS architecture interfaces and tools. In: 1st European Conference on Model Driven Software Engineering, Nuremberg, Germany, December 2003, pp. 1–11 (2003)

27. Jard, C., Jéron, T.: TGV: theory, principles and algorithms. In: The Sixth World Conference on Integrated Design and Process Technology, IDPT 2002, Pasadena, California (June 2002)

28. Kuliamin, V.V., Petrenko, A.K., Kossatchev, A.S., Bourdonov, I.B.: UniTesK: Model based testing in industrial practice. In: 1st European Conference on Model Driven Software Engineering, Nuremberg, Germany, December 2003, pp. 55–63 (2003)

29. Lee, D., Yannakakis, M.: Principles and methods of testing finite state machines – a survey. In: Proceedings of the IEEE, Berlin, August 1996, vol. 84, pp. 1090–1123. IEEE Computer Society Press, Los Alamitos (1996)

30. Nachmanson, L., Veanes, M., Schulte, W., Tillmann, N., Grieskamp, W.: Optimal strategies for testing nondeterministic systems. In: ISSTA 2004, July 2004. Software Engineering Notes, vol. 29, pp. 55–64. ACM, New York (2004)

31. Petrenko, A., Yevtushenko, N., Bochmann, G.v.: Testing deterministic implementations from nondeterministic FSM specifications. In: Baumgarten, B., Burkhardt, H.-J., Giessler, A. (eds.) IFIP TC6 9th International Workshop on Testing of Communicating Systems, pp. 125–140. Chapman & Hall, Boca Raton (1996)

32. Puterman, M.L.: Markov Decision Processes: Discrete Stochastic Dynamic Programming. Wiley-Interscience, New York (1994)

33. Tretmans, J., Belinfante, A.: Automatic testing with formal methods. In: EuroSTAR 1999: 7th European Int. Conference on Software Testing, Analysis & Review. EuroStar Conferences, Barcelona, Spain, Galway, Ireland, November 8–12 (1999)

34. Tretmans, J., Brinksma, E.: TorX: Automated model based testing. In: 1st European Conference on Model Driven Software Engineering, Nuremberg, Germany, December 2003, pp. 31–43 (2003)

35. van der Bij, M., Rensink, A., Tretmans, J.: Compositional testing with ioco. In: Petrenko, A., Ulrich, A. (eds.) FATES 2003. LNCS, vol. 2931, pp. 86–100. Springer, Heidelberg (2004)

36. Veanes, M., Campbell, C., Schulte, W., Kohli, P.: On-the-fly testing of reactive systems. Technical Report MSR-TR-2005-03, Microsoft Research (January 2005)

37. Veanes, M., Roy, P., Campbell, C.: Online testing with reinforcement learning. In: Havelund, K., Núñez, M., Roşu, G., Wolff, B. (eds.) FATES 2006 and RV 2006. LNCS, vol. 4262, pp. 240–253. Springer, Heidelberg (2006)

38. Veanes, M., Campbell, C., Schulte, W., Tillmann, N.: Online testing with model programs. In: ESEC/FSE-13: Proceedings of the 10th European Software Engineering Conference held jointly with 13th ACM SIGSOFT International Symposium on Foundations of Software Engineering, pp. 273–282. ACM, New York (2005)

39. Yannakakis, M.: Testing, optimization, and games. In: Proceedings of the Nineteenth Annual IEEE Symposium on Logic In Computer Science, LICS 2004, pp. 78–88. IEEE Computer Society Press, Los Alamitos (2004)

40. Yi, W., Larsen, K.G.: Testing probabilistic and nondeterministic processes. In: Testing and Verification XII, pp. 347–361. North-Holland, Amsterdam (1992)

Testing Real-Time Systems Using UPPAAL

Anders Hessel[1], Kim G. Larsen[2], Marius Mikucionis[2], Brian Nielsen[2],
Paul Pettersson[1], and Arne Skou[2]

[1] Department of Information Technology, Uppsala University, P.O. Box 337,
SE-751 05 Uppsala, Sweden
{hessel,paupet}@it.uu.se
[2] Department of Computer Science, Aalborg University, Fredrik Bajersvej 7E,
DK-9220 Aalborg, Denmark
{kgl,marius,bnielsen,ask}@cs.aau.dk

Abstract. This chapter presents principles and techniques for model-based black-box conformance testing of real-time systems using the UPPAAL model-checking tool-suite. The basis for testing is given as a network of concurrent timed automata specified by the test engineer. Relativized input/output conformance serves as the notion of implementation correctness, essentially timed trace inclusion taking environment assumptions into account. Test cases can be generated offline and later executed, or they can be generated and executed online. For both approaches this chapter discusses how to specify test objectives, derive test sequences, apply these to the system under test, and assign a verdict.

1 Introduction

Many computer-based systems monitor and control a physical environment through sensors and actuators. The physical laws governing the environment induce a set of real-time constraints which the system must obey in order to achieve satisfactory or safe operation. Thus the computer system must not only produce correct result or reaction, but must do so at the correct time; neither too early nor too late. For a *real-time system* the timely reaction is just as important as the kind of reaction.

Testing real-time systems is even more challenging than testing untimed reactive systems, because the tester must now consider *when* to stimulate system, *when* to expect responses, and how to assign verdicts to the observed timed event sequence. Further, the test cases must be executed in real-time, i.e., the test execution system itself becomes a real-time system.

In this chapter we introduce a formal approach to model-based black-box conformance testing of real-time systems. We aim both at introducing timed testing to readers that are new in the area by giving many examples, and to more experienced readers by being formally precise and by touching on more advanced topics.

1.1 Approach and Chapter Outline

Real-time influences all aspects of test generation: The specification language must allow for the specification of real-time constraints. The conformance

R.M. Hierons et al. (Eds.): Formal Methods and Testing, LNCS 4949, pp. 77–117, 2008.

(implementation) relation must define what real-time behavior should be considered correct. It should be possible to specify what parts of the specified behavior should be tested. This can be done through test purposes, coverage criteria, or random exploration. Finally, the test generation algorithm must analyze the real-time specification, select and instantiate test cases, and output these in a timed test notation language. This computation must be done efficiently in order to handle large and complex specifications.

The timed automata formalism has become a popular and widespread formalism for specifying real-time systems. We adopt the particular UPPAAL style of timed automata. UPPAAL style timed automata have proven very expressive and convenient, but can still be analyzed efficiently. Section 2 introduces timed automata, their formal semantics in terms of timed labeled transition systems, and how to use timed automata to model and specify the behavior of real-time systems.

In the timed testing research community there is still no consensus on the exact conformance relation to use to evaluate the correctness of an implementation compared to its specification. Timed trace inclusion captures many of our intuitive expectations as well as having desired formal properties and is consistent with the widely accepted untimed input/output conformance-relation of Tretmans. We propose relativized timed input/output conformance relation between model and implementation under test (IUT) which coincides with timed trace inclusion taking assumptions about the environment behavior explicitly into account. In addition to allowing explicit and independent modelling of the environment, it also has some nice theoretical properties that allow testing effort to be reused when the environment or system requirements change. Relativized real-time input-output conformance is presented in Section 3.

Common approaches to test selection include test purposes or coverage criteria. When a model-checker is to be used to generate test sequences, the model is typically explicitly annotated with auxillary variables or automata that allow the test purpose or coverage criterion to be formulated as a reachability property that can be issued to the model-checker. In this chapter we present a more elegant approach where test purposes and coverage criteria can be formulated as *observer automata* that can be automatically superimposed on the model. This avoids explicit changes to the model, and allows the user to specify his own coverage criteria with relative ease. Observers and test generation using model-checking are presented in Section 4.

Given the model and observer automata, the problem becomes how to implement a test generator that efficiently can generate the required test suite. In Section 4.4 we propose an efficient algorithm that extends the basic reachability algorithm in UPPAAL with a compact bit-vector encoding of the specified coverage criteria.

The chapter illustrates two different approaches to timed testing which can be viewed as two extremes in a spectrum of possible approaches, offline and online testing, as depicted in Figure 1. In between these extremes are approaches that precompute a strategy or reduced specification (with particular test purpose in

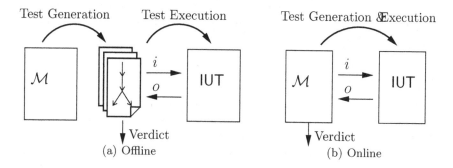

Fig. 1. Online vs. Offline Test Generation

mind) later to be executed online. Offline and online testing are compared below and discussed in detail in Sections 4 and 5.

1.2 Offline Test Generation

In *offline test generation* the test suite is pre-computed completely from the specification before it is executed on the implementation under test. Offline test generation inherits a general advantage of automated model-based testing such that when the requirements or model change, test cases can be automatically re-generated to reflect the change, rather than manually updating every test case and test script.

The advantages of offline test generation are that test cases are easier, cheaper, and faster to execute because all time constraints in the specification have been resolved at test generation time, and in addition, that the test suite can be generated with some a-priori guarantees, e.g., that the specification is structurally covered, or that a given set of test-objectives are met as fast or with as few resources as possible.

There are two main disadvantages of offline test generation. One is that the specification must be analyzed in its entirety, which often results in a state-explosion which limits the size of the specification that can be handled. Another problem is non-deterministic implementations and specifications. In this case, the output (and output timing) cannot be predicted, and the test case must be adaptive. Typically, the test case takes the form of a test-tree that branches for all possible outcomes. This may lead to very large test cases. In particular for real-time systems the test case may need to branch for all time instances where an output could arrive.

Offline test generators therefore often limit the expressiveness and amount of non-determinism of the specification language. This has been a particular problem for offline test generation from timed automata specifications, because the technique of determinizing the specification cannot be directly applied.

Given a restricted class of deterministic and output urgent timed automata we show in Section 4 how it is possible to use the unmodified UPPAAL model-checker to synthesize test cases that are guaranteed to take the least possible time to execute. We also define a language for defining test purposes and coverage criteria, and present an efficient test generation algorithm.

1.3   Online Testing

Another testing approach is *online (on-the-fly) testing* that combines test generation and execution. Here the test generator interactively interprets the model, and stimulates and observes the IUT. Only a single test input is generated from the model at a time which is then immediately executed on the IUT. Then the produced output (if any) by the IUT as well as its time of occurrence are checked against the specification, a new input is produced and so forth until it is decided to end the test, or an error is detected. Typically, the inputs and delays are chosen randomly. An observed test run is a trace consisting of an alternating sequence of (input or output) actions and time delays.

There are several advantages of online testing. Testing may potentially continue for a long time (hours or even days), and therefore long, intricate test cases that stress the IUT may be executed. The state-space-explosion problem experienced by many offline test generation tools is reduced because only a limited part of the state-space needs to be stored at any point in time. Further, online test generators often allow more expressive specification languages, especially wrt. allowed non-determinism in real-time models: Since they are generated event-by-event they are automatically adaptive to the non-determinism of the specification and implementation. Online testing has proven an effective error detection technique [59, 62, 6].

A disadvantage is that the specification must be analyzed online and in real-time which require very efficient test generation algorithms to keep up with the implementation and specified real-time requirements. Also the test runs are typically long, and consequently the cause of a test failure may be difficult to diagnose. Although some guidance is possible, test generation is typically randomized which means that satisfaction of coverage criteria cannot be a priory guaranteed, but must instead be evaluated post mortem.

In Section 5 we present a sound and complete algorithm for online testing of real-time systems from timed automata specifications allowing full non-determinism. We describe an extension of UPPAAL, named TRON, that implements this algorithm, and give an application example. We furthermore show how testing can be viewed as the two sub-problems of environment emulation and system monitoring, and we show how TRON can be configured to perform both combined or independently.

2   Specification of Real-Time Systems

This section formally presents our semantic framework, and introduces timed input/output transition systems (TIOTS), timed automata (TA), and our relativized timed input/output conformance relation.

2.1   Environment and System Modelling

An embedded system interacts closely with its environment which typically consists of the controlled physical equipment (the plant) accessible via sensors and actuators, other computer based systems or digital devices accessible via communication networks using dedicated protocols, and human users. A major development task is to ensure that an embedded system works correctly in its real operating environment. Due to lack of resources it is not feasible to validate the system for all possible (imaginary) environments. Also it is not necessary if the environments are known to a large extent. However, the requirements and the assumptions of the environment should be clear and explicit.

We denote the system being developed IUT, and its real operating environment RealENV. These communicate by exchanging *input* and *output* signals (seen from the perspective of IUT). Using a model-based development approach, the environment assumptions and system requirements are captured through abstract behavioral models denoted $\mathcal{E}$ and $\mathcal{S}$ respectively, communicating on abstract signals $i \in A_{in}$ and $o \in A_{out}$ corresponding (via a suitable abstraction) to the real *input* and *output*, see Figure 2.

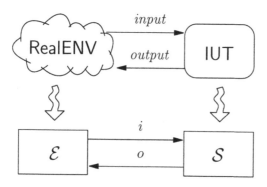

Fig. 2. Abstraction of a system

Modelling the environment explicitly and separately and taking this into account during test generation has several advantages: 1) the test generation tool can synthesize only relevant and realistic scenarios for the given type of environment, which in turn reduces the number of required tests and improves the quality of the test suite; 2) the engineer can guide the test generator to specific situations of interest; 3) a separate environment model avoids explicit changes to the system model if testing must be done under different assumptions or use patterns.

2.2   Timed I/O Transition Systems

To define our testing framework formally we need to introduce a semantic foundation for real-time systems. We use it to model systems and to define the formal semantics of timed automata. A timed input/output transition system (TIOTS) is a labelled transition system where actions have been classified as inputs or outputs, and where dedicated delay labels model the progress of time. In our case we use the set of positive real-numbers to model time. Below we also extend commonly used notation for labeled transition systems to TIOTS.

Formal Definition of TIOTS. We assume a given set of actions A partitioned into two disjoint sets of output actions A_{out} and input actions A_{in}. In addition we assume that there is a distinguished unobservable action $\tau \notin A$. We denote by A_τ the set $A \cup \{\tau\}$.

A *timed I/O transition system* (TIOTS) $\mathcal{S}$ is a tuple $(S, s_0, A_{in}, A_{out}, \rightarrow)$, where

- S is a set of states, $s_0 \in S$,
- and $\rightarrow \subseteq S \times (A_\tau \cup \mathbb{R}_{\geq 0}) \times S$ is a transition relation satisfying the usual constraints of *time determinism* (if $s \xrightarrow{d} s'$ and $s \xrightarrow{d} s''$ then $s' = s''$), *time additivity* (if $s \xrightarrow{d_1} s'$ and $s' \xrightarrow{d_2} s''$ then $s \xrightarrow{d_1 + d_2} s''$), and *zero-delay* (for all states $s \xrightarrow{0} s$). $d, d_1, d_2 \in \mathbb{R}_{\geq 0}$, and $\mathbb{R}_{\geq 0}$ denotes non-negative real numbers.

Notation for TIOTS. Let $a, a_{1...n} \in A$, $\alpha \in A_\tau \cup \mathbb{R}_{\geq 0}$, and $d, d_{1...n} \in \mathbb{R}_{\geq 0}$. We write $s \xrightarrow{\alpha}$ iff $s \xrightarrow{\alpha} s'$ for some s'. We use $\Rightarrow$ to denote the τ-abstracted transition relation such that $s \xRightarrow{a} s'$ iff $s \xrightarrow{\tau}{}^* \xrightarrow{a} \xrightarrow{\tau}{}^* s'$, and $s \xRightarrow{d} s'$ iff $s \xrightarrow{\tau}{}^* \xrightarrow{d_1} \xrightarrow{\tau}{}^* \xrightarrow{d_2} \xrightarrow{\tau}{}^* \ldots \xrightarrow{\tau}{}^* \xrightarrow{d_n} \xrightarrow{\tau}{}^* s'$ where $d = d_1 + d_2 + \cdots d_n$. We extend $\Rightarrow$ to sequences in the usual manner.

$\mathcal{S}$ is *strongly input enabled* iff $s \xrightarrow{i}$ for all states s and for all input actions i. It is *weakly input enabled* iff $s \xRightarrow{i}$ for all states s and for all input actions i. We assume that input actions (seen from the system point of view) are controlled by the environment and outputs are controlled by the system. An input enabled system cannot refuse input actions. However it may decide to ignore the input by executing a transition that results in the same state.

$\mathcal{S}$ is *non-blocking* iff for any state s and any $t \in \mathbb{R}_{\geq 0}$ there is a timed output trace $\sigma = d_1 o_1 \ldots o_n d_{n+1}$, $o_i \in A_{out}$, such that $s \xRightarrow{\sigma}$ and $\sum_i d_i \geq t$. Thus $\mathcal{S}$ will not block time in any input enabled environment. This property ensures that a system will not force or rush its environment to deliver an input, and vice versa, the environment will never force outputs from the system. Time is common for both the system and its environment, and neither controls it.

To model potential implementations it is useful to define the properties of *isolated outputs* and *determinism*. $\mathcal{S}$ is *deterministic* if for all delays or actions $\alpha \in A_\tau \cup \mathbb{R}_{\geq 0}$, and all states s, whenever $s \xrightarrow{\alpha} s'$ and $s \xrightarrow{\alpha} s''$ then $s' = s''$. That is, the successor state of an action is always uniquely known.

We say that $\mathcal{S}$ has *isolated outputs* if whenever $s \xrightarrow{o}$ for some output action o, then $s \xcancel{\xrightarrow{\tau}}$ and $s \xcancel{\xrightarrow{d}}$ for all $d > 0$ and whenever $s \xrightarrow{o'}$ then $o' = o$. A system with isolated outputs will only offer one output at a time, and will never retract an offered output by performing internal actions or delays.

Finally, a TIOTS exhibits *output urgency* iff whenever an output (or τ) is enabled, it will occur immediately, i.e., whenever $s \xrightarrow{\alpha}$, $\alpha \in A_{out} \cup \{\tau\}$ then

$s \not\xrightarrow{d}, d \in \mathbb{R}_{\geq 0}$. An output urgent system will deliver the output immediately when ready.

An observable *timed trace* $\sigma \in (A \cup \mathbb{R}_{\geq 0})^*$ is of the form $\sigma = d_1 a_1 d_2 \ldots a_k d_{k+1}$. We define the observable timed traces $\mathsf{TTr}(s)$ of a state s as:

$$\mathsf{TTr}(s) = \{ \sigma \in (A \cup \mathbb{R}_{\geq 0})^* \mid s \xRightarrow{\sigma} \} \tag{1}$$

For a state s (and subset $S' \subseteq S$) and a timed trace σ, s After σ is the set of states that can be reached after σ:

$$s \text{ After } \sigma = \{ s' \mid s \xRightarrow{\sigma} s' \}, \quad S' \text{ After } \sigma = \bigcup_{s \in S'} s \text{ After } \sigma \tag{2}$$

The set $\mathsf{Out}(s)$ of observable outputs or delays from states $s \in S' \subseteq S$ is defined as:

$$\mathsf{Out}(s) = \{ a \in A_{out} \cup \mathbb{R}_{\geq 0} \mid s \xRightarrow{a} \}, \quad \mathsf{Out}(S') = \bigcup_{s \in S'} \mathsf{Out}(s) \tag{3}$$

TIOTS Composition. Let $\mathcal{S} = (S, s_0, A_{in}, A_{out}, \rightarrow)$ and $\mathcal{E} = (E, e_0, A_{out}, A_{in}, \rightarrow)$ be TIOTSs. Here E is the set of environment states and the set of input (output) actions of $\mathcal{E}$ is identical to the output (input) actions of $\mathcal{S}$. The parallel composition of $\mathcal{S}$ and $\mathcal{E}$ forms a *closed system* $\mathcal{S} \parallel \mathcal{E}$ whose observable behavior is defined by the TIOTS $(S \times E, (s_0, e_0), A_{in}, A_{out}, \rightarrow)$ where $\rightarrow$ is defined as

$$\frac{s \xrightarrow{a} s' \quad e \xrightarrow{a} e'}{(s,e) \xrightarrow{a} (s',e')} \quad \frac{s \xrightarrow{\tau} s'}{(s,e) \xrightarrow{\tau} (s',e)} \quad \frac{e \xrightarrow{\tau} e'}{(s,e) \xrightarrow{\tau} (s,e')} \quad \frac{s \xrightarrow{d} s' \quad e \xrightarrow{d} e'}{(s,e) \xrightarrow{d} (s',e')} \tag{4}$$

2.3 Timed Automata

Timed automata [2] is an expressive and popular formalism for modelling real-time systems. Essentially a timed automaton is an extended finite state machine equipped with a set of real-valued clock-variables that track the progress of time and that can guard when transitions are allowed.

Formal Definition of Timed Automata. Let X be a set of $\mathbb{R}_{\geq 0}$-valued variables called *clocks*. Let $\mathcal{G}(X)$ denote the set of *guards* on clocks being conjunctions of constraints of the form $x \bowtie c$, and let $\mathcal{U}(X)$ denote the set of *updates* of clocks corresponding to sequences of statements of the form $x := c$, where $x \in X$, $c \in \mathbb{N}$, and $\bowtie \in \{\leq, <, =, >, \geq\}$. A *timed automaton* over (A, X) is a tuple (L, ℓ_0, I, E), where

- L is a set of locations, $\ell_0 \in L$ is an initial location,
- $I : L \rightarrow \mathcal{G}(X)$ assigns invariants to locations, and
- E is a set of edges such that $E \subseteq L \times \mathcal{G}(X) \times A_\tau \times \mathcal{U}(X) \times L$.

We write $\ell \xrightarrow{g, a, u} \ell'$ iff $(\ell, g, \alpha, u, \ell') \in E$.

The semantics of a TA is defined in terms of a TIOTS over states of the form $s = (\ell, \bar{v})$, where ℓ is a location and $\bar{v} \in \mathbb{R}_{\geq 0}^X$ is a clock valuation satisfying the invariant of ℓ. Intuitively, a timed automaton can either progress by executing an edge or by remaining in a location and letting time pass:

$$\frac{\forall d' \leq d. \; I_\ell(d')}{(\ell, \bar{v}) \xrightarrow{d} (\ell, \bar{v} + d)} \quad \frac{\ell \xrightarrow{g, \alpha, u} \ell' \wedge g(\bar{v}) \wedge I_{\ell'}(\bar{v}'), \; \bar{v}' = u(\bar{v})}{(\ell, \bar{v}) \xrightarrow{\alpha} (\ell', \bar{v}')} \tag{5}$$

In delaying transitions, $(\ell, \bar{v}) \xrightarrow{d} (\ell, \bar{v} + d)$, the values of all clocks of the automaton are incremented by the amount of the delay d, denoted $\bar{v} + d$. The automaton may delay in a location ℓ as long as the invariant I_ℓ for that location remains true. Discrete transitions $(\ell, \bar{v}) \xrightarrow{\alpha} (\ell', \bar{v}')$ correspond to execution of edges $(\ell, g, \alpha, u, \ell')$ for which the guard g is satisfied by $\bar{v}$, and for which the invariant of the target location $I_{\ell'}$ is satisfied by the updated clock valuation $\bar{v}'$. The target state's clock valuation $\bar{v}'$ is obtained by applying clock updates u on $\bar{v}$.

Uppaal Timed Automata. Throughout this chapter we use UPPAAL syntax to illustrate TA, and the figures are direct exports from UPPAAL. UPPAAL allows construction of large models by composing timed automata in parallel and lets these communicate using shared discrete and clock variables and synchronize (rendezvous-style) on complementary input and output actions, as well as broadcast actions.

Initial locations are marked using a double circle. Edges are by convention labeled by the triple: guard, action, and assignment in that order. The internal τ-action is indicated by an absent action-label. Committed locations are indicated by a location with an encircled "C". A committed location must be left immediately by the next transition taken in the system. An urgent location (encircled "U") must be left without letting time pass, but allows interleaving by other automata. Finally, bold-faced clock conditions placed under locations are location invariants. In addition to clocks, UPPAAL also allows integer variables to be used in guards and assignments.

The latest version further supports a safe subset of C-code in assignments and guards, and C-data-structures.

Example 1. Fig. 3 shows a TA modelling the behavior of a simple light-controller. The user interacts with the controller by touching a touch sensitive pad. The light has three intensity levels: OFF, DIMMED, and BRIGHT. Depending on the timing

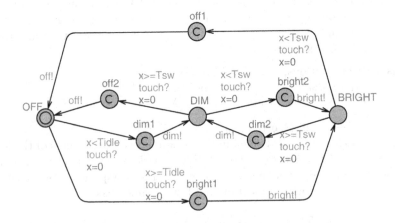

Fig. 3. Light Controller

between successive touches (recorded by the clock x), the controller toggles the light levels. For example, in dimmed state, if a second touch is made quickly (before the switching time $T_{sw} = 4$ time units) after the touch that caused the controller to enter dimmed state (from either off or bright state), the controller increases the level to bright. Conversely, if the second touch happens after the switching time, the controller switches the light off. If the light controller has been in off state for a long time (longer than or equal to $T_{idle} = 20$), it should reactivate upon a touch by going directly to bright level.

The simple light controller can perform the execution sequence $(\texttt{OFF}, x = 0) \xrightarrow{5} (\texttt{OFF}, x = 5) \xrightarrow{touch?} (\texttt{dim1}, x = 0) \xrightarrow{dim!} (\texttt{DIM}, x = 0) \xrightarrow{3.14} (\texttt{DIM}, x = 3.14) \xrightarrow{touch?} (\texttt{bright2}, x = 0) \xrightarrow{bright!} (\texttt{BRIGHT}, x = 0)$ resulting in the observable trace $\sigma = 5 \cdot touch? \cdot dim! \cdot 3.14 \cdot touch! \cdot bright!$. Note that $\{(\texttt{OFF}, x = 0)\}$ After $\sigma = \{(\texttt{BRIGHT}, x = 0)\}$, $\mathsf{Out}(\{(\texttt{OFF}, x = 0)\}$ After $\sigma) = \mathbb{R}_{\geq 0}$, but $\mathsf{Out}((\texttt{bright2}, x = 0)) = \{bright!\} \cup \{0\}$.

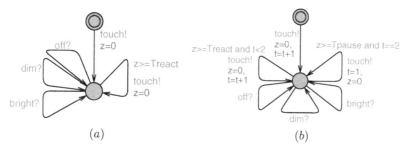

(a)   (b)

Fig. 4. Two possible environment models for the simple light switch

Figure 4 shows two possible environment models for the simple light controller. Figure 4(a) models a user capable of performing any sequence of touch actions. When the constant T_{react} is set to zero he is arbitrarily fast. A more realistic user is only capable of producing touches with a limited rate; this can be modeled setting T_{react} to a non-zero value. Figure 4(b) models a different user able to make two quick successive touches (counted by integer variable t), but which then is required to pause for some time (to avoid cramp), e.g., $T_{pause} = 5$.

The TA shown in Figure 3 and Figure 4 respectively can be composed in parallel on actions $A_{in} = \{\texttt{touch}\}$ and $A_{out} = \{\texttt{off}, \texttt{dim}, \texttt{bright}\}$ forming a closed network (to avoid cluttering the figures we may sometimes omit making them explicitly input enabled; for the unspecified inputs there is a non-drawn self looping edge that merely consumes the input without changing the location).

Example 2. Figure 5(a) shows a timed automaton specification C^r for a controller whose goal is to control and keep the room temperature in *Med* range by turning *On* and *Off* the room cooling device. The controller is required: 1) to turn *On* the cooling device within an allowed reaction time r when the room temperature reaches *High* range, and 2) to turn it *Off* within r when the temperature drops to *Low* range. Observe how location invariants are used to force the automaton to

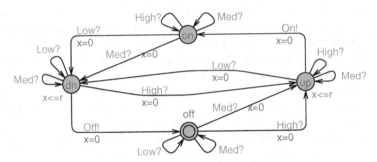

(a) $\mathcal{C}^r$: simple cooling controller with reaction time r.

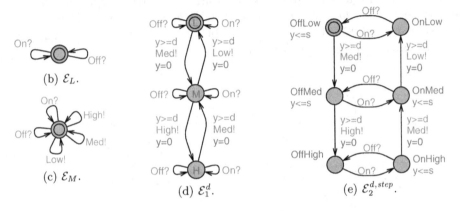

(b) $\mathcal{E}_L$.

(c) $\mathcal{E}_M$.

(d) $\mathcal{E}_1^d$.

(e) $\mathcal{E}_2^{d,step}$.

Fig. 5. Timed automata of simple controller and various environments

leave the **dn** and **up** locations before the reaction time has elapsed, in consequence producing the output at some time before the required reaction time. When the room temperature is medium the cooling is allowed to be either on or off.

This specification is non-deterministic in two ways. First, there are several next states to a *Med* temperature, e.g.,

$$\{(\texttt{off}, x = 0)\} \text{ After } 5 \cdot Med? = \{(\texttt{off}, x = 5), (\texttt{up}, x = 0)\}. \tag{6}$$

Second, the controller switches state *within* the reaction time r, but it is unknown when. Thus from e.g., state $(\texttt{up}, x = 0)$ the controller may execute any of the observable traces, $d \cdot On!, 0 \leq d \leq r$. Note that

$$\mathsf{Out}((\texttt{up}, x = 0)) = \{On!\} \cup \{d \mid 0 \leq d \leq r\}. \tag{7}$$

The intention of this specification (given our conformance relation) is to allow implementation freedom to the manufacturer wrt. exact functionality, speed, timing tolerances, etc..

The Uppaal Tool. In the UPPAAL tool it is possible to edit, simulate and check properties of UPPAAL timed automata in a graphical environment. The property specification language supports safety, liveness, deadlock, and response properties.

In this chapter we use the UPPAAL tool for offline test generation by expressing the test case generation problem as a safety property that can be solved by reachability analysis. Safety properties are used to expresses requirements of the form "the model can never reach an undesired state". The dual properties like "the system can reach a desired state", are usually referred to as reachability properties.

When checking a safety property, the UPPAAL tool performs symbolic reachability analysis of the network of timed automata to search for reachable states where the property is satisfied (or not satisfied). If a state that satisfies the property is found, UPPAAL generate a diagnostic traces witnessing a submitted safety property. Currently UPPAAL supports three options for diagnostic trace generation: *some trace* leading to the goal state, the *shortest trace* with the minimum number of transitions, and *fastest trace* with the shortest accumulated time delay. The underlying algorithm used for finding time-optimal traces is a variation of the A*-algorithm [5,39]. Hence, to improve performance it is possible to supply a heuristic function estimating the remaining cost from any state to the goal state.

To perform reachability analysis of (densely) timed automata UPPAAL uses a (finite) symbolic representation of the state space and symbolic computation steps.

A *symbolic state* is of the form (ℓ, D), where ℓ is a control location of a timed automaton and D is a convex subset of $\mathbb{R}_{\geq 0}^{|X|}$, i.e. it represents the (potentially infinite) set of concrete states $\{(\ell', \bar{v}) \mid \ell' = \ell \wedge \bar{v} \in D\}$. The initial symbolic state is (ℓ_0, D_0), where $D_0 = \{ \bar{v} \mid (\ell_0, \bar{v}_0) \xrightarrow{d} (\ell_0, \bar{v}) \}$ and $\bar{v}_0$ is the clock valuation assigning all clocks to zero.

A *symbolic computation step* $(\ell, D) \xrightarrow{\alpha} (\ell', D')$ consists of performing an action followed by some delay, and can be performed iff $(\ell, \bar{v}) \xrightarrow{\alpha} (\ell', \bar{v}')$, and

$$D' = \left\{ \bar{v}'' \mid (\ell, \bar{v}) \xrightarrow{\alpha} (\ell', \bar{v}') \wedge (\ell', \bar{v}') \xrightarrow{d} (\ell', \bar{v}'') \wedge \bar{v} \in D \right\}.$$

It is possible to represent a convex subset D as a so-called *difference bounded matrix* [21] that can be efficiently manipulated by constraint-solving techniques [53], implemented as model-checking tools such as UPPAAL and Kronos [20].

3   Relativized Timed Conformance

In this section we define our notion of conformance between TIOTSs. Our notion derives from the input/output conformance relation (ioco) of Tretmans and de Vries [58,63] by taking time and environment constraints into account. Under assumptions of weak input enabledness our relativized timed conformance relation (denoted rtioco$_e$) coincides with relativized timed trace inclusion. Like ioco, this relation ensures that the implementation has only the behavior allowed by the specification. In particular, 1) it is not allowed to produce an output at a time when one is not allowed by the specification, 2) it is not allowed to omit producing an output when one is required by the specification.

The ioco relation operates with the concept of *quiescence* allowing (eternal) absence of outputs to be observed by means of a finite time out, and be equalized with a special observable action, resulting in a more discriminating relation. It is debatable whether the same abstraction is reasonable in real-time systems. Briones et al. have proposed relations that allows this [12], see also the discussion in Section 6.1. Our relation takes the view that only finite progress of time can be observed in a real-time system. Thus, $rtioco_e$ offers the notion of time-bounded (finite) quiescence, that—in contrast to ioco's conceptual eternal quiescence—can be observed in a real-time system.

Formal Definition of $rtioco_e$. Let $\mathcal{S} = (S, s_0, A_{in}, A_{out}, \rightarrow)$ be an weak-input enabled and non-blocking TIOTS. An *environment* for $\mathcal{S}$ is itself a weak-input enabled and non-blocking TIOTS $\mathcal{E} = (E, e_o, A_{out}, A_{in}, \rightarrow)$ with reversed inputs and outputs.

Given an environment $e \in E$ the e-relativized timed input/output conformance relation $rtioco_e$ between system states $s, t \in S$ is defined as:

$$s\ rtioco_e\ t \quad \text{iff} \quad \forall \sigma \in \mathsf{TTr}(e).\,\mathsf{Out}\big((s,e)\ \mathsf{After}\ \sigma\big) \subseteq \mathsf{Out}\big((t,e)\ \mathsf{After}\ \sigma\big)$$

Whenever $s\ rtioco_e\ t$ we will say that s is a correct implementation (or refinement) of the specification t under the environmental constraints expressed by e. Under the assumption of weak input-enabledness of both $\mathcal{S}$ and $\mathcal{E}$ we may characterize relativized conformance in terms of trace-inclusion as follows:

Lemma 1. *Let $\mathcal{S}$ and $\mathcal{E}$ be input-enabled with states $s, t \in S$ and $e \in E$ resp., then*

$$s\ rtioco_e\ t \quad \text{iff} \quad \mathsf{TTr}(s) \cap \mathsf{TTr}(e) \subseteq \mathsf{TTr}(t) \cap \mathsf{TTr}(e)$$

Thus if $s\ rtioco_e\ t$ does not hold then there exists a trace σ of e such that $s \overset{\sigma}{\Rightarrow}$ but $t \overset{\sigma}{\nRightarrow}$. Given the notion of relativized conformance it is natural to consider the preorder on environments based on their discriminating power, i.e. for environments e and f:

$$e \sqsubseteq f \quad \text{iff} \quad rtioco_f \subseteq rtioco_e \tag{8}$$

(to be read f is more discriminating than e). It follows from the definition of rtioco that $e \sqsubseteq f$ iff $\mathsf{TTr}(e) \subseteq \mathsf{TTr}(f)$. In particular there is a most (least) discriminating (weakly) input enabled and non-blocking environment U (O) given by $\mathsf{TTr}(U) = (A \cup \mathbb{R}_{\geq 0})^*$ $\big(\mathsf{TTr}(O) = (A_{out} \cup \mathbb{R}_{\geq 0})^*\big)$. The corresponding conformance relation $rtioco_U$ ($rtioco_O$) specializes to simple timed trace inclusion (timed output trace inclusion) between system states.

Moreover, because we treat environment constraints explicitly and separately, $rtioco_e$ has some nice theoretical and practical attractive properties that allows the tester to re-use testing effort if either the environment assumption is strengthened, or if the system specification is weakened. Assume that $i\ rtioco_e\ s$, then without re-testing

$$if\ s \sqsubseteq s'\ then\ i\ rtioco_e\ s' \tag{9}$$

$$if\ e' \sqsubseteq e\ then\ i\ rtioco_{e'}\ s \tag{10}$$

In the following we exemplify how our conformance relation discriminates systems, and illustrate the potential power of environment assumptions and how this can help to increase the relevance of the generated tests for a given environment.

Example 3. Consider the simple cooling controller C^r of Figure 5(a), where r is a parameter r with its reaction time, and the environment in Figure 5(c).

Take C^{10} to be the specification and assume that the implementation behaves like C^{12}. Clearly, C^8 rtioco$_{\mathcal{E}_M}$ C^6 because $\sigma = 0 \cdot Med! \cdot 7 \cdot On! \in \mathsf{TTr}(C^8)$, but $\sigma \notin \mathsf{TTr}(C^6)$, or alternatively, $\mathsf{Out}(C^8$ After $0 \cdot Med! \cdot 7) = \{On!\} \cup \mathbb{R}_{\geq 0} \not\subseteq \mathsf{Out}(C^6$ After $0 \cdot Med! \cdot 7) = \mathbb{R}_{\geq 0}$ (recall that C^r may remain in location *off* on input *Med* and not produce any output). The implementation can thus perform an output at a time not allowed by the specification.

Next, suppose C^r is implemented by a timed automaton C'^r equal to C^r, except the transition $up \xrightarrow{Low} dn$ is missing, and replaced by a self loop $up \xrightarrow{Low} up$.

They are distinguishable by the timed trace $0 \cdot Med? \cdot 0 \cdot High? \cdot 0 \cdot Low? \cdot 0 \cdot On!$ in the implementation that is not in the specification (switches the compressor *Off* instead).

Example 4. Figure 5(c) shows the universal (most general) and completely unconstrained environment $\mathcal{E}_M$ where room temperature may change unconstrained and may change (discretely) with any rate. This may not be realistic in the given physical environment, and there may be less need to test the controller in such an environment, as temperature normally evolves slowly and continuously, e.g., it cannot change drastically from *Low* to *High* and back unless through *Med*. Similarly, most embedded and real-time systems also interact with physical environments and other digital systems that— depending on circumstances—can be assumed to be correct and correctly communicate using well defined interfaces and protocols.

Figures 5(b) to 5(e) show four possible environment assumptions for C^r. Figure 5(c) and Figure 5(b) shows respectively the most discriminating and least discriminating environments. Figure 5(d) shows the environment model $\mathcal{E}_1^d$ where the temperature changes through *Med* range and with a speed bounded by d. Figure 5(e) shows an even more constrained environment $\mathcal{E}_2^{d,s}$ that assumes that the cooling device works, e.g., temperature changes with an upper and lower speed bounded by d and s.

Notice that $\mathcal{E}_2$ and $\mathcal{E}_1$ have less discriminating power and thus may not reveal faults found under more discriminating environments. However, if the erroneous behavior is impossible in the actual operating environment the error may be irrelevant. Consider again the implementation C'^r from above. This error can be detected under $\mathcal{E}_0$ and $\mathcal{E}_1^k$ if $k = 3d$ and $r > k$, via the timed trace that respects $d \cdot Med? \cdot d \cdot High? \cdot d \cdot Med? \cdot d \cdot Low? \cdot \varepsilon \cdot On!$, $\varepsilon \leq r$. The specification would produce *Off*. The error cannot be detected under $\mathcal{E}_1$ if it is too slow $3d > r$, and never under $\mathcal{E}_2$ for no value of d.

In the extreme the environment behavior can be so restricted that it only reflects a single test scenario that should be tested. In our view, the environment assumptions should be specified explicitly and separately.

4   Offline Test Generation

In this section, we describe an offline test generation approach for real-time systems specified as timed automata. In order to specify that a certain level of thoroughness is achieved in the testing we shall require that a generated test suite satisfies a given coverage criterion. For untimed systems coverage criteria have been studied by researchers for many years, and a number specific coverage criteria have been proposed in the literature, including [45,52,14,15,17,26,41,51, 49,23,54]. In comparison, research in real-time coverage criteria is still a more immature area where not many general results are available. Therefore, most of the coverage criteria and test generation techniques described in this section were originally proposed for testing of untimed systems. However, they can often be adopted for the domain of real-time system. For example, the well-known all-definitions use-pair coverage criterion [26,41] (described in Sections 4.2 and 4.3), can be applied to definitions and uses of timers, as well as data variables.

We will see in Section 4.2 how test case generation can be performed by reformulating the problem as a model-checking problem that can be solved by a model-checking tool like UPPAAL. This will require that the original system is annotated with variables that are needed to formulate the test case generation problem as a model-checking problem. For intricate coverage criteria, it can be cumbersome to find and manually do the right model annotations. The auxiliary variables also add extra complexity to the timed automata model. In Section 4.3 we present a formal language to specify coverage criteria and we review an algorithm which handles the extra information directly in the algorithm. In this way the process becomes more user friendly, and the coverage information can be dealt with more efficiently using a bit-vector representation.

In order to make offline test case generation applicable to timed automata specifications, we shall assume that the underlying TIOTS is *deterministic*, *weakly input enabled*, *output urgent*, with *isolated outputs* as defined in Section 2.2. This means that the S is assumed to react deterministically to any input provided, and will always be able to accept input from the test case. At any state, the S is also assumed to always have at most one output action that will occur immediately.

Further, as discussed in Section 2, we shall assume that the test specification is given as a closed network of TA that can be partitioned into one subnetwork S specifying the required behavior of the IUT, and one subnetwork $\mathcal{E}$ modelling the behavior of its intended environment RealENV, as depicted in Fig. 2.

4.1   Test-Case Generation by Model-Checking

When generating test cases by model-checking, the idea is to formulate the problem as a reachability problem that can be solved with an existing model-checking tool. As mentioned, we will use the UPPAAL tool introduced in Section 2.3 to perform reachability analysis of timed automata. More precisely, we shall use a boolean combination of comparisons between integer constants and variables in the model to characterise a desired state to be reached.

In Section 4.2, we will describe in more details how UPPAAL's ability to produce traces witnessing a posed reachability property can be used to produce test cases for a given test purpose or coverage criteria. First, we describe how diagnostic traces can be interpreted as test cases.

From Diagnostic Traces to Test Cases. Let A be a TA composition of an IUT model S and a model $\mathcal{E}$ of its intended environment RealENV. A diagnostic trace produced by UPPAAL for a given reachability question on A demonstrates the sequence of moves to be made by each of the system components and the required clock constraints needed to reach the target location. A (concrete) diagnostic trace will have the form:

$$(s_0, e_0) \xrightarrow{\gamma_0} (s_1, e_1) \xrightarrow{\gamma_1} (s_2, e_2) \xrightarrow{\gamma_2} \cdots (s_n, e_n)$$

where s_i, e_i are states of the S and $\mathcal{E}$, respectively, and γ_i are either time-delays or synchronization (or internal) actions. The latter may be further partitioned into purely S or $\mathcal{E}$ transitions (hence invisible for the other part) or synchronizing transitions between the IUT and the RealENV (hence observable for both parties).

A *test sequence* is an alternating sequence of concrete delay actions and observable actions. From the diagnostic trace above a *test sequence*, $\lambda \in A_{in} \cup A_{out} \cup \mathbb{R}_{\geq 0}$, may be obtained simply by projecting the trace to the $\mathcal{E}$-component, while removing invisible transitions, and summing adjacent delay actions. Finally, a *test case* to be executed on the real IUT implementation may be obtained from λ by the addition of *verdicts*.

First note that with the assumptions made on the underlying TIOTS made above, the conformance relation specializes to timed trace inclusion, as discussed in Section 3. Thus, after any input sequence, the implementation is allowed to produce an output only if the specification is also able to produce that output. Similarly, the implementation may delay (thereby staying silent) only if the specification also may delay. The test sequences produced by our techniques are derived from diagnostic traces, and are thus guaranteed to be included in the specification.

To clarify the construction we may model the test case itself as a TA A_λ for the test sequence λ. Locations in A_λ are labelled using two distinguished labels, PASS and FAIL. The execution of a test case is now formalized as the composition of the test case automaton A_λ and IUT A_I.

$$\text{IUT } \textbf{passes } \lambda \;\; \textit{iff} \;\; A_\lambda \parallel A_I \;\not\rightarrow^* \text{FAIL}$$

A_λ is constructed such that a *complete execution* terminates in a FAIL state if the IUT cannot perform λ and such that it terminates in a PASS state if the IUT can execute all actions of λ. The construction is illustrated in Figure 6.

4.2 Coverage-Based Test Case Generation

We shall see how test cases satisfying a given *coverage criterion* can be generated by model-checking. A common approach to the generation of test cases is to first

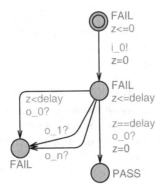

Fig. 6. Test case automaton for the sequence $i_0! \cdot delay \cdot o_0?$

manually formulate a set of informal test purposes and then to formalize these such that the model can be used to generate one or more test cases for each test purpose.

Test Purposes. A test purpose is a specific test objective (or property) that the tester would like to observe on the IUT. We will formulate the test purpose as a property that can be checked by reachability analysis of the combined $\mathcal{E}$ and $\mathcal{S}$ model. Different techniques can be used for this purpose. Sometimes the test purpose can be directly transformed into a simple model-checking property expressed as a boolean combination of automata locations. In other cases it may require decoration of the model with auxiliary flag variables. Another technique is to replace the environment model with a more restricted one that matches the behavior of the test purpose only.

Example 5. We exemplify these two approaches using the following two test purposes expressing test objectives of the simple light controller in Example 1.

TP1: Check that the light can become bright.
TP2: Check that the light switches off after three successive touches.

   The test purpose **TP1** can be formulated as a simple reachability property requiring that eventually the `lightContoller` can enter location `BRIGHT`. Generating the *shortest* diagnostic trace results in the test sequence:

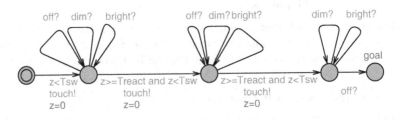

Fig. 7. Test Environment for TP2

$$20 \cdot touch! \cdot 0 \cdot bright?$$

However, the *fastest sequence* satisfying the test purpose is

$$0 \cdot touch! \cdot 0 \cdot dim? \cdot 0 \cdot touch! \cdot 0 \cdot bright?$$

The test purpose **TP2** can be formulated by a reachability property requiring that a location in a specific environment automaton can be reached. In Figure 7 an environment automaton tpEnv for **TP2** is shown. The automaton restricts the possible user input so that there is at least Treact time units in between two consecutive touches. The fastest test sequence satisfying the test purpose is:

$$0 \cdot touch! \cdot 0 \cdot dim? \cdot Treact \cdot touch! \cdot 0 \cdot bright? \cdot Treact \cdot touch! \cdot 0 \cdot off?$$

Coverage Criteria. Often the tester is interested in creating a test suite that ensures that the specification or implementation is covered in a certain way. This ensures that a certain level of thoroughness has been achieved in the test generation process. Here we explain how test sequences with guaranteed coverage of the IUT model can be computed by model-checking, effectively giving automated tool support.

A large suite of coverage criteria have been proposed in the literature, such as statement, transition, and definition-use coverage, each with its own merits and application domain. We explain how to apply some of these to TA models (more coverage criteria will be introduced in Section 4.3).

Edge Coverage: A test sequence satisfies the *edge-coverage criterion* [45] if, when executed on the model, it traverses every edge of the selected TA-components. Edge coverage can be formulated as a reachability property in the following way: add an auxiliary variable e_i of type boolean (initially false) for each edge to be covered (typically realized as a bit array in UPPAAL), and add to the assignments of each edge i an assignment $e_i :=$ **true**; a test suite can be generated by formulating a property requiring that a state can be reached in which all e_i variables are true, i.e., $(e_0 ==$**true** $\wedge e_1 ==$**true** $\wedge \ldots \wedge e_n ==$**true**$)$. The auxiliary variables are needed to enable formulation of the coverage criterion as a reachability property using the UPPAAL property specification language which is a restricted subset of *timed computation tree logic* (TCTL) [3].

Location Coverage: A test sequence satisfies the *location-coverage criterion* [45] if, when executed on the model, it visits every location of the selected TA-components. To generate test sequences with location coverage, we introduce an auxiliary variable b_i of type boolean (initially false for all locations except the initial) for each location ℓ_i to be covered. For every edge with destination ℓ_i: $\ell' \xrightarrow{g,a,u} \ell_i$ add to the assignments u $b_i :=$**true**; the reachability property will then require all b_i variables to be true.

Definition-Use Pair Coverage: The definition-use pair criterion [17] is a data-flow coverage technique where the idea is to cover paths in which a variable is *defined*, i.e. appears in the left-hand side of an assignment, and later is *used*, i.e. appears in a guard or the right-hand side of an assignment.

We use (v, e_d, e_u) to denote a *definition-use pair* (DU-pair) for variable v if e_d is an edge where v is defined and e_u is an edge where v is used. A DU-pair (v, e_d, e_u) is valid if e_u is reachable from e_d and v is not redefined in the path from e_d to e_u. A test sequence covers (v, e_d, e_u) iff (at least) once in the sequence, there is a valid DU-pair (v, e_d, e_u). A test sequence satisfies the (all-uses) DU-pair coverage criterion of v if it covers all valid DU-pairs of v.

To generate test sequences with definition-use pair coverage, we assume that the edges for a model are enumerated, so that e_i is the number of edge i. We introduce an auxiliary data-variable v_d (initially **false**) with value domain $\{$**false**$\} \cup \{1 \ldots |E|\}$ to keep track of the edge at which variable v was last defined, and a two-dimensional boolean array du of size $|E| \times |E|$ (initially **false**) to store the covered pairs. For each edge e_i at which v is defined we add $v_d := e_i$, and for each edge e_j at which v is used we add the conditional assignment *if* $(v_d \neq$ **false**$)$ *then* $du[v_d, e_j] :=$ **true**. Note that if v is both used and defined on the same edge, the array assignment must be made before the assignment of v_d.

The reachability property will then require all $du[i, j]$ representing valid DU-pairs to be true for the (all-uses) DU-pair criterion. Note that a test sequence satisfying the DU-pair criterion for several variables can be generated using the same encoding, but extended with one auxiliary variable and array for each covered variable.

Example 6. The light switch in Figure 3 requires a bit-array of 12 elements (one per edge). When the environment can touch arbitrarily fast the generated fastest edge covering test sequence has the accumulated execution time 28. The solution (there might be more traces with the same fastest execution time) generated by UPPAAL is:

$$0 \cdot touch! \cdot 0 \cdot dim? \cdot 0 \cdot touch! \cdot 0 \cdot bright? \cdot$$
$$0 \cdot touch! \cdot 0 \cdot off? \cdot 20 \cdot touch! \cdot 0 \cdot bright? \cdot$$
$$4 \cdot touch! \cdot 0 \cdot dim? \cdot 4 \cdot touch! \cdot 0 \cdot off?$$

4.3   Test Case Generation Using Observers

As described in the previous section, it is in principle possible to generate test cases by annotating UPPAAL timed automata with auxiliary variables, and solve the problem by reachability analysis. However, for more intricate coverage criteria it can be cumbersome and very time-consuming to find the proper model annotations. Another problem with using model-checking algorithms and tools to generate test cases is that they are not really tailored for the problem, which may lead to problems with performance.

In this section, we shall present another approach to offline test case generation for real-time systems modeled as timed automata. Instead of using model annotations and reachability properties to specify coverage criteria, we shall present a language of *observers* as a generic and formal specification language for coverage criteria. We shall further see how to adapt a model-checking algorithm to internally handle information about coverage, so that test-case generation can be performed in a more efficient way.

The observers presented here are based on the notion of observers described by Blom et.al., in [7]. In their setting, observers are used to express coverage criteria of test cases generated from system specification described as extended finite state machines (EFSMs). In this section, we shall review their work and adapt the results to our setting, i.e., for timed automata specifications of real-time systems. We first describe how observers are used to specify coverage criteria.

The Observer Language. As we have seen, a coverage criterion typically consists of a (rather large) set of items that should be "covered" or examined by the test suite. The set of items to be covered is derived from a more general criterion, requiring that some property ψ should be fulfilled, where ψ is a logical property characterizing the items to be covered. For example, ψ could be satisfied for all locations or edges of a model, to characterize the location of edge coverage criteria mentioned in the previous section. In the following, we will use the term *coverage item* for an item satisfying ψ, and assume that a coverage criterion is to cover as many coverage items ψ as possible of a model.

Using standard techniques from model-checking and run-time verification it is possible to represent a coverage item by an observer that monitors how a timed automaton executes. Whenever a coverage item characterized by the observer is fulfilled, the observer will "accept" the trace. We shall assume that an observer can observe the actions in a trace of an automaton, and also other details about the timed automata performing the action, such as the source and target locations, and the values of its state variables. This will make it possible to characterise a wide range of coverage criteria as observers.

Formally, an *observer* of a timed automaton $\mathcal{S} = (L, \ell_0, I, E)$ is a tuple (Q, q_0, Q_f, B) where

- Q is a finite set of *observer locations*
- q_0 is the *initial observer location.*
- $Q_f \subseteq Q$ is a set of *accepting observer locations.*
- B is a set of edges, each of form $q \xrightarrow{b} q'$ where $q, q' \in Q$ and b is a predicate that depend on the $\mathcal{S}$ transition $(\ell, \bar{v}) \xrightarrow{\alpha} (\ell', \bar{v}')$. The evaluation of b can depend on an input/output action α, and/or the syntactic edge $\ell \xrightarrow{g,\alpha,u} \ell'$ the $\mathcal{S}$ transition is derived from.[1]

In many cases, the initial location q_0 has an edge to itself with the predicate **true**. We use the symbol ● to represent q_0 together with such a self-loop. Similarly, we assume that each $q_f \in Q_f$ has an edge to itself with the predicate **true**. We use the symbol ◎ to represent accepting locations. Intuitively, the loop in q_0 is often used to allow the observer to "non-deterministically" start monitoring at any point in a timed trace. The loop in each q_f is used to allow an observer to stay in an accepting location.

---

[1] For UPPAAL timed automata extended by variables, b can also depend on the variables.

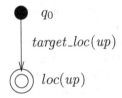

Fig. 8. An observer for location coverage of location *up*

Example 7. As a very simple example, consider the observer shown in Figure 8 characterizing the coverage item *"visit location up of the automaton"*. It has an initial location q_0 and an accepting location $loc(up)$. The predicate $target\_loc(up)$ is satisfied when location *up* is reached in the monitored timed automata. Hence, the observer could e.g., be used to express that location *up* should be covered in automaton C^r of Figure 5.

Intuitively, observers have the following semantics: At any specific instant an observer operates in one or *serveral* of its locations, say $Q_i \subseteq Q$. At each transition, the observer traverses all outgoing edges from each location $q \in Q_i$, whose predicates are satisfied (enabled) due to the monitored transition of S. Note that more than one (or none) of the outgoing edges can be enabled. Thus the possible successors of a single location q can be zero or more locations. This means that, if there is a path to an accepting location q_f, that can be reached by choosing the "right" enabled edge after each transition of S, the observer will find that path, like a non-deterministic automaton would do. In that sense, an observer will monitor and find all possible coverage items. Later in this section, we will define formally how observers monitor coverage criteria.

Since, a coverage criterion typically stipulates that a set of coverage items should be covered, the notion of observers is extended with a parameterization mechanism so that they can specify a *set of* coverage items. Parameterized observers are observers, in which locations and edges may have parameters that range over given domains. Each possible instantiation of a parameter gives a certain observer location or edge. For each specified coverage item, the observer has an *accepting* (possibly parameterized) location which (for convenience) is given the name of the corresponding coverage item. When the accepting location is reached, the trace has covered the corresponding coverage item.

Example 8. The coverage criterion *"visit all locations of C^r"* can be represented by a parameterized observer with one initial state, and one parameterized accepting location, named $loc(\mathtt{L})$, where L is a parameter that ranges over locations in automaton C^r. For each value ℓ of L, the location $loc(\ell)$ is entered when the automaton enters location ℓ. A parameterized observer for location coverage is shown in Figure 9(a).

Without loss of generality we will, in the following description of observers, use a single timed automaton corresponding to the TIOTS S in Section 2. Internal actions of the $\mathcal{E}$ will not affect the observer and the extension to a network of timed automata is straight forward.

How Observers Monitor Coverage Criteria. In test case generation an observer observes the transitions of the timed automaton monitored. Reached accepting locations correspond to covered coverage items. We formally define the execution of an observer in terms of a composition between a timed automaton and an observer, which has the form of a *superposition* of the observer onto the timed automaton. Each state of this superposition consists of a state of the timed automaton, together with a set of currently occupied observer locations.

If a predicate b on an observer edge is satisfied by a timed automaton transition $(\ell, \bar{v}) \xrightarrow{\alpha} (\ell', \bar{v}')$ we write $(\ell, \bar{v}) \xrightarrow{\alpha} (\ell', \bar{v}') \models b$. Formally, the superposition of an observer (Q, q_0, Q_f, B) onto a timed automaton S is defined as follows:

- *States* are of the form $\langle (\ell, \bar{v}) | Q \rangle$, where $(\ell, \bar{v})$ is a state of the timed automaton, and Q is a set of locations of the observer.
- The *initial state* is the tuple $\langle (\ell_0, \bar{v}_0) | \{q_0\} \rangle$, where $(\ell_0, \bar{v}_0)$ is the initial state of the timed automaton, and q_0 is the initial location of the observer.
- A *computation step* is defined by the following two rules
  - $\langle (\ell, \bar{v}) | Q \rangle \xrightarrow{\alpha} \langle (\ell', \bar{v}') | Q' \rangle$ if $(\ell, \bar{v}) \xrightarrow{\alpha} (\ell', \bar{v}')$ and
    $$Q' = \left\{ q' \mid q \xrightarrow{b} q' \text{ and } q \in Q \text{ and } (\ell, \bar{v}) \xrightarrow{\alpha} (\ell', \bar{v}') \models b \right\}$$
  - $\langle (\ell, \bar{v}) | Q \rangle \xrightarrow{d} \langle (\ell, \bar{v}') | Q \rangle$ if $(\ell, \bar{v}) \xrightarrow{d} (\ell, \bar{v}')$
- A state $\langle (\ell, \bar{v}) | Q \rangle$ of the superposition *covers* the coverage item represented by the location $q_f \in Q_f$ if $q_f \in Q$.

Note that the way the set Q is updated essentially results in an (on-the-fly) subset construction of the parameterized observer. Initially, Q contains only the initial observer location q_0. In the subsequent computation steps, Q contains the set of all occupied observer locations, representing already covered and partially covered coverage items. In each discrete action step, the set of occupied observer locations Q' is obtained by generating all possible successors to the locations in Q, i.e. all q' such that there exists a $q \in Q$ and an edge $q \xrightarrow{b} q' \in B$ with b satisfied by the computation step of the timed automaton. The observer set Q is not affected by delay transitions, indicating that the the notion of observers presented in this chapter can not observe time delays.

Both the initial and all accepting observer locations (most commonly) have implicit self-loops with predicate *true*. This means that in the superposition of the observer onto a timed automaton, the initial observer location q_0 is always occupied and all reached accepting observer locations (representing covered coverage items) are guaranteed to remain in Q. As mentioned before, The fact that q_0 is always occupied can be intuitively understood as allowing for the observer to non-deterministically start monitoring a timed automaton (or an IUT) at *any* computation step of a run (or at any point during test execution).

Example 9. Figure 9 shows observers specifying a number of coverage criteria described in the literature [17].

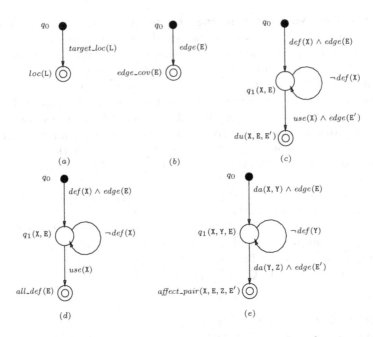

Fig. 9. Five examples of coverage criteria expressed as observers

The *all-locations* [45] coverage criteria is specified by the observer shown in Figure 9(a), where the parameter L is any location in a timed automaton (if restricted to one automaton). If the observer is superposed onto a TIOTS consisting of the timed automaton C^r in Figure 5, we have that L = $\{on, dn, off, up\}$ and the edge of the parameterized observer represents one edge for each location in the automaton C^r i.e. an edge guarded by $target\_loc(on)$ with target location $loc(on)$ etc. Here $target\_loc(L)$ is a predicate which evaluates to true if the observer monitors an edge of the timed automaton C^r with the target location L. The set of possible coverage items is thus $\{loc(on), loc(dn), loc(off), loc(up)\}$.

The *all-edges* [45] coverage observer in Figure 9(b) is similar to the all-location coverage observer. Here $edge(E)$ is a predicate which evaluates to true if the observer monitors edge E of the timed automaton C^r. The edges of the timed automaton C^r in Figure 5 are E=$\{e_0, \ldots, e_{15}\}$[2], and thus the set of possible coverage items when the observer is superposed onto the timed automaton is $\{edge\_cov(e_i) \mid e_i \in E\}$.

The *all-definition* use-pairs (all-uses [17], reach coverage [26, 41]) coverage observer is shown in Figure 9(c). It uses the two predicates $def(X)$ and $use(X)$ that are true if X is defined and used on the monitored edge, respectively (as defined in Section 4.2). The observer has an accepting location $du(X, E, E')$, where X is a variable name, E is an edge on which X is defined, and E' an edge on which X is used. Variable X may not be redefined in the trace between E and E'. If the

---

[2] We assume that the edges can be referred to by indexes 0 to 15.

observer monitors the execution sequence $(\texttt{OFF}, x = 0) \xrightarrow{5} (\texttt{OFF}, x = 5) \xrightarrow{touch?}$ $(\texttt{dim1}, x = 0) \xrightarrow{dim!} (\texttt{DIM}, x = 0) \xrightarrow{3.14} (\texttt{DIM}, x = 3.14) \xrightarrow{touch?} (\texttt{bright2}, x = 0) \xrightarrow{bright!} (\texttt{BRIGHT}, x = 0)$ of the timed automaton in Figure 3 the only covered coverage item is $du(x, \texttt{OFF} \xrightarrow{touch?} \texttt{dim1}, \texttt{DIM} \xrightarrow{touch?} \texttt{bright2})$.

The *all-definitions* [51] coverage observer of Figure 9(d) is similar to the all-definition use-pairs coverage except that only the defining edges are required to be covered. When the observer is superposed with the timed automaton in Figure 3 the set of accepting locations is { $all\_def(\texttt{OFF} \xrightarrow{touch?} \texttt{bright1})$, $all\_def(\texttt{BRIGHT} \xrightarrow{touch?} \texttt{dim2})$, $all\_def(\texttt{DIM} \xrightarrow{touch?} \texttt{bright2})$, $all\_def(\texttt{OFF} \xrightarrow{touch?} \texttt{dim1})$, $all\_def(\texttt{DIM} \xrightarrow{touch?} \texttt{off2})$, $all\_def(\texttt{BRIGHT} \xrightarrow{touch?} \texttt{off1})$ }. The *all affect-pairs* (Ntafos' required k-Tuples [49]) coverage observer is shown in Figure 9(e). It uses the predicate $da(x, y)$ that is true if the observer monitors a transition in which the value of variable x affects the value of variable y. The observer accepts whenever a variable x affects a variable z via another variable y. In this case we require that x directly affects y which, without redefinition, directly affects z.

A Symbolic Semantics of Observers. The way observers monitor coverage criteria, as defined above for timed automata, will result in an infinite state space due to the dense representation of time. Therefore, before presenting the test case generation algorithm, we shall introduce a finite-state *symbolic* semantics based on the symbolic semantics of timed automata described in Section 2.3.

Formally, the symbolic semantics of observers superposed onto a timed automaton is defined as follows:

- *Symbolic states* are of the form $\langle (\ell, D) | \mathcal{Q} \rangle$, where (ℓ, D) is a symbolic state of the timed automaton, and $\mathcal{Q}$ is a set of observer locations.
- A *initial symbolic state* is a tuple $\langle (\ell_0, D_0) | \{q_0\} \rangle$, where (ℓ_0, D_0) is the initial symbolic state of the timed automaton, and q_0 is the initial observer location.
- A computation step is a triple $\langle (\ell, D) | \mathcal{Q} \rangle \stackrel{\alpha}{\Rightarrow} \langle (\ell', D') | \mathcal{Q}' \rangle$ for ℓ' and α such that $(\ell, \bar{v}) \stackrel{\alpha}{\rightarrow} (\ell', \bar{v}')$,

$$D' = \left\{ \bar{v}'' \mid (\ell, \bar{v}) \stackrel{\alpha}{\rightarrow} (\ell', \bar{v}') \wedge (\ell', \bar{v}') \stackrel{d}{\rightarrow} (\ell', \bar{v}'') \wedge \bar{v} \in D \right\}, \text{ and}$$
$$\mathcal{Q}' = \left\{ q' \mid q \stackrel{b}{\longrightarrow} q' \wedge q \in \mathcal{Q} \wedge (\ell, \bar{v}) \stackrel{\alpha}{\rightarrow} (\ell', \bar{v}') \models b \right\}.$$

Note that the evaluation of b does not depend on the clock values of the observed timed automata. Thus, if $(\ell, \bar{v}) \stackrel{\alpha}{\rightarrow} (\ell', \bar{v}')$ is a valid transition satisfying b, then any valid transition $(\ell, \bar{v}'') \stackrel{\alpha}{\rightarrow} (\ell', \bar{v}''')$ in $(l, D) \stackrel{\alpha}{\rightarrow} (l', D')$ will also satisfy b.

4.4   Test Case Generation with Observers

In test case generation with observers, we use the superposition of an observer onto a timed automaton, and view the test case generation problem as a state-space exploration problem. To cover a single coverage item q_f is the problem of finding a trace

$$tr = \langle(\ell_0, \bar{v}_0)|\{q_0\}\rangle \overset{d}{\rightsquigarrow} \overset{\alpha}{\rightsquigarrow} \ldots \overset{d'}{\rightsquigarrow} \overset{\alpha'}{\rightsquigarrow} \overset{d''}{\rightsquigarrow} \langle(\ell, \bar{v})|\mathcal{Q}\rangle \text{ such that } q_f \in \mathcal{Q} \qquad (11)$$

It can be shown, that the problem can also be stated based on the symbolic semantics as

$$tr = \langle(\ell_0, D_0)|\{q_0\}\rangle \overset{\alpha}{\Rightarrow} \ldots \overset{\alpha'}{\Rightarrow} \langle(\ell, D)|\mathcal{Q}\rangle \text{ such that } q_f \in \mathcal{Q} \qquad (12)$$

We will use $\omega(tr) = \alpha \ldots \alpha'$ to denote the *word* of the trace tr, or just ω whenever tr is clear from the context. In general, a single trace tr may cover several accepting locations of the observer. We say that the trace ω covers n accepting observer states if there are n accepting states in $\mathcal{Q}$, and we use $|Q_f \cap \mathcal{Q}|$ to denote the number of accepting states in $\mathcal{Q}$.

Algorithm 1. Test generation for maximum coverage.

---

1 PASS:= $\emptyset$; MAX := 0; $\omega_{max} := \omega_0$;
2 WAIT:= $\{\langle\langle(\ell_0, D_0)|\{q_0\}\rangle, \omega_0\rangle\}$;
3 **while** WAIT$\neq \emptyset$ **do**
4   select $\langle\langle(\ell, D)|\mathcal{Q}\rangle, \omega\rangle$ from WAIT;
5   **if** $|Q_f \cap \mathcal{Q}| > $ MAX **then**
6          $\llcorner$ $\omega_{max} := \omega$; MAX := $|Q_f \cap \mathcal{Q}|$;
7   **if** *for all* $\langle(\ell, D')|\mathcal{Q}'\rangle$ *in* PASS: $\mathcal{Q} \not\subseteq \mathcal{Q}'$ *or* $D \not\subseteq D'$ **then**
8   add $\langle(\ell, D)|\mathcal{Q}\rangle$ to PASS;
9   **for all** $\langle(\ell'', D'')|\mathcal{Q}''\rangle$ such that $\langle(\ell, D)|\mathcal{Q}\rangle \overset{\alpha}{\Rightarrow} \langle(\ell'', D'')|\mathcal{Q}''\rangle$ **do**
10             $\llcorner$ add $\langle\langle(\ell'', D'')|\mathcal{Q}''\rangle, \omega\alpha\rangle$ to WAIT;

11 **return** ω_{max} and MAX;

We are now ready to describe the test case generation algorithm [7]. We shall restrict the presentation to an algorithm generating a single trace. The same technique can be used to produce sets of traces to cover many coverage items. Alternatively, the timed system model $\mathcal{S}$ can be annotated with edges that reset the system to its initial state. A generated trace can then be interpreted as a set of test cases separated by the reset edges [27].

An abstract algorithm to compute test case is shown in Algorithm 1. The algorithm computes the maximum number of coverage items that can be visited (MAX), and returns a trace with maximum coverage (ω_{max}). The two main data structures WAIT and PASS are used to keep track of the states waiting to be explored, and the states already explored, respectively.

Initially, the set of already explored states is empty and the only state waiting to be explored is the *extended state* $\langle\langle(\ell_0, D_0)|\{q_0\}\rangle, \omega_0\rangle$, where ω_0 is the empty trace. The algorithm then repeatedly examines extended states from WAIT. If a state $\langle(\ell, D)|\mathcal{Q}\rangle$ found in WAIT is included in a state $\langle(\ell, D')|\mathcal{Q}'\rangle$ in PASS, then obviously $\langle(\ell, D)|\mathcal{Q}\rangle$ does not need to be further examined. If not, all successor states that are reachable from $\langle(\ell, D)|\mathcal{Q}\rangle$ in one computation step are put on WAIT, with their traces extended with the action of the computation step from

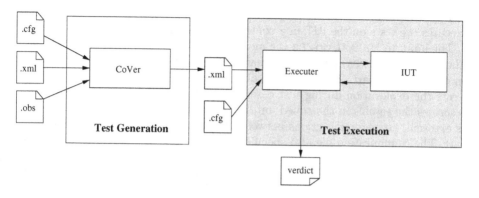

Fig. 10. UPPAAL CO✓ER setup

which they are generated. The state $\langle(\ell, D)|\mathcal{Q}\rangle$ is saved in PASS. The algorithm terminates when WAIT is empty.

The variables ω_{max} and MAX are initially set to the empty trace and 0, respectively. They are updated whenever an extended state is found in WAIT which covers a higher number of coverage items than the current value of MAX. Throughout the execution of the algorithm, the value of MAX is the maximum number of coverage items that have been covered by a single trace, and ω_{max} is one such trace. When the algorithm terminates, the two values MAX and ω_{max} are returned.

It has been shown in e.g. [40] how to extract a concrete diagnostic trace from traces generated by symbolic model-checkers for timed automata. The same technique can be directly applied to extract concrete traces with Algorithm 1. Thus, we can compute traces like Equation 11 from traces like Equation 12 generated by the algorithm. The results on soundness and completeness of symbolic model-checking for timed automata also applies to Algorithm 1 since the number of possible elements in the sets $\mathcal{Q}$ is guaranteed to be finite.

4.5   Tool Implementation

The concept of observers and the test case generation algorithm presented in this section have been implemented in a version of the UPPAAL tool, called UPPAAL CO✓ER [3][28,29]. The current implementation uses bit-vector analysis techniques to represent and manipulate coverage, and supports an extended version of the observer language described in this section [7]. For a given coverage criterion (a set of) test cases can be generated from system specifications described as a network of UPPAAL timed automata [27].

A typical setup in which UPPAAL CO✓ER is used to test an IUT is shown in Figure 10. The setup is divided in two parts, a test *generation* part for generating

---

[3] More information about UPPAAL CO✓ER is available at the web site http://user.-it.uu.se/~hessel/CoVer/.

and transforming test cases into XML-format, and a test *execution* part that executes the tests on the IUT in a controlled environment.

The input to UPPAAL CO√ER is a model, an observer, and a configuration file. The model is an UPPAAL timed automata network (.xml) with a system part and an environment part. The observer (.obs) expresses the coverage criterion that steers the exploration during test case generation. The configuration file (.cfg) describes the signals in the timed automata network that should be considered as external, i.e. the interactions between the system part and the environment part. The configuration file also specifies the variables that should be passed as parameters in the input/ output signals.

The UPPAAL CO√ER tool produces a test suite consisting of a set of test cases (.xml) that are timed traces where each input and output signal has a list of parameters with values (according to the configuration file). An *Executer* interprets the test cases, executes them, and returns a verdict for each test case.

UPPAAL CO√ER has been used in a large case study in collaboration with Ericsson, in which model-based testing was applied to test a WAP gateway [29]. In the case study, the session and transaction layers of the WAP protocol were modeled in detail as UPPAAL timed automata, and observers were used to specify the coverage criteria the test suites should satisfy. The UPPAAL CO√ER tool was applied to generate test suites that were automatically translated into executable test scripts that revealed several discrepancies between the model and the actual implementation.

The observer techniques presented in this section have also been implemented in a tool operating on a subset of the functional language Erlang [8]. The tool has been applied in a case study in collaboration with the Swedish tele communication company Mobile Arts AB.

5   Online Testing

The previous section described offline test generation from timed automata specifications given test purposes or coverage criteria specified as observer automata or reachability properties, but was limited to deterministic specifications. However, for many real-time systems the ordering or timing of events cannot be known a priory, and hence its behavior can not be appropriately captured by a deterministic model.

Moreover, as elaborated in Section 6.3, timed automata cannot be determinized, and hence using determinization as intermediate step as is done by many untimed test generators is infeasible for timed automata, and other approaches are necessary. Here we present online testing which is a promising approach. We present a real-time online testing algorithm, its soundness, completeness and implementation.

5.1   Non-determinism and Time

In general non-determinism in specification is used as a means of *abstraction*. It may be that the exact circumstances in the implementation that lead to different event orderings or timings are not known or would require a model with too many details. It may also be that the implementation internally exhibits non-determinism which cannot be observed or controlled by the tester, e.g., the exact arrival order and timings of external interrupts. A further typical use of non-determinism is to model *optional* behavior that is permitted, but not required by all implementations.

Non-determinism plays a particular role in real-time systems because it is used to express timing uncertainty. A typical real-time requirement is that the IUT must deliver an output within a given time bound, but as long as the deadline is satisfied, the IUT conforms. In TIOTS, this is specified as a non-deterministic choice between letting time pass and producing an output. In timed automata this is described syntactically by using an invariant on a location with the outgoing edge producing the output (see e.g., location l_2 of Figure 5(a) where the compressor is required to switch on (and off) within r time units.

Further, outputs from the IUT may be delayed by an unpredictable amount of time in the communication software between the test host and IUT. Some timing tolerance on most output actions is often required.

A non-deterministic model may reach/occupy several possible states after having executed an action, and as a consequence it may have different possible next behaviors. This possible set of states represents the uncertainty the tester has about the exact state of a (conforming) IUT, and the tester must be prepared to accept any legal next behavior according to the state set.

Example 10. As examples, consider the simple compressor controller of Figure 5(a). Upon receiving a medium temperature reading the controller may either stay off or switch on the compressor, see Equation 6. Further consider the timed automata in Figure 11. The following equations list the states that can be reached after an observable action and a delay. Note that in the second case even a single transition can result in more (infinite with dense time) states. In this example it is not known when the clock x is reset on the internal transition.

$$\{\langle l_0, x = 3\rangle\} \text{ After } a = \{\langle l_2, x = 3\rangle, \langle l_4, x = 3\rangle, \langle l_3, x = 0\rangle\}$$

$$\{\langle l_5, x = 0\rangle\} \text{ After } 4 = \{\langle l_5, x = 4\rangle, \langle l_6, 0 \le x \le 4\rangle\}$$

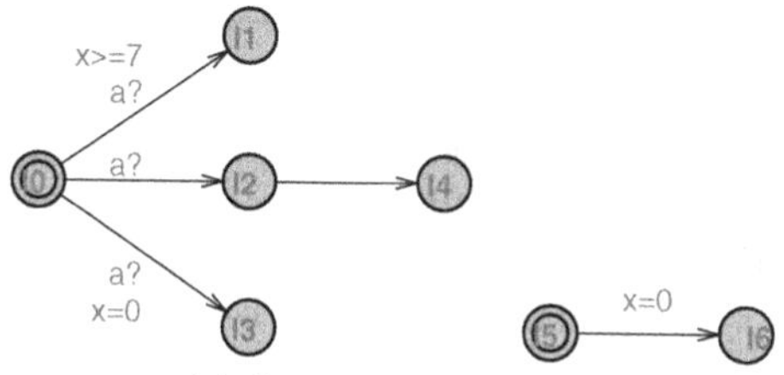

(a) S1   (b) S2

Fig. 11. Two non-deterministic timed automata

Such non-deterministic timed specifications are algorithmically and computationally more complex to analyze than their untimed counter parts because they require symbolic manipulation of sets of infinite sets of states.

5.2   A Real-Time Online Testing Algorithm

The test specification input to Algorithm 2 consists of two *weakly input enabled* and *non-blocking* TIOTSs $\mathcal{S} \parallel \mathcal{E}$ respectively modelling the IUT and its environment. It maintains the current reachable state set $\mathcal{Z} \subseteq S \times E$ that the test specification can possibly occupy after the timed trace σ observed so far. Knowing this state-set allows it to choose appropriate inputs and to validate IUT outputs. Moreover, if the computed state set becomes empty ($\mathcal{S} \parallel \mathcal{E}$ After $\sigma = \emptyset$), the IUT has exhibited a timed trace not in the test specification, and the IUTcannot be rtioco conforming, see Section 3. The possible set of states is computed incrementally event by event.

Algorithm 2. Test generation and execution: $TestGenExe(\mathcal{S}, \mathcal{E}, \text{IUT}, T)$.

```
 1  Z := {(s₀, e₀)};              // initialize the state set with initial state
 2  while Z ≠ ∅ ∧ ♯iterations ≤ T do
 3  │  switch between action, delay and restart randomly do
 4  │  │  case action:                              // offer an input
 5  │  │  │  if EnvOutput(Z) ≠ ∅ then
 6  │  │  │  │  randomly choose i ∈ EnvOutput(Z);
 7  │  │  │  │  send i to IUT,;
 8  │  │  │  └  Z := Z After i;
 9  │  │  case delay:                               // wait for an output
10  │  │  │  randomly choose d ∈ Delays(Z);
11  │  │  │  sleep for d time units or wake up on output o at d' ≤ d;
12  │  │  │  if o occurs then
13  │  │  │  │  Z := Z After d';
14  │  │  │  │  if o ∉ ImpOutput(Z) then  return fail ;
15  │  │  │  └  else Z := Z After o
16  │  │  └  else  Z := Z After d;              // no output within d delay
17  │  └  case restart:  Z := {(s₀, e₀)}; reset IUT;    // reset and restart
18  if Z = ∅ then return fail else return pass;
```

The tester can perform three basic actions: either send an input (enabled environment output) to the IUT, wait for an output for some time, or reset the IUT and restart. If the tester observes an output or a time delay it checks whether this is legal according to the state set. The state set is updated whenever an input is given, or an output or a delay is observed.

Illegal occurrence or absence of an output is detected if the state set becomes empty which is the result if the observed trace is not in the specification. The functions used in Algorithm 2 are defined as: $\mathsf{EnvOutput}(\mathcal{Z}) = \{a \in A_{in} \mid \exists(s, e) \in \mathcal{Z}.e \xrightarrow{a}\}$, $\mathsf{ImpOutput}(\mathcal{Z}) = \{a \in A_{out} \mid \exists(s, e) \in \mathcal{Z}.s \xrightarrow{a}\}$, and $\mathsf{Delays}(\mathcal{Z}) = \{d \mid \exists(s, e) \in \mathcal{Z}.e \xRightarrow{d}\}$ [4]. Note that $\mathsf{EnvOutput}$ is empty if the environment has no outputs to offer. Similarly, the Delays function cannot pick at random from the entire domain of real-numbers if the environment must produce an input to the IUT model before a certain moment in time.

5.3   Soundness and Completeness

Algorithm 2 constitutes a randomized algorithm for providing stimuli to (in terms of input and delays) and observing resulting reactions from (in terms of output) a given IUT. Under a testing hypothesis about the behavior of the IUT and given that the TIOTSs $\mathcal{S}$ and $\mathcal{E}$ satisfy the below given assumptions, the randomization used in Algorithm 2 may be chosen such that the algorithm is both complete and sound in the sense that it (eventually with probability one) gives the verdict "fail" in all cases of non-conformance and the verdict "pass" in cases of conformance.

The hypothesis is based on the results on digitization techniques in [57][5] which allow the dense-time trace inclusion problem between two sets of timed traces to be reduced to discrete time. In particular it suffices to choose unit delays in Algorithm 2 (assuming that the models and the IUT share the same magnitude of a time unit).

Moreover, if the behavior of the IUT is a non-blocking, input enabled, deterministic TIOTS with isolated outputs the reaction to any given timed input trace $\sigma = d_1 i_1 \ldots d_k i_k d_{i+1}$ is completely deterministic. More precisely, given the stimuli σ there is a unique $\rho \in \mathsf{TTr}(\mathsf{IUT})$ such that $\rho \uparrow A_{in} = \sigma$, where $\rho \uparrow A_{in}$ is the natural projection of the timed trace ρ to the set of input actions. If the IUT is allowed to be non-deterministic it cannot be guarenteed that all its behavior have been revealed.

Theorem 1. *Assume that the behavior of* IUT *may be modeled[6] as a weakly input enabled, non-blocking, deterministic TIOTS with isolated outputs,* $\mathsf{TTr}(\mathsf{IUT})$ *and* $\mathsf{TTr}(\mathcal{E})$ *are closed under digitization and that* $\mathsf{TTr}(\mathcal{S})$ *is closed under inverse digitization. Then Algorithm 2 with only unit delays is sound and complete in the following senses:*

---

[4] According to the definition of rtioco_e given in Section 3, all environment traces and delays must be considered, not only the delays that can occur in the parallel composition of $\mathcal{S}$ and $\mathcal{E}$; in a parallel composition a delay is only permitted if both components agree. Therefore $\mathsf{Delays}(\mathcal{Z})$ extracts the possible delays from the environment component e of the system state (s,e) to ensure that the algorithm will try to wait beyond the specified deadlines before supplying a new input.

[5] We refer the reader to [57] for the precise definition of digitization and inverse digitization.

[6] The assumption that the IUT can be modeled by a formal object in a given class is commonly referred to as the *test hypothesis*. Only its existence is assumed, not a known instance.

1. *Whenever TestGenExe*$(\mathcal{S}, \mathcal{E}, \mathsf{IUT}, T) = fail$ *then* IUT rtiόcοε $\mathcal{S}$.
2. *Whenever* IUT rtiόcοε $\mathcal{S}$ *then* $\mathsf{Prob}\big(TestGenExe(\mathcal{S}, \mathcal{E}, \mathsf{IUT}, T) = fail\big) \xrightarrow{T \to \infty}$ 1

   where T is the maximum number of iterations of the while-loop before exiting.

Proof. The proof can be found in [38]. □

From [57, 34] it follows that the closure properties required in Theorem 1 are satisfied if the behavior of the IUT and the $\mathcal{E}$ are TIOTSs induced by closed timed automata (i.e. where all guards and invariants are non-strict) and $\mathcal{S}$ is a TIOTS induced by an open timed automaton (i.e. with guards and invariants being strict). In practice these requirements are not restrictive, e.g. for strict guards one can always scale the clock constants to obtain arbitrary high precision.

5.4   Tool Implementation

The online testing algorithm Algorithm 2 is implemented in a tool named UP-PAAL-TRON [38]: UPPAAL extended for Testing Real-time systems ONline. It implements the setup shown in Figure 12.

We assume that the IUT is a black-box whose state is not directly observable, i.e., only physical *input* and *output* actions are observable. The *adapter* is an IUT specific hardware/software component that connects the IUT to TRON and is responsible for translating abstract input *"in"* test events into physical stimuli and physical IUT output observations into abstract model outputs *"out"*. All events are time-stamped at testing tool side, meaning that the adapter model should be included as part of implementation specification. TRON *engine* loads the test specification which is a network of timed automata partitioned into *models* of the *environment* and the IUT. The goal of TRON is to emulate and replace the environment of the IUT: stimulate the IUT with input that is deemed relevant by the environment part of the model, based on the timed sequence of input and output actions performed so far.

Because TRON executes on platforms whose execution cannot be entirely predicted and controlled (e.g. due to operating system scheduling and tool analysis performance issues), Algorithm 2 is implemented in such a way that TRON checks the validity of output with timing and also the actual timing of input

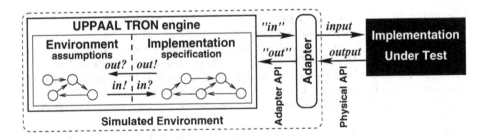

Fig. 12. TRON test setup

execution. TRON provides an application programming interface to enable programming of adapters, and provides the means for loading this as a dynamically linked library.

Internally, TRON uses matured efficient timed automata symbolic reachability algorithm from UPPAAL [4] to compute the symbolic state set which means that the model semantics is preserved and analysis is efficient for online testing. Thus, to compute the operator After the online testing algorithm manipulates sets of symbolic states (ℓ, D), see Section 2.3, and is constructed such that it terminates even if the model contains τ action loops. Further information about the implementation of the required symbolic operations can be found in [38].

To evaluate online testing we have created a number of small academic specifications and implementation (and mutants thereof). The results regarding both performance and error detection capability are promising. More details can be found in [38]. We have also evaluated online testing on an industrial case [44], an electronic refrigeration controller provided by the Danish manufacturer Danfoss A/S. Besides temperature based compressor regulation it has numerous features for handling alarms and defrosting cycles, etc.

We found that real-time online testing is an effective means of detecting discrepancies between the model and the implementation in practice. It also appears feasible performance-wise for such realistic models.

However, large and very non-deterministic models can run into a state explosion making it problematic to update the state-set in real-time which may limit the granularity of time constraints that can be checked in real-time. In a typical test run in the Danfoss case, the state-set varied typically between a few symbolic states and a few hundred symbolic states. Exploring these is unproblematic for the modern model-checking engine employed by TRON. Updating even medium sized state-sets with around a 100 states requires only a few milli-seconds of CPU-time on a modern PC. The largest encountered state-sets (around 3000 states) were very infrequent, and required around 300 milli-seconds.

Real-time online testing thus appears feasible for a large range of embedded systems.

5.5 Testing = Environment Emulation + Implementation Monitoring

On closer inspection it turns out that online testing consists of two logically different functions, namely *environment emulation* and IUT *monitoring*:

Environment Emulation: An environment emulator (completely or partly) replaces the real environment of the IUT, and stimulates the IUT with new inputs based on the history of previous inputs and observed outputs. An environment emulator thus executes online in real-time and actively stimulates the IUT, but does not assign verdicts to the observed trace.

IUT Monitoring: A monitor passively observes the timed input/output sequence produced between the IUT and its real-environment, and determines whether this behavior is (relativized input/output) conforming to the specification. Hence, the monitor functions as a test oracle. Monitoring is also sometimes called *passive testing*.

The monitor can be executed in three different ways. It may run *real-time online* in which case non-conformance is reported immediately. This requires that the monitor has sufficient computational resources to analyze the model at the pace dictated by the IUT. Alternatively the monitor may be executed online, but at its own pace (virtual time). Events that are unprocessed are buffered until the monitor becomes ready. Non-conformance will be reported while the IUT is running, but typically some time after it has occurred. Finally, the monitor can be executed offline (post-mortem) on a collected (finite) trace.

Until now we have presented our framework, test-generation and execution algorithm, and TRON as a tool that performs environment emulation and online real-time monitoring as an integrated program.

However, in some situations it is beneficial to separate the two functions in different parts/tools. For example, the two functions can be performed by dedicated tools specialized for the particular function or executed on dedicated platforms (e.g., a hard real-time operating system/computer for environment emulation and a fast (soft-real-time) number-crunching computer for monitoring). Another example is performance. It may not be possible to evaluate a large detailed model of the IUT online in real-time (models of the IUT tends to be larger and much more detailed than the environment model). With a separate monitoring function this can be done afterwards or on a separate dedicated computer.

The explicit separation of the test specification into an environment part and an IUT part allows TRON to be configured easily to perform both pure emulation and monitoring as described in the following.

We denote the behavioral model of the IUT with input actions A_{in} and output actions A_{out} by $S(A_{in}, A_{out})$. Similarly, we denote the environment by $\mathcal{E}(A_{out}, A_{in})$. Also let $U(A_{in}, A_{out})$ and $O(A_{in}, A_{out})$ denote respectively the most (universal) and least (passive) discriminating timed automata, see Section 3. The universal timed automaton is capable of performing any trace. The passive timed automata silently consume input actions.

To use TRON for pure environment emulator use the intended environment model $\mathcal{E}(A_{out}, A_{in})$ and replace the IUT-model $S(A_{in}, A_{out})$ by $U(A_{in}, A_{out})$. In consequence TRON will produce timed traces only in $\mathcal{E}(A_{out}, A_{in})$. Non-conformance will never be reported because $U(A_{in}, A_{out})$ allows any timed trace. This configuration is depicted in Figure 13(a).

Similarly, pure monitoring can be achieved using a slightly modified IUT-model $S' = S(\emptyset, A_{in} \cup A_{out})$ where all input actions are changed to output actions, see Figure 13(b). This model contains the same traces (ignoring i/o labeling) as the original. The environment model must be completely passive and not contain any inputs (as seen from the IUT point of view), $O' = O(A_{in} \cup A_{out}, \emptyset)$. Thus, with no essential modification to TRON or Algorithm 2 the monitoring can be executed in simulated time or offline. If the monitor is uncertain about

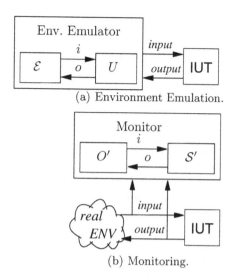

(a) Environment Emulation.

(b) Monitoring.

Fig. 13. Model based emulation and monitoring

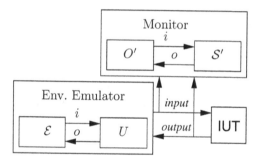

Fig. 14. Model-based Testing via Combined Environment Emulation and Monitoring

the state of the IUT when started, Algorithm 2 can be started with a different (over-approximated) state-set instead of the initial state.

Finally, we observe that online testing can be obtained by running two instances of TRON, one performing monitoring and the other environment emulation, see Figure 14. The two instances may possibly run on different computers.

6   Discussion and Future Work

Model-based test generation for real-time specifications has been investigated by others (see e.g., [50, 43, 11, 30, 22, 13, 56, 47, 36, 27, 42]), but remain relatively immature. In this section we discuss our approach to timed testing and compare to important related work. Also we mention topics for future work in the area.

6.1 Conformance Relations

The choice of conformance relation is important for both theoretical and practical reasons, yet there is still no wide spread consensus in the community about its definition.

Our relativized timed input/output conformance relation is a timed and environment-relativized extension of a solid and widespread implementation relation used in model based conformance testing of untimed systems, namely the input/output conformance relation by Tretmans [58]. Informally, input/output conformance requires for all specification traces that the implementation never produces an output not allowed by the specification, and that it never refuses to produce an output (forever stays quiescent) when the specification requires one. As also noted in [36, 42] a timed input/output conformance relation can be obtained (assuming input enabledness) as timed trace inclusion between the implementation and its specification.

A fundamental question is how quantitative properties like real-time can be observed of the physical IUT. E.g., can event occurrences be observed at time points or only within error bounds, and should such fundamental physical uncertainties be an explicit part of the theory? Similarly, does a concept like quiescence make sense in a real-time system, or are only time bounded (finite time) observations possible? New alternative timed implementation relations have been formulated by Briones and Brinksma in [12].

Another question is related to the goal of real-time testing. Timed trace inclusion does not allow the implementation to be faster than the specification. In some cases this may be unsafe. However, in many other cases it seems natural that the implementation should be allowed to be as fast as possible. Therefore faster-than type relations have been proposed [19, 46]. Thus there seem to be a unclear cut boundary between real-time correctness testing and performance testing.

6.2 Specification of Tests

The test cases to be executed on the IUT can be selected by different means. Typical approaches are test purposes, model-coverage criteria, fault-models (see e.g., [30, 22]) , or randomly.

Test purposes are specific observation objectives formulated by the test engineer, see e.g. [23, 54]. Another popular approach is to cover the model in the hope that a covering test suite is also thorough. Further, model coverage is an important measure for estimating the confidence the developers can have in the executed tests.

In typical approaches, the selection of test cases follows some particular coverage criterion, such as coverage of control states, edges, etc. For finite-state machines several approaches focus on particular coverage criteria, e.g., Bouquet and Legeard [9] synthesize test cases corresponding to combinations of choices of control flow and boundary values of state variables. Nielsen and Skou [48] generate test cases from timed automata that cover different time-domains represented as reachable symbolic states.

Since different coverage criteria are suitable in different situations, and satisfy different constraints on fault detection capability, cost, information about where potential faults may be located, etc., it is highly desirable that a test generation tool is able to generate test suites in a flexible manner, for a wide variety of different coverage criteria. In other words, a test generation tool should accept a simple specification of a coverage criterion, given in a language that can easily specify a large set of coverage criteria, and be able to generate test suites accordingly. Hong et al [32, 31] describe how flow-based coverage criteria can be expressed in temporal logic. Friedman et al [24] specifies coverage by giving a set of projections of the state space (e.g., on individual state variables, components of control flow) that should be covered, possibly under some restrictions.

The observer approach described in this chapter generalizes these approaches and provides such a flexible language. Test purposes can in some sense be regarded as coverage observers, but are not used to specify more generic coverage criteria and do not make use of parameterization, as we do.

Where offline test generation uses symbolic and constraint solving algorithms to satisfy a coverage criterion, online test generators typically uses cheap randomized choice techniques, and can thus not guarantee satisfaction of the coverage criteria, or only provide a probabilistic guarantee provided (unrealistic) long execution time. The achieved coverage of an online testing session can easily be evaluated post-mortem by comparing the collected timed trace with the model. This can for instance be done by executing the timed trace on the model suitably extended with auxiliary coverage or meta-variables, as described in Section 4.2. Another approach is to dynamically collect coverage information during the test run and use this to guide (reduce the random choices) toward uncovered parts of the model.

Except for the obvious extensions of untimed coverage criteria, there exists very little research [48, 16] that deals explicitly with real-time coverage criteria, i.e., criteria that tries to cover the time domain and timer/clock values of a timed specification. Future work includes formulating such real-time coverage criteria and extending the observer approach to allow easy specification of these.

6.3   Test Generation Algorithms

Many model-checker based test generators that generate tests from a coverage criterion invoke the model checker for each coverage item resulting in a single test case per coverage item, see e.g., [25]. This not only results in many test cases and a large test generation overhead, but also a large test execution overhead because many sub-sequences will be identical. It may be more efficient to cover several items by the same test, and generate a test suite that covers the model as much as possible, as our algorithm in Section 4.4. However, this requires that the model checker is extended with dedicated search and pruning algorithms and efficient bit vector encodings of the coverage criteria. We also expect such efficient encodings to play an important role in monitoring and guiding the online test generator toward a coverage goal.

Moreover, whereas most other work on optimizing test suites, e.g. [1, 60, 33], focus on minimizing the length of the test suite, our technique may also reduce the actual execution time, because it considers that some events take longer to produce or and take real-time constraints into account. It may even produce the time optimal test sequences.

Most offline algorithms explicitly determinize the specification [18, 35, 47] as an intermediate step. However, for expressive formalisms like TA this approach is problematic because in general they cannot be determinized.

It is well-known that from the theory of timed automata that non-deterministic timed automata (unlike finite automata) cannot be determinized to a language equivalent deterministic timed automata [2]. It is also not in general possible to remove internal transitions from a timed automata (and when they can, it may be very costly) [61]. Much work on timed test generation from TA therefore restrict the amount and type of allowed non-determinism: [56, 22, 27] completely disallow non-determinism, [36, 47] restrict the use of clocks, guards or clock resets. This gives a less expressive and less flexible specification language. In contrast, online testing is automatically adaptive and only implicitly determinizes the specification, and only partially up to the concrete trace observed so far.

Our approach to online testing is inspired by the (untimed) algorithm proposed by Tretmans et. al. in [63, 6]. They have implemented online testing from Promela [63] and LOTOS specifications in the TORX [62] tool, and practical application to real case studies show promising results [59, 62, 6]. However, TORX provides no support for real-time. Similarly to Krichen and Tripakis [55, 42] we use symbolic reachability computation algorithms to track the current state-set for timed automata with unrestricted non-determinism. We extend the UPPAAL model-checker resulting in an integrated and mature testing and verification tool.

It seems likely that a combination of the strengths of offline and online testing will require the notion of games. In a two-player game one player is trying to reach a winning state by performing controllable game-moves while being affected by uncontrollable moves by the opponent. Translated into testing this corresponds to the situation where the tester is trying reach a state where the test purpose (or coverage criterion) is satisfied by giving controllable inputs to the IUT (the opponent) that responds by making uncontrollable and unpredictable output actions. The goal of the test generator is to compute a winning strategy that will partly be computed statically and partly be interpreted and computed dynamically. Although promising work is in progress on such timed games [10] the required concepts are not sufficiently well developed yet.

The UPPAAL framework is perfectly suited for exploring timed properties of the model, but there is little effort done toward combining it with more complicated test data generation. The recent release of UPPAAL supports C-like data declarations which would enable to combine and implement ideas from [37].

6.4   Real-Time Test Execution and Diagnostics

The execution of real-time test cases is also a challenge, both for online and offline generated tests, because the test execution system is a real-time system with deadlines and potential narrow tolerances. There are two main problems. One is that the host platform may cause unpredictable real-time performance of the tester because of scheduling latency, competing processes, i/o activity and disturbances from competing processes. The other is that there is communication media between the tester and the IUT that must be factored into the test generation or execution. It introduces latency and uncertainty on the order and timing of observations. These problems are not only technical engineering problems, but also seem to require clarification at a semantic and theoretical level.

When non-conformance has been detected the next step is to diagnose why the run failed. It may be an error in the specification, the adaptor layer, or the implementation. If the error is in the implementation the exact cause has to be found and corrected, and regression testing must be performed.

For online testers these issues are especially problematic, because test sequences are typically very long and randomly generated, and hence are difficult to diagnose and reproduce for regression testing. The current TRON implementation assumes that the fault appears in the last testing step and gives a hint about what output was expected and when, and prints information about the last known non-empty state-set. While very helpful, it does not necessarily indicate the cause of the fault, which may have been caused by an internal fault executed by the IUT much earlier. Also TRON allows a recorded timed trace to be replayed against the implementation. However, doing so for long traces with narrow timing tolerances is technically very challenging.

In the future we plan to combine coverage facts with information about passed and failed test runs, in the hope that difference in coverage (of the model or code) could help locate the cause of the error, an approach inspired by the concept of delta-debugging [64].

7   Conclusions

In this chapter we reviewed progress on formal model-based testing of real-time systems. We presented a testing framework consisting of a formal, timed specification language, timed automata, and a formal real-time correctness relation, relativized input/output conformance. We conclude that this framework is solid, technically sound and works well in practice. Based on this common framework we demonstrated two extreme approaches to timed test generation. In offline (optimal) satisfaction of test purpose or coverage criterion is the aim, while online testing ensures thoroughness through volume and brute-force.

These approaches are implemented by (substantially) extending the efficient algorithms and data structures from the UPPAAL model-checker. We find such a mature tool and efficient machinery important for the practical use of the test generation techniques.

Overall, we conclude that significant progress has been made in the area of timed testing, but also that many exciting and important challenges remain. These range from technical engineering problems to principal semantic (and perhaps philosophical) ones.

Acknowledgements

We would like to thank the anonymous reviewers for their detailed and constructive comments that greatly helped improving this presentation.

References

1. Aho, A.V., Dahbura, A.T., Lee, D., Uyar, M.Ü.: An Optimization Technique for Protocol Conformance Test Generation Based on UIO Sequences and Rural Chinese Postman Tours. IEEE Transactions on Communications 39(11), 1604–1615 (1991)
2. Alur, R., Dill, D.L.: A Theory of Timed Automata. Theoretical Computer Science 126(2), 183–235 (1994)
3. Alur, R., Courcoubetis, C., Dill, D.: Model-checking for Real-Time Systems. In: Proc. of Logic in Computer Science, Jun 1990, pp. 414–425. IEEE Computer Society Press, Los Alamitos (1990)
4. Behrmann, G., Bengtsson, J., David, A., Larsen, K.G., Pettersson, P., Yi, W.: Uppaal implementation secrets. In: Damm, W., Olderog, E.-R. (eds.) FTRTFT 2002. LNCS, vol. 2469, pp. 3–22. Springer, Heidelberg (2002)
5. Behrmann, G., Fehnker, A., Hune, T., Larsen, K.G., Pettersson, P., Romijn, J.: Efficient Guiding Towards Cost-Optimality in UPPAAL. In: Margaria, T., Yi, W. (eds.) ETAPS 2001 and TACAS 2001. LNCS, vol. 2031, pp. 174–188. Springer, Heidelberg (2001)
6. Belinfante, A., Feenstra, J., de Vries, R.G., Tretmans, J., Goga, N., Feijs, L., Mauw, S., Heerink, L.: Formal test automation: A simple experiment. In: Csopaki, G., Dibuz, S., Tarnay, K. (eds.) 12th Int. Workshop on Testing of Communicating Systems, pp. 179–196. Kluwer Academic Publishers, Dordrecht (1999)
7. Blom, J., Hessel, A., Jonsson, B., Pettersson, P.: Specifying and generating test cases using observer automata. In: Grabowski, J., Nielsen, B. (eds.) FATES 2004. LNCS, vol. 3395, pp. 125–139. Springer, Heidelberg (2005)
8. Blom, J., Jonsson, B.: Automated test generation for industrial erlang applications. In: Proc. 2003 ACM SIGPLAN workshop on Erlang, Uppsala, Sweden, pp. 8–14 (August 2003)
9. Bouquet, F., Legeard, B.: Reification of executable test scripts in formal specification-based test generation: The java card transaction mechanism case study. In: Araki, K., Gnesi, S., Mandrioli, D. (eds.) FME 2003. LNCS, vol. 2805, pp. 778–795. Springer, Heidelberg (2003)
10. Bouyer, P., Cassez, F., Fleury, E., Larsen, K.G.: Optimal Strategies in Priced Timed Game Autoamata. In: Lodaya, K., Mahajan, M. (eds.) FSTTCS 2004. LNCS, vol. 3328, Springer, Heidelberg (2004)
11. Braberman, V., Felder, M., Marré, M.: Testing Timing Behaviors of Real Time Software. In: Quality Week 1997, San Francisco, USA, pp. 143–155 (April-May 1997)
12. Briones, L.B., Brinksma, E.: A Test Generation Framework for Quiescent Real-Time Systems. In: Grabowski, J., Nielsen, B. (eds.) International workshop on Formal Approaches to Testing of Software. Co-located with IEEE Conference on Automates Software Engineering 2004, Linz, Austria, pp. 64–78 (September 2004)
13. Cardell-Oliver, R.: Conformance Testing of Real-Time Systems with Timed Automata. Formal Aspects of Computing 12(5), 350–371 (2000)

14. Chilenski, J.J., Miller, S.P.: Applicability of modified condition/decision coverage to software testing. Software Engineering Journal 9(5), 193–200 (1994)
15. Chow, T.S.: Testing software design modeled by finite-state machines. IEEE Transactions on Software Engineering 4(3), 178–187 (1978)
16. Clarke, D., Lee, I.: Testing Real-Time Constraints in a Process Algebraic Setting. In: 17th International Conference on Software Engineering (1995)
17. Clarke, L.A., Podgurski, A., Richardsson, D.J., Zeil, S.J.: A formal evaluation of data flow path selection criteria. IEEE Trans. on Software Engineering 15(11), 1318–1332 (1989)
18. Cleaveland, R., Hennessy, M.: Testing Equivalence as a Bisimulation Equivalence. Formal Aspects of Computing 5, 1–20 (1993)
19. Cleaveland, R., Zwarico, A.E.: A Theory of Testing for Real-Time. In: Sixth Annual IEEE Symposium on Logic in Computer Science, pp. 110–119 (1991)
20. Daws, C., Olivero, A., Yovine, S.: Verifying ET-LOTOS programs with Kronos. In: Hogrefe, D., Leue, S. (eds.) Proc. of 7th Int. Conf. on Formal Description Techniques, North-Holland, Amsterdam (1994)
21. Dill, D.: Timing Assumptions and Verification of Finite-State Concurrent Systems. In: Sifakis, J. (ed.) CAV 1989. LNCS, vol. 407, pp. 197–212. Springer, Heidelberg (1990)
22. En-Nouaary, A., Dssouli, R., Khendek, F., Elqortobi, A.: Timed Test Cases Generation Based on State Characterization Technique. In: 19th IEEE Real-Time Systems Symposium (RTSS 1998), December 2–4 1998, pp. 220–229 (1998)
23. Fernandez, J.-C., Jard, C., Jéron, T., Viho, C.: An experiment in automatic generation of test suites for protocols with verification technology. Science of Computer Programming 29 (1997)
24. Friedman, G., Hartman, A., Nagin, K., Shiran, T.: Projected state machine coverage for software testing. In: Proc. ACM SIGSOFT International Symposium on Software Testing and Analysis, pp. 134–143 (2002)
25. Heimdahl, M.P.E., Rayadurgam, S., Visser, W., Devaraj, G., Gao, J.: Auto-generating Test Sequences Usiong Model Checkers: A Case Study. In: Petrenko, A., Ulrich, A. (eds.) FATES 2003. LNCS, vol. 2931, Springer, Heidelberg (2004)
26. Herman, P.M.: A data flow analysis approach to program testing. Australian Computer J. 8(3) (November 1976)
27. Hessel, A., Larsen, K.G., Nielsen, B., Pettersson, P., Skou, A.: Time-Optimal Real-Time Test Case Generation using UPPAAL. In: Petrenko, A., Ulrich, A. (eds.) FATES 2003. LNCS, vol. 2931, pp. 136–151. Springer, Heidelberg (2004)
28. Hessel, A., Pettersson, P.: A test generation algorithm for real-time systems. In: Ehrich, H.-D., Schewe, K.-D. (eds.) Proc. of 4th Int. Conf. on Quality Software, September 2004, pp. 268–273. IEEE Computer Society Press, Los Alamitos (2004)
29. Hessel, A., Pettersson, P.: Model-Based Testing of a WAP Gateway: an Industrial Study. In: Brim, L., Haverkort, B.R., Leucker, M., van de Pol, J. (eds.) FMICS 2006 and PDMC 2006. LNCS, vol. 4346, Springer, Heidelberg (2007)
30. Higashino, T., Nakata, A., Taniguchi, K., Cavalli, A.R.: Generating Test Cases for a Timed I/O Automaton Model. In: Csopaki, G., Dibuz, S., Tarnay, K. (eds.) Testing of Communicating Systems: Method and Applications, IFIP TC6 12th International Workshop on Testing Communicating Systems (IWTCS), Budapest, Hungary, September 1–3, 1999. IFIP Conference Proceedings, vol. 147, pp. 197–214. Kluwer, Dordrecht (1999)
31. Hong, H.S., Cha, S.D., Lee, I., Sokolsky, O., Ural, H.: Data flow testing as model checking. In: ICSE 2003: 25th Int. Conf. on Software Engineering, May 2003, pp. 232–242 (2003)

32. Hong, H.S., Lee, I., Sokolsky, O., Ural, H.: A temporal logic based theory of test coverage. In: Katoen, J.-P., Stevens, P. (eds.) ETAPS 2002 and TACAS 2002. LNCS, vol. 2280, pp. 327–341. Springer, Heidelberg (2002)
33. Hong, H.S., Lee, I., Sokolsky, O., Ural, H.: A Temporal Logic Based Theory of Test Coverage and Generation. In: Katoen, J.-P., Stevens, P. (eds.) ETAPS 2002 and TACAS 2002. LNCS, vol. 2280, pp. 327–341. Springer, Heidelberg (2002)
34. Ouaknine, J., Worrell, J.: Revisiting digitization, robustness, and decidability for timed automata. In: 18th IEEE Symposium on Logic in Computer Science (LICS 2003), Ottawa, Canada, June 2003, pp. 198–207. IEEE Computer Society Press, Los Alamitos (2003)
35. Jéron, T., Morel, P.: Test generation derived from model-checking. In: Halbwachs, N., Peled, D.A. (eds.) CAV 1999. LNCS, vol. 1633, pp. 108–122. Springer, Heidelberg (1999)
36. Khoumsi, A., Jéron, T., Marchand, H.: Test cases generation for nondeterministic real-time systems. In: Petrenko, A., Ulrich, A. (eds.) FATES 2003. LNCS, vol. 2931, Springer, Heidelberg (2004)
37. Koopman, P.W.M., Alimarine, A., Tretmans, J., Plasmeijer, M.J.: Gast: Generic automated software testing. In: Peña, R., Arts, T. (eds.) IFL 2002. LNCS, vol. 2670, pp. 84–100. Springer, Heidelberg (2003)
38. Larsen, K., Mikucionis, M., Nielsen, B.: Online Testing of Real-time Systems using Uppaal. In: Grabowski, J., Nielsen, B. (eds.) International workshop on Formal Approaches to Testing of Software. Co-located with IEEE Conference on Automates Software Engineering 2004, Linz, Austria (September 2004)
39. Larsen, K.G., Behrmann, G., Brinksma, E., Fehnker, A., Hune, T., Pettersson, P., Romijn, J.: As cheap as possible: Efficient cost-optimal reachability for priced timed automat. In: Berry, G., Comon, H., Finkel, A. (eds.) CAV 2001. LNCS, vol. 2102, pp. 493–505. Springer, Heidelberg (2001)
40. Larsen, K.G., Pettersson, P., Yi, W.: Diagnostic Model-Checking for Real-Time Systems. In: Proc. of Workshop on Verification and Control of Hybrid Systems III, October 1995. LNCS, vol. 1066, pp. 575–586. Springer, Heidelberg (1995)
41. Laski, J.W., Korel, B.: A data flow oriented program testing strategy. IEEE Transactions on Software Engineering SE-9(3), 347–354 (1983)
42. Krichen, M., Tripakis, S.: Black-box Conformance Testing for Real-Time Systems. In: Graf, S., Mounier, L. (eds.) SPIN 2004. LNCS, vol. 2989, Springer, Heidelberg (2004)
43. Mandrioli, D., Morasca, S., Morzenti, A.: Generating Test Cases for Real-Time Systems from Logic Specifications. ACM Transactions on Computer Systems 13(4), 365–398 (1995)
44. Mikucionis, M., Larsen, K.G., Nielsen, B., Skou, A.: Testing rea-time embedded software using uppaal-tron —an industrial case study. In: Embedded Software (EMSOFT), New Jersey, USA (September 2005)
45. Myers, G.: The Art of Software Testing. Wiley-Interscience, Chichester (1979)
46. Núñez, M., Rodríguez, I.: Conformance Testing Relations for Timed Systems. In: Grieskamp, W., Weise, C. (eds.) International workshop on Formal Approaches to Testing of Software, Co-located with Computer Aided Verification, Edinburgh, Scotland, UK (July 2005)
47. Nielsen, B., Skou, A.: Automated Test Generation from Timed Automata. In: Tools and Algorithms for the Construction and Analysis of Systems, April 2001, pp. 343–357 (2001)
48. Nielsenand, B., Skou, A.: Automated test generation from timed automata. International Journal on Software Tools for Technology Transfer 5, 59–77 (2003)

49. Ntafos, S.: A comparison of some structural testing strategies. IEEE Transaction on Software Engineering 14, 868–874 (1988)

50. Peleska, J., Amthor, P., Dick, S., Meyer, O., Siegel, M., Zahlten, C.: Testing Reactive Real-Time Systems. In: Material for the School – 5th International School and Symposium on Formal Techniques in Real-Time and Fault-Tolerant Systems (FTRTFT 1998), Lyngby, Denmark (1998)

51. Rapps, S., Weyuker, E.J.: Selecting software test data using data flow information. IEEE Transactions on Software Engineering 11(4), 367–375 (1985)

52. RCTA, Washington D.C., USA. RTCA/DO-178B, Software Considerations in Airborne Systems and Equipment Certifications (December 1992)

53. Rokicki, T.G., Myers, C.J.: Automatic verification of timed circuits. In: Dill, D.L. (ed.) CAV 1994. LNCS, vol. 818, pp. 468–480. Springer, Heidelberg (1994)

54. Rusu, V., du Bousquet, L., Jéron, T.: An approach to symbolic test generation. In: Grieskamp, W., Santen, T., Stoddart, B. (eds.) IFM 2000. LNCS, vol. 1945, pp. 338–357. Springer, Heidelberg (2000)

55. Tripakis, S.: Fault Diagnosis for Timed Automata. In: Damm, W., Olderog, E.-R. (eds.) FTRTFT 2002. LNCS, vol. 2469, Springer, Heidelberg (2002)

56. Springintveld, J., Vaandrager, F., D'Argenio, P.R.: Testing Timed Automata. Theoretical Computer Science 254(1–2), 225–257 (2001)

57. Henzinger, T.A., Manna, Z., Pnueli, A.: What good are digital clocks? In: Kuich, W. (ed.) ICALP 1992. LNCS, vol. 623, pp. 545–558. Springer, Heidelberg (1992)

58. Tretmans, J.: Testing concurrent systems: A formal approach. In: Baeten, J.C.M., Mauw, S. (eds.) CONCUR 1999. LNCS, vol. 1664, pp. 46–65. Springer, Heidelberg (1999)

59. Tretmans, J., Belinfante, A.: Automatic testing with formal methods. In: EuroSTAR 1999: 7th European Int. Conference on Software Testing, Analysis & Review. Barcelona, Spain. EuroStar Conferences, Galway, Ireland, November 8–12 (1999)

60. Ümit Uyar, M., Fecko, M.A., Sethi, A.S., Amar, P.D.: Testing Protocols Modeled as FSMs with Timing Parameters. Computer Networks: The International Journal of Computer and Telecommunication Networking 31(18), 1967–1998 (1999)

61. Diekert, V., Gastin, P., Petit, A.: Removing epsilon-Transitions in Timed Automata. In: Reischuk, R., Morvan, M. (eds.) STACS 1997. LNCS, vol. 1200, pp. 583–594. Springer, Heidelberg (1997)

62. de Vries, R., Tretmans, J., Belinfante, A., Feenstra, J., Feijs, L., Mauw, S., Goga, N., Heerink, L., de Heer, A.: Côte de resyste in PROGRESS. In: STW Technology Foundation, editor, PROGRESS 2000 – Workshop on Embedded Systems, October 2000, pp. 141–148. The Netherlands, Utrecht (2000)

63. de Vries, R.G., Tretmans, J.: On-the-fly conformance testing using SPIN. Software Tools for Technology Transfer 2(4), 382–393 (2000)

64. Zeller, A., Hildebrandt, R.: Simplifying and Isolating Failure-Inducing Input. IEEE Transactions on Software Engineering 28(2), 183–200 (2002)

Coverage Criteria for State Based Specifications

Paul Ammann, Jeff Offutt, and Wuzhi Xu

Department of Information and Software Engineering
George Mason University, USA
{pammann,offutt,wxu2}@gmu.edu

Abstract. Test engineers often face the task of developing a set of test cases that are appropriate for a given software artefact. The software testing literature is replete with testing methods tailored to the various specification, design, and implementation methods used in software engineering. This chapter takes a novel inverted view. Instead of starting with the specific artefact at hand, we identify two general sets of coverage criteria – one based on graphs and the other based on predicates. We then ask two questions with respect to the specific artefact under test: (1) What graphs are suitable abstractions of the artefact for the purpose of testing? (2) What predicates should be extracted from this artefact for the purpose of testing? Combining the answers to these two questions with the standard graph-based and logic-based coverage criteria yields test requirements. The test engineer can then proceed to identify test cases that satisfy the various requirements. This chapter illustrate this technique in the context of testing software that is modelled by state-based specifications. We present a representative sample of graph-based and logic-based test coverage criteria. We extract appropriate graphs and predicates from state based specifications and apply the coverage criteria.

1 Overview

This chapter describes two kinds of test criteria. One kind is based on graphs, the most common source of tests in use today, and the other is based on logic expressions. The use of logic coverage criteria has been steadily growing in recent years. One major cause for their use in practice has been the requirement by the US Federal Aviation Administration (FAA) that the logic coverage criteria MCDC be used for safety critical parts of the avionics software in commercial aircraft.

Each section, Section 2 for graphs and Section 3 for logic expressions, starts out in a very theoretical way, but a firm grasp of the theoretical aspects of coverage makes the remainder of the chapter simpler. The first subsection in each section emphasizes generic views of graphs and logic expressions without regard to the their source or what aspect of the software they model. After this model and the criteria are established, the next subsections turn to practical applications by demonstrating how generic versions of the criteria are adapted to specific graphs and expressions from various software artefacts, including code, specifications, and finite state machines. References to the research literature

R.M. Hierons et al. (Eds.): Formal Methods and Testing, LNCS 4949, pp. 118–156, 2008.
© Springer-Verlag Berlin Heidelberg 2008

are postponed to the end of the chapter, and appear as a separate bibliographic notes section.

1.1   Graphs and Test Paths

Directed graphs form the foundation for many coverage criteria. Given some artefact under test, the idea is to obtain some graph abstraction of that artefact. For example, the most common graph abstraction for source maps statements to a control flow graph. It is important to understand that the graph is not the same as the artefact, and that, indeed, artefacts typically have several useful, but nonetheless quite different, graph abstractions. The same abstraction that produces the graph from the artefact also maps test cases for the artefact to paths in the graph. Accordingly, a graph-based coverage criterion evaluates a test set for an artefact in terms of how the paths corresponding to the test cases "cover" the artefact's graph abstraction.

We give our basic notion of a graph below and add additional structures as necessary. A graph G formally is:

- a set N of *nodes*, where $N \neq \emptyset$
- a set N_0 of *initial nodes*, where $N_0 \subseteq N$ and $N_0 \neq \emptyset$
- a set N_f of *final nodes*, where $N_f \subseteq N$ and $N_f \neq \emptyset$
- a set E of *edges*, where E is a subset of $N \times N$

Note that there may be more than one initial node; that is, N_0 is a set. This is necessary for some software artefacts, for example, if a class has multiple entry points, but sometimes we will restrict the graph to having one initial node. Edges are considered to be *from* one node and *to* another and written as (n_i, n_j). The edge's initial node n_i is sometimes called the *predecessor* and n_j is called the *successor*.

We always identify final nodes, and there is always at least one final node. The reason is that every test must start in some initial node, and end in some final node. The concept of a final node depends on the kind of software artefact the graph represents. Some test criteria require tests to end in a particular final node. Other test criteria are satisfied with any node for a final node, in which case the set N_f is the same as the set N.

The term "node" has various synonyms. Graph theory texts sometimes call a node a *vertex*, and testing texts typically identify a node with the structure it represents, often a statement or a basic block. Similarly, graph theory texts sometimes call an edge an *arc*, and testing texts typically identify an edge with the structure it represents, often a branch. This section discusses graph criteria in a generic way; thus we stick to general graph terms.

Graphs are often depicted with bubbles and arrows. Figure 1 shows three example graphs. The nodes with incoming edges but no predecessor nodes are the initial nodes. The nodes with heavy borders are final nodes. Figure 1(a) has a single initial node and no cycles. Figure 1(b) has three initial nodes, as well as a cycle ($[n_1, n_4, n_8, n_5, n_1]$). Figure 1(c) has no initial nodes, and so does not meet the requirements of our definition of a graph.

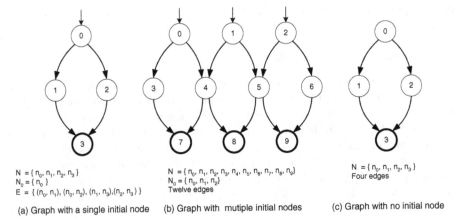

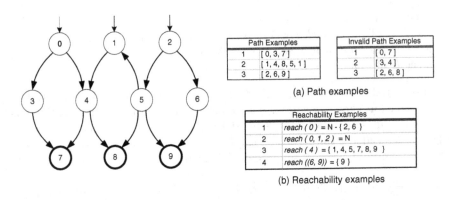

Fig. 1. Graph (a) has a single initial node, graph (b) multiple initial nodes, and graph (c) (rejected) with no initial nodes

Fig. 2. Example of paths

A *path* is a sequence $[n_1, n_2, \ldots, n_M]$ of nodes, where each pair of adjacent nodes, (n_i, n_{i+1}), $1 \leq i < M$, is in the set E of edges. The length of a path is defined as the number of edges it contains and we sometimes consider paths and subpaths of length zero. A *subpath* of a path p is a subsequence of p (possibly p itself). Following the notation for edges, we say a path is *from* the first node in the path and *to* the last node in the path. It is also useful to be able to say that a path is *from* (or *to*) an edge e, which simply means that e is the first (or last) edge in the path.

Figure 2 shows a graph along with several example paths, and several examples that are not paths. For instance, the sequence $[n_0, n_7]$ is not a path because there is not a direct edge between the two nodes.

Some test criteria require traversing a path that starts at a specific node and ends at another. This is only possible if there is a path in the graph between those nodes. When we apply these criteria on specific graphs, we sometimes find that we have asked for a path that for some reason cannot be executed. For example, a path may demand that a loop be executed zero times in a situation where the program always executes the loop at least once. This kind of problem is based on the semantics of the software artefact that the graph represents.

The graphs are models of the software in some abstract way and it is convenient to assume that they *correspond* to an actual program in some way. Likewise, paths in the graph are assumed to correspond to execution paths in the program. So the graphs are used to derive tests, which are then run on an executable program. In this chapter, we use the concept "executing a path in the graph" synonymously with "executing statements in the program that correspond with a path in the graph", with an implicit understanding that some translation from graph model to program statements are needed. How this translation works in practice depends on how the graph is modelling the program.

We say that a node n (or an edge e) is *syntactically reachable* from node n_i if there exists a path from node n_i to n (or edge e). A node n (or edge e) is also "semantically reachable" if it is possible to execute at least one of the execution paths with some input. We can define the function $reach_G(x)$ as the portion of a graph that is syntactically reachable from the parameter x. The parameter for $reach_G()$ can be a node, an edge, or a set of nodes or edges. Then $reach_G(n_i)$ is the set of nodes and edges (*subset* of G) that is syntactically reachable from node n_i, $reach_G(N_0)$ is the subset of G that is syntactically reachable from any initial node, $reach_G(e)$ is the subset of G that is syntactically reachable from edge e, and so on. Some graphs have nodes that cannot be syntactically reached from any initial nodes. These graphs frustrate attempts to satisfy a coverage criterion, so we typically restrict our attention to $reach_G(N_0)$.[1]

Consider the examples in Figure 2. From n_0, it is possible to reach all nodes except for n_2 and n_6. From the entire set of initial nodes $\{n_0, n_1, n_2\}$, it is possible to reach all nodes. If we start at n_4, it is possible to reach all nodes except n_0, n_2, n_3, and n_6. If we start at edge (n_6, n_9), it is only possible to reach n_9. Note that we assume that it is always possible to reach a node from itself via a path of length zero. In addition, some graphs (such as finite state machines) have explicit edges from a node to itself, that is, (n_i, n_i). Basic graph algorithms can be used to compute syntactic reachability.

A test path represents the execution of a test case on the program that the graph models. The reason test paths must start in N_0 is that test cases always begin from an initial node. It is important to note that a single test path in the graph may correspond to a very large number of test cases on the software. It is also possible that a test path may correspond to zero test cases if the test path happens to be infeasible.

Definition 1. Test path: *A test path is a path, possibly of length zero, that starts at some node in N_0 and ends at some node in N_f.*

---

[1] By way of example, typical control flow graphs have very few if any syntactically unreachable nodes, but call graphs, especially for object-oriented programs, often do.

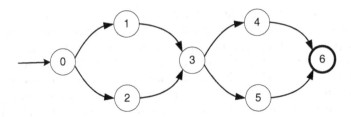

Fig. 3. A Single-Entry Single-Exit graph. This example is sometimes called the "double-diamond" graph.

For some graphs, all test paths start at the same node and end at the same node. We call these *single entry/single exit* or *SESE* graphs. For SESE graphs, the set N_0 has exactly one node, called n_0, and the set N_f also has exactly one node, called n_f. We require that n_f be syntactically reachable from every node in N, and that no node in N (except n_f) be syntactically reachable from n_f. In other words, no edges start at n_f.

Figure 3 is an example of a SESE graph. This particular structure is sometimes called a "double-diamond" graph, and corresponds to the control flow graph for a sequence of two `if-then-else` statements. The initial node, n_0, is designated with an incoming arrow (remember that there is only one), and the final node, n_6, is designated with a thick circle. There are exactly four test paths in the double-diamond graph: $[n_0, n_1, n_3, n_4, n_6]$, $[n_0, n_1, n_3, n_5, n_6]$, $[n_0, n_2, n_3, n_4, n_6]$, and $[n_0, n_2, n_3, n_5, n_6]$.

We need some terminology to express the notion of nodes, edges, and subpaths that appear in test paths, and choose familiar terminology from travelling. A test path p is said to *visit* node n if n is in p. Test path p is said to *visit* edge e if e is in p. The term visit applies well to single nodes and edges, but sometimes we want to turn our attention to subpaths. For subpaths, we use the term **tour**. Test path p is said to *tour* subpath q if q is a subpath of p. The first path of Figure 3, $[n_0, n_1, n_3, n_4, n_6]$, visits nodes n_0 and n_1, visits edges (n_0, n_1) and (n_3, n_4), and tours the subpath $[n_1, n_3, n_4]$.

We define a mapping $path_G$ for tests, so for a test case t, $path_G(t)$ is the test path in graph G that is executed by t. Since it is usually obvious which graph we are discussing, we omit the subscript G. We also define the set of paths toured by a set of tests. For a test set T, $path(T)$ is the set of test paths in T: $path_G(T) = \{path_G(t) \mid t \in T\}$.

1.2   Logic Predicates and Clauses

The other model that we use to generate tests is logic predicates. We formalize logical expressions in a common mathematical way. A *predicate* is an expression that evaluates to a boolean value, and is our topmost structure. A simple example is: $((a > b) \vee C) \wedge p(x)$. Predicates may contain boolean variables, non-boolean variables that are compared with the comparator operators $\{ >, <, =, \geq, \leq, \neq \}$, and function calls. The internal structure is created by the logical operators:

- ¬ – the *negation* operator
- ∧ – the *and* operator
- ∨ – the *or* operator
- → – the *implication* operator
- ⊕ – the *exclusive or* operator
- ↔ – the *equivalence* operator

Some of these operators ($\oplus$, $\rightarrow$, $\leftrightarrow$) may seem unusual for readers with a bias toward source code, but they turn out to be common in some specification languages and very handy for our purposes. Short circuit versions of the *and* and *or* operators are also sometimes useful, and will be addressed when necessary. We adopt a typical precedence, which, from highest to lowest, matches the order listed above. When there is doubt, we use parentheses for clarity.

A *clause* is a predicate that does not contain any of the logical operators. For example, the predicate $(a > b) \lor C \land p(x)$, contains three clauses; a relational expression $(a > b)$, a boolean variable C and the function call $p(x)$. Because they may contain a structure of their own, relational expressions require special treatment.

A predicate may be written in a variety of logically equivalent ways. For example, the predicate $((a = b) \lor p(x)) \land (C \lor p(x))$ is logically equivalent to the predicate given in the previous paragraph, but $((a = b) \land p(x)) \lor (C \land p(x))$ is not. The usual rules of boolean algebra (not reviewed here) may be used to convert boolean expressions into equivalent forms. Many of our examples are given in disjunctive normal form for convenience, but this is not necessary.

Logical expressions come from a variety of sources. The most familiar to most readers will probably be source code of a program. For example, the following if statement:

```
if ((a > b) || C) && (x < y)
    o.m();
else
    o.n();
```

will yield the expression given previously: $((a > b) \lor C) \land (x < y)$. Other sources of logical expressions include transitions in finite state machines. A transition such as: button2 = true (when gear = park) will yield the expression $gear = park \land button2 = true$. Similarly, a precondition in a specification such as "pre: stack Not full AND object reference parameter not null" will result in a logical expression such as $\neg\ stackFull() \land newObj \neq null$.

Next, this chapter turns to test criteria that are defined on graphs, and Section 3 describes test criteria that are defined on logical expressions.

2   Graph Coverage

The structure described in Section 1.1 is adequate to define coverage on graphs. As is usual in the testing literature, we divide these criteria into two types.

The first are commonly referred to as *control flow coverage* criteria. Because we generalize this situation, we call them *structural graph coverage criteria*. The other set of criteria are based on the flow of data through the software artefact represented by the graph, and are called *data flow coverage* criteria. Data flow is not widely studied for specifications, thus these criteria are not relevant to this chapter. We identify the appropriate test requirements and then define each criterion in terms of the test requirements. In general, for any graph-based coverage criterion, the idea is to identify the test requirements in terms of various structures in the graph.

For graphs, coverage criteria define test requirements, TR, in terms of properties of test paths in a graph G. A typical test requirement is *met* by *visiting* a particular node or edge or by *touring* a particular path. The definitions in Section 1 far for a *visit* are adequate, but the notion of a *tour* requires more development.

Definition 2. Satisfaction: *Given a set TR of test requirements for graph coverage criterion C, test set T satisfies C coverage on graph G if and only if for every test requirement tr in $\overline{TR}$, there is a test path p in path(T) such that p meets the test requirement tr.*

This is a very general statement that now must be refined for individual kinds of coverage.

2.1   Graph Coverage Criteria

We specify graph coverage criteria by specifying a set of test requirements, TR. We will start by defining criteria to visit every node and then every edge in a graph. The first criterion is probably familiar and is based on the old notion of executing every statement in a program. This concept has variously been called "statement coverage," "block coverage," "state coverage," and "node coverage." We use the general graph term "node coverage." Although this concept is familiar and simple, we introduce some additional notation. The notation initially seems to complicate the criterion, but ultimately has the effect of making subsequent criteria cleaner and mathematically precise, avoiding confusion with more complicated situations.

The requirements that are produced by a graph criterion are technically predicates that can have either the value true (the requirement has been met) or false (the requirement has **not** been met). For the double-diamond graph in Figure 3, the test requirements for node coverage are: $TR = \{visit\ n_0,\ visit\ n_1,\ visit\ n_2,\ visit\ n_3,\ visit\ n_4,\ visit\ n_5,\ visit\ n_6\}$. That is, we must satisfy a predicate for each node, where the predicate asks whether the node has been visited or not.

We choose to use a simple formulation of the definition that abstracts the issue of predicates in the test requirements.

CRITERION 1. **Node Coverage (NC):** *TR contains each reachable node in G.*

With this definition, it is left as understood that the term "contains" actually means "contains the predicate $visit_n$." This simplification allows us to simplify the writing of the test requirements for Figure 3 to only contain the nodes: $TR = \{n_0, n_1, n_2, n_3, n_4, n_5, n_6\}$. Test path $p_1 = [n_0, n_1, n_3, n_4, n_6]$ meets the first, second, fourth, fifth, and seventh test requirements, and test path $p_2 = [n_0, n_2, n_3, n_5, n_6]$ meets the first, third, fourth, sixth and seventh. Therefore if a test set T contains $\{t_1, t_2\}$, where $path(t_1) = p_1$ and $path(t_2) = p_2$, then T satisfies node coverage on G.

Node Coverage is implemented in many commercial testing tools, most often as statement coverage. So is the next common criterion of edge coverage, usually implemented as branch coverage:

CRITERION 2. **Edge Coverage (EC):** *TR contains each reachable path of length up to 1 in G.*

The reader might wonder why the test requirements for edge coverage also explicitly include the test requirements for node coverage – that is, why the phrase "up to" is included in the definition. In fact, all the graph coverage criteria are developed in this way. The motivation is subsumption for graphs that do not contain more complex structures. For example, consider a graph with a node that has no edges. Without the "up to" clause in the definition, edge coverage would not cover that node. Intuitively, we would like edge testing to be at least as demanding as node testing. The chosen style of definition seems to be the best way to achieve this property. To make our TR sets readable, we list only the maximal length paths.

Figure 4 illustrates the difference between node and edge coverage. In program statement terms, this is a graph of the common "if-else" structure.

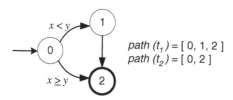

$path\ (t_1) = [\ 0,\ 1,\ 2\ ]$
$path\ (t_2) = [\ 0,\ 2\ ]$

t_1 satisfies node coverage on the graph, but not edge coverage
t_2 satisfies edge coverage

Fig. 4. A graph showing Node and Edge Coverage

There are other coverage criteria that only use the graph definitions introduced so far. For example, one requirement is that each path of length (up to) two be toured in some test path. With this context, Node Coverage could be redefined to contain each path of length zero. Clearly, this idea can be extended to paths of any length, although possibly with diminishing returns. We formally define one of these criteria.

CRITERION **3. Edge-Pair Coverage (EPC):** *TR contains each reachable path of length up to 2 in G.*

One useful testing criterion is to start the software in some state (for example, a node in the finite state machine) and then follow transitions (that is, edges) so that the last state is the same as the start state. This type of testing is used to verify that the system is not changed by certain inputs. Shortly, we will formalize this notion as round trip coverage.

Before proceeding, a few more definitions are needed. A path from n_i to n_j is *simple* if no node appears more than once on the path, with the exception that the first and last nodes may be identical. That is, there are no internal loops in a simple path, although the entire path itself may wind up being a loop. One aspect of simple paths is that all non-simple paths can be created by composing simple paths.

A *round trip* path is a simple path of nonzero length that starts and ends at the same node. One type of round trip test coverage requires at least one round trip path to be taken for each node, and another requires all possible round trip paths.

CRITERION **4. Simple Round Trip Coverage (SRTC):** *TR contains at least one round-trip path for each reachable node in G that begins and ends a round-trip path.*

CRITERION **5. Complete Round Trip Coverage (CRTC):** *TR contains all round-trip paths for each reachable node in G.*

Next is path coverage, which is traditional in the testing literature.

CRITERION **6. Complete Path Coverage (CPC):** *TR contains all paths in G.*

Sadly, Complete Path coverage is useless if a graph has a cycle, since there are an infinite number of paths, and hence an infinite number of test requirements. A variant of this criterion is, however, useful. Suppose that instead of requiring all paths, we consider a specified set of paths. For example, these paths might be given by the customer in the form of usage scenarios.

CRITERION **7. Specified Path Coverage (SPC):** *TR contains a set S of test paths, where S is supplied as a parameter.*

2.2   Graph Coverage for Specification

The general graph criteria defined in Section 2.1 can be used on many kinds of graphs, the most familiar to developers probably being control flow graphs. However, the criteria are independent from where the graphs come from, so this section turns to the question of where to obtain the graphs by discussing two specific aspects of software that are commonly modelled by graphs.

The literature has a large proliferation of techniques for generating graphs and criteria for covering those graphs, but most of them are in fact very similar. This section begins by looking at graphs based on *sequencing constraints* among methods in classes, then graphs that represent state behavior of software. Both aspects of programs can be modelled in many languages; this treatment tries to stay as language-neutral as possible.

Testing Sequencing Constraints. It was pointed out in Section 1.1 that call graphs for classes often wind up being disconnected and in many cases (such as with small Abstract Data Types or ADTs), there are no calls at all between methods in a class. However, there are almost always rules that constrain the order of calls. For example, many ADTs must be initialized before being used, it is invalid to *pop* an element from a stack until something has been *pushed* onto it, and an element cannot be removed from a queue until an element has been put on. These rules impose constraints on the order in which methods may be called. Generally, a *sequencing constraint* is a rule that imposes some restriction on the order in which certain methods may be called.

Sequencing constraints are sometimes explicitly expressed, sometimes implicitly expressed, and sometimes not expressed at all. Sometimes they are encoded as a precondition or other specification, but not directly as a sequencing condition. For example, consider the following informal precondition for DeQueue():

```
public int DeQueue ()
{
// Pre: At least one element must be on the queue.
.
:
public EnQueue (int e)
{
// Post: e is on the end of the queue.
```

Although it is not said explicitly, a clever programmer can infer that the only way an element can "be on the queue" is if EnQueue() has previously been called. Thus there is an implicit sequencing constraint between EnQueue() and DeQueue().

Of course formal specifications can help make the relationships more precise. Wise testers will certainly use formal specifications when available, but responsible testers must look for formal relationships even when they are not explicitly stated. Also note that sequencing constraints do not capture all the behavior, but only abstract certain key aspects. The sequence constraint that EnQueue() must be called before DeQueue() does not capture the fact that if we only EnQueue() one item, and then try to DeQueue() two items, the queue will be empty. The precondition may capture this fact, but usually not in a formal way that automated tools can use. This kind of relationship is beyond the ability of a simple sequencing constraint but can be dealt with by some of the state behavior techniques in the next subsection.

This relationship is used during testing in two different ways. They are illustrated with a small example of a class that encapsulates operations on a cache. The class `Cache` has three methods:

- `loadCache (File F)` // loads the cache from the file with name F
- `saveCache (File F)` // Saves the cache to disk and makes it unavailable
- `writeCache (Object O)` // Writes an object into the cache

This class has several sequencing constraints that can be inferred even from the informal descriptions. The statements use "must" and "should" in very specific ways. When "must" is used, it implies that violation of the constraint is a fault. When "should" is used, it implies that violation of the constraint is a potential fault, but not necessarily. Explicit sequencing constraints can be written as follows:

1. A `loadCache (f)` must be executed before every `writeCache (f)`
2. A `loadCache (f)` must be executed before every `saveCache (f)`
3. A `writeCache (f)` may not be executed after a `saveCache (f)` unless there is a `loadCache (f)` in between
4. A `writeCache (f)` should be executed before every `saveCache (f)`

Constraints are used in testing in two ways to evaluate software that uses the class (a "client"), based on the Control Flow Graph (CFG). Consider the two (partial) CFGs in Figure 5, representing two units that use `Cache`. This graph can be used to test the use of the `Cache` class by checking for sequence violations. This can be done both statically and dynamically.

Static checks (not considered to be traditional testing) proceed by checking each constraint. First consider the `writeCache ()` statements at nodes 2 and 5 in graph (a). First check to see whether there are paths from the `loadCache ()`

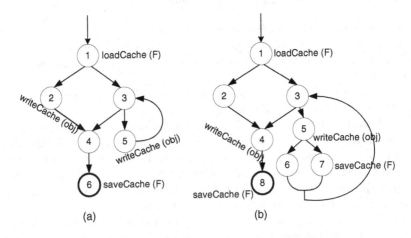

(a)   (b)

Fig. 5. Control flow graph using the File ADT

at node 1 to nodes 2 and 5 (constraint 1). Next check whether there is a path from the loadCache () at node 1 to the saveCache () at node 6 (constraint 2). For constraints 3 and 4, check to see if there is a path from the saveCache () at node 6 to any of the writeCache () statements, and see if there exists a path from the loadCache () to the saveCache () that does not go through at least one writeCache (). This will uncover one possible problem, the path [1, 3, 4, 6] goes from a loadCache () to a saveCache () with no intervening writeCache () calls.

This process will find a more serious problem with graph (b) in 5. There is a path from the saveCache () at node 7 to the writeCache () at node 5 and to the writeCache () at node 4. While this may seem simple enough not to require formalism for such small graphs, this process is quite difficult with large graphs containing dozens or hundreds of nodes.

Dynamic testing follows a slightly different approach. Consider the problem in graph (a) where there is no writeCache () on the possible path [1, 3, 4, 6]. It is quite possible that the logic of the program dictates that the edge (3, 4) can *never* be taken unless the loop [3, 5, 3] is taken at least once. Because deciding whether the path [1, 3, 4, 6] can be taken or not is a formally undecidable problem, this situation can only be checked by dynamic execution. Thus test requirements are generated to try to *violate* the sequencing constraints. For the Cache class, generate the following sets of test requirements:

1. Cover every path from the start node to every node that contains a write Cache () such that the path does not go through a node containing a loadCache ().
2. Cover every path from the start node to every node that contains a save Cache () such that the path does not go through a node containing a loadCache ().
3. Cover every path from every node that contains a saveCache () to every node that contains a writeCache ().
4. Cover every path from every node that contains a loadCache () to every node that contains a saveCache () such that the path does not go through a node containing a writeCache ().

Of course, in a well written program, all of these test requirements will be infeasible. However, any tests that are created as a result of these requirements will almost certainly reveal a sequencing fault if one exists.

Testing State Behavior of Software. Another major use of graphs based on specifications is to model state behavior of the software by developing some form of finite state machine (FSM). Over the last 25 years, there have been many suggestions for creating FSMs and how to test software based on the FSM. The topic of how to create, draw, and interpret an FSM has filled entire textbooks, and authors have gone into great depth and effort to define what exactly goes into a state, what can go onto edges, and what causes transitions. Rather than using any particular notation, this chapter defines a very generic model for FSMs that can be adapted to virtually any notation. These FSMs are essentially graphs, and the graph testing criteria already defined are used to test software based on the FSM.

One advantage of basing tests on FSMs is that huge numbers of practical software applications are based on a finite state machine model, or can be modelled as a finite state machine. Virtually all embedded software fits in this category, including software in remote controls, household appliances, watches, cars, cell phones, airplane flight guidance, traffic signals, railroad control systems, network routers and factory automation. Indeed, most software can be modelled with FSMs, the primary limitation being the number of states needed to model the software. Word processors, for example, contain so many commands and states that modelling them as an FSM is probably impractical.

There is often great value in creating FSMs. If the test engineer creates an FSM to describe existing software, he or she will almost certainly find faults in the software. Some would even argue the converse; if the designers created FSMs, the testers should not bother creating them because problems will be rare.

A *Finite State Machine* is a graph whose nodes represent states in the execution behavior of the software and edges represent transitions among the states. A *state* represents a recognizable situation that remains in existence over some period of time. A state is defined by specific values for a set of variables; as long as those variables have those values the software is considered to be in that state. (Note that these variables are defined at the modelling/design level and may not necessarily correspond to variables in the software.) A *transition* is thought of as occurring in zero time and represents a change to the values of one or more variables. When the variables change, the software is considered to move from the transition's *pre-state* (predecessor) to its *post-state* (successor). FSMs often define *preconditions* or *guards* on transitions, which define values that specific variables must have for the transition to be enabled, and *triggering events*, which are changes in variable values that cause the transition to be taken. A trigger event "triggers" the change in state. For example, the modelling language SCR calls these WHEN conditions and triggering events. The values the triggering events have before the transition are sometimes called *before-values*, and the values after the transition are sometimes called *after-values*. When graphs are drawn, transitions are often annotated with the guards and or the values that change.

Figure 6 illustrates this model with a simple transition that opens an elevator door. If the elevator button is pressed (the trigger event), the door opens only if the elevator is not moving (the precondition, $elevSpeed = 0$).

Given this type of graph, many of the previous criteria can be defined directly. Node Coverage requires that each state in the FSM be visited at least once. In the context of FSMS, node coverage is sometimes called *State Coverage*. Edge Coverage is applied by requiring that each transition in the FSM be visited at least once, which has been called *Transition Coverage*. The Edge-Pair Coverage criterion was originally defined for FSMs and is also called *transition-pair* and *two-trip*.

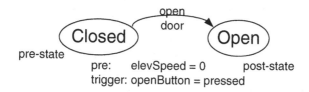

Fig. 6. Elevator door open transition

3 Logic Coverage

Logical expressions show up in all sorts of places in software and are essential in some form or another to most specification languages, formal and informal. This section discusses criteria on generic logical expressions, then how logical expressions can be obtained from specifications.

3.1 Logic Expression Coverage Criteria

Clauses and predicates are used to introduce a variety of coverage criteria. Let P be a set of predicates and C be a set of clauses in the predicates in P. For each predicate $p \in P$, let C_p be the clauses in p, that is $C_p = \{c | c \in p\}$. Typically, C is the union of the clauses in each predicate in P, that is $C = \bigcup_{p \in P} C_p$.

CRITERION 8. **Predicate Coverage (PC):** *For each $p \in P$, TR contains two requirements: p evaluates to true, and p evaluates to false.*

This is where the graph criteria conceptually overlap the logic expression criteria; the graph version of Predicate Coverage was introduced in Section 2.1 as Edge Coverage. For control flow graphs where P is the set of predicates associated with branches, Predicate Coverage and Edge Coverage are the same. For the predicate given above, $((a > b) \lor C) \land p(x)$, two tests that satisfy Predicate Coverage are $(a = 5, b = 4, C = true, p(x) = true)$ and $(a = 5, b = 6, C = false, p(x) = false)$.

An obvious failing of this criterion is that the individual clauses are not always exercised. Predicate coverage for the above clause could also be satisfied with the two tests $(a = 5, b = 4, C = true, p(x) = true)$ and $(a = 5, b = 4, C = true, p(x) = false)$, in which the first two clauses never have the value *false*! The solution to this problem is to move to the clause level.

CRITERION 9. **Clause Coverage (CC):** *For each $c \in C$, TR contains two requirements: c evaluates to true, and c evaluates to false.*

The predicate $((a > b) \lor C) \land p(x)$ requires different values to satisfy CC. Clause Coverage requires that $(a > b) = true$ and *false*, $C = true$ and *false*, and $p(x) = true$ and *false*. These requirements can be satisfied with two tests: $((a = 5, b = 4), (C = true), p(x) = true)$ and $((a = 5, b = 6), (C = false), p(x) = false))$.

Clause Coverage does not subsume Predicate Coverage, and Predicate Coverage does not subsume Clause Coverage, as shown by the predicate $p = a \lor b$. Formally, the clauses C are those in p: $C = C_p = \{a, b\}$. Consider the four test inputs that enumerate the combinations of logical values for the clauses:

$$p = a \lor b$$
$$t_1 = (a = true, \ b = true) \rightarrow p = true$$
$$t_2 = (a = true, \ b = false) \rightarrow p = true$$
$$t_3 = (a = false, \ b = true) \rightarrow p = true$$
$$t_4 = (a = false, \ b = false) \rightarrow p = false$$

The pair of test cases $T_1 = \{t_1, t_2\}$ satisfies neither Clause Coverage (because a is never false) nor Predicate Coverage (because p is never false). Test set $T_2 = \{t_2, t_3\}$ satisfies Clause Coverage, but not Predicate Coverage (because p is never false). Test set $T_3 = \{t_2, t_4\}$ satisfies Predicate Coverage, but not Clause Coverage (because b is never true). Test set $T_4 = \{t_1, t_4\}$ is the only pair that satisfies both Clause Coverage and Predicate Coverage. These test sets demonstrate that neither Predicate Coverage nor Clause Coverage subsume the other.

From the testing perspective, a coverage criterion should test individual clauses and also the predicate. The most direct approach to rectify this problem is to try all combinations of clauses:

CRITERION **10. Combinatorial Coverage (CoC):**   *For each $p \in P$, TR has test requirements for the clauses in C_p to evaluate to each possible combination of truth values.*

Combinatorial Coverage is also called Multiple Condition Coverage. For the predicate $((A \lor B) \land C)$, the complete truth table contains eight elements:

	A	B	C	$(A \lor B) \land C$
1	T	T	T	T
2	T	T	F	F
3	T	F	T	T
4	T	F	F	F
5	F	T	T	T
6	F	T	F	F
7	F	F	T	F
8	F	F	F	F

A predicate p with n independent clauses has 2^n possible assignments of truth values. This may be okay with three or four clauses, but a predicate with five clauses has 32 possible assignments, making Combinatorial Coverage unwieldy at best, and possibly impractical. What is needed is a criterion that captures the effect of each clause, but does so in a reasonable number of tests. These observations lead, after some thought[2], to a powerful collection of test criteria that are based on the notion of making individual clauses "active" as defined in the next subsection.

Active Clause Coverage. The lack of subsumption between Clause and Predicate Coverage is unfortunate, but there are deeper problems with Clause and Predicate Coverage. Specifically, tests at the clause level, should have an effect on the predicate. When debugging, we say that one fault *masks* another if the second fault cannot be observed until the first fault is corrected. There is a similar notion of masking in logical expressions. In the predicate $p = a \wedge b$, if $b = false$, b can be said to mask a, because no matter what value a has, p will still be $false$. To avoid masking when tests are constructed, it is necessary to consider the circumstances under which a clause affects the value of a predicate.

Definition 3. Determination: *Given a clause c_i in predicate p, called the* <u>*major clause*</u>, *c_i determines p if the remaining* <u>*minor*</u> *clauses $c_j \in p$, $j \neq i$ have values so that changing the truth value of c_i changes the truth value of p.*

Note that this definition explicitly does **not** require that $c_i = p$. This issue has been left ambiguous by previous definitions, some of which require the predicate and the major clause to have the same value. This interpretation is not practical. When the negation operator is used, for example, if the predicate is $p = \neg a$, it becomes impossible for the major clause and the predicate to have the same value.

Consider the example above, where $p = a \vee b$. If b is false, then clause a determines p, because then the value of p is exactly the value of a. However if b is true, then a does not determine p, since p is true regardless of the value of a.

From the testing perspective, we would like to test each clause under circumstances where the clause determines the predicate. Consider again the predicate $p = a \vee b$. If b is not varied under circumstances where b determines p, then there is no evidence that b is used correctly. For example, test set T_4, which satisfies both Clause and Predicate Coverage, tests neither a nor b effectively. In fact, if the *or* operator uses short circuit evaluation, test case t_1 does not even cause b to be evaluated!

CRITERION **11. Active Clause Coverage (ACC):**   *For each $p \in P$ and each major clause $c_i \in C_p$, choose minor clauses c_j, $j \neq i$ so that c_i determines p. TR has two requirements for each c_i: c_i evaluates to true and c_i evaluates to false.*

For example, for $p = a \vee b$, TR has a a total of four requirements, two for clause a and two for clause b. Clause a determines p if and only if b is false. This results

---

[2] In practice, this "thought" turned out to be the collective effort of over a dozen researchers, who published tens of papers over a 15 to 20 year period, as detailed in Section 5.

in the two test requirements $\{(a = true, b = false), (a = false, b = false)\}$. Clause b determines p if and only if a is false. This results in the two test requirements $\{(a = false, b = true), (a = false, b = false)\}$. This concept is summarized in the partial truth table below, (the values for the major clauses are in bold face).

$$
\begin{array}{c|c|c}
 & a & b \\
\hline
c_i = a & \mathbf{T} & \text{f} \\
 & \mathbf{F} & \text{f} \\
\hline
c_i = b & \text{f} & \mathbf{T} \\
 & \text{f} & \mathbf{F} \\
\end{array}
$$

Two of these requirements are identical, resulting in three distinct test requirements for Active Clause Coverage for the predicate $a \vee b$, namely, $\{(a = true, b = false), (a = false, b = true), (a = false, b = false)\}$. Such overlap always happens, and it turns out that for a predicate with n clauses, $n + 1$ distinct test requirements, rather than the $2n$ one might expect, are sufficient to satisfy Active Clause Coverage.

ACC is almost identical to the way early papers described another technique called MCDC. It turns out that this criterion has some ambiguity, which has led to a fair amount of confusion of interpretation of MCDC over the years. The most important question is whether the minor clauses c_j need to have the same values when the major clause c_i is true as when c_i is false. Resolving this ambiguity leads to three distinct and interesting flavours of Active Clause Coverage. For a simple predicate such as $p = a \vee b$, the three flavours turn out to be identical, but differences appear for more complex predicates. The most general flavour allows the minor clauses to have different values.

CRITERION 12. **General Active Clause Coverage (GACC):** *For each $p \in P$ and each major clause $c_i \in C_p$, choose minor clauses c_j, $j \neq i$ so that c_i determines p. TR has two requirements for each c_i: c_i evaluates to true and c_i evaluates to false. The values chosen for the minor clauses c_j do not need to be the same when c_i is true as when c_i is false, that is, $c_j(c_i = true) = c_j(c_i = false) \; \forall \; c_j$ OR $c_j(c_i = true) \neq c_j(c_i = false) \; \forall \; c_j$.*

Unfortunately, it turns out that General Active Clause Coverage does not subsume Predicate Coverage, as the following example shows.

Consider the predicate $p = a \leftrightarrow b$. Clause a determines p for any assignment of truth values to b. So, let us choose for the case where a is true, b to be true as well, and for the case where a is false, b false as well. For clause b, make the same selections. This results in only two test requirements, $TR = \{(a = true, b = true), (a = false, b = false)\}$. p evaluates to *true* for both of these cases, so Predicate Coverage is not achieved.

Many testing researchers have a strong feeling that ACC should subsume PC, thus the second flavour of ACC insists that p evaluates to true for one assignment of values to the major clause c_i, and false for the other. Note that c_i

and p do not have to have the same values, as discussed with the definition for determination.

CRITERION **13. Correlated Active Clause Coverage (CACC):** *For each $p \in P$ and each major clause $c_i \in C_p$, choose minor clauses c_j, $j \neq i$ so that c_i determines p. TR has two requirements for each c_i: c_i evaluates to true and c_i evaluates to false. The values chosen for the minor clauses c_j must cause p to be true for one value of the major clause c_i and false for the other, that is, it is required that $p(c_i = true) \neq p(c_i = false)$.*

Consider the example $p = a \wedge (b \vee c)$. For a to determine the value of p, the expression $b \vee c$ must be true. There are three ways to achieve this: b true and c false, b false and c true, and both b and c true. So, it would be possible to satisfy Correlated Active Clause Coverage with respect to clause a with the two test requirements: $\{(a = true, b = true, c = false), (a = false, b = false, c = true)\}$. There are other possible test requirements with respect to a. The following truth table helps enumerate them. The row numbers are taken from the complete truth table for the predicate given previously. Specifically, CACC can be satisfied for a by choosing one test requirement from rows 1, 2 and 3, and the second from rows 5, 6 and 7. There are, of course, nine possible ways to do this.

	a	b	c	$a \wedge (b \vee c)$
1	T	T	T	T
2	T	T	F	T
3	T	F	T	T
5	F	T	T	F
6	F	T	F	F
7	F	F	T	F

The final flavour forces the value for clause c_j to be identical for both assignments of truth values to c_i.

CRITERION **14. Restricted Active Clause Coverage (RACC):** *For each $p \in P$ and each major clause $c_i \in C_p$, choose minor clauses c_j, $j \neq i$ so that c_i determines p. TR has two requirements for each c_i: c_i evaluates to true and c_i evaluates to false. The values chosen for the minor clauses c_j must be the same when c_i is true as when c_i is false, that is, it is required that $c_j(c_i = true) = c_j(c_i = false) \, \forall \, c_j$.*

For the example $p = a \wedge (b \vee c)$, only three of the nine sets of test requirements that satisfy Correlated Active Clause Coverage with respect to clause a will satisfy Restricted Active Clause Coverage with respect to clause a. In terms of the previously given complete truth table, row 2 can be paired with row 6, row 3 with row 7, or row 1 with row 5. Thus, instead of the nine ways to satisfy CACC, only three can satisfy RACC.

	a	b	c	$a \wedge (b \vee c)$
1	T	T	T	T
5	F	T	T	F
2	T	T	F	T
6	F	T	F	F
3	T	F	T	T
7	F	F	T	F

CACC versus RACC. Examples of satisfying a predicate for each of these three criteria are given later. One point that may not be immediately obvious is how CACC and RACC differ in practice.

It turns out that some logical expressions can be completely satisfied under CACC, but have infeasible test requirements under RACC. These expressions are a little subtle and only exist if there are dependency relationships among the clauses, that is, some combinations of values for the clauses are prohibited. Since this often happens in real programs – because program variables frequently depend upon one another – it is useful to consider such an example.

Consider a system with a valve that might be either open or closed, and several modes, two of which are "Operational" and "Standby." Suppose that there are two constraints:

1. The valve must be open in "*Operational*" and closed in all other modes.
2. The mode cannot be both "*Operational*" and "*Standby*" at the same time.

This leads to the following clause definitions:

$$a = \textit{"The valve is closed"}$$
$$b = \textit{"The system status is Operational"}$$
$$c = \textit{"The system status is Standby"}$$

Suppose that a certain action can only be taken if the valve is closed and the system status is either in *Operational* or *Standby*. That is:

$$p = \textit{valve is closed AND (system status is Operational OR}$$
$$\textit{system status is Standby)}$$
$$= a \wedge (b \vee c)$$

This is exactly the predicate that was analyzed above. The constraints above can be formalized as:

$$1 \ \neg a \leftrightarrow b$$
$$2 \ \neg(b \wedge c)$$

These constraints limit the feasible values in the truth table. As a reminder, the complete truth table for this predicate is:

	a	b	c	$a \wedge (b \vee c))$	
1	T	T	T	T	violates constraints 1 & 2
2	T	T	F	T	violates constraint 1
3	T	F	T	T	
4	T	F	F	F	
5	F	T	T	F	violates constraint 2
6	F	T	F	F	
7	F	F	T	F	violates constraint 1
8	F	F	F	F	violates constraint 1

Recall that for a to determine the value of P, either b or c or both must be true. Constraint 1 rules out the rows where a and b have the same values, that is, rows 1, 2, 7, and 8. Constraint 2 rules out the rows where b and c are both true, that is, rows 1 and 5. Thus the only feasible rows are 3, 4, and 6. Recall that CACC can be satisfied by choosing one from rows 1, 2 or 3 and one from rows 5, 6 or 7. But RACC requires one of the pairs 2 and 6, 3 and 7, or 1 and 5. Thus RACC is infeasible for a in this predicate.

Inactive Clause Coverage. The Active Clause Coverage Criteria focus on making sure the major clauses <u>do</u> affect their predicates. A complementary criterion to Active Clause Coverage ensures that changing a major clause that should *not* affect the predicate does not, in fact, affect the predicate.

CRITERION **15. Inactive Clause Coverage:** *For each $p \in P$ and each major clause $c_i \in C_p$, choose minor clauses c_j, $j \neq i$ so that c_i does <u>not</u> determine p. TR has four requirements for c_i under these circumstances: (1) c_i evaluates to true with p true, (2) c_i evaluates to false with p true, (3) c_i evaluates to true with p false, and (4) c_i evaluates to false with p false.*

Although Inactive Clause Coverage (ICC) has some of the same ambiguity as does ACC, there are only two distinct flavours, namely *General Inactive Clause Coverage (GICC)* and *Restricted Inactive Clause Coverage (RICC)*. The notion of correlation is not relevant for Inactive Clause Coverage because c_i cannot correlate with p since c_i does not determine p. Also, Predicate Coverage is guaranteed in all flavours due to the structure of the definition.

The formal versions of GICC and RICC are as follows.

CRITERION **16. General Inactive Clause Coverage (GICC):** *For each $p \in P$ and each major clause $c_i \in C_p$, choose minor clauses c_j, $j \neq i$ so that c_i does <u>not</u> determine p. The values chosen for the minor clauses c_j do not need to be the same when c_i is true as when c_i is false, that is, $c_j(c_i = true) = c_j(c_i = false) \; \forall \; c_j$ OR $c_j(c_i = true) \neq c_j(c_i = false) \; \forall \; c_j$.*

CRITERION **17. Restricted Inactive Clause Coverage (RICC):** *For each $p \in P$ and each major clause $c_i \in C_p$, choose minor clauses c_j, $j \neq i$ so that c_i does <u>not</u> determine p. The values chosen for the minor clauses c_j must be the same when c_i is true as when c_i is false, that is, it is required that $c_j(c_i = true) = c_j(c_i = false) \; \forall \; c_j$.*

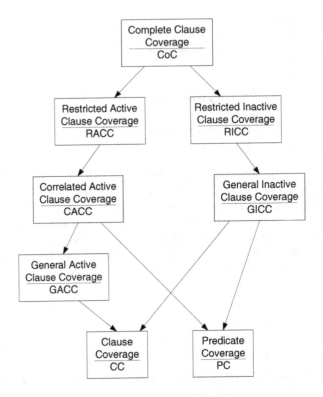

Fig. 7. Subsumption relations among logic coverage criteria

Figure 7 shows the subsumption relationships among the logic expression criteria. Note that the Inactive Clause Coverage Criteria do not subsume any of the Active Criteria, and vice versa.

Making a Clause Determine a Predicate. So, how does one go about finding values for the minor clauses c_j so that the major clause c_i determines the value of p? The authors are aware of three different methods presented in the literature; a direct definitional approach is given here. Pointers to the other two, one of which is an algorithmic version of the definitional approach, are given in the bibliographic notes.

For a predicate p with clause (or boolean variable) c, let $p_{c=true}$ represent the predicate p with every occurrence of c replaced by $true$ and $p_{c=false}$ be the predicate p with every occurrence of c replaced by $false$. The rest of this development assumes there are no duplicates (that is, p contains only one occurrence of c). Note that neither $p_{c=true}$ nor $p_{c=false}$ contains any occurrences of the clause c. Now connect the two expressions with an exclusive or:

$$p_c = p_{c=true} \oplus p_{c=false}$$

It turns out that p_c describes the exact conditions under which the value of c determines that of p. That is, if values for the clauses in p_c are chosen so that p_c is true, then the truth value of c determines the truth value of p. If the clauses in p_c are chosen so that p_c evaluates to false, then the truth value of p is independent of the truth value of c. This is exactly what is needed to implement the various flavours of Active and Inactive Clause Coverage.

As a first example, try $p = a \vee b$. p_a is, by definition:

$$
\begin{aligned}
p_a &= p_{a=true} \oplus p_{a=false} \\
&= (true \vee b) \oplus (false \vee b) \\
&= true \oplus b \\
&= \neg b
\end{aligned}
$$

That is, for the major clause a to determine the predicate p, the only minor clause b must be false. This should make sense intuitively, since the value of a will have any effect on the value of p only if b is false. By symmetry, it is clear that p_b is $\neg a$.

Changing the predicate to $p = a \wedge b$ results in

$$
\begin{aligned}
p_a &= p_{a=true} \oplus p_{a=false} \\
&= (true \wedge b) \oplus (false \wedge b) \\
&= b \oplus false \\
&= b
\end{aligned}
$$

That is, $b = true$ is needed to make a determine p. By a similar analysis, $p_b = a$.

The equivalence operator is a little less obvious and brings up an interesting point. Consider $p = a \leftrightarrow b$.

$$
\begin{aligned}
p_a &= p_{a=true} \oplus p_{a=false} \\
&= (true \leftrightarrow b) \oplus (false \leftrightarrow b) \\
&= b \oplus \neg b \\
&= true
\end{aligned}
$$

That is, for any value of b, a determines the value of p **without regard to the value for b**! This means that for a predicate p, such as this one, where the value of p_c is the constant true, the Inactive Clause Criteria are infeasible with respect to c. Inactive Clause Coverage cannot be applied to expressions that use the equivalence operator.

A more general version of this conclusion can be drawn that applies to the Active Criteria as well. If a predicate p contains a clause c such that p_c evaluates to the constant false, the Active Criteria are infeasible with respect to c. The ultimate reason is that the clause in question is redundant; the predicate can be rewritten without it. While this may sound like a theoretical curiosity, it is actually a very useful result for testers. If a predicate contains a redundant clause, that is a very strong signal that something is wrong with the predicate!

Consider $p = a \wedge b \vee a \wedge \neg b$. This is really just the predicate $p = a$; b is irrelevant. Computing p_b yields

$$
\begin{aligned}
p_b &= p_{b=true} \oplus p_{b=false} \\
&= (a \wedge true \vee a \wedge \neg true) \oplus (a \wedge false \vee a \wedge \neg false) \\
&= (a \vee false) \oplus (false \vee a) \\
&= a \oplus a \\
&= false
\end{aligned}
$$

so it is impossible for b to determine p.

Now consider how to make clauses determine predicates for more complicated expressions. The expression $p = a \wedge (b \vee c)$ yields

$$
\begin{aligned}
p_a &= p_{a=true} \oplus p_{a=false} \\
&= (true \wedge (b \vee c)) \oplus (false \wedge (b \vee c)) \\
&= (b \vee c) \oplus false \\
&= b \vee c
\end{aligned}
$$

This example ends with an undetermined answer, which points out the key difference between CACC and RACC. Three choices of values make $b \vee c$ true, ($b = c = true$), ($b = true, c = false$), and ($b = false, c = true$). Correlated Active Clause Coverage allows one pair of values to be used when a is true and another when a is false. Restricted Active Clause Coverage requires the same pair to be used for both values of a.

The derivation for b and equivalently for c is slightly more complicated:

$$
\begin{aligned}
p_b &= p_{b=true} \oplus p_{b=false} \\
&= (a \wedge (true \vee c)) \oplus (a \wedge (false \vee c)) \\
&= (a \wedge true) \oplus (a \wedge c) \\
&= a \oplus (a \wedge c) \\
&= a \wedge \neg c
\end{aligned}
$$

Finding Satisfying Values. The final step in applying the logic coverage criteria is, of course, to choose values that satisfy the criteria. This step can be automated fairly easily, although sometimes arbitrary choices can be made. This section shows how to generate values for one example. The example is from the first section of the chapter:

$$
p = (a \vee b) \wedge c
$$

Finding values for **Predicate Coverage** is easy and was already shown in Section 3. There are two test requirements:

$$
TR_{PC} = \{p = true, p = false\}
$$

and they can be satisfied with the following values for the clauses:

$$
\begin{array}{c|c|c|c}
 & a & b & c \\
\hline
p = true & t & t & t \\
p = false & t & t & f
\end{array}
$$

To run the test cases, of course, we need to refine these truth assignments to create values for clauses a, b, and c. Suppose that clauses a, b, and c were defined in terms of Java program variables as follows:

a	`x < y`, a relational expression for program variables `x` and `y`
b	`done`, a primitive boolean value
c	`list.contains(str)`, for `List` and `String` objects

Thus, the complete expanded predicate is actually:

$$p = (x < y \lor done) \land list.contains(str)$$

Then the following values for the program variables satisfy the test requirements for predicate coverage.

	a	b	c		
$p = true$	x=3 y=5	done = true	list=["Rat","Cat","Dog"]	str = "Cat"
$p = false$	x=0 y=7	done = true	list=["Red","White"]	str = "Blue"

Note that the values for the program variables need not be the same in a particular test case if the goal is to set a clause to a particular value. For example, clause a is true in both tests, even though program variables x and y have different values.

Values to satisfy **Clause Coverage** were also shown in Section 3. There are six test requirements: $TR_{CC} = \{a = true, a = false, b = true, b = false, c = true, c = false\}$
and they can be satisfied with the following values for the clauses (blank cells represent "don't-care" values):

$$
\begin{array}{c|c|c|c}
 & a & b & c \\
\hline
a = true & t & & \\
a = false & f & & \\
b = true & & t & \\
b = false & & f & \\
c = true & & & t \\
c = false & & & f
\end{array}
$$

Refining the truth assignments to create values for program variables x, y, b, $list$, and str is similar and straightforward.

Values for minor clauses to ensure the major clauses will determine the values for p, as given in Section 3.1, are:

p_a	$\neg b \land c$
p_b	$\neg a \land c$
p_c	$a \lor b$

The next criterion is **Combinatorial Coverage**, which requires all combinations of values for the clauses. CoC has eight test requirements, which can be satisfied with the following values:

	a	b	c	$(a \vee b) \wedge c$
1	t	t	t	t
2	t	t	f	f
3	t	f	t	t
4	t	f	f	f
5	f	t	t	t
6	f	t	f	f
7	f	f	t	f
8	f	f	f	f

Recall that **General Active Clause Coverage** requires that each major clause be true and false and the minor clauses be such that the major clause determines the value of the predicate. Similarly to Clause Coverage, there are three pairs of test requirements:

$$TR_{GACC} = \{(a = true \wedge p_a, a = false \wedge p_a), (b = true \wedge p_b, b = false \wedge p_b), (c = true \wedge p_c, c = false \wedge p_c)\}$$

The test requirements can be satisfied with the following values for the clauses. Note that these can be the same as with Clause Coverage with the exception that the blank cells from Clause Coverage are replaced with the values from the determination analysis. In the following table, values for major clauses are indicated with upper case letters in bold-face.

	a	b	c	p
$a = true \wedge p_a$	**T**	f	t	t
$a = false \wedge p_a$	**F**	f	t	f
$b = true \wedge p_b$	f	**T**	t	t
$b = false \wedge p_b$	f	**F**	t	f
$c = true \wedge p_c$	t	f	**T**	t
$c = false \wedge p_c$	f	t	**F**	f

Note the duplication; the first and fifth rows are identical, and the second and fourth are identical. Thus only four tests are needed to satisfy GACC.

A different way of looking at GACC considers all of the possible pairs of test inputs for each pair of test requirements. Recall that the active clause coverage criteria always generate test requirements in pairs, with one pair generated for each clause in the predicate under test. The row numbers from the truth table are used to identify these test inputs. Hence, the pair $(3, 7)$ represents the first two tests listed in the table above.

It turns out that $(3, 7)$ is the only pair that satisfies the GACC test requirements with respect to clause a, and $(5, 7)$ is the only pair that satisfies the GACC test requirements with respect to clause b. For clause c, the situation is more interesting. Nine pairs satisfy the GACC test requirements for clause c, namely

$$\{(1,5),(1,6),(1,7),(2,5),(2,6),(2,7),(3,5),(3,6),(3,7)\}$$

Recall that **Correlated Active Clause Coverage** requires that each major clause be true and false, the minor clauses be such that the major clause determines the value of the predicate, and the predicate must have both the value true and false. As with GACC, there are three pairs of test requirements: For clause a, the pair of test requirements is:

$$a = true \wedge p_a \wedge p = x$$

$$a = false \wedge p_a \wedge p = \neg x$$

where x may be either true or false. The point is that p must have a different truth value in the two test cases. The CACC test requirements with respect to b and c are similar.

For the example predicate p, a careful examination of the pairs of test cases for GACC reveals that p takes on both truth values in each pair. Hence, there is no difference between GACC and CACC for predicate p, and the same pairs of test inputs apply. This is not, of course, true in general.

The situation for RACC is quite different, however, for the example p. Recall that **Restricted Active Clause Coverage** is the same as CACC except that it requires the values for the minor clauses c_j to be identical for both assignments of truth values to the major clause. For clause a, the pair of test requirements that RACC generates is:

$$a = true \wedge p_a \wedge b = B \wedge c = C$$

$$a = false \wedge p_a \wedge b = B \wedge c = C$$

for some boolean constants B and C. An examination of the pairs given above for $GACC$ reveal that with respect to clauses a and b, there is no change. Namely, pair $(3,7)$ satisfies RACC with respect to clause a and pair $(5,7)$ satisfies RACC with respect to b. However, with respect to c, only three pairs satisfy RACC, namely,

$$\{(1,5),(2,6),(3,7)\}$$

This example leaves one question about the different flavours of Active Coverage, namely, what is the practical difference among them? That is, beyond the subtle difference in the arithmetic, how do they affect practical testers? The real differences do not show up very often, but when they do they can be dramatic and quite annoying.

GACC does not require that Predicate Coverage be satisfied, so use of that flavour may mean the program is not tested as thoroughly as it should be. In practical use, it is easy to construct examples where GACC is satisfied but Predicate Coverage is not when the predicates are very small (one or two terms), but difficult with three or more terms.

The restrictive nature of RACC, on the other hand, can sometimes make it hard to satisfy the criterion. This is particularly true when there are dependencies among the clauses. Consider a case where in the predicate used above, when $x < y$ is true, the semantics of the program force *done* to be true, and when $x < y$ is false, *done* must be false. When this happens, the two clauses are said to be *correlated*. Then RACC cannot be 100% satisfied (that is, there are infeasible test requirements), but CACC can. Thus, the authors recommend that Correlated Active Clause Coverage is usually the most practical flavour of ACC.

Complicating Issues. A variety of technical issues have been identified that complicate the Active Clause Coverage criteria. As with many criteria, the most important is the issue of infeasibility. Infeasibility is often a problem because clauses are sometimes related to one another. That is, choosing the truth value for one clause may affect the truth value for another clause. Consider, for example, a common loop structure, which assumes short circuit semantics:

```
while (i < n and a[i] != 0) {do something to a[i]}
```

The idea here is to avoid evaluating a[i] if i is out of range, and short circuit evaluation is not only assumed, but depended on. Clearly, it is not going to be possible to develop a test case where i < n is false and a[i] != 0 is true.

In principle, the issue of infeasibility for clause and predicate criteria is no different from that for graph criteria. In both cases, the solution is to satisfy test requirements that are feasible, and then identify and remove from consideration test requirements that are infeasible.

It is also worth noting that this development treats clauses semantically, rather than using the syntactic treatment that is common in the literature. That is, the following predicate:

$$a \wedge b \vee \neg a \wedge \neg b$$

is treated as having two clauses – a and b. The fact that both of these clauses show up multiple times is ignored. The advantage of this approach is that exactly the same test requirements are developed, no matter how the predicate is expressed.

3.2   Logic Coverage for Specifications

Software specifications, both formal and informal, appear in a variety of forms and languages. They almost invariably include logical expressions, allowing the logic coverage criteria to be applied. The first subsection looks at their application to simple preconditions on methods, then other forms of specifications.

Specification-based Logic Coverage. Programmers often include preconditions as part of their methods. The preconditions are sometimes written as part of the design, and sometimes added later as documentation. Many formal specification languages (such as Z) have explicit preconditions. Some sort of precondition is always valid, although they are often not written explicitly. A tester may still consider using this technique when the preconditions are not explicit, by developing the preconditions as part of the testing process.

Consider the cal method in Figure 3.2. The method lists explicit preconditions in natural language, which can be translated into predicate form as follows:

$$month1 >= 0 \wedge month1 <= 12 \wedge month2 >= 0 \wedge month2 <= 12 \wedge month1 <= month2$$

$$\wedge day1 >= 1 \wedge day1 <= 31 \wedge day2 >= 1 \wedge day2 <= 31 \wedge year >= 1 \wedge year <= 10000$$

The comment about $day1$ and $day2$ being in the same year can be safely ignored, because that prerequisite is enforced syntactically by the fact that only one parameter appears for $year$. It is probably also clear that these preconditions are not complete. Specifically, a day of 31 is only valid for some months. This requirement should be reflected in the specifications or in the program.

This predicate has a very simple structure. It has eleven clauses (which sounds like a lot!) but the only logical operator is "and," so it is in disjunctive normal form. Satisfying predicate coverage for `cal()` is simple – all clauses need to be true for the true case and all clauses need to be false for the false case. So ($month1 = 4$, $month2 = 4$, $day1 = 12$, $day2 = 30$, $year = 1961$) and ($month1 = 6, month2 = 4, day1 = 12, day2 = 30, year = 1961$) satisfy predicate coverage. Clause coverage requires all clauses to be true and false. It is reasonable to try to satisfy this requirement with only two tests, but some clauses are related and cannot both be false at the same time. For example, $month1$ cannot be less than 0 and greater than 12 at the same time. The true test for predicate coverage allows all clauses to be positive, then the following tests make each clause negative. ($month1 = -1$, $month2 = -2$, $day1 = 0$, $day2 = 0$, $year = 0$) and ($month1 = 13$, $month2 = 13$, $day1 = 32$, $day2 = 32$, $year = 10500$).

```
public static int cal (int month1, int day1, int month2,
                       int day2, int year)
{
//*************************************************************
// Calculate the number of Days between the two given days in
// the same year.
// preconditions : day1 and day2 must be in same year
//                 1 <= month1, month2 <= 12
//                 1 <= day1, day2 <= 31
//                 month1 <= month2
//                 The range for year: 1 ... 10000
//*************************************************************
```

Fig. 8. Header for calendar method

Making each clause determine the predicate with disjunctive normal form predicates is simple – each minor clause must be true. To find the remaining tests, each other predicate is made to be false in turn. Therefore, CACC (and also RACC) is satisfied by the tests that are specified in Table 1. (Abbreviations of the variable names are used to save space.)

Logic Coverage of Finite State Machines. Section 2.1 discussed the application of graph coverage criteria to Finite State Machines. Recall that FSMs are graphs with nodes that represent states and edges that represent transitions,

Table 1. Correlated Active Clause Coverage for `cal()` Preconditions

	$m1 \geq 0$	$m1 \leq 12$	$m2 \geq 0$	$m2 \leq 12$	$m1 \leq m2$	$d1 \geq 1$	$d1 \leq 31$	$d2 \geq 1$	$d2 \leq 31$	$y \geq 1$	$y \leq 10000$
1. $m1 \geq 0 = T$	T	t	t	t	t	t	t	t	t	t	t
2. $m1 \geq 0 = F$	F	t	t	t	t	t	t	t	t	t	t
4. $m1 \leq 12 = F$	t	F	t	t	t	t	t	t	t	t	t
5. $m2 \geq 0 = F$	t	t	F	t	t	t	t	t	t	t	t
6. $m2 \leq 12 = F$	t	t	t	F	t	t	t	t	t	t	t
7. $m1 \leq m2 = F$	t	t	t	t	F	t	t	t	t	t	t
8. $d1 \geq 1 = F$	t	t	t	t	t	F	t	t	t	t	t
9. $d1 \leq 31 = F$	t	t	t	t	t	t	F	t	t	t	t
10. $d2 \geq 1 = F$	t	t	t	t	t	t	t	F	t	t	t
11. $d2 \leq 31 = F$	t	t	t	t	t	t	t	t	F	t	t
12. $y \geq 1 = F$	t	t	t	t	t	t	t	t	t	F	t
13. $y \leq 10000 = F$	t	t	t	t	t	t	t	t	t	t	F

with pre-states and a post-states. FSMs usually model behaviour of the software and can be more or less formal and precise, depending on the needs and inclinations of the developers. This section treats FSMs in a generic way, as graphs. Differences in notations are considered only in terms of the effect they have on applying the criteria.

The most common way to apply logic coverage criteria to FSMs is to use logical expressions from the transitions as predicates. In the Elevator example in the Section 2.1, the trigger and thus the predicate is *openButton = pressed*. Tests are created by applying the criteria from Section 3 to these predicates.

Consider the slightly larger example in Figure 9. This FSM models the behavior of the memory seat in a car. The memory seat has two configurations for two separate drivers and controls the side mirrors (`sideMirrors`), the vertical height of the seat (`seatBottom`), the horizontal distance of the seat from the steering wheel (`seatBack`), and the lumbar support (`lumbar`). The intent is to remember the configurations so that the drivers can conveniently switch configurations with the press of a button. Each state in the figure has a number for efficient reference.

The initial state of the FSM is whichever configuration it was in when the system was last shut down, either Driver 1 or Driver 2. The drivers can modify the configuration by manipulating one of the four controls; changing the side mirrors, moving the seat backward or forward, raising or lowering the seat, or modifying the lumbar support (triggering events). These controls only work if the `ignition` is on (a guard). The driver can also change to the other configuration by pressing either `Button1` or `Button2`. In these cases, the guards only allow the configuration to be changed if the `Gear` is in `Park` or the `ignition` is off. These are *safety constraints*, because it would be dangerous to allow the driver's seat to go flying around when the car is moving.

When the driver changes one of the controls, the memory seat is put into the modified configuration state. The new state can be saved by simultaneously pressing the `Reset` button and either `Button1` or `Button2`. The new configuration is permanently saved when the ignition is turned off.

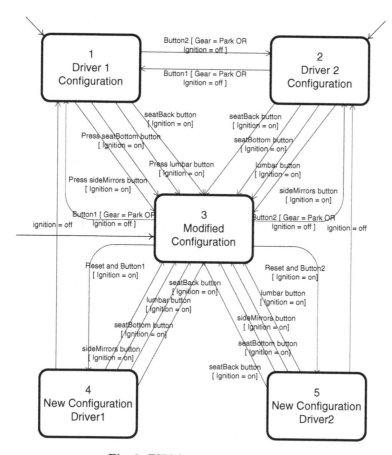

Fig. 9. FSM for a memory car seat

This type of FSM provides an effective model for testing software, although several issues must be understood and dealt with when creating predicates and then test values. Guards are not always explicitly listed as conjuncts, but they are conjuncts in effect and so should be combined with the triggers using the AND operator. In some specification languages, for example SCR, the triggers actually imply two values. In SCR, if an event is labeled as triggering, it means that the value of the resulting expression must explicitly change. This implies two values – a before and after value, and is modelled by introducing a new variable. For example, in the memory seat example, the transition from New Configuration Driver 1 to Driver 1 Configuration is taken when the ignition is turned off. If that is a triggering transition in the SCR sense, then the predicate needs to have two parts: $ignition = on \ \land \ ignition' = off$. $ignition'$ is the after value.

The transitions from Modified Configuration to the two New Configuration states demonstrate another issue. The two buttons Reset and Button1 (or Button2) must be pressed **simultaneously**. In practical terms for this example, it is important to test for what happens when one button is pressed slightly prior to the other. Unfortunately, the mathematics of logical expressions used here do not have an explicit way to represent this requirement, thus this situation is not handled explicitly. The two buttons are connected in the predicate with the AND operator. This is a simple example of the general problem of timing, and needs to be addressed in the context of real-time software.

The predicates for the memory seat example are in Table 2 (using the state numbers from Figure 9).

The tests to satisfy the various criteria are fairly straightforward and are left to the exercises. Several issues must be addressed when choosing values for test cases. The first is that of reachability; the test case must include *prefix* values to reach the pre-state. For most FSMs, this is just a matter of finding a path from an initial state to the pre-state (using a depth first search), and the predicates associated with the transitions are solved to produce inputs. The memory seat example has two initial states, and the tester cannot control which one is entered because it depends on the last state the system was in when it was last shut down. In this case, however, an obvious solution presents itself. Every test can begin by putting the Gear in park and pushing Button 1 (part of the prefix). If the system is in the Driver 2 state, these inputs will cause the system to transition to the Driver 1 state. If the system is in the Driver 1 state, these inputs will have no effect. In either case, the system will effectively start in the Driver 1 state.

Some FSMs also have exit states that must be reached with postfix values. Finding these values is essentially the same as finding prefix values; that is, finding a path from the post-state to a final state. In the memory seat example, there is no exit state so this step can be skipped. The results of the test case (*verification values*) must also be made visible. This might be possible by giving an input to the program to print the current state, or causing some other output that is dependent on the state. The exact form and syntax this takes depends on the implementation, so cannot be finalized until the input-output behaviour syntax of the software is designed.

One major advantage of this form of testing is determining the expected output. It is simply the post-state of the transition for the test case values that cause the transition to be true, and the pre-state for the test case values that cause the transition to be false (the system should remain in the current state). The only exception to this rule is that occasionally a false predicate might coincidentally be a true predicate for another transition, in which case the expected output should be the post-state of the alternate transition. This situation can be recognized automatically.

The final problem is that of converting a test case (composed of prefix values, test case values, postfix values, and expected output) into an executable test script. The potential problem here is that the variable assignments for the predicates must be converted into inputs to the software. This has been called the *mapping problem* with FSMs and is analogous to the internal variable problem of automatic test data generation for programs. Sometimes this step is a simple syntactic rewriting predicate assignments (Button1 to program input *button1*).

Table 2. Predicates from Memory Seat Example

Pre-state	Post-state	Predicate
1	2	$Button2 \wedge (Gear = Park \vee ignition = off)$
1	3	$sideMirrors \wedge ignition = on$
1	3	$seatButton \wedge ignition = on$
1	3	$lumbar \wedge ignition = on$
1	3	$seatBack \wedge ignition = on$
2	1	$Button1 \wedge (Gear = Park \vee ignition = off)$
2	3	$sideMirrors \wedge ignition = on$
2	3	$seatButton \wedge ignition = on$
2	3	$lumbar \wedge ignition = on$
2	3	$seatBack \wedge ignition = on$
3	1	$Button1 \wedge (Gear = Park \vee ignition = off)$
3	2	$Button2 \wedge (Gear = Park \vee ignition = off)$
3	4	$Reset \wedge Button1 \wedge ignition = on$
3	5	$Reset \wedge Button2 \wedge ignition = on$
4	1	$ignition = off$
4	3	$sideMirrors \wedge ignition = on$
4	3	$seatButton \wedge ignition = on$
4	3	$lumbar \wedge ignition = on$
4	3	$seatBack \wedge ignition = on$
5	2	$ignition = off$
5	3	$sideMirrors \wedge ignition = on$
5	3	$seatButton \wedge ignition = on$
5	3	$lumbar \wedge ignition = on$
5	3	$seatBack \wedge ignition = on$

Other times the input values can be directly encoded as method calls and embedded into a program (for example, Button1 becomes *pressButton1()*). Other times, however, this problem is much greater and can involve turning seemingly small inputs at the FSM modelling level into long sequences of inputs or method calls. The exact situation depends on the software implementation, thus a general solution to this problem is at present elusive.

4   Summary

This chapter describes two kinds of test criteria suitable for software modelled by state-based specifications. One kind is based on graphs, and the other is based on logic expressions. After we present a representative sample of graph-based and logic-based test coverage criteria, we extract appropriate graphs and predicates from state-based specifications and apply the coverage criteria. The unusual part of our presentation is the identification of the coverage criteria first, followed by the application of the criteria to software artefact at hand. In contrast, most treatments of software testing criteria identify the artefact first, and then develop the criteria. The approach used here has the advantage of focusing on the common aspects of coverage criteria across all software artefacts.

The overall result of the chapter is a guide that helps test engineers in the task of developing a set of test cases that are appropriate for a state-based specification.

5   Bibliographic Notes

During the research for this paper, one thing that became abundantly clear is that this field has had a significant amount of parallel discovery of the same techniques by people working independently. Some individuals have discovered various aspects of the same technique, which was subsequently polished up into test criteria. Others have invented the same techniques, but based them on different types of graphs or used different names. Thus, ascribing credit for these testing criteria is a perilous task. This section is a sincere effort, but the authors only claim that the bibliographic notes in this chapter are starting points for further study in the literature.

5.1   Graph Coverage Criteria

The research into covering graphs seems to have started with generating tests from finite state machines (FSM), which has a long and rich history. Some of the earliest papers were in the 1970s [15,29,31,41,49]. The primary focus of most of these papers was on using FSMs to generate tests for telecommunication systems that are defined with standard finite automata, although much of the work pertained to general graphs. The control flow graph seems to have been invented either by Kosaraju in 1974 [38] or by Legard in 1975 [40]. In papers published in 1975, Huang [31] suggested covering each edge in a FSM, and Howden [29] suggested covering complete trips through a FSM, but without looping. In a similar paper from the same year [47,48] (as cited by Zhu [59]), Paige defined "level-i path coverage." Informally, the level-i criterion starts with testing all paths that have no duplicate nodes from a start node to an end node. Then, subpaths that have no duplicate nodes that have not yet been covered must be covered. Gourlay's extension was *length-n coverage* [27], which requires coverage of all subpaths of length less than or equal to n.

In 1976, McCabe [41] suggested the same idea on control flow graphs as the primary application of his cyclomatic complexity metric. In 1976, Pimont and Rault [49] suggested covering pairs of edges, using the term "switch cover." In 1978, Chow [15] suggested generating a spanning tree from the FSM and then basing test sequences on paths through this tree. In 1991, Fujiwara [25] extended Pimont and Rault's pairs of edges to arbitrary lengths, and used the term "n-switch" to refer to a sequence of edges. He also attributed "1-switch," or switch cover, to Chow and called it the "W-method," an inaccuracy that has been repeated in numerous papers. The idea of covering pairs of edges was rediscovered in the 1990s and included in the British Computer Society Standard for Software Component Testing and called *two-trip* [9] and by Offutt et al. [46], who called it *transition-pair*.

Other test generation methods based on FSMs include tour [44], the distinguished sequence method [26], and unique input-output method [52]. Their objectives are to detect output errors based on state transitions driven by inputs. FSM based test generation has been used to test a variety of applications including lexical analyzers, real-time process control software, protocols, data processing, and telephony. One important observation in this chapter is that the criteria for covering finite state machines are not substantially different from criteria for other graphs.

Several later papers focused on automatic test data generation to cover structural elements in the program [6,7,16,21,24,30,36,37,45,50]. Much of this work was based on the analysis techniques of symbolic evaluation [10,17,18,21,23,29]. and slicing [53,55]. Recently, researchers have been trying to use search-based algorithms (such as genetic and evolutionary algorithms) to address the automatic test data generation problem [42].

The problem of handling loops has plagued graph-based criteria from the beginning. It seems obvious that paths should be covered, but loops create infinite numbers of paths. In Howden's 1975 paper [29], he specifically addressed loops by covering complete paths "without looping," and Chow's 1978 suggestion to use spanning trees was an explicit attempt to avoid having to execute loops [15]. Binder's book [5] used the technique from Chow's paper, but changed the name to *round trip*, which is the name that used here.

Another early suggestion was based on testing loop free programs [11], which is certainly interesting from a theoretical view, but not totally practical.

White and Wiszniewski [58] suggested limiting the number of loops that need to be executed based on specific patterns. Weyuker, Weiss and Hamlet tried to choose specific loops to test based on data definitions and uses [57].

Kim, Hong, Cho, Bae and Cha used a graph-based approach to generate tests from UML state diagrams [34]. SCR was first discussed by Henninger [28] and its use in model checking and testing was introduced by Atlee [3]. Constructing tests from UML use case diagrams is a more recent development, though relatively straightforward. It was first suggested by Briand and Labiche [8]. This chapter does not include this idea explicitly.

5.2   Logic Coverage Criteria

The active clause criteria seem to have their beginnings in Myers' 1979 book [43]. A more accessible paper is by Zhu [59]. He defined decision and condition coverage, which Chilenski and Miller later used as a conceptual basis for MCDC [12,51]. The definitions as originally given correspond to GACC in this book and did not address whether minor clauses had to have the same value for both values of the major clause. Most members of the aviation community interpreted MCDC to mean that the values of the minor clauses had to be the same, an interpretation that is called "unique-cause MCDC" [14]. Unique-cause MCDC corresponds to RACC. More recently, the FAA has accepted the view that the minor clauses can differ, which is called "masking MCDC" [13]. Masking MCDC corresponds to CACC. A previous paper [2] clarified the definitions in the form used here and introduced the term "CACC."

The inactive clause criteria are adapted from the RC/DC method of Vilkomir and Bowen [54]. This chapter treats the criteria differently by viewing them as complementary to the ACC criteria instead of competitive.

Jasper et al. presented techniques for generating tests to satisfy MCDC [32]. They took the definition of MCDC from Chilenski and Miller's paper with the "default" interpretation that the minor clauses must be the same for both values of the major clauses. They went on to modify the interpretation so that if two clauses are coupled, which implies it is impossible to satisfy determination for both, the two clauses are allowed to have different values for the minor clauses. The fact that different values are allowed only when clauses are coupled puts their interpretation of MCDC between RACC and CACC.

Weyuker, Goradia and Singh presented techniques for generating test data for software specifications that are limited to boolean variables [56]. The techniques were compared in terms of the ability of the resulting test cases to kill mutants [20,21]. The results were that their technique, which is closely related to MCDC, performed better than any of the other techniques. Weyuker et al. incorporated syntax as well as meaning into their criteria. They presented a notion called *meaningful impact* which is related to the notion of determination, but which has a syntactic basis rather than a semantic one. The concepts in that paper described subsets of the mutation operators for logical expressions used in previous mutation systems such as Mothra [21,35,19].

Kuhn investigated methods for generating tests to satisfy various decision-based criteria, including MCDC tests [39]. He used the definition from Chilenski and Miller [51,12], and proposed the boolean derivative to satisfy MCDC. In effect, this interpreted MCDC in such a way to match CACC.

Dupuy and Leveson's 2000 paper evaluated MCDC experimentally [22]. They presented results from an empirical study that compared pure functional testing with functional testing augmented by MCDC. The experiment was performed during the testing of the attitude control software for the HETE-2 (High Energy Transient Explorer) scientific satellite. The definition of MCDC from their paper is the traditional definition given in the FAA report and Chilenski and Miller's paper: "Every point of entry and exit in the program has been invoked at least once, every condition in a decision in the program has taken on all possible outcomes at least once, and each condition has been shown to affect that decision outcome independently. A condition is shown to affect a decision's outcome independently by varying just that decision while holding fixed all other possible conditions."

Note the typo in last line: "varying just that decision" should be "varying just that condition". This does not say that the decision has a different value when the condition's value changes. "Holding fixed" can be assumed to imply that the minor clauses cannot change with different values for the major clause (that is, RACC, not CACC).

The full predicate method of Offutt, Liu, Abdurazik and Ammann [46] explicitly relaxed the requirement that the major clauses have the same value as the predicate. This is equivalent to CACC and almost the same as masking MCDC.

Jones and Harrold have developed a method for reducing the regression tests that were developed to satisfy MCDC [33]. They defined MCDC as follows: "MC/DC is a stricter form of decision (or branch) coverage. ... MC/DC requires that each condition in a decision be shown by execution to independently affect the outcome of the decision". This is taken directly from Chilenski and Miller's original paper, and their interpretation of the definition is the same as CACC.

SCR was first discussed by Henninger [28] and its use in model checking and testing was introduced by Atlee [4,3].

The method of determining p_c given in this book uses the boolean derivative developed by Akers [1]. Both Chilenski [13] and Kuhn [39] applied Akers's derivative to exactly the problem given in this chapter. The other methods are the pairs table method of Chilenski and Miller and the tree method, independently discovered by Chilenski [13] and Offutt [46]. The tree method implements the boolean derivative method in a procedural way.

Ordered Binary Decision Diagrams (OBDDs) offer another way of determining p_c. In particular, consider any OBDD in which clause c is ordered last. Then any path through the OBDD that reaches a node labeled c (there will be exactly zero, one, or two such nodes) is, in fact, an assignment of values to the other variables so that c determines p. Continuing the path on to the constants T and F yields a pair of test satisfying $RACC$ with respect to c. Selecting two different paths that reach the same node labeled c, and then extending each so that one reaches T and the other reaches F yields a pair of tests that satisfy $CACC$, but not $RACC$, with respect to c. Finally, if there are two nodes labeled c, then it is possible to satisfy $GACC$ but not $CACC$ with respect to c: Select paths to each of the two nodes labeled c, extend one path by choosing c true, and the other by choosing c false. Both paths will necessarily end up in the same node, namely, either T or F. ICC tests with respect to c can be derived by considering paths to T and F in and OBDD where the paths do not include variable c. The attractive aspect of using OBDDs to derive ACC or ICC tests is that a variety of existing tools can handle a relatively large number of clauses. The unattractive aspect is that for a predicate with N clauses, N different OBDDs for a given function are required, since the clause being attended to needs to be the last in the ordering. To the knowledge of the authors, the use of OBDDs to derive ACC or ICC tests does not appear in the literature.

References

1. Akers, S.B.: On a theory of boolean functions. Journal Society Industrial Applied Mathematics 7(4), 487–498 (1959)
2. Ammann, P., Offutt, J., Huang, H.: Coverage criteria for logical expressions. In: Proceedings of the 14th International Symposium on Software Reliability Engineering, Denver, CO, November 2003, pp. 99–107. IEEE Computer Society Press, Los Alamitos (2003)
3. Atlee, J.M.: Native model-checking of SCR requirements. In: Fourth International SCR Workshop (November 1994)
4. Atlee, J.M., Gannon, J.: State-based model checking of event-driven system requirements. IEEE Transactions on Software Engineering 19(1), 24–40 (1993)

5. Binder, R.: Testing Object-oriented Systems. Addison-Wesley Publishing Company Inc., New York (2000)
6. Borzovs, J., Kalniņš, A., Medvedis, I.: Automatic construction of test sets: Practical approach. In: Barzdins, J., Bjorner, D. (eds.) Baltic Computer Science. LNCS, vol. 502, pp. 360–432. Springer, Heidelberg (1991)
7. Boyer, R.S., Elpas, B., Levitt, K.N.: Select–a formal system for testing and debugging programs by symbolic execution. In: Proceedings of the International Conference on Reliable Software, June 1975, SIGPLAN Notices, vol. 10(6) (1975)
8. Briand, L., Labiche, Y.: A UML-based approach to system testing. In: Gogolla, M., Kobryn, C. (eds.) UML 2001. LNCS, vol. 2185, pp. 194–208. Springer, Heidelberg (2001)
9. Special Interest Group in Software Testing British Computer Society. Standard for Software Component Testing, Working Draft 3.3. British Computer Society (1997), http://www.rmcs.cranfield.ac.uk/~cised/sreid/BCS_SIG/
10. Cheatham, T.E., Holloway, G.H., Townley, J.A.: Symbolic evaluation and the analysis of programs. IEEE Transactions on Software Engineering 4 (July 1979)
11. Cherniavsky, J.C.: On finding test data sets for loop free programs. Information Processing Letters 8(2), 106–107 (1979)
12. Chilenski, J.J., Miller, S.P.: Applicability of modified condition/decision coverage to software testing. Software Engineering Journal 9(5), 193–200 (1994)
13. Chilenski, J., Richey, L.A.: Definition for a masking form of modified condition decision coverage (MCDC). Technical report, Boeing, Seattle, WA (1997), http://www.boeing.com/nosearch/mcdc/
14. Chilenski, J.J.: Personal communication (March 2003)
15. Chow, T.: Testing software designs modeled by finite-state machines. IEEE Transactions on Software Engineering SE-4(3), 178–187 (1978)
16. Clarke, L.A.: A system to generate test data and symbolically execute programs. IEEE Transactions on Software Engineering 2(3), 215–222 (1976)
17. Clarke, L.A., Richardson, D.J.: Applications of symbolic evaluation. The Journal of Systems and Software 5(1), 15–35 (1985)
18. Darringer, J.A., King, J.C.: Applications of symbolic execution to program testing. IEEE Computer 4 (April 1978)
19. DeMillo, R.A., Guindi, D.S., King, K.N., McCracken, W.M., Offutt, J.: An extended overview of the Mothra software testing environment. In: Proceedings of the Second Workshop on Software Testing, Verification, and Analysis, Banff, Alberta, July 1988, pp. 142–151. IEEE Computer Society Press, Los Alamitos (1988)
20. DeMillo, R.A., Lipton, R.J., Sayward, F.G.: Hints on test data selection: Help for the practicing programmer. IEEE Computer 11(4), 34–41 (1978)
21. DeMillo, R.A., Offutt, J.: Constraint-based automatic test data generation. IEEE Transactions on Software Engineering 17(9), 900–910 (1991)
22. Dupuy, A., Leveson, N.: An empirical evaluation of the MC/DC coverage criterion on the HETE-2 satellite software. In: Proceedings of the Digital Aviations Systems Conference (DASC) (October 2000)
23. Fairley, R.E.: An experimental program testing facility. IEEE Transactions on Software Engineering SE-1, 350–3571 (1975)
24. Ferguson, R., Korel, B.: The chaining approach for software test data generation. ACM Transactions on Software Engineering Methodology 5(1), 63–86 (1996)
25. Fujiwara, S., Bochman, G., Khendek, F., Amalou, M., Ghedasmi, A.: Test selection based on finite state models. IEEE Transactions on Software Engineering 17(6), 591–603 (1991)

26. Gonenc, G.: A method for the design of fault-detection experiments. IEEE Transactions on Computers C-19, 155–558 (1970)
27. Gourlay, J.S.: A mathematical framework for the investigation of testing. IEEE Transactions on Software Engineering 9(6), 686–709 (1983)
28. Henninger, K.: Specifying software requirements for complex systems: New techniques and their applications. IEEE Transactions on Software Engineering SE-6(1), 2–12 (1980)
29. Howden, W.E.: Methodology for the generation of program test data. IEEE Transactions on Software Engineering SE-24 (May 1975)
30. Howden, W.E.: Symbolic testing and the DISSECT symbolic evaluation system. IEEE Transactions on Software Engineering 3(4) (July 1977)
31. Huang, J.C.: An approach to program testing. ACM Computing Surveys 7(3), 113–128 (1975)
32. Jasper, R., Brennan, M., Williamson, K., Currier, B., Zimmerman, D.: Test data generation and feasible path analysis. In: Proceedings of the 1994 International Symposium on Software Testing, and Analysis, August 1994, August 1994, pp. 95–107. ACM Press, New York (1994)
33. Jones, J.A., Harrold, M.J.: Test-suite reduction and prioritizaion for modified condition / decision coverage. IEEE Transactions on Software Engineering 29(3), 195–209 (2003)
34. Kim, Y.G., Hong, H.S., Cho, S.M., Bae, D.H., Cha, S.D.: Test cases generation from UML state diagrams. IEE Proceedings – Software 146(4), 187–192 (1999)
35. King, K.N., Offutt, J.: A Fortran language system for mutation-based software testing. Software – Practice and Experience 21(7), 685–718 (1991)
36. Korel, B.: Automated software test data generation. IEEE Transactions on Software Engineering 16(8), 870–879 (1990)
37. Korel, B.: Dynamic method for software test data generation. Software Testing, Verification, and Reliability 2(4), 203–213 (1992)
38. Kosaraju, S.: Analysis of structured programs. Journal of Computer Systems and Science 9, 232–255 (1974)
39. Kuhn, D.R.: Fault classes and error detection capability of specification-based testing. ACM Transactions on Software Engineering Methodology 8(4), 411–424 (1999)
40. Legard, H., Marcotty, M.: A generalogy of control structures. Communications of the ACM 18, 629–639 (1975)
41. McCabe, T.J.: A complexity measure. IEEE Transactions on Software Engineering SE-2(4), 308–320 (1976)
42. McMinn, P.: Search-based software test data generation: A survey. Software Testing, Verification, and Reliability 13(2), 105–156 (2004)
43. Myers, G.: The Art of Software Testing. John Wiley and Sons, New York (1979)
44. Naito, S., Tsunoyama, M.: Fault detection for sequential machines by transition tours. In: Proceedings Fault Tolerant Computing Systems, pp. 238–243. IEEE Computer Society Press, Los Alamitos (1981)
45. Offutt, J., Jin, Z., Pan, J.: The dynamic domain reduction approach to test data generation. Software – Practice and Experience 29(2), 167–193 (1999)
46. Offutt, J., Liu, S., Abdurazik, A., Ammann, P.: Generating test data from state-based specifications. Software Testing, Verification, and Reliability 13(1), 25–53 (2003)
47. Paige, M.R.: Program graphs, an algebra, and their implication for programming. IEEE Transactions on Software Engineering SE-1(3), 286–291 (1975)
48. Paige, M.R.: In: Proc. of IEEE 2nd Annual International Computer Software and Applications Conference (COMPSAC 1978), pp. 527–532 (1978)

49. Pimont, S., Rault, J.C.: A software reliability assessment based on a structural behavioral analysis of programs. In: Proceedings of the Second International Conference on Software Engineering, San Francisco, CA (October 1976)

50. Ramamoorthy, C.V., Ho, S.F., Chen, W.T.: On the automated generation of program test data. IEEE Transactions on Software Engineering 2(4), 293–300 (1976)

51. RTCA-DO-178B. Software considerations in airborne systems and equipment certification (December 1992)

52. Sabnani, K., Dahbura, A.: A protocol testing procedure. Computer Networks and ISDN Systems 14(4), 285–297 (1988)

53. Tip, F.: A survey of program slicing techniques. Technical report CS-R-9438, Computer Science/Department of Software Technology, Centrum voor Wiskunde en Informatica (1994)

54. Vilkomir, S.A., Bowen, J.P.: Reinforced condition/decision coverage (RC/DC): A new criterion for software testing. In: Bert, D., P. Bowen, J., C. Henson, M., Robinson, K. (eds.) B 2002 and ZB 2002. LNCS, vol. 2272, pp. 295–313. Springer, Heidelberg (2002)

55. Weiser, M.: Program slicing. IEEE Transactions on Software Engineering SE-10(4), 352–357 (1984)

56. Weyuker, E., Goradia, T., Singh, A.: Automatically generating test data from a boolean specification. IEEE Transactions on Software Engineering 20(5), 353–363 (1994)

57. Weyuker, E.J., Weiss, S.N., Hamlet, R.G.: Data flow-based adequacy analysis for languages with pointers. In: Proceedings of the Fourth Symposium on Software Testing, Analysis, and Verification, Victoria, British Columbia, Canada, October 1991, pp. 74–86. IEEE Computer Society Press, Los Alamitos (1991)

58. White, L., Wiszniewski, B.: Path testing of computer programs with loops using a tool for simple loop patterns. Software – Practice and Experience 21(10), 1075–1102 (1991)

59. Zhu, H., Hall, P.A.V., May, J.H.R.: Software unit test coverage and adequacy. ACM Computing Surveys 29(4), 366–427 (1997)

Testing in the Distributed Test Architecture

J. Chen[1], R.M. Hierons[2], and H. Ural[3]

[1] School of Computer Science, University of Windsor
Windsor, Ontario, Canada N9B 3P4
xjchen@uwindsor.ca

[2] Department of Information Systems and Computing, Brunel University
Uxbridge, Middlesex, UB8 3PH, United Kingdom
rob.hierons@brunel.ac.uk

[3] School of Information Technology and Engineering, University of Ottawa
Ottawa, Ontario, Canada K1N 6N5
ural@site.ottawa.ca

Abstract. The introduction of multiple remote testers to apply a test or checking sequence introduces the possibility of controllability and observability problems. These problems can require the use of external coordination message exchanges among testers. It is desirable to construct a test or checking sequence from the specification of the system under test such that it is free from these problems without requiring the use of external coordination messages. Here we define criteria on the specification of the system under test for this to be possible. For specifications satisfying the criteria, algorithms for constructing subsequences that eliminate the need for external coordination messages are given.

1 Introduction

Testing an implementation of a system under test (SUT) N is often carried out by constructing an input sequence from the specification M of the system, applying the input sequence in a test architecture, and analyzing the resulting output sequence to determine whether the implementation *conforms to* the specification on this input sequence. Conformance testing has been extensively studied in the context where M is a Finite State Machine (FSM) and N is a state-based system whose externally observable behaviour can also be represented by an FSM. This is motivated by the fact that FSMs are used to model a number of classes of systems including communications protocols [23] and control circuits [16]. The focus of much of the previous work has been on automatically generating input sequences from FSMs (see, for example, [1,12,13,29,28]). According to different test criteria, such an input sequence can be a test sequence [20,21] or a checking sequence [9,11,17].

The widespread use of distributed systems has led to interest in FSM-based testing when the SUT is a distributed system. A distributed system may have multiple sources of input and multiple destinations for output, often spread over a wide area across the machine boundary. This may lead to a *distributed test architecture* in which there is one tester at each interface/*port*. For example,

R.M. Hierons et al. (Eds.): Formal Methods and Testing, LNCS 4949, pp. 157–183, 2008.
© Springer-Verlag Berlin Heidelberg 2008

when testing a layer of a protocol stack we can use one tester at the upper port and one tester at the lower port [4].

The application of a test or checking sequence in the distributed test architecture introduces the possibility of controllability and observability problems. The controllability problem manifests itself when a tester is required to send the current input and because it did not send the previous input and did not receive the previous output it cannot determine when to send the input. The observability problem manifests itself when a tester is expecting an output in response to either a previous input or the current input and because it is not the sender of the current input, it cannot determine when to start and stop waiting for the output. Suppose, for example, that a transition t_2 follows a transition t_1 in testing and that t_1 should send output o to port p and t_2 should send no output to port p. We get an output shift fault if in N t_1 sends no output to p and t_2 send o to p. This is a potentially *undetectable output shift fault* if t_2 does not involve input at p in which case all of the testers observe the expected sequences of inputs and outputs if this output shift fault occurs: the faults in t_1 and t_2 mask one another in this test or checking sequence.

It is desirable to construct a test or checking sequence that causes no controllability or observability problems during its application in a distributed test architecture (see, for example, [2,8,10,14,18,22,24,30]). For some specifications, there exists such an input sequence in which the coordination among testers is achieved indirectly via their interactions with N [21,19]. However, for some other specifications, there may not exist an input sequence in which the testers can coordinate solely via their interactions with N [2,22]. In this case it is necessary for testers to communicate directly by exchanging external coordination messages among themselves over a dedicated channel during the application of the input sequence [3].

Both controllability and observability problems may be overcome through the use of external coordination messages among remote testers [3]. However, using external coordination messages introduces the necessity to set up a separate communications network. In addition, external coordination messages introduce delays and these delays can cause problems if we have timing issues in our testing. This is particularly problematic if the SUT responds rapidly to inputs, relative to the network used for external coordination messages.

In this chapter, we summarize the literature on resolving these controllability and observability problems. We present conditions on M under which these problems can be overcome and algorithms for constructing subsequences that eliminate the controllability and observability problems. First we give a necessary and sufficient condition on M so that each transition *involved in a potentially undetectable output shift fault* can be *independently verified at port p*. By *verified at port p*, we mean we are able to conclude that the output of this transition at port p is correct if we observe the correct output sequence on a certain transition path. By *independently*, we mean that the above conclusion regarding the output at port p for a transition does not rely on the correctness of any other transitions. Independence here can be helpful for fault diagnoses. Sometimes we do not require this notion of independence. If this is the case then the above condition on M can be weakened. We present an algorithm that determines whether M satisfies this weaker condition and when it does so constructs subsequences that check the transitions.

The rest of this chapter is organized as follows. Section 2 introduces the preliminary terminology. Section 3 gives a formal definition of the controllability problem and a brief overview of related work. In Section 4 we give a formal definition of the observability problem and summarize previous work. Sections 5 - 9 contain our work regarding overcoming the controllability and observability problems. This includes the procedure to identify observability problems (Section 5), the formal definition of verifiability of potentially undetectable output shift faults (Section 6), a necessary and sufficient condition to independently resolve all potentially undetectable output shift faults in our context (Section 7), a general approach to check for the satisfiability of the criterion in a given specification to resolve all potentially undetectable output shift faults in our context (Section 8), as well as the comparison between these two approaches (Section 9). Conclusions are given in Section 10.

2   An n-Port FSM and Its Graphical Representation

When a system interacts with its environment at more than one port it is necessary to extend the FSM notation. This can be achieved through having input and output alphabets associated with each port. A transition is triggered by input from one port and sends output to zero or more ports. Thus, the output of a transition can be represented by a set or vector [3].

An n-port Finite State Machine M (simply called an FSM M) is defined as $M = (S, I, O, \delta, \lambda, s_0)$ where S is a finite set of states of M; $s_0 \in S$ is the initial state of M; $I = \bigcup_{i=1}^{n} I_i$, where I_i is the input alphabet of port i, and $I_i \cap I_j = \emptyset$ for $i, j \in [1, n]$, $i \neq j$; $O = \prod_{i=1}^{n} (O_i \cup \{-\})$, where O_i is the output alphabet of port i, and $-$ means null output; δ is the transition function that maps $S \times I$ to S; and λ is the output function that maps $S \times I$ to O. Each $y \in O$ is a vector of outputs, i.e., $y = \langle o_1, o_2, ..., o_n \rangle$ where $o_i \in O_i \cup \{-\}$ for $i \in [1, n]$. We use $*$ to denote any possible output, including $-$, at a port and $+$ to denote non-empty output. We also use $*$ to denote any possible input or any possible vector of outputs.

We will use 2-port FSMs in all examples. In a 2-port FSM, ports U and L stand for the upper interface and the lower interface of the FSM. An output vector $y = \langle o_1, o_2 \rangle$ on the label of a transition of a 2-port FSM is a pair of outputs with $o_1 \in O_1$ at U and $o_2 \in O_2$ at L.

Example 1. Figure 1 shows a 2-port FSM. Suppose s_0 is the initial state. In this state, the FSM M can receive from port L an input request *initReq* to start a conversation. Upon this request, it gives output *initReqToU* to inform the upper layer at port U, and enters state s_1. This request may either be rejected or be accepted: In state s_1, i) if there is an input *initRej* from port U to reject the request, then there will be a message *initRejToL* sent to L and the machine will

initRej, initAcc, data, end are input at U
initReq is input at L

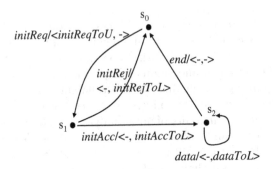

Fig. 1. A 2-port finite state machine

return back to the inital state; ii) if there is an input *initAcc* from port U to accept the request, then there will be a message *initAccToL* sent to port L and the machine will be in state s_2 for the conversation. In state s_2 we can recursively receive input *data* from port U and send *dataToL* to port L, until a special input *end* is received and the machine returns back to the initial state.

In the following, $p \in [1, n]$ is a port. A *transition* of an FSM M is a triple $t = (s_1, s_2, x/y)$, where $s_1, s_2 \in S$, $x \in I$, and $y \in O$ such that $\delta(s_1, x) = s_2$, $\lambda(s_1, x) = y$. s_1 and s_2 are called the *starting state* and the *ending state* of t respectively. The *input/output pair* x/y is the *label* of t and t will also be denoted as $s_1 \xrightarrow{x/y} s_2$. We use $y\,|_p$ or $t\,|_p$ to denote the output at port p in output vector y or in transition t respectively. We use $\mathcal{T}$ to denote the set of all transitions in M.

A *path* $\rho = t_1\ t_2\ \cdots\ t_k\ (k \geq 0)$ is a finite sequence of transitions such that for $k \geq 2$, the ending state of t_i is the starting state of t_{i+1} for all $i \in [1, k-1]$. When the ending state of the last transition of path ρ_1 is the starting state of the first transition of path ρ_2, we use $\rho_1@\rho_2$ to denote the *concatenation* of ρ_1 and ρ_2. The *label* of a path $(s_1, s_2, x_1/y_1)\ (s_2, s_3, x_2/y_2) \cdots (s_k, s_{k+1}, x_k/y_k)$ $(k \geq 1)$ is the sequence of input/output pairs $x_1/y_1\ x_2/y_2 \cdots x_k/y_k$ which is an *input/output sequence*. The *input portion* of a path $(s_1, s_2, x_1/y_1)\ (s_2, s_3, x_2/y_2)$ $\cdots (s_k, s_{k+1}, x_k/y_k)$ $(k \geq 1)$ is the input sequence $x_1 x_2 \dots x_k$. We say t is *contained in* ρ if t is a transition along path ρ.

When ρ is non-empty, we use *first*(ρ) and *last*(ρ) to denote the first and last transitions of path ρ respectively and *pre*(ρ) to denote the path obtained from ρ by removing its last transition.

A *same-port-output-cycle* in an FSM is a path $(s_1, s_2, x_1/y_1)\ (s_2, s_3, x_2/y_2) \cdots$ $(s_k, s_{k+1}, x_k/y_k)$ $(k \geq 2)$ such that $s_1 = s_{k+1}$, $s_i \neq s_{i+1}$ for $i \in [1, k]$, and there exists a port p with $y_i\,|_p \neq\ -$ and $x_i \notin I_p$ for all $i \in [1, k]$. An *isolated-port-cycle* in an FSM is a path $(s_1, s_2, x_1/y_1)\ (s_2, s_3, x_2/y_2) \cdots (s_k, s_{k+1}, x_k/y_k)$ $(k \geq 2)$

$$o_1 \neq -$$
$$o_2 \neq -$$
i_1, i_2 are input at U i_3, i_4 are input at L

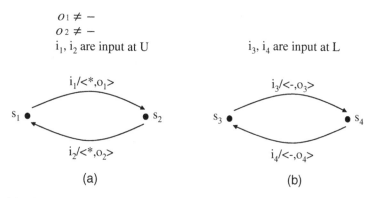

(a)   (b)

Fig. 2. (a): A 2-port FSM with same-port-output-cycle; (b): A 2-port FSM with isolated-port-cycle

such that $s_1 = s_{k+1}$, $s_i \neq s_{i+1}$ for $i \in [1, k]$, and there exists a port p with $y_i \mid_p = -$ and $x_i \notin I_p$ for all $i \in [1, k]$.

Example 2. In the FSM in Figure 2(a), i_1 and i_2 are input at U while o_1 and o_2 are non-empty output at L. So path $(s_1, s_2, i_1/\langle *, o_1 \rangle)$ $(s_2, s_1, i_2/\langle *, o_2 \rangle)$ is a *same-port-output-cycle*. In the FSM in Figure 2(b), i_3 and i_4 are input at L, so path $(s_3, s_4, i_3/\langle -, o_3 \rangle)$ $(s_4, s_3, i_4/\langle -, o_4 \rangle)$ is an *isolated-port-cycle* as the output of these transitions at U are all empty.

3   Controllability Problems

When testing a system with multiple ports, there is one tester at each port. Let us suppose that testing involves the input of x_i at port p and then x_{i+1} at port $p' \neq p$. In order for the tester at p' to know when to input x_{i+1} it must know when x_i has been input. If the tester at p' does not know when x_i has been input because it does not receive output from the transition triggered by x_i, then we encounter a *controllability problem*.

Formally, given an FSM M and an input/output sequence x_1/y_1 x_2/y_2 ... x_k/y_k of M a *controllability* (also called *synchronization*) problem occurs when, in the labels x_i/y_i and x_{i+1}/y_{i+1} of two consecutive transitions, there exists $p \in [1, n]$ such that $x_{i+1} \in I_p$, $x_i \notin I_p$, $y_i \mid_p = -$ ($i \in [1, k-1]$).

Consecutive transitions t_i and t_{i+1} form a *synchronizable pair* of transitions if t_{i+1} can follow t_i without causing a synchronization problem. In this case, t_{i+1} is said to be an *eligible successor* of t_i.

Example 3. In Figure 1, let

$$t_1 = (s_0, s_1, initReq/\langle initReqToU, - \rangle),$$
$$t_2 = (s_1, s_0, initRej/\langle -, initRejToL \rangle),$$
$$t_3 = (s_1, s_2, initAcc/\langle -, initAccToL \rangle),$$

$$t_4 = (s_2, s_2, data/\langle -, dataToL\rangle),$$

$$t_5 = (s_2, s_0, end/\langle -, -\rangle).$$

t_1 and t_2 form a synchronizable pair of transitions. The tester at port U knows that input $initRej$ of t_2 should be given after it has received the output $initReq$-ToU of the previous transition t_1.

By contrast, t_5 and t_1 do not form a synchronizable pair of transitions, because the tester at port L neither gives the input of the first transition t_5 nor receives its output, so it does not know *when* it should give input $initReq$ of the second transition t_1.

Any path in which every pair of transitions is synchronizable is a *synchronizable path*. An input/output sequence is *synchronizable* if it is the label of a synchronizable path.

We assume that for every pair of transitions (t, t') there is a synchronizable path that starts with t and ends with t'. If this condition does not hold, then the FSM is said to be *intrinsically non-synchronizable* [2].

The methods proposed in [24,8,10] are based on heuristic techniques for the solution of the synchronization problem. They construct what is called an auxiliary graph from the given FSM and a tour of this auxiliary graph yields a synchronizable test sequence [24,8] or checking sequence [10]. These methods assume that there are two ports in the SUT and thus two testers, namely U and L. They also require that for each state s of M there are two sequences, called synchronizable unique input/output sequences (SUIOs), $SUIO^U(s)$ and $SUIO^L(s)$ such that for $p \in \{U, L\}$ $SUIO^p(s)$ has the following property: $SUIO^p(s)$ starts with input at p and for every state $s' \neq s$ the expected output from applying $SUIO^p(s)$ in states s and s' are different. SUIOs are used to check the final states of transitions, synchronization problems between a SUIO and its predecessor being eliminated by an appropriate choice of SUIO. A digraph $G = (V, E)$ is said to be *order-specified* if for each edge $e_{i,j} = (v_i, v_j, x/y) \in E$, a subset of the edges leaving vertex v_j is specified as eligible successors of $e_{i,j}$, and a path in G is said to be *correctly ordered* if for every consecutive pair of edges $e_{j,k} = (v_j, v_k; x_j/y_j)$ and $e_{k,l} = (v_k, v_l; x_k/y_k)$, $e_{k,l}$ is an eligible successor of $e_{j,k}$. Given a 2p-FSM M, a test sequence can be constructed from the order-specified digraph $G = (V, E)$ and a set of SUIOs [24].

The method proposed in [10] assumes the existence of a reliable reset feature[1] and aims to construct a checking sequence. The solution is based on the construction of a correctly-ordered digraph $G' = (V', E')$ such that all edges of G are in one-to-one correspondence with edges in G', and all paths in G' are correctly ordered paths in G and thus correspond to synchronized paths in M. SUIO sequences are used to construct test subsequences that start at the initial state and these are connected by a reset. The checking sequence constructed by

---

[1] A reset feature is an operation that returns the specification M to its initial state irrespective of its current state. A reliable reset feature is a reset feature that is known to have been correctly implemented in the SUT.

this method is minimized by eliminating redundant subsequences and using the judicious choice of transition sequences and SUIOs.

The literature proposes several methods for constructing a synchronizable test or checking sequence. A key point here is to construct a synchronizable path that starts with a given transition t and ends with another given transition t'. This can be achieved by searching for an appropriate path in the correctly-ordered digraph G'.

The methods described above make the assumption that the testers may only communicate with each other indirectly via their interactions with the SUT. It is recognized that these methods will not yield synchronizable input/output sequences for all FSMs because some FSMs are intrinsically non-synchronizable.

Alternatively, we can assume that the testers may communicate with each other directly over some dedicated channels. Suppose that a synchronization problem occurs in two consecutive transitions with labels x_j/y_j and x_{j+1}/y_{j+1}. Let U (or L) be the tester that sends x_j. A typical solution is to insert an external coordination message exchange $\langle -C_{L(U)}, +C_{U(L)} \rangle$ relating to controllability between x_j/y_j and x_{j+1}/y_{j+1} where "$-C_{L(U)}$" denotes the sending of an external coordination message C (informing the tester at L (or U) that it can send input x_{j+1}) to tester L (or U) from tester U (or L), and "$+C_{U(L)}$" denotes the receipt of C from tester U (or L) by tester L (or U) [3].

The method presented in [8] supports an additional communication channel that facilitates external coordination message exchanges related to controllability amongst the testers, and the cost of these messages is included in the minimization algorithm. The use of such external coordination messages allows for the construction of a synchronizable test sequence for any FSM, including those which are intrinsically non-synchronizable. The solution proposed in [3] also uses external coordination messages to resolve controllability problems.

Tai and Young [22] introduce an alternative definition of synchronizable which depends on the current state and eligible transitions of the FSM as well as the transitions in the test sequences. Specifically, their definition states that a test sequence is synchronizable if any execution of M and the testers according to the test sequence is deterministic (i.e., the current state of M has at most one eligible transition). Tai and Young refer to the synchronization problem as it is defined in this section as the *pair-wise synchronization problem*. The authors also discuss both port-based testing, which allows testers to communicate with each other only indirectly via their interactions with the SUT, and group-based testing, which divides the ports of the SUT into groups and allows the testers for ports in the same group to communicate with each other directly using external coordination messages.

4   Observability Problems

One of the difficulties in dealing with distributed systems comes from the absence of a global clock. This complicates testing in a distributed test architecture [18] in the sense that, with multiple ports, it is hard to determine the global order of the input and output and in particular, which input triggered a particular output

initRej, initAcc, data, end are input at *U*
initReq is input at *L*

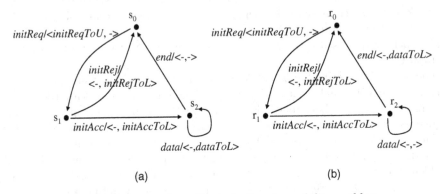

(a)   (b)

Fig. 3. An example to illustrate the observability problem

value. As a consequence, it is difficult to detect output being shifted along the path while applying a test or checking sequence.

Suppose we have the FSM in Figure 1 as the specification FSM which is also given in Figure 3(a) for convenience. Recall that $t_4 = (s_2, s_2, data/\langle -, dataToL \rangle)$, and $t_5 = (s_2, s_0, end/\langle -, - \rangle)$, as defined in Example 3.

In t_4, the input of *data* at port U is expected to lead to *dataToL* being output at port L. In t_5, the input of *end* at port U does not invoke any output. t_4 and t_5 form a synchronizable pair of transitions as the tester at port U inputs *end* after it has given input *data*.

It is possible that in the implementation N, however, these two transitions are incorrectly implemented as shown in Figure 3(b): there is no output in response to the input of *data* while the input of *end* leads to output *dataToL* at port L. In this case by applying the input sequence of t_4t_5, each tester observes the correct behaviour: the tester at U observes input *data* followed by input *end*, and the tester at port L observes output *dataToL*. While the inputs of *data* and *end* lead to the wrong output in N, the testers do not observe a failure since the two faults mask one another in this sequence. Since this can occur, we say that the two transitions t_4 and t_5 in Figure 3(a) are involved in a *potentially undetectable output shift fault* in the sense that it is possible that the SUT has an output shifted to/from another transition and this fault cannot be detected by the test or checking sequence.

We distinguish between *forward* and *backward* output shift faults. The former refers to the possible output shifts *along* the path while we apply a test or checking sequence, and the latter refers to possible output shifts *against* the path while we apply a test or checking sequence. In the above example, we have a potentially undetectable *forward* output shift. Suppose that M is as shown in Figure 3(b). Then M contains a potentially undetectable output shift fault in the same pair of transitions: it is possible that N is the same as M except that this sequence is implemented as shown in Figure 3(a). This fault is a *backward* output shift.

initRej, initAcc, data, end are input at *U*
initReq is input at *L*

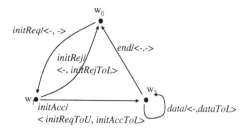

Fig. 4. An example to illustrate the detectable output shift

Note that not all output shifts are undetectable. Again, suppose that we have a specification M shown in Figure 3(a): the tester at port L inputs *initReq*, which is expected to lead to *initReqToU* being output at port U. Tester at U then inputs *initAcc*, which is expected to lead to output of *initAccToL* at port L. It is possible that N is the same as M except that this pair of transitions is implemented as Figure 4 shows. However, this output shift is *detectable* at U because the tester at port U can realize that there is no output *initReqToU* in response to input *initReq* before it gives input *initAcc*.

Potentially undetectable output shift faults represent possible fault masking in a given test or checking sequence. In this chapter, we are interested in avoiding potentially undetectable output shift faults, because the faults that are masked in testing might lead to problems when the system is used since these transitions could be used in different sequences that reveal the faults.

Before reviewing related work we formally define output shift faults.

Definition 1. *A transition t is involved in a potentially undetectable output shift fault at p if and only if there exists a transition t' and a transition path ρ such that at least one of the following holds.*

1. *$t\rho t'$ is a synchronizable path, no transition in $\rho t'$ contains input at p, the outputs at p in all transitions contained in ρ are empty, $t\mid_p = -$ and $t'\mid_p \neq -$. In this case an undetectable output shift fault can occur between t and t' in $t\rho t'$ and we call this a* backward *output shift fault.*
2. *$t'\rho t$ is a synchronizable path, no transition in ρt contains input at p, the outputs at p in all transitions contained in ρ are empty, $t\mid_p = -$ and $t'\mid_p \neq -$. In this case an undetectable output shift fault can occur between t' and t in $t'\rho t$ and we call this a* forward *output shift fault.*

When ρ is empty, we also say that t is involved in a potentially undetectable 1-shift output fault.

The observability problem occurs when we have potentially undetectable output shift faults in the specification FSM and this is a problem we wish to avoid in test or checking sequence generation.

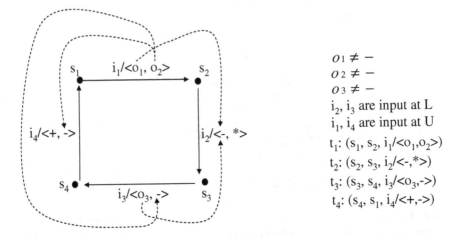

$$O_1 \neq -$$
$$O_2 \neq -$$
$$O_3 \neq -$$

i_2, i_3 are input at L
i_1, i_4 are input at U

t_1: $(s_1, s_2, i_1/<o_1,o_2>)$
t_2: $(s_2, s_3, i_2/<-,*>)$
t_3: $(s_3, s_4, i_3/<o_3,->)$
t_4: $(s_4, s_1, i_4/<+,->)$

Fig. 5. Illustration of observability problem

Example 4. The specification given in Figure 5 is free from *same-port-output-cycles* and *isolated-port-cycles*. Any two consecutive transitions in it form a *synchronizable pair*. However, it contains observability problems. Let $t = t_3$, $\rho = t_4$ and $t' = t_1$. We have (i) $t\rho t'$ is a synchronizable path; (ii) since i_1 and i_4 are input at port U, no transition in $\rho t'$ contains input at port L; (iii) the output at port L in the transition contained in ρ is empty; (iv) t has empty output at L while t' has nonempty output at L so transition t_3 is involved in a potentially undetectable backward output shift fault at port L.

The dashed arrows in Figure 5 illustrates all potentially undetectable output shift faults in this example:

- t_1 and t_2 are involved in potentially undetectable 1-shift forward output shift fault at port U;
- t_2 and t_3 are involved in potentially undetectable 1-shift backward output shift fault at port U;
- t_1 and t_4 are involved in potentially undetectable 1-shift backward output shift fault at port L;
- t_3 is involved in a potentially undetectable backward output shift fault at port L.

Let U (or L) be the tester that sends x_{j+1}. As with the controllability problems, some solutions in the literature assume the possibility of inserting an external coordination message exchange $\langle -B_{L(U)}, +B_{U(L)} \rangle$ relating to observability between x_j/y_j and x_{j+1}/y_{j+1} where "$-B_{L(U)}$" denotes the sending of an external coordination message B to tester L (or U) from tester U (or L), and "$+B_{U(L)}$" denotes the receipt of B from tester U (or L) by tester L (or U) [3]. Through this exchange of the external coordination message B, tester U (or L) informs tester L (or U) that it should expect to receive an output from N (in the case of a backward shift) or that it should have received an output from N by now (in the case of a forward shift).

Many researchers have studied the observability problem, very often together with the controllability problem. Earlier studies on the observability problem proposed solutions where first a synchronizable test sequence or checking sequence is generated and then this is inspected for observability problems. These problems are then resolved by augmenting the sequence with additional sequences or direct communication between testers, depending on the test architecture. Solutions that assume only indirect communication among testers generate additional synchronizable subsequences for the purpose of resolving observability problems. Those solutions which support direct communication resolve such problems by inserting external coordination message exchanges into the test sequence.

Young and Tau [30] assumes that testers may communicate only indirectly via their interactions with the SUT. Their strategy is to validate the transitions in the test sequence one at a time, i.e. given a test sequence consisting of transitions $t_1, t_2, t_3, \ldots, t_n$ for a given FSM M and the implementation N of M, first test N by using t_1. If this test is successful, test N using t_1, t_2, then t_1, t_2, t_3, and so on.

Luo *et al.* [19] proposes an approach that adds specific transitions to the synchronizable test sequence, with the intent of detecting all 1-shift output faults during the application of the sequences in the distributed test architecture. They proposes the following algorithm to accomplish this:

- generate a synchronizable test sequence Π by using one of the test generation methods for FSMs;
- find a set Ω of consecutive pairs of transition along the path caused by applying Π, where each pair may have a potential undetectable 1-shift output fault;
- if Ω is empty, stop. Otherwise, add a set of additional synchronizable test subsequences to Π such that Π can ensure the absence of potential undetectable 1-shift output faults in the transition pairs of Π.

Hierons and Ural [15] propose a method for generating a checking sequence based on UIO sequences[2]. It is assumed in [15] that testers may communicate only indirectly via their interactions with the SUT. To verify the uniqueness of state s_i, the input portion of the UIO sequence for every state must be applied at s_i. Therefore, the method requires that the input portion of every UIO sequence can be applied at every state without causing synchronization problems. Potential 1-shift output faults are detected by adding specific transitions to the synchronizable checking sequence, as in [19].

Cacciari and Rafiq [3] propose the use of external coordination messages to resolve problems relating to controllability and observability. They show in [3] how a minimal set of messages can be added to a given test sequence to produce

---

[2] An input/output sequence x/y is a UIO for a state s of M if the response of M to x is y if and only if M was in state s.

a synchronised test sequence that detects the potentially undetectable output shift faults. This approach can be adopted only when the test generation is separated into two phases: the generation of the initial test sequence that satisfies certain test criterion, and the insertion of the external coordination messages into the initial test sequence. Apparently, the separation of the test generation into two phases may lead to a suboptimal test: a short initial sequence may require the addition of many messages. To overcome this problem, Hierons [14] and Whittier [25] show how a single phase can be used to construct test sequences that are free from controllability and observability problems, and they resolve the optimization problem in doing so. The method in [14] generates a minimal length test sequence, while the method in [25] generates a test sequence that is minimal in terms of both the length of the test sequence and the number of external coordination message exchanges.

In the methods described in [3,19,30,25], the fault model[3] assumed consists of only output faults in which a transition could produce the wrong output vector. These synchronizable test sequences may not detect faults in an implementation that also has transfer faults in which the end state of a transition is incorrect. The checking sequence method presented in [15] assumes a remote test architecture in which testers can only communicate via their interactions with the SUT. As a result, the method must make restrictive assumptions regarding the existence of synchronizable UIO sequences, and requires additional input sequences to address problems related to observability.

Ural and Williams propose two methods based on distinguishing sequences[4] that will detect the presence of any output and/or transfer fault(s) in an implementation of an FSM [26,27]. The first method assumes the presence of a reliable reset that returns the implementation to its initial state, while the second method does not. Both methods take into consideration both external coordination and input/output costs and consist of a set of transformation rules that construct modified digraphs from the specification of a given 2p-FSM M, allowing for the construction of a synchronizable checking sequence that verifies every state and transition. This synchronizable checking sequence will ensure also that no 1-shift output fault remain undetected. Both methods attempt to reduce the total number of external coordination message exchanges by taking their cost into consideration during the construction of the checking sequence.

5   Identifying Observability Problems

To resolve the observability problems, i.e. to verify that the SUT is free from undetectable output shift faults, we need to verify the output of transition t at

---

[3] A fault model describes the set of possible faulty SUTs and given a fault model F we can aim to find a test or checking sequence that will lead to failures for any faulty members of F.

[4] An input sequence x is a distinguishing sequence for M if no two states of M lead to the same response to x.

port p for each t which is involved in a potentially undetectable output fault at p. First of all, we need to identify all such transitions for each port p.

We will use $\mathcal{T}_p$ to denote the set of transitions that are involved in potentially undetectable output shift faults at p. Let $\mathcal{T}'_p = \mathcal{T}_p \cap \{t \mid t|_p \neq -\}$ denote the set of transitions that are involved in potentially undetectable output shift faults at p and whose output at p is non-empty. Similarly, $\mathcal{T}_p - \mathcal{T}'_p$ denotes the set of transitions that are involved in potentially undetectable output shift faults at p and whose output at p is empty.

Example 5. In the given specification in Figure 6, there is an undetectable output shift fault in $t_1 t_3$ at port U, because the input of t_3 is not at U while there is a potential output shift of o from t_3 to t_1. In fact, $\mathcal{T}_U = \{t_1, t_3\}$, $\mathcal{T}'_U = \{t_3\}$, $\mathcal{T}_L = \mathcal{T}'_L = \emptyset$.

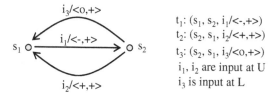

$t_1: (s_1, s_2, i_1/<-,+>)$
$t_2: (s_2, s_1, i_2/<+,+>)$
$t_3: (s_2, s_1, i_3/<o,+>)$
i_1, i_2 are input at U
i_3 is input at L

Fig. 6. An example where $\mathcal{T}_p$ is verifiable at U

To calculate $\mathcal{T}'_p$ and $\mathcal{T}_p - \mathcal{T}'_p$, we can first determine all transitions involved in potentially undetectable *1-shift* output faults. This can be done by comparing every synchronizable pair of transitions $s_1 \xrightarrow{x_1/y_1} s_2$ and $s_2 \xrightarrow{x_2/y_2} s_3$ where x_2 is not at p. If y_1 has non-empty output at p while y_2 does not, or vice versa, then t_1 and t_2 are involved in potentially undetectable 1-shift output fault and we can put them into $\mathcal{T}'_p$ and $\mathcal{T}_p - \mathcal{T}'_p$ respectively. In particular, for the purpose of the next step of the calculation, we can mark each transition put into $\mathcal{T}_p - \mathcal{T}'_p$ as *backward* or *forward* to indicate whether it is involved in a potentially undetectable backward or forward output shift. Note that a transition can be marked as both *forward* and *backward*. This step takes $\mathcal{O}(v^2)$ time where v is the number of transitions in M. At the end of this step, the set $\mathcal{T}'_p$ calculated is what we want. Then we can find all of the other transitions in $\mathcal{T}_p - \mathcal{T}'_p$ that have empty output at p and are involved in potentially undetectable output shift faults. We can keep adding transitions $s_1 \xrightarrow{x_1/y_1} s_2$ into $\mathcal{T}_p - \mathcal{T}'_p$ if the output of y_1 at p is empty and one of the following holds:

- There exists $s_2 \xrightarrow{x_2/y_2} s_3$ in $\mathcal{T}_p - \mathcal{T}'_p$ marked as *backward*, x_2 is not at p, and $s_2 \xrightarrow{x_2/y_2} s_3$ is an eligible successor of $s_1 \xrightarrow{x_1/y_1} s_2$. In this case, the added transition is also marked as *backward*.
- There exists $s_3 \xrightarrow{x_2/y_2} s_1$ in $\mathcal{T}_p - \mathcal{T}'_p$ marked as *forward*, x_1 is not at p, and $s_1 \xrightarrow{x_1/y_1} s_2$ is an eligible successor of $s_3 \xrightarrow{x_2/y_2} s_1$. In this case, the added transition is also marked as *forward*.

This step also takes $\mathcal{O}(v^2)$ time.

6   Verifiability of Outputs

Now that we have identified all the transitions that are involved in potentially undetectable output shift fault, we want to produce test or checking sequences that verify the output of transition t at port p for each $t \in \mathcal{T}_p$. Without using external coordination messages, we reach this goal by constructing a subsequence for each transition in $\mathcal{T}_p$ so that if these subsequences appear in the test or checking sequence, and the output observed when the test or checking sequences is applied to the SUT is correct, then it is guaranteed that the SUT is free from undetectable output shift faults.

Now suppose that $t \in \mathcal{T}_p$. If we can find a synchronizable path ρ containing t such that the following conditions hold, then the input portion of ρ can serve as such a subsequence for (t, p).

- ρ is synchronizable;
- we are able to determine the output sequence of ρ at p from applying the input portion of ρ from the starting state of ρ;
- from the correct output sequence of ρ at p we can deduce that the output of t at p is correct.

We require that $first(\rho)$ and $last(\rho)$ have input at p in order to identify a certain output sequence: no matter how ρ is concatenated with other subsequences, we can always determine the output sequence produced at p in response to the first $|pre(\rho)|$ inputs of ρ since this output sequence is immediately preceded and followed by input at p.

To determine the correct output of (t, p) from the correct output sequence of ρ at p, we require that

- If the output of (t, p) is nonempty, then all the outputs at p in $pre(\rho)$ are either also nonempty or already known to be correct.
- If the output of (t, p) is empty, then all the outputs at p in $pre(\rho)$ are either also empty or already known to be correct.

We say that transitions t_1 and t_2 have the same *type* of output at p when the output of t_1 and t_2 at p are either both empty or both non-empty.

Example 6. In the specification in Figure 6, we know that there is an undetectable output shift fault in $t_1 t_3$ at port U. We are interested in constructing a path to verify that the output of transition t_1 and t_3 at this port are correct.

$\rho_1 = t_1 t_2$ is such a synchronizable path for t_1: it has input at U in t_1 ($first(\rho)$) and input at U in t_2 ($last(\rho)$), and if the correct the output is observed at U between these two inputs when ρ_1 is applied as a subsequence, we are able to deduce that the output of t_1 at U is correct.

If we know that the output of t_1 at U is correct, then $\rho_2 = t_1 t_3 t_1$ is also a sufficient synchronizable path for t_3: it has input at U in t_1 (for both $first(\rho)$ and $last(\rho)$), and if the correct output is observed at U between these two inputs when ρ_2 is applied then we are able to deduce that the output of t_3 at U is correct since we already know that the output of t_1 at U is correct.

Formally, we introduce the following concept.

Definition 2. *Let t be a transition and v a set of transitions in M. ρ is an absolute verifying path upon v for (t, p) if*

- *ρ is a synchronizable path;*
- *t is contained in $pre(\rho)$;*
- *$first(\rho)$ and $last(\rho)$ and only these two transitions in ρ have input at p;*
- *$t \notin v$ and for all t' contained in $pre(\rho)$, either $t' \in v$ or $t' \mid_p = - \Leftrightarrow t \mid_p = -$.*

Note that given t and ρ we will typically consider a minimal *set v that satisfies the above conditions: if $t' \mid_p = - \Leftrightarrow t \mid_p = -$ then $t' \notin v$.*

Example 7. In Figure 6,

- $t_1 t_2$ is an absolute verifying path upon $\emptyset$ for (t_1, U).
- $t_1 t_3 t_1$ is an absolute verifying path upon $\{t_1\}$ for (t_3, U).

Directly from this definition, we have:

Proposition 1. *If ρ is an absolute verifying path upon v for (t, p) and v is a minimal such set, then ρ is an absolute verifying path upon v for (t', p) for any t' contained in $pre(\rho)$ such that $t' \mid_p = - \Leftrightarrow t \mid_p = -$.*

No matter how ρ is concatenated with other subsequences, we can always determine the output sequence produced at p in response to the first $|\rho| - 1$ inputs of ρ since this output sequence is immediately preceded and followed by input at p. By checking the correctness of this output sequence, we would like to conclude that the output of t at p is correct. This is expressed in the following proposition:

Proposition 2. *Let v be a set of transitions in M, ρ an absolute verifying path upon v for (t, p). If for every transition t' in v, the output at p of t' in the SUT is correct, then the correct output sequence at p in response to the first $|pre(\rho)|$ inputs of ρ implies the correct output of (t, p).*

Proof. Suppose $t \mid_p \neq -$ (The proof for the case when $t \mid_p = -$ is analogous).

Suppose that m inputs from $pre(\rho)$ lead to non-empty output at p in M. Thus, if we observe the correct output sequence in response to the first $|pre(\rho)|$ inputs of ρ then we must observe m outputs at p in response to these inputs.

Since $t \mid_p \neq -$, and ρ is an absolute verifying path upon v for (t, p), we know by definition that for all t' in ρ' such that $t' \mid_p = -$, the output of t' at p is correct (and so is $-$) in the SUT. So, we know that the corresponding $|pre(\rho)| - m$ inputs in $pre(\rho)$ lead to empty output at p in the SUT. Thus we can map the observed outputs at p, in response to the input portion of $pre(\rho)$, to the inputs that caused them and so if the correct output sequence is observed then the output of p at t must be correct.

7   Finding an Absolute Verifying Path Upon ∅

To verify the output of (t, p), we try to find a path ρ that is an absolute verifying path upon v for (t, p) for some set v such that the output at p for every transition in v is verified. As a special case, we would like to know if there exists an absolute verifying path upon $\emptyset$ for each $t \in \mathcal{T}_p$. Of course, if this is possible then the input portion of these paths can be used as the subsequences we want. The advantage in doing so is that we can *independently* verify each output of a transition in the sense that we are able to conclude that the output of this transition at port p is correct from observing the correct output sequence on a certain transition path, and that the above conclusion does not rely on assuming the correctness of any other transitions. Independence here can be helpful for fault diagnoses: in the case that the SUT contains only undetectable output shift faults, we will be able to identify them.

Below, we present a necessary and sufficient condition on M for (t, p) to have an absolute verifying path upon $\emptyset$ for each p and each $t \in \mathcal{T}_p$. This condition is presented in terms of potentially undetectable 1-shift output faults as in [6] while it holds also for general potentially undetectable output shift faults.

7.1   Condition

If $\rho_1 @ t @ \rho_2$ is an absolute verifying path upon $\emptyset$ for (t, p), then ρ_1 and ρ_2 are called an *absolute leading path* and an *absolute trailing path* respectively [6]. Suppose that M is an FSM which is not intrinsically non-synchronizable, has no same-port-output-cycles, and has no isolated-port-cycles. The following is a necessary and sufficient condition on M to guarantee the existence of an absolute leading path and an absolute trailing path for (t, p) for each t involved in a potentially undetectable output shift fault.

Given an FSM M which is not intrinsically non-synchronizable and has neither same-port-output-cycles nor isolated-port-cycles, there exist absolute verifying paths upon $\emptyset$ for all of its potentially undetectable 1-shift output faults if and only if for any synchronizable pair of transitions $t_1 = s_1 \xrightarrow{*/*} s$ and $t_2 = s \xrightarrow{*/*} s_2$ in M,

a *if there exists a potentially undetectable forward shift of an output at port p, then there exists at least one transition to s with a null output at port p that forms a synchronizable pair of transitions with t_2, and at least one transition from s with either an input or a non-empty output at port p that forms a synchronizable pair of transitions with t_1.*

b *if there exists a potentially undetectable backward shift of an output at port p, then there exists at least one transition to s with a non-empty output at port p that forms a synchronizable pair of transitions with t_2, and at least one transition from s with either an input or a null output at port p that forms a synchronizable pair of transitions with t_1.*

$o_2 \neq -$
i_1, i_2 are input at L
i_3 is input at U

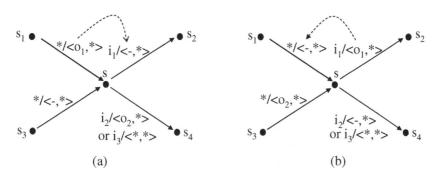

$$(a) \qquad\qquad\qquad\qquad (b)$$

Fig. 7. illustration of the condition

Figure 7 illustrates the condition in a 2-port FSM setting. In this figure, we have potentially undetectable forward output shift fault in (a) and potentially undetectable backward output shift fault in (b), as the dashed arrows show. For such potential faults, we have a transition from s_3 to s and a transition from s to s_4, so the condition holds. In fact, in (a), the transition from s to s_4 will be used to check if there is a missing output o_1 in transition $s_1 \xrightarrow{*/<o_1,*>} s$, as a result of a forward output shift. The transition from s_3 to s will be used to check if there is an extra output in transition $s \xrightarrow{i_1/<-,*>} s_2$ as a result of a forward output shift. The transitions from s_3 to s and from s to s_4 in (b) will be used analogously.

Theorem 1. *Let M be a given FSM which is not intrinsically non-synchronizable and has no same-port-output-cycles and has no isolated-port-cycles. Let p be any port of M. There is an absolute verifying path upon $\emptyset$ for every $t \in T_p$, if and only if for any synchronizable pair of transitions $t_1 = s_1 \xrightarrow{x_1/y_1} s$ and $t_2 = s \xrightarrow{x_2/y_2} s_2$ in the FSM,*

$$(x_2 \notin I_p \wedge y_1|_p = - \Leftrightarrow y_2|_p \neq -) \text{ implies}$$

$\exists s_3, x_3, y_3, s_4, x_4, y_4$ s.t. $t_3 = s_3 \xrightarrow{x_3/y_3} s$, $(y_3|_p = - \Leftrightarrow y_1|_p \neq -)$, $t_4 = s \xrightarrow{x_4/y_4} s_4$, $(x_4 \in I_p \vee (y_4|_p = - \Leftrightarrow y_2|_p \neq -))$, t_1 and t_4 form a synchronizable pair of transitions, and t_3 and t_2 form a synchronizable pair of transitions.

Proof. $(\Rightarrow)$ Let $t_1 = s_1 \xrightarrow{x_1/y_1} s$ and $t_2 = s \xrightarrow{x_2/y_2} s_2$ be any synchronizable pair of transitions in M.

Suppose $x_2 \notin I_p$, and $y_1|_p = - \Leftrightarrow y_2|_p \neq -$, i.e. t_1 and t_2 are involved in a potentially undetectable output shift. By the hypothesis there exists absolute verifying paths upon $\emptyset$ for t_1 and t_2 respectively.

Let ρ_1 be an absolute leading path for t_2. Since $x_2 \notin I_p$, $\rho_1 \neq \varepsilon$. Let $t_3 = s_3 \xrightarrow{x_3/y_3} s$ be the last transition of ρ_1 then we have $(y_3|_p = - \Leftrightarrow y_1|_p \neq -)$ and by definition t_3 and t_2 form a synchronizable pair of transitions as required.

Let ρ_2 be an absolute trailing path for t_1 and so $\rho_2 \neq \varepsilon$. Let $t_4 = s \xrightarrow{x_4/y_4} s_4$ be the first transition of ρ_2 then we have $(x_4 \in I_p$ or $(y_4|_p = - \Leftrightarrow y_2|_p \neq -))$ and by definition t_1 and t_4 form a synchronizable pair of transitions.

($\Leftarrow$) Let t be any transition in $\mathcal{T}_p$. We prove that there is an absolute leading path ρ_1 for (t, p). The part for absolute trailing path follows in the same way.

If the input of t is at p, then ε is an absolute leading path. Suppose instead that the input of t is not at p. Let ρ' be a longest synchronizable path ending in t in which every transition has the same type of output at p as t, and no transition has input at p. Since M has a finite number of states and has neither same-port-output-cycles or isolated-port-cycles, the existence of such a (finite) ρ' is guaranteed. Let t_1' be the first transition of ρ'. Let $t_2' = s_2' \xrightarrow{x_2/y_2} s_1'$ be any transition ending at the starting state of t_1' such that t_2' and t_1' form a synchronizable pair of transitions. If $y_2|_p = - \Leftrightarrow t|_p = -$, then $t_2'@\rho'$ is an absolute leading path as by the maximality of ρ' we have that $x_2 \in I_p$. If $y_2|_p = - \Leftrightarrow t|_p \neq -$, then t_2' and t_1' are involved in a potentially undetectable output shift fault. According to the condition, there exists $t_3' = s_3' \xrightarrow{x_3/y_3} s_1'$ such that $y_3|_p = - \Leftrightarrow t|_p = -$ and t_3' and t_1' form a synchronizable pair of transitions. Again, $x_3 \in I_p$, so $t_3'@\rho'$ is a absolute leading path as required.

7.2   Algorithm

In Section 5 we showed how one can identify all pairs of transitions that are involved in a potentially undetectable output shift fault. For each such pair, we can determine in constant time whether the above condition is satisfied. Once we know that a given specification satisfies the condition, we can use the algorithm in Figure 8 to construct an absolute verifying path upon $\emptyset$ for (t, p) for a given transition $t \in \mathcal{T}_p$.

This algorithm is composed of two parts: lines 3-13 find an absolute leading path ρ_1 and the rest of the algorithm produces an absolute trailing path ρ_2. Here we briefly describe the first of these two parts as they are quite similar.

If the input of transition t is at p then we can terminate with $\rho_1 = \varepsilon$. Otherwise, we check if there exists a transition ending at the starting state v of $\rho_1@t$ that can form a synchronizable path with $\rho_1@t$ and which has input at p and the same type of output at p as t. If there is such a transition, the current ρ_1 preceded by this transition suffices. Otherwise we precede ρ_1 with a transition ending at the starting state of $\rho_1@t$ that can form a synchronizable path with $\rho_1@t$ and which has the same type of output at p as t, and repeat the procedure. Such a transition is guaranteed to exist: if there exists v''. $v'' \xrightarrow{x'/y'} v$ that can form a synchronizable path with $\rho_1@t$ where the type of the output of y at p is different from that of t, then there exists a potentially undetectable output shift between $v'' \xrightarrow{x'/y'} v$ and the first transition of $\rho_1@t$. By our condition, $\exists v'$. $v' \xrightarrow{x/y} v$ that

1: **input**: an FSM M that satisfies the above condition, a port p of M, and a transition
   $t \in \mathcal{T}_p$ of M where the output of t at p is y^*
2: **output**: $\rho_1@t@\rho_2$ which is an absolute verifying path upon $\emptyset$ for (t,p)
3: let $\rho_1 := \varepsilon$
4: **if** the input of t is not at port p **then**
5:     let $v :=$ the starting state of t
6:     **while** $\neg\exists v'$ s.t. $v' \xrightarrow{x/y} v$, $v' \xrightarrow{x/y} v@\rho_1@t$ is a synchronizable path, $x \in I_p$ and
       $(y \mid_p= - \Leftrightarrow y^* \mid_p= -)$ **do**
7:         let v' be a state s.t. $v' \xrightarrow{x/y} v$, $v' \xrightarrow{x/y} v@\rho_1@t$ is a synchronizable path, $(y \mid_p=$
           $- \Leftrightarrow y^* \mid_p= -)$
8:         let $\rho_1 := (v', v, x/y)@\rho_1$
9:         let $v := v'$
10:     **end while**
11:     let v' be a state s.t. $v' \xrightarrow{x/y} v$, $v' \xrightarrow{x/y} v@\rho_1@t$ is a synchronizable path, $x \in I_p$
       and $(y \mid_p= - \Leftrightarrow y^* \mid_p= -)$
12:     let $\rho_1 := (v', v, x/y)@\rho_1$
13: **end if**
14: let $\rho_2 = \varepsilon$
15: let $v :=$ the ending state of t
16: **while** $\neg\exists v'$ s.t. $v \xrightarrow{x/y} v'$, $t@\rho_2@v' \xrightarrow{x/y} v$ is a synchronizable path, and $x \in I_p$
    do
17:     let v' be a state s.t. $v \xrightarrow{x/y} v'$, $t@\rho_2@v \xrightarrow{x/y} v'$ is a synchronizable path, and
       $(y \mid_p= - \leftrightarrow y^* \mid_p= -)$
18:     let $\rho_2 := \rho_2@(v, v', x/y)$
19:     let $v := v'$
20: **end while**
21: let v' be a state s.t. $v \xrightarrow{x/y} v'$, $t@\rho_2v \xrightarrow{x/y} v'$ is a synchronizable path, and $x \in I_p$
22: let $\rho_2 := \rho_2@(v, v', x/y)$

Fig. 8. Algorithm 1: generating absolute verifying paths upon $\emptyset$

forms a synchronizable path path with $\rho_1@t$ such that the type of the output of
y at p is the same as that of t.

Termination is guaranteed because M must be free from same-port-output-cycles and isolated-port-cycles. Furthermore, since M has no same-port-output-cycles or isolated-port-cycles, this procedure cannot repeat a state of M and thus, if M has m states, ρ_1 can have length at most $m - 1$.

8   Finding an Absolute Verifying Path Upon a Set v

When the given specification does not satisfy the above criterion, we are not able to construct subsequences to *independently* verify the output of each transition involved in a potentially undetectable output shift fault at port p. However, there may still exists a set of subsequences such that when these subsequences are included into the test or checking sequence and the observed output is correct, we have confidence that the implementation is free from undetectable output shift faults. In this section, we describe this general approach. As in [7], the results are applicable to any potentially undetectable output shift faults, not restricted to only potentially undetectable *1-shift* output faults.

8.1   Constructing Absolute Verifying Path Upon Set v

To verify the output of each transition involved in a potentially undetectable output shift fault at port p, we try to find a path ρ that is an absolute verifying path upon v for (t, p) for some (possibly empty) set v such that the output at p for every transition in v is verified by some other path that has been chosen. In doing so, we need to search for an acyclic digraph of transitions such that each transition in this digraph has an absolute verifying path upon a set of transitions that appear as its successors in the digraph. Such an acyclic graph can be represented as a *partial order* in the following way.

A *relation R* between elements of a set A and elements of a set B is a subset of $A \times B$. If (a, b) is an element of relation R then a is related to b under R and we also write aRb. The set of elements related to $a \in A$ under R is denoted $R(a)$ and thus $R(a) = \{b \in B | (a, b) \in R\}$.

Given a set A, a relation R between A and A is a *partial order* if it satisfies the following conditions.

1. For all $a \in A$, aRa.
2. If aRa' and $a'Ra$ then $a = a'$.
3. If a_1Ra_2 and a_2Ra_3 then a_1Ra_3.

Definition 3. *Suppose that $\mathcal{U}$ is a set of transitions of M, $\mathcal{R}$ is a relation from $\mathcal{U}$ to $\mathcal{U}$, and $\mathcal{P}$ is a function from $\mathcal{U}$ to synchronizable paths of M. Let p be any port in M. The set $\mathcal{U}$ of transitions is verifiable at p under $\mathcal{R}$ and $\mathcal{P}$ if the following hold.*

(a) For all $t \in \mathcal{U}$, $\mathcal{P}(t)$ is an absolute verifying path upon $\mathcal{R}(t)$ for (t, p);
(b) $\mathcal{R} \cup \{(t, t) | t \in \mathcal{U}\}$ is a partial order.

Where such $\mathcal{R}$ and $\mathcal{P}$ exist we also say that $\mathcal{U}$ is verifiable at p.

Suppose that $\mathcal{U}$ is verifiable at p under $\mathcal{R}$ and $\mathcal{P}$ and we observe correct output sequence corresponding to the first $|pre(\mathcal{P}(t))|$ output of $\mathcal{P}(t)$ for each $t \in \mathcal{U}$. Then according to Proposition 2, we know that the output of t at p is correct for each $t \in \mathcal{U}$. So our goal is to find a set $\mathcal{U}$ that is verifiable at p such that $\mathcal{T}_p \subseteq \mathcal{U}$.

Example 8. In Figure 6, for port U, we have $\mathcal{T}_U = \{t_1, t_3\}$. $\mathcal{T}_U$ is verifiable at U because

- t_1t_2 is an absolute verifying path upon $\emptyset$ for (t_1, U).
- $t_1t_3t_1$ is an absolute verifying path upon $\{t_1\}$ for (t_3, U).

So let $\mathcal{P}(t_1) = t_1t_2$, $\mathcal{P}(t_3) = t_1t_3t_1$, $\mathcal{R}(t_1) = \emptyset$, $\mathcal{R}(t_3) = \{t_1\}$ (i.e. $\mathcal{R} = \{(t_3, t_1)\}$), then $\mathcal{T}_p = \{t_1, t_3\}$ is verifiable at U under $\mathcal{P}$ and $\mathcal{R}$.

Proposition 3. *If ρ is an absolute verifying path upon v for (t,p) and v is a minimal such set then $v \subseteq \mathcal{T}_p$.*

Proof. Let $\rho = t_1 \ldots t_k$ (for $k \geq 2$) where $t = t_i$ for some $i \in [1, k-1]$. Suppose $t_i \mid_p \neq -$ (the case for $t_i \mid_p = -$ is analogous). Consider an arbitrary transition $t' \in v$: it is sufficient to prove that $t' \in \mathcal{T}_p$.

By the minimality of v we have that t' is contained in $pre(\rho)$ and so $t' = t_j$ for some $j \in [1, k-1]$. Since ρ is an absolute verifying path upon v for (t_i, p), $t_i \notin v$ and so $j \neq i$. Suppose $i < j$ (the case for $i > j$ is analogous).

Since $t_j \in v$, by the minimality of v we have that $t_j \mid_p = -$. Now as $i < j$, $t_i \mid_p \neq -$, $t_j \mid_p = -$, there exists some maximal l with $i \leq l < j$ such that $t_l \mid_p \neq -$. Let $\rho' = t_l \ldots t_j$. By Definition 2, no transition in ρ' has input at p. By considering ρ' we see that $t_j \in \mathcal{T}_p$.

This result allows us to consider only transitions in $\mathcal{T}_p$ for $\mathcal{U}$.

Proposition 4. *Suppose that M is an FSM that is not intrinsically non-synchronizable, p is a port of M and $\mathcal{U}$ is a set of transitions verifiable at port p. If $\mathcal{T}_p' \subseteq \mathcal{U}$ or $\mathcal{T}_p - \mathcal{T}_p' \subseteq \mathcal{U}$, then $\mathcal{T}_p$ is verifiable at p.*

Proof. Suppose $\mathcal{U}$ is verifiable under $\mathcal{R}$ and $\mathcal{P}$ and that $\mathcal{R}$ is a minimal such relation (i.e. $\mathcal{U}$ is not verifiable using a relation that contains fewer pairs).

First, consider the case that $\mathcal{T}_p' \subseteq \mathcal{U}$. According to Theorem 2 in [5], there exists an absolute verifying path upon $\mathcal{T}_p'$ for (t, p) for every $t \notin \mathcal{T}_p'$. Since $\mathcal{T}_p' \subseteq \mathcal{U}$, there exists $\rho'_{p,t}$, the absolute verifying path upon $\mathcal{T}_p'$ for (t, p), for $t \in \mathcal{T}_p - \mathcal{U}$. Now define relation $\mathcal{R}'$ and function $\mathcal{P}'$ in the following way.

1. $\mathcal{R}' = \mathcal{R} \cup \{(t, t') \mid t \in \mathcal{T}_p - \mathcal{U} \wedge t' \in \mathcal{T}_p'\}$
2. $\mathcal{P}' = \mathcal{P} \cup \{(t, \rho'_{p,t}) \mid t \in \mathcal{T}_p - \mathcal{U}\}$

It is easy to check that $\mathcal{T}_p$ is verifiable at p under $\mathcal{R}'$ and $\mathcal{P}'$ as required.

Now consider the case that $\mathcal{T} - \mathcal{T}_p' \subseteq \mathcal{U}$. Similar to Theorem 2 in [5], we can prove that there exists an absolute verifying path upon $\mathcal{T}_p - \mathcal{T}_p'$ for (t, p) for every $t \notin \mathcal{T} - \mathcal{T}_p'$. The proof is then similar to that for the case where $\mathcal{T}_p' \subseteq \mathcal{U}$.

8.2 Algorithm

Now we consider an algorithm:

- to check if $\mathcal{T}_p$ is verifiable at p. According to Proposition 4, this amounts to checking whether there exists $\mathcal{U}$ such that $\mathcal{U}$ is verifiable at p and $\mathcal{T}_p' \subseteq \mathcal{U}$ or $\mathcal{T}_p - \mathcal{T}_p' \subseteq \mathcal{U}$;
- when $\mathcal{T}_p$ is verifiable at p, construct absolute verifying paths for each transition in $\mathcal{T}_p$.

Figure 9 gives such an algorithm. Here, $\mathcal{U}$ is a set of transitions that are verifiable at p. It is initially set to empty. We search for transitions to be added into $\mathcal{U}$ and try to make $\mathcal{U} \supseteq \mathcal{T}_p$. According to Proposition 3, we only need to

1: **input:** M and a port p of M
2: **output:** whether $\mathcal{T}_p$ is verifiable at p, and if so, provide $\rho_{p,t}$ for each transition $t \in \mathcal{T}_p$
3: $\mathcal{U} := \emptyset$
4: **for all** $t \in \mathcal{T}_p$ **do**
5:     $\mathcal{P}(t) := null$
6: **end for**
7: **if** $\mathcal{T}_p = \emptyset$ **then**
8:     $success := true$
9:     goto line 27
10: **end if**
11: $success := false$
12: $checkset := \mathcal{T}_p$
13: $checkset' := \emptyset$
14: **while** $checkset \neq \emptyset \wedge checkset' \neq checkset$ **do**
15:     $checkset' := checkset$
16:     **if** we can find an absolute verifying path $\rho_{p,t}$ upon $\mathcal{U}$ for (t,p) for some $t \in checkset$ **then**
17:         **for** t' contained in $pre(\rho_{p,t})$ such that $(t' \notin \mathcal{U})$ and $(t'|_p = - \Leftrightarrow t|_p = -)$ **do**
18:             add t' to $\mathcal{U}$
19:             $\mathcal{P}(t') := \rho_{p,t}$
20:         **end for**
21:         $checkset := \mathcal{T}_p - \mathcal{U}$
22:         **if** $checkset = \emptyset$ **then**
23:             $success := true$
24:         **end if**
25:     **end if**
26: **end while**
27: **if** $success$ **then**
28:     output("success", $\mathcal{P}$)
29: **else**
30:     output("no such set of sequences exists.")
31: **end if**

Fig. 9. Algorithm 2: generating a set of paths

consider transitions in $\mathcal{T}_p$ to be added into $\mathcal{U}$, so in fact, we seek a set $\mathcal{U}$ such that $\mathcal{U} = \mathcal{T}_p$.

If we succeed, we have an absolute verifying path $\rho_{p,t}$ in $\mathcal{P}(t)$ for each $t \in \mathcal{U}$. Of course, if we do not need the absolute verifying paths but just want to check whether $\mathcal{T}_p$ is verifiable at p, the algorithm can be easily modified so that it stops whenever $\mathcal{T}_p \subseteq \mathcal{U}$ or $\mathcal{T}'_p \subseteq \mathcal{U}$ (Proposition 4).

If $\mathcal{T}_p$ is empty, then we do not need to do anything (lines 7-10). If $\mathcal{T}_p \neq \emptyset$, then we start to check if there exists a transition $t \in \mathcal{T}_p$ that has an absolute verifying path (upon $\emptyset$) for (t,p). We use $checkset$ to denote the current set of transitions that we need to search for absolute verifying paths and initially $checkset = \mathcal{T}_p$. Thus if $checkset$ becomes $\emptyset$ then we terminate the loop and the algorithm has found a sufficient set of paths. At the end of an iteration the set $checkset'$ denotes the value of *checkset* before the iteration of the while loop and thus if there is no progress (*checkset'* = *checkset* at this point) the algorithm terminates with failure.

Whenever we find an absolute verifying path $\rho_{p,t}$ upon $\mathcal{U}$, we can add t' to $\mathcal{U}$ for all t' contained in *pre*(ρ) and $t'|_p = - \Leftrightarrow t|_p = -$. This is based on Proposition 1. At the same time, we update *checkset*.

Recall that G' is a correctly ordered directed graph in which paths correspond to synchronizable paths in M [10]. To find an absolute verifying path ρ upon $\mathcal{U}$ for (t, p), we can construct $G'[t, \mathcal{U}]$ which is obtained from G' by removing all edges except those corresponding to a transition t' in one of the following cases:

- t' has input at p;
- $t'|_p = - \Leftrightarrow t|_p = -$;
- $t' \in \mathcal{U}$.

We then search for a synchronizable path in $G'[t, \mathcal{U}]$ that contains t, starts with input at p, and ends with input at p. It is natural to search for such a path using a breadth-first search in order to find a shortest such path. Note that we do not need to consider cycles in $G'[t, \mathcal{U}]$: if there exists an absolute verifying path with a cycle then there is such a path that has no cycles.

The following two results show that Algorithm 2 is correct.

Theorem 2. *Suppose that Algorithm 2 outputs "success" and $\mathcal{P}$. Then there exists a relation $\mathcal{R}$ such that $\mathcal{T}_p$ is verifiable at p under $\mathcal{R}$ and $\mathcal{P}$.*

Proof. Define a relation $\mathcal{R}$ in the following way. Given a transition $t \in \mathcal{T}_p$ consider the iteration in which t is added to $\mathcal{U}$ and let $\mathcal{U}_t$ denote the value of $\mathcal{U}$ at the beginning of this iteration. Then, since we could add t to $\mathcal{U}$ on this iteration, there is an absolute verifying path upon $\mathcal{U}_t$ for (t, p). Thus, we let $\mathcal{R}$ be the relation such that for all $t \in \mathcal{T}_p$, $\mathcal{R}(t) = \mathcal{U}_t$. Clearly $\mathcal{T}_p$ is verifiable at p under $\mathcal{R}$ and $\mathcal{P}$ as required.

Theorem 3. *Suppose that Algorithm 2 does not output "success". Then $\mathcal{T}_p$ is not verifiable at p.*

Proof. Proof by contradiction: suppose that there exists $\mathcal{R}$ and $\mathcal{P}$ such that $\mathcal{T}_p$ is verifiable at p under $\mathcal{R}$ and $\mathcal{P}$ and that Algorithm 2 terminates with a set $\mathcal{U}$ such that $\mathcal{T}_p \not\subseteq \mathcal{U}$.

Define a function *depth* from $\mathcal{T}_p$ to the integers in the following way. The base case is $depth(t) = 1$ if $\mathcal{R}(t) = \emptyset$. The recursive case is if $\mathcal{R}(t) \neq \emptyset$ then $depth(t) = 1 + max_{t' \in \mathcal{R}(t) \setminus \{t\}} depth(t')$. Let t denote an element of $\mathcal{T}_p \setminus \mathcal{U}$ that minimises $depth(t)$. But, every element of $\mathcal{R}(t)$ is in $\mathcal{U}$ and thus there exists an absolute verifying path upon $\mathcal{R}(t)$ for (p, t). This contradicts the algorithm terminating with set $\mathcal{U}$ such that $\mathcal{T}_p \not\subseteq \mathcal{U}$ as required.

Now we turn to the complexity of the algorithm.

Let $m = |\mathcal{T}_p|$ be the number of transitions involved in output shift faults at p. For each while-loop (line 14-26), we construct an absolute verifying path upon $\mathcal{U}$

for one of the transitions in *checkset*, and we can remove at least one transition from *checkset*. As initially $|checkset| = m$, the while-loop will be executed at most m times.

Within each while-loop in lines 14-26, we check whether we can find an absolute verifying path $\rho_{p,t}$ upon $\mathcal{U}$ for (t, p) for some $t \in checkset$. This can be realized by trying to construct $\rho_{p,t}$ for each $t \in checkset$ until such a $\rho_{p,t}$ is found. This involves at most $|checkset| \leq m$ time for each iteration.

For each attempt to construct an absolute verifying path upon $\mathcal{U}$ for a given transition t, it takes $\mathcal{O}(wv)$ time to construct a path where w is the number of vertices in G' and v is the number of transitions in M.

For the for-loop in lines 17-20, we can keep a set α of all transitions t' contained in $pre(\rho_{p,t})$ such that $t' \notin \mathcal{U}$ and $t'|_p = - \Leftrightarrow t|_p = -$ during the construction of $\rho_{p,t}$. This does not affect our estimated time $\mathcal{O}(wv)$. After we have found such an $\rho_{p,t}$ successfully, we can move all transitions in α from *checkset* to $\mathcal{U}$. For each such move, there will be one less while-loop executed, and thus the time for the operation of the for-loop in lines 17-20 can be ignored.

In summary, the time complexity of Algorithm 1 is $\mathcal{O}(m^2wv)$.

9   Comparison

To make sure that each transition involved in a potentially undetectable output shift fault can be *independently* verified at port p, we need to have an absolute verifying path upon $\emptyset$ for (t, p) for all transition t involved in a potentially undetectable output shift fault. We have presented a necessary and sufficient condition on the specification FSM for this to be possible. This condition is sufficient for $\mathcal{T}_p$ to be verifiable. However, it is not necessary for $\mathcal{T}_p$ to be verifiable.

Example 9. In Figure 6 we have shown that $\mathcal{T}_p$ is verifiable at U. However, the condition in Section 7 does not hold. This is because for (t_3, U), t_3 does not have input at U and there is no transition ending at s_2 with non-empty output at U.

The following shows another more elaborated example where $\mathcal{T}_p$ is verifiable at U while the condition in Section 7 does not hold.

Example 10. In Figure 10, there are undetectable output shift faults at port U in t_1t_2 and in t_2t_5. $\mathcal{T}_U = \{t_1, t_2, t_5\}$. $\mathcal{T}'_U = \{t_1, t_5\}$.

The condition in Section 7 does not hold because for (t_1, U), there is no transition starting from s_2 that has either input at U or non-empty output at U.

However, $\mathcal{T}_U$ is verifiable at U:

- $t_4t_5t_1$ is an absolute verifying path upon $\emptyset$ for (t_5, U).
- $t_3t_2t_5t_1$ is an absolute verifying path upon $\{t_5\}$ for (t_2, U).
- $t_1t_2t_5t_1$ is an absolute verifying path upon $\{t_2, t_5\}$ for (t_1, U).

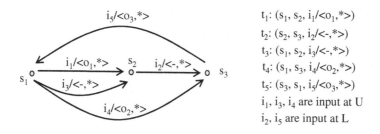

$$t_1: (s_1, s_2, i_1/<o_1,*>)$$
$$t_2: (s_2, s_3, i_2/<-,*>)$$
$$t_3: (s_1, s_2, i_3/<-,*>)$$
$$t_4: (s_1, s_3, i_4/<o_2,*>)$$
$$t_5: (s_3, s_1, i_5/<o_3,*>)$$
i_1, i_3, i_4 are input at U
i_2, i_5 are input at L

Fig. 10. Comparing the two conditions

10 Conclusion

This chapter has presented a sound procedure to check for the possibility of constructing a test or checking sequence that will not cause controllability and observability problems and will not require external coordination message exchanges among remote testers during its application in a distributed test architecture. This is realized by constructing a path that can help check the output of a transition t at a given port p, for each transition t involved in a potentially undetectable output shift fault. The effectiveness of this path, for checking the output of transition t at port p, must not be affected by controllability and observability problems. The correct output of transition t at port p is deduced from observing the correct output sequence when applying the input portion of this path. There remains the open problem of producing an *efficient* test or checking sequence from an FSM, that is guaranteed to determine the correctness of the SUT for the considered fault model.

Acknowledgements

This work was supported in part by Engineering and Physical Sciences Research Council grant number GR/R43150, Formal Methods and Testing (FORTEST), Natural Sciences and Engineering Research Council (NSERC) of Canada under grant RGPIN 976 and 209774, and Leverhulme Trust grant number F/00275/D, Testing State Based Systems.

References

1. Aho, A.V., Dahbura, A.T., Lee, D., Uyar, M.U.: An optimization technique for protocol conformance test generation based on UIO sequences and Rural Chinese Postman Tours. In: Protocol Specification, Testing, and Verification VIII, Atlantic City, pp. 75–86. Elsevier, North-Holland (1988)
2. Boyd, S., Ural, H.: The synchronization problem in protocol testing and its complexity. Information Processing Letters 40, 131–136 (1991)
3. Cacciari, L., Rafiq, O.: Controllability and observability in distributed testing. Information and Software Technology 41, 767–780 (1999)

4. Chanson, S.T., Lee, B.P., Parakh, N.J., Zeng, H.X.: Design and implementation of a Ferry Clip test system. In: Protocol Specification, Testing and Verificaion, IX, pp. 101–118. Elsevier, North-Holland (1990)
5. Chen, J., Hierons, R.M., Ural, H.: Overcoming observability problems in distributed test architectures. Information Processing Letters 98, 177–182 (2006)
6. Chen, J., Hierons, R.M., Ural, H.: Conditions for resolving observability problems in distributed testing. In: de Frutos-Escrig, D., Núñez, M. (eds.) FORTE 2004. LNCS, vol. 3235, pp. 229–242. Springer, Heidelberg (2004)
7. Chen, J., Hierons, R.M., Ural, H.: Resolving observability problems in distributed test architecture. In: Wang, F. (ed.) FORTE 2005. LNCS, vol. 3731, pp. 219–232. Springer, Heidelberg (2005)
8. Chen, W., Ural, H.: Synchronizable checking sequences based on multiple UIO sequences. IEEE/ACM Transactions on Networking 3, 152–157 (1995)
9. Gill, A.: Introduction to the Theory of Finite-State Machines. McGraw-Hill, New York (1962)
10. Guyot, S., Ural, H.: Synchronizable checking sequences based on UIO sequences. In: Proc. of IFIP IWPTS 1995, Evry, France, September 1995, pp. 395–407 (1995)
11. Hennie, F.C.: Fault detecting experiments for sequential circuits. In: Proc. of Fifth Ann. Symp. Switching Circuit Theory and Logical Design, Princeton, N.J., pp. 95–110 (1964)
12. Hierons, R.M.: Extending test sequence overlap by invertibility. The Computer Journal 39, 325–330 (1996)
13. Hierons, R.M.: Testing from a finite state machine: Extending invertibility to sequences. The Computer Journal 40, 220–230 (1997)
14. Hierons, R.M.: Testing a distributed system: generating minimal synchronised test sequences that detect output-shifting faults. Information and Software Technology 43(9), 551–560 (2001)
15. Hierons, R.M., Ural, H.: Synchronized checking sequences based on UIO sequences. Information and Software Technology 45(12), 793–803 (2003)
16. Iyengar, V., Chakrabarty, K.: An efficient finite-state machine implementation of Huffman decoders. Information Processing Letters 64, 271–275 (1998)
17. Lee, D., Yannakakis, M.: Principles and methods of testing finite–state machines – a survey. Proceedings of the IEEE 84(8), 1089–1123 (1996)
18. Luo, G., Dssouli, R., Bochmann, G.v.: Generating synchronizable test sequences based on finite state machine with distributed ports. In: The 6th IFIP Workshop on Protocol Test Systems, pp. 139–153. Elsevier, North-Holland (1993)
19. Luo, G., Dssouli, R., Bochmann, G.v., Venkataram, P., Ghedamsi, A.: Test generation with respect to distributed interfaces. Computer Standards and Interfaces 16, 119–132 (1994)
20. Sabnani, K.K., Dahbura, A.T.: A protocol test generation procedure. Computer Networks 15, 285–297 (1988)
21. Sarikaya, B., Bochmann, G.v.: Synchronization and specification issues in protocol testing. IEEE Transactions on Communications 32, 389–395 (1984)
22. Tai, K.C., Young, Y.C.: Synchronizable test sequences of finite state machines. Computer Networks 13, 1111–1134 (1998)
23. Tanenbaum, A.S.: Computer Networks, 3rd edn. Prentice-Hall, Englewood Cliffs (1996)
24. Ural, H., Wang, Z.: Synchronizable test sequence generation using UIO sequences. Computer Communications 16, 653–661 (1993)
25. Ural, H., Whittier, D.: Distributed testing without encountering controllability and observability problems. Information Processing Letters 88(3), 133–141 (2003)

26. Ural, H., Williams, C.: Generating checking sequences for a distributed test architecture. In: IFIP TestCom, Sophia Antipolis, France, pp. 146–162 (2003)
27. Ural, H., Williams, C.: Constructing checking sequences for distributed testing. Formal Aspects of Computing 18(1), 84–101 (2006)
28. Ural, H., Wu, X., Zhang, F.: On minimizing the lengths of checking sequences. IEEE Transactions on Computers 46, 93–99 (1997)
29. Yang, B., Ural, H.: Protocol conformance test generation using multiple UIO sequences with overlapping. In: ACM SIGCOMM 1990: Communications, Architectures, and Protocols, Twente, The Netherlands (September 1990)
30. Young, Y.C., Tai, K.C.: Observation inaccuracy in conformance testing with multiple testers. In: Proc. of IEEE WASET, pp. 80–85 (1998)

Testing from X-Machine Specifications

Kirill Bogdanov

Department of Computer Science, The University of Sheffield
Regent Court, 211 Portobello Street, Sheffield S1 4DP, UK
K.Bogdanov@dcs.shef.ac.uk

Abstract. The chapter describes how to model software containing complex data using X-machines and how test generation can be performed from such models. Testing using X-machines can be used to demonstrate specific results by testing: one may even claim that an implementation is behaviourally-equivalent to a specification if testing did not reveal defects. The ability to make such claims requires a tester to be precise in what is actually being tested and what has to be assumed. A number of assumptions underlying the testing method are described including what can be done when they cannot be satisfied.

1 Introduction

Finite-state machines are useful for modelling systems which do not rely on rich data. Many real systems use numerous variables, each of which may take many different values; directly representing such systems as finite-state machines leads to a known problem of state explosion, in that the number of states in a finite-state machine representing such a system becomes too big for model-checking or testing methods to complete in realistic amount of time. For this reason, a lot of existing papers seek to simplify a system in some way, but not to over-simplify, so that results of model-checking or testing from a simplified system can be related to the original one. This chapter describes a specific approach to such a simplification and the related testing method, advocated in papers devoted to X-machines and shows its relation to the existing work. The presentation is deliberately informal, introducing the ideas of how things work and why; a purely formal description can be found in [BHI+06].

1.1 Software Testing

Software testing has been traditionally viewed as a way to exercise a system in an attempt to break it [Mye79]. Identification of the number of faults remaining in a program once testing is complete gave rise to software fault estimation models [Woo96] which use the number of defects found during development and aim to estimate the number left. One may reasonably expect that both a highly-complex subsystem and the one with a large number of defects previously detected in it will be relatively error-prone, however models estimating the number of defects left do not provide any information on the type of remaining defects. They serve

R.M. Hierons et al. (Eds.): Formal Methods and Testing, LNCS 4949, pp. 184–208, 2008.

as a risk-management tool for a business to decide when to ship a product rather than a guide to developers.

Exhaustive testing, in other words, the one where all possible sequences of inputs are attempted, will be able to find all faults, but it is also too time-consuming to be of a practical value. For instance, there is an infinite number of possible sequences of button presses for programs with a user interface, hence exhaustive testing of most programs will never terminate. Choosing the 'relevant' inputs from an infinite set of them is the problem of testing. Since not all possible sequences will be attempted, it is necessary to extrapolate from results of executing a small sample of possible inputs, to other possible sequences.

A lot of software testing is based on the coverage concept: a program which is more thoroughly tested is the one which has more constructs of it visited (covered) during testing. This idea makes it possible to test software for which no specification or any kind of model exists, only the source code. At the same time, it does not permit one to draw definite conclusions about the quality of software once testing is complete. There is nothing like 'such and such faults are not present', it is more like 'covered so much, seems ok'. In the area where latent faults may cause a very costly failure, such as in telecommunications, there was a demand for better testing methods. It turned out that many network protocols can be modelled as finite-state machines (*FSM*) and a lot of work has been done in testing from FSM, in relation to testing of such protocols. Due to their simplicity, very powerful testing methods from FSM exist, permitting one, for instance, to demonstrate by testing that an implementation is equivalent to a specification, under specific conditions.

Given a specification and an implementation, the problem whether they have the same behaviour is not decidable in general; testing aims to look into a specific part of each of the two systems (i.e., a small decidable part of the overall problem). The rest (necessarily undecidable) has to be contained in the *assumptions*. These assumptions are known in different papers under the name of *test hypothesis* [Gau95] or *fault model* (described, for instance, in paper [Pet00]). How good or bad a testing method is can be judged from two perspectives: mathematical and practical. The former is to do with (1) whether equivalence or conformance of an implementation to a specification can be demonstrated by testing (subject to assumptions) (2) the range of systems which can be tested using any given method and (3) how easy it is to justify the assumptions of this method. From a practical point of view, it all depends on the range of systems a particular company needs to test, how hard it is to apply a method and whether the method does a better job than methods already in use by the said company.

1.2   The Problem of Abstraction

Many real systems tend to be rather complex, which stems from the complexity of tasks they have to complete. For instance, an email client has to be able to retrieve messages from a server in response to user requests, decode different types of messages, format them for presentation, include a text editor to compose messages and send them. This may seem like a very brief description, but even retrieving messages could be a complex problem on its own: the client has to utilise a specific protocol to talk to a server (perhaps even negotiate the one to use), the server may respond with a valid message, with garbage, respond with either of this multiple times, return an error or fail to respond at all. It is important to be able to check whether an email system is capable of handling these errors without loss of data, regardless of the order in which they appear. Methods developed for finite-state machines are very powerful in this respect, so it seems like a good idea to apply them to such a complex system. This in turn requires a system to be represented as a finite-state machine (FSM) in which every combination of values of program's variables has to be represented by a state. Even for a program with a hundred 32-bit variables, the total state space is $2^{32*100} \approx 10^{963}$. In testing of such a system, one cannot realistically expect to explore the whole of this state space directly; moreover, this may often be unnecessary. For instance, when testing network protocols, such as handshake or quality of service, it may not matter which data is being transmitted; in testing from a user interface, one may expect the network to work reliably. In addition, some parts of the email application will be provided by an operating system, which could make them 'trustworthy' and hence details of their operation could be omitted from the model used as a basis for test generation. This leads to an important question: where do we draw boundaries between the parts to include in FSM model and those not to? If one attempts to test a subsystem which is too complex, it may take too long in practice to explore even 10^{10} states; moreover, a complex system is a lot more difficult to control and observe than a simple one. Finally, a failing test may be notoriously hard to debug. One may consider splitting a system into a number of parts and testing each of them using the best method available. The conclusion of correctness of an implementation can then be drawn from results of testing and the approach taken to decomposition, provided the assumptions (mentioned above) made by each of the testing methods utilised are satisfied. This is not the only way to test a system with a large state space. A possible alternative is to limit testing to specific parts of a system a developer is interested in. This is the idea behind testing using a test purpose [GP05]; the paper [PBG04] considers both limiting state identification (Section 4.3) to relevant subsets of states and usage of an abstraction technique.

In a similar way to finite-state machines, X-machines contain a transition diagram, but labels of transitions in X-machines are names of functions which perform computations, this way X-machines describe possible sequences in which these functions can be executed. The X-machine testing method was developed to demonstrate absence of specific control-flow defects in an implementation (specifically, to check the equivalence of transition diagrams between a specification and an implementation), under assumptions that (a) an implementation can be modelled with an X-machine containing the same functions (which also have to be tested) and (b) certain conditions on both a specification and an implementation are satisfied. These conditions are not always possible to ensure; in situations where they do not hold, the method can be modified to take specific properties of a system into account in order not to weaken the conclusions of testing [Van02, BH01]. If a system is being built in consideration that it will have to be tested (a rather desirable expectation!), one may introduce facilities into it, in order to make testing easier. The splitting of testing into that of functions and a transition diagram provided by X-machines offers a possible method to structure testing of a complex system; transition diagram testing corresponds to an integration testing of functions [Pre94].

2   Introduction to X-Machines

Consider a simple email client which communicates with an email server. A complete email client has to have an interface, including message view and composition windows and many other parts; for simplicity, only the message-retrieving part is described here. A user is presented with a list of messages from which he or she can request any to be retrieved and the client will request this message from the server and display it on a screen. It takes time to retrieve a message, so an impatient user may click again, instructing the client to obtain a new message. A transition diagram of an X-machine describing such a system is shown in Figure 1; this diagram only contains labels which give names to computations. The computations themselves (called *functions*) have to be described elsewhere and in the case of the email client, they are shown in Table 1.

The initial state is the idle **I** state, corresponding to the email client waiting for user's clicks; this state is denoted by an arrow pointing at it out of nowhere. If a user clicks on the message already being displayed, the transition with the *sel_same* label is taken to ignore the click, otherwise, *sel_diff* records the number (ID) of the new message to display, sends a request to the email server and displays the 'loading' message. The **R** state corresponds to the client waiting for the server to respond; upon receipt of the body of the requested message, the *retr_curr* transition is taken to the **I** state and the message is displayed to a user. The server may take time to respond and an impatient user may click again on the same or a different message. In the first case, the *sel_same* transition is taken and the click is ignored; in the latter, a new request is sent to a server by *sel_diff*. If the server does not report an error in response to the new request, the previous one is assumed to have been cancelled, and the server starts retrieving the new message; when finished, the new message is returned by the server causing *retr_curr* to be taken from **R** to **I**. If an error is reported, the *retr_fail* transition is taken to the **W** state; this is the case when the client has to wait until the server has finished fetching the old message before resubmitting the request for the new one, once again. The client waits in the **W** state, recording the number of the last message clicked upon by a (very impatient) user. Once the server responds, one of the *retr_prev* or the *retr_curr* transitions is taken. The former corresponds to the server responding with the previously-requested message and the client responds by requesting the most recent message asked for by a user to be retrieved; the latter corresponds to the situation where a user clicked on the message he/she asked for before and the one the server fetched.

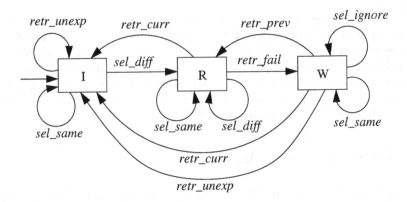

Fig. 1. A simple email message retrieving system

It is theoretically possible for the server to return a failure in the **I** or **W** states, which is a sign of some kind of internal problem with the server; the client reports this error.

So far, the transitions in the model have only been described informally, without any details of communication between the email client and the outside world, as well as the kind of data the client should store. Now we turn to the formal description of the behaviour. Let us assume that the input from a user is a message number to retrieve and the client has to output the text of a message it receives from the server; communication with the server is by sending a message number and the response is either the body of the message or a failure report. For this reason, commands sent to the server are outputs of the client and responses from the server are client's inputs. It is assumed that a failure may only be reported by the server if a request is submitted before the server had a chance to respond to the previous request. Traditionally, a set of inputs (*input alphabet*) of an X-machine is denoted by Σ and the set of outputs is denoted by Γ. For the client $\Sigma = (\mathbb{N} \cup \{\bot\}) \times (\text{TEXT} \times \mathbb{N} \cup \{\text{'FAIL'}, \bot\}) \setminus \{(\bot, \bot)\}$, where the first part $\mathbb{N} \cup \{\bot\}$ reflects the number of a message a user has clicked on and the second part $\text{TEXT} \times \mathbb{N} \cup \{\text{'FAIL'}, \bot\}$ reflects a response from the server. The response can either contain a body of a message retrieved together with its number or an error flag received from the server. The number of the retrieved message is necessary in the case when multiple requests are sent to the server by the repeated execution of the *sel_diff* transition from the **R** state, followed by the *retr_fail* transition, because in this case it is not known which of those requests have been honoured by the server. $\bot$-values are included to indicate that no data is received from either a user or the email server. The value $(\bot, \bot)$ is excluded from the input alphabet because there is no need to consider the case when no input is received. The only situation when this may be useful is when timeouts are considered, but they seem best dealt with using special 'timeout' inputs. The set of possible outputs (*output alphabet*) of the considered X-machine is $\Gamma = \text{TEXT} \times (\mathbb{N} \cup \{\bot\})$, describing text to display on the screen for a user to see and the request to the email server. It is assumed that the email client always updates the screen, but does not always send a request to the email server (indicated using the $\perp$ value in the second part of the output tuple). In the model of the client, the source of an input (a user or the server) and the destination of an output corresponds to a particular element in the input/output tuples.

The email system has to store the currently selected message and the total number of messages in a user's mailbox (the simple model considered does not account for retrieving or updating the total number). This way, it can detect when a user chose a different message to the one which was requested last. As has been hinted above, transitions of an X-machine can perform non-trivial computations; in practice they have to be both computable and easy to test (described in Section 4.4). Data stored by an X-machine is called *Memory*; it can be accessed and modified by all functions; for the email client, memory has to contain a number of a message last selected by a user, text to be displayed to the user and the total number of messages in the user's mailbox. The type for such a memory is $M = \mathbb{N} \times \textbf{TEXT} \times \mathbb{N}$. Text stored in memory is primarily intended to store an email message shown to a user; in a more complex email reader, there would be functions to perform a search within a message. When a message is being retrieved, a user may be confused to see an old message when the new one has been selected and *sel_same* executes; for this reason, this text is replaced with the '`loading`' message by the *sel_diff* function.

Both finite-state machines and X-machines are idle in states; when an input is received from an environment, they instantly perform a computation and produce an output. In the actual fact, a computation may take time, but this should be imperceptible to an environment, which should see a response arrive instantly. Every transition can be described as a function $\Sigma \times M \to M \times \Gamma$, taking an input and the current value of memory and producing an output and the new value of memory. The set of functions used in a given X-machine is denoted by Φ and for the email client $\Phi = \{sel\_same, sel\_diff, sel\_ignore, retr\_curr, retr\_prev, retr\_fail, retr\_unexp\}$. The same name can label more than one transition, as evidenced by the *sel_same* function. Given that transitions compute functions, the term 'precondition' used in the table can be replaced with 'domain' (denoted $\textbf{dom}$) and a more mathematical treatment of X-machines later in this chapter will use $\textbf{dom}$. In order to complete the X-machine model of the email client, one only needs to define the initial value of memory, $m_0 = (0, ``", total)$, assuming that $total > 0$ denotes the total number of messages in the mailbox. Formally, an X-machine is defined as a tuple $Z = (\Sigma, \Gamma, Q, M, \Phi, F, q_0)$. Most elements of this tuple have been defined above, the rest are Q, denoting the set of states $Q = \{\textbf{I}, \textbf{R}, \textbf{W}\}$, $q_0 = \textbf{I}$ denoting the initial state and F describing the next-state function $F : Q \times \Phi \to Q$. Function F is most commonly depicted graphically as a transition diagram, and such a diagram is typically expected to contain all states Q and the initial state q_0, $\forall q \in Q . \exists \phi \in \Phi . (q, \phi) \in \textbf{dom}\, F$, $q_0 \in Q$. With these definitions, it is possible to express what it means for an X-machine to take a transition from a state $q \in Q$ with memory $m \in M$ in response to an input $\sigma \in \Sigma$: the transition taken will be labelled by some function $\phi \in \Phi$ from the current state such that a precondition of this function is satisfied,

Table 1. Functions of the email client X-machine

function name	input Σ (user, server)	precondition on input and current value of memory (curr, msg, total)	new memory value	output Γ (user, server)
sel_same	$(n, \perp)$	$n = curr \vee$ $n \geq total$	$(curr, msg, total)$	$(msg, \perp)$
sel_diff	$(n, \perp)$	$n \neq curr \wedge$ $n < total$	$(n, \text{'loading'}, total)$	$(\text{'loading'}, n)$
sel_ignore	$(n, \perp)$	$n \neq curr \wedge$ $n < total$	$(n, msg, total)$	$(\text{'loading'}, \perp)$
retr_curr	$(\perp, (txt, m))$	$txt \neq \text{'FAIL'} \wedge$ $curr = m$	$(m, txt, total)$	$(txt, \perp)$
retr_prev	$(\perp, (txt, m))$	$txt \neq \text{'FAIL'} \wedge$ $curr \neq m$	$(curr, msg, total)$	$(\text{'loading'}, curr)$
retr_fail	$(\perp, \text{'FAIL'})$	true	$(curr, msg, total)$	$(\text{'loading'}, \perp)$
retr_unexp	$(\perp, \text{'FAIL'})$	true	$(curr, \text{'error'}, total)$	$(\text{'error'}, \perp)$

$(q, \phi) \in \text{dom} \, F \wedge (\sigma, m) \in \text{dom} \, \phi$. The new state will be $q' = F(q, \phi)$; the output γ and the new memory m' will satisfy $(m', \gamma) = \phi(\sigma, m)$.

As has been mentioned above, every label of an X-machine computes a function; the transition diagram of an X-machine determines which sequences of these functions can be executed. Execution of a sequence of functions is similar to a computation of a composition of these functions, because each of them operates on the value of memory updated by the previous function; such a composition takes a sequence of input symbols (each from a set Σ) and computes a sequence of outputs (each of which is from set Γ). For this reason, one may consider an X-machine to compute a function $\Sigma^* \rightarrow \Gamma^*$ (where A^* is a Kleene star, i.e., for some set A, A^* denotes a set of all finite sequences with elements from set A; set A^* contains an infinite number of elements). In order to define this function, one has to start by defining possible paths through a transition diagram: a *path* from a state q is a sequence of functions $\phi_1 \ldots \phi_k$ such that for every $i \in 1..k \, . \, (q_i, \phi_i) \in \text{dom} \, F \wedge q_{i+1} = F(q_i, \phi_i); \, q_1 = q$. Intuitively, it is a sequence of functions such that one can take a transition from q labelled with ϕ_1, from the target state of this transition, there is a transition labelled with ϕ_2 and so on. A function $\|\phi_1 \ldots \phi_k\|$ computed by a sequence of functions $\phi_1 \ldots \phi_k$ can be defined inductively as follows. First, for an empty input sequence ϵ, the result is an empty sequence of outputs and the starting memory value $\|\epsilon\|(\epsilon, m) = (m, \epsilon)$. Second, assume that for a sequence of inputs $\sigma_1 \ldots \sigma_k$, an X-machine executes a sequence $\phi_1 \ldots \phi_k$ of functions such that $\|\phi_1 \ldots \phi_k\|(\sigma_1 \ldots \sigma_k, m) = (m_k, \gamma_1 \ldots \gamma_k)$ ($k = 0$ corresponds to an empty sequence). In this case, $\|\phi_1 \ldots \phi_k \phi_{k+1}\|(\sigma_1 \ldots \sigma_k \sigma_{k+1}, m_k) = (m_{k+1}, \gamma_1 \ldots \gamma_k \gamma_{k+1})$ where $(\sigma_{k+1}, m_k) \in \text{dom} \, \phi_{k+1}$ and $(m_{k+1}, \gamma_{k+1}) = \phi_{k+1}(m_k, \sigma_{k+1})$. Combining the notion of paths with that of functions $\|\phi_1 \ldots \phi_k\|$, it is possible to define a function $f_Z : \Sigma^* \rightarrow \Gamma^*$ computed by an X-machine Z in the following way: $f_Z(\epsilon) = \epsilon$ and for $k > 0$, $f_Z(\sigma_1 \ldots \sigma_k) = \gamma_1 \ldots \gamma_k$ if there is a path $\phi_1 \ldots \phi_k$ from state q_0 such that $(\sigma_1 \ldots \sigma_k, m_0) \in \mathrm{dom}\,\|\phi_1 \ldots \phi_k\|$ and $\|\phi_1 \ldots \phi_k\|(\sigma_1 \ldots \sigma_k, m_0) = (m, \gamma_1 \ldots \gamma_k)$.

Since an X-machine computes a function, there is no reason why it cannot be used as a function of another X-machine. The idea of X-machines as functions has been developed in [Sta02, Sta06] where a behaviour of an X-machine is considered to be a union of compositions of its functions, over all paths through its transition diagram (typically an infinite number of paths). In a sense, this is how X-machines were originally introduced by Eilenberg [Eil74], where transition functions operated on a data structure called X, comprising a sequence of inputs, a sequence of outputs and memory. Behaviour of X-machines was a composition of such functions along possible paths; this explains the reason why the term 'X-machines' was introduced. The same idea can be expressed as a Kleene algebra [Koz94] where · is interpreted as function composition and + as a union. Many different types of X-machines were introduced in the literature, such as those which may spontaneously take transitions without consuming an input or those producing a sequence of output symbols rather than a single symbol. For simplicity, this chapter focuses on 'stream' X-machines which consume exactly one input per transition they take and produce exactly one output symbol.

Most of the work on testing from X-machines considers functions used on transitions to be defined separately from a transition diagram and satisfy properties which are convenient for testing. Unlike extended finite-state machines (EFSM) [CK93, PBG04], Harel statecharts [HN96] and UML [OMG03], there is no specific language defined in order to describe the behaviour of such functions in X-machines: any language is in principle good enough. Treatment of transition functions as abstract entities satisfying specific properties is the key difference between most papers on X-machines and papers on extended finite-state machines: the latter tend to consider EFSM as a compact representation of a corresponding FSM; for X-machines, the aim is not to delve into the structure of functions.

3   Well-Formedness of X-Machines

3.1   Features of a Transition Diagram

If the diagram of the email client did not have a transition with *retr_fail* label, the state **W** would be unreachable and hence redundant. Another example of a redundant state is shown in Figure 2. The X-machine on the left of the figure has a redundant state, because states **B** and **C** are equivalent: from either of them, the only possible sequence of functions is an infinite sequence of *b*s. By

Fig. 2. An example of a non-minimal X-machine

associating every state with a set of paths which can be taken from it, it is possible to remove redundant states; for example, an X-machine on the right of Figure 2 is equivalent to the one on the left of that figure. A transition diagram which does not have redundant states is further called *minimal*. It is also possible to have a nondeterministic X-machine, where there are two transitions with the same label from a state, leading to two different states. Standard finite-state automata minimisation approach [Coh96] can be used here to turn a nondeterministic X-machine into a behaviourally-equivalent deterministic one. The described problems correspond to properties of F, encoding the transition diagram; for instance, if F is a function (many-to-one), then the transition diagram is necessarily deterministic.

At this point, it is necessary to mention that the above discussion only considered a transition diagram, with no attention paid to computations performed by functions; in the situation where b has a condition which the value of memory produced by a violates, both machines in Figure 2 would have redundant transitions. Unfortunately, it is not in general possible to determine if there is a sequence of inputs such that a given sequence of arbitrary computations can be followed; for this reason, it is *assumed* for testing that an arbitrary sequence of functions can always be attempted. This can be accomplished if a system under construction is built to be testable; a rather direct approach [IH97] to this problem is to introduce a special input per function, so that if that input arrives, the precondition of the corresponding function will be true. In response to such an input, a function may have no choice but do nothing at all since the value of memory may be such that this function cannot perform its computation. The described condition is called *input-completeness* and the details are provided in Section 4.4. The described separation of computations of functions from a transition diagram has both advantages and disadvantages; an advantage is that methods developed for finite-state machines can be applied to X-machines, including FSM testing methods and minimisation. The two main disadvantages are that (1) the model may be harder to build since developers have to make a decision what to hide in functions and what is to be included on the diagram, and (2) for testing, it is necessary to ensure that an implementation can be modelled as an X-machine with the same set of functions. Both of these problems are described in the testing section (Section 4).

3.2   Nondeterminism Associated with Functions

X-machines can be nondeterministic not only in the FSM sense described above, where there are multiple transitions with the same label from the same state. First, transitions may actually compute relations rather than functions, hence an output and a new memory value from such a relation may not be uniquely determined by a current memory and an input. For example, the *retr_fail* label can be defined to either report an error ('please wait') or keep the 'loading' message. For the email system, either could be appropriate, hence an X-machine specification can include both options, leaving it to an implementor to make the final decision.

The *sel_same* function can be defined so as to ignore a click on the same message but occasionally clear the screen if a click is received on a message number beyond the current number of messages ($n \geqslant total$). This does not seem to be an unreasonable choice given that the graphical user interface for this client should never make it possible to click on messages with numbers above the current total number of messages. With such a function and an interface, the email client will nevertheless be deterministic; i.e., f_Z will be a function when restricted to inputs supplied by an interface.

The second cause of nondeterminism is that domains of relations/functions may intersect, hence for some inputs and memory values any of a number of possible transitions may execute. For example, if the condition that $n < total$ was missing from the definition of the *sel_diff* label, in the case when a user chose $n > total$, preconditions of both *sel_same* and *sel_diff* would be satisfied. If in this situation the X-machine was in the **I** state, then either of the two transitions could be taken. Often, nondeterministic specifications are considered erroneous, however there are many cases when they may have to be nondeterministic, such as when an implementer is given a choice as to what to do or when modelling an inherently nondeterministic system. Most implementations are deterministic, but some are not, such as network protocols where timing may play a role in messages arriving in a different order. There are known testing methods which permit testing *conformance* of an implementation to a specification, even for nondeterministic specifications and/or implementations. Checking for determinism is easy at the level of the transition diagram, but this problem is not in general decidable for functions.

Further in this chapter it is assumed that X-machines are deterministic, this means that (1) F is a function, (2) each of the elements of Φ computes a function and (3) $\forall q \in Q; \phi_1, \phi_2 \in \Phi$. $\phi_1 \neq \phi_2 \wedge (q, \phi_1) \in \mathrm{dom}\, F \wedge (q, \phi_2) \in \mathrm{dom}\, F \Rightarrow \mathrm{dom}\, \phi_1 \cap \mathrm{dom}\, \phi_2 = \emptyset$. The last statement says that any two different functions on transitions from the same state have to have non-intersecting domains. Every deterministic X-machine Z computes a function f_Z, however it is possible to build a nondeterministic X-machine computing a function if a composition of transition relations is a function. An example of this is an X-machine with only two possible paths, $\phi_a\phi_b\phi_c$ and $\phi_b\phi_a\phi_c$ and functions defined for all values of memory and input. Function ϕ_a can be defined to increment a memory variable by 1 and ϕ_b increment it by 2; with ϕ_c producing the value of this variable as an output, both of these paths produce the same output.

3.3   Completeness Associated with Computations of Labels of Transitions

It is perhaps most annoying to click a button on a screen, see it depress and release, and for nothing to change, especially if this is a 'delete message' button, since if clicked too many times, it may delete important messages (granted, undo facilities are usually available). This problem boils down to the following: can a system ignore an input? For the email system described, it is possible for both a response from the email server and a click from a user to arrive at the same time, in which case the input becomes $(n, (txt, m))$. No transitions are defined for such an input from any state of the email client. In order to ensure that there is a defined behaviour from the **R** state, the machine can be improved by extending the definition of *retr_curr* and introducing the new *retr_sel_diff* function. The former will have to accept the $(n, (txt, m))$ input under the condition that $n = m \land txt \neq$ 'FAIL' and if so behave as it is currently defined. Function *retr_sel_diff* will have to accept such an input too, under the condition the $n \neq m \land n < total \land txt \neq$ 'FAIL' and in response output ('loading', n) and make the new value of memory $(n, \text{'loading'}, total)$; such a new function has to label a transition from **R** to **R**, in a similar way to *sel_diff*. Finally, *retr_fail* can be extended to respond to $(n, \text{'FAIL'})$ and store the newly-requested message number as *curr*. In a similar way, one can extend functions on transitions from the **I** and **W** states. Beyond these ideas, formal definitions of these functions are not provided here since they are not important for the subsequent elaboration of the ideas of testing from X-machines. It is expected that the email server will never spontaneously report a failure, thus the *retr_unexp* cannot realistically be expected to be taken. Nevertheless, it has been included in the specification for completeness. When the email server responds with a message body in the **R** state, $curr = m$ is always true if the server can be expected not to retrieve messages it was not asked to and hence although there is no behaviour defined from this state when $curr \neq m$, this cannot occur in the course of operation of the client.

One may argue that a specification has to be *completely defined*, i.e., defined for arbitrary sequences of inputs. For this reason, it is typical to assume that when an input arrives for which no behaviour is defined, the system will do nothing in response; in terms of X-machines, this means that it has to remain in the same state with the same value of memory. An alternative way to make a system completely defined is to introduce a special error state which is entered whenever an input is received when no transition can be taken in response. These two cases are known as 'implicitly defined' transitions in protocol testing [BP94]. Many specifications may be deliberately defined to be incomplete, to offer freedom for an implementer to add arbitrary extra functionality, as long as everything specified is properly implemented ('undefined by default' in protocol testing [BP94]). This may or may not be desirable; there are 'easter eggs' in some well-known programs such as the one in a spreadsheet application where entering a specific number in a specific column eventually leads to portraits of developers being displayed to a bemused user.

An implementation is often inherently complete, hence a possible way to implement an incompletely-defined specification is to ignore all 'unexpected' inputs. When an input arrives which cannot be ignored (such as when a method of an object is unexpectedly called and has to return another object), an implementer has to make decisions as to what behaviour to implement. Some of the choices made by the implementer could be wrong. One of such errors has been discussed above, where in a situation when a mouse click and a response from a server arrive both at the same time, the two may be ignored and hence the email client 'locks up', indefinitely waiting for a response from the server. Such an error could be rather hard to detect during developer testing since the probability of this happening under test is rather low and the lock-up may be very hard to reproduce using reports from users. For these reasons, it is important to develop specifications which are complete; the problem here is that since functions of X-machines are not constrained, checking for completeness is undecidable in the general case.

In order to define completeness, it is not appropriate to simply state that for every state and input there has to be a transition defined, because everything depends on memory. There could be no transitions defined for some values of it, but if such values are never reached in the course of execution of an X-machine, it does not matter. Using the definition of computation performed by a deterministic X-machine, one can define completeness by requiring $\forall k \in \mathbb{N}, (\sigma_1 \ldots \sigma_k) \in \text{dom } f_Z$ where $\sigma_i \in \Sigma$.

3.4   All States Are Terminal States

It is assumed in this chapter that all states of X-machines are terminal states. For finite-state machines, an output is only produced if an input sequence ends when a machine is in a terminal state. Same applies to X-machines and makes testing in the presence of non-terminal states rather more complex since state identification can depend on whether a particular sequence of functions can be followed or not. If a machine happens to enter a non-terminal state, no output will be produced by it, even if a particular sequence of functions can be followed. This is additionally complicated by the fact that a faulty implementation can have any state in it implemented as a non-terminal one. For this reason, it is assumed in this chapter that all states of both a specification and an implementation are terminal; the case when this is not so is considered by [Sta02] where a machine is expected to be modified so as to report (as an output) whether or not it has reached a terminal state.

4   X-Machine Testing Method

4.1   The Strategy of X-Machine Testing Method

The X-machine testing method [HI98, IH97] has originally been developed to test the transition diagram using the well-known FSM testing method, called the W method [Vas73, Cho78]. The X-machine testing method aims to test for the equivalence of the behaviour of an implementation, to a specification. This work has been subsequently extended to conformance testing of a deterministic implementation to a nondeterministic specification [HH04] as well as for equivalence testing of a nondeterministic implementation to a nondeterministic specification [IH00]. The [HH04] is the adaptation of the FSM state-counting method [PYB96] to X-machines; in the context of labelled-transition systems, conformance testing methods include [Tre96, LMN04].

The assumptions and the kinds of faults considered differ between different X-machine testing methods, but the fundamental abstraction assumption remains: it is assumed that an implementation can be modelled by an X-machine using the same (or conforming) functions as those in a specification. It is this assumption which makes it possible to use finite-state machine testing methods to check the equivalence or conformance of transition diagrams (the q_0 and F parts of the definition of an X-machine) between a specification and an implementation. If transition diagrams are equivalent and functions Φ behave the same, it essentially follows that an implementation computes the same function f_Z as a specification.

When the testing method was initially developed, it was assumed that functions used by an implementation are accessible to a tester and hence can be tested before testing a transition diagram. Testing of such functions can be done using, for instance, the category-partition testing method [OB88]; if a function on a transition is itself modelled by an X-machine, it can also be tested using the X-machine testing method. The condition that functions are available for separate testing can be hard to satisfy, for instance, the email client could be implemented as a single procedure, querying an operating system for events and using if-then-else or switch statements to branch to different parts of the procedure depending on an input and a state. This way, an implementation is essentially monolithic and hence it is impossible to 'extract' functions such as sel_diff out of it to check if these functions operate correctly. For this reason, an extension to the X-machine testing method was developed [Ipa04] in order to test functions 'together' with testing a transition diagram. This is not a perfect solution: functions are still required to satisfy a specific condition, but they no longer have to be tested in isolation.

4.2   The Approach to Testing X-Machines Using the W Method

This section focuses on how X-machines can be tested using the W method, for details refer to [HI98, IH97]; the same approach can be used to adapt other finite-state machine testing methods such as Wp [FBK+91], HSI [LPB94] or UIO and others, described in [RDT95]. As described above, the idea is to use an FSM testing method to test that a transition diagram of an implementation is equivalent to the one of a specification. One can start testing by attempting to visit every state and checking that the correct state has been entered. For instance, one would like to enter the **W** state and verify that such a state has actually been implemented. Afterwards, it is necessary to check all transitions from every state; for each function on a transition from it, this involves (1) supplying an input satisfying a precondition of the function and (2) verifying that the target state of the corresponding transition has been entered.

For the email client, testing of the retr_curr transition from the **R** state to the **I** one involves entering the **R** state by taking the sel_diff transition, then attempting the retr_curr transition and finally checking that the **I** state has been reached. Starting from the initial state and initial memory value, for sel_diff, the corresponding input is a mouse-click on any message with a number above zero. When sel_diff is executed, a tester has to verify that the correct request has been sent to an email server and the 'loading' message is displayed on a screen. For testing, one may replace a server with a *stub* and a user with a *driver* [Pre94]. Transition *retr_curr* has to follow *sel_diff* in this test, so an input which is a 'success' response from a stub of a server has to be supplied; *retr_curr* should display the message provided by the stub, on a screen. If a different output is produced to each of these two inputs, the implementation is considered to have failed the test. How to check whether the correct state was entered is described below.

Finally, it is necessary to check that no unexpected transitions are present from any states; for this type of testing to be carried out, one has to attempt all other functions from every state. For instance, one would like to verify that a transition with the *retr_fail* label is not implemented from the **I** state.

4.3 State Verification

State verification involves checking that the system under test has entered the expected state. There are two overall approaches to performing this task, attempting to retrieve values of a system's variables and by attempting further transitions. For the email client, the current state may be stored in a variable and a developer may add a special method to be used during testing to retrieve a value of it. Identifying a state by taking further transitions involves attempting sequences of functions from each state and checking whether a particular sequence can be followed or not, the same idea as state identification for a finite-state acceptor. For every pair of states, one may identify a path which exists from one of them but not from the other. For instance, a sequence consisting of a singleton function *retr_unexp* distinguishes between **R** and the other two states. Likewise, *retr_prev* distinguishes between **W** and all other states. In some cases, more than a single sequence may have to be used to distinguish a state from all other states. A W set is a set of such sequences for every pair of states. It can only be generated if the transition diagram of an X-machine does not contain behaviourally-equivalent states, which is the case for minimal X-machines (Section 3.1). The algorithm for construction of the W set is described in [Gil62].

Identification of states by accessing variables requires access to the internal data of a system under test, but produces fewer test sequences. The same problem exists in finite-state machine testing. Accessing system's variables tends to be used in testing of object-oriented software [MK94], where it is expected to be easy to obtain values of member variables of objects. Taking sequences of transitions is used in protocol testing, such as to check compatibility of some vendor's implementation of a protocol where internal data of such an implementation is not accessible. It is also possible to use a combination of the two, where some state-related data of an implementation is available [Car00, BH02]. The X-machine testing has been originally developed as a pure black-box testing method (verifying states by taking transitions); it has subsequently been used for testing of VHDL designs where states were identified by observation of internal data [Van02].

Having described the idea of the testing method, the formal definition of a test set is $T = C * W \cup C * \Phi * W$. Here the C set (called a *state cover* set) is a set of paths such that for every state Q, there is a path in C which leads from q_0 to that state. For two sets A and B, $A * B = \{ab \mid a \in A, b \in B\}$ is a set of sequences where every sequence from A is concatenated with every sequence of B. The idea of the $C * W$ part is to visit every state and verify it; $C * \Phi * W$ attempts every function from every state and verifies the entered state. The test set can be re-written as $T = C * (\{\epsilon\} \cup \Phi) * W$. Some functions are not expected to be implemented from every state, in this case, it is enough to confirm this; for this reason, it is not necessary to attempt elements of W after attempting every function which is not expected to label a transition from a state under test.

Compared to the W method, there are FSM testing methods [FBK+91, LPB94] which produce smaller test suites without weakening conclusions obtained by testing. In order to reduce the number of test sequences, these methods use smaller sets than W to identify states and can be used for testing of X-machines in a similar way to the W method.

4.4   Design for Test Conditions

Regardless which testing method is used to produce test sequences from an X-machine transition diagram, the result is a set of sequences of functions, not sequences of inputs. For instance, inputs necessary to follow *sel_diff retr_curr* were described above. For each sequence $\phi_1 \ldots \phi_k$ generated by an X-machine testing method, one has to find $\sigma_1 \ldots \sigma_k$ such that $(\sigma_1 \ldots \sigma_k, m_0) \in \mathrm{dom} \|\phi_1 \ldots \phi_k\|$. It is important to note that test sequences of functions are generated with the aim to explore a transition diagram rather than explore the expected behaviour of an implementation. As a result, such sequences could be difficult to follow, for instance, a test method is likely to generate a sequence of *sel_diff retr_fail* from the **I** state. Such a sequence cannot occur in practice because a server may only report a failure if it is sent an unexpected request, and only if it cannot cope with it. For the email client, *retr_fail* can be attempted by getting a stub to send test messages, including a 'FAIL' to the client. Preconditions of functions can make certain paths difficult to follow and the problem whether an arbitrary sequence of functions can be attempted is undecidable in general. There are three possible ways to tackle this:

1. Assume that if a tester cannot find inputs to follow a particular sequence of functions, such a sequence cannot be followed even in a faulty implementation. This assumption requires changes to the testing method since one is no longer assuming that an implementation may contain an essentially arbitrary transition diagram.
2. Attempt to take a longer sequence of transitions, so that memory is set to a value such that the function of interest can be attempted. In this case, one has to ensure that even in a faulty implementation both memory and a state will be set to the expected values before a function of interest is attempted. This is only easy to ensure if variables contributing to both memory and state are easily accessible to a tester, as has been the case in [Van02].
3. Develop both a specification and an implementation in order to make it easy to perform testing. This may require adding extra inputs to functions which

contain complex preconditions, so as to force those preconditions to become true when such inputs are supplied under test. This circumvents the problem of finding the appropriate inputs.

Testing of a transition diagram involves running sequences of functions in much the same way as integration testing of multiple units of software involves running these units. For this reason, testing of a transition diagram can reveal defects in processing functions. This way of testing is substantially less effective if extra test inputs are used because such inputs are going to be used when preconditions of functions cannot be satisfied and hence functions will have to perform dummy rather that real computations.

Formally, the *input-completeness* condition can be defined such that $\forall \phi \in \varPhi; m \in M . \exists \sigma \in \varSigma . (\sigma, m) \in \mathsf{dom}\, \phi$. This is a rather strict condition: most of the time, values of memory attained during testing will not cover the whole of M; one may deliberately choose a set of inputs for testing so as to limit the set of attained memory values to a value known to a tester (which can be conservatively approximated). As a consequence, it is possible to limit the condition of input-completeness only to values of memory which are going be reached during testing. The result is called *testing context*, refer for instance to [BHI$^+$06] for details.

There could be a number of functions which are attempted using the same input, such as *retr_fail* and *retr_unexp*, so there has to be a way to determine which of them has actually fired in an implementation in response to a common input. The former function displays 'loading' on a screen while the latter displays 'error'. Likewise, *retr_curr* and *retr_prev* are easy to tell apart by whether any data is sent to the server stub. If instead of displaying the 'loading' text, the old email message was displayed instead by *sel_ignore*, it would be difficult to tell the *sel_same* function from *sel_ignore*, because they would produce the same output for the same input. To distinguish them, one could add test outputs to these functions. The condition that every pair of functions can be distinguished based on their outputs is called *output-distinguishability* and is defined by $\forall \phi_1, \phi_2 \in \varPhi . \exists \sigma \in \varSigma; m, m_a, m_b \in M; \gamma \in \varGamma . \phi_1(\sigma, m) = (\gamma, m_a) \wedge \phi_2(\sigma, m) = (\gamma, m_b) \Rightarrow \phi_1 = \phi_2$. It says that if for any input and memory two functions produce the same output then these two are actually the same function. The notion of test context applies here too. For deterministic X-machines considered here, $m_a = m_b$; in testing of nondeterministic X-machines with relations on transitions [IH00, HH04], different values of memory may be produced.

Adding distinct test outputs may be impossible if multiple functions are supposed to be implemented by the same piece of code, but in this case such functions are not really distinct. Let a *retr* function be used instead of *retr_curr* on a transition from the **R** state to the **I** one. *retr* can be defined to be only different from *retr_curr* in the precondition, so that *retr* is taken upon a receipt of $(\perp, (txt, m))$. In this case, function *retr_curr* is a special case of *retr* with a more complex precondition, hence the two are indistinguishable and mostly implemented by the same code. In this case, testing whether each of the two is implemented from each state has to focus on testing whether the common part exists from every state and whether the extra part of *retr_curr* is implemented.

It is hence suggested that such functions be split, so that *retr_curr* becomes *retr* and *retr_the_rest*.

A possible way to automate checking if design for test conditions are satisfied is to convert the whole X-machine into an FSM. This can be done using the tool developed to analyse EFSM and perform test generation from them [IF06] or the tool targeting X-machines [PKS03]. The downside is that the conversion may yield too many states for a meaningful analysis.

As described above, testing involves attempting every function from every state; this requires a way to enter those states after every test sequence. In a faulty implementation, it may not be known where test sequences end and a synchronising sequence [LY96] to enter a specific state may traverse untested transitions and hence may fail to work in a faulty implementation. For this reason, the testing method described requires a reliable reset to be implemented, which is used to bring an implementation to an initial state with an initial value of memory. It is then possible to use a sequence from the state cover set C to re-enter a state of interest. In FSM testing, it is possible to perform testing even when no reset is available [HU02, IU99], however this can produce relatively long test sequences. An extension of the work on FSM testing without reset to X-machines has not yet been done.

4.5   Extra States

An implementation may potentially contain more states than a specification. This may be related to how a system is implemented, such as when some code is copy-and-pasted. If an implementation is correct, every 'extra' state has to be behaviourally-equivalent to some state in a specification. For instance, the machine on the right of Figure 2 can be considered a specification and the one on the left an implementation with one extra state. Checking that all the extra states behave the same way as the corresponding states in a specification is also the task of testing, but it is made rather more difficult by the fact that extra states can be everywhere, in other words, any transition may potentially lead to such an extra state. Without a known upper bound on the potential number of such states, testing cannot find all faults in the transition diagram. For this reason, it is typically assumed that such a number is known before test generation commences; although it is possible to choose a higher number 'just in case', the amount of testing grows exponentially with the increase in this number. Let us assume that there could be only one extra state, but any transition from every state may lead into it. In this case, one has to try every possible function from every state in order to make sure that this state is entered. In order to verify that the extra state is behaviourally-equivalent to one of the states in a specification, it is necessary to attempt every function from it and verify that for each transition which fires, the entered state is correct. If there are two extra states, the only way to get to the second one could be from the first one, hence one has to attempt every pair of functions from every state.

If a minimal specification contains n states and a tester assumes that an implementation can have at most m states, the test set is

$$C * (\{\epsilon\} \cup \Phi \cup \Phi^2 \cup \ldots \cup \Phi^{m-n+1}) * W$$

where $\Phi^0 = \{\epsilon\}$ and $\Phi^p = \Phi * \Phi^{p-1}$. Compared to the test set from Section 4.3, higher powers of Φ are used to attempt to enter and test the behaviour of potential extra states. The described test set, when converted to sequences of inputs, is proven to be capable of detecting all faults [IH97], subject to the following conditions: (1) a specification is a deterministic and completely defined X-machine with a minimal transition diagram, satisfying input-completeness and output-distinguishability; (2) an implementation can be modelled as a deterministic X-machine with the same input and output alphabets, a known upper bound to the number of states and the same initial memory as a specification; (3) for every function of an implementation, there is a behaviourally-equivalent function in a specification; (4) both a specification and implementation feature a reliable reset.

4.6   Testing of Functions

As mentioned above, functions can be tested separately from a transition diagram. In cases where this is not possible, one may still perform the testing following [Ipa04]; it is assumed that functions are output-distinguishable.

Consider the problem of testing *retr_curr* from the **R** state: not only one has to attempt *retr_curr* with various inputs in order to test it, but this also has to be done from a specific state and with a predictable memory value. Indeed, for testing of a function $\Sigma \times M \to M \times \Gamma$, one has to control both memory and inputs. In a faulty implementation, *sel_diff* may be absent or lead to the wrong state. This is a problem faced by a tester. The solution is to start by testing functions from the initial state and initial memory value. Output-distinguishability guarantees that a tester will be confident that the right functions fire in response to inputs, hence functions leaving the **I** state can be tested. Afterwards, it is possible to attempt *sel_diff*, which should enter the **R** state and then attempt *retr_curr*. If following *sel_diff*, function *retr_curr* can be executed (and this will be known from output-distinguishability), then it can be tested, even if the state entered by *sel_diff* is wrong. Since *sel_diff* has been tested in advance, the memory value used during testing of *retr_curr* is known. With this, *retr_curr* can be tested. By repeating the process of testing functions further and further away from the initial state, but entering states to exercise those functions using only previously-tested functions, all functions of an implementation can be tested. Subsequently, a transition diagram can be tested as described above. This is the idea of the testing method. The problem of setting the memory value for testing functions is not considered by [Ipa04]; testing of functions can be expected to be performed entirely using inputs/outputs from a known memory value. If access to elements of memory necessary for testing of functions is not available, one may modify functions such that both an input and a representation of a memory value are supplied to a function as a part of a test input.

The first part, testing of functions, is performed using a *function cover* set V which is used to 'access' functions for testing of them, rather like *sel_diff* was used to access *retr_curr*. Formally, V is sequence of paths $v_1 \ldots v_k$, such that all of them can be followed from an initial state of a specification and one can introduce an order $\phi_1 \ldots \phi_k$ in which functions of an X-machine are tested, such that (1) $v_1 = \epsilon$ in order to access ϕ_1 from the initial state and (2) every v_i accesses ϕ_i using previously tested functions, $v_i \in \{\phi_1 \ldots \phi_{i-1}\}^*$ and $v_i \phi_i$ is a path which can be followed.

4.7   Building X-Machine Specifications That Are Useful for Testing

Deciding what to include in functions and what has to be a part of a transition diagram is precisely the problem of abstraction this chapter has started with. It is worth considering a few extreme cases in order to illustrate what to strive for.

The number of states can be chosen to be small or large. In the former case, the extreme situation is an X-machine with a single state and a number of transitions looping in this state, perhaps even a single transition encompassing all possible computations of a system. Since the X-machine testing method aims to test a transition diagram, all it can tell one is whether all transitions of a specification and no others are implemented, but since functions are expected to have been tested in advance, this is likely to be already known. For this reason, testing such a system using the X-machine testing method is unlikely to reveal anything new. On the other extreme, when every combination of values of memory variables is a part of a state, the end result is a huge finite-state machine, untestable due to its size. By constraining ranges of values of variables, it may be possible to reduce the number of states of the resulting automaton.

In general, the choice of what to include in a state and what in memory has to be governed by factors such as what kind of control needs testing. Indeed, if a subsystem under test only performs a simple computation, such as an addition, one can expect a category-partition testing method [OB88] to be enough. For this reason, one might wish to use a state-based testing method only where there is a non-trivial control flow.

The number of functions can also affect the model and how easy it is to test. On one extreme, there could be only one (or few) functions, packing a substantial complexity; on the other, every path through code in an implementation could be described by a separate function. The problem associated with testing from an X-machine with few functions lies with a (1) (likely) a small state-transition diagram and (2) difficulty of following sequences of them prescribed by the testing method, since given complex preconditions and data transformations performed by functions, it may be hard to devise a sequence of inputs to force a system to follow test sequences. Too many functions means a lot more testing, since the method assumes that any of them can erroneously be implemented from any state. For this reason, it may introduce substantially more test sequences than a tester may consider reasonable; a way to combat this problem is to constrain possible faulty implementations to those where only some functions may be erroneously implemented from some states.

Finally, one may attempt to decompose lengthy computations into sequences of functions, triggered by *tick*-inputs. In this case, the X-machine starts to resemble a flow-chart, where each stage of a computation is separated by a state.

For instance, the *retr_curr* label could be decomposed into *decompose* and *format* functions, with *decompose* splitting an email message received into parts (html, plain text parts and attachments) and decoding them; *format* could take html and 'simplify' it by removing links or perhaps even removing all html tags. Such flowchart models appear relatively artificial, in that even if an implementation performs a computation in similar stages, it is not likely to wait in every state for a tester to initiate the following stage of the computation. What's more important, is that from each state, it may be next to impossible to attempt functions other than those which are present from such a state in a specification. With design for test conditions consequently not satisfied, testing reduces to following specific paths rather than verifying that from every state, those transitions which are present in a specification, are actually implemented and there are no other transitions leaving those states.

4.8   Testing of Incomplete Systems

A specification and/or an implementation may be incomplete, in other words with no defined behaviour for specific combinations of states, memory values and inputs. This can make testing substantially more complex.

One of the problems testing from an incomplete system has been described in Section 3.3. Whoever decides to verify by testing that inputs in situations when no behaviour has been specified, are ignored, faces a difficult task: there (1) could be an infinite number of possible values of memory when certain inputs have to be ignored and (2) there is no indication as to which combinations of memory and input to choose and which not to. This is exactly the overall problem of software testing, described in Section 1.1; the fact that X-machines consist of functions and a transition diagram, makes it possible to test functions before testing a diagram and assume that if a function is executed in response to an input, such a function will fire in response to any other input in the domain of that function. There is no such structure for inputs which are expected to be ignored; for this reason, one may have to make an extra assumption that no functions beyond those specified may be present in a potentially faulty implementation. Such an assumption means that once one verifies that for every state, transitions with the expected functions are present and transitions with other specification functions are absent, upon receipt of an input for which no behaviour has been specified, an implementation will not have a function it can fire, hence such an input will be ignored.

Test sequence execution can be performed step-by-step or a whole sequence at a time. In the former case, one attempts and input and checks an output, then the next input is attempted and so on. In the latter case, a whole sequence of inputs is attempted and the output is compared with the expected one. In testing of an incomplete system which ignores unexpected inputs, the latter approach yields substantially less information: if inputs are applied one at a time, it is known which of them are ignored, if the whole input sequence is attempted and a shorter sequence of outputs is received, it is not known which inputs were ignored. This is the reason why [BGIH03] includes an empty sequence in the W set, to ensure that before checking that an implementation has entered a correct state, it is verified that the system under test has actually executed a path which is supposed to lead to that state.

Both the W method and its improvements [FBK+91, LPB94] expect every sequence from a state identification set to be attempted from every state to be identified, with a subsequent reset. If an implementation ignores an attempt to fire a transition with a particular label, it may be possible to assume that it remained in the same state with the same memory value and hence another function be attempted, without having to reset a system and re-run a test sequence to enter a state to be identified. This is the idea behind adaptive testing, where every test input may depend on the history of outputs received from a system under test. Nondeterministic systems may follow any of a number of different paths in response to a specific sequence of inputs, because for every input received an implementation may nondeterministically fire one of the available transitions. For this reason, in testing of nondeterministic X-machines [IH00, HH04], it is assumed that outputs provided by an implementation can be used to determine both the function executed and the new memory value each time such a nondeterministic decision is made; as a consequence, one would expect such tests to be adaptive. More recent work in the context of adaptive FSM testing [Hie04] has not yet been adapted for testing of X-machines.

It is also possible that situations in which a specification does not have a defined behaviour cannot occur in practice (this corresponds to 'forbidden transitions' in protocol testing [BP94]). For instance, if all events are collected in some kind of a queue and hence multiple of them cannot arrive simultaneously, it is not possible for both a button press and a server response to be received by the considered email client at the same time. The observation that a particular input or a sequence of inputs cannot arrive in practice can be used to reduce the amount of testing dramatically. For instance, one may assume that in a system containing a number of concurrently-executing X-machines, most functions of any of these X-machines cannot be used in any other X-machine. In terms of the email client, this means that *retr_fail* function cannot be used in the server. Another assumption could be that in any path through a transition diagram, specific labels can never follow others, even in a faulty implementation. For example, *retr_prev* cannot be immediately followed by *retr_fail*.

The problem of testing a system embedded in an environment which never supplies specific sequences of inputs and/or transforms output sequences from a system under test is known in FSM testing as *testing in context* [PYBD96]. In testing of timed input-output transition systems (TIOTS), the idea of context is known as environment [LMN04].

Finally, specific inputs may be impossible to apply in some states and hence states which would otherwise be distinguishable, will not be such. It is important to note that the amount of testing for such an incomplete system can be immense: in the context of FSM, testing of an implementation with a maximum of m states against a specification with n states can require a test set of Σ^{mn} [LPB94]. In the realm of finite-state machine testing, testing of incomplete systems has led to the development of specific testing methods [PY05, LPB94].

5   Conclusion and Applications

X-machines permit one to specify complex systems and at the same time manage the complexity of testing since a transition diagram and operations executed when transitions are taken can be tested separately. An adaptation of FSM testing methods to X-machines allows one to ascertain by testing that an implementation behaves the same as a specification (or conforms to it), subject to a number of assumptions described in this chapter.

Considering the 'usefulness' conditions of a testing method, mentioned in Section 1.1, it seems reasonable to claim that X-machine testing method (1) can be used to demonstrate equivalence/conformance of the behaviour of an implementation, to a specification; (2) is useful for testing software with a non-trivial control behaviour, where it is possible to draw a parallel between functions in a specification and those in an implementation. The conditions for applicability of the method (3) may be more or less hard to satisfy, but they are clearly defined. In practice, the X-machine testing method has been used for testing integrated circuits from VHDL source, for six months in the context of a major embedded microcontroller developer. As described in [BHI⁺06], not only X-machine tests took rather less time to develop than tests used by the company, they also executed in a much shorter span of time and found many more mutants of the source VHDL.

Compared to the one described here, a similar approach to abstraction has been applied to Harel statecharts in [BH01, BH02]; it turned out that relatively weak additional assumptions can reduce the amount of testing by many orders of magnitude [BH04]. A complex system may consist of a number of communicating parts; in the context of X-machines, one can represent each communicating subsystem with an X-machine, with a matrix holding the data being exchanged between them. Every cell ij can represent data being passed from the ith X-machine to the jth one. A system of communicating X-machines has a number of constraints imposed on it, which makes testing easier and stops communicating X-machines from engaging in an infinite sequence of communications. As a consequence, such a system behaves as a nondeterministic X-machine with a cross-product of states and transitions of the communicating X-machines. The testing method has been extended to testing of such systems in [IH02]; the main limitation is the size of the resulting test set.

References

[BGIH03] Bălănescu, T., Gheorghe, M., Ipate, F., Holcombe, M.: Formal black box testing for partially specified deterministic finite state machines. Foundations of Computing and Decision Systems 28(1) (2003)

[BH01]   Bogdanov, K., Holcombe, M.: Statechart testing method for aircraft control systems. Software Testing, Verification and Reliability 11(1), 39–54 (2001)

[BH02]   Bogdanov, K., Holcombe, M.: Testing from statecharts using the Wp method. In: CONCUR 2002 Satellite Workshop on Formal Approaches To Testing (FATES), pp. 19–33 (2002)

[BH04]   Bogdanov, K., Holcombe, M.: Refinement in statechart testing. Software
           Testing, Verification and Reliability 14, 189–211 (2004)
[BHI⁺06]   Bogdanov, K., Holcombe, M., Ipate, F., Seed, L., Vanak, S.: Testing meth-
           ods for X-machines, a review. Formal Aspects of Computing 18(1) (2006)
[BP94]   Bochmann, G., Petrenko, A.: Protocol testing: review of methods and rel-
           evance for software testing. In: 1994 ACM International Symposium on
           Software Testing and Analysis (ISSTA 1994), pp. 109–124 (1994)
[Car00]   Cardell-Oliver, R.: Conformance tests for real-time systems with timed au-
           tomata specifications. Formal Aspects of Computing 12(5), 350–371 (2000)
[Cho78]   Chow, T.: Testing software design modeled by finite-state machines. IEEE
           Transactions on Software Engineering SE-4(3), 178–187 (1978)
[CK93]   Cheng, K., Krishnakumar, A.: Automatic functional test generation using
           the extended finite state machine model. In: ACM-SIGDA; IEEE. Proceed-
           ings of the 30th ACM/IEEE Design Automation Conference, Dallas, TX,
           June 1993, pp. 86–91. ACM Press, New York (1993)
[Coh96]   Cohen, D.: Introduction to Computer Theory, 2nd edn. John Wiley & Sons,
           New York (1996)
[Eil74]   Eilenberg, S.: Automata, languages and machines, vol. A. Academic Press,
           London (1974)
[FBK⁺91]   Fujiwara, S., von Bochmann, G., Khendek, F., Amalou, M., Ghedamsi, A.:
           Test selection based on finite state models. IEEE Transactions on Software
           Engineering 17(6), 591–603 (1991)
[Gau95]   Gaudel, M.: Testing can be formal, too. In: Mosses, P.D., Schwartzbach,
           M.I., Nielsen, M. (eds.) CAAP 1995, FASE 1995, and TAPSOFT 1995.
           LNCS, vol. 915, pp. 82–96. Springer, Heidelberg (1995)
[Gil62]   Gill, A.: Introduction to the Theory of Finite-State Machines. McGraw-Hill,
           New York (1962)
[GP05]   Gunter, E., Peled, D.: Model checking, testing and verification working
           together. Formal Aspects of Computing 17(2), 201–221 (2005)
[HH04]   Hierons, R., Harman, M.: Testing conformance of a deterministic imple-
           mentation against a non-deterministic stream X-machine. Theoretical Com-
           puter Science 4, 191–233 (2004)
[HI98]   Holcombe, M., Ipate, F.: Correct Systems: building a business process so-
           lution. Springer, Heidelberg (1998)
[Hie04]   Hierons, R.: Testing from a nondeterministic finite state machine using
           adaptive state counting. IEEE Trans. Computers 53(10), 1330–1342 (2004)
[HN96]   Harel, D., Naamad, A.: The STATEMATE Semantics of Statecharts. ACM
           Transactions on Software Engineering and Methodology 5(4), 293–333
           (1996)
[HU02]   Hierons, R., Ural, H.: Reduced length checking sequences. IEEETC: IEEE
           Transactions on Computers 51, 1111–1117 (2002)
[IF06]   IF tool (2006),
           http://www-verimag.imag.fr/~async/IF/
[IH97]   Ipate, F., Holcombe, M.: An integration testing method that is proved to
           find all faults. International Journal of Computer Mathematics 63, 159–178
           (1997)
[IH00]   Ipate, F., Holcombe, M.: Generating test sequences from non-deterministic
           generalized stream X-machines. Formal Aspects of Computing 12(6), 443–
           458 (2000)
[IH02]   Ipate, F., Holcombe, M.: Testing conditions for communicating stream X-
           machine systems. Formal Aspects of Computing 13(6), 431–446 (2002)

[Ipa04]   Ipate, F.: Complete deterministic stream X-machine testing. Formal Aspects of Computing 16(4), 374–386 (2004)
[IU99]   Inan, K., Ural, H.: Efficient checking sequences for testing finite state machines. Information and Software Technology 41, 799–812 (1999)
[Koz94]   Kozen, D.: A completeness theorem for Kleene algebras and the algebra of regular events. Information and Computation 110(2), 366–390 (1994)
[LMN04]   Larsen, K., Mikucionis, M., Nielsen, B.: Online testing of real-time systems using Uppaal. In: Grabowski, J., Nielsen, B. (eds.) FATES 2004. LNCS, vol. 3395, pp. 79–94. Springer, Heidelberg (2005)
[LPB94]   Luo, G., Petrenko, A., von Bochmann, G.: Selecting test sequences for partially specified nondeterministic finite state machines. In: IFIP Seventh International Workshop on Protocol Test Systems, Japan, pp. 95–110 (1994)
[LY96]   Lee, D., Yannakakis, M.: Principles and methods of testing finite state machines – A survey. In: Proceedings of the IEEE, August 1996, vol. 84, pp. 1090–1123 (1996)
[MK94]   McGregor, J.D., Korson, T.D.: Integrated object-oriented testing and development processes. Communications of the ACM 37(9), 59–77 (1994)
[Mye79]   Myers, G.: The art of software testing. John Wiley and Sons, Chichester (1979)
[OB88]   Ostrand, T.J., Balcer, M.J.: The category-partition method for specifying and generating functional tests. Communications of the ACM 31(6), 676–686 (1988)
[OMG03]   OMG. Unified Modeling Language specification, version 1.5 (March 2003), http://www.omg.org/technology/documents/formal/uml.htm
[PBG04]   Petrenko, A., Boroday, S., Groz, R.: Confirming configurations in EFSM testing. IEEE Transactions on Software Engineering 30(1), 29–42 (2004)
[Pet00]   Petrenko, A.: Fault model-driven test derivation from finite state models: Annotated bibliography. In: Cassez, F., Jard, C., Rozoy, B., Dermot, M. (eds.) MOVEP 2000. LNCS, vol. 2067, pp. 19–23. Springer, Heidelberg (2001)
[PKS03]   Eleftherakis, G., Kefalas, P., Sotiriadou, A.: Developing tools for formal methods. In: 9th Panhellenic Conference on Informatics, Thessaloniki, Greece, November 2003, pp. 625–639 (2003)
[Pre94]   Pressman, R.: Software Engineering, a practitioner's approach, 3rd edn. McGraw-Hill, London (1994)
[PY05]   Petrenko, A., Yevtushenko, N.: Testing from partial deterministic FSM specifications. IEEE Transactions on Computers 54(9), 1154–1165 (2005)
[PYB96]   Petrenko, A., Yevtushenko, N., von Bochmann, G.: Testing deterministic implementations from nondeterministic FSM specifications. In: Proc. of 9th International Workshop on Testing of Communicating Systems (IWTCS 1996), pp. 125–140 (1996)
[PYBD96]   Petrenko, A., Yevtushenko, N., von Bochmann, G., Dssouli, R.: Testing in context: framework and test derivation. Computer Communications 19, 1236–1249 (1996)
[RDT95]   Ramalingam, T., Das, A., Thulasiraman, K.: On testing and diagnosis of communication protocols based on the FSM model. Computer communications 18(5), 329–337 (1995)
[Sta02]   Stannett, M.: Complete behavioural testing (two extensions to state-machine testing. In: CONCUR 2002 Satellite Workshop on Formal Approaches To Testing (FATES), pp. 51–64 (2002)

[Sta06]   Stannett, M.: The theory of X-machines. Technical Report CS-05-09, The University of Sheffield, UK (2006)

[Tre96]   Tretmans, J.: Test generation with inputs, outputs and repetitive quiescence. Software – Concepts and Tools 17(3), 103–120 (1996)

[Van02]   Vanak, S.: Complete functional testing of hardware descriptions. PhD thesis, The University of Sheffield, UK (2002)

[Vas73]   Vasilevskii, M.: Failure diagnosis of automata, vol. 4, pp. 653–665. Cybernetics, Plenum Publ. Corporation, New York (1973)

[Woo96]   Wood, A.: Predicting software reliability. Computer 29(11), 69–77 (1996)

Testing Data Types Implementations from Algebraic Specifications

Marie-Claude Gaudel[1] and Pascale Le Gall[2]

[1] Université de Paris-Sud 11, LRI CNRS UMR 8623,
Bat. 490, F-91405 Orsay Cedex, France
mcg@lri.fr
[2] Université d'Évry-Val d'Essonne, IBISC CNRS FRE 2873,
523 pl. des Terrasses F-91025 Évry Cedex, France
pascale.legall@ibisc.univ-evry.fr

Abstract. Algebraic specifications of data types provide a natural basis for testing data types implementations. In this framework, the conformance relation is based on the satisfaction of axioms. This makes it possible to state formally the fundamental concepts of testing: exhaustive test set, testability hypotheses, oracle. Various criteria for selecting finite test sets have been proposed. They depend on the form of the axioms, and on the possibilities of observation of the implementation under test. This last point is related to the well-known oracle problem. As the main interest of algebraic specifications is data type abstraction, testing a concrete implementation raises the issue of the gap between the abstract description and the concrete representation. The observational semantics of algebraic specifications bring solutions on the basis of the so-called observable contexts. After a description of testing methods based on algebraic specifications, the chapter gives a brief presentation of some tools and case studies, and presents some applications to other formal methods involving data types.

1 Introduction

Deriving test cases from some descriptions of the Implementation Under Test (the IUT) is a very old and popular idea. In their pioneering paper [36], Goodenough and Gerhart pointed out that the choice of test cases should be based both on code coverage, and on specifications expressed by condition tables. One of the first papers where software testing was based on some formal description of the system under test, was by Chow [23]: software was modelled by finite state machines. It has been very influential on all the subsequent works on testing based on formal specifications.

Most approaches in this area are based on behavioural descriptions: for instance the control graph of the program, or some finite state machine or labelled transition system. In such cases, it is rather natural to base the selection of test scenarios on some coverage criteria of the underlying graph.

Algebraic specifications are different: abstract data types are described in an axiomatic way [5,14,57]. There is a signature Σ, composed of a finite set S of sorts

R.M. Hierons et al. (Eds.): Formal Methods and Testing, LNCS 4949, pp. 209–239, 2008.

and a finite set F of function names over the sorts in S, and there is a finite set of axioms Ax. The correctness requirement is no more, as above, the ability (or the impossibility) for the IUT to exhibit certain behaviours: what is required by such specifications is the satisfaction of the axioms by the implementation of the functions of F. As a consequence, a natural way for testing some IUT is to choose some instantiations of the axioms (or of some consequences of them) and to check that when computed by the IUT, the terms occurring in the instantiations yield results that satisfy the corresponding axiom (or consequence). This approach was first proposed by Gannon et al. [33], and Bougé et al. [15,16], and then developed and implemented by Bernot et al. [10].

Since these foundational works, testing from algebraic specifications has been investigated a lot. Numerous works have addressed different aspects.

Some authors as in [6] or [24] focus on a target programming language (Ada or Haskell). Testing from algebraic specifications has also been successfully adapted for testing object-oriented systems [22,31,55]. Besides, methods inspired from algebraic testing have been applied to some other kinds of specifications like model-based specifications, first by Dick et al. [28], and more recently in [25]. Some other works explore links between test and proof [7,18,32].

Some tools [18,24,49] based either on resolution procedures or on specialised tactics in a proof engine, have been developed and used.

Extensions of algebraic specifications have also been studied, for instance, bounded data types [4] or partial functions [3]. More recently, some contributions [30,46,47] have been done to take into account structured or modular specifications aiming at defining structured test cases and at modelling the activity of both unit testing and integration testing.

Another special feature of algebraic specifications is the abstraction gap between the abstract specification level and the concrete implementation. This raises problems for interpreting the results of test experiments with respect to the specification. This characteristic is shared with other formal methods that allow the description of complex data types in an abstract way, for instance VDM, Z, and their object oriented extensions.

As a consequence, in the area of testing based on algebraic specifications, a special emphasis has been put on the oracle problem [3,8,43,45,58]. The oracle problem concerns the difficulty of defining reliable decision procedures to compare values of terms computed by the IUT. Actually, implementations of abstract data types may have subtle or complex representations, and the interface of the concrete data types is not systematically equipped with an equality procedure to compare values. In practice, only some basic data types provide a reliable decision procedure to compare values. They are said to be observable. The only way to define (partial) decision procedure for abstract data types is to observe them by applying some (composition of) functions yielding an observable result: they are called observable contexts. Observational approaches of algebraic specifications bring solutions to define an appropriate notion of correctness taking into account observability issues.

The chapter is organised as follows: Section 2 presents some necessary basic notions of algebraic specifications; Section 3 gives the basic definitions of *test* and *test experiment* against an algebraic specification; Section 4 introduces in a progressive way the notions of *exhaustive test set* and *testability hypothesis* in a simple case. Then Section 5 addresses the issue of the selection of a finite test set via the so-called *uniformity* and *regularity* selection hypotheses. Section 6 develops further the theory, addressing the case where there are observability problems: this leads to a reformulation of the definitions mentioned above, and to a careful examination of the notion of correctness. Section 7 presents some of the most significant related pieces of work. The last section is devoted to brief presentations of some case studies, and to the descriptions of some transpositions of the framework to some other formal methods where it is possible to specify complex data types.

2 Preliminaries on Algebraic Specifications

Algebraic specifications of data types, sometimes called axiomatic specifications, provide a way of defining abstract data types by giving the properties (axioms) of their operations. There is no explicit definition of each operation (no pre- and post-condition, no algorithm) but a global set of properties that describes the relationship between the operations. This idea comes from the late seventies [35,37]. It has been the origin of numerous pieces of work that have converged on the definition of CASL, the Common Algebraic Specification Language [14].

An example of an algebraic specification is given in Figure 1: it is a CASL specification of containers of natural numbers, i.e., a data structure that contains possibly duplicated numbers with no notion of order. This specification states that there are three sorts of values, namely Natural Numbers, Booleans and Containers. Among the operations, there is, for instance, a function named *isin* which, given two values, resp. of sort natural number and container, returns a boolean value. The operations must satisfy the axioms that are the formulas itemised by big bullets.

The sorts, operation names, and profiles of the operations are part of the *signature* of the specification. The signature gives the interface of the specified data type. Moreover, it declares some sorted variables that are used for writing the axioms.

An *(algebraic) signature* $\Sigma = (S, F, V)$ consists of a set S of sorts, a set F of function names each one equipped with an arity in $S^* \times S$ and a set of variables V, each of them being indexed by a sort. In the sequel, a function f with arity $(s_1 \ldots s_n, s)$, where $s_1 \ldots s_n, s \in S$, will be noted $f : s_1 \times \ldots \times s_n \to s$.

In Figure 1, the sorts of the signature are *Nat* and *Bool* (specified in some OUR/NUMBERS/WITH/BOOLS specification, not given here), and *Container*; the functions are [] (the empty container), _ :: _ (addition of a number to a container), *isin* that checks for the belonging of a number to a container, and *remove* that takes away one occurrence of a number from a container; the variables are x, y of *Nat* sort, and c of *Container* sort.

from OUR/NUMBERS/WITH/BOOLS **version** 0.0 **get** NAT, BOOL

spec CONTAINERS =
     NAT, BOOL
then
     generated type $Container ::= [] \mid \_::\_(Nat;\ Container)$
     op $isin : Nat \times Container \rightarrow Bool$
     op $remove : Nat \times Container \rightarrow Container$
     $\forall\ x,\ y: Nat;\ c: Container$
     • $isin(x, []) = false$ %(isin_empty)%
     • $eq(x, y) = true \Rightarrow isin(x, y :: c) = true$ %(isin_1)%
     • $eq(x, y) = false \Rightarrow isin(x, y :: c) = isin(x, c)$ %(isin_2)%
     • $remove(x, []) = []$ %(remove_empty)%
     • $eq(x, y) = true \Rightarrow remove(x, y :: c) = c$ %(remove_1)%
     • $eq(x, y) = false \Rightarrow remove(x, y :: c) = y :: remove(x, c)$ %(remove_2)%
end

Fig. 1. An Algebraic specification of containers of natural numbers

Given a signature $\Sigma = (S, F, V)$, $T_\Sigma(V)$ is the set of *terms with variables in V* freely generated from variables and functions in Σ and preserving arity of functions. Such terms are indexed by the sort of their result. We note $T_\Sigma(V)_s$ the subset of $T_\Sigma(V)$ containing exactly those terms indexed by s.

T_Σ is the set $T_\Sigma(\emptyset)$ of the *ground terms* and we note $T_{\Sigma,s}$ the set of ground terms of sort s.

Considering the CONTAINER specification, an example of a ground term t of *Container* sort is $0 :: 0 :: []$. An example of a term t' with variables is $isin(x, 0 :: c)$ that is of *Bool* sort.

A *substitution* is any mapping $\rho : V \rightarrow T_\Sigma(V)$ that preserves sorts. Substitutions are naturally extended to terms with variables. The result of the application of a substitution ρ to a term t is called an *instantiation* of t, and is noted $t\rho$. In the example, let us consider the substitution $\sigma : \{x \rightarrow 0, y \rightarrow 0, c \rightarrow y :: []\}$, the instantiation $t'\sigma$ is the term with variable $isin(0, 0 :: y :: [])$.

Σ-*equations* are formulae of the form $t = t'$ with $t, t' \in T_\Sigma(V)_s$ for $s \in S$. An example of an equation on containers is $remove(x, []) = []$.

A *positive conditional Σ-formula* is any sentence of the form $\alpha_1 \wedge \ldots \wedge \alpha_n \Rightarrow \alpha_{n+1}$ where each α_i is a Σ-equation ($1 \leq i \leq n+1$). $Sen(\Sigma)$ is the set of all positive conditional Σ-formulae.

A *(positive conditional) specification* $SP = (\Sigma, Ax, C)$ consists of a signature Σ, a set Ax of positive conditional formulae often called *axioms*, and some *constraints* C, which may restrict the interpretations of the declared symbols (some examples are given below). When C is empty, we note $SP = (\Sigma, Ax)$ instead of $SP = (\Sigma, Ax, \emptyset)$.

Specifications can be structured as seen in the example: a specification SP can use some other specifications $SP_1, \ldots, SP_n$. In such cases, the signature is the union of signatures, and there are some *hierarchical* constraints that require the semantics of the used specifications to be preserved (for more explanations see [57]).

In the CONTAINERS specification, there are six axioms, named $isin\_empty$, $isin\_1$, $isin\_2$, $remove\_empty$, $remove\_1$, and $remove\_2$, and there is a so-called *generation* constraint, expressed at the line beginning by **generated type**, that all the containers are computable by composition of the functions $[]$ and $\_ :: \_$. Such constraints are also called *reachability constraints*. The functions $[]$ and $\_ :: \_$ are called the *constructors* of the *Container* type.

In some algebraic specification languages, axioms can be formulae of first-order logic, as in CASL. However, in this chapter we mainly consider positive conditional specifications[1].

A Σ-*algebra* $\mathcal{A}$ is a family of sets A_s, each of them being indexed by a sort; these sets are equipped, for each $f : s_1 \times \ldots \times s_n \rightarrow s \in F$, with a mapping $f^{\mathcal{A}} : A_{s_1} \times \ldots \times A_{s_n} \rightarrow A_s$. A Σ-morphism μ from a Σ-algebra $\mathcal{A}$ to a Σ-algebra $\mathcal{B}$ is a mapping $\mu : A \rightarrow B$ such that for all $s \in S$, $\mu(A_s) \subseteq B_s$ and for all $f : s_1 \times \ldots \times s_n \rightarrow s \in F$ and all $(a_1, \ldots, a_n) \in A_{s_1} \times \ldots \times A_{s_n}$ $\mu(f^{\mathcal{A}}(a_1, \ldots, a_n)) = f^{\mathcal{B}}(\mu(a_1), \ldots, \mu(a_n))$.
$Alg(\Sigma)$ is the class of all Σ-algebras.

Intuitively speaking, an implementation of a specification with signature Σ is a Σ-algebra: it means that it provides some sets of values named by the sorts, and some way of computing the functions on these values without side effect.

The set of ground terms T_Σ can be extended into a Σ-algebra by providing each function name $f : s_1 \times \ldots \times s_n \rightarrow s \in F$ with an application $f^{T_\Sigma} : (t_1, \ldots, t_n) \mapsto f(t_1, \ldots, t_n)$. In this case, the function names of the signature are simply interpreted as the syntactic constructions of the ground terms.

Given a Σ-algebra $\mathcal{A}$, we note $\_^{\mathcal{A}} : T_\Sigma \rightarrow A$ the unique Σ-morphism that maps any $f(t_1, \ldots, t_n)$ to $f^{\mathcal{A}}(t_1^{\mathcal{A}}, \ldots, t_n^{\mathcal{A}})$. A Σ-algebra $\mathcal{A}$ is said *reachable* if $\_^{\mathcal{A}}$ is surjective.

A Σ-*interpretation* in A is any mapping $\iota : V \rightarrow A$. It is just an assignment of some values of the Σ-algebra to the variables. Given such an interpretation, it is extended to terms with variables: the value of the term is the result of its computation using the values of the variables and the relevant $f^{\mathcal{A}}$.

A Σ-algebra $\mathcal{A}$ *satisfies* a Σ-formula $\varphi : \bigwedge_{1 \leq i \leq n} t_i = t_i' \Rightarrow t = t'$, noted $\mathcal{A} \models \varphi$, if and only if for every Σ-interpretation ι in A, if for all i in $1..n$, $\iota(t_i) = \iota(t_i')$ then $\iota(t) = \iota(t')$. Given a specification $SP = (\Sigma, Ax, C)$, a Σ-algebra $\mathcal{A}$ is a SP-*algebra* if for every $\varphi \in Ax$, $\mathcal{A} \models \varphi$ and $\mathcal{A}$ fulfils the C constraint. $Alg(SP)$ is the subclass of $Alg(\Sigma)$ exactly containing all the SP-algebras.

A Σ-formula φ is a *semantic consequence* of a specification $SP = (\Sigma, Ax)$, noted $SP \models \varphi$, if and only if for every SP-algebra $\mathcal{A}$, we have $\mathcal{A} \models \varphi$.

3   Testing Against an Algebraic Specification

Let SP be a positive conditional specification and IUT be an Implementation Under Test. In dynamic testing, we are interested in the properties of the

---

[1] The reason is that most tools and case studies we present have been performed for and with this kind of specifications. An extension of our approach to first order logic, with some restrictions on quantifiers, was proposed by Machado in [46].

computations by IUT of the functions specified in SP. IUT provides some procedures or methods for executing these functions. The question is whether they satisfy the axioms of SP.

Given a ground Σ-term t, we note t^{IUT} the result of its computation by IUT. Now we define how to test IUT against a Σ-equation.

Definition 1 (: Test and Test Experiment). *Given a Σ-equation ϵ, and IUT which provides an implementation for every function name of Σ,*

- *a test for ϵ is any ground instantiation $t = t'$ of ϵ;*
- *a test experiment of IUT against $t = t'$ consists in the evaluation of t^{IUT} and t'^{IUT} and the comparison of the resulting values.*

Example 1. One test of the *isin_empty* equation in the CONTAINERS specification of Figure 1 is $isin(0, []) = false$.

The generalization of this definition to positive conditional axioms is straightforward.

In the following, we say that a test experiment is successful if it concludes to the satisfaction of the test by the IUT, and we note it IUT *passes* τ where τ is the test, i.e., a ground formula. We generalise this notation to test sets: IUT *passes* TS means that $\forall \tau \in TS$, IUT *passes* τ.

Deciding whether IUT *passes* τ is the oracle problem mentioned in the introduction. In the above example it is just a comparison between two boolean values. However, such a comparison may be difficult when the results to be compared have complex data types. We postpone the discussion on the way it can be realised in such cases to Section 6. Actually, we temporarily consider in the two following sections that this decision is possible for all sorts, i.e., they are all "observable".

Remark 1. Strictly speaking, the definition above defines a tester rather than a test data: a test $t = t'$ is nothing else than the abstract definition of a program that evaluates t and t' via the relevant calls to the IUT and compares the results; a test experiment is an execution of this tester linked to the IUT.

We can now introduce a first definition of an exhaustive test of an implementation against an algebraic specification. A natural notion of correctness, when all the data types of the specification are observable, is that the IUT satisfies the axioms of the specification. Thus we start with a first notion of exhaustive test inspired from the notion of satisfaction as defined in Section 2.

4   A First Presentation of Exhaustivity and Testability

Definition 2 (: Exhaustive Test Set, first version). *Given a positive conditional specification $SP = (\Sigma, Ax)$, an exhaustive test set for SP, denoted as $Exhaust_{SP}$, is the set of all well-sorted ground instantiations of the axioms in Ax:*

$$Exhaust_{SP} = \{\phi\rho \mid \phi \in Ax, \rho \in V \to T_{\Sigma}\}$$

An exhaustive test experiment of some IUT against SP is the set of all the test experiments of the IUT against the formulas of $Exhaust_{SP}$. As stated above, this definition is very close to (and is derived from) the notion of satisfaction of a set of Σ-axioms by a Σ-algebra. In particular, the fact that each axiom can be tested independently comes from this notion.

However, an implementation's passing once all the tests in the exhaustive test set does not necessarily mean that it satisfies the specification: first, this is true only if the IUT is deterministic; second, considering all the well-sorted ground instantiations is, a priori, not the same thing as considering all the Σ-interpretations in the values of the IUT. It may be the case that some values are not expressible by ground terms of the specification.

In other words, the above test set is exhaustive with respect to the specification, but may be not with respect to the values used by the program. Thus some *testability hypotheses* on the implementation under test are necessary: the success of the exhaustive test set ensures the satisfaction of the specification by the implementation only if this implementation behaves as a reachable Σ-algebra (cf. Section 2).

Practically, this means that:

- There is a realisation of every function of Σ that is supposed to be deterministic; the results do not depend on some hidden, unspecified, internal state.
- The implementation is assumed to be developed following good programming practices; any computed value of a data type must always be a result of the specified operations of this data type.
- There is a comparison procedure for the values of every sort of the signature.

Note that, explicitly or not, all testing methods make assumptions on IUT: a totally erratic system, or a diabolic one, may pass some test set and fail later on[2]. In our case these hypotheses are static properties of the program. Some of them are (or could be) checkable by some preliminary static analysis of the source code.

Definition 3 (: Σ-Testability). *Given a signature Σ, an IUT is Σ-testable if it defines a reachable Σ-algebra $\mathcal{A}_{IUT}$. Moreover, for each τ of the form $t = t'$, there exists a way of deciding whether it passes or not.*

The Σ-testability of the IUT is called the minimal hypothesis H_{min} on the IUT.

Let us note $Correct(IUT, SP)$ the correctness property that a given IUT behaves as a reachable SP-algebra (i.e., the axioms are satisfied and all the values

---

[2] Testing methods based on Finite State Machine descriptions rely on the assumption that the IUT behaves as a FSM with the same number of states as the specification; similarly, methods based on IO-automata or IO-Transition Systems assume that the IUT behaves as an IO-automata: consequently, it is supposed input-enabled, i.e., always ready to accept any input.

are specified). The fundamental link between exhaustivity and testability is given
by the following formula:

$$H_{min}(IUT) \Rightarrow (\forall \tau \in Exhaust_{SP}, IUT\ passes\ \tau \Leftrightarrow Correct(IUT, SP))$$

$Exhaust_{SP}$ is obviously not usable in practice since it is generally infinite. Actually, the aim of the definitions of $Exhaust_{SP}$ and H_{min} is to provide frameworks for developing theories of black-box testing from algebraic specifications.
Practical test criteria (i.e., those which correspond to finite test sets) will be described as stronger hypotheses on the implementation. This point is developed in
Sections 5 and 6.

Before addressing the issue of the selection of finite test sets, let us come back
to the definition of $Exhaust_{SP}$. As it is defined, it may contain useless tests,
namely those instantiations of conditional axioms where the premises are false:
such tests are always successful, independently of the fact that their conclusion
is satisfied by the IUT or not. Thus they can be removed.

Example 2. Assuming that $eq(0,0) = true$ is a semantic consequence of the
OUR/NUMBERS/WITH/BOOLS specification, we can derive an equational test
for the *remove_1* conditional axiom in the CONTAINERS specification of Figure
1. This test is simply the ground equation:
$remove(0, 0 :: 0 :: []) = 0 :: []$.

In the example of Figure 1, we have distinguished a subset of functions as constructors of the *Container* type (namely [] and ::). Under some conditions, the
presence of constructors in a specification makes it possible to characterise an
equational exhaustive test set.

A *signature with constructors* is a signature $\Sigma = < S, F, V >$ such that a subset
C of elements of F are distinguished as constructors. Let us note $\Omega = < S, C, V >$
the corresponding sub-signature of Σ, and T_Ω the corresponding ground terms.
A specification $SP = < \Sigma, Ax >$ where Σ is a signature with constructors C is
complete with respect to its constructors if and only if both following conditions
hold:

- $\forall t \in T_\Sigma, \exists t' \in T_\Omega$ such that $SP \models t = t'$
- $\forall t, t' \in T_\Omega, SP \models t = t' \Rightarrow < \Sigma, \emptyset > \models t = t'$, i.e., t and t' are syntactically
  identical

Example 3. The CONTAINERS specification of Figure 1 is complete with respect
to the constructors $C = \{[], ::\}$ of the *Container* sort: from the axioms, any
ground term of *Container* sort containing some occurrence of the (non constructor) *remove* function is equal to some ground term containing only occurrences
of [] and ::. Moreover, there is only one such ground term.

For such specifications and under some new hypotheses on the IUT, it is possible
to demonstrate that the set of ground conclusions of the axioms is exhaustive.
When removing premises satisfied by the specification, we should be careful not
to remove some other premises that the IUT could interpret as true, even if they

are not consequences of the specification. A sufficient condition is to suppose that the IUT correctly implements the constructors of all the sorts occurring in the premises. Let us introduce the new testability hypothesis $H_{min,C}$ for that purpose. Intuitively, $H_{min,C}$ means that the IUT implements data types with a syntax very close to their abstract denotation. It may seem to be a strong hypothesis, but in fact, it only applies to basic types, often those provided by the implementation language. As soon as the data type implementation is subtle or complex, the data type is then encapsulated and thus considered as non observable for testing (cf. Section 6).

Definition 4. *IUT satisfies $H_{min,C}$ iff IUT satisfies H_{min} and :*

$$\forall s \in S, \forall u, v \in T_{\Omega,s}, \text{ IUT passes } u = v \Leftrightarrow SP \models u = v$$

Definition 5

$$EqExhaust_{SP,C} = \{\, \epsilon\rho \mid \exists \alpha_1 \wedge \ldots \wedge \alpha_n \Rightarrow \epsilon \in Ax,$$
$$\rho \in V \to T_\Omega, SP \models (\alpha_1 \wedge \ldots \wedge \alpha_n)\rho\}$$

Under $H_{min,C}$ and for specifications complete with respect to their constructors $EqExhaust_{SP,C}$ is an exhaustive test set. A proof can be found in [42] or in [1]. Its advantage over $Exhaust_{SP}$ is that it is made of equations. Thus the test experiments are simpler.

Some other approaches for the definitions of exhaustivity and testability are possible. For instance, as suggested in [11] and applied by Dong and Frankl in the ASTOOT system [31], a different possibility is to consider the algebraic specification as a term rewriting system, following a "normal-form" operational semantics. Under the condition that the specification defines a ground-convergent rewriting system, it leads to an alternative definition of the exhaustive test set:

$$Exhaust'_{SP} = \{t = t \downarrow \mid t \in T_\Sigma\}$$

where $t \downarrow$ is the unique normal form of t. The testability hypothesis can be weakened to the assumption that the IUT is deterministic (it does not need anymore to be reachable). In [31], an even bigger exhaustive test set was mentioned (but not used), which contained for every ground term the inequalities with other normal forms, strictly following the definition of initial semantics.

Actually, this is an example of a case where the exhaustive test set is not built from instantiations of the axioms, but more generally from an adequate set of semantic consequences of the specification. Other examples are shown in Section 6.

5   Selection Hypotheses: Uniformity, Regularity

5.1   Introduction to Selection Hypotheses

A black-box testing strategy can be formalised as the selection of a finite subset of some exhaustive test set. In the sequel, we work with $EqExhaust_{SP,C}$, but what we say is general to the numerous possible variants of exhaustive test sets.

Let us consider, for instance, the classical partition testing strategy[3]. It consists in defining a finite collection of (possibly non-disjoint) subsets that covers the exhaustive test set. Then one element of each subset is selected and submitted to the implementation under test. The choice of such a strategy corresponds to stronger hypotheses than H_{min} on the implementation under test. We call such hypotheses *selection hypotheses*. In the case of partition testing, they are called *uniformity hypothesis*, since the implementation under test is assumed to behave uniformly on some test subsets UTS_i (as Uniformity Test Subset):

$$UTS_1 \cup \ldots \cup UTS_p = EqExhaust_{SP,C}, \text{ and}$$

$$\forall i = 1, \ldots, p, (\forall \tau \in UTS_i, IUT \text{ passes } \tau \Rightarrow IUT \text{ passes } UTS_i)$$

Various selection hypotheses can be formulated and combined depending on some knowledge of the program, some coverage criteria of the specification and ultimately cost considerations. Another type of selection hypothesis is *regularity hypothesis*, which uses a size function on the tests and has the form "if the subset of $EqExhaust_{SP,C}$ made up of all the tests of size less than or equal to a given limit is passed, then $EqExhaust_{SP,C}$ also is"[4].

All these hypotheses are important from a theoretical point of view because they formalise common test practices and express the gap between the success of a test strategy and correctness. They are also important in practice because exposing them makes clear the assumptions made on the implementation. Thus, they give some indication of complementary verifications, as used by Tse et al. in [20]. Moreover, as pointed out by Hierons in [40], they provide formal bases to express and compare test criteria and fault models.

5.2   How to Choose Selection Hypotheses

As said above, the choice of the selection hypotheses may depend on many factors. However, in the case of algebraic specifications, the text of the specification provides useful guidelines. These guidelines rely on coverage of the axioms and composition of the cases occurring in premise of the axioms via unfolding as stated first in [10], and extended recently in [1].

We recall that axioms are of the form $\alpha_1 \wedge \ldots \wedge \alpha_n \Rightarrow \alpha_{n+1}$ where each α_i is a Σ-equation $t_i = t_i'$, $(1 \leq i \leq n + 1)$.

From the definition of $EqExhaust_{SP,C}$, a test of such an axiom is some $\alpha_{n+1}\rho$ where $\rho \in V \to T_\Sigma$ is a well-typed ground substitution of the variables of the axiom such that the premise of the axiom, instantiated by ρ, is true: it is a semantic consequence of the specification ($SP \models (\alpha_1 \wedge \ldots \wedge \alpha_n)\rho$).

One natural basic testing strategy is to cover each axiom once, i.e., to choose for every axiom one adequate substitution ρ only. The corresponding uniformity hypothesis is

---

[3] More exactly, it should be called sub-domain testing strategy.

[4] As noticed by several authors, [31], [20], and from our own experience [53], such hypotheses must be used with care. It is often necessary to choose this limit taking in consideration some "white-box knowledge" on the implementation of the data types: array bounds, etc.

$\forall \rho \in V \rightarrow T_\Sigma$ such that $SP \models (\alpha_1 \wedge \ldots \wedge \alpha_n)\rho$, IUT passes $\alpha_{n+1}\rho \Rightarrow$
(IUT passes $\alpha_{n+1}\rho'$, $\forall \rho' \in V \rightarrow T_\Sigma$ such that $SP \models (\alpha_1 \wedge \ldots \wedge \alpha_n)\rho'$)

It defines a so-called *uniformity sub-domain* for the variables of the axiom that is the set of ground Σ-terms characterised by $SP \models (\alpha_1 \wedge \ldots \wedge \alpha_n)$.

Example 4. In the example of Figure 1, covering the six axioms requires six tests, for instance the following six ground equations:

- $isin(0, [\,]) = false$, with the whole Nat sort as uniformity sub-domain;
- $isin(1, 1 :: 2 :: [\,]) = true$, with the pairs of Nat such that $eq(x, y) = true$ and the whole $Container$ sort as uniformity sub-domain;
- $isin(1, 0 :: 3 :: [\,]) = false$, with the pairs of Nat such that $eq(x, y) = false$ and the whole $Container$ sort as uniformity sub-domain;
- $remove(1, [\,]) = [\,]$, with the Nat sort as uniformity sub-domain;
- $remove(0, 0 :: 1 :: [\,]) = 1 :: [\,]$, with the pairs of Nat such that $eq(x, y) = true$ and the $Container$ sort as uniformity sub-domain;
- $remove(1, 0 :: [\,]) = 0 :: [\,]$, with the pairs of Nat such that $eq(x, y) = false$ and the $Container$ sort as uniformity sub-domain.

Such uniformity hypotheses are often too strong. A method for weakening them, and getting more test cases, is to compose the cases occurring in the axioms. In the full general case, it may involve tricky pattern matching on the premises and conclusions, and even some theorem proving. However, when the axioms are in a suitable form one can use the classical unfolding technique defined by Burstall and Darlington in [19]. It consists in replacing a function call by its definition. Thus, for unfolding to be applicable, the axioms must be organised as a set of functions definitions: every function is defined by a list of conditional equations such as:

$$\wedge_{1 \leq i \leq m} \alpha_i \Rightarrow f(t_1, \ldots, t_n) = t$$

where the domain of the function must be covered by the disjunction of the premises of the list.

Example 5. In the example of Figure 1, the $isin$ function is defined by:

- $isin(x, [\,]) = false$ %(isin_empty)%
- $eq(x, y) = true \Rightarrow isin(x, y :: c) = true$ %(isin_1)%
- $eq(x, y) = false \Rightarrow isin(x, y :: c) = isin(x, c)$ %(isin_2)%

It means that every occurrence of $isin(t_1, t_2)$ can correspond to the three following sub-cases:

- $t_2 = [\,]$: in this case $isin(t_1, t_2)$ can be replaced by $false$;
- $t_2 = y :: c$ and $eq(t_1, y) = true$: in this case, it can be replaced by $true$;
- $t_2 = y :: c$ and $eq(t_1, y) = false$: in this case, it can be replaced by $y :: isin(t1, c)$.

A way of partitioning the uniformity sub-domain induced by the coverage of an axiom with some occurrence of $f(t_1, \ldots, t_n) = t$ is to introduce the sub-cases stated by the definition of f, and, of course, to perform the corresponding replacements in the conclusion equation to be tested. This leads to a weakening of the uniformity hypotheses.

Example 6. Let us consider the *isin_2* axiom. Its coverage corresponds to the uniformity sub-domain "pairs of *Nat* such that $eq(x, y) = false$" $\times$ "the *Container* sort". Let us unfold in this axiom the second occurrence of *isin*, i.e., $isin(x, c)$. It leads to three sub-cases for this axiom:

- $c = []$:
  $eq(x, y) = false \wedge c = [] \Rightarrow isin(x, y :: []) = isin(x, [])$, i.e, false;
- $c = y' :: c'$ and $eq(x, y') = true$:
  $eq(x, y) = false \wedge c = y' :: c' \wedge eq(x, y') = true \Rightarrow isin(x, y :: y' :: c') = isin(x, y' :: c')$, i.e., true;
- $c = y' :: c'$ and $eq(x, y') = false$:
  $eq(x, y) = false \wedge c = y' :: c' \wedge eq(x, y') = false \Rightarrow isin(x, y :: y' :: c') = y :: isin(x, y' :: c')$, i.e., $isin(x, c')$.

The previous uniformity sub-domain is partitioned in three smaller sub-domains characterised by the three premises above. Covering these sub-cases leads to test bigger containers, and to check that *isin* correctly behaves independently of the fact that the searched number was the last to be added to the container or not. Applying the same technique to the *remove_2* axiom leads to test that in case of duplicates, one occurrence only is removed.

Of course, unfolding can be iterated: the last case above can be decomposed again into three sub-cases. Unbounded unfolding leads generally to infinite test sets[5]. Limiting the number of unfoldings is generally sufficient for ensuring the finiteness of the test set. Experience has shown (see Section 8) that in practice one or two levels of unfolding are sufficient for ensuring what test engineers consider as a good coverage and a very good detection power. In some rare cases, this limitation of unfolding does not suffice for getting a finite test set: then, it must be combined with regularity hypotheses, i.e., limitation of the size of the ground instantiations.

Unfolding has been implemented by Marre within the tool LOFT [10,48,49] using logic programming. There are some conditions on the specifications manipulated by LOFT:

- they must be complete with respect to constructors;
- when transforming the specification into a conditional rewriting system (by orienting each equation $t = t'$ occuring in an axiom from left to right $t \rightarrow t'$), the resulting conditional rewrite system must be confluent and terminating;
- each equation $t = t'$ that is the conclusion of an axiom must be such that t may be decomposed as a function f, not belonging to the set of constructors, applied to a tuple of terms built on constructors and variables only.

Under these conditions, the LOFT tool can decompose any uniformity domain into a family of uniformity sub-domains. It can also compute some solutions into

---

[5] Actually, as it is described here, unbounded unfolding yields an infinite set of equations very close to the exhaustive test set. The only remaining variables are those that are operands of functions without definitions, namely, in our case, constructors.

a given uniformity sub-domain. These two steps correspond respectively to the computation of the uniformity hypotheses based on unfolding subdomains and to the generation of an arbitrary test case per each computed subdomain. The unfolding procedure is based on an equational resolution procedure involving some unification mechanisms. Under the conditions on the specifications given above, the unfolding procedure computes test cases such that: sub-domains are included in the domain they are issued from (soundness), and the decomposition into subdomains covers the split domain (completeness).

In [1], Aiguier et al. have extended the unfolding procedure for positive conditional specifications without restrictions. This procedure is also sound and complete. However, the price to pay is that instead of unfolding a unique occurrence of a defined function, the extended unfolding procedure requires to unfold all occurrences of the defined functions in a given equation among all the equations characterising the domain under decomposition. This may result in numerous test cases.

We have seen that conditional tests can be simplified into equational ones by solving their premises. It can be done in another way, replacing variables occurring in the axiom by terms as many times as necessary to find good instantiations. This method amounts to draw terms as long as the premises are not satisfied. This is particularly adapted in a probabilistic setting. In [9], Bouaziz et al. give some means to build some distributions on the sets of values.

6 Exhaustivity and Testability Versus Observability

Until now, we have supposed that a test experiment $t = t'$ of the IUT may be successful or not depending on whether the evaluations of t and t' yield the same resulting values. Sometimes, comparing the test outputs may be a complex task when some information is missing. It often corresponds to complex abstract data types encapsulating some internal concrete data representations. Some abstract data types (sets, stacks, containers, etc.) do not always provide an equality procedure within the implementation under test and we reasonably cannot suppose the existence of a finite procedure, the oracle, to correctly interpret the test results as equalities or inequalities. The so-called *oracle problem* in the framework of testing from algebraic specifications amounts to deal with equalities between terms of non observable sorts.

In this section, we distinguish a subset S_{Obs} of observable sorts among the set S of all sorts. For example, it may regroup all the sorts equipped with an equality predicate within the IUT environnement, for instance equality predicates provided by the programming language and considered as reliable. The minimal hypothesis H_{min} is relaxed to the weaker hypothesis H_{min}^{Obs} expressing that the the IUT still defines a reachable Σ-algebra but that the only remaining elementary tests which may be interpreted by the IUT as a verdict success/failure are the ground equality $t = t'$ of observable sort. The set Obs of all observable formulae is the subset of $Sen(\Sigma)$ of all formulae built over observable ground equalities. Any formula of Obs may be considered as a test experiment, and reciprocally.

The oracle problem in the case of non observable sorts may be tackled by two distinct but related questions. How to turn non observable equalities under test into test experiments tractable by an *IUT* only satisfying H_{min}^{Obs}? How far can we still talk about correctness when dealing with observability issues? Roughly speaking, the answers lie respectively in using observable contexts and in defining correctness up to some observability notion. We present these two corresponding key points in the following sections.

6.1   Observable Contexts

In practice, non observable abstract data types can be observed through successive applications of functions leading to an observable result. It means that properties related to non observable sorts can be tested through observable contexts:

Definition 6 (: Context and Observable context).

An observable context c for a sort s is a term of observable sort with a unique occurrence of a special variable of sort s, generically denoted by z.

Such a context is often denoted c[z] or simply c[.] and c[t] denotes cσ where σ is the substitution associating the term t to the variable z.

An observable context is said to be minimal if it does contain an observable context as a strict subterm[6].

Only minimal observable contexts are meaningful for testing. Indeed, if a context c has an observable context c' as a strict subterm, then $c[z]$ may be decomposed as $c_0[c'[z]]$. It implies that for any terms t and t', $c[t] = c[t']$ iff $c'[t] = c'[t']$. Both equalities being observable, the simpler one, $c'[t] = c'[t']$, suffices to infer whether $c[t] = c[t']$ holds or not. In the sequel, all the observable contexts will be considered as minimal by default.

For example, we can use set cardinality and element membership to observe some set data type as well as the height and the top of all successive popped stacks for some stack data type. Thus, a non observable ground equality of the form $t = t'$ is observed through all observable contexts $c[.]$ applied to both t and t'. From a testing point of view, it amounts to apply to both terms t and t' the same successive application of operations yielding an observable value, and to compare the resulting values.

Example 7. With the CONTAINERS specification of Figure 1, we now consider that the sort *Container* is no more an observable sort while *Nat* and *Bool* are observable ones. Ground equalities of sort *Container* should be observed through the observable sorts *Nat* and *Bool*. An abstract test like $remove(3, []) = []$ is now observed through observable contexts. Each observable context of sort *Container* gives rise to a new (observable) test belonging by construction to *Obs*. For example, the context $isin(3, z)$ applied to the previous abstract test leads to the test: $isin(3, remove(3, [])) = isin(3, [])$.

---

[6] A subterm of a term t is t itselt or any term occurring in it. In particular, if t is of form $f(t_1, \ldots, t_n)$ then $t_1, \ldots$ and t_n are subterms of t. A strict subterm of t is any subterm of t which differs from t.

In practice, there is often an infinity of such observable contexts. In the case of the CONTAINERS specification, we can build the following observable contexts[7]

$$isin(x, x_1 :: (x_2 :: \ldots (x_n :: z))), \; isin(x, remove(x_1, remove(x_2, \ldots, remove(x_n, z))))$$

or more generally, any combination of the operations $remove$ and $::$ surrounded by the $isin$ operation. As a consequence, we are facing a new kind of selection problem: to test an equality $t = t'$ of $Container$ sort, one has to select among all these observable contexts a subset of finite or even reasonable size.

Bernot in [8] gives a counter-example based on the stack data type to assess that without additional information on the IUT, all the contexts are a priori necessary to test a non observable equality, even those involving constructors such as $::$. More precisely, a context of the form $isin(x, x_1 :: z)$ may appear useless since it leads to build larger $Container$ terms instead of observing the terms replacing z. In [8], it is shown that those contexts may reveal some programming errors depending on a bad use of state variables. From a theoretical point of view, let us consider a specification reduced to one axiom $a = b$ expressing that two non observable constants are equal. Then for any given arbitrary minimal context c_0, one can design a program P_{c_0} making $c[a] = c[b]$ true for all minimal observable contexts except c_0. This fact means that in general, any minimal context is needed to "fully" test non observable equalities. This is a simplified explanation of a proof given by Chen et al. in [20].

Let us point out that replacing an equation $t = t'$ by the (infinite) set of $c[t] = c[t']$ with c an observable context is classical within the community of algebraic specifications. Different observational approaches [13,54] have been proposed to cope with refinement of specifications based on abstract data types. They have introduced the so-called behavioural equalities, denoted by $t \approx t'$. The abstract equality is replaced by the (infinite) set of all observables contexts applying to both terms. More precisely, an algebra $\mathcal{A}$ satisfies $t \approx t'$ if and only if for every Σ-interpretations ι in A, for all observable contexts c, we have $\iota(c[t]) = \iota(c[t'])$. Behavioural equalities allow the specifier to refine abstract data types with concrete data types that do not satisfy some properties required at the abstract level. For example, the Set abstract data type with some axioms stating the commutativity of the element insertion, can be refined into the $List$ abstract data type where the addition of an element by construction cannot be commutative. The refinement of Set by $List$ is ensured by requiring that equalities on sets hold in the list specification only up to the behavioural equality. It amounts to state that observable operations (here the membership operation) behave in the same way at the abstract level of sets and at the implementation level of lists and to ignore those properties of the implementation that are not observable.

Considering an infinity of contexts is possible using context induction as defined by Hennicker in [39]. This is useful to prove a refinement step, but is useless

---

[7] For convenience, we use the variables x, x_1, ..., x_n to denote arbitrary ground terms of sort Nat in a concise way.

in order to define an oracle. So, how can we select a finite set of observable contexts? Below we give some hints:

- The selection hypotheses presented in Section 5 to choose particular instantiations of axiom variables can be transposed to choose observable contexts. In particular, a rather natural way of selecting contexts consists in applying a regularity hypothesis. The size of a context is often defined in relation with the number of occurrences of non observable functions occurring in it.
- If one can characterise the equality predicate by means of a set of axioms, then one can use this axiomatisation, as proposed by Bidoit and Hennicker in [12], to define the test of non observable equalities. To give an intuition of how such an axiomatisation looks like, we give below the most classical one. It concerns the specification of abstract data types like sets, bags or containers, for which two terms are equal if and only if they exactly contain the same elements. Such an axiomatisation looks like:

$$c \approx c' \text{ iff } \forall e, isin(e, c) = isin(e, c')$$

where c and c' are variables of the abstract data type to be axiomatised, and e is a variable of element sort. $c \approx c'$ denotes the behavioural equality that is axiomatised. The axiomatisation simply expresses that the subset of contexts of the form $isin(e, z)$ suffices to characterize the behavioural equality. This particular subset of contexts can then be chosen as a suitable starting point to select observable contexts to test non observable equalities. Such an approach has two main drawbacks. First, such a finite aximatisation may not exist[8] or be difficult to guess. Second, selecting only from the subset of observable contexts corresponding to a finite axiomatisation amounts to make an additional hypothesis on the IUT, which has been called the *oracle hypothesis* in [8]. In a few words, it consists in supposing that the IUT correctly implements the data type with respect to the functions involved in the axiomatisation. In the example of Containers, two containers are supposed to be behaviourally equal if and only if the membership operation *isin* applied on the containers always gives the same results. In other words, by using axiomatisation to build oracles, we are exactly supposing what we are supposed to test. Clearly, it may appear as a too strong hypothesis.
- Chen, Tse and others in [20] point out that some static analysis of the IUT may help to choose an adequate subset of observable contexts. When testing whether $t = t'$ holds or not, the authors compare their internal representations r and r' within the IUT. If r and r' are equal, then they can conclude[9] that the IUT passes $t = t'$. Otherwise, if r and r' are not equal, then they study which data representation components are different in r and r' and which are the observations which may reveal the difference. This makes it possible to build a subset of observable contexts which has

---

[8] For example, the classical stack specification has no finite axiomatisation of stack equality.

[9] [45] is partially based on this same idea: if the concrete implementations are identical, then necessarily their corresponding abstract denotations are equal terms.

a good chance to observationally distinguishes t and t'. The heuristic they have proposed has been successfully applied in an industrial context [56].

6.2   Correctness with Observability Issues

We have seen in Section 6.1 that the test of a non observable equality may be approached by a finite subset of observable contexts. More precisely, a non observable ground equality $t = t'$ may be partially verified by submitting a finite subset of the test set:

$$Obs(t = t') = \{c[t] = c[t'] \mid c \text{ is a minimal observable context}\}.$$

The next question concerns testability issues: can we adapt the notions of correctness and exhaustivity when dealing with observability? For example, one may wonder whether the set $Obs(t = t')$ may be considered as an exhaustive test set for testing the non observable (ground) equality $t = t'$. More generally, by taking inspiration from the presentation given in Section 4, we look for a general property linking the notions of exhaustive test set and testability such as:

$$H_{min}^{Obs}(IUT) \Rightarrow (\forall \tau \in Exhaust_{SP}^{Obs}, IUT \text{ passes } \tau \Leftrightarrow Correct^{Obs}(IUT, SP))$$

6.2.1   Equational Specifications
If SP is an equational specification[10], then following Section 6.1, the test set

$$Exhaust_{SP}^{Obs} = \{ c[t]\rho = c[t']\rho \mid t = t' \in Ax, \rho \in V \to T_\Sigma, $$
$$c \text{ minimal observable context}\}$$

is a good candidate[11] since it simply extends the $Obs(t = t')$ sets to the case of equations with variables. Actually, $Exhaust_{SP}^{Obs}$ is an exhaustive test set provided that we reconsider the definition of correctness taking into account observability.

By definition of observability, the IUT does not give access to any information on non observable sorts. Considering a given IUT as correct with respect to some specification SP should be defined up to all the possible observations and by discarding properties directly expressed on non observable sorts. Actually, observational correctness may be defined as: IUT is observationally correct with respect to SP according to the set of observations Obs, if there exists an SP-algebra $\mathcal{A}$ such that IUT and $\mathcal{A}$ exactly behave in the same way for all possible observations.

To illustrate, let us consider the case of the Container specification enriched by a new axiom of commutativity of element insertions:

$$x :: (y :: c) = y :: (x :: c)$$

---

[10] Axioms of an equational specification are of the form $t = t'$ where t and t' are terms with variables and of the same sort.

[11] Let us remark that if t and t' are of observable sort s, then the only minimal observable context is z_s such that $t\rho = t'\rho$ are the unique tests associated to the axiom $t = t'$.

The *Container* data type is classically implemented by the *List* data type. However, elements in lists are usually stored according to the order of their insertion. In fact, the *List* data type is observationally equivalent to the *Container* data type as soon as the membership element is correctly implemented in the *List* specification. It is of little matter whether the *List* insertion function satisfies or not the axioms concerning the addition of elements in Containers.

This is formalised by introducing equivalence relations between algebras defined up to a set of Σ-formulae.

Definition 7. *Let $\Psi \subset Sen(\Sigma)$ and $\mathcal{A}$ and $\mathcal{B}$ be two Σ-algebras.*

$\mathcal{A}$ is said to be Ψ-equivalent to $\mathcal{B}$, denoted by $\mathcal{A} \equiv_\Psi \mathcal{B}$, if and only if we have $\forall \varphi \in \Psi, \mathcal{A} \models \varphi \Longleftrightarrow \mathcal{B} \models \varphi$.

$\mathcal{A}$ is said to be observationally equivalent to $\mathcal{B}$ if and if $\mathcal{A} \equiv_{Obs} \mathcal{B}$.

We can now define observational correctness:

Definition 8. *Let IUT be an implementation under test satisfying H_{min}^{Obs}.*

IUT is observationally correct with respect to SP and according to Obs, denoted by $Correct^{Obs}(IUT, SP)$ if and only if

$$\exists \mathcal{A} \text{ reachable } SP\text{-algebra}, IUT \equiv_{Obs} \mathcal{A}$$

Remark 2. This notion of observational correctness has been first recommended for testing purpose by Le Gall and Arnould in [42,43] for a large classe of specifications and observations[12]. With respect to the observational approaches in algebraic specifications [13], it corresponds to abstractor specifications for which the set of algebras is defined as the set of all algebras equivalent to at least an algebra of a kernel set, basically the set of all algebras satisfying the set of axioms.

From a testing point of view, each reachable SP-specification is obviously observationally correct with respect to SP. Reciprocally, an implementation IUT is observationally correct if it cannot be distinguished by observations from at least a reachable SP-algebra, say IUT_{SP}. So, nobody can say whether the implementation is the SP-algebra IUT_{SP}, and thus intrinsically correct, or the IUT is just an approximation of one reachable Σ-algebra up to the observations Obs. Thus, under the hypothesis H_{min}^{Obs}, any observationally correct IUT should be kept. Finally, $Correct^{Obs}(IUT, SP)$ captures exactly the set of all implementations which look like SP-algebras up to the observations in Obs. With this appropriate definition of $Correct^{Obs}(IUT, SP)$, the test set $Exhaust_{SP}^{Obs}$ is exhaustive. A sketch of the proof is the following. For each IUT passing $Exhaust_{SP}^{Obs}$, let us consider the quotient algebra $\mathcal{Q}$ built from IUT with the axioms of SP. We can then show that $\mathcal{Q}$ is a SP-algebra and is observationally equivalent to IUT.

---

[12] For interested readers, [10,42,43] give a generic presentation of formal testing from algebraic specifications in terms of institutions.

6.2.2 Positive Conditional Specifications with Observable Premises

We also get an exhaustive test set when considering axioms with observable premises. For each axiom of the form $\alpha_1 \wedge \ldots \wedge \alpha_n \Rightarrow t = t'$ with all α_i of observable sort, it suffices to put in the corresponding exhaustive test set all the tests of the form $\alpha_1\rho \wedge \ldots \wedge \alpha_n\rho \Rightarrow c[t]\rho = c[t']\rho$ for all substitutions $\rho : V \rightarrow T_\Sigma$ and for all minimal observable contexts c.

Moreover, if we want to have an exhaustive test set involving equations only, as it has been done in Section 4, we should restrict to specifications with observable premises and complete with respect to the set $\mathcal{C}_{Obs}$ of constructors of observable sorts. As in Section 4, we also consider that the IUT correctly implements the constructors of all the sorts occurring in the premise, here the observable sorts[13]. That is to say, IUT satisfies $H_{min,\mathcal{C}_{Obs}}$ iff IUT satisfies H_{min} and:

$$\forall s \in S_{Obs}, \forall u, v \in T_{\Omega,s} IUT \; passes \; u = v \Leftrightarrow SP \models u = v$$

Under $H_{min,\mathcal{C}_{Obs}}$ and for the considered restricted class of specifications (i.e., observable premises and completeness with respect to $\mathcal{C}_{Obs}$),

$$EqExhaust_{SP}^{Obs} = \{c[t]\rho = c[t']\rho \mid \exists \alpha_1 \wedge \ldots \wedge \alpha_n \Rightarrow t = t' \in Ax, \rho \in V \rightarrow T_\Sigma,$$
$$c \; min. \; obs. \; context, SP \models (\alpha_1 \wedge \ldots \wedge \alpha_n)\rho\}$$

is an exhaustive test set with respect to observational correctness.

6.2.3 Generalisation to Non-observable Premises

Is it possible to generalise such a construction of an exhaustive test set for specifications with positive conditional formulas comprising non-observable premises? A first naive solution would consist in replacing each non-observable equation $t = t'$ occurring either in the premise or in the conclusion of the axioms by a subset of $Obs(t = t')$. Unfortunately, such an idea cannot be applied, unless one accepts to submit biased tests[14]. This fact has been reported by Bernot and others in [8,10]. To give an intuition, let us consider a new axiom

$$x :: x :: l = x :: l \Rightarrow true = false$$

which means that if addition to a container is idempotent, then[15] it would lead to $true = false$. Let us try to test the ground instance $0 :: 0 :: [] = 0 :: [] \Rightarrow true = false$ by considering a test ϕ in Obs of the form

$$\bigwedge_{\substack{\psi_i \in Obs(0 :: 0 :: [] = 0 :: []) \\ i \in I, I \; finite \; index}} \psi_i \Rightarrow u = v$$

---

[13] When observable sorts coincide with the basic data types of the programming language, such an hypothesis is quite plausible. Thus, this is a weak hypothesis.

[14] A test is said to be biased when it rejects at least a correct implementation.

[15] This is no more than a positive conditional way of specifying $x :: x :: l \neq x :: l$. Actually, as the trivial algebra (with one element per sort) is satisfying all the conditional positive specifications, the inconsistency of specifications is often expressed by the possibility of deriving the boolean equation $true = false$.

then the IUT may pass the premise

$$\bigwedge_{\substack{\psi_i \in Obs(0 :: 0 :: [] = 0 :: []) \\ i \in I, I \text{ finite index}}} \psi_i$$

without $0 :: 0 :: [] = 0 :: 0 :: []$ being a consequence of the specification. In that case, the IUT passes the test ϕ by passing the conclusion $true = false$. Thus, observing non observable premises through a finite set of contexts leads to require an observable equality, here $true = false$, which in fact is not required by the specification. This is clearly a bad idea.

It is now widely recognised that non-observable equations may be observed through some subset of observable contexts only when their position in the test is positive[16]. For example, the disjunctive normal form of $0 :: 0 :: [] = 0 :: [] \Rightarrow true = false$ is $\neg(0 :: 0 :: [] = 0 :: []) \lor true = false$ and thus $0 :: 0 :: [] = 0 :: []$ has a negative position in the test. In particular, Machado in [45,46] considers any first order formula whose Skolem form does not contain existential quantifiers. Every non-observable equations in positive positions are observed by means of observable contexts while those in negative positions are observed by using concrete equality in the implementation. In that sense, Machado's approach is not a pure black-box approach deriving test cases and oracles from specifications but an approach mixing black-box and white-box where test cases are derived from the specifications and the oracle procedure is built from both the specification and the IUT.

We have shown that to deal with axioms with non-observable premises, it is not possible to apply observable contexts. However, can we do something else to handle such axioms? A tempting solution is to use the specification to recognise some ground instances of the axiom for which the specification requires the non observable premise to be true.

Let us come back to the axiom

$$x :: x :: l = x :: l \Rightarrow true = false$$

If it stands alone, nothing can be done to test it. Let us introduce a new axiom stating the idempotence law on the element insertion:

$$eq(x, y) = true \Rightarrow x :: y :: l = y :: l$$

Any ground instance of $x :: x :: l = x :: l$ is then a semantic consequence of the specification such that $true = false$ also becomes a semantic consequence. In such a case, one would like to consider $true = false$ as a test and even more, it seems rather crucial to submit this test precisely! This small example illustrates clearly why in this case, tests cannot be only ground instances of axioms but

---

[16] Roughly speaking, an atom $t = t'$ is said to be in a positive position if by putting the test into disjunctive normal form, then the $t = t'$ is not preceded by a negation.

shoud be selected among all the observable semantic consequences of the specification[17] (see the end of Section 2 for the definition of semantic consequence.). Let us remark that according to the form of the specifications, one can use the unfolding technique described in Section 5 in order to solve the premise in the specification. In [42], Le Gall has shown that when the specification is complete with respect to the set $\mathcal{C}_{Obs}$ of constructors of observable sorts and under $H_{min, \mathcal{C}_{Obs}}$,

$$EqExhaust_{SP}^{Obs} = \{c[t]\rho = c[t']\rho \mid \exists \alpha_1 \wedge \ldots \wedge \alpha_n \Rightarrow t = t' \in Ax, \rho \in V \to T_\Sigma,$$
$$c \text{ min. obs. context}, SP \models (\alpha_1 \wedge \ldots \wedge \alpha_n)\rho\}$$

is an exhaustive test set with respect to observational correctness. Curiously, whether there are non-observable premises or not in the specification, the corresponding equational exhaustive test set is not modified.

7 Related Work

7.1 Related Work on Selection

In [24], Claessen and Hughes propose the QuickCheck tool for randomly testing Haskell programs from algebraic specifications. Axioms are encoded into executable Haskell programs whose arguments denote axiom variables. Conditional properties are tested by drawing data until finding a number, given as parameter, of cases which satisfy the premises. Of course, the procedure is stopped when a too large number of values is reached. The QuickCheck tool provides the user with test case generation functions for any arbitrary Haskell data type, and in particular, also for functional types. The user can observe how the random data are distributed over the data type carrier. When he considers that the distribution is not well balanced on the whole domain, for instance if the premises are satisfied by data of small size only, it is possible to specialise the test case generation functions to increase the likelihood to draw values ensuring a better coverage of the domain of premise satisfaction. This last feature is very useful for dealing with dependent data types. In [7], Berghofer and Nipkow use Quickcheck to exhibit counter-examples for universally quantified formulae written in executable Isabelle/HOL. This is a simple way to rapidly debug formalisation of a theory. In [32], Dydjer et al. develop a similar approach of using functional testing technics to help the proof construction by analysing counter-examples.

In [18], Brucker and Wolff use the full theorem proving environment Isabelle/HOL to present a method and a tool HOL-TestGen for generating test cases. They recommend to take benefit of the Isabelle/HOL proof engine equipped with tactics to transform a test domain (denoted as some proof goal) into test subdomains (denoted as proof subgoals). Selection hypotheses are expressed as proof hypotheses and the user can interact to guide the test data generation. Both the Quickcheck

---

[17] Observable semantic consequences are just those semantic consequences that belong to *Obs*. By construction, selecting a test outside this set would reject at least one correct implementation.

and TestGen tools present the advantage of offering an unified framework to deal with the specification, the selection and the generation of test cases, and even the submission of the test cases and the computation of the test verdict.

7.2   Related Work on Observability

We have given a brief account of observability considerations and their important impact on testability issues. In particular, there does not always exist an exhaustive test set, since such an existence depends on some properties of the specification and the implementation: namely, restrictions on the specification and hypotheses on the implementation.

The importance of observability issues for the oracle problem as been first raised by Bougé [16] and then Bernot, Gaudel and Marre in [8,10]. It has been studied later on by Le Gall and Arnould [43] and Machado [3,45]. Depending on the hypotheses on the possible observations and on the form or the extensions of the considered specifications, the oracle problem has been specialised. For example, in [4], Arnould et al. define a framework for testing from specifications of bounded data types. To some extent, bounds of data types limit the possible observations: any data out of the scope of the bound description should not be observed when testing against such specifications. The set of observable formulae are formulae which are observable in the classical sense, where all terms are computed as being under the specified bound.

As soon as partial function are considered in the specification, it must be observable whether a term is defined or not. In [3], Arnould and Le Gall consider specifications with partial functions where definedness can be specified using an unary predicate def. The specification of equalities are declined with two predicates, strong equality $=$ allowing two undefined terms to be equal; existential equality $\overset{e}{=}$ for which only defined terms may be considered as equal. As the predicate $\overset{e}{=}$ may be expressed in term of $=$ and def, testing from specification with partiality naturally introduces two kinds of elementary tests directly related to the predicates def and $=$. Testing with partial functions requires to take into account the definition predicate: intuitively, testing whether a term is defined or not systematically precedes the following testing step, that is testing about equality of terms. Some initial results about testability and exhaustive test sets can be found in [3].

7.3   Variants of Exhaustivity

Most exhaustive test sets presented here are made of tests directly derived from the axioms: tests are ground instances of (conclusions of) axioms, some equalities being possibly surrounded by observable contexts. Such tests do not necessarily reflect the practice of testing. Actually, the usual way of testing consists in applying the operation under test to some tuples of ground constructor terms and to compare the value computed by the IUT to a ground constructor term denoting the expected result. This can be described by tests of the form:

$$f(u_1, \ldots, u_n) = v$$

with f the function to be tested, and $u_1, \ldots, u_n, v$ ground constructor terms. The underlying intuition is that the constructor terms can denote all the concrete values manipulated by the implementation (reachability constraint). To illustrate this point of view, in the case of the CONTAINERS specification and by considering again that the sort $Container$ is observable, for the axiom $remove\_2$, instead of testing $remove(2, 3 :: []) = 3 :: remove(2, [])$ by solving the premise $eq(2, 3) = false$, a test of the good form would be $remove(2, 3 :: []) = 3 :: []$. Such a test may be obtained by applying the $remove\_1$ axiom to the occurrence $remove(2, [])$. In particular, LOFT [48,49] computes tests of this reduced form. In [1,3,4], Arnould et al. present some exhaustive tests built from such tests involving constructor terms as much as possible.

7.4   The Case of Structured Specifications

Until now, we have considered flat specifications which consist of a signature, a set of axioms, and possibly reachability constraints. Moreover, we have studied the distinction between observable and non observable sorts. Observable sorts often correspond to the basic types provided by the programming environment, and non observable sorts to the type of interest for the specification. However, algebraic specifications may be structured using various primitives allowing to import, combine, enrich, rename or forget (pieces of) imported specifications. Such constructions should be taken into account when testing.

As a first step to integration testing of systems described by structured algebraic specifications, Machado in [46,47] shows how to build a test set whose structure is guided by the structure of the specification. The main and significant drawback of this approach is that hidden operations are ignored. As soon as an axiom involves an hidden operation, the axiom is not tested. Depending on the organisation of the specification, this can mean that a lot of properties are removed from the set of properties to be tested.

In [30], Doche and Wiels define a framework for composing test cases according to the structure of the specification. Their approach may be considered as modular since the IUT should have the same structure as the specification and the tests related to the sub-specifications are composed together. These authors have established that correctness is preserved under some hypotheses[18] and have applied their approach to an industrial case study reported in [29].

8   Case Studies and Applications to Other Formal Methods

This part of the paper briefly reports some case studies and experiments related to the theory presented here. Some of them were performed at LRI, some of

---

[18] For interested readers, the hypotheses aim at preserving properties along signature morphisms and thus, are very close to the satisfaction condition of the institution framework.

them elsewhere. The first subsection is devoted to studies based on algebraic specifications. The next one reports interesting attempts to transpose some aspects of the theory to other formal approaches, namely VDM, Lustre, extended state machines and labelled transition systems. A special subsection presents some applications to object-oriented descriptions.

8.1   First Case Studies with Algebraic Specifications

A first experiment, performed at LRI by Dauchy and Marre, was on the on-board part of the driving system of an automatic subway[19] in collaboration with a certification agency. An algebraic specification was written [27]. Then two critical modules of the specification were used for experiments with LOFT: the overspeed controller and the door opening controller. These two modules shared the use of eight other specification modules that described the state of the on-board system. The number of axioms for the door controller was 25, with rather complex premises. The number of axioms of the speed controller was 34. There where 108 function names and several hundred axioms in the shared modules. Different choices of uniformity hypotheses were experienced for the door controller: they led to 230, 95, and 47 tests. For the over-speed controller, only one choice was sensible and led to 95 tests. The experiment is reported in details in [26]. In a few words, these tests were used by the certification team as a sort of checklist against the tests performed by the development team. This approach led to the identification of a tricky combination of conditions that had not been tested by the developers.

A second experiment is reported in [53] and was performed within a collaboration between LRI and the LAAS laboratory in Toulouse. The experiment was performed on a rather small piece of software written in C, which was extracted from a nuclear safety shutdown system. The piece of software contained some already known bugs that were discovered but one: it was related to some hidden shared variable in the implementation, and required rather large instantiations, larger than the bound chosen a priori for the regularity hypothesis. On a theoretical point of view, this can be analysed as a case where the testability hypothesis was not ensured. More practically, the fault was easy to detect by "white-box" methods, either static analysis or structural testing with branch coverage. This is coherent with the remark in Section 4 on the possibility of static checking of the testability hypothesis, and with the footnote 4 in Section 5 on the difficulties to determine adequate bounds for regularity hypotheses.

An experiment of "intensive" testing of the EPFL library of Ada components was led by Buchs and Barbey in the Software Engineering Laboratory at EPFL [6]. First an algebraic specification of the component was reengineered: the signature was derived from the package specifications of the family, and the axioms were written manually. Then the LOFT system was used with a standard choice of hypotheses.

LOFT has been also used for the validation of a transit node algebraic specification [2]. Generating test cases was used for enumerating scenarios with a given

---

[19] Precisely, the train controller on line D in Lyon that has been operating since 1991.

pattern. It led to the identification of one undesirable, and unexpected, scenario in the formal specification.

It was also used for the test of the data types of an implementation of the Two-Phase-Commit protocol [34] without finding any fault: this was probably due to the fact that the implementation had been systematically derived from a formal specification. Other aspects of this case study are reported in the next subsection.

The specifications and test sets of these case studies are too large to be given here. Details can be found in [27] and [26] for the first one, in [2] and [50] for the transit node, and in [41] for the Two-Phase-Commit protocol.

8.2   Applications to Other Methods

Actually, the approach developed here for algebraic data types is rather generic and presents a general framework for test data selection from formal specifications. It has been reused for, or has inspired, several test generation methods from various specification formalisms: VDM, Lustre, full LOTOS.

The foundational paper by Jeremy Dick and Alain Faivre on test case generation from VDM specifications [28] makes numerous references to some of the notions and techniques presented here, namely uniformity and regularity hypotheses, and unfolding. The formulae of VDM specifications are relations on states described by operations (in the sense of VDM, i.e., state modifications). They are expressed in first-order predicate calculus. These relations are reduced to a disjunctive normal form (DNF), creating a set of disjoint sub-relations. Each sub-relation yields a set of constraints which describe a single test domain. The reduction to DNF is similar to axiom unfolding: uniformity and regularity hypotheses appear in relation with this partition analysis. As VDM is state-based, it is not enough to partition the operations domains. Thus the authors give a method of extracting a finite state automaton from a specification. This method uses the results of the partition analysis of the operations to perform a partition analysis of the states. This led to a set of disjoint classes of states, each of which corresponds either to a precondition or a postcondition of one of the above sub-relations. Thus, a finite state automaton can be defined, where the states are some equivalence classes of states of the specifications. From this automaton, some test suites are produced such that they ensure a certain coverage of the automaton paths. The notion of test suites is strongly related to the state orientation of the specification: it is necessary to test the state evolution in presence of sequences of data, the order being important.

Test generation from Lustre descriptions has been first studied jointly at CEA and LRI. The use of the LOFT system to assist the test of Lustre programs has been investigated. Lustre is a description language for reactive systems which is based on the synchronous approach [38]. An algebraic semantics of Lustre was stated and entered as a specification in LOFT. Lustre programs were considered as enrichments of this specification, just as some specific axiom to be tested. After this first experience, GATEL, a specific tool for Lustre was developed by Marre at CEA (Commissariat à l'Énergie Atomique). In GATEL, a Lustre specification of the IUT, and some Lustre descriptions of environment constraints and test purpose are interpreted via Constraint Logic Programming. Unfolding is the basic technique, coupled with a specific constraint solving library [51,52]. GATEL is used at IRSN (Institut de Radioprotection et Sûreté Nucléaire) for identifying those reachable classes of tests covering a given specification, according to some required coverage criteria. The functional tests performed by the developers are then compared to these classes in order to point out uncovered classes, i.e., insufficient testing. If it is the case, GATEL provides test scenarios for the missing classes.

LOTOS is a well known formal specification language, mainly used in the area of communication protocols. There are two variants: basic LOTOS makes it possible to describe processes and their synchronisation, with no notion of data type; full LOTOS, where it is possible to specify algebraic data types and how their values can be communicated or shared between specified processes. In the first case, the underlying semantics of a basic LOTOS specification is a finite labelled transition system. There is an extremely rich corpus of testing methods based on such finite models (see [17] for an annotated bibliography). However, there are few results on extending them to infinite models, as it is the case when non trivial data types are introduced. In [34], Gaudel and James have stated the underlying notions of testability hypotheses, exhaustive test sets, and selection hypotheses for full LOTOS.

This approach has been used by James for testing an implementation of the Two-Phase-Commit Protocol developed from a LOTOS specification into Concert/C. The results of this experiment are reported in [41]. As said in the previous sub-section, tests for the data types were obtained first with the LOFT system. Then a set of testers was derived manually from the process part of the specification. The submission of these tests, was preceded by a test campaign of the implementations of the atomic actions of the specification by the Concert/C library, i.e., the communication infrastructure (the set of gates connecting the processes), which was developed step by step. It was motivated by the testability hypothesis: it was a way of ensuring the fact that the actions in the implementation were the same as in the specification, and that they were atomic. No errors were found in the data types implementations, but an undocumented error of the Concert/C pre-processor was detected when testing them. Some errors were discovered in the implementation of the main process. They were related to memory management, and to the treatment of the time-outs. There are always questions on the interest of testing pieces of software, which have been formally specified and almost directly derived from the specification. But this experiment shows that problems may arise: the first error-prone aspect, memory management, was not expressed in the LOTOS specification because of its abstract nature; the second one was specified in a tricky way due to the absence of explicit time in classical LOTOS. Such unspecified aspects are unavoidable when developing efficient implementation.

8.3   Applications to Object-Oriented Software

It is well known that there is a strong relationship between abstract data types and object orientation. There is the same underlying idea of encapsulation of the concrete implementation of data types. Thus it is not surprising that the testing methods presented here for algebraic specifications has been adapted to the test of object oriented systems. We present two examples of such adaptations.

The ASTOOT approach was developed by Dong and Frankl at the Polytechnic University in New-York [31]. The addressed problem was the test of object-oriented programs: classes are tested against algebraic specifications. A set of tools had been developed. As mentioned at the end of Section 4, a different choice was made for the exhaustive test set, which is the set of equalities of every ground term with its normal form, and it was also suggested to test inequalities of ground terms As normal forms are central in the definition of tests, there was a requirement that the axioms of the specification must define a convergent term rewriting system. Moreover, there is a restriction to classes such that their operations have no side effects on their parameters and functions have no side effects: it corresponds to a notion of testability. The oracle problem was addressed by introducing a notion of observational equivalence between objects of user-defined classes, which is based on minimal observational contexts, and by approximating it. Similarly to Section 5, the test case selection was guided by an analysis of the conditions occurring in the axioms; the result was a set of constraints that was solved manually. The theory presented here for algebraic data types turned out to cope well with object-orientation, even when different basic choices were made.

This had been confirmed by further developments by Tse and its group at the university of Hong Kong [20,22,56]. In their approach, object-oriented systems are described by algebraic specifications for classes and contract specification for clusters of related classes: contracts specify interactions between objects via message-passing rules. As in our approach, some tests are fundamental pairs of equivalent ground terms obtained via instantiations of the axioms. As in ASTOOT non equivalent pairs of terms are also considered. Some white-box heuristic for selecting relevant observable contexts makes it possible to determine whether the objects resulting from executing such test cases are observationally equivalent. Moreover, message passing test sequences are derived from the contract specification and the source code of the methods. This method has been recently applied for testing object-oriented industrial software [56].

9   Conclusion

Algebraic specifications have proved to be an interesting basis for stating some theory of black-box testing and for developing methods and tools. The underlying ideas have turned out to be rather general and applicable to specification methods including data types, whatever the formalism used for their description. It is the case of the notions of uniformity hypothesis, and regularity hypotheses that have been reused in other contexts.

In presence of abstraction and encapsulation, the oracle problem raises difficult issues due to the limitations on the way concrete implementations can be observed and interpreted. This is not specific to algebraic specifications and abstract data types: the same problems arise for embedded and/or distributed systems. It is interesting to note the similarity between the observable contexts presented here, and the various ways of distinguishing and identifying the state reached after a test sequence in finite state machines [44], namely separating families, distinguishing sequences, characterising sets, and their variants.

The methodology presented here has been applied, as such or with some adjustments, in a significant number of academic and industrial case studies. In most cases, they have been used for some a posteriori certification of critical systems that had already been intensively validated and verified, or for testing implementations that have been developed from some formal specification. This is not surprising: in the first case, the risks are such that certification agencies are ready to explore sophisticated methods; in the second case, the availability of the formal specification encourages its use for test generation. In both circumstances, it was rather unlikely to find errors. However, some were discovered and missing test cases were identified. In some cases, the detection of these were welcome and prevented serious problems. This is an indication of the interest in test methods based on formal specifications and of the role they can play in the validation and verification process.

References

1. Aiguier, M., Arnould, A., Boin, C., Le Gall, P., Marre, B.: Testing from algebraic specifications: Test data set selection by unfolding axioms. In: Grieskamp, W., Weise, C. (eds.) FATES 2005. LNCS, vol. 3997, pp. 203–217. Springer, Heidelberg (2006)
2. Arnold, A., Gaudel, M., Marre, B.: An experiment on the validation of a specification by heterogeneous formal means: The transit node. In: 5th IFIP Working Conference on Dependable Computing for Critical Applications (DCCA5), pp. 24–34 (1995)
3. Arnould, A., Le Gall, P.: Test de conformité: une approche algébrique. Technique et Science Informatiques, Test de logiciel 21(9), 1219–1242 (2002)
4. Arnould, A., Le Gall, P., Marre, B.: Dynamic testing from bounded data type specifications. In: Hlawiczka, A., Simoncini, L., Silva, J.G.S. (eds.) EDCC 1996. LNCS, vol. 1150, pp. 285–302. Springer, Heidelberg (1996)
5. Astesiano, E., Kreowski, H.-J., Krieg-Bruckner, B.: Algebraic Foundations of Systems Specification. In: IFIP State-of-the-Art Reports, Springer, Heidelberg (1999)
6. Barbey, S., Buchs, D.: Testing Ada abstract data types using formal specifications. In: 1st Int. Eurospace-Ada-Europe Symposium. LNCS, vol. 887, pp. 76–89. Springer, Heidelberg (1994)
7. Berghofer, S., Nipkow, T.: Random testing in isabelle/hol. In: SEFM, pp. 230–239 (2004)
8. Bernot, G.: Testing against formal specifications: A theoretical view. In: Abramsky, S. (ed.) TAPSOFT 1991, CCPSD 1991, and ADC-Talks 1991. LNCS, vol. 494, pp. 99–119. Springer, Heidelberg (1991)

9. Bernot, G., Bouaziz, L., Le Gall, P.: A theory of probabilistic functional testing. In: ICSE 1997: Proceedings of the 19th international conference on Software engineering, pp. 216–226. ACM Press, New York (1997)

10. Bernot, G., Gaudel, M.-C., Marre, B.: Software testing based on formal specifications: A theory and a tool. Software Engineering Journal 6(6), 387–405 (1991)

11. Bernot, G., Gaudel, M.-C., Marre, B.: A formal approach to software testing. In: 2nd International Conference on Algebraic Methodology and Software Technology (AMAST). Worshops in Computing Series, vol. 670, pp. 243–253. Springer, Heidelberg (1992)

12. Bidoit, M., Hennicker, R.: Behavioural theories and the proof of behavioural properties. Theoretical Computer Science 165(1), 3–55 (1996)

13. Bidoit, M., Hennicker, R., Wirsing, M.: Behavioural and abstractor specifications. Science of Computer Programming 25(2-3), 149–186 (1995)

14. Bidoit, M., Mosses, P.D.: CASL user manual. LNCS, vol. 2900. Springer, Heidelberg (1998)

15. Bougé, L.: Modélisation de la notion de test de programmes, application à la production de jeux de test. Ph. D. thesis, Université de Paris 6 (1982)

16. Bougé, L., Choquet, N., Fribourg, L., Gaudel, M.-C.: Test set generation from algebraic specifications using logic programming. Journal of Systems and Software 6(4), 343–360 (1986)

17. Brinksma, E., Tretmans, J.: Testing transition systems: An annotated bibliography. In: Cassez, F., Jard, C., Rozoy, B., Dermot, M. (eds.) MOVEP 2000. LNCS, vol. 2067, pp. 187–195. Springer, Heidelberg (2001)

18. Brucker, A.D., Wolff, B.: Symbolic test case generation for primitive recursive functions. In: Grabowski, J., Nielsen, B. (eds.) FATES 2004. LNCS, vol. 3395, pp. 16–32. Springer, Heidelberg (2005)

19. Burstall, R.M., Darlington, J.: A transformation system for developing recursive programs. Journal of the Association for Computing Machinery 24(1), 44–67 (1977)

20. Chen, H.Y., Tse, T.H., Chan, F.T., Chen, T.Y.: In black and white: an integrated approach to class-level testing of object-oriented programs. ACM transactions on Software Engineering and Methodology 7(3), 250–295 (1998)

21. Chen, H.Y., Tse, T.H., Chan, F.T., Chen, T.Y.: In black and white: an integrated approach to class-level testing of object-oriented programs. ACM transactions on Software Engineering and Methodology 7(3), 250–295 (1998)

22. Chen, H.Y., Tse, T.H., Chen, T.Y.: TACCLE: A methodology for object-oriented software testing at the class and cluster levels. ACM Transactions on Software Engineering and Methodology 10(1), 56–109 (2001)

23. Chow, T.S.: Testing software design modeled by finite-state machines. IEEE Transactions on Software Engineering SE-4(3), 178–187 (1978)

24. Claessen, K., Hughes, J.: Quickcheck: A lightweight tool for random testing of haskell programs. In: International Conference on Functional Programming, pp. 268–279 (2000)

25. Dan, L., Aichernig, B.K.: Combining algebraic and model-based test case generation. In: ICTAC 2004 (2004)

26. Dauchy, P., Gaudel, M.-C., Marre, B.: Using algebraic specifications in software testing: A case study on the software of an automatic subway. Journal of Systems and Software 21(3), 229–244 (1993)

27. Dauchy, P., Ozello, P.: Experiments with formal specifications on MAGGALY. In: Second International Conference on Applications of Advanced Technologies in Transportation Engineering, Mineapolis (1991)

28. Dick, J., Faivre, A.: Automating the generation and sequencing of test cases from model-based specifications. In: Formal Methods Europe 1993. LNCS, vol. 670, pp. 268–284. Springer, Heidelberg (1993)
29. Doche, M., Seguin, C., Wiels, V.: A modular approach to specify and test an electrical flight control system. In: FMICS-4 (1999)
30. Doche, M., Wiels, V.: Extended institutions for testing. In: Rus, T. (ed.) AMAST 2000. LNCS, vol. 1816, pp. 514–528. Springer, Heidelberg (2000)
31. Dong, R.K., Frankl, Ph.G.: The ASTOOT approach to testing object-oriented programs. ACM Transactions on Software Engineering and Methodology 3(2), 103–130 (1994)
32. Dybjer, P., Haiyan, Q., Takeyama, M.: Combining testing and proving in dependent type theory. In: Basin, D., Wolff, B. (eds.) TPHOLs 2003. LNCS, vol. 2758, pp. 188–203. Springer, Heidelberg (2003)
33. Gannon, J., McMullin, P., Hamlet, R.: Data abstraction implementation, specification and testing. ACM Transactions on Programming Languages and Systems 3(3), 211–223 (1981)
34. Gaudel, M.-C., James, P.J.: Testing algebraic data types and processes: A unifying theory. Formal Aspects of Computing 10(5-6), 436–451 (1998)
35. Goguen, J.A., Thatcher, J.W., Wagner, E.G.: An initial algebra approach to the specification, correctness and implementation of abstract data types. In: Current Trends in Programming Methodology IV: Data structuring, pp. 80–144. Prentice Hall, Englewood Cliffs (1978)
36. Goodenough, J.B., Gerhart, S.: Toward a theory of test data selection. IEEE Transactions on Software Engineering SE-1(2), 156–173 (1975)
37. Guttag, J.V., Horning, J.J.: The algebraic specification of abstract data types. Acta Informatica 10(1), 27–52 (1978)
38. Halbwachs, N., Caspi, P., Raymond, P., Pilaud, D.: The synchronous data-flow programming language LUSTRE. Proceedings of the IEEE 79(9), 1305–1320 (1991)
39. Hennicker, R.: Context induction: a proof principle for behavioural abstractions and algebraic implementations. Formal Aspects of Computing 3(4), 326–345 (1991)
40. Hierons, R.M.: Comparing test sets and criteria in the presence of test hypotheses and fault domains. ACM Trans. Softw. Eng. Methodol. 11(4), 427–448 (2002)
41. James, P.R., Endler, M., Gaudel, M.-C.: Development of an atomic broadcast protocol using LOTOS. Software Practice and Experience 29(8), 699–719 (1999)
42. Le Gall, P.: Les algèbres étiquetées : une sémantique pour les spécifications algébriques fondée sur une utilisation systématique des termes. Application au test de logiciel avec traitement d'exceptions. PhD thesis, Université de Paris XI, Orsay (1993)
43. Le Gall, P., Arnould, A.: Formal specification and test: correctness and oracle. In: 11th WADT joint with the 9th general COMPASS workshop, Oslo, Norway. LNCS, vol. 1130, pp. 342–358. Springer, Heidelberg (1996)
44. Lee, D., Yannakakis, M.: Principles and methods of testing finite state machines - A survey. Proceedings of the IEEE 84, 1090–1126 (1996)
45. Machado, P.: On oracles for interpreting test results against algebraic specifications. In: Haeberer, A.M. (ed.) AMAST 1998. LNCS, vol. 1548, Springer, Heidelberg (1998)
46. Machado, P.: Testing from structured algebraic specifications. In: Rus, T. (ed.) AMAST 2000. LNCS, vol. 1816, pp. 529–544. Springer, Heidelberg (2000)
47. Machado, P., Sannella, D.: Unit testing for CASL architectural specifications. In: Diks, K., Rytter, W. (eds.) MFCS 2002. LNCS, vol. 2420, pp. 506–518. Springer, Heidelberg (2002)

48. Marre, B.: Toward an automatic test data set selection using algebraic specifications and logic programming. In: Furukawa, K. (ed.) Eight International Conference on Logic Programming (ICLP 1991), pp. 25–28. MIT Press, Cambridge (1991)

49. Marre, B.: Loft: a tool for assisting selection of test data sets from algebraic specifications. In: Mosses, P.D., Schwartzbach, M.I., Nielsen, M. (eds.) CAAP 1995, FASE 1995, and TAPSOFT 1995. LNCS, vol. 915, pp. 799–800. Springer, Heidelberg (1995)

50. Marre, B., Arnold, A., Gaudel, M.C.: Validation d'une spécification par des formalismes différents: le noeud de transit. Revue Technique et Science Informatiques 16(6), 677–699 (1997)

51. Marre, B., Arnould, A.: Test sequences generation from LUSTRE descriptions: GATEL. In: 15h I.E.E.E. International Conference on Automated Software Engineering, pp. 229–237 (2000)

52. Marre, B., Blanc, B.: Test selection strategies for lustre descriptions in gatel. In: MBT 2004 joint to ETAPS 2004. ENTCS, vol. 111, pp. 93–111 (2004)

53. Marre, B., Thévenod-Fosse, P., Waeselink, H., Le Gall, P., Crouzet, Y.: An experimental evaluation of formal testing and statistical testing. In: SAFECOMP 1992, pp. 311–316 (1992)

54. Orejas, F., Navarro, M., Sanchez, A.: Implementation and behavioural equivalence: A survey. In: Bidoit, M., Choppy, C. (eds.) Abstract Data Types 1991 and COMPASS 1991. LNCS, vol. 655, pp. 144–163. Springer, Heidelberg (1993)

55. Péraire, C., Barbey, S., Buchs, D.: Test selection for object-oriented software based on formal specifications. In: IFIP Working Conference on Programming Concepts and Methods (PROCOMET 1998), Shelter Island, New York, USA, June 1998, pp. 385–403. Chapman Hall, Boca Raton (1998)

56. Tse, T.H., Lau, F.C.M., Chan, W.K., Liu, P.C.K., Luk, C.K.F.: Testing object-oriented industrial software without precise oracles or results. Communications of the ACM (accepted, 2006)

57. Wirsing, M.: Handbook of Theoretical Computer Science. In: Formal models and semantics, chapter Algebraic Specification, vol. B, Elsevier, Amsterdam (1990)

58. Zhu, H.: A note on test oracles and semantics of algebraic specifications. In: QSIC 2003, pp. 91–99. IEEE Computer Society, Los Alamitos (2003)

From MC/DC to RC/DC: Formalization and Analysis of Control-Flow Testing Criteria[*]

Sergiy A. Vilkomir[1] and Jonathan P. Bowen[2]

[1] Software Quality Research Laboratory (SQRL)
Department of Electrical Engineering and Computer Science
The University of Tennessee, 203 Claxton Complex, Knoxville, TN 37996-3450, USA
vilkomir@cs.utk.edu
[2] Centre for Research on Evolution, Search and Testing (CREST)
Department of Computer Science, Kings College London
Strand, London WC2R 2LS, UK
jpbowen@gmail.com
http://www.jpbowen.com

Abstract. This chapter describes an approach to the formalization of existing criteria used in computer systems software testing and proposes a Reinforced Condition/Decision Coverage (RC/DC) criterion. This criterion has been developed from the well-known Modified Condition/Decision Coverage (MC/DC) criterion and is more suitable for the testing of safety-critical software where MC/DC may not provide adequate assurance. As a formal language for describing the criteria, the Z notation has been selected. Formal definitions in the Z notation for RC/DC, as well as MC/DC and other criteria, are presented. Specific examples of using these criteria for specification-based testing are considered and some features are formally proved. This characterization is helpful in the understanding of different types of testing and also the correct application of a desired testing regime.

1 Introduction

Software testing criteria (or alternatively, test data adequacy criteria or coverage criteria) play an important role in the whole testing process. These criteria are used as [65]:

- stopping rules that determine whether sufficient testing has been done;
- measurements of test quality, when a degree of adequacy is associated with each test set;
- generators, for test data selection. Test sets are considered as equivalent if they satisfy the same criterion.

The use of testing criteria as regulatory requirements during software certification and licensing also has its own specific features and benefits. At the time of

---

[*] This chapter was previously published as [55] and is reproduced here in a slightly modified form with permission.

R.M. Hierons et al. (Eds.): Formal Methods and Testing, LNCS 4949, pp. 240–270, 2008.

regulatory assessment, the stage of testing assessment is one of the most important where efforts of experts should be concentrated [58].

The methods and criteria of testing are traditionally divided into structural (or white-box) and functional (or black-box) aspects [41,47]. Structural testing criteria (i.e., criteria that take into account an internal structure of the program) are in turn divided into data-flow and control-flow criteria, although the combination of the two has been considered [44,51]. Data-flow criteria are based on the investigation of the ways in which values are associated with variables and how these associations can affect the execution of the program [65]. Control-flow criteria, in particular, examine logical expressions, which determine the branch and loop structure of the program. This group of criteria is considered in this chapter. The aim of these criteria is to help in testing *decisions* (the program points at which the control flow can divide into various paths) and *conditions* (atomic predicates which form component parts of decisions) in a program.

If software is developed based on formal (mathematical) specifications, control-flow criteria might be used to examine logical expressions from specifications. In other words, the same criteria might be used for code-based and specification-based testing. Both applications have their own specific features. The use of control-flow criteria for code-based testing has been studied in detail. In this chapter, we consider using these criteria mainly from the specification-based point of view.

In the scientific literature, criteria definitions are typically informal (in natural language). Sometimes these definitions are not clear enough and this can lead to inaccurate understanding. However, formal methods [10] can be helpful both in clarifying testing criteria and also aiding in the testing process itself [8]. In this chapter, the task of producing formal criteria definitions is considered. As a formal language for describing the criteria, the Z notation [30,49] has been selected, which is used not only in an academic context but also for industrial development of high-integrity systems such as safety-critical software [9].

This chapter is based on our previous results [52,53] and is structured as follows. Section 2 presents a brief review and then formal definitions of various control-flow criteria. Criteria such as statement coverage (SC), decision coverage (DC), condition coverage (CC), decision/condition coverage (D/CC), multiple-condition coverage (MCC) and full predicate coverage (FPC) are addressed.

Section 3 presents a detailed analysis of the Modified Condition/Decision Coverage (MC/DC) criterion. A definition in the Z notation is proposed and an explanation of how this formal approach can eliminate the ambiguity of informal definitions is given. A specific example using MC/DC is considered, illustrating the interdependence of the conditions and decisions. We analyze a major shortcoming of the MC/DC criterion, namely the deficiency of requirements for the testing of the "false operation" type of failures. Examples of situations when failures of this type are present are considered, to illustrate the problem. These have an especially vital importance for safety-critical applications.

To eliminate the shortcoming of MC/DC, we propose a Reinforced Condition/Decision Coverage (RC/DC) criterion, which is considered in Section 4. The central idea is that the MC/DC criterion can be improved if it is extended to require that each condition in a decision is shown to be varied without changing the outcome of the decision (RC/DC). Z schemas for the formal definition of RC/DC and examples of its application are provided. Some features of RC/DC as well as MC/DC are formally proved. An example when RC/DC reveals faults that are not revealed by MC/DC is considered. General conclusions and directions for future work are addressed in Section 5.

2   Control-Flow Criteria

2.1   General Definitions of Control-Flow Criteria

In the testing of control-flow criteria, the concepts of 'decision' and 'condition' are important. A decision is a program point at which the control flow can divide into various paths. An example of a decision is the **if. . . then. . . else** construct in typical imperative programming languages. A decision is a Boolean expression consisting of one or more conditions, combined by logical connectives. A condition is an elementary Boolean expression (atomic predicate) that cannot be divided into further Boolean expressions.

The simplest control-flow criteria were formulated in the 1960s and 1970s. The following are based on the well-known book by G. Myers [41]:

- SC: every statement in the program has been executed at least once;
- DC: every statement in the program has been executed at least once, and every decision in the program has taken all possible outcomes at least once;
- CC: every statement in the program has been executed at least once, and every condition in each decision has taken all possible outcomes at least once;
- D/CC: every statement in the program has been executed at least once, every decision in the program has taken all possible outcomes at least once, and every condition in each decision has taken all possible outcomes at least once;
- MCC: every statement in the program has been executed at least once, and all possible combinations of condition outcomes in each decision have been invoked at least once.

All the above-mentioned definitions involve the SC criterion as a component. However, this inclusion is slightly artificial because pure decision or condition coverage is not connected with SC. The purpose of this inclusion is to establish the following partial ordering of the control flow criteria: criterion A is stronger (subsumes) criterion B if every test set that satisfies A also satisfies B. Other relations between testing criteria have been also considered [23].

The MCC criterion is the strongest and requires the use of various combinations of conditions values. However, an excessive number of test cases can be required. If the number of conditions in a decision is equal to n, then the number of test cases to satisfy this criterion is at most 2^n; the use of so many test cases is not normally possible in practice even for relatively moderate values of n. The other criteria mentioned above are weaker and require considerably fewer test patterns. Thus, CC requires two tests for each condition and the total number of tests is at most $2n$. However, in this connection, the testing of combinations of condition values is missing and a resultant test suite may not be sufficient for safety-critical software [21].

The FPC criterion [43] is based on the use of specifications. The original definition uses different terms (for example, 'clause' instead 'condition'). However, it is possible to reformulate it in a manner that is consistent with the previous definitions. FPC requires that the value of a decision is directly correlated with the value of a condition.

The hierarchy of the above-mentioned control-flow criteria is given in Figure 1. The definitions and analysis of these criteria are considered in [41,43,47,52,65].

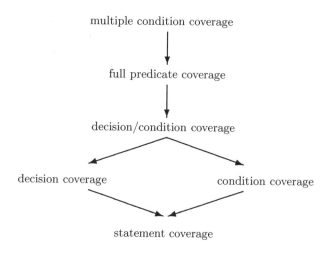

Fig. 1. The hierarchy of control-flow criteria

Traditionally, control-flow criteria are considered as code-based (program-based). In this case, decisions and conditions are considered as a part of the code (program). However, we can also consider decisions and conditions more generally as logical expressions. Similar logical expressions might be used in software specifications as well as in the software itself. In this case, the control-flow criteria can be regarded as being specification-based. Examples of using some criteria for specification-based testing are addressed later in Section 2.2, 3.4 and 4.3.

In addition to those mentioned above, other control-flow criteria have been introduced (for example, LCSAJ [64], DD-path [45] and Object Level [25] coverage criteria). Diagrams, which show the interrelationship between control-flow and data-flow criteria, are considered in [25,42,46,65].

The most complicated control-flow criterion is MC/DC. Thus, detailed consideration of MC/DC is addressed later in Section 3.

2.2 An Example for the Criteria Application

The following example illustrates the application of the testing criteria for a decision, containing three conditions and implementing the principle of the logical *majorization* '2 from 3': the decision is true if and only if any two conditions are true. This principle is widely used for data processing in many safety-critical systems [60]. Note that this example of the use of the testing criteria is given only to provide a simple explanation. It is of no great practical value because the number of conditions is small and thus it is feasible to use all combinations.

Let d be the decision and A, B and C be conditions. Then

$$d = (A \wedge B) \vee (A \wedge C) \vee (B \wedge C)$$

The values of conditions are 1 (*TRUE*) or 0 (*FALSE*). Eight combinations of the values of the conditions exist. The combinations, which satisfy the criteria, are given in Table 1.

Table 1. Combinations satisfied the criteria

combination	values				CC, D/CC,	MCC
number	A	B	C	d	DC	+
1	1	1	1	1		+
2	1	1	0	1		+
3	1	0	1	1	+	+
4	0	1	1	1		+
5	1	0	0	0		+
6	0	1	0	0	+	+
7	0	0	1	0		+
8	0	0	0	0		+

For MCC, the set containing all eight combinations is required. For DC, CC, and D/CC, two combinations are sufficient (for example, numbers 3 and 6). Other variants are also possible. Pairs $(1,8)$, $(2,7)$ and $(4,5)$ also satisfy these criteria. At the same time, pair $(2,6)$ satisfies DC criterion but is not sufficient for CC and D/CC, as conditions B and C do not vary their values.

It is necessary to remember that values of conditions depend on values of input variables. Further (in Section 3.3) we consider an example where condition A depends on variable x; $A = 1$ when $x > 20$ and $A = 0$ when $x \leq 20$.

2.3 Formalization of Control-Flow Criteria in Z

The criteria such as FPC and MC/DC are quite complicated and require additional explanation. Various interpretations of these definitions are possible giving rise to ambiguity. To help alleviate this situation, formal definitions of testing criteria are presented here.

Formalization of various testing criteria (mainly, the simple ones: SC, DC, CC) has been carried out using, for example, set theory [23], graph theory [44], predicate logic [37,51] and temporal logic [2]. In this chpater, the Z notation [30,49] is used for the formal definition of the simple criteria above as well as more complicated ones (MC/DC and RC/DC).

Some reasons for choosing the Z notation are as follows. Z has been used for a number of digital systems in a variety of ways to improve the specification of computer-based systems [6]. Advantages of Z are the existence of software tools that can automatically perform checking to eliminate certain types of errors and well-defined semantics of the language that reduces ambiguity and inaccuracy. Many textbooks on Z are now available (e.g., [31]) and Z is taught on many university computer science courses [7]. Concerning software testing, the Z notation has been used to derive tests from model-based specifications [13,50], for the testing of abstract data types (modules, classes, package, clusters) [26], automatic test case generation [11,12], and the selection of test cases and evaluation of test results [29]. So, when Z is used for software development and testing, it is expedient to use testing criteria that have also been formulated in Z.

We considered the formal definitions in the Z notation for some control-flow criteria in [52]. In this chapter, a slightly different approach is proposed. Within the framework of this approach, we distinguish between input variables for a whole program and input variables for an individual decision. It allows us to consider possible changes of values of input variables and the repeated execution of a decision in a loop. A more precise definition of the notion of a decision is introduced gradually and used in the next section for the formulation of a formal definition for MC/DC and RC/DC.

For defining the criteria, the given sets *STATEMENT* and *INPUT* are used:

[*STATEMENT*, *INPUT*]

The *STATEMENT* set contains all separately identifiable statements from a given program to be tested. The term 'statement' is understood here in the broad sense, as an explicit statement, a control statement (branch point), or an entry/exit point. An accurate definition depends on the programming language used. For our purpose, further details are not needed and it is sufficient to model *STATEMENT* as a given set. Lists of all statements that are covered by MC/DC for the C, C++ and Ada'83 programming languages are given in [17].

The *INPUT* set corresponds to all the possible states of the program during its execution. For example, we could define *INPUT* = *Variable* $\nrightarrow$ *Value*, where *Variable* is the set of all input, output and internal variables of the program and *Value* is the set of all possible values of those variables. However, the formalization used throughout this chapter does not rely on the structure of *INPUT*, so we prefer to leave it abstract. Note that we sometimes use an element of *INPUT* to represent a test case (the initial value of all the input variables), while other times we use an element of *INPUT* to represent an intermediate state of the program just before a particular decision or condition is executed. We use the name *INPUT* to emphasize the fact that the members of this set are the input data of decisions and conditions in the program.

Now we can create the Z schema[1] *StatementCoverage* for the SC criterion, which is a component of all other control-flow criteria including MC/DC and RC/DC. Since we want to analyse the internal behaviour of the program (decisions and conditions, etc.), it is not sufficient to record only the input states and output states of each execution – we also record snapshots of the internal state of the program before the execution of each statement.

The set *startinput* is the set of all *possible* input states of the program (values of the input variables). That is, it corresponds to the precondition of the program. The *starttest* variable models all the test cases that were actually executed using the program. Since each test case must satisfy the precondition of the program, *starttest* is a subset of *startinput*.

The *statementinput* function describes the internal state of the program in a concise form that is useful for analysis of coverage criteria. For each statement in the program and each possible input to the program, it gives all the possible states of the program *just before* that statement is executed. The result can be not only one specific element of *INPUT* but several different elements (a subset) of *INPUT* because of potential repeated execution of the statement in a loop. For example, if we have the statement x := x+1 within a loop, and the initial state with $x = 3$ causes this loop to be executed three times, then we might have

$$statementinput = \{(\texttt{x:=x+1}, \{x \mapsto 3\}) \mapsto \{\{x \mapsto 3\}, \{x \mapsto 4\}, \{x \mapsto 5\}\}\}$$

Another reason for having multiple states in the output of *statementinput* would be when the program is non-deterministic.

StatementCoverage _____

$startinput, starttest : \mathbb{P}\, INPUT$
$statementinput : STATEMENT \times INPUT \nrightarrow \mathbb{P}\, INPUT$

$starttest \subseteq startinput$
$\text{dom}\, statementinput = STATEMENT \times startinput$
$\forall st : STATEMENT \bullet \bigcup\{i : starttest \bullet statementinput(st, i)\} \neq \varnothing$

An alternative type for *statementinput* could be $STATEMENT \rightarrow (INPUT \leftrightarrow INPUT)$. This is a more typical formulation in Z specifications, but the (isomorphic) encoding we have chosen is nearer to the intuition of most testers.

If, for some statement *st*, the value of *statementinput* is the empty set for all testing data, this means that this statement is never executed during test runs of a program; i.e., the testing data does not satisfy the SC criterion. As the SC criterion is a component part of all other criteria, its schema is in the signature of all other schemas used for defining testing criteria.

We now introduce some definitions. The *Bool* set contains values for logical variables: 1 (*TRUE*) and 0 (*FALSE*):

---
[1] All schemas in this chapter have been checked using the ZTC type-checker package [33].

$Bool == \{0, 1\}$

We encode this as numbers since this is a standard nomenclature used by many testers. We use the elements of this set as values of $cond$, a set of partial logical functions on $INPUT$:

$cond == INPUT \nrightarrow Bool$

Another equivalent encoding more attuned to the way Z is often used could have been $cond == \mathbb{P}\, INPUT$, but again we use a formulation more familiar to those involved with testing.

The relation $InputPairs$ describes pairs of data from $INPUT$. It is convenient to use this type because we always apply a pair of test cases for testing when varying each condition or decision.

$InputPairs == INPUT \leftrightarrow INPUT$

The following schema describes a decision. According to our broad understanding of the notion of a 'statement', we consider a decision as a program statement ($decst$). This means that the decision can be executed (i.e., be covered during a program execution). The decision can be considered as a logical function ($value$) and is presented as a logical expression where arguments are conditions ($argdec$).

Dec

$StatementCoverage$
$decst : STATEMENT$
$value : cond$
$decinput, decinput0, decinput1, testset : \mathbb{P}_1\, INPUT$
$argdec : \mathbb{P}_1\, cond$
$changedec : cond \nrightarrow InputPairs$

$decinput = \mathrm{dom}\, value = \bigcup\{i : startinput \bullet statementinput(decst, i)\}$
$decinput0 = \{i : decinput \mid value\ i = 0\}$
$decinput1 = \{i : decinput \mid value\ i = 1\}$
$\langle decinput0, decinput1 \rangle$ partitions $decinput$
$testset = \bigcup\{i : starttest \bullet statementinput(decst, i)\}$
$argdec \subseteq \{c : cond \mid \mathrm{dom}\, c = decinput \wedge \mathrm{ran}\, c = Bool\}$
$\mathrm{dom}\, changedec = argdec$
$\mathrm{ran}\, changedec \subseteq decinput \leftrightarrow decinput$
$\forall c : cond \mid c \in argdec \bullet$
$\quad changedec\ c = \{i_0, i_1 : decinput \mid value\ i_0 \neq value\ i_1 \wedge c\ i_0 \neq c\ i_1\}$

The $decinput$ set contains data (values of input, output and internal variables), which activates the given decision.

The $argdec$ set contains all conditions (atomic predicates), which make a decision. For example, if a decision is $A_1 \vee B_1$, then the A_1 and B_1 conditions form the decision and *argdec* is $\{A_1, B_1\}$ (see also an example in Section 3.3). These conditions are the arguments of the logical formula; this formula determines the decision *value* function uniquely. A condition may have multiple occurrences in a decision and such occurrences are treated as one condition.

The *testset* set contains data from *INPUT*, which activating the given decision during testing of a program. The *testset* set is the only field that depends upon the actual test cases (that is, upon *starttest*). It gives the set of all the program states (immediately before the given decision was executed) that occurred during the actual test runs. So the members of *testset* are testing data for the decision. If a decision statement is executed multiple times inside a loop, one test case for the whole program from *starttest* (one test run) may generate several test cases for the decision from *testset*.

The set *changedec c* is a set of pairs of data that simultaneously vary the decision and condition c (i.e., condition c equals 0 for one element of the pair and equals 1 for another element). Consider again the decision $d = A_1 \vee B_1$, but now with conditions A_1 and B_1 depending on the input variable x; $A_1 = 1$ when $x < 5$ and $B_1 = 1$ when $x > 10$. Then the pair of input values (4, 6) is a member of the range of *changedec*(A_1); $d = 1$ and $A_1 = 1$ when $x = 4$ and $d = 0$ and $A_1 = 0$ when $x = 6$ (i.e., d and A_1 are simultaneously varied).

The following schema determines a formal definition of the DC criterion based on the fact that for any specific decision, the set *testset* should contains a pair of data that vary this decision (i.e., for which this decision takes different values, both 0 and 1).

DecisionCoverage _____

StatementCoverage
_____

$\forall\, Dec \bullet (testset \times testset) \cap \{i_0, i_1 : decinput \mid value\ i_0 \neq value\ i_1\} \neq \varnothing$

The following schema determines the CC criterion and is analogous with the previous schema. It claims that a pair of input data from the testing set should exist, for which the condition takes different values.

ConditionCoverage _____

StatementCoverage
_____

$\forall\, Dec;\ c : cond \mid c \in argdec \bullet$
$(testset \times testset) \cap \{i_0, i_1 : decinput \mid c\ i_0 \neq c\ i_1\} \neq \varnothing$

The formal description of the D/CC criterion uses the fact that this criterion is the union of the decision criterion and the condition criterion. Therefore, the schema of this criterion contains only references to two previous schemas, effectively conjoined using schema inclusion:

DecisionConditionCoverage _____

DecisionCoverage

ConditionCoverage

The last scheme determines the MCC criterion:

$$
\begin{array}{l}
\underline{MultipleConditionCoverage}\\
StatementCoverage\\[4pt]
\hline
\forall\,Dec;\ condset : \mathbb{P}\,cond \mid condset \in \mathbb{P}\,argdec\ \bullet\\
(\exists\,comb : \mathbb{P}_1\,decinput \bullet (\forall\,i : comb \bullet (\forall\,c : condset \bullet c\ i = 1)\ \wedge\\
(\forall\,c : argdec \mid c \notin condset \bullet c\ i = 0))) \Rightarrow (testset \cap comb \neq \varnothing)
\end{array}
$$

The definition claims that the testing data set (*testset*) should contain the data for testing every combination of the values of conditions in a decision, if such a combination is possible in principle (i.e., if there are input data for which the value of conditions make up the given combination). In the schema given above, each combination of the values of the conditions is clearly defined by the subset *condset* of the conditions, which equal 1 for this combination. Accordingly, the other conditions from *argdec*, which are not members of *condset*, equal 0 for this combination.

The subset of input data, which display this combination, is denoted as *comb*. If such a non-empty subset *comb* exists, then at least one of its elements should be a member of the test set.

3   MC/DC

3.1   General Definition of MC/DC

The definition of the MC/DC criterion, according to [48], is the following:

Every point of entry and exit in the program has been invoked at least once, every condition in a decision in the program has taken on all possible outcomes at least once, every decision in the program has taken all possible outcomes at least once, and each condition in a decision has been shown to affect the decision's outcome independently. A condition is shown to affect a decision's outcome independently by varying just that condition while holding fixed all other possible conditions.

The maximum number of required tests for a decision with n conditions is $2n$. The first part of the MC/DC definition (*every point of entry and exit in the program has been invoked at least once*) is just the standard SC criterion. This part is traditionally added to all control-flow criteria and is not directly connected with the main point of MC/DC.

The second and the third parts of the definition are just the CC and DC criteria. The inclusion of these parts in the definition of MC/DC could be considered excessive because satisfiability of CC and DC results from the main part of the MC/DC definition: *each condition has been shown to affect the decision's outcome independently.*

The key word in this definition is 'independently'; i.e., the aim of MC/DC is the elimination during testing of the mutual influence of the individual conditions and the testing of the correctness of each condition separately.

Investigation of MC/DC has initially been considered in [15,16,32]. Detailed consideration of the different aspects of this criterion was carried out more recently in [5,20,24,27,28,57,63]. The successful practical application of MC/DC for satellite control software has been evaluated [21] though the difficulties during the analysis of this type of coverage (e.g., it is extremely expensive to carry out and can affect staff morale and time) were also addressed [14]. The application of this criterion in the testing of digital circuits was considered in [40], test-suite reduction and prioritization algorithms for MC/DC – in [34]. A number of software tools (CodeTEST [4], DACS-Object Coverage Tools [19], LDRA Testbed [39], etc.) support the MC/DC criterion.

However, it should be noted that the original definition of the MC/DC criterion allows different interpretations and understanding during the application of the criterion. The informal definition gives no precise answer to the following practical questions (some possible answers are considered in Section 3.2):

- How to handle the situation when it is impossible to vary a condition and a decision while holding fixed all other conditions (see Section 3.3 for an example of such a situation). To assume that such a condition does not satisfy the MC/DC criterion is probably a poor way of dealing with this situation. In any case, such conditions should be checked during testing.
- How to understand multiple occurrences of a condition in a decision. For example, for a decision of the form $(A \wedge B) \vee (\neg A \wedge C)$, should we assume three conditions (A, B and C) or four (the first A, B, C and the second A) conditions? Both approaches have been used [15,27] but the last one seems unnatural for many situations.
- How to treat degenerate conditions and decisions, which are either always 0 or always 1. Of course, the appearance of such conditions should attract the attention of the tester and be justified. But if it is valid for some reason, does it mean that in this case MC/DC is not satisfied because such conditions cannot be varied?
- How to consider coupled conditions (i.e., conditions that cannot be varied independently). According to [15], two or more conditions are strongly coupled if varying one always varies the other, and weakly coupled if varying one sometimes, but not always, varies the others. However, it is questionable whether strongly coupled conditions logically differ.

Imperfection in the original definition of MC/DC caused the appearance of different forms of this criterion (e.g., Masking MC/DC) that try to solve the above-mentioned problems [17,18]. For eliminating inaccuracies and answering the above questions, a more precise formal definition of the MC/DC criterion is essential. Mathematical definitions in terms of the Boolean Difference were considered in [17,38]. Here, we propose a formal definition of MC/DC using the Z notation.

3.2   Formal Definition of MC/DC

Consider *DecModified*, an extended version of the *Dec* schema. A new set *change decfix c* of pairs of data are considered for each condition.

DecModified
_____

Dec
changedecfix : *cond* $\nrightarrow$ *InputPairs*

---
dom *changedecfix* = *argdec*
ran *changedecfix* $\subseteq$ *decinput* $\leftrightarrow$ *decinput*
$\forall c : cond \mid c \in argdec \bullet$
  changedecfix $c = \{i_0, i_1 : decinput \mid (i_0, i_1) \in changedec\ c\ \wedge$
  $(\forall othercond : argdec \mid othercond \neq c \bullet othercond\ i_0 = othercond\ i_1)\}$

The *changedecfix c* set contains pairs of data that vary the decision and given condition c (i.e., for all other conditions from the decision), the condition value for the first element of the pair coincides with the condition value for the second element. Obviously, *changedecfix* $c \subseteq changedec\ c$.

For the definition of MC/DC (and, later, RC/DC), the *choice* function is used.

---
choice : *InputPairs* $\times$ *InputPairs* $\rightarrow$ *InputPairs*

$\forall a, b : InputPairs \bullet$
$(a \neq \varnothing \Rightarrow choice(a, b) = a) \wedge (a = \varnothing \Rightarrow choice(a, b) = b)$

The arguments are two sets. If the first one is not empty, the function just returns that set; otherwise, the second set is returned.

Now it is possible to create a formal definition of MC/DC. For each condition in each decision, the aim of this criterion is to have, as a part of the testing data, pairs of input data that vary this condition simultaneously with the decision while, if it is possible, fixing all other conditions. The following Z schema captures MC/DC:

MC_DC
_____

StatementCoverage

$\forall DecModified;\ c : cond \mid c \in argdec \bullet$
$(testset \times testset) \cap choice(changedecfix\ c, changedec\ c) \neq \varnothing$

Let us prove that it is always possible to choose testing data to satisfy MC/DC (i.e., that *choice(changedecfix c, changedec c)* $\neq \varnothing$), using the method of the proof by contradiction.

Lemma 1

$MC\_DC;\ c : cond \vdash choice(changedecfix\ c, changedec\ c) \neq \varnothing$

Proof

$choice(changedecfix\ c, changedec\ c) = \varnothing$ [assumption]

$\Leftrightarrow changedec\ c = \varnothing$ [definition of $choice$]

$\Leftrightarrow \neg\,(\exists\, i_0, i_1 : decinput \mid c\ i_0 \neq c\ i_1 \bullet$ [definition of $changedec$]
$value\ i_0 \neq value\ i_1)$

$\Leftrightarrow \forall\, i_0, i_1 : decinput \mid c\ i_0 = 0 \wedge c\ i_1 = 1 \bullet$ [logic]
$value\ i_0 = value\ i_1$

$\Rightarrow \forall\, i_0, i_1 : decinput \mid$ [$decinput0, decinput1 : \mathbb{P}_1\ INPUT$]
$c\ i_0 = 0 \wedge c\ i_1 = 1 \bullet \exists\, i_2 : decinput \bullet$
$value\ i_2 \neq value\ i_0 \wedge value\ i_2 \neq value\ i_1$

$\Rightarrow \forall\, i_0, i_1 : decinput \mid c\ i_0 = 0 \wedge c\ i_1 = 1 \bullet$ [$c\ i_2 = 0 \vee c\ i_2 = 1$]
$\exists\, i_2 : decinput \bullet (c\ i_2 = 0 \wedge value\ i_2 \neq value\ i_1)\ \vee$
$(c\ i_2 = 1 \wedge value\ i_2 \neq value\ i_0)$

$\Rightarrow \exists\, i_0, i_1, i_2 : decinput \bullet$ [$c\ i_1 = 1 \wedge c\ i_0 = 0$]
$(c\ i_2 \neq c\ i_1 \wedge value\ i_2 \neq value\ i_1)\ \vee$
$(c\ i_2 \neq c\ i_0 \wedge value\ i_2 \neq value\ i_0)$

$\Rightarrow \exists\, n, m : decinput \bullet$ [$n = i_2 \wedge (m = i_0 \vee m = i_1)$]
$c\ n \neq c\ m \wedge value\ n \neq value\ m$

$\Leftrightarrow changedec\ c \neq \varnothing$ [definition of $changedec$]

$\Leftrightarrow choice(changedecfix\ c, changedec\ c) \neq \varnothing$ [definition of $choice$]

$\Rightarrow false$ [contradiction]$\square$

Let us consider how the proposed formal definition of MC/DC answers the questions formulated in Section 3.1:

- *How to handle the situation when it is impossible to vary a condition and a decision while holding fixed all other conditions.* The main point here is how to understand "while holding fixed all other *possible* conditions" from the original definition of MC/DC. One could attempt to hold fixed the maximum number of other conditions but finding such test cases could be a nontrivial optimisation task. Another approach is Masking MC/DC, to assure that no other condition influences the outcome, even if some conditions change values [22]. Both approaches significantly impede using MC/DC. According to our formal definition of MC/DC, if it is impossible to find such testing data (i.e., *changedecfix* $c = \varnothing$), we can vary the condition and the decision without fixing other conditions (i.e., take testing data from *changedec* c).
- *How to understand multiple occurrences of a condition in a decision.* In the original MC/DC paper [15] and the definition in the Federal Aviation Administration standard DO-178B [48], multiple occurrences of the same condition

are intentionally considered as different conditions. One of the reasons for this is that MC/DC was designed to be a source-code level criterion, ensuring a proper level of object code coverage. However, this controversial approach considerably complicates using MC/DC and makes no sense for specification-based testing. That is why, according to our definition of a decision (in the *Dec* schema), we consider a set (*argdec*) of conditions that make a decision. This means that each condition is considered only once. This approach is more mathematically valid and corresponds with understanding a decision as a function of conditions.

– *How to treat degenerate conditions and decisions.* According to the definition of a decision (again in the *Dec* schema), both of the sets *decinput0* and *decinput1* are non-empty. This means that every decision should take the value of both 0 and 1 and the degenerate decisions are excluded from consideration. The *Dec* schema also ensures that the range of every condition is equal to *Bool*; i.e., every condition should take both 0 and 1 values and thus degenerate conditions are excluded from consideration. The reason for this approach is that degenerate conditions and decisions are always covered by any testing data. So, we consider them as satisfying MC/DC because it does not make demands on such decisions and conditions. In this aspect our approach is similar to [17] where only 'non-constant' conditions and decisions are applied in the Masking MC/DC definition.

– *How to consider the coupled conditions.* The coupled conditions [15] cause problems in selecting the testing data satisfying the MC/DC criterion. However, these problems exist only for weakly coupled conditions. As we show below (see Lemma 2), if one condition, A, always varies another condition, B, then $A = B \lor A = \neg B$, where $\neg$ is formally defined as follows:

$$\begin{array}{|l}
\hline
\neg : cond \rightarrowtail cond \\
\hline
\forall c : cond \bullet \neg c = c \mathbin{\S} \{0 \mapsto 1, 1 \mapsto 0\}
\end{array}$$

Thus we can consider A and B as entering the same condition in a decision. In other words, strongly coupled conditions as mentioned in [15] do not logically differ. Any two strongly coupled conditions can by syntactically different as expressions but must be logically equivalent or negated as logical functions.

Lemma 2

$MC\_DC; \ A, B : cond \vdash$

$(\forall i_0, i_1 : decinput \bullet A \ i_0 \neq A \ i_1 \Rightarrow B \ i_0 \neq B \ i_1) \Rightarrow (A = B \lor A = \neg B)$

Proof

$\neg ((\forall i_0, i_1 : decinput \bullet$ [assumption]

    $A \ i_0 \neq A \ i_1 \Rightarrow B \ i_0 \neq B \ i_1) \Rightarrow (A = B \lor A = \neg B))$

$\Leftrightarrow (\forall i_0, i_1 : decinput \bullet$ [logic]

    $A \ i_0 \neq A \ i_1 \Rightarrow B \ i_0 \neq B \ i_1) \land (A \neq B \land A \neq \neg B)$

$\Rightarrow (\exists i_0, i_1 : decinput \bullet$

$$A \; i_0 = 0 \wedge A \; i_1 = 1 \wedge B \; i_0 \neq B \; i_1) \wedge \qquad \text{[ran } A = Bool]$$

$$(A \neq B \wedge A \neq \neg B)$$

[**CASE 1** : $B \; i_0 = 1, \; B \; i_1 = 0$]

$\Rightarrow A \neq \neg B$ \hfill [logic]

$\Leftrightarrow \exists \, i_2 : decinput \bullet A \; i_2 = B \; i_2$ \hfill [logic]

[**CASE 1.1** : $A \; i_2 = 0, \; B \; i_2 = 0$]

$\Rightarrow A \; i_2 \neq A \; i_1$ \hfill $[A \; i_1 = 1]$

$\Rightarrow B \; i_2 \neq B \; i_1$ \hfill $[A \; i_2 \neq A \; i_1 \Rightarrow B \; i_2 \neq B \; i_1]$

$\Rightarrow B \; i_2 = 1$ \hfill $[B \; i_1 = 0]$

$\Rightarrow false$ \hfill [contradiction with **CASE 1.1**]

[**CASE 1.2** : $A \; i_2 = 1, \; B \; i_2 = 1$]

$\Rightarrow A \; i_2 \neq A \; i_0$ \hfill $[A \; i_0 = 0]$

$\Rightarrow B \; i_2 \neq B \; i_0$ \hfill $[A \; i_2 \neq A \; i_0 \Rightarrow B \; i_2 \neq B \; i_0]$

$\Rightarrow B \; i_2 = 0$ \hfill $[B \; i_0 = 1]$

$\Rightarrow false$ \hfill [contradiction with **CASE 1.2**]

[**CASE 2** : $B \; i_0 = 0, \; B \; i_1 = 1$]

$\Rightarrow A \neq B$ \hfill [logic]

$\Leftrightarrow \exists \, i_2 : decinput \bullet A \; i_2 \neq B \; i_2$ \hfill [logic]

[**CASE 2.1** : $A \; i_2 = 0, \; B \; i_2 = 1$]

$\Rightarrow A \; i_2 \neq A \; i_1$ \hfill $[A \; i_1 = 1]$

$\Rightarrow B \; i_2 \neq B \; i_1$ \hfill $[A \; i_2 \neq A \; i_1 \Rightarrow B \; i_2 \neq B \; i_1]$

$\Rightarrow B \; i_2 = 0$ \hfill $[B \; i_1 = 1]$

$\Rightarrow false$ \hfill [contradiction with **CASE 2.1**]

[**CASE 2.2** : $A \; i_2 = 1, \; B \; i_2 = 0$]

$\Rightarrow A \; i_2 \neq A \; i_0$ \hfill $[A \; i_0 = 0]$

$\Rightarrow B \; i_2 \neq B \; i_0$ \hfill $[A \; i_2 \neq A \; i_0 \Rightarrow B \; i_2 \neq B \; i_0]$

$\Rightarrow B \; i_2 = 1$ \hfill $[B \; i_0 = 0]$

$\Rightarrow false$ \hfill [contradiction with **CASE 2.2**]$\Box$

3.3 An Example for MC/DC

The contents of the proposed formal definitions are considered below. Different examples of MC/DC use that have been presented previously (for example, see [15]) have often considered only simple decisions containing two or three conditions. Using MC/DC for such decisions has no great practical use since it is feasible to achieve full multiple condition coverage. Furthermore, such examples do not reflect complicated situations, which are typical in realistic practical examples of use of this criterion. We consider a more complex example (but one that is still far from a real practical problem because of space considerations), which takes into account the following factors:

- Dependence of the values of the conditions and decisions on input data;
- Dependence of the specific decision on its place in the computer program, i.e., on the values of other decisions in the program;
- Dependence of the conditions in the specific decision on each other (i.e., the possibility that one condition takes a value depending on the value of other conditions in this decision).

This example uses a computer program fragment, whose graph is given in Figure 2.

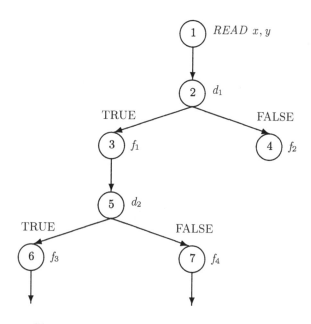

Fig. 2. Flow graph of a program fragment

In this fragment, the input data x and y are read; let the value of both x and y be between 0 and 100. For this simple example, we could consider $INPUT$ as just pairs of values:

$$INPUT == (0 .. 100) \times (0 .. 100)$$

Then, depending on the values of x and y, the computation by one from four formulae $f_1 - f_4$ is implemented.

The control flow of this program is determined by two decisions: d_1 and d_2. Let d_1 depend on conditions A_1 and B_1 and d_2 depend on conditions A, B, C and D, as it is shown below:

$d_1, d_2 : DecModified$
$A, B, C, D, A_1, B_1 : cond$
$x, y : 0 .. 100$

$A\ (x, y) = 1 \Leftrightarrow x > 20$
$B\ (x, y) = 1 \Leftrightarrow y < 60$
$C\ (x, y) = 1 \Leftrightarrow x > 40$
$D\ (x, y) = 1 \Leftrightarrow y < 80$
$A_1\ (x, y) = 1 \Leftrightarrow x > 20$
$B_1\ (x, y) = 1 \Leftrightarrow y > 60$
$d_1.decinput = INPUT$
$d_2.decinput = \{x, y : 0 .. 100 \mid x > 20 \lor y > 60\}$
$d_1.argdec = \{A_1, B_1\}$
$d_2.argdec = \{A, B, C, D\}$
$d_1.value\ (x, y) = 1 \Leftrightarrow A_1\ (x, y) = 1 \lor B_1\ (x, y) = 1$
$d_2.value\ (x, y) = 1 \Leftrightarrow$
$\quad ((A\ (x, y) = 1 \land B\ (x, y) = 1) \lor (C\ (x, y) = 1 \land D\ (x, y) = 1))$

For the d_1 decision, $d_1.decinput$ is all possible $INPUT$s and both conditions A_1 and B_1 are independent. The examples of the testing data satisfy the MC/DC criterion for d_1 are given in Table 2.

Table 2. Testing data satisfied the MC/DC criterion for d_1

num	values			testing data	variations		MC/DC
	A_1	B_1	$d_1.value$	(x, y)	A_1	B_1	
1	1	1	1	$(50, 70)$			
2	1	0	1	$(50, 50)$	*		+
3	0	1	1	$(10, 70)$		*	+
4	0	0	0	$(10, 50)$	*	*	+

For the d_2 decision, the set $d_2.decinput$ is more restrictive than the full set of possible $INPUT$s because of the interdependency of d_1 and d_2. The members of $d_2.decinput$ are only the input data for which d_1 equals 1 (i.e., is TRUE).

The conditions in d_2 are interdependent in pairs. For conditions A and C the situation $(A = 0 \land C = 1)$ is impossible because $(C = 1) \Rightarrow (A = 1)$. For conditions B and D the situation $(B = 1 \land D = 0)$ is impossible because $(B = 1) \Rightarrow (D = 1)$.

As it is shown in Table 3, only 8 of the 16 combinations of condition values are possible.

The combinations $(0, 1, 1, 1)$, $(0, 1, 1, 0)$, $(0, 0, 1, 1)$ and $(0, 0, 1, 0)$ are impossible because of the value of the condition A. Combinations $(1, 1, 1, 0)$, $(1, 1, 0, 0)$ and $(0, 1, 0, 0)$ are impossible because of the value of the condition D. The combination $(0, 1, 0, 1)$ is impossible because of the value of the decision d_1.

Testing data satisfying the MC/DC criterion for the conditions B, C and D are shown in Table 3 marked as '*'.

Table 3. Testing data satisfied the MC/DC criterion for d_2

num	values					testing data	variations				MC/DC
	A	B	C	D	$d_2.value$	(x, y)	A	B	C	D	
1	1	1	1	1	1	$(50, 50)$					
2	1	1	1	0	-	impossible					
3	1	1	0	1	1	$(30, 50)$	•	*			+
4	1	0	1	1	1	$(50, 70)$			*	*	+
5	0	1	1	1	-	impossible					
6	1	1	0	0	-	impossible					
7	1	0	1	0	0	$(50, 90)$				*	+
8	1	0	0	1	0	$(30, 70)$		*	*		+
9	0	1	1	0	-	impossible					
10	0	1	0	1	-	impossible					
11	0	0	1	1	-	impossible					
12	1	0	0	0	0	$(30, 90)$					
13	0	1	0	0	-	impossible					
14	0	0	1	0	-	impossible					
15	0	0	0	1	0	$(10, 70)$	•				+
16	0	0	0	0	0	$(10, 90)$					

For the condition A it is impossible to choose similar combinations, i.e., combinations for which the values of A and d_2 are changed and the values of B, C and D are fixed. So, following the formal definition of MC/DC, in this case for the condition A it is sufficient to take any combinations that vary A and d_2 without fixing other conditions. For example, it is possible to take combinations $(1, 1, 0, 1)$ and $(0, 0, 0, 1)$, for which the values of A and d_2 vary simultaneously (marked '•' in Table 3). The test set satisfying the MC/DC criterion for the decision d_2 consists of five pairs of the input data (marked '+' in Table 3).

3.4   The Main Shortcoming of MC/DC

As already mentioned earlier, the MC/DC criterion is used mainly for testing of safety-critical avionics software [48]. The main aim of MC/DC is testing situations when changing a condition implies a change in a decision. Often a decision can be associated with some safety-critical operation of a system. In such cases, MC/DC requires the testing of situations when changing one condition has some consequence on the operation of the system. A software error in such situations could involve *non-operation* (inability to operate on demand) type of failures. Such situations are extremely important and the MC/DC requirements are entirely reasonable.

However, as we show below, this criterion has one substantial shortcoming, not previously mentioned in the literature, namely deficiency of requirements for testing of the *false actuation* (operation without demand) type of failures. This could make this criterion insufficient for many safety-critical applications.

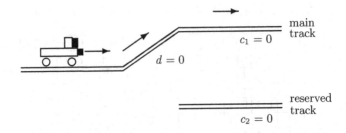

Fig. 3. Railway points: The initial situation

The false actuation of a system could be invoked by a software error in situations when changing a condition should not imply changing a decision. We now consider several examples, mainly from the specification-based point of view.

Railway points. Consider a computer control system for a railway that is responsible for switching over the points by which trains can be routed in one direction to another.

Let there be two tracks (main and reserved); conditions c_1 and c_2 determine track states (which may be either occupied or clear) and decision d determines changing the route from the main track to the reserved track and vice versa. Decision d may depend on many other conditions (not shown here), not only on c_1 and c_2, i.e., $d = f(c_1, c_2, \ldots)$. The logical function f may be quite complicated and using MC/DC is advisable. We consider using MC/DC only for c_1 and c_2.

The initial situation is shown in Figure 3. In this situation the main (upper) track is clear ($c_1 = 0$), the reserved (lower) track is clear ($c_2 = 0$), the points are set for the main track ($d = 0$). Consider two situations; the first one is tested by MC/DC and the second one is not.

The first situation (Figure 4) is when the main track becomes occupied (varying the condition c_1 from 0 to 1) and, therefore, it is necessary to switch over the points to the reserved track (varying the decision d from 0 to 1).

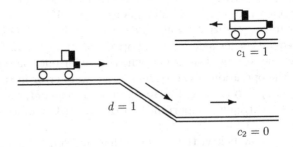

Fig. 4. Railway points: The situation that is tested by MC/DC (normal operation)

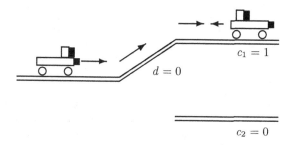

Fig. 5. Railway points: The situation that is tested by MC/DC (non-operating failure)

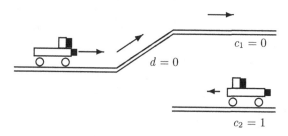

Fig. 6. Railway points: The situation that is not tested by MC/DC (normal operation)

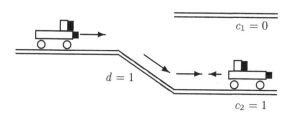

Fig. 7. Railway points: The situation that is not tested by MC/DC (false actuation failure)

Such a situation must be tested by MC/DC. To understand its importance, consider what will happen if a failure occurs. The failure in this situation (Figure 5) involves keeping the value of the decision ($d = 0$) instead of varying it; this means non-operation of the system, leaving the points positioned for the occupied track, and could result in a possible crash. So testing this situation is very important.

The second situation (Figure 6) is when the reserved track becomes occupied (varying the condition c_2 from 0 to 1) and, therefore, it is necessary to keep the main track as a route (keeping the decision d equal 0).

This situation need not be tested by MC/DC but let us again examine consequences of a failure. The failure in this situation (Figure 7) involves varying the value of the decision d from 0 to 1 instead of keeping it fixed at 0. This means false operation of the system, switching the points towards the occupied track and the possibility of a crash. So testing this situation is also very important.

Thus, from the safety point of view, these situations are symmetrical and both can lead to a crash. Therefore, both types of failures should be considered and both situations should be tested with the same degree of importance.

Protection system for a nuclear reactor. Consider a decision that is responsible for actuating a reactor protection system at a nuclear power plant (i.e., the reactor shutdown) and a condition that describes some criterion for the actuation (e.g., excessive pressure over some specified level). Varying this decision because of variation of the condition should be tested since failure in this situation means the non-operation of the system in case of emergency conditions and can lead to the nuclear accident.

Nevertheless, keeping the value of the decision is also important. The failure in this situation means the false actuation of the system during normal operating and can lead to non-forced reactor shutdown, the deterioration of the physical equipment, and the underproduction of electricity.

The typical architecture of nuclear reactor protection systems (three channels with '2 from 3' logical voting) takes into account this particular problem. The use of three identical channels decreases the probability of the system not operating correctly. However, if it is only required to consider this factor, the '1 from 3' logic is more reliable. The aim of using '2 from 3' voting is to provide protection against false actuation of a system as in this case the false signal from one channel does not lead to system actuation.

Thus, during software testing for the reactor protection system, it is necessary to include test cases for both varying and keeping a decision's outcomes.

Planned halt of a computer control system. Sometimes specific situations are possible, when keeping a decision is much more important for safety than varying a decision. Consider a decision that is responsible for a planned (non-emergency) halt of a continuous process control system, e.g., for planned maintenance. Conditions describe when this process is in a safe state allowing the control system to be switched off. Again consider two situations.

The first situation is when the state of the process becomes safe (because of varying the condition) and it is possible to switch the system off (varying the decision). The failure in this situation does not have grave consequences and means only a delay of the system halt.

The second situation is when the state of the process remains unsafe (despite varying the condition) and the control system should continue in operation (keeping the decision). The failure in this situation means that the system is erroneously switched off. Such a fault leads to loss of control and this is important with respect to safety. So it is important to test the keeping of the value of this decision.

The examples considered above demonstrate that for many cases testing only varying a decision when varying a condition (i.e., using MC/DC) is insufficient from the safety point of view. To eliminate this shortcoming, we propose the use of a new RC/DC criterion in critical applications.

4 RC/DC

4.1 General Definition of RC/DC

As we have shown in Section 3, MC/DC does not require testing some situation, which can be important for safety. The main idea of RC/DC is for future development of MC/DC with the purpose of making it more effective. Testing according to RC/DC should include test cases required by MC/DC and additional test cases for testing important situations when a false actuation of a system is possible. In that way, all requirements of MC/DC are valid and a new requirement for keeping the value of a decision when varying a condition is added to the testing regime.

With the objective of ensuring compatibility and continuity with the MC/DC definition, we define RC/DC as follows:

> Every point of entry and exit in the program has been invoked at least once, each condition in a decision has been shown to affect the decision's outcome independently, *and each condition in a decision has been shown to keep the decision's outcome independently.* A condition is shown to affect *and keep* a decision's outcome independently by varying just that condition while holding fixed *(if it is possible)* all other conditions.

The reservation "if it is possible" is used because it may not be possible to affect or keep the value of a decision independently. For more accurate consideration and analysis of all possible situations, we propose the formal definition of RC/DC using the Z notation in the next section.

4.2 Formal Definition of RC/DC

For elaboration of the formal definition of RC/DC, we carry out further development of the Z schema, describing the notion of the decision. The *DecReinforced* schema below differs from the *DecModified* schema by adding four new functions: *keep0*, *keep1*, *keep0fix* and *keep1fix*. Each of these functions connects conditions with pairs of input data.

$\_\_ DecReinforced _____$
DecModified
$keep0, keep1, keep0fix, keep1fix : cond \rightarrow\!\!\!\rightarrow InputPairs$

$_____$
$\mathrm{dom}\, keep0 = \mathrm{dom}\, keep1 = \mathrm{dom}\, keep0fix = \mathrm{dom}\, keep1fix = argdec$
$\mathrm{ran}\, keep0 \cup \mathrm{ran}\, keep1 \cup \mathrm{ran}\, keep0fix \cup \mathrm{ran}\, keep1fix \subseteq decinput \leftrightarrow decinput$
$\forall\, c : cond \mid c \in argdec \bullet$
$\quad keep0\ c = \{i_0, i_1 : decinput \mid value\ i_0 = value\ i_1 = 0 \land c\ i_0 \neq c\ i_1\} \land$
$\quad keep1\ c = \{i_0, i_1 : decinput \mid value\ i_0 = value\ i_1 = 1 \land c\ i_0 \neq c\ i_1\} \land$
$\quad keep0fix\ c = \{i_0, i_1 : decinput \mid (i_0, i_1) \in keep0\ c \land$
$\quad\quad (\forall\, othercond : argdec \mid othercond \neq c \bullet othercond\ i_0 = othercond\ i_1)\} \land$
$\quad keep1fix\ c = \{i_0, i_1 : decinput \mid (i_0, i_1) \in keep1\ c \land$
$\quad\quad (\forall\, othercond : argdec \mid othercond \neq c \bullet othercond\ i_0 = othercond\ i_1)\}$

The functions $keep0$ and $keep1$ assign for each condition the subset of pairs of input data that vary the condition but keep the value of the decision equal to 0 (for $keep0$) or 1 (for $keep1$). The difference between the $keep0fix/keep1fix$ functions and the $keep0/keep1$ functions is that, for the $keep0fix/keep1fix$ functions, all the other conditions are kept fixed. This is similar to the difference between $changedecfix$ and $changedec$ in the $DecModified$ schema.

The introduced functions allow formulation of the formal definition of the RC/DC criterion:

$$
\begin{array}{|l|}
\hline
\textit{RC\_DC} \\
\;\;MC\_DC \\
\hline
\;\;\forall\, DecReinforced;\;\; c : cond \mid c \in argdec \bullet \\
\;\;(\textbf{let}\; target0 == choice(keep0fix\; c, keep0\; c); \\
\;\;\;\;\; target1 == choice(keep1fix\; c, keep1\; c) \bullet \\
\;\;\;\;\;(target0 \neq \varnothing \Rightarrow (testset \times testset) \cap target0 \neq \varnothing) \wedge \\
\;\;\;\;\;(target1 \neq \varnothing \Rightarrow (testset \times testset) \cap target1 \neq \varnothing)) \\
\hline
\end{array}
$$

This criterion contains MC/DC as a component and in addition includes the requirements for testing of invariability of the decision when a condition varies. In this way, the set of test cases should contain pairs of input data from two sets $target0$ and $target1$, which keep (if it is possible) the value of the decision and fix (if it is possible) all other conditions. If holding other conditions is not possible, the test cases that keep the value of the decision without fixing other conditions should be used.

Let us prove that if the decision does not coincide with the condition or the condition's negation, it is always possible to choose testing data that satisfies RC/DC; i.e., $(target0 \neq \varnothing) \vee (target1 \neq \varnothing)$.

Lemma 3

$RC\_DC;\; c, value : cond \vdash$

$(value \neq c \wedge value \neq \neg\, c) \Rightarrow (target0 \neq \varnothing \vee target1 \neq \varnothing)$

Proof

$\neg\,((value \neq c \wedge value \neq \neg\, c) \Rightarrow$ \hfill [assumption]
$\;\;\;\;(target0 \neq \varnothing \vee target1 \neq \varnothing))$

$\Leftrightarrow value \neq c \wedge value \neq \neg\, c \wedge target0 = \varnothing \wedge target1 = \varnothing$ \hfill [logic]

$\Rightarrow choice(keep0fix\; c, keep0\; c) = \varnothing \wedge$ \hfill [definition of $target0$ and $target1$]
$\;\;\;\; choice(keep1fix\; c, keep1\; c) = \varnothing$

$\Leftrightarrow keep0\; c = \varnothing \wedge keep1\; c = \varnothing$ \hfill [definition of $choice$]

$\Leftrightarrow \neg\,(\exists\, i_0, i_1 : decinput \bullet$ \hfill [definition of $keep0$ and $keep1$]
$\;\;\;\; c\; i_0 \neq c\; i_0 \wedge value\; i_0 = value\; i_1)$

$\Leftrightarrow \forall\, i_0, i_1 : decinput \bullet c\; i_0 \neq c\; i_1 \Rightarrow value\; i_0 \neq value\; i_1$ \hfill [logic]

$\Rightarrow c = value \vee c = \neg\, value$ \hfill **[Lemma 2]**

$\Rightarrow false$ \hfill [contradiction]$\square$

It should be noted that there are decisions that do not keep one of the values (0 or 1) when varying a condition. For example, $A \vee B$ does not keep 0 and $A \wedge B$ does not keep 1.

4.3   Examples for RC/DC

Example 1. Consider the following rule for the actuation of the protection system of the VVER-1000 type [61] nuclear reactor: the system should shut down a reactor in the case of decrease of the pressure in the first circuit to less than 150 kg/cm^2 under the coolant temperature of more than $260°$ centigrade and reactor capacity equal or more than 75% of the rated capacity or decrease of the pressure in the first circuit to less than 140 kg/cm^2 under the coolant temperature more than $280°$ centigrade. For measurement of each input parameter (pressure p and temperature t), three sensors are used (inputs p_1, p_2, p_3 and t_1, t_2, t_3) with majority voting of inputs.

Hence, 13 conditions are used for determination of necessity of the system actuation:

$$P_{11} = p_1 < 150 \qquad P_{21} = p_2 < 150$$
$$P_{31} = p_3 < 150 \qquad P_{12} = p_1 < 140$$
$$P_{22} = p_2 < 140 \qquad P_{32} = p_3 < 140$$
$$T_{11} = t_1 > 260 \qquad T_{21} = t_2 > 260$$
$$T_{31} = t_3 > 260 \qquad T_{12} = t_1 > 280$$
$$T_{22} = t_2 > 280 \qquad T_{32} = t_3 > 280$$
$$NR = N \geq 0.75 N_r$$

The decision that is responsible for this actuation criterion is:

$$(((P_{11} \wedge P_{21}) \vee (P_{11} \wedge P_{31}) \vee (P_{21} \wedge P_{31})) \wedge$$
$$((T_{11} \wedge T_{21}) \vee (T_{11} \wedge T_{31}) \vee (T_{21} \wedge T_{31})) \wedge NR) \vee$$
$$(((P_{12} \wedge P_{22}) \vee (P_{12} \wedge P_{32}) \vee (P_{22} \wedge P_{32})) \wedge$$
$$((T_{12} \wedge T_{22}) \vee (T_{12} \wedge T_{32}) \vee (T_{22} \wedge T_{32})))$$

The number of all possible combinations of values of the 13 conditions equals $2^{13} = 8192$. Not all combinations are possible because of coupled conditions. Thus, it is impossible to have $P_{i1} = 0 \wedge P_{i2} = 1$ and also $T_{i1} = 1 \wedge T_{i2} = 0$, $i = 1, 2, 3$. This means that there are three possible outcomes for the every pair of conditions (P_{i1}, P_{i2}) and (T_{i1}, T_{i2}). The maximum number of possible tests is 3^6 (for these six pairs of conditions) times 2 (for possible values of NR) that equals 1458. However, this number of possible combinations is still too large to be completely checked during practical testing.

The RC/DC criterion requires a maximum of 6 test cases for each condition (two for varying the decision, two for keeping it 0 and two for keeping it 1). Therefore, not more than 78 combinations are required for this decision. However, this number is overestimated since the same combinations can be used for testing different conditions. The minimization of the number of test cases for

RC/DC could demand special analysis and be a hard task. The cost of this analysis could exceed the obtained benefit from the minimization. Nevertheless, if further reduction of test cases is not very important, the selection of test cases presents no difficulty. For testing maintaining the value 0 for the decision during variation of the condition P_{11}, it is sufficient to select combinations of input data, for which $T_{11} = 0$ and $T_{21} = 0$. This ensures that the decision equals 0; therefore, any possible values of the other conditions could be fixed. For testing maintaining the value 1 for the decision during variation of the condition P_{11}, it is sufficient to fix, for example, $P_{12} = P_{22} = T_{12} = T_{22} = 1$ and any allowed values of the other conditions.

Example 2. Using RC/DC could be expedient during specification-based testing. For this type of testing, the basis for test generation is software specifications and data for testing results analysis (oracle data) are also drawn from specifications. Then a computer program is tested as a black box and testing results are compared with the oracle data.

Using RC/DC during specification-based testing might allow revealing not only accidental single errors in logical expressions (like Operator Reference Fault, Variable Negation Fault, etc. [62]) but also more general errors. One of the possible examples is mistakenly using a different specification when the specification for one mode of a computer system is used by mistake for another mode. Consider an example when RC/DC reveals such error while MC/DC fails to do it.

Let the correct specification d_3 be $A \wedge B \wedge C \wedge D$. The test cases in Table 4 satisfy the MC/DC criterion (the only one possible test set).

Table 4. Testing data satisfied the MC/DC criterion for d_3

num	values					variations			
	A	B	C	D	$d_3.value$	A	B	C	D
1	1	1	1	1	1	*	*	*	*
2	0	1	1	1	0	*			
3	1	0	1	1	0		*		
4	1	1	0	1	0			*	
5	1	1	1	0	0				*

The test cases in Table 5 could be added to satisfy the RC/DC criterion (one from the several possibilities). All these test cases keep d_3 value equal to 0; it is not possible to keep 1 for this decision.

Let us suppose that the following incorrect specification d_4 has been used by mistake instead of d_3 in the program: $A \wedge B \wedge C \wedge D \vee (\neg A \wedge \neg B) \vee (\neg C \wedge \neg D)$. Consider how test cases according MC/DC and RC/DC can reveal this fault.

Results of all test combinations for d_3 and d_4 are given in Table 6.

As is shown in Table 6, the values of d_3 and d_4 coincide for test combinations 1–5. This means that this test set, created according MC/DC, does not reveal the fault. On the other hand, $d_3.value \neq d_4.value$ for combinations 6–10. Thus,

Table 5. Testing data satisfied the RC/DC criterion for d_3

num	values					variations			
	A	B	C	D	$d_3.value$	A	B	C	D
6	1	0	0	0	0	*			
7	0	1	0	0	0		*		
8	0	0	1	0	0			*	
9	0	0	0	1	0				*
10	0	0	0	0	0	*	*	*	*

Table 6. Testing results for d_3 and d_4

num	values					
	A	B	C	D	$d_3.value$	$d_4.value$
1	1	1	1	1	1	1
2	0	1	1	1	0	0
3	1	0	1	1	0	0
4	1	1	0	1	0	0
5	1	1	1	0	0	0
6	1	0	0	0	0	1
7	0	1	0	0	0	1
8	0	0	1	0	0	1
9	0	0	0	1	0	1
10	0	0	0	0	0	1

the test cases, created according RC/DC, detect the difference between correct and incorrect specifications (i.e., reveal this fault).

5 Conclusions and Future Work

The subject of this chapter has been the formalization of criteria for software testing. Control-flow criteria (i.e., criteria using logical expressions), which relate to the branch and loop structure of the program, have been considered. If mathematical (logical) specifications of software are used, these criteria can be applied for specification-based testing as well. The Z notation [6,30,49] has been utilized for the formal definition of the criteria. Z schemas formally describing all the major control-flow testing criteria have been presented. These definitions help to eliminate the possibility of ambiguities, which is likely for definitions in natural language.

The Modified Condition/Decision Coverage (MC/DC) criterion [48] has been analyzed in detail. The formal definition in the Z notation allows us not only to make some problems regarding MC/DC clearer, but also to prove some features of this criterion formally. In particular, we have considered situations when it is impossible to vary a condition and a decision while holding all other conditions fixed and have proposed to vary the condition without fixing others for these cases. Then we formally proved that, in the framework of the proposed approach, it is always possible to choose testing data to satisfy MC/DC.

In this chapter, we have also proposed and formalized the Reinforced Condition/Decision Coverage (RC/DC) criterion for software testing, which strengthens the requirements of the MC/DC criterion. The MC/DC criterion does not include requirements for testing of 'false operation' type failures. Such failures, as we have shown in several examples, can be highly important in safety-critical computer systems.

The proposed RC/DC criterion aims to eliminate this shortcoming and requires the consideration of situations when varying a condition keeps the value of a decision constant. Using RC/DC gives an advantage for specification-based testing since it requires testing safety-important situations when a false actuation of a system is possible. Although the number of required test cases rises, the growth remains linear compared to the number of conditions in a decision, making the approach practicable. We have illustrated the application of the RC/DC criterion in the testing of nuclear reactor protection system software. An important area of application of the RC/DC criterion could be using it as a regulatory requirement in standards, especially in safety-related areas [56,54,59].

The further application of the main idea of RC/DC was suggested by Ammann, Offutt and Huang [3]. They introduced Inactive Clause Coverage criteria (ICC). These criteria consider situations when changing a condition does not affect the decision. Thus, RC/DC is one of the possible realizations of ICC.

The basis of many testing criteria, including MC/DC and RC/DC, is an empirical understanding of testing aims. That is why an experimental investigation is important and we consider it as a major direction for further work in studying the effectiveness of testing criteria [35,36]. A set of software tools is envisaged, for insertion of different types of faults into decisions, and then to apply test cases according to different testing criteria. Experimental results of the detection of faults could be used for the comparison of the effectiveness of testing criteria and for practical recommendations of employment of MC/DC and RC/DC in industry.

Other possibilities for future investigation include:

- using RC/DC for specification-based testing;
- using RC/DC for integration testing of a whole computer system;
- automated generation of test inputs in line with the RC/DC criterion;
- formalization of other testing criteria (e.g., data-flow control criteria).

In summary, we have developed and formalized the RC/DC testing criterion, building on the existing MC/DC criterion, which we believe could be important in the testing of safety-critical application, as illustrated by a number of examples here. The role of formal methods in aiding testing still has great potential and it is hoped that the research in this chapter goes some way to demonstrating the beneficial relationship between these two complementary aspects of software engineering.

References

1. Abdurazik, A., Amman, P., Ding, W., Offutt, J.: Evaluation of Three Specification-based Testing Criteria. In: 6th IEEE International Conference on Engineering of Complex Computer Systems (ICECCS 2000), Tokyo, Japan (September 2000)
2. Ammann, P.E., Black, P.E.: Test Generation and Recognition with Formal Methods. In: The First International Workshop on Automated Program Analysis, Testing and Verification, Limerick, Ireland (June 2000)
3. Ammann, P., Offutt, J., Huang, H.: Coverage Criteria for Logical Expressions. In: Proceedings of the 14th International Symposium on Software Reliability Engineering (ISSRE 2003), Denver, Colorado, USA, November 17–20, 2003, pp. 99–107 (2003)
4. Applied Microsystems Corporation. DO-178B & ED-12B Software Verification using CodeTEST, http://www.amc.com/news/
5. Bishop, P.G.: MC/DC based estimation and detection of residual faults in PLC logic networks. In: Supplementary Proceedings 14th International Symposium on Software Reliability Engineering (ISSRE 2003, Fast Abstracts, Denver, Colorado, USA, November 17–20, 2003, pp. 297–298 (2003)
6. Bowen, J.P.: Formal Specification and Documentation using Z: A Case Study Approach. International Thomson Computer Press (1996)
7. Bowen, J.P.: Experience Teaching Z with Tool and Web Support. ACM SIGSOFT Software Engineering Notes 26(2), 69–75 (2001)
8. Bowen, J.P., Bogdanov, K., Clark, J., Harman, M., Hierons, R.: FORTEST: Formal Methods and Testing. In: Proceedings of 26th Annual International Computer Software and Applications Conference (COMPSAC 2002), Oxford, UK, August 26–29, 2002, pp. 91–101. IEEE Computer Society Press, Los Alamitos (2002)
9. Bowen, J.P., Hinchey, M.G.: Industrial-Strength Formal Methods in Practice. FACIT series. Springer, Heidelberg (1999)
10. Bowen, J.P., Hinchey, M.G.: Formal Methods. In: Tucker, A.B. (ed.) Computer Science Handbook, 2nd edn., Ch. 106, pp. 1–25. Chapman & Hall/CRC, Boca Raton (2004)
11. Burton, S., Clark, J., Galloway, A., McDermid, J.: Automated V&V for High Integrity Systems, A Target Formal Methods Approach. In: Proceedings of the 5th NASA Langley Formal Methods Workshop (June 2000)
12. Burton, S., Clark, J., McDermid, J.: Proof and Automation: An Integrated Approach. In: Proceedings of the 1st International Workshop of Automated Program Analysis, Testing and Verification (June 2000)
13. Carrington, D., Stocks, P.: A Tale of Two Paradigms: Formal Methods and Software Testing. In: Bowen, J.P., Hall, J.A. (eds.) Z User Workshop, Cambridge, 1994, Workshops in Computing, pp. 51–68. Springer, Heidelberg (1994)
14. Chapman, R.: Industrial Experience with SPARK. In: Proceedings of ACM SIGAda Annual International Conference (SIGAda 2000), Johns Hopkins University/Applied Physics Laboratory, Laurel, Maryland, USA November 12–16 (2000)
15. Chilenski, J., Miller, S.: Applicability of Modified Condition/Decision Coverage to Software Testing. Software Engineering Journal, 193–200 (September 1994)
16. Chilenski, J., Newcomb, P.H.: Formal Specification Tool for Test Coverage Analysis. In: Proceedings of the Ninth Knowledge-Based Software Engineering Conference, September 20–23, 1994, pp. 59–68 (1994)
17. Chilenski, J., Richey, L.: Definition for a Masking form of Modified Condition Decision Coverage (MCDC), Boeing Report (December 1997)

18. Chilenski, J.: An Investigation of Three Forms of the Modified Condition Decision Coverage (MCDC) Criterion, Report DOT/FAA/AR-01/18 (April 2001)

19. DDC-I, Inc. The DACS-Object Coverage tools. MC/DC and the DACS-Object Coverage Tools, http://www.ddci.com/

20. DeWalt, M.: MCDC: A Blistering Love/Hate Relationship. In: FAA National Software Conference, Long Beach, California, USA, April 6–9(1999)

21. Dupuy, A., Leveson, N.: An Empirical Evaluation of the MC/DC Coverage Criterion on the HETE-2 Satellite Software. In: Proceedings of the Digital Aviation Systems Conference (DASC), Philadelphia, USA (October 2000)

22. FAA Certification Authorities Software Team (CAST). Position Paper CAST-6, Rationale for Accepting Masking MC/DC in Certification Projects (August 2001)

23. Frankl, P.G., Weyuker, E.J.: A Formal Analysis of the Fault-Detecting Ability of Testing Methods. IEEE Transactions on Software Engineering 19(3), 202–213 (1993)

24. Galloway, A., Paige, R.F., Tudor, N.J., Weaver, R.A., Toyn, I., McDermid, J.: Proof vs testing in the context of safety standards. In: Proceedings of the 24th Digital Avionics Systems Conference (DASC 2005), Washington DC, USA, October 30 – November 3, vol. 2 (2005)

25. Haworth, B.: Adequacy Criteria for Object Testing. In: Proceedings of the 2nd International Software Quality Week Europe 1998, Brussels, Belgium (November 1998)

26. Hayes, I.J.: Specification Directed Module Testing. IEEE Transactions on Software Engineering SE-12(1), 124–133 (1986)

27. Hayhurst, K.J., Veerhusen, D.S., Chilenski, J.J., Rierson, L.K.: A Practical Tutorial on Modified Condition/Decision Coverage, Report NASA/TM-2001-210876, NASA, USA (May 2001)

28. Hayhurst, K.J., Veerhusen, D.S.: A Practical Approach to Modified Condition/Decision Coverage. In: 20th Digital Avionics Systems Conference (DASC), Daytona Beach, Florida, USA, October 14–18, 2001, pp. 1B2/1–1B2/10 (2001)

29. Hörcher, H.-M.: Improving Software Tests using Z Specifications. In: P. Bowen, J., Hinchey, M.G. (eds.) ZUM 1995. LNCS, vol. 967, pp. 152–166. Springer, Heidelberg (1995)

30. ISO/IEC. Information technology – Z formal specification notation – Syntax, type system and semantics. ISO/IEC 13568, International Organization for Standardization (2002)

31. Jacky, J.: The Way of Z: Practical Programming with Formal Methods. Cambridge University Press, Cambridge (1997)

32. Jasper, R., Brennan, M., Williamson, K., Currier, B., Zimmerman, D.: Test Data Generation and Feasible Path Analysis. In: Proceedings of 1994 International Symposium on Software Testing and Analysis, Seattle, Washington, USA, August 17–19, 1994, pp. 95–107 (1994)

33. Jia, X.: ZTC: A Type Checker for Z Notation. User's Guide. Version 2.03, August 1998. Division of Software Engineering, School of Computer Science, Telecommunication and Information Systems, DePaul University, USA (1998)

34. Jones, J., Harrold, M.: Test-Suite Reduction and Prioritization for Modified Condition/Decision Coverage. In: Proceedings of the IEEE International Conference on Software Maintenance (ICSM 2001), Florence, Italy, November 7–9, 2001, pp. 92–101 (2001)

35. Kapoor, K., Bowen, J.P.: Experimental Evaluation of the Variation in Effectiveness for DC, FPC and MC/DC Test Criteria. In: Proceedings of ACM-IEEE 2003 International Symposium on Empirical Software Engineering (ISESE 2003), Rome, Italy, September 30 – October 1, 2003, pp. 185–194. IEEE Computer Society Press, Los Alamitos (2003)

36. Kapoor, K., Bowen, J.P.: A Formal Analysis of MCDC and RCDC Test Criteria. Software Testing, Verification and Reliability 15(1), 21–40 (2005)

37. Kaufman, A.V., Chernonozhkin, S.K.: Testing Criteria and a System for Evaluation of the Completeness of a Test Set. Programming and Computer Software 6, 301–311 (1998)

38. Kuhn, D.: Fault Classes and Error Detection Capability of Specification-Based Testing. ACM Transactions On Software Engineering and Methodology 8(4), 411–424 (1999)

39. LDRA Ltd. Modified Condition/Decision Coverage with LDRA Testbed, http://www.ldra.co.uk/pages/mcdc.asp

40. Li, Y.Y.: Structural Test Cases Analysis and Implementation. 42nd Midwest Symposium on Circuits and Systems 2(8–11), 882–885 (1999)

41. Myers, G.: The Art of Software Testing. Wiley-Interscience, Chichester (1979)

42. Ntafos, S.: A Comparison of Some Structural Testing Strategies. IEEE Transactions on Software Engineering 14(6), 868–874 (1988)

43. Offutt, A.J., Xiong, Y., Liu, S.: Criteria for Generating Specification-Based Tests. In: Proceedings of Fifth IEEE International Conference on Engineering of Complex Computer Systems (ICECCS 1999), Las Vegas, Nevada, USA, October 18–21, 1999, pp. 119–129 (1999)

44. Podgurski, P., Clarke, L.: A Formal Model of Program Dependences and its Implications for Software Testing, Debugging and Maintenance. IEEE Transactions on Software Engineering 16(9), 965–979 (1990)

45. Prather, R.E.: Theory of Program Testing – An Overview. Bell System Technical Journal 62(10), 3073–3105 (1984)

46. Rapps, S., Weyuker, E.J.: Selecting Software Test Data Using Data Flow Information. IEEE Transactions on Software Engineering SE-11(4), 367–375 (1985)

47. Roper, M.: Software Testing. McGraw-Hill, New York (1994)

48. RTCA. Software Considerations in Airborne Systems and Equipment Certification. DO-178B, RTCA, Washington DC, USA (1992)

49. Spivey, J.M.: The Z Notation: A Reference Manual, 2nd edn. International Series in Computer Science. Prentice-Hall, Englewood Cliffs (1992)

50. Stocks, P., Carrington, D.: A Framework for Specification-Based Testing. IEEE Transactions on Software Engineering 22(11), 777–793 (1996)

51. Tai, K.-C.: Theory of Fault-Based Predicate Testing for Computer Programs. IEEE Transactions on Software Engineering 22(8), 552–562 (1996)

52. Vilkomir, S.A., Bowen, J.P.: Formalization of Software Testing Criteria Using the Z Notation. In: Proceedings of COMPSAC 2001: 25th IEEE Annual International Computer Software and Applications Conference, Chicago, Illinois, USA, October 8–12, 2001, pp. 351–356. IEEE Computer Society Press, Los Alamitos (2001)

53. Vilkomir, S.A., Bowen, J.P.: Reinforced Condition/Decision Coverage (RC/DC): A New Criterion for Software Testing. In: Bert, D., Bowen, J.P., C. Henson, M., Robinson, K. (eds.) B 2002 and ZB 2002. LNCS, vol. 2272, Springer, Heidelberg (2002)

54. Vilkomir, S.A., Bowen, J.P.: Establishing Formal Regulatory Requirements for Safety-Critical Software Certification. In: Proceedings of AQuIS 2002: 5th International Conference on Achieving Quality In Software and SPICE 2002: 2nd International Conference on Software Process Improvement and Capability Determination, Venice, Italy, March 13–15, 2002, pp. 7–18 (2002)
55. Vilkomir, S.A., Bowen, J.P.: From MC/DC to RC/DC: Formalization and Analysis of Control-Flow Testing Criteria. Formal Aspects of Computing, Vol. 18 (2006), DOI: 10.1007/s00165-005-0084-7
56. Vilkomir, S.A., Ghose, A.: Development of a normative package for safety-critical software using formal regulatory requirements. In: Bomarius, F., Iida, H. (eds.) PROFES 2004. LNCS, vol. 3009, pp. 523–537. Springer, Heidelberg (2004)
57. Vilkomir, S.A., Kapoor, K., Bowen, J.P.: Tolerance of Control-Flow Testing Criteria. In: Proceedings of 27th IEEE Annual International Computer Software and Applications Conference (COMPSAC 2003), Dallas, Texas, USA, November 3–6, 2003, pp. 182–187. IEEE Computer Society Press, Los Alamitos (2003)
58. Vilkomir, S.A., Kharchenko, V.S.: An 'Asymmetric' Approach to the Assessment of Safety-Critical Software during Certification and Licensing. In: Project Control: The Human Factor, Proceedings of ESCOM–SCOPE 2000 Conference, Munich, Germany, April 18–20, 2000, pp. 467–475 (2000)
59. Vilkomir, S.A., Kharchenko, V.S.: Methodology of the Review of Software for Safety Important Systems. In: Safety and Reliability. Proceedings of ESREL 1999 – The Tenth European Conference on Safety and Reliability, Munich-Garching, Germany, September 13–17, 1999, vol. 1, pp. 593–596 (1999)
60. Voas, J., Ghosh, A., Charron, F., Kassab, L.: Reducing Uncertainty About Common-Mode Failures. In: Proceedings of the Eighth International Symposium on Software Reliability Engineering (ISSRE 1997), Albuquerque, New Mexico, USA (November 1997)
61. Voznessensky, V., Berkovich, V.: VVER 440 and VVER-1000: Design Features in Comparison with Western PWRS. In: International Conference on Design and Safety of Advanced Nuclear Power Plants, vol. 4 (October 1992)
62. Weyuker, E., Goradia, T., Singh, A.: Automatically Generating Test Data from a Boolean Specification. IEEE Transactions on Software Engineering 20(5), 353–363 (1994)
63. White, A.L.: Comments on Modified Condition/Decision Coverage for Software Testing. In: 2001 IEEE Aerospace Conference Proceedings, Big Sky, Montana, USA, March 10–17, 2001, vol. 6, pp. 2821–2828 (2001)
64. Woodward, M.R., Hedley, D., Hennell, M.A.: Experience with Path Analysis and Testing of Programs. IEEE Transactions on Software Engineering SE-6(3), 278–286 (1980)
65. Zhu, H., Hall, P.A., May, H.R.: Software Unit Test Coverage and Adequacy. ACM Computing Surveys 29(4), 336–427 (1997)

Comparing the Effectiveness of
Testing Techniques

Elaine J. Weyuker

AT&T Labs – Research
180 Park Avenue, Florham Park, NJ 07932, USA
weyuker@research.att.com

Abstract. Testing software systems requires practitioners to decide how to select test data. This chapter discusses what it means for one test data selection criterion to be more effective than another. Several proposed comparison relations are discussed, highlighting the strengths and weaknesses of each. Also included is a discussion of how these relations evolved and argue that large scale empirical studies are needed.

1 Introduction

When we speak about someone or something being better than something else, we all have an intuitive sense of what is meant. For example, when we say that Mary is a better singer than John, it means that she sings more sweetly or is better able to stay on tune, has a better sense of rhythm or is more dynamic and connects better with the audience. Of course, in some cases the basis for comparison is clear, but in other cases the ranking might be highly subjective and very much a matter of personal taste. Thus when I say that this is the best book I have ever read, or even the best book on a particular subject, you might reasonably disagree even if you have read exactly the same books as I have, and have equal expertise in the subject matter. Again, there may be a significant component of subjectivity and reasonable people might disagree. One reason is that these comparisons might be made using different implicit assumptions about what the most important dimensions are. For me, the better book is the one that is clearer and more concise; for you, the most important criteria are plot and character development. Even when we clearly articulate and agree on the characteristics that we are using to make the comparison, we might reasonably disagree because we simply have different aesthetic tastes. I like purple, you like green.

When it comes to making comparisons about technical issues such as which is the better operating system or programming language, we might again see some of the issues alluded to above arising. These might include such things as the intended use, one's previous experience, available tools, and again, subjective likes and dislikes. For some things it probably does not matter which programming language is selected. If the programmer is proficient in Java but not C++, then in many cases the decision is clear: use the language that the programmer is most proficient in, and that should increase the chances that the software will be

R.M. Hierons et al. (Eds.): Formal Methods and Testing, LNCS 4949, pp. 271–291, 2008.

produced quickly and correctly. Of course there might be interoperability issues relating to other system components which have to be taken into account, or organizational standards.

Now what about software testing methods? It is important to use a method that is effective. But what exactly does "effective" mean? Presumably it means that if the tester uses the method to select test cases, then "most" of the "important" or "critical" 'faults will be exposed, allowing them to be removed, yielding highly dependable software. Since the ultimate goal of testing is to improve or assess the dependability of the software under test, the testing strategy that does this most successfully should be considered best. But as we will see, even this is not entirely straight-forward since different testers using the same testing strategy might select different test sets and therefore expose different faults. This might lead to different degrees of dependability while using the same testing strategy properly.

Much of the literature on comparing testing methods is predicated on an underlying assumption that we all know what it means for one test selection criterion to be more effective than another, and the definitions proposed and relations suggested try to codify the underlying intuition about just what "more effective" should mean.

But do we really have a single dimension on which we can all agree that if one test case selection method A is more effective than another test case selection method B in this dimension, then A is a better way to test programs than B? There are many testing stages: unit, feature, integration, system, load, stress, performance, end-to-end, operations readiness to name just some of the levels. Would it matter whether the testing strategy is intended for unit testing or system testing, for example? What if the intended level is not specified? Are there testing methods that are appropriate for all development stages? Can there be a universally most effective testing method? Can we even say that method A is *always more effective* than method B? These are some of the issues that we will investigate in this chapter.

For many people, the first and most critical issue when assessing testing criteria is finding *faults*, by which we mean a mistake in the software which, when executed, may cause the software to *fail* or behave incorrectly. If strategy A is guaranteed to find all the faults that strategy B does plus some additional ones, then many people would agree that A is a more effective testing method than B. But what if, using that criterion, it is not the case that A is more effective than B nor that B is more effective than A? Does that mean that we ca not say anything about their relative goodness? What if it is possible that A will find all the faults that B does with particular test sets selected to satisfy the two criteria for a given program, but that other test sets that satisfy A and B do not have that property? In that case the effectiveness of a testing strategy might be dependent on how it was being used, or the tester who was using the strategy. Is it possible that A will find all the faults that B does in program P_1, but the reverse is true for program P_2, so that the effectiveness of a testing method varies with the program?

What if A and B find all the same faults in a set X, and in addition, A also finds faults $F_1, F_2, \ldots, F_N$ for some large number N, while B finds fault F_{N+1} in addition to the faults in X. A finds almost all the same faults as B, plus many more, but it does not find F_{N+1}. Is one of the criteria more effective than the other? Strategy A finds many more faults than strategy B, but suppose F_{N+1} is a really critical fault, while all of the faults $F_1, F_2, \ldots, F_N$ are in some sense trivial? Is there a clear winner? Given that the goal of testing is to improve the dependability of the software, the mere number of faults uncovered may be less important than the severity of the faults uncovered.

Another dimension to consider is how frequently a particular fault will be triggered when used in the environment in which it will be deployed, with a given workload or input distribution. If fault F_{N+1} will be triggered repeatedly, while faults $F_1, F_2, \ldots, F_N$ are never triggered, does this affect our perception of which testing strategy is more effective?

Although it is not clear that there is a single correct answer to these questions, I will nonetheless consider them and discuss the degree to which they are important or unimportant. Again, much may be subjective and I will try to state when that is the case.

In this chapter I will focus on how to compare the effectiveness of testing strategies to help us determine which is the best approach for a given program, or for all programs in general. I will describe various false attempts at defining comparison relations, and describe where we are now. I will discuss why many of the proposed relations were not satisfactory. I hope this will challenge some readers to think about this important issue in new ways, and lead to a renewed interest in the problem, and some exciting new insights.

2   Comparison Relations

Probably the first suggestion for how to compare software testing strategies used the subsumption relation. Intuitively, subsumption is a very natural way to compare strategies. It really seems like it captures the essence of what we mean when we say that one testing strategy is more effective or more comprehensive than another.

Formally, test selection criterion C_1 *subsumes* test selection criterion C_2 if for every program P, every test suite that satisfies C_1 also satisfies C_2.

In [23] and [24], Rapps and Weyuker introduced a new family of data flow-based test case selection strategies, and several control flow-based and data flow-based criteria were compared using the subsumption relation. It was firmly believed that this relation indicated that the subsumed relations were less good than the subsuming relations because it was harder to satisfy the subsuming relation.

However, it was later recognized that subsumption had definite deficiencies when used to compare testing strategies. The first deficiency was recognized and pointed out by Rapps and Weyuker in [23], namely that many testing criteria are incomparable using subsumption, in the sense that neither subsumes the other.

An even more serious limitation associated with subsumption is that it can be misleading. It is easy to come up with examples of testing strategies such that C_1 subsumes C_2 but there are test suites that satisfy C_2, the "less effective" testing strategy, that expose faults, while test suites that satisfy C_1, the "more effective" strategy, do not expose any faults. The problem arises because there are typically many different test suites that satisfy a given strategy and generally there is little or no guidance as to which of these test suites to choose. Therefore, the tester may be lucky when selecting the test suite for C_2 and unlucky when selecting the C_1 test suite, or it may even be that the "natural" test suite to select for C_2 is more effective at uncovering faults than the "natural" test suite that one would select to satisfy C_1. This issue was pointed out in a number of papers including Hamlet's discussion in [15].

With the weaknesses associated with subsumption in mind, Gourlay [13] introduced the power relation. A test selection criterion is said to *detect* a failure if *every* test set that satisfies that criterion contains an input that causes program P to fail, and there is at least one test set satisfying the criterion for P. Then, criterion C_1 is at least as *powerful* as criterion C_2 if for every program P, if C_2 detects a failure in P, then so does C_1. In the sequel I will refer to an input for which the output produced by P on that input does not agree with the specified output, as a *failure-causing* input.

While subsumption is purely a set inclusion relation (and Rapps and Weyuker initially discussed the relationship between their data flow and control flow criteria in terms of *inclusion*) and does not associate the "more effective" criterion with fault identification, Gourlay specifically tied the notion of a more powerful criterion to its ability to identify faults. Although intuitively this did make a positive step towards addressing the weaknesses associated with subsumption, it also wound up introducing a new set of problems without entirely eliminating subsumption's deficiencies.

In particular, the incomparability problem remains an issue for Gourlay's power relation since many criteria are still incomparable under the power relation. In addition, the power relation does not entirely eliminate the situation in which the "less effective" relation exposes faults while the "more effective" one does not. The central problem here is that the power relation is based on the definition of "detecting" a failure which is a very demanding one. If C_1 is at least as powerful as C_2, there can still be failures that will more often be exposed by C_2 than C_1 even though neither criterion (always) detects them in the formal sense. And it may also be the case that the ones more frequently exposed by the "less effective" criterion are in some sense "more important" or "more critical" than the ones frequently exposed by the "more effective" criterion, and hence the use of the "less effective" criterion will often lead to more dependable programs than the use of the more powerful criterion.

It may also happen that P contains faults but neither C_1 nor C_2 detects any failures in this formal sense because of the stringent requirements associated with the notion of detection. As discussed relative to the subsumption relation, most test selection criteria do not *require* the selection of specific test cases, so a criterion will be satisfied by many different test sets, some of which will include inputs that fail, while others will not include any inputs that fail. Since this is the case, it is possible that the test set selected for the criterion deemed less effective by the power relation will expose more faults than the one selected for the criterion deemed more effective by the power relation.

In addition, most criteria are *monotonic* as defined in [26]. This means that for most criteria, adding additional test cases to a test suite does not prevent the test suite from continuing to satisfy a given test selection criterion. The minimal set that satisfies a criterion might not include a test case that fails, but when some additional test cases are added, the test set does include a failing input. In a sense, Gourlay's notion of detecting a failure, and therefore the power relation, tried to deal with this problem explicitly by only considering faults for which every test set satisfying the criterion must include an input that will exercise the fault and cause a failure. However, by so doing, it makes it very difficult, if not impossible, to identify faults that will be *detected* by a criterion, and consequently to show that one criterion is more powerful than another. I will discuss this issue further when other comparison relations are considered since this is a fundamental problem shared by other proposed comparison relations.

In [32], Weyuker, Weiss, and Hamlet introduced the BETTER relation in an attempt to address the weaknesses associated with both the subsumption and power relations. They first defined the notion of a test case being *required* by a criterion C to test a program P, if every test set that satisfies C for that program must include that test case. This addressed the issue of monotonicity mentioned above so that the authors only considered the relevant test suites, rather than ones created by adding additional (non-essential) test cases.

They next introduced the BETTER relation, and said criterion C_1 is *BETTER* than criterion C_2 if for every program P, any failure-causing input *required* by C_2 is also *required* by C_1.

They showed that:

$$(C_1 \; subsumes \; C_2) \Rightarrow (C_1 \; BETTER \; C_2) \Rightarrow (C_1 \; at \; least \; as \; powerful \; as \; C_2)$$

They also proved that the converse did not hold. It therefore follows that these three relations are all distinct relations.

Again the newly-defined relation that was designed to solve the previously-defined relations' problems, had its own problems. As before, the incomparability problem had not been solved, and very few criteria actually *require* the selection of specific test cases. This means that the set of failure-causing inputs *required* by a criterion will typically be empty, even though P contains faults. It is also very difficult to show that one criterion is BETTER than another criterion directly. Often the easiest or only way to show this is to show that the subsumption relation holds, and hence by the above theorem, that the BETTER and power relations hold too.

So we see that although several formal ways of comparing software testing strategies have been proposed and used to do the comparison, reflection indicates that they do not really tell us what we would like them to tell us about the relative effectiveness of different strategies.

There is another way of noticing that the above-cited types of comparison relations fall short of ideal, and this helped us focus our attention in a different direction. Consider the following simple example. Calling the set of possible inputs to a program, the *input domain*, let P be a program with domain $D = \{0,1,2,3,4\}$. Assume there is only one failure-causing input in the domain, namely 0; all of the other possible inputs are treated correctly by P. The domain may be divided into subsets called *subdomains*.

Assume that C_1 requires the selection of one test case from the subdomain $\{0,1,2\}$ and one test case from the subdomain $\{3,4\}$, while C_2 requires the selection of one test case from the subdomain $\{0,1,2\}$ and one test case from the subdomain $\{0,3,4\}$. Then six test sets satisfy criterion C_1: $\{0,3\}$, $\{0,4\}$, $\{1,3\}$, $\{1,4\}$, $\{2,3\}$, and $\{2,4\}$, of which two, ($\{0,3\}$ and $\{0,4\}$), or one-third of the test sets expose the fault. Nine test sets satisfy criterion C_2: $\{0,0\}$, $\{0,3\}$, $\{0,4\}$, $\{1,0\}$, $\{1,3\}$, $\{1,4\}$, $\{2,0\}$, $\{2,3\}$, and $\{2,4\}$, of which five expose the fault, or more than one-half of the possible test sets expose the fault. Therefore, if each test set determined by a criterion is equally likely to be selected, C_1 subsumes C_2 but the *probability* that a test set selected using C_2 will expose a fault is higher than that for a test set selected by C_1. That is, if the tester is just as likely to select the test set $\{1,3\}$ to satisfy C_2 as they are to select test set $\{0,4\}$, then we have this sort of problem.

The reason that this counter-intuitive situation occurred was that 0, the only input that failed, was a member of both of C_2's subdomains, but was in only one of C_1's subdomains. This meant that 0 could be selected as the representative of either or both of C_2's subdomains, but as the representative of only one of C_1's subdomains. Therefore, although C_1 subsumes C_2, and is therefore intuitively a more demanding criterion, in practice using C_2 is more likely to do what we hope to do when testing: expose the problem in the software, so that it can be removed thereby making the software more dependable.

What we have seen so far is that for each of the formal relations that were proposed for comparing testing strategies, there were fundamental flaws that prevented them from allowing testers to use them to make meaningful comparisons. The example discussed above for which a subsumed selection criterion was more likely to expose a fault than the subsuming criterion, led us to consider using probabilities as the basis for comparing testing strategies. This will be discussed in the next section.

3   Using Probabilistic Measures

The observation described in the previous section that it was possible for C_1 to subsume C_2 but the probability that C_2 exposes faults is higher than the probability that C_1 does, led Frankl and Weyuker to consider defining relations that would address problems of this nature. Several researchers had previously used a probabilistic measure M to assess the ability of a testing approach to expose faults and determine whether one criterion was more effective at finding faults than another, including [4,16,30]. In [9], Frankl and Weyuker introduced the covers and universally covers relations and used M as a way of assessing whether testing strategies related by these relations were guaranteed to be more effective at detecting faults. M was formally defined for program P whose sub-domains are $\{D_1, D_2, \ldots, D_n\}$, specification S and test selection criterion C as follows: Denoting the size of subdomain D_i by d_i, and letting m_i be the number of failure-causing inputs in D_i, then

$$M(C, P, S) = 1 - \prod_{i=1}^{n}(1 - \frac{m_i}{d_i}).$$

Assuming the independent selection of one test case from each subdomain using a uniform distribution, M is the probability that a test suite will expose at least one fault.

Frankl and Weyuker formally defined the covers relation as follows: Let C_1 and C_2 be criteria, and let $\mathcal{SD}_C(P, S)$ denote the nonempty multiset of subdomains from which test cases are selected to satisfy criterion C for program P and specification S. C_1 covers C_2 for (P, S) if for every subdomain $D \in \mathcal{SD}_{C2}(P, S)$ there is a collection $\{D_1, \ldots, D_n\}$ of subdomains belonging to $\mathcal{SD}_{C1}(P, S)$ such that $D_1 \cup \ldots \cup D_n = D$. C_1 universally covers C_2 if for every program, specification pair (P, S), C_1 covers C_2 for (P, S). Thus, the covers relation attempts to determine which criterion is more appropriate for a particular program and specification pair, while the universally covers relation aims at classifying the quality of a testing strategy in general.

Frankl and Weyuker showed in [9], that a number of well-known criteria are related by the covers relation, but that even if C_1 covers C_2 for (P, S), it is possible for $M(C_1, P, S) < M(C_2, P, S)$. This is similar to the situation described in the last section for subsumption. For the covers relation, they showed that this sort of inversion can happen when a subdomain of the covering criterion is used to cover more than one subdomain of the covered criterion.

This led Frankl and Weyuker to define a new relation, the properly covers relation, in [9]. To solve the problem observed for the covers relation, this new relation requires that this sort of "inversion" cannot happen. Formally we have: Let $\mathcal{SD}_{C1}(P, S) = \{D_1^1, \ldots, D_m^1\}$, and $\mathcal{SD}_{C2}(P, S) = \{D_1^2, \ldots, D_n^2\}$. C_1 properly covers C_2 for (P,S) if there is a multi-set

$$\mathcal{M} = \{D_{1,1}^1, \ldots, D_{1,k_1}^1, \ldots, D_{n,1}^1, \ldots, D_{n,k_n}^1\}$$

such that $\mathcal{M}$ is a sub-multi-set of $\mathcal{SD}_{C1}(P, S)$ and

$$D_1^2 = D_{1,1}^1 \cup \ldots \cup D_{1,k_1}^1$$

$$\vdots$$

$$D_n^2 = D_{n,1}^1 \cup \ldots \cup D_{n,k_n}^1$$

Informally this says that if C_1 properly covers C_2 then each of C_2's subdomains can be "covered" by C_1 subdomains (expressed as a union of some C_1 subdomains). In addition, it must be done in such a way that none of C_1's subdomains occurs more often in the covering than it does in $\mathcal{SD}_{C1}$, thereby preventing the sort of misleading view of the criteria's effectiveness that we saw in the earlier example.

C_1 *universally properly covers* C_2 if for every program P and specification S, C_1 properly covers C_2 for (P, S).

It was proved in [9] that if C_1 properly covers C_2 for program P and specification S, then $M(C_1, P, S) \geq M(C_2, P, S)$. Again, just as the covers relation considered the effectiveness of criteria for a specific program while the universally covers relations assessed them relative to all programs, the properly covers relation is also program-specific while the universally properly covers relation assesses criteria relative to any program.

The above-cited theorem allowed Frankl and Weyuker to say in a concrete way that criterion C_1 is more effective at finding faults than criterion C_2, for a specific program P. Generalizing this theorem by using the universally properly covers relation, Frankl and Weyuker also showed that there were many well-known test selection criteria that were related by the universally properly covers relation, and hence these criteria could in a sense be ranked.

In a follow-up paper [10], Frankl and Weyuker investigated whether there were other appropriate ways of assessing the fault-detecting ability of a criterion, and therefore considered E, the *expected number of failures detected*. Again, letting $\mathcal{SD}_C(P, S) = \{D_1, \ldots D_n\}$, and assuming independent random selection of one test case from each subdomain using a uniform distribution, E was defined to be:

$$E(C, P, S) = \sum_{i=1}^{n} \frac{m_i}{d_i}.$$

Frankl and Weyuker proved that it is also true that if C_1 properly covers C_2 for program P and specification S, then $E(C_1, P, S) \geq E(C_2, P, S)$. In addition they provided examples that showed that in the case in which C_1 subsumes C_2, but *does not* properly cover C_2, this is not necessarily the case.

Thus, by using the universally properly covers relation, Frankl and Weyuker were able to rank testing criteria using both the probability of detecting at least one fault and the expected number of faults exposed, and did so for roughly a dozen well-known testing criteria. This is shown in Figure 1 which is reproduced from [10].

It is important to notice, however, that they clearly pointed out that the fact criterion C_1 universally properly covers criterion C_2 does not guarantee that C_1 will find more faults than criterion C_2. However it is true that a testing practitioner is guaranteed to be *more likely* to detect a fault using C_1 than C_2 provided that test cases are selected using a somewhat artificial selection method. On the other hand, if C_1 does not universally properly cover criterion C_2 then even if C_1 requires substantially more test cases than C_2, it may still be less likely to detect a fault.

Although these papers are of theoretical interest, and provide an interesting way of ranking testing strategies, the primary weaknesses of these papers become apparent if they are to be used pragmatically. As alluded to above, the method

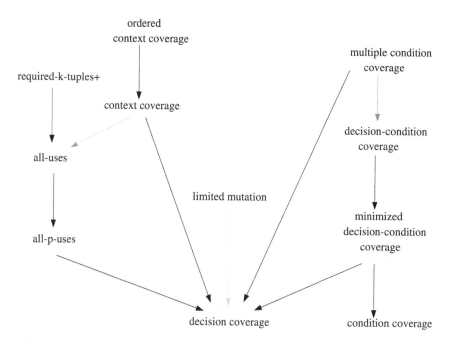

Fig. 1. Summary of Relations between criteria. A solid arrow from C_1 to C_2 indicates that C_1 universally properly covers C_2, a dotted arrow from C_1 to C_2 indicates that C_1 subsumes but does not universally properly cover C_2; any relation that is not explicitly shown in the figure and that does not follow from transitivity along with the fact that universally properly covers implies subsumption, does not hold.

of test case selection is artificial, as are the criteria definitions used. As discussed in earlier sections, testing practitioners tend to use test selection criteria in very personalized ways, relying on intuition and experience to help select test cases even when using a particular test case selection strategy. The Frankl/Weyuker results assume instead that random selection from within the subdomains defined by the selection criterion is done.

In [6], a different approach was taken to comparing testing criteria. First, instead of comparing specific testing strategies, the authors analytically compared what they refer to as debug testing and operational testing. In *debug testing*, the tester aims at selecting test cases that will cause failures to occur. *Operational testing*, on the other hand, subjects the software to a statistical distribution of inputs that is intended to be representative of the inputs that the software is expected to be subjected to during operation.

The goal of this research was to see whether higher software dependability could be achieved using debug testing, which they equated to looking for failures, or by selecting test cases based on the expected field usage (operational testing). Therefore, instead of basing the comparison on the probability of finding one or more faults or failures, or the number of faults detected, their goal is to base their assessment of a testing criterion on the reliability of the program under test after it has been tested using a given strategy. Although the intuition on which this assessment is based is interesting, and adds to the overall picture provided by this sort of analytic research, there are limitations to the applicability of the authors' observations to real development projects.

In order to facilitate the assessment, the authors made simplifying assumptions. For example, they assumed that all testers will respond to a given failure with modifications that will have exactly the same effect, regardless of the type of testing being done. In addition, they assumed that such fixes are always successful. Based on my experience working with production programs, these seem to be highly unrealistic assumptions. Another assumption made is that when a failure occurs, all testers will recognize it, which also is not consistent with my experience working with professional testers. Other assumptions include that all software have single inputs (rather than complex vectors) and when the software is run on the input, a single result is produced. Furthermore, it is assumed that the software's response to the input in no way affects later runs of the software. This implies that whenever a program is run on a given input, exactly the same output will be produced regardless of earlier runs. Again this is not at all consistent with software problems that testing groups I have worked with have encountered. In many cases, it is only after the software has run for significant periods of time that a given input will trigger a failure. This is particularly true for performance-related problems such as memory leaks, which tend to account for significant percentages of field faults.

The stated goal of operational testing, is primarily to assess the dependability of the software, according to the authors, and faults are found only incidentally as part of this assessment. The authors note that during debug testing, test cases are generally selected without regard to the severity of the failure that a test case is likely to expose or the frequency with which the failure is likely to occur in the field. In other words, that testers generally do not perform any sort of risk analysis when selecting test cases for debug testing. My experience working with many industrial testing organizations is that it is absolutely standard for testing practitioners to assign a severity to every fault uncovered which is used as the basis for prioritizing debugging efforts. A brief relevant discussion of risk analysis as it relates to testing is included in Section 5 of this chapter.

One further point: I have found that it is not uncommon in some production environments to base debug testing on an operational distribution [1] blurring the distinction between debug and operational testing.

Hierons [17] introduced the use of test hypotheses and fault domains to facilitate the comparison of testing strategies. A *test hypothesis* describes a property that the software tester believes holds for the software that is being tested. Hierons gives the example of the situation when the tester believes that if the software behaves correctly on one positive integer, then it will also work correctly when any positive integer is used as input. Clearly then, if the tester is correct, there is no need to test the software on more than one positive integer since no additional information about the software's correctness will be gleaned from additional positive integer inputs. This is often described as *partitioning* the input domain into subdomains, such that all of the elements of a given subdomain are related in some way. In this case the basis for being in a given subdomain is whether or not the tester believes the elements will fail or succeed similarly. There are many different testing techniques described in the literature that fall into this category of division into subdomains. [16,30,31].

Hierons also defined a *fault domain* to be a set F of functional behaviors such that the tester believes that the functional behavior of the software being tested is equivalent to some member of F, and notes that there is a relationship between fault domains and test hypotheses. After introducing test hypotheses and fault domains, Hierons then explored the types of statements that can be made regarding the fault detecting ability of different testing techniques if one is willing to assume the existence of fault domains and fault hypotheses. In particular he defined what it means for a test set T_1 to be at least as strong as another test set T_2 in the presence of a test hypothesis H. If for every incorrect program implementation P satisfying H, if whenever P fails on T_2, P also fails on T_1, then T_1 is *at least as strong as* T_2. Therefore this definition compares the ability of test sets to expose faults regardless of how the test sets were selected, rather than comparing the fault detecting ability of different test set selection methods.

He then extended the use of test hypotheses to compare testing criteria rather than just test sets. Because of the monotonicity issue discussed earlier, he defined a *non-reducible* test set T relative to a criterion C, program P, and specification s to be one such that T satisfies C and no proper subset of T satisfies C. Then criterion C_1 is at *least as strong* as criterion C_2 if and only if for every faulty program for which hypothesis H holds, if there is a non-reducible test set T_2 that satisfies C_2 that can show that P is faulty, then every test set that satisfies C_1 can show that P is faulty.

Again this work is highly interesting theoretically, but has definite limitations when trying to apply the ideas in a real production setting. First, how will the assumptions regarding fault domains and test hypotheses made and how will test cases be generated using the assumptions? Again it is not clear what this formal analysis tells us about how practitioners can use these ideas to assess testing criteria and decide which one is most appropriate for testing their systems.

4   Limitations of Formal Analysis

Although the universally properly covers relation seemed like a very natural and promising way of assessing the effectiveness of testing strategies proposed to date, there are still a number of limitations associated with any such analysis that should be recognized.

One important problem that was not considered by Frankl and Weyuker is that all of these relations were applied to compare idealized versions of testing strategies which are virtually never used in practice. In a sense, that is the chronic problem associated with formal approaches to software processes. The ultimate goal of comparing testing methods is to be able to tell testing practitioners how best to test their software and what to expect if it is tested using some particular strategy. But if the testing strategies that we are able to compare are not the ones that practitioners use, are we really telling them anything useful at all?

When we determine that a theoretical version of criterion C_1 is more effective that a theoretical version of criterion C_2, does it tell us anything about how the real similarly-named versions of these criteria that are used by practitioners, relate?

Similar types of issues are associated with all of the comparison relations that I have discussed above. For example, one commonly considered testing criterion is *branch testing*, also known as *decision coverage*. Informally, branch testing requires that sufficient test cases be included so that every branch or outcome of a decision statement in the program under test be exercised at least once. No mention is made of how those test cases are to be selected. More formally, in order to prove the sorts of theorems that we have discussed above, it was necessary to make the process more precise. For this reason, the formal definition of branch testing assumes that the domain is first divided into subdomains, each containing exactly those members of the input domain that cause a given branch in the program to be exercised. Then it is assumed that one element of each subdomain is randomly selected using a uniform distribution.

It is difficult to imagine that this process would ever be followed in practice. Pragmatically, branch testing tends to be used more often as a way of assessing the thoroughness of testing, rather than as a basis for selecting test cases. A tester typically selects test cases based on intuition and experience until they believe they have done a comprehensive job. They might then use a branch coverage tool that determines the percentage of the branches of the program that have been exercised by the test suite they have assembled so far. If the percentage is high, the tester might then see which branches had not been covered and try to determine an input that would cause each of the uncovered branches to be exercised. If the percentage was low, then the tester would likely continue to use ad hoc methods of selecting test cases and then reassess the branch coverage achieved, iterating until the percentage of branches covered exceeded a prescribed level or the tester believed that they had done enough.

If branch testing is used in that manner, then we know *nothing whatsoever* about how its effectiveness compares to other testing strategies, because we did not assess *that* version of branch testing, we assessed an entirely different testing method that we are calling branch testing. The same is true for all of the testing strategies compared – they were not the *real* strategies that testers use to select test cases, they were idealized versions. So we are left with the question: Does knowing that idealized test case selection method A is superior to idealized test case selection method B, tell us anything about the relative effectiveness of "real" methods A and B? And given that the real methods A and B are not formally defined, is there in fact a single "real" method A or B, or do different practitioners each have their own ways of using them?

Another limitation of the work described above is that there is no provision for human variability. Each tester comes to the table with their own set of experiences, expertises, and acquired intuition, and so two different testers using exactly the same approach to test a given software system will generally select different sets of test cases. This is *not* because of the variability due to random selection – it is because of individualized human behavior and the latitude provided by the testing criteria in the selection of elements of a subdomain. How can we codify this behavior so that we can say meaningful things about the effectiveness of using different testing methods?

There are similar pragmatic issues associated with Hierons' work, particularly how the assumptions underlying fault domains and test hypotheses are made and how test cases will be generated using the assumptions. Once again we have the situation in which it is not clear what this formal analysis tells us about reality or how the concepts introduced in these research papers can be used by practitioners.

A different kind of issue is related to the appropriateness of relying on the measures M and E as a basis for feeling confident that one testing strategy does a more effective job than another. Neither of these measures differentiates at all between high consequence faults and trivial faults. Therefore, if criterion C_1, the criterion that properly covers criterion C_2, exposes trivial faults while C_2 exposes catastrophic faults, then the fact that the program was tested using C_1 does not really indicate that it is more dependable than it would have been if it had been tested using C_2. This is true in spite of the fact that more faults were uncovered using C_1, and there was a higher likelihood of exposing faults, since the ones that were being exposed were of little consequence.

And what about the cost of doing the testing itself? Suppose C_1 *does* do a somewhat more effective job of testing than C_2, and exposes more faults of equivalent or higher severity than C_2 does. But what if C_1 costs orders of magnitude more to use than C_2? Is the added benefit worth the added cost?

Perhaps the biggest problem is that when we are done testing the software using a given criterion, even if it really is the most effective of the ones being considered, what do we know about the dependability of the tested software? Do we know anything about how many faults remain in software or whether the resulting software is dependable enough for the given application? These problems have not been addressed at all by this research. Are there concrete ways that we can determine that information? Without such an assessment is the theoretical research comparing testing techniques of any practical value?

5   Other Issues

The relations that I considered viewed effectiveness from the perspective of the test selection criterion's ability to find faults. That is certainly one important dimension of effectiveness. Of course, a testing criterion that uncovers many faults but also leaves many faults undetected is less desirable than one that uncovers almost all faults, provided the ones left behind are not the critical ones. Similarly, criteria that lead to higher dependability are more desirable than ones that do not consider the overall dependability of the system.

Thus, a good measure of effectiveness would rely not only on the number of faults a test suite uncovers, but also the percentage of faults that remain undetected. Of course, pragmatically, one can count how many faults were uncovered, although there may be technical difficulties determining exactly how to count such faults, but we generally do not know what faults are in a system, and hence we ca not determine, in practice, what percentage were left undetected. Therefore, we may have to settle for comparing the numbers of faults found by different criteria. Alternatively, we could base our assessments on the degree to which the system reliability has been improved assuming that there is an agreed-upon definition of reliability.

Another issue already alluded to is that not all faults were created equal. That is, some faults have disastrous results, while others are barely a nuisance. If a fault causes an airplane to crash or large amounts of money to be diverted from one account to another, then the fault has substantial consequences. On the other hand, if the desired shade of the background of a website is slightly off, it may be aesthetically less pleasing to some, but obviously far less catastrophic than one of the faults mentioned above. If we are able to associate a cost of failure with potential faults, and a probability of that fault's occurrence, then we could do a risk analysis. [28] This might allow us to compare testing strategies based on how many high risk faults they uncover or the amount of risk reduction they guarantee. But, of course, that is inherently a system-specific sort of comparison and therefore just because the strategy will do a more effective job for *this* system, we are not able to extrapolate to other systems.

In an attempt to address this sort of issue, Frankl and Weyuker [11] extended their earlier work on comparing testing strategies discussed in Section 3 [10]. First they generalized the test selection strategies considered to make them somewhat less artificial. They also introduced two new measures of test effectiveness that were related to risk. The first compared strategies based on the expected risk detected, while the second considered the expected risk reduction. They then investigated whether it was possible to compare testing strategies using either of these new measures. Again they used the properly covers relation and showed that if C_1 properly covers C_2 then under very constrained circumstances, C_1 was guaranteed to perform at least as well as C_2 by both of these measures. This seems to be a positive step on the road to more realistic comparisons, but still involves the use of not entirely realistic definitions of testing strategies.

6   Comparing Criteria Empirically

So far I have discussed formal analytic ways of comparing software testing criteria. It is also possible to compare these criteria empirically, and, in fact, there are two distinct sorts of empirical studies that could be performed. The first involves doing a formal scientific experiment, while the second involves a far less formal case study.

Formal experiments generally involve applying the technique under consideration to a substantial population of software systems and observing various characteristics of this application, such as cost, effectiveness, or ease of use. Formal experiments have the advantage that you can extrapolate from the results observed during the experiment to other systems, because the subjects of the experiment were supposedly representative of the larger population which is your universe.

But true scientific experiments are rarely if ever done in this area for several reasons. First, it would require that there be a clear understanding of what is meant by a "typical" program containing "typical" faults, and we generally do not have that sort of information, even in limited domains such as medical or telecommunications applications. In addition, the cost of doing a significant experiment on multiple large systems would generally be completely prohibitive, as would be the time to complete such an experiment.

Several papers describing small "experiments" that aim to compare the effectiveness of different testing strategies have been published. However, there has generally been no validation or even plausible arguments made that the subject software are in any way representative of software systems in use. Similarly there has been no evidence that the faults, which have frequently been *seeded* or deliberately inserted, are in any way representative of real faults that occur in large software systems. For these reasons, even when the authors have referred to these empirical studies as experiments, I do not believe that they meet the standards used in most scientific fields of being a scientific experiment. I will therefore refer to them in this section simply as empirical studies.

Examples of published empirical studies comparing two or more testing strategies include [4,5,7,8,12,14,18,19,20,21,25] These studies have generally used small programs, specifically written for experimentation, which have not been shown to be representative of any particular system, or program type. In addition, for most of these studies, the faults are synthetic and have been seeded into the software. Even for the few studies that did use large systems and/or naturally-occurring faults, they failed to satisfy the "representative" criterion for being considered a true scientific experiment that would allow us to extrapolate widely from observations made for the subject faults and software in terms of the effectiveness of the studied testing strategies.

Although a second type of empirical study involves the use of one or more large industrial software system, containing real faults, it is still sometimes of limited value for other software projects because it is necessary to *model* the system. This involves designing a simplified version of the system which is close enough to reality that the observations made about the model are believed to be valid for the full system, yet simple enough to make the mathematics tractable. Our experience has been that most software testers find modeling very difficult or impossible to do. In addition, when the study is completed for the simplified system or systems, one does not necessarily have an accurate picture of how effective the testing strategies considered for the system model will be for real systems.

In general, case studies examine the application of one or more testing strategy or characteristics of testing strategies for one or a few specific systems. They acknowledge that these systems and the faults they contain may not be representative of a wider class of programs. By recognizing the importance of replicating case studies on many different large systems, with many different characteristics, we are able to build up a significant amount of evidence, that individually may not be persuasive, that some testing strategy is more effective than another. By showing similar experiences with many different software systems, we are able to draw conclusions about the effectiveness of one or more testing strategy. For the purposes of this chapter, when I refer to a case study, I am referring to one performed on a "real" system, produced by professional programmers to accomplish a real task in a production environment. I am also referring to the situation in which whatever faults occur in the system occurred naturally, as opposed to the case in which they were seeded, or synthetically inserted into the software.

Although it is difficult to perform case studies well, and expensive to design and perform these studies, it is nonetheless typically much more feasible to perform carefully crafted case studies than formal experiments using real deployed software systems. Of course, it is generally impossible to directly extrapolate from results observed for one or two specific systems that served as subjects of a case study to systems in general since the subjects were typically *not* selected because they were especially representative, but rather because there were project personnel who were willing to participate in the study, or management support, or because the project itself initiated the study to find out information about *their* project.

Nonetheless, by repeating similar case studies we build up a body of knowledge that can allow us to conclude that because of the similarity of results for different sorts of systems, developed in different languages, with different development and test personnel, and different development environments, we can in fact deduce that the observations made for the specific systems, can in fact be applied to other types of systems. By carefully replicating case studies, with different specific systems and different types of systems, we see more pieces of the puzzle, and therefore we can be more convinced that we have a general solution of the puzzle.

Besides the limitation that case study results might not be generalizable, there are other problems that may be similar to those associated with the formal analytic comparison relations. For example, case studies may also involve the use of idealized ways of using the criterion or other behavior that does not reflect how the development project normally behaves. That is one of the reasons that I restrict attention to real production systems, developed by professionals to perform a real, mission-critical task. My assumption further, is that testing strategies under consideration are also being used as intended.

Nonetheless, for some testing strategies, there may not be any provision to account for individualized behavior. Therefore, one professional tester might correctly use a strategy and select test suite X while another professional tester might correctly use the same strategy and select test suite Y, where X and Y are entirely disjoint. For that reason, the testing strategy might perform very well in a case study done using the first tester, yet poorly in a case study using the second tester. For that reason, it is even more essential that case studies be replicated. If we see large amounts of variability in the success of using certain testing strategies, that might point us in the direction of removing this variability by in some way codifying what the more successful tester is doing.

Furthermore, if the case study is just intended to assess the effectiveness of different test case selection strategies, then cost may not have been evaluated during the case study and no cost-benefit analysis may have been performed. This might mean that the pragmatic usefulness of the strategies studied might not have been assessed. Similarly, since the severity of faults uncovered by testing strategies is generally not an integral part of test case selection criteria, a case study designed to compare the effectiveness of different strategies might not even consider the fault severity dimension or the degree to which the removal of detected faults improves the overall system dependability.

In addition, an assessment of the overall state of the software may not have been made at the end of the case study, so although the case study may have indicated that testing strategy A was more effective for a given system or systems than testing strategy B, it may still be the case that neither strategy is really acceptable because the required level of dependability may not have been met.

But even small or limited case studies do have some real positive character-istics too. They can provide a "proof of concept" which may be sufficient to encourage practitioners to try the technique being investigated, in the field. It may be considered too big a risk to try a new testing technique or other software development strategy on a large production software project because of time and reliability constraints. However, if it can be shown in a case study that other similar production projects have used the technique and gotten better results than the currently-used process that the project or organization has been using, that might be sufficient to convince management of the usefulness of the new approach.

Additionally, case studies can provide an estimate of the difficulty of using the test selection criterion. Often it may seem to project personnel that the learning curve will be too steep to make the adoption of the new technique worthwhile. By showing how other projects have adopted the use of the criterion, and including a description of the experience of testers, it might be possible to convince a project to try using it too. I have found that to be the case for other validation and dependability-related activities.

For example, once production projects saw the way we used operational dis-tributions describing the expected workload of the system once it is operational in the field, as the basis for selection of test cases for several large industrial software projects, as documented in case studies described in [1], they were will-ing or even eager to try basing their test case selection strategies on operational distributions.

Other examples in which large-scale case studies were used to help convince projects to move a strategy or approach to some software development stage from a research environment into production use include a performance testing strategy described in [2], the use of architecture reviews as a means of predicting likely project success [3], the use of a technique designed to predict system scalability [29], and the use of a statistical model that predicts which files of a large software system are likely to contain the largest number of faults in the next release of the system [22].

Another issue that may serve as a roadblock to the adoption of a new test case selection criterion is the perceived or actual cost of using it. Estimates of this cost can be essential in convincing management of the practicality or feasibility of using the strategy. Thus, one test case selection strategy may find 10% more faults than another, but if it costs one hundred times more, or it is *feared* that it will cost much more to use, then it might be dismissed out of hand. I have found that a comprehensive case study that includes an accurate assessment of its cost to use on one or more real projects may be sufficient to win acceptance for the strategy.

One other useful potential payoff of doing a large industrial case study to determine the effectiveness of a software test selection criterion relates to modeling. It is often difficult to determine an effective granularity for modeling the software. When it is necessary to model a system, particularly when the system is very large, the task can sometimes seem overwhelming to practitioners. In these situations, case studies that include a description of the level of granularity at which the modeling was done can be extremely helpful, serving as a sort of a template.

Our personal experience has been that large industrial case studies are difficult and expensive but very valuable for the reasons mentioned above, and therefore well worth the time and effort. In many cases they provide information that cannot be determined any other way.

7   Conclusions

We have studied a variety of proposed ways of comparing software testing criteria, and found that many of the formal comparison relations had profound problems associated with them, even though they initially appeared to be intuitively reasonable.

Of central importance was the fact that all of the testing criteria that were compared by the relations were idealized versions of the way practitioners actually test software. So, even though we know precisely how these idealized criteria are related based on the expected number of faults detected and the probability of finding faults, we are not able to state conclusively how the versions of these strategies actually used in practice stack up.

Also, none of the proposed comparison relations took the cost into account. If we knew that one criterion was a little bit more effective at finding faults than another but that it cost many times as much, would the more effective strategy still be attractive or even feasible to use? That would likely depend heavily on the application and its reliability requirements. And if criterion C_1 was deemed more effective than criterion C_2 by some relation, but all the faults that were being detected by C_1 were trivial faults, while C_2 found profound and potentially catastrophic faults, would we still consider C_1 a more effective criterion? By all the relations we investigated, C_1 might be considered in some way stronger, since there is no way to factor in the severity or consequence of the faults.

Perhaps most important is that there is no indication whatsoever of how dependable the software will be when it has been thoroughly tested according to some criterion. Even knowing that criterion C_1 always does a more effective job of testing than criterion C_2, does not imply that C_1 does a *good* job of testing.

So what are the implications of all this? First, this is a call for new thought and more important, new types of thought to be put into attacking this problem. We saw that the initial proposals for comparison relations seemed reasonable at first glance, but turned out to be flawed because they really did not properly capture the essence of what it means for one testing strategy to be more effective at finding faults than another.

Then there was the insight that using probabilistic measures would be more appropriate, and in fact they *are* more appropriate in certain ways. But there are still serious flaws. It is very difficult to imagine how to formalize what is in practice a very individualized process. Testing practitioners often develop their own versions of the test selection criteria introduced in textbooks or develop ways of testing software based on their experience, intuition, available tools, application domains, project norms, project deadlines, and many other factors.

I believe that the research performed so far provides us with insights and although I have described serious flaws associated with these analytic assessments, I nonetheless firmly believe that they are valuable. Each time a new perspective is proposed, especially if designed to address weaknesses identified in earlier proposals, I believe that we, as a community move closer to greater understanding. Perhaps instead of comparing testing strategies in general, we may need to relativize the comparisons to particular domains, programming languages, or environments.

There is also a very important role for empirical studies. They can tell us things that all the theorems in the world cannot tell us – how something really works in practice. Comparing and assessing software testing strategies is a very important and essential problem that must be solved in order to elevate the practice of testing. I think the best hope for a solution will be the combination of carefully thought out theory, done by people who understand both theory and practice, along with carefully thought out case studies.

In closing I note that in earlier papers, I tried to identify properties of software test data adequacy criteria [26] and software complexity measures [27] as a way of evaluating the effectiveness of proposed criteria. An important future direction of research in the area of comparing testing strategies might involve the identification and codification of the characteristics that make comparison relations either appropriate or inappropriate. In this way we can try to make progress in defining good comparison relations. If we knew what properties a comparison relation *should* possess and which ones they definitely *should not* have, we might be able to say in concrete terms whether the comparisons they make were important.

For example, one might argue that it should be possible to compare all or most testing strategies using a proposed relation. We saw, however, that this was not true for relations such as subsumption and power. Another requirement might be that the relation should never give misleading results. Again, this was not true for the subsumption and power relations. As outlined above, we have already identified several other properties that proposed comparison relations should have but do not. Perhaps we can come to some agreement about these desirable properties and that will point us in exciting new directions.

Fundamentally, progress in this area will involve a great deal of ingenuity, some essential insights, and a great deal of effort, but hopefully it will all be worth the trouble. Perhaps some day in the future we will be able to tell testing practitioners how to test their software and we will know in concrete ways, the state of the resulting software. But I think that is still a while off.

References

1. Avritzer, A., Weyuker, E.J.: The automatic generation of load test suites and the assessment of the resulting software. IEEE Transactions on Software Engineering, 705–716 (September 1995)
2. Avritzer, A., Weyuker, E.J.: Deriving workloads for performance testing. Software Practice and Experience 26(6), 613–633 (1996)
3. Avritzer, A., Weyuker, E.J.: Metrics to assess the likelihood of project success based on architecture reviews. Empirical Software Engineering Journal 4(3), 197–213 (1999)
4. Duran, J.W., Ntafos, S.C.: An evaluation of random testing. IEEE Transactions on Software Engineering 10(7), 438–444 (1984)
5. Thévenod-Fosse, P., Waeselynck, H., Crouzet, Y.: An Experimental Study on Software Structural Testing: Deterministic Versus Random Input Generation. In: IEEE Fault-Tolerant Computing: The Twenty-First International Symposium, Montreal, Canada, June 1991, pp. 410–417 (1991)
6. Frankl, P.G., Hamlet, D., Littlewood, B., Strigini, L.: Evaluating testing methods by delivered reliability. IEEE Transactions on Software Engineering 24(8), 586–601 (1998)
7. Frankl, P.G., Weiss, S.N.: An Experimental Comparison of the Effectiveness of Branch Testing and Data Flow Testing. IEEE Transactions on Software Engineering 19(8), 774–787 (1993)
8. Frankl, P.G., Weiss, S.N., Hu, C.: All-Uses versus Mutation Testing: An Experimental Comparison of Effectiveness. Journal of Systems and Software 38(3), 235–253 (1997)
9. Frankl, P.G., Weyuker, E.J.: A formal analysis of the fault detecting ability of testing methods. IEEE Transactions on Software Engineering, 202–213 (March 1993)
10. Frankl, P.G., Weyuker, E.J.: Provable improvements on branch testing. IEEE Transactions on Software Engineering 19(10), 962–975 (1993)
11. Frankl, P.G., Weyuker, E.J.: Testing Software to Detect and Reduce Risk. Journal of Systems and Software 53(3), 275–286 (2000)
12. Girgis, M.R., Woodward, M.R.: An Experimental Comparison of the Error Exposing Ability of Program Testing Criteria. In: Proceedings of the IEEE Workshop on Software Testing, July 1986, pp. 64–73 (1986)

13. Gourlay, J.S.: A mathematical framework for the investigation of testing. IEEE Transactions on Software Engineering SE-9(6), 686–709 (1983)
14. Grindal, M., Lindström, B., Offutt, J., Andler, S.F.: An Evaluation of Combination Testing Strategies. Empirical Software Engineering 11(4), 583–611 (2006)
15. Hamlet, D.: Theoretical comparison of testing methods. In: Proceedings Third Symposium on Testing, Analysis and Verification, Key West, pp. 28–37 (1989)
16. Hamlet, D., Taylor, R.: Partition testing does not inspire confidence. IEEE Transactions on Software Engineering 16(12), 1402–1411 (1990)
17. Hierons, R.M.: Comparing test sets and criteria in the presence of test hypotheses and fault domains. ACM Transactions of Software Engineering and Methodology 11(4), 427–448 (2002)
18. Hutchins, M., Foster, H., Goradia, T., Ostrand, T.: Experiments on the effectiveness of dataflow- and controlflow-based test adequacy criteria. In: Proceedings of the 16th International Conference on Software Engineering, May 1994, pp. 191–200 (1994)
19. Kuhn, D.R.: An Investigation of the Applicability of Design of Experiments to Software Testing. In: Proceedings of the 27th NASA/IEEE Software Engineering Workshop (December 2002)
20. Ntafos, S.: A comparison of some structural testing strategies. IEEE Transactions on Software Engineering 14(6), 868–874 (1988)
21. Offutt, A.J., Pan, J., Tewary, K., Zhang, T.: An Experimental Evaluation of Data Flow and Mutation Testing. Software-Practice and Experience 26(2), 165–176 (1996)
22. Ostrand, T., Weyuker, E., Bell, R.: Predicting the location and number of faults in large software systems. IEEE Transactions on Software Engineering 31(4) (April 2005)
23. Rapps, S., Weyuker, E.J.: Data flow analysis techniques for program test data selection. In: Proceedings Sixth International Conference on Software Engineering, Tokyo, Japan, pp. 272–278 (September 1982)
24. Rapps, S., Weyuker, E.J.: Selecting software test data using data flow information. IEEE Transactions on Software Engineering SE-14(4), 367–375 (1985)
25. Pizza, M., Strigini, L.: Comparing the effectiveness of testing methods in improving programs: the effect of variations in program quality. In: Proc. 9th International Symp. on Software Reliability Engineering, ISSRE 1998, Paderborn, Germany (November 1998)
26. Weyuker, E.J.: Axiomatizing software test data adequacy. IEEE Transactions on Software Engineering SE-12(12), 1128–1138 (1986)
27. Weyuker, E.J.: Evaluating Software Complexity Measures. IEEE Transactions on Software Engineering 14(9), 1357–1365 (1988)
28. Weyuker, E.J.: Using failure cost information for testing and reliability assessment. ACM Transactions on Software Engineering and Methodology 5(2), 87–98 (1996)
29. Weyuker, E.J., Avritzer, A.: A metric to predict software scalability. In: Proc. 8th IEEE Symposium on Metrics (METRICS 2002), June 2002, pp. 152–158 (2002)
30. Weyuker, E.J., Jeng, B.: Analyzing partition testing strategies. IEEE Transactions on Software Engineering 17(7), 703–711 (1991)
31. Weyuker, E.J., Ostrand, T.J.: Theories of Program Testing and the Application of Revealing Subdomains. IEEE Transactions on Software Engineering, 236–245 (May 1980)
32. Weyuker, E.J., Weiss, S.N., Hamlet, D.: Comparison of program testing strategies. In: Proceedings Fourth Symposium on Software Testing, Analysis, and Verification, October 1991, pp. 1–10. ACM Press, New York (1991)

The Test Technology TTCN-3

Ina Schieferdecker[1], Jens Grabowski[2], Theofanis Vassiliou-Gioles[3],
and George Din[4]

[1] Technical University Berlin/Fraunhofer FOKUS
ina@cs.tu-berlin.de
[2] University of Goettingen
grabowski@informatik.uni-goettingen.de
[3] Testing Technologies
vassiliou@testingtech.de
[4] Fraunhofer FOKUS
din@fokus.fraunhofer.de

Abstract. The Testing and Test Control Notation (TTCN-3) is a widely established test technology traditionally used in the telecommunication domain. In its new version, TTCN-3 has a wider scope and applicability. It can be applied not only for testing the conformance and interoperability of communication protocols but also for testing the functionality, interoperation and performance of software-based systems in general. Therefore, TTCN-3 is nowadays used in other domains such as automotive, railways, avionics, or security systems. This chapter introduces the concepts of the TTCN-3 language and provides examples of its practical use.

1 Overview

Despite of automated on-the fly test generation as, for example, advocated in [3], the explicit specification of tests is needed as the majority of tests is still developed manually [16,20,22]. For that, the use of a standardized and well-defined test notation is recommended as the tests can be defined in a precise, well-understood and widely accepted format. Furthermore, automatically generated tests are often extended and adapted manually as current test generation techniques still bear several limitations. In order to keep track of those adaptations, the resulting tests should be explicitly denoted as well. Another advantage of standardized test specifications is the ability to provide test platforms for automated test execution, which could be used across domains – provided that there are domain-specific adapters for the different target technologies.

TTCN-3 is the successor language of the Tree and Tabular Combined Notation (TTCN) [14,17] which was developed due to the imperative necessity to have a universally understood test (specification and implementation) language able to describe test data and test behaviours with sophisticated test concepts. TTCN-3 [15] is a powerful test technology which allows to specify and execute

R.M. Hierons et al. (Eds.): Formal Methods and Testing, LNCS 4949, pp. 292–319, 2008.
© Springer-Verlag Berlin Heidelberg 2008

detailed test descriptions for several kinds of testing on different levels of abstraction including, for example, component level, integration level, and system level testing.

TTCN-3 has been specifically developed for the design and definition of test systems. The syntax and operational semantics of TTCN-3 tests is commonly understood and not related to a particular programming language or technology of systems to be tested. TTCN-3 tests concentrate on the purpose of the test and abstract from particular test system details. Off the shelf tools for TTCN-3 and TTCN-3-based test systems are readily available [34]. Many successful test solutions and applications have been realised with TTCN-3 also beyond the traditional telecommunication domain [2,13,31].

The development of TTCN-3 was driven by industry and academia with the objective to obtain one test notation for black-box and grey-box testing. In contrast to earlier test technologies, TTCN-3 encourages the use of a common methodology and style which leads to a simpler maintenance of test suites and increases their reuse. When using TTCN-3, a test designer develops test cases at an abstract level. She can focus on the test logic for checking a system against given test purposes. She does not have to deal with test system specifics and test execution details. A standardized test notation provides a lot of advantages to test solution providers, testers and other users of test specifications and test results: the use of a standardized test notation reduces the costs for education and training as a large amount of documentation, examples, and predefined test suites is available. In 2007, a TTCN-3 certification procedures has been established, so that people's TTCN-3 knowledge can be examined and certified along internationally agreed rules [4]. It is obviously preferred to use wherever possible the same notation for testing than learning different technologies for different test projects. The constant use and collaboration between TTCN-3 vendors and users ensure a continuous maintenance and further development of the base technology.

TTCN-3 enables systematic, specification-based testing for functional, interoperability, robustness, regression, scalability, and load testing on component, integration and system level. It supports the definition of test procedures for local and distributed *test configurations* via homogeneous or heterogeneous interfaces (so called *ports*) to the *system under test* (the SUT). It allows the definition of simple and complex *test behaviours* in terms of sequences, alternatives, and loops of system stimuli and observations. Test behaviours can be executed in parallel on a number of *test components*. Configurations of test components can be fixed or can vary during test execution, i.e. test components may be created dynamically depending on the conditions along a test run.

The interaction with the SUT can be realised either by *asynchronous, message-based* or *synchronous, procedure-based* communication. The test system provides stimuli to the SUT and receives and checks the SUT reactions. The observed SUT reactions are checked against expected reactions by using *templates*. Templates are defined in terms of *matching mechanisms* which allow to define expected responses in a detailed manner by concrete values, by ranges or sets of values, or by logical properties of value sets. Based on the comparison between expected and observed reaction, the SUT is assessed and *test verdicts* are assigned. Basically, all test data and test behaviours can be *parameterized*, even parameters for complete test suites can be defined.

The concepts of TTCN-3 outlined above are defined by a well-defined syntax and operational semantics, which provide a precise meaning and execution semantics to TTCN-3. Figure 1 presents the architecture of the TTCN-3 technology. TTCN-3 is based on a *core language* which has a look and feel similar to a general purpose programming language like C, C++ or Java. The predefined tabular and graphical presentation formats address users preferring a tabular or Message Sequence Chart (MSC) [19] like presentation of test specifications. TTCN-3 allows to import data types and data values specified in the Abstract Syntax Notation One (ASN.1) [18], the Interface Definition Language (IDL) [23] or the Extended Markup Language (XML) [38]. Further presentation formats like, e.g. a state machine-based presentation format, and interfaces to data type and data value notations like, e.g. defining the import of C and C++ data types and data values are under discussion or even under development. They may be standardized in future version of the TTCN-3 standard.

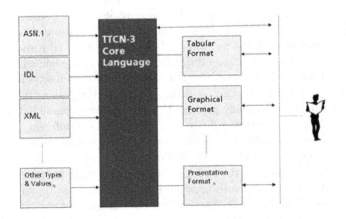

Fig. 1. The TTCN-3 Language Architecture

The rest of the chapter is structured as follows: Section 2 reviews the history of TTCN-3 and enumerates the different parts of the TTCN-3 standard series. In Section 3, the main concepts of TTCN-3 such as test case, test behaviour, verdict, or alt statement are described. The presentation formats are explained in Section 4. Section 5 introduces a web-server test example to demonstrate the application of the TTCN-3 concepts. Section 6 presents the execution interfaces of TTCN-3 and explains how TTCN-3 test systems can be realized by use of these interfaces. The import and usage of external data into TTCN-3 test suites is explained in Section 7. A comparison with the UML Testing Profile [24] is given in Section 8. Finally, a summary and an outlook conclude the chapter.

2   The Standard and Its History

TTCN-3 has been developed by the European Telecommunication Standards Institute (ETSI). The TTCN-3 standard comprises currently seven parts and two additional technical reports. The technical reports will become the parts 7 and 9 of the TTCN-3 standard and specify the use of ASN.1 and XML in TTCN-3. The already standardized seven parts of the TTCN-3 standard [6,7,8,9,10,11,12] contain the following information:

Part 1: TTCN-3 Core Language. This document specifies the textual syntax of TTCN-3.

Part 2: Tabular Presentation Format. The tabular presentation format presents a TTCN-3 specification within a collection of tables.

Part 3: Graphical Presentation Format. The graphical presentation format is used to represent TTCN-3 tests as interactions between the SUT and the test system. This presentation format is based on the Message Sequence Chart (MSC) [19] language.

Part 4: Operational semantics. The operational semantics describes the meaning of TTCN-3 behaviour by providing a state oriented view on the execution of TTCN-3 tests.

Part 5: TTCN-3 Runtime Interfaces (TRI). A complete test system implementation requires a platform specific adaptation layer. TRI contains the specification of a common Application Programming Interface (API) interface to adapt TTCN-3 test systems to an SUT.

Part 6: TTCN-3 Control Interfaces (TCI). This part of the TTCN-3 standard contains the specification of the APIs, which a TTCN-3 execution environment should implement for the encoding and decoding of test data, test management, component handling, external data control and logging.

Part 8: Use of IDL in TTCN-3. This document provides guidelines and mappings rules for the combined use of IDL and TTCN-3.

TTCN-3 evolved from the Tree and Tabular Combined Notation (TTCN) which was developed for conformance testing of telecommunication protocols. TTCN was first published in 1992 as part 3 of the international ISO/IEC standard 9646 "OSI Conformance Testing Methodology and Framework" [17]. Since then, TTCN has been intensively used to specify tests for different technologies like Global System for Mobile Communication (GSM), Digital Enhanced Cordless Technologies (DECT), Intelligent Network Application Protocol (INAP), and Integrated Services Digital Network (N-ISDN, B-ISDN). Small extensions of TTCN [14] addressed test modules, parallel test setups and the use of ASN.1 in TTCN. Although TTCN was improved, it implements the concepts of OSI conformance testing and is therefore only of limited usability for other kinds of testing such as interoperability, robustness, regression, or system testing. Since TTCN was designed for testing OSI protocols, it is also difficult to apply TTCN to other technologies like for mobile systems or CORBA-based applications.

In 1998, ETSI was asked by its members to develop a new test language, namely TTCN-3, addressing current and upcoming test requirements. The development of TTCN-3 was encouraged by key players of the telecommunication industry and by researchers to overcome the limitations of TTCN. The standardization process, lead by the ETSI Protocol and Testing Competence Center (PTCC), completed in 2000 the first version of TTCN-3. Since then TTCN-3 is a continuously maintained test technology. For this, ETSI provides a well-defined change request procedure (see http://www.ttcn-3.org/TTCN3cr.htm), to which everybody can contribute. This allows corrections and extensions to TTCN-3 resulting in revised versions of the standard. In February 2007 TTCN-3 v3.2.1 has been approved by ETSI. From its first version in 2000 until its latest version in 2007, TTCN-3 has evolved to a powerful basis for test development and can serve as a target for test generation and other means of efficient test development [27,37].

3   The Concepts of TTCN-3

The TTCN-3 core language is a modular language which has a similar look and feel to a typical programming language like, e.g. C or C++. In addition to the typical programming language constructs, it contains all important features necessary to specify test procedures and campaigns like test verdicts to assess test runs, matching mechanisms to compare the reactions of the SUT with the expected outputs, timer handling to specify time restrictions, the handling of test components to support distributed testing, the ability to specify encoding information, support for different kinds of communication (i.e. synchronous and asynchronous communication) and the possibility to log test information during a test run.

3.1   TTCN-3 Module

A TTCN-3 test specification is defined by a set of modules. As shown in Figure 2, a module typically contains imports from other modules; data type definitions, test data descriptions, definitions for test configuration, test behaviour specifications and a module control part to specify the ordering, selection and execution of test cases.

The top-level building-block of TTCN-3 is the module. A module cannot contain sub-modules, but may import partially or completely definitions from other modules and contains further definitions necessary for a test. A module definition starts with the keyword **module**. A module can be parameterized; a parameter is a data value that is supplied by the test environment at runtime. It is possible to initialize a parameter with a default value.

A TTCN-3 module has two parts: the module definitions part and the module control part. The module definitions part contains definitions specified by that module. These definitions can be used everywhere in the module and may be imported from other modules. The module control part is the main program

Module

Module Definitions	
Imports	Importing definitions from other modules defined in TTCN-3 or other languages
Data Types	User defined data types (messages, PDUs, information elements, ...)
Test Data	Test data transmitted/received during test execution (templates, values)
Test Configuration	Definition of the test components and communication ports
Test Behavior	Specification of the dynamic test behavior

Module Control	Defining the sequence, loops, conditions, etc. for the execution of test cases

Fig. 2. The TTCN-3 Module Structure

of a module. It describes the execution sequence of the test cases. The control part can use the verdicts delivered by test cases to select the next test case to be executed. The control part of a module can call any test case known in the module, i.e. locally defined in the module or imported from another module.

3.2 TTCN-3 Test System and Test Cases

A test case (TTCN-3 keyword **testcase**) is executed by a test system. TTCN-3 allows the specification of local and distributed test systems with static and dynamic test configurations. A test system may consist of a single test component or of a set of interconnected test components. It has well-defined communication ports and an explicit test system interface, which defines the boundaries to the test system. The set of test components together with their connections to the SUT and to other test components constitute the test configuration.

Within every test system, there is one Main Test Component (MTC). All other test components are called Parallel Test Components (PTCs). The MTC is created and started automatically at the beginning of each test case execution. The behaviour of the MTC is specified in the body of the test case definition. A test case terminates when the MTC terminates. This implies also the termination of all PTCs. During the execution of a test case, PTCs can be created, started and stopped dynamically. A test component may stop itself or can be stopped by another test component.

For communication purposes, each test component owns a set of local communication ports. Each port has an in- and an out-direction. The in-direction is modelled as an infinite FIFO queue, which stores the incoming information until it is processed by the test component owning the port. The out-direction is directly linked to the communication partner which can be another test component or the SUT. This means that that outgoing information is not buffered.

During test execution, TTCN-3 distinguishes between connected and mapped ports. Connected ports are used for the communication with other test components. If two ports are connected, the in-direction of one port is linked to the out-direction of the other, and vice versa. A mapped port is used for the communication with the SUT. In TTCN-3, connections and mappings can be created and destroyed dynamically at runtime. There are no restrictions on the number of connections and mappings a component may have. A component may be connected to itself. One-to-many connections are allowed. For the communication among test components and between test components and the SUT, TTCN-3 supports message-based and procedure-based communication. Message-based communication is based on an asynchronous message exchange. The principle of procedure-based communication is to call procedures in remote entities. This allows a test component to emulate the client or server side during a test. Furthermore, unicast, multicast and broadcast communication are also supported by TTCN-3.

Test cases define test behaviours which can be executed to check whether the SUT passes the test or not. A test case is considered to be a self-contained and complete specification of a test procedure that checks a given test purpose. The result of a test case execution is a test verdict.

TTCN-3 provides a special test verdict mechanism for the interpretation of test runs. This mechanism is implemented by a set of predefined verdicts, local and global test verdicts and operations for reading and setting local test verdicts. The predefined verdicts are **pass**, **inconc**, **fail**, **error** and **none**. They can be used for the judgment of complete and partial test runs. A **pass** verdict denotes that the SUT behaves according to the test purpose, a fail indicates that the SUT violates its specification. An **inconc** (inconclusive) describes a situation where neither a pass nor a fail can be assigned. The verdict **error** indicates an error in the test devices. The verdict none is the initial value for local and global test verdicts, i.e. no other verdict has been assigned yet.

During test execution, each test component maintains its own local test verdict. A local test verdict is an object that is instantiated automatically for each test component at the time of component creation. A test component can retrieve and set its local verdict. The verdict **error** is not allowed to be set by a test component. It is set automatically by the TTCN-3 run-time environment, if an error in the test equipment occurs. When changing the value of a local test verdict, special overwriting rules apply. The overwriting rules only allow that a test verdict becomes worse. For example, a **pass** may change to **inconc** or **fail**, but a **fail** cannot change to a **pass** or **inconc**. All local test verdicts contribute to the final global test verdict of the test case. For this, the overwriting rules explained above are also used, i.e. the worst local verdict will become the final global verdict of the test case.

3.3   Test Behaviour

TTCN-3 allows an easy and efficient description of simple and complex, sequential and parallel test behaviours in terms of sequences, alternatives, loops, stimuli and responses. Stimuli and responses are exchanged at the interfaces of the SUT, which are defined as a collection of ports. The test system can use a single test component for sequential test procedures or a number of test components to perform test procedures in parallel. Likewise to the interfaces of the SUT, the interfaces of the test components are described as ports.

An **alt** statement describes an ordered set of alternatives, i.e. an ordered set of alternative branches of behaviour. Each alternative has a guard. A guard consists of several preconditions, which may refer to the values of variables, the status of timers, the contents of port queues and the identifiers of components, ports and timers. The same precondition can be used in different guards. An alternative becomes executable, if the corresponding guard is fulfilled. If several alternatives are executable, the first executable alternative in the list of alternatives will be executed. If no alternative becomes executable, the **alt** statement will be executed as a loop until one of the guards will permit entering an alternative.

In TTCN-3, a **default** mechanism can be used to handle communication events which may occur, but which do not contribute to the test objective. A **default** behaviour can be specified by an **altstep** which then can be activated as a default behaviour. It is possible to define complex default behaviour by having activated several altsteps at the same time. For each test component, the defaults, i.e. activated altsteps, are stored in a list of defaults in the order of their activation. The default behaviours can be activated or deactivated through the TTCN-3 operations **activate** and **deactivate**. These operations operate on the list of defaults. An **activate** operation appends a new default to the beginning of the list and a **deactivate** operation removes a default from that list.

The default mechanism is invoked at the end of each **alt** statement, if the default list is not empty and if due to the current state none of the alternatives is executable. The default mechanism invokes the first altstep in the list of defaults, i.e. the altstep which has been lastly activated, and waits for the result of its termination. The termination can be successful or unsuccessful. Unsuccessful means that none of the alternatives of the altstep defining the default behaviour is executable, successful means that one of the alternatives has been executed.

In case of an unsuccessful termination, the default mechanism invokes the next default in the list. If the last default in the list has terminated unsuccessfully, the default mechanism will return to the **alt** statement and indicate an unsuccessful default execution. An unsuccessful default execution causes the **alt** statement to be executed again.

In case of a successful termination, the default may either stop the test component by means of a **stop** statement, the main control flow of the test component will continue immediately after the **alt** statement from which the default mechanism was called or the test component will execute the **alt** statement again. The latter has to be specified explicitly by means of a **repeat** statement.

3.4 TTCN-3 Communication and Test Data

For the communication among test components and between test components and the SUT, TTCN-3 supports message-based and procedure-based communication.

Message-based communication is based on the exchange of messages via buffers. This kind of communication is often called asynchronous communication, because the sending and receiving of a message are decoupled. A sender continues its execution after sending the message without waiting for an answer. Procedure-based communication uses remote procedure calls for communication. This kind of communication is often also called synchronous communication, because the caller of a remote procedure is normally blocked during the treatment of the call, i.e. caller and callee are synchronized via the call.

TTCN-3 offers the following operations for procedure-based communication:

- **call**: to invoke a remote procedure;
- **getcall**: to accept a call from remote;
- **reply**: to reply to a previously received call;
- **getreply**: to accept a reply;
- **raise**: to report an exception to a previously received call;
- **catch**: to collect an exception reported by a remote procedure invocation.

For message-based communication, TTCN-3 offers the following operations:

- **send**: to send a message;
- **receive**: to receive a message;
- **trigger**: to discard all messages until the specified message is received.

TTCN-3 offers different possibilities to specify test data. The structure of test data can be described by means of pre- and user-defined data types and signatures (for procedure-based communication. Data values, value sets and value ranges can be specified by means of constants, variables, data templates and signature templates. Besides this, TTCN-3 offers also the possibility to import data described in other languages like, for example, ASN.1, IDL or XML.

Most of the predefined data types of TTCN-3 are similar to the basic data types known from programming languages like C, C++ or Java. However, some of them are special to TTCN-3:

- Port types define the characteristics communication ports, i.e. kind of communication, communication direction, data to be exchanged via a port of this type.
- Component types define the properties of test components, i.e. ports and local variables, timers and constants owned by a component of that type.
- The **verdicttype** is an enumeration type which defines the possible test verdicts, i.e. **pass**, **fail**, **inconc**, **error** and **none**.
- The **anytype** is a union of all known TTCN-3 types of a TTCN-3 module; an instance of anytype is used as a generic object which is evaluated when the value is known.
- The **default** type is used for default handling. A value of this type is a reference to a default.

For the definition of structured data types, TTCN-3 supports ordered and unordered structured types such as **record** (ordered structure), **record of** (ordered list), **set** (unordered structure), **set of** (unordered list), **enumerated** and **union**. Furthermore, for procedure-based communication, TTCN-3 offers the possibility to define procedure signatures. Signatures are characterized by their name, an optional list of parameters, an optional return value and an optional list of exceptions.

Templates are the main means to represent test data in TTCN-3. A template is a data structures used to define a pattern for a data item sent or received over a port. A template may describe a distinct value, a range of values or a set of values. Distinct values may be transmitted over a port, whereas templates describing ranges or sets of values may be matched with data received from the SUT or other test components. Such a match is successful, if the received data is an element of the data values described by the template. Templates can be specified for arbitrary data types (data templates) and for signatures (signature templates). Furthermore, they can be parameterized, extended and in other template definitions.

4   TTCN-3 Presentation Formats

TTCN-3 offers its core language and two standardized presentation formats to serve the needs of different application domains and users. The textual core language suits best to persons familiar with a general purpose programming language. A core language based test development allows using a text editor of the users' choice and, thus, enables an easy integration into a test environment.

The tabular presentation format for TTCN-3 (TFT) is defined in part 2 of the TTCN-3 standard series. It is designed for users that prefer to use tables for test specification. TFT presents a TTCN-3 module as a collection of tables. TFT highlights the structural aspects of a TTCN-3 module – in particular type and template structures.

Part 3 of the TTCN-3 standard series defines the graphical presentation format for TTCN-3 (GFT) [29]. GFT provides a visualization of TTCN-3 behaviour definitions in an MSC-like manner [19]. It eases the reading, documentation and discussion of test procedures. It is also well suited to describe of test traces and for analyzing of the test results. For each kind of TTCN-3 behaviour definition, GFT provides a special diagram type, i.e. function diagrams for representing functions, altstep diagrams for the visualization of altsteps, test case diagrams for showing test cases and control diagrams for showing the control part of a module.

However, the work on presentation formats is not finished. Where needed, additional presentation formats to represent specific aspects of TTCN-3 test suites can be defined and seamlessly integrated into a TTCN-3 development environment.

5   TTCN-3 Example

The use of TTCN-3 is demonstrated by a small example to test a web server's functionality. A single request represented by a Uniform Resource Locator (URL) is sent to the web server. After receiving the request, the web server should respond by sending an XML file back containing a list of **dinosaurs**. We expect that the list must contain a dinosaur whose name is **Brachiosaurus**. If there is such a dinosaur in the list, the test verdict is **pass**.

5.1   Core Language Example

In the following, we present the TTCN-3 module for testing the Web server described above. The module is split into several parts. We first present a part and describe its contents afterwards.

Listing 1.

```
module dinolistTest {                                      1
  modulepar integer NUMBER_OF_PTCS := 1
  with {
  extension (NUMBER_OF_PTCS)                                4
  "Description: Default number of PTCs";
  }
  type record urlType {                                     7
   charstring protocol ,
   charstring host ,
   charstring file                                          10
  }
  template urlType urlTemplate := {
   protocol := "http://",                                   13
   host := "www.testingtech.de",
   file := "/TTCN-3_Example/dinolist.xml"
  }                                                         16
  :
```

In the lines 7 to 11 of Listing 1, we specify the structure of a URL by defining the **record** urlType. The urlType consists of fields for a **protocol** (line 8), a **host** (line 9), and a **file** (line 10). All fields are of type **charstring** since the request to a Web server also is a string. Until now, we specified only which fields a URL is composed of. We did not specify the values of the fields. This is done within the template declaration with name urlTemplate (lines 12 to 16). In this template, the protocol field is set to http://, the host field is set to www.testingtech.de and the file is set /TTCN-3_Example/dinolist.xml. This means, the complete URL sent to the Web server is URL http://www.testingtech.de/TTCN-3_Example/dinolist.xml.

Listing 2.

```
:
type set of dinosaurType dinolistType;                            2
type record dinosaurType {
  charstring name,
  charstring len ,                                                5
  charstring mass,
  charstring time,
  charstring place                                                8
}
template dinosaurType BrachiosaurusTemplate := {
  name := "Brachiosaurus",                                       11
  len := ?,
  mass := ?,
  time := ?,                                                     14
  place := ?
}
template dinolistType DinoListTemplate := {                      17
  ?,
  ?,
  BrachiosaurusTemplate,                                         20
  ?,
  ?,
  ?,                                                             23
  ?
}
:                                                                26
```

In the next step, we define the answer that we expect from the Web server during the test. As already mentioned, we expect a list of dinosaurs, where one of them must have the name Brachiosaurus. As we don't know at which position of the list our expected dinosaur is, we define a type dinolistType (line 2), which is a **set of** dinosaurs.

A dinosaur represented by the **record** type dinosaurType (lines 3 to 9). It consists of the fields name (line 4) which specifies the name of the dinosaur, len (line 5) which specifies the length (length is a keyword in TTCN-3 and can therefore not used as field name), mass specifying the weight (line 6), time describing when the dinosaur lived (line 7) and place specifying the place where the dinosaur lived (line 8).

A template for dinosaurs with the name BrachiosaurusTemplate is defined in the lines 10 to 16. As it is not important which length and mass the dinosaur had or when and where it lived, these fields were filled with a ? wildcard meaning any value is accepted as valid, i.e. these fields must be filled with a **charstring** but the concrete values do not matter.

For the list of dinosaurs, the template DinoListTemplate is defined (lines 17 to 25). During the test we expect to receive a list of seven dinosaurs from the Web server. The third dinosaurs in the list must be a `Brachiosaurus`. For this, the template `BrachiosaurusTemplate` is reference in the `DinoListTemplate` template (line 20). The other fields of `DinoListTemplate` must be valid dinosaurs, but their kind is is irrelevant. This is specified again by using the matching for any value symbol ?.

Listing 3.

```
:
type component ptcType {                                            2
  port httpPortType httpPort;
  timer localTimer := 3.0;
                                                                   5

}
type port httpPortType message {
  out urlType;                                                     8
  in dinolistType;
}
type component mtcType {}                                          11
type component systemType {
  port httpPortType httpPortArray[NUMBER_OF_PTCS];
                                                                   14

}
:
```

After defining the messages that will be exchanged, test components have to be specified (Listing 3). We start with the type for the PTCs that will send requests to the Web server and check the received messages (lines 2 to 6). This component type has the name `ptcType` and owns a port and a timer. The port is named `httpPort` (line 3) and of type `httpPortType`. The timer has the name `localTimer` and its default expiration time is set to `3.0` seconds (line 4). The port type definition `httpPortType` of `httpPort` can be found in the lines 7 to 10. It is a port for message-based communication (keyword **message**) and it allowed to send messages of type `urlType` (line 8) and to receive messages of type `dinolistType` (line 9).

In a next step, we define the component type `mtcType` (line 11). This component type describes the type of the MTC. The MTC is created by the test system automatically at the start of each test case execution. The behaviour of an MTC is the body of a test case definition. As in the example test case, presented afterwards, the whole communication with the SUT is done only via PTCs, there is no need to define ports, variables or timers for the MTC. Hence, the component type `mtcType` is empty.

Finally, a test component is needed that represents the interfaces to the SUT (lines 12 to 15). It is necessary to define the interfaces where the ports of the PTCs can be mapped to, so that communication can take place. Therefore, an array of ports is created with a size of the given module parameter `NUMBER_OF_PTCS` (Listing 1, lines 2 to 5). Module parameters give the possibility to change parameter settings during a test campaign, without the need to change the TTCN-3 module definitions and to recompile it. Every module parameter can have a default value; in our case it is set to 1.

Listing 4.

```
:
testcase DinoListTest_1 ()
runs on mtcType system systemType {                                3
  var ptcType ptcArray [NUMBER_OF_PTCS];
  var integer i := 0;
  for (i := 0; i < NUMBER_OF_PTCS; i := i + 1) {                   6
    ptcArray[i] := ptcType.create;
    map (ptcArray[i]: httpPort, system: httpPortArray[i]);
  }                                                                 9
  for (i := 0; i < NUMBER_OF_PTCS; i := i + 1) {
    ptcArray[i].start (ptcBehaviour());
  }                                                                 12
  all component.done;
}
:                                                                   15
```

Now, the **testcase** itself and by that the behaviour of the MTC has to be specified (Listing 4, lines 2 to 14). The name of the test case is `DinoListTest_1`. The test case body starts with the definition of an array of components of type `ptcType` (line 4). The size of this array is defined by the module parameter `NUMBER_OF_PTCS`.

Then, the PTCs are created within a **for** loop (lines 6 to 9). In each cycle of the loop, a test component is created and its reference is stored in the array of PTCs (line 7). Furthermore, the port of the newly created test component is mapped to the system port in the system array of ports `httpPortArray`.

Once the test configuration is set up in a second **for** statement (lines 10 to 12), the behaviour of each PTC is started with the function `ptcBehaviour()`.

With the **all component.done** statement (line 13), the termination of all parallel test components is awaited. This ensures that every test component contributes to the overall test case verdict.

Listing 5.

```
:                                                                   1
function ptcBehaviour() runs on ptcType {
  httpPort.send (urlTemplate);
  localTimer.start;                                                 4
  alt {
    [] httpPort.receive (DinoListTemplate) {
      localTimer.stop;                                              7
      setverdict (pass);
    }
```

```
[] httpPort.receive {                                    10
 localTimer.stop;
 setverdict (fail);
}                                                        13
[] localTimer.timeout {
 setverdict (fail);
}                                                        16
}
}                                                        19
:
```

The behaviour of a PTC is described by the function `ptcBehaviour()` shown in the lines 2 to 18 of Listing 5. Firstly, a request (the template `urlTemplate` defined in Listing 1) is sent via `httpPort` (line 3). The `httpPort` is the port of a PTC and has been mapped to a port of the SUT by the MTC in the test case definition. This means that messages send on port `httpPort` are forwarded to the SUT.

Immediately after sending the request, a `localTimer` is started (line 4) as a watch dog to avoid infinite waiting for responses. The timer will run `3.0` seconds as this is the default value of `localTimer` in the `ptcType` type definition (Listing 3).

After the start of the timer, an **alt** statement is used to describe the potential reactions of the SUT:

1. The expected dinosaur list that matches the `DinoListTemplate` is received (line 6). Then the timer is stopped (line 7) and the verdict is set to **pass** (line 8).
2. Something else is received that does not match the expected response. This is specified by using a **receive** operation without a parameter (line 10). In this case, the timer will also be stopped (line 11), but the verdict will be set to **fail** (line 12) as the SUT responded incorrectly.
3. If nothing is received within `3.0` seconds, a **timeout** message from the timer `localTimer` occurs (line 14). Then, the verdict will also be set to fail (line 15).

After that, the PTC terminates. If during test case execution no further PTCs are running, the MTC terminates also. The final verdict of the test case is the accumulated test verdicts of all PTCs.

Listing 6.

```
:
control {                                                3
 execute (DinoListTest_1());
}
}
```

In the lines 2 to 4 of Listing 6, the module control part for our example module is specified. If the control part is called from the test management, the testcase `DinoListTest_1` will be executed (line 3).

5.2 GFT Example

The test behaviour definitions of the TTCN-3 module described in the previous section can be visualized by means of the Graphical Presentation Format for TTCN-3 (GFT). Figure 3 visualizes the test case `DinoListTest_1`. A comparison with the textual description provided in Listing 4 shows that the information in both presentations is identical.

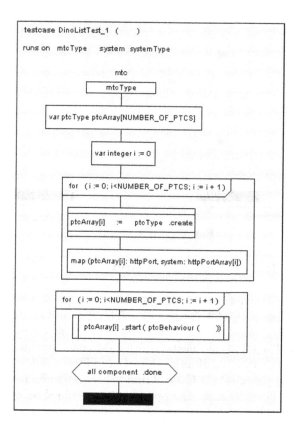

Fig. 3. A GFT Testcase

The GFT diagram in Figure 4 presents the behaviour of the PTCs. It shows that after sending the URL request the positive case when receiving the expected answer and the two negative cases when receiving a wrong or no response.

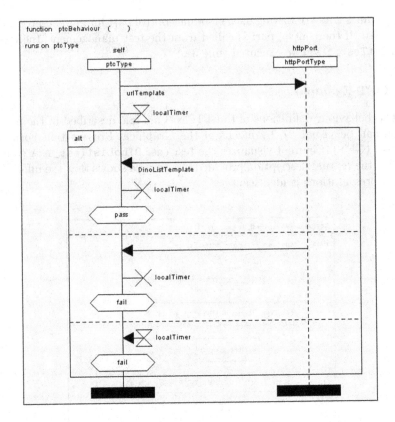

Fig. 4. A GFT Function

6   TTCN-3 Based Test Execution

TTCN-3 standardizes not only the language but also the architecture of an execution environment for TTCN-3 test suites. The standard architecture of a test system consists of several entities which communicate mutually through predefined interfaces. The ETSI specification of the test system architecture is given in two documents: the TTCN-3 Runtime Interfaces (TRI) which is the fifth part of the standard and the TTCN-3 Control Interfaces (TCI) which is the sixth part of the standard. The TRI and TCO provide with a defined set of APIs a unified model to realise the TTCN-3 based test systems. Further extension beyond a pure TTCN-3 based test system are possible [36].

The general structure of a TTCN-3 test system is depicted in Figure 5. A TTCN-3 test system is built-up of a set of interacting entities which manage the test execution (by interpreting or executing the TTCN-3 code), realise the communication with the SUT, implement external functions and handle timer operations.

The TTCN-3 Executable (TE) contains the executable code produced by the compilation of TTCN-3 modules and the TTCN-3 run-time itself. The TE

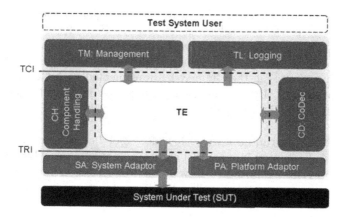

Fig. 5. TTCN-3 Test System Architecture

communicates with the Test Management (TM), the Component Handling (CH) and the Codec (CD) via TCI. The communication with the SUT is realised by using the TRI which defines the interfaces between the TE, the System Adapter (SA) and the Platform Adapter (PA). The different components of a test system have the following functions:

- The TE interprets or executes the compiled TTCN-3 code. It manages the different TTCN-3 entities like test control, test behaviour, test components, types, values and queues.
- The CH handles the communication between components. The CH API contains operations to create, start, stop test components, to establish the connection between test components, to handle the communication operations and to manage the verdicts. The information about the created components and their physical locations is stored in a repository within the test execution environment.
- The TM manages the test execution. It implements operations to execute tests, to provide and set module parameters and external constants. The TTCN-3 logging mechanismis also realised by this component.
- The CD encodes and decodes values according to their types. The TTCN-3 values are encoded into bit strings which are sent to the SUT. The received data is decoded back into TTCN-3 values.
- The SA realises the communication with the SUT. The TTCN-3 communication operations used to interact with the SUT, are implemented by the SA.
- The PA implements timers and external functions. Timers are platform specific elements and have to be implemented outside the pure TTCN-3 test system. The PA provides operations in to handle timers by means of create, start and stop operations. External functions are only declared in a TTCN-3 module. They are implemented in the PA.

The TCI and TRI operations are defined in IDL [23]. They are mapped to the test system specific technology. Particularly, TRI and TCI handle aspects like inter-component communication and timer handling which need to be implemented out-side the TE. This approach allows the use of different test system implementations, e.g. the CH may be implemented with CORBA, Remote Method Invocation (RMI) or another technology. The implementation of the CH is transparent to TE. The TE calls the operations provided by CH which finally handle the requests.

TTCN-3 tests can run on a single test device or be distributed over several test devices and executed in a parallel and coordinated manner [28,33].

Figure 6 provides a distributed view of the test system architecture. The TE is instantiated on each test device. The handling of test components, which may be created on different nodes, is realised by the CH.

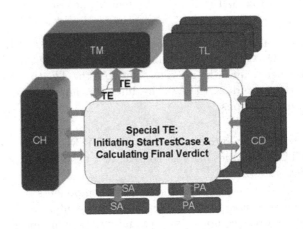

Fig. 6. Realisation of Distributed TTCN-3 Test Systems

The TM is executed the test device from which the test runs are being managed by the user. It is responsible for the user control of the test execution, for the logging of the distributed tests and for the presentation of the results to the user. The CD, SA and PA entities are instantiated on each device because their implementation may differ depending on the underlying, potentially heterogeneous test devices.

7   TTCN-3 External Data

As illustrated in Figure 1, TTCN-3 supports the import of foreign data objects, i.e. defined in other languages than TTCN-3, into TTCN-3 modules. Such foreign data objects can only be used in TTCN-3 modules, if they have a TTCN-3 meaning.

The term TTCN-3 view can be best explained by considering a case where the definition of a TTCN-3 object refers to another TTCN-3 object; the information content of the referenced object shall be available and is used for the new definition. For example, when a template is defined based on a structured type, the identifiers and types of fields of the base type shall be accessible and are used for the template definition. In a similar way, when the referenced type is a foreign object, it shall provide the same information content as if it has been declared as TTCN-3 type. A foreign object, may contain more information than required by TTCN-3. In such a case, the additional information has no meaning in TTCN-3 and is therefore not accessible.

The use of foreign objects in TTCN-3 modules is supported by two concepts: Firstly, the language allows to **import** and use them like TTCN-3 definitions. Secondly, special **attribute** strings are defined which assure that a TTCN-3 module referring to foreign objects will be portable to any tool supporting the external language.

To make declarations of foreign object visible in TTCN-3 modules, their names shall be imported just like declarations from other TTCN-3 modules. When imported, only the TTCN-3 meaning of the object will be seen in the importing TTCN-3 module. There are two main differences between importing TTCN-3 items and objects defined in other languages:

- When importing non-TTCN-3 definitions, the **import** statement shall contain an appropriate language identifier.
- Only foreign objects with a TTCN-3 meaning can be imported into a TTCN-3 module.

Importing can be done automatically using the **all** directive, in which case all importable objects are automatically imported, or done manually by listing the names of items to be imported.

In several important application domains that are amongst the first users of TTCN-3, ASN.1 is used to describe the data structure of messages. For this reason, TTCN-3 provides sophisticated support to use ASN.1 together with TTCN-3. It allows the reference to ASN.1 definitions from within TTCN-3 modules and the specification of encoding rules for imported ASN.1 definitions including the dynamic control of encoding options.

An increasing number of distributed applications use the XML to exchange data These data exchanges follow very precise rules for data format description in the form of Document Type Descriptions (DTDs) or XML Schemas. There are also XML based communication protocols like, for example, the Simple Object Access Protocol (SOAP), that are based on XML Schemas. Like any other communication system, XML based systems are also candidates for testing using TTCN-3. The XML mapping rules provide a definition for the use of XML with TTCN-3. It enables the combined use of XML types defining XML based protocols, interfaces, Web services, applications or documents with TTCN-3 based testing [32].

Last but not least, object-based technologies such as CORBA, the Distributed Component Object Model (DCOM), or the Distributed Computing Environment

(DCE) and component-based technologies such as the CORBA Component Model (CCM), the Enterprise Java Beans (EJB), or the .Net framework use interface specifications to describe the structure of object- and component-based systems including operations and capabilities to interact with the environment. These interface specifications support interoperability and reusability of objects and components. The techniques used for interface specifications are often IDL-based, for example, CORBA IDL, Microsoft IDL or DCE IDL. These languages are comparable in their abilities to define system interfaces, operations at system interfaces and system structures. They only differ in details of the object or component model. When considering the test of object- and component-based systems with TTCN-3, one is faced with the problem of accessing the systems to be tested via the system interfaces described in form of an IDL specification. TTCN-3 supports the import of IDL definitions into TTCN-3 modules by providing standardized IDL to TTCN-3 mapping rules.

8   U2TP and TTCN-3

The OMG (Object Management Group) has initiated the development of a UML 2.x testing profile (U2TP) to make the Unified Modelling Language (UML) also applicable for the design of test systems. It addresses typical testing concepts in model-based system development and for integrated system and test development processes [1]. Compared with TTCN-3, U2TP also addresses test design and can be mapped to TTCN-3 [16,25,39].

U2TP defines a language for designing, visualizing, specifying, analyzing, constructing and documenting the artefacts of test systems. It is a test modelling language that can be used with all major object and component technologies and be applied to test systems in various application domains. U2TP can be used stand alone for test artefacts only or in an integrated manner with UML for handling system and test artefacts together.

U2TP extends UML 2.x with test specific concepts like test components, verdicts, defaults, etc. These concepts are grouped into concepts for test architecture, test data, test behaviour and time. As a UML profile, U2TP seamlessly integrates into UML. It is based on the UML 2.x meta-model and reuses UML 2.x syntax. The U2TP test concepts are structured into

- *Test architecture* concepts defining concepts related to test structure and test configuration, i.e. the elements and their relationships involved in a test;
- *Test behaviour* concepts defining concepts related to the dynamic aspects of test procedures and addressing stimuli, observations and activities during a test;
- *Test data* concepts defining concepts for test data used in test procedures, i.e. the structures and meaning of values to be processed in a test;
- *Time* concepts defining concepts for a time quantified definition of test procedures, i.e. the time constraints and time observation for test execution.

Architecture concepts	Behaviour concepts	Data concepts	Time Concepts
SUT	Test objective	Wildcards	Timer
Test components	Test case	Data pools	Time zone
Test context	Defaults	Data partitions	
Test configuration	Verdicts	Data selectors	
Arbiter	Test control	Coding rules	
Scheduler			

Fig. 7. Overview of Basic Testing Profile Concepts

	U2TP	TTCN-3
Test Design	✓	—
Test Specification	✓	✓
Test Execution	(—)	✓
Test Meta Modelling	✓	(✓)
Format	Graphical	Textual and graphical
Transformation	U2TP to TTCN-3 (✓)	TTCN-3 to U2TP ✓

Fig. 8. Comparison of U2TP and TTCN-3

U2TP was an ideal opportunity to bring TTCN-3 in form of GFT to the attention of the UML world [26]. In fact, GFT is the archetype for U2TP. U2TP uses several concepts being developed in GFT. Still, TTCN-3 and U2TP differ in several respects: U2TP is based on the object oriented paradigm of UML where behaviours are bound to objects only, while TTCN-3 is based on the TTCN-3 test behaviour concept of functions and binding of functions to test components. U2TP uses additional diagrams to define, e.g. the test architecture, test configuration and test deployment. Test behaviour can be defined as interaction diagrams (as in TTCN-3) but also as state machines or activity diagrams. While TTCN-3 supports dynamic test configurations, U2TP uses static configurations where only the number of test components may vary but not the structure of the connections between test components. In addition, U2TP has only one FIFO queue per test component, while TTCN-3 uses a FIFO queue per test component port. New concepts in U2TP as compared to TTCN-3 are the arbiter, the validation action, the test trace and the data pool, data partition and data selector.

However, above all, U2TP and TTCN-3 address different phases in test development as shown in Figure 8. U2TP addresses primarily test design and test specification, while TTCN-3 addresses test specification and test execution. U2TP can also support test execution, but this needs still to be worked out along the approaches towards executable UML.

Test design is out of scope for TTCN-3. U2TP has by definition a meta-model (as an extension of the UML 2.0 meta-model). For TTCN-3, proprietary meta-models exist only. Both have graphical presentation formats, while TTCN-3 has also a textual notation.

The transformation from TTCN-3 to U2TP is always possible; the other way works only, if the U2TP specifies implementable and executable tests. Mapping rules have been defined accordingly. Currently, TTCN-3 is widely supported by tools and test solutions. For U2TP, first tools e.g. [35] exist, further tools are under development.

9   Summary

In this chapter, a detailed introduction into TTCN-3 is provided. The chapter explains the concepts behind TTCN-3, the TTCN-3 core language as well as the implementation and execution of TTCN-3 test systems. It also discusses how TTCN-3 can be integrated with other technologies such as by reusing external data or mappings to and from U2TP.

TTCN-3 has been designed especially for testing purposes and provides powerful testing constructs. These make it the technology of choice for a wide variety of testing needs. Over the last years, the TTCN-3 technology has been used in different areas of testing including telecommunication or data communication as well as automotive, railways, avionics or security systems.

One of the most important characteristics of TTCN-3 is its technology and platform independence. This allows testers to concentrate on the test logic, while the complexity of the test realization on a given test device (e.g. operating system, hardware configuration, etc.) is moved to the TTCN-3 platform. Complex test behaviours which involve multiple interacting test entities are easier to specify in TTCN-3 than in other test frameworks such as JUnit [21] since technical aspects are hidden behind the abstract language artefacts.

Typical applications of TTCN-3 include functional, conformance, and interoperability testing of various systems on component, integration and system level. There is also an increasing interest in applying TTCN-3 to performance, load and scalability testing — one example is the application of TTCN-3 for IMS (IP Multimedia Subsystem) benchmarking [5]. TTCN-3 has gained also special attention in the context of testing embedded systems [30]. Future work on TTCN-3 will include specializations of TTCN-3 in further application areas such as financial or medical systems.

References

1. Baker, P., Dai, Z.R., Grabowski, J., Haugen, O., Lucio, S., Samuelsson, E., Schieferdecker, I., Williams, C.: The UML 2.0 Testing Profile. In: Proceedings by ASQF Press, Nuremberg, Germany (September 2004) (conquest 2004)
2. Burton, S., Baresel, A., Schieferdecker, I.: Automated testing of automotive telematics systems using TTCN-3. In: Proceedings by Fraunhofer IRB Verlag, 3rd Workshop on System Testing and Validation (SV 2004), Paris, France (December 2004)
3. de Vries, R.G., Tretmans, J.: On-the-fly conformance testing using SPIN. International Journal on Software Tools for Technology Transfer (STTT) 2(4), 382–393 (2000)
4. Schieferdecker, I., et al. The TTCN-3 Certificate: An ETSI/GTB Certification Scheme for TTCN-3 (2007), http://www.german-testing-board.info
5. ETSI TISPAN. IMS/NGN Performance Benchmark, Technical Standard (TS) 186 008, Sophia-Antipolis, France (February 2007)
6. ETSI Standard (ES) 201 873-1 V3.2.1 (2007–02): Methods for Testing and Specification (MTS); The Testing and Test Control Notation version 3; Part 1: TTCN-3 Core Language. European Telecommunications Standards Institute (ETSI), Sophia-Antipolis France (February 2007)
7. ETSI Standard (ES) 201 873-2 V3.2.1 (2007–02): Methods for Testing and Specification (MTS); The Testing and Test Control Notation version 3; Part 2: TTCN-3 Tabular presentation Format (TFT). European Telecommunications Standards Institute (ETSI), Sophia-Antipolis France (February 2007)
8. ETSI Standard (ES) 201 873-3 V3.2.1 (2007–02): Methods for Testing and Specification (MTS); The Testing and Test Control Notation version 3; Part 3: TTCN-3 Graphical presentation Format (GFT). European Telecommunications Standards Institute (ETSI), Sophia-Antipolis France (February 2007)
9. ETSI Standard (ES) 201 873-4 V3.2.1 (2007–02): Methods for Testing and Specification (MTS); The Testing and Test Control Notation version 3; Part 4: TTCN-3 Operational Semantics. European Telecommunications Standards Institute (ETSI), Sophia-Antipolis France (February 2007)
10. ETSI Standard (ES) 201 873-5 V3.2.1 (2007–02): Methods for Testing and Specification (MTS); The Testing and Test Control Notation version 3; Part 5: TTCN-3 Runtime Interface (TRI). European Telecommunications Standards Institute (ETSI), Sophia-Antipolis France (February 2007)
11. ETSI Standard (ES) 201 873-6 V3.2.1 (2007–02): Methods for Testing and Specification (MTS); The Testing and Test Control Notation version 3; Part 6: TTCN-3 Control Interface (TCI). European Telecommunications Standards Institute (ETSI), Sophia-Antipolis France (February 2007)
12. ETSI Standard (ES) 201 873-8 V3.2.1 (2007–02): Methods for Testing and Specification (MTS); The Testing and Test Control Notation version 3; Part 8: Using IDL with TTCN-3. European Telecommunications Standards Institute (ETSI), Sophia-Antipolis France (February 2007)
13. TTCN-3 User Conference Series (2004-2007), http://www.ttcn-3.org
14. ETSI Technical Report (TR) 101 666 (1999–2005): Information Technology — Open Systems Interconnection Conformance testing methodology and framework; The Tree and Tabular Combined Notation (TTCN) (Ed. 2++). European Telecommunications Standards Institute (ETSI), Sophia-Antipolis France (May 1999)
15. Grabowski, J., Hogrefe, D., Rethy, G., Schieferdecker, I., Wiles, A., Willcock, C.: An Introduction into the Testing and Test Control Notation (TTCN-3). Computer Networks Journal (2003)

16. Gross, H.-G., Schieferdecker, I., Din, G.: Model-Based Built-In Tests. In: ITM 2004, International workshop on Model Based Testing, co-located with ETAPS 2004, Barcelona, Spain, January 2004. Electronic Notes in Theoretical Computer Science, vol. 111 (2004)

17. ISO/IEC IS 9646. Information Technology - OSI Conformance Testing Methodology and Framework. International Multipart Standard 9646, Geneva, Switzerland (February 1992-1996)

18. ITU-T Recommendations X.680-683 (2002): Information Technology — Abstract Syntax Notation One (ASN.1):
    - X.680: Specification of Basic Notation
    - X.681: Information Object Specification
    - X.682: Constraint Specification
    - X.683: Parameterization of ASN.1 Specifications.
    ITU Telecommunication Standards Sector, Geneva Switzerland (2002)

19. ITU-T Recommendation Z.120: Message Sequence Chart (MSC). ITU Telecommunication Standards Sector, Geneva Switzerland (1999)

20. Kaner, C., Falk, J., Nguyen, H.Q.: Testing Computer Software, 2nd edn. John Wiley & Sons, Ltd, Chichester (1999)

21. Martin, R.C.: Agile Software Development: Principles, Patterns, and Practices, Upper Saddle River, NJ, USA. Prentice Hall PTR, Englewood Cliffs (2003)

22. Myers, G.J. (Revised by C. Sandler, T. Badgett, and T.M. Thomas): The Art of Software Testing, 2nd edn. John Wiley & Sons, Ltd, Chichester (2004)

23. Object Management Group (OMG). Common Object Request Broker Architecture (CORBA): Core Specification, Version 3.0.3 (16.08.2005) (March 2004),
    http://www.omg.org/docs/formal/04-03-01.pdf

24. Object Management Group (OMG). UML 2.0 Testing Profile (April 2004),
    http://www.omg.org/cgi-bin/doc?ptc/2004-04-02

25. Schieferdecker, I.: The UML 2.0 Test Profile as a Basis for Integrated System and Test Development. In: Proceedings by Köllen Druck+Verlag GmbH, Jahrestagung der Gesellschaft für Informatik, Bonn, Germany, vol. 35 (September 2005)

26. Schieferdecker, I., Dai, Z.R., Grabowski, J., Rennoch, A.: The UML 2.0 Testing Profile and its Relation to TTCN-3. In: Hogrefe, D., Wiles, A. (eds.) TestCom 2003. LNCS, vol. 2644, Springer, Heidelberg (2003)

27. Schieferdecker, I., Din, G.: A Metamodel for TTCN-3. In: Núñez, M., Maamar, Z., Pelayo, F.L., Pousttchi, K., Rubio, F. (eds.) FORTE 2004. LNCS, vol. 3236, Springer, Heidelberg (2004)

28. Schieferdecker, I., Din, G., Apostolidis, D.: Distributed Functional and Load tests for Web services. International Journal on Software Tools for Technology Transfer (STTT) (2004)

29. Schieferdecker, I., Grabowski, J.: The Graphical Format of TTCN-3 and its Relation to UML and MSC. In: Sherratt, E. (ed.) SAM 2002. LNCS, vol. 2599, Springer, Heidelberg (2003)

30. Schieferdecker, I., Grossmann, J.: Testing Embedded Control Systems with TTCN-3. In: Obermaisser, R., Nah, Y., Puschner, P., Rammig, F.J. (eds.) SEUS 2007. LNCS, vol. 4761, pp. 7–9. Springer, Heidelberg (2007)

31. Schieferdecker, I., Rennoch, A., Hoefig, E.: TTCN-3 — A Test Technology for the Automotive Domain. In: Proceedings by expert Verlag. Simulation und Test in der Funktions- und Softwareentwicklung für die Automobilelektronik, Berlin, Germany (March 2005)

32. Schieferdecker, I., Stepien, B.: Automated Testing of XML/SOAP based Web Services. In: Informatik Aktuell, Fachkonferenz der Gesellschaft für Informatik (GI) Fachgruppe Kommunikation in verteilten Systemen (KiVS), Leipzig, vol. 13 (February 2003)
33. Schieferdecker, I., Vassiliou-Gioles, T.: Realizing distributed TTCN-3 test systems with TCI. In: Hogrefe, D., Wiles, A. (eds.) TestCom 2003. LNCS, vol. 2644, Springer, Heidelberg (2003)
34. Schieferdecker, I., Vassiliou-Gioles, T.: Tool Supported Test Frameworks in TTCN-3. In: ENTCS (80). 8th Intern. Workshop in Formal Methods in Industrial Critical Systems, Røros, Norway (June 2003)
35. Eclipse Test & Performance Tools Platform Project (2004-2007), http://www.eclipse.org/tptp/
36. Vassiliou-Gioles, T., Din, G., Schieferdecker, I.: Execution of External Applications using TTCN-3. In: Groz, R., Hierons, R.M. (eds.) TestCom 2004. LNCS, vol. 2978, Springer, Heidelberg (2004)
37. Vouffo-Feudjio, A., Schieferdecker, I.: Test Pattern with TTCN-3. In: Grabowski, J., Nielsen, B. (eds.) FATES 2004. LNCS, vol. 3395, Springer, Heidelberg (2005)
38. World Wide Web Consortium (W3C) Recommendation: Extensible Markup Language (XML) 1.1 (2004), http://www.w3.org/TR/2004/REC-xml11-20040204/
39. Zander, J., Dai, Z.R., Schieferdecker, I., Din, G.: From U2TP Models to Executable Tests with TTCN-3 — An Approach to Model Driven Testing. In: Khendek, F., Dssouli, R. (eds.) TestCom 2005. LNCS, vol. 3502, Springer, Heidelberg (2005)

Glossary

Acronym	Explanation
ASN.1	http://www.asn1.org/) Abstract Syntax Notation One: an ITU standardized data type specification and coding language, which is used particularly in telecommunications
ATS	Abstract Test Suite: a collection of abstractly defined, thus system-, test system-, and implementation-independent test cases, typically described in TTCN-3, U2TP or other proprietary test notations
ETS	Executable Test Suite: a collection of executable test cases, which are typically generated automatically from abstract test cases
ETSI	http://www.etsi.org) European Telecommunication Standards Institute: an independent, non-profit organization, whose mission is to produce telecommunications standards
FIFO	Queuing Discipline First-In-First-Out
GFT	Graphical Presentation Format of TTCN-3: the graphical format of TTCN-3, especially for the visualization, development and documentation of test behaviours
IDL	http://www.omg.org/gettingstarted/omg_idl.htm) Interface Definition Language: IDL is an OMG standardized specification language for object interfaces
ISO	http://www.iso.org International Organization for Standardization: the world's largest developer of standards with its principal activity being the development of technical standards
ITU	http://www.itu.ch International Telecommunication Union: an international organization within the United Nations System where governments and the private sector coordinate global telecom networks and services
MSC	http://www.sdl-forum.org/MSC/ Message Sequence Charts: a language standardized by ITU for the description and specification of the interactions between system components based on sequence diagrams, which is adopted to a big extend in UML 2.0
MTC	Main Test Component: the main test component of a TTCN-3 test case, which steers and controls the test configuration and test run
OMG	http://www.omg.org Object Management Group: an open membership, not-for-profit consortium that produces and maintains computer industry specifications for interoperable enterprise applications
PTC	Parallel Test Component: a parallel test component of a TTCN-3 test case, which performs test behaviour in parallel to other test components and which determines its own, local verdict about the correctness of the tested system
SUT	System Under Test: the system to be tested - in dependence of the testing level a system component, a set of system components, a subsystem, a system or a composition of systems, which is/are to be tested
TCI	TTCN-3 Control Interfaces: the control interfaces of TTCN-3, which support the test management, the handling of test components and the coding/decoding of test data

Acronym	Explanation
TFT	Graphical Presentation Format of TTCN-3: the graphical format of TTCN-3, especially for the visualization, development and documentation of test data and type structures
TRI	TTCN-3 Runtime Interfaces: the run time interfaces of TTCN-3, which support the communication with the SUT, the time handling during test execution and the integration of external functionalities
TSI	Test System Interface: the interface to the SUT, which is taken as black box or grey box when testing with TTCN-3, and over that the interaction with the test system for the evaluation of functionality, the efficiency, the scaling, etc. of the SUT is performed
TTCN-3	http://www.ttcn-3.org) Testing and Test Control Notation: standardized test specification and implementation technology by ETSI (ES 201 873 series) and by ITU (Z.140 series). TTCN-3 is a technology for the development, specification, visualization and documentation of detailed test specifications
UML	http://www.uml.org/ Unified Modelling Language: UML is a non-proprietary modelling and specification language. The use of UML is not restricted to software modelling. It can, for example, be used for modelling hardware and is commonly used for business process modelling and organizational structure modelling. The UML is an open method used to specify, visualize, construct and document the system artefacts. The current version is UML 2.0
U2TP	http://www.fokus.fraunhofer.de/u2tp UML 2.0 Testing Profile: the standardized testing profile of UML 2.0 by OMG. U2TP defines a language for designing, visualizing, specifying, analyzing, constructing and documenting the artefacts of test systems. It is a test modelling language that can be used with all major object and component technologies and applied to testing systems in various application domains. U2TP can be used stand alone for the handling of test artefacts or in an integrated manner with UML for a handling of system and test artefacts together
XML	http://www.w3.org/XML/ Extended Markup Language: XML is a standardized markup language for documents containing structured information by the World Wide Web Consortium

Testability Transformation – Program Transformation to Improve Testability

Mark Harman[1], André Baresel[2], David Binkley[3], Robert Hierons[4], Lin Hu[1], Bogdan Korel[5], Phil McMinn[6], and Marc Roper[7]

[1] King's College London, Strand, London WC2R 2LS, UK
Mark.Harman@kcl.ac.uk
[2] DaimlerChrysler, Alt Moabit 96a, Berlin, Germany
[3] Loyola College, 4501 North Charles Street, Baltimore, MD 21210-2699, USA
[4] Brunel University, Uxbridge, Middlesex UB8 3PH, UK
[5] Illinois Institute of Technology, 10 W. 31st Street, Chicago, IL 60616, USA
[6] University of Sheffield, Regent Court, 211 Portobello Street, Sheffield S1 4DP, UK
[7] Strathclyde University, 26 Richmond Street, Glasgow G1 1XH, UK

Abstract. Testability transformation is a new form of program transformation in which the goal is not to preserve the standard semantics of the program, but to preserve test sets that are adequate with respect to some chosen test adequacy criterion. The goal is to improve the testing process by transforming a program to one that is more amenable to testing while remaining within the same equivalence class of programs defined by the adequacy criterion. The approach to testing and the adequacy criterion are parameters to the overall approach. The transformations required are typically neither more abstract nor are they more concrete than standard "meaning preserving transformations". This leads to interesting theoretical questions. but also has interesting practical implications. This chapter provides an introduction to testability transformation and a brief survey of existing results.

1 Introduction

A *testability transformation* (TeTra) is a source-to-source program transformation that seeks to improve the performance of a previously chosen test data generation technique [28]. Testability transformation uses the familiar notion of program transformation in a novel context (testing) that requires the development of novel transformation definitions, novel transformation rules and algorithms, and novel formulations of programming language semantics, in order to reason about testability transformation.

This chapter presents an overview of the definitions that underpin the concept of testability transformation and several areas of recent work in testability transformation, concluding with a set of open problems. The hope is that the chapter will serve to encourage further interest in this new area and to stimulate research into the important formalizations of test-adequacy oriented semantics, required in order to reason about it.

R.M. Hierons et al. (Eds.): Formal Methods and Testing, LNCS 4949, pp. 320–344, 2008.

As with traditional program transformation [12,36,43], TeTra is an automated technique that alters a program's syntax. However, TeTra differs from traditional transformations in two important ways:

1. The transformed program is merely a "means to an end", rather than an 'end' in itself. The transformed program can be discarded once it has served its role as a vehicle for adequate test data generation. By contrast, in traditional transformation, it is the original program that is discarded and replaced by the transformed version.

2. The transformation process need not preserve the traditional meaning of a program. For example in order to cover a chosen branch, it is only required that the transformation preserves the set of test-adequate inputs for the branch. That is, the transformed program must be guaranteed to execute the desired branch under the same initial conditions. By contrast, traditional transformation preserves functional equivalence, a much more demanding requirement.

These two observations have three important implications:

1. **There is no psychological barrier to transformation.** Tradition transformation requires the developer to replace familiar code with machine-generated, structurally altered equivalents. It is part of the fokelore of the program transformation community that developers are highly resistant to the replacement of the familiar by the unfamiliar. There is no such psychological barrier for testability transformation: the developer submits a program to the system and receives test data. There is no replacement requirement; the developer need not even be aware that transformation has taken place.

2. **Considerably more flexibility is available in the choice of transformations to apply.** Guaranteeing functional equivalence is demanding, particularly in the presence of side effects, goto statements, pointer aliasing and other complex language features. By contrast, merely ensuring that a particular branch is executed for an identical set of inputs is comparatively less demanding.

3. **Transformation algorithm correctness is less important.** Traditional transformation replaces the original program with the transformed version, so correctness is paramount. The cost of 'incorrectness' for testability transformation is much lower; the test data generator may fail to generate adequate test data. This situation is one of degree and can be detected, trivially, using coverage metrics. By contrast, functional equivalence is *undecidable*.

2   Testability Transformation

Testability transformation seeks to transform a program to make it easier to generate test data (i.e., it seeks to improve the original program's 'testability'). There is an apparent paradox at the heart of this notion of testability transformation:

Structural testing is based upon structurally defined test adequacy criteria. The automated generation of test data to satisfy these criteria can be impeded by properties of the software (for example, flag variables, side effects, and unstructured control flow). Testability transformation seeks to remove the problem by transforming the program so that it becomes easier to generate adequate test data. However, transformation alters the structure of the program. Since the program's structure is altered and the adequacy criterion is structurally defined, it would appear that the original test adequacy criterion may no longer apply.

The solution to this apparent paradox is to allow a testability transformation to co-transform the adequacy criterion. The transformation of the adequacy criterion ensures that adequacy for the transformed program with the transformed criterion implies adequacy of the original program with the original criterion. These remarks are made more precise in the following three definitions.

First, a *test adequacy criterion* is any set of syntactic constructs to be covered during testing. Typical examples include a set of nodes, a set of branches, a set of paths, etc. For example, to achieve "100% branch coverage", this set would be the set of all branches of the program. Observe that the definition also allows more fine grained criteria, such as testing to cover a particular branch or statement.

Second, a *testing-oriented transformation* is a partial function that maps a program and test adequacy criteria to an updated program and updated test adequacy criteria [20]. (In general, a program transformation is a partial function from programs to programs.) Finally, a *testability transformation* is a testing-oriented transformation, τ such that for all programs p and criteria c, $\tau(p, c) = (p', c')$ implies that for all test sets T, T is adequate for p according to c if T is adequate for p' according to c' [20].

A simple example of a testability-transformation is the removal of code that does not impact a target statement or branch. One approach to such a removal is program slicing [46,6]. Removing code allows existing techniques to better focus on the statement of branch of interest. A more involved example is given in Section 4.3.

3   Test Data Generation

One of the most pressing problems in the field of software testing revolves around the issue of automation. Managers implementing a testing strategy are soon confronted with the observation that large parts of the process need to be automated in order to develop a test process that has a chance to scale to meet the demands of existing testing standards and requirements [8,39].

Test data must be generated to achieve a variety of coverage criteria to assist with rigorous and systematic testing. Various standards [8,39] either require or recommend branch coverage adequate testing, and so testing to achieve this is a mission-critical activity for applications where these standards apply. Because generating test data by hand is tedious, expensive, and error-prone, automated test data generation has remained a topic of interest for the past three decades [9,16,24].

Several techniques for automated test data generation have been proposed, including symbolic execution [9,23], constraint solving [13,34], the chaining method [16], and evolutionary testing [40,22,32,33,35,37,42]. This section briefly reviews two currently used techniques for automating the process of test data generation, in order to make the work presented on testability transformation for automated test data generation in this chapter self contained.

3.1 Evolutionary Testing

The general approach to evolutionary test data generation is depicted in Figure 1[1]. The outer circle in Figure 1 provides an overview of a typical procedure for an evolutionary algorithm. First, an initial population of solution guesses is created, usually at random. Each individual within the population is evaluated by calculating its *fitness*: a measure of how close the individual comes to being a solution (fitness is formalized later in this section). The result is a spread of solutions ranging in fitness.

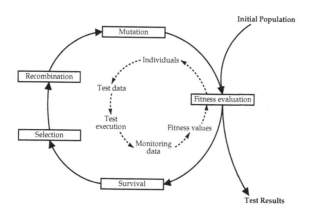

Fig. 1. Evolutionary Algorithm for Testing

In the first iteration all individuals survive. Pairs of individuals are selected from the population, according to a pre-defined selection strategy, and combined to produce new solutions. At this point mutation is applied. This models the role of mutation in genetics, introducing new information into the population. The evolutionary process ensures that productive mutations have a greater chance of survival than less productive ones.

The new individuals are evaluated for fitness. Survivors into the next generation are chosen from parents and offspring with regard to fitness. The algorithm

---

[1] This style of evolutionary test data generation is based on the DaimlerChrysler Evolutionary Testing System [44].

is iterated until the optimum is achieved or some other stopping condition is satisfied.

In order to automate software test data generation using evolutionary algorithms, the problem must first be transformed into an optimization task. This is the role of the inner circle of the architecture depicted in Figure 1. Each generated individual represents a test datum for the system under test. Depending on which test aim is pursued, different fitness functions emerge for test data evaluation.

If, for example, the temporal behaviour of an application is being tested, the fitness evaluation of the individuals is based on the execution times measured for the test data [38,45]. For safety tests, the fitness values are derived from pre- and post-conditions of modules [41], and for robustness tests of fault-tolerance mechanisms, the number of controlled errors forms the starting point for the fitness evaluation [40].

For structural criteria, such as those upon which this chapter focuses, a fitness function is typically defined in terms of the program's predicates [4,7,22,32,35,44]. It determines the fitness of candidate test data, which in turn determines the direction taken by the search. The fitness function essentially measures how close a candidate test input drives execution to traversing the desired (target) path or branch.

Typically, the test-data generation tool first instruments each predicate to capture fitness information, which guides the search to the required test data. For example if a branching condition a == b needs to be executed as true, the values of a and b are used to compute a fitness value using abs(a-b). The closer this "branch distance" value is to zero, the closer the condition is to being evaluated as true, and the closer the search is to finding the required test data.

As a simple example, consider trying to test the true branch of the predicate a > b. While typical execution of a genetic algorithm might include an initial population of hundreds of test inputs, for the purposes of this example, consider two such individuals, i_1 and i_2. Suppose that, when executed on the input i_1, a equals b, and when run on i_2, a is much less than b, then i_1 would have a greater chance of being selected for the next generation. It would also have a better chance of being involved in (perhaps multiple) crossover operations with other potential solutions to create the children that form the next generation.

3.2   The Chaining Method

The chaining approach uses data flow information derived from a program to guide the search when problem statements (conditional statements in which a different result is required) are encountered [16]. The chaining approach is based on the concept of an event sequence (a sequence of program nodes) that needs to be executed prior to the target. The nodes that affect problem statements are added to the event sequence using data flow analysis.

The alternating variable method [25] is employed to execute an event sequence. It is based on the idea of 'local' search. An arbitrary input vector is chosen at random, and each individual input variable is probed by changing its value by a small amount, and then monitoring the effects of this on the branches of the program.

The first stage of manipulating an input variable is called the *exploratory* phase. This probes the neighbourhood of the variable by increasing and decreasing its original value. If either move leads to an improved objective value, a *pattern* phase is entered. In the pattern phase, a larger move is made in the direction of the improvement. A series of similar moves is made until a minimum for the objective function is found for the variable. If the target structure is not executed, the next input variable is selected for an exploratory phase.

For example, consider again, the predicate a > b. Assuming a is initially less than b, a few small increases in a improves the objective value (the difference between a and b). Thus, the pattern phase is entered, during which the iteration of ever-larger increases to the value of a finally produce a value of a that is greater than b, satisfying the desired predicate and locating an input that achieves coverage of the desired branch.

4   Three Application Areas for Testability Transformation

The effectiveness of test data generation methods, such as the evolutionary method and the chaining method, can be improved through the use of testability transformation (TeTra). This section presents three case studies that illustrate the wide range of testability transformation's applicability. The first two subsections concern applications to evolutionary testing, while the third concerns the chaining method.

4.1   TeTra to Remove Flags for Evolutionary Testing

Testability Transformation was first applied to the *flag problem* [19]. This section considers the particularly difficult variant of the flag problem where the flag variable is assigned within a loop. Several authors have also considered this problem [7,4]; however, at present, testability transformation offers the most generally applicable solution. Furthermore, this solution is applicable to other techniques such as the chaining method and symbolic execution [11], which are known to perform poorly in the presence of loop assigned flags.

A *flag* variable is any boolean variable used in a predicate. Where the flag only has relatively few input values (from some set S) that make it adopt one of its two possible values, it will be hard for any testing technique to uncover a value from S. This problem typically occurs with internal flag variables, where the input state space is reduced, with relatively few "special values" (those in S) being mapped to one of the two possible outcomes and all others (those not in S) being mapped to the other.

The fitness function for a predicate that tests a flag yields either maximal fitness (for the "special values") or minimal fitness (for any other value). In the landscape induced by the fitness function, there is no guidance from lower fitness to higher fitness. This is illustrated by the landscape at the right of Figure 2.

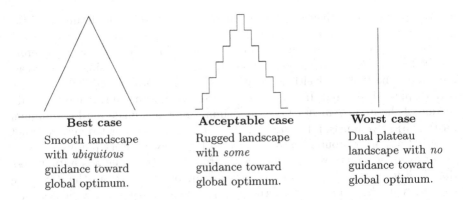

Best case	**Acceptable case**	**Worst case**
Smooth landscape with *ubiquitous* guidance toward global optimum.	Rugged landscape with *some* guidance toward global optimum.	Dual plateau landscape with *no* guidance toward global optimum.

Fig. 2. The flag landscape: the needle in a haystack problem. The y-axis measures fitness while each x-axis represents the input space.

A similar problem is observed with any k-valued enumeration type, whose fitness landscape is determined by k discrete values. As k becomes larger the program becomes progressively more testable; provided there is an ordering on the k elements, the landscape becomes progressively more smooth as k increases. The landscapes in the centre and then left of Figure 2 illustrate the effect of increasing k.

The problem of flag variables is particularly acute where the flag is assigned a value in a loop and then used later outside the loop. For example, consider the variable flag in the upper left of Figure 3. In this situation, the fitness function computed at the test outside the loop may depend upon values of "partial fitness" computed at each and every iteration of the loop. Many previous approaches to the flag problem breakdown in the presence of loop-assigned flags [4,7,20]. These simpler techniques are effective with non-loop-assigned flags.

The aim of the loop-assigned flag removal algorithm is to replace the use of a flag variable with an expression that provides better guidance. The algorithm has two steps. The first adds two variables: a new induction variable, counter, is added to the loop to count the number of iterations that take place. The second new variable, fitness, is a real-valued variable that collects a cumulative fitness score for the assignments that take place during the loop. When applied to code from the upper left of Figure 3, the result of the first step is shown in the upper right of Figure 3. Where "if (flag)" has been replaced with "if (counter == fitness)".

The variable counter measures the number of times the loop passes down the desired path (the one which executes the assignment to flag in a way that gives the desired final value for flag). This gives rise to the improved but coarse grained landscape as shown in the centre of Figure 2 [2]. The coarseness comes because loop iteration is deemed either to traverse the desired path (with a consequent increase in accumulated fitness) or to miss this path (with no change in accumulated fitness).

void f(char a[ELEMCOUNT])	void f(char a[ELEMCOUNT])
| ```c
{
  int i;
  int flag = 1;


  for (i=0; i<ELEMCOUNT; i++)
  {
    if (a[i] != 0)
    {
      flag = 0;

    }



  }
  if (flag)
    /* target */
}
``` | ```c
{
  int i;
  int flag = 1;
  int counter = 0;
  double fitness = 0.0;

  for (i=0; i<ELEMCOUNT; i++)
  {
    if (a[i] != 0)
    {
      flag = 0;

    }
    else
      fitness += 1.0;
      counter++;
  }
  if (counter == fitness)
    /* target */
}
``` |
| **Original Untransformed Program** | **Coarse-Grained Transformation** |

```c
void f(char a[ELEMCOUNT])
{
  int i;
  int flag = 1;
  int counter = 0;
  double fitness = 0.0;
  for (i=0; i<ELEMCOUNT; i++)
  {
    if (a[i] != 0)
    {
      flag = 0;
      fitness = fitness + local(a[i] != 0);
    }
    else
      fitness += 1.0;
      counter++;
  }
  if (counter == fitness)
    /* target */
}
```

Fine-Grained Transformation

Fig. 3. Illustration of the coarse and fine grain loop-flag removal transformation

A further improvement is possible using an additional transformation that instruments the program to compute, for iterations that fail to traverse the described path, how close the iteration comes to traversing the desired path. The transformed code, shown it the lower section of Figure 3, employs the computation of a "local fitness calculation" (the function local), which captures the proximity of each loop iteration to the desired branch. This produces the smoothest fitness landscape (shown at the left of Figure 2).

The function local is a macro expansion that implements a different 'local' or 'branch' fitness [28]. The particular expansion applied depends upon the predicate to be optimized and can, as such, be viewed as a parameter to the overall approach.

Once the transformation has added these variables, the algorithm's second step slices [46,6] the resulting program with respect to the transformed predicate. Slicing removes parts of the program that do not influence the predicate. The result is a program specialized to the calculation of a smooth fitness function targeting the single branch of interest. In this way, the algorithm has essentially transformed the original program into a fitness function, tailor-made to have a smooth fitness landscape with a global optimum at the point where the variable `flag` has the desired value.

To provide empirical data as to the impact of loop assigned flag removal, the three programs depicted in Figure 3 were studied. (The effect of the slicing step is not shown in the figure to facilitate comparisons between the three versions of the program.) because it distills the worst possible case. That is, test data generation needs to find a single value (all array elements set to zero) in order to execute the branch marked /* `target` */. This single value must be found in a search space which is governed by the size of the array. The program is thus a template and 20 different versions were experimented with for each technique. In each successive version, the array size is increased, from an initial value of 1, through to a maximum size of 40. As the size of the array increases, the difficultly of the search problem increases; the needle is sought in an increasingly large haystack.

The DaimlerChrysler Evolutionary Testing system was used to obtain the results [5,44]. This system generates test data for C programs using a variety of white box criteria. It is a proprietary system, developed in-house and provided to DaimlerChrysler developers through a web portal.

For each technique, the evolutionary algorithm was run ten times to ensure robustness of the results reported and to allow comparison of the variations between the runs for each of the three techniques. An upper limit was set on the number of possible fitness evaluations allowed; thus, some runs failed to find any solution.

The ten-run averages for each of the three approaches are depicted in Figure 4. As can be seen, the fine-grained technique outperforms the coarse-grained technique. The coarse-grained technique achieves some success, but the test effort is noticeably worse than for the fine-grained technique. Both do considerably better than the no transformation approach which fails to find suitable test data on most runs.

The data from all 10 runs of each program are depicted in Figure 5. The no transformation approach fails to find any test data to cover the branch in all but two situations. The first is where the array is of size one. In this instance there is a high chance of finding the "special value" by random search, and all ten runs achieve this. At array size two, the chances of hitting the right value at random have diminished dramatically; only one of the ten runs manages to find a solution. For all other runs, no solution is found. In all cases, without transformation, the evolutionary search degenerates to a random search. Such a random search has a minuscule chance of finding the "needle in the haystack".

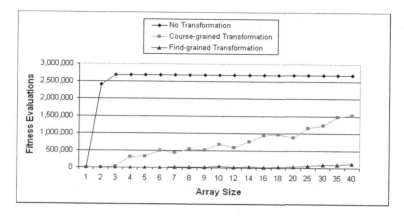

Fig. 4. Ten-run averages of the evolutionary search for each of the three approaches

The data for the course grained approach shows success for all runs with a steady increase in effort required. Perhaps more importantly, as seen in the middle graph of Figure 5, there is an increase in variability (the height difference from fewest to most fitness evaluations is growing as the problem becomes more difficult). This is a tell-tale sign of the partially random nature of search. That is, where the landscape provides guidance, the evolutionary algorithm can exploit it, but when it does not, the search becomes a locally random search until a way of moving off the local plateau is found.

Finally, the only interesting aspect of the data for the fine-grained transformation are two spikes (at array size 10 and 40). These are essentially the mirror image of the "good luck" the untransformed algorithm had finding a solution randomly. Here, the algorithm gets to test data in which all but one array entry is zero, but then through random "bad luck" takes longer to find the solution. In this case it only serves to slow the search. It does not prevent the search from finding the desired test data.

Statistically, the claim that the fine-grained approach is better than the coarse-grained approach, which in turn, is better than the no transformation approach was confirmed using a Mann-Whitney test [1]. This test is a non-parametric test for statistical significance in the differences between two data sets. Because the test is non-parametric, the data is not required to be normally distributed for the test to be applicable. Both comparisons report high statistically significant difference ($p < 0.0001$).

4.2 TeTra for Nested Predicates to Assist Evolutionary Testing

The second example considers the problem that predicate nesting causes evolutionary test data generation. Evolutionary techniques face two key problems when encountering nested predicates: first, constraints on the input are only revealed as each individual predicate is satisfied, and second, the information guiding the search is treated locally at each predicate. For example, consider the

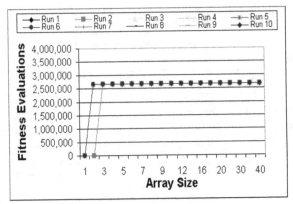

(a) With No Transformation

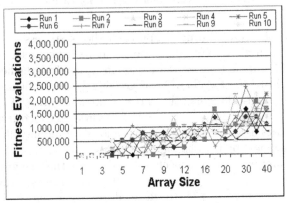

(b) With Coarse-Grained Transformation

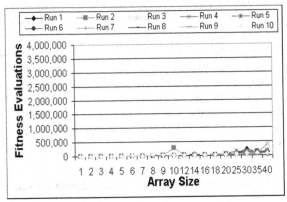

(c) With Fine-Grained Transformation

Fig. 5. The ten runs of the evolutionary search for each of the three approaches. For a given array size, each chart shows the total number of fitness evaluation required to find a solution or reaching the fixed limit.

code shown in Figure 6a. Here the condition c == 0 is not encountered until after a equals b. Thus, the search does not find out that c is important until a == b is satisfied. Furthermore, while attempting to make c == 0 true, the search must operate in the smaller search space defined by the predicate a == b. Any adjustment in the values of a or b could potentially put the search back at 'square one'. Thus, once test data has been found to execute a conditional in a certain way, the outcome at that condition must be maintained so that the path to the current condition is also maintained.

The latter problem causes problems for the search when predicates are not mutually exclusive. For example, in Figure 6a, variable c must be made zero without changing the values of a and b. However c is actually b+1 (Statement 2). Therefore b needs to be -1 for Statement 3 to be executed as true. If values other than -1 have been selected for a and b, the search has no chance of making the condition at Statement 3 true. That is unless of course it backtracks to reselect values of a and b. However, if it were to do this, the fact that c needs to be zero at Statement 3 will be 'forgotten,' as Statement 3 is no longer reached, and its fitness is not computed.

This phenomenon is captured in a plot of the fitness landscape (Figure 6c). The shift from satisfying the predicate of Statement 1 to the secondary satisfaction of the predicate of Statement 2 is characterized by a sudden drop in the landscape down to spikes of local optima. Any move to input values where a is not equal to b yanks the search up out of the optima and back to the area where Statement 1 is evaluated as false again.

McMinn et al. proposed a solution to the nested predicate problem based on testability transformation [31]. In essence, their approach evaluates all the conditions leading to the target at the same time. This is done by flattening the nesting structure in which the target lies and is non-trivial when code intervenes between conditionals (for example, it could contain a loop). The transformation takes the original program and removes decision statements on which the target is control dependent. In this way, when the program is executed, it is free to proceed into originally nested regions, regardless of whether the original branching predicate would have allowed that to happen.

In place of each predicate an assignment to a new variable _dist is added. These assignments compute the branch distance based on the original predicate. At the end of the program, the value of _dist reflects the summation of each of the individual branch distances. This value may then be used as the fitness value for the test data input. This inline accumulation of fitness information within the program body is not unlike the fine-grained transformation method employed by Baresel et al. [2] for collecting information in loop bodies involving assignments to flags.

Figure 6 shows an example of this transformation where the original program, shown in Figure 6a, is transformed into the program seen in Figure 6b. The benefit of the transformation is seen by comparing the fitness landscapes shown in Figures 6c and 6d where the sharp drop into local minima of the original landscape is replaced with smooth planes sloping down to the global minimum.

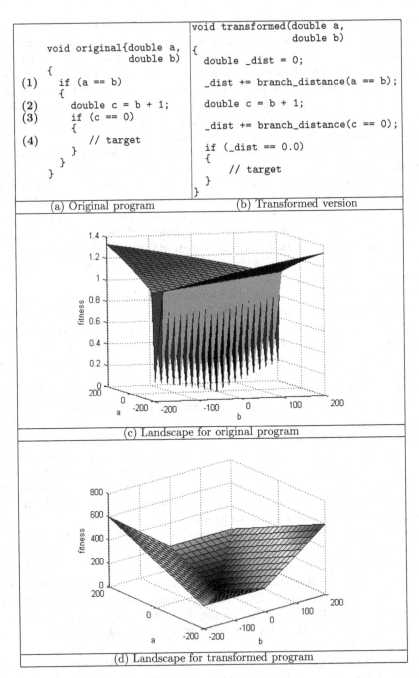

```
                                    void transformed(double a,
                                                     double b)
        void original{double a,    {
                       double b)       double _dist = 0;
        {
(1)        if (a == b)                 _dist += branch_distance(a == b);
           {
(2)           double c = b + 1;        double c = b + 1;
(3)           if (c == 0)
              {                        _dist += branch_distance(c == 0);
(4)              // target
              }                        if (_dist == 0.0)
           }                           {
        }                                 // target
                                       }
                                    }
```

(a) Original program   (b) Transformed version

(c) Landscape for original program

(d) Landscape for transformed program

Fig. 6. Case study showing (a) the original and (b) the transformed versions of the code. The transformation removes the sharp drop into points of local minima prevalent in the fitness landscape of the original program seen in part (c), with the more directional landscape of the transformed program, seen in part (d).

The improvement comes because the search can concentrate on both conditionals at the same time and is in possession of all the facts required to make them both true at the very beginning of the search.

The solution is not free of challenges, as the transformed program can potentially have issues with the removal of certain types of predicates that prevent the occurrence of run-time errors. One example of this is a predicate that tests and then references heap allocated storage. For example, transformation of the conditional if (p != NULL) { if (p->x > 0) ··· } would include, in the computation of _dist, the dereferencing of the potentially NULL pointer p.

Therefore the transformed test object must be evaluated in its own 'sandbox' to prevent any potential abnormal termination from affecting the rest of the test data generation system. The fitness function is calculated using all fitness information that was successfully accumulated. In this way, search performance is unlikely to be worse than if the original version of the program were being used. Improving the treatment of such predicates forms one area for future work, while the issue of nesting within a loop body forms another.

In their study of nested if statements McMinn et al. provide two key empirical results from a collection of forty real-world programs [31]. The first result shows the prevalence of nested predicates in real-world code (on average 3 nested predicate pairs per 100 lines of non-comment non-blank code). Over 80% of these include intervening code two-thirds of which affected the second predicate and thus cannot simply be reordered out of the way. The second result compares finding test data for the original and transformed versions of two programs. The first program is that of Figure 6. TeTra allowed the evolutionary search to find test data using half the effort (test data evaluations) of the untransformed program. The second program studied included three levels of nesting. For the original version of this program, the evolutionary algorithm failed to find test data, while it succeeded every time using the transformed version.

4.3   TeTra for Data Dependence Transformation to Assist the Chaining Method

The third case study, considers the speculative application of testability transformation to the chaining method [16]. Existing test data generation methods use different types of information about a program in order to guide the search process (e.g., a control flow graph, control dependencies, data flows, etc). Although existing methods work well for many programs, complex logic and intricate dependence relationships between program elements can pose a challenge to test generators. Thus, without transformation, test data is hard for a data-flow technique to generate. Transformation is used in this case is to remove the barrier created by control dependencies in discovering a good 'chain'.

This third case study, exploits the fact that testability transformation need not preserve the standard semantics. In this more radical form of testability transformation, the transformations may yield programs for which it is known that the wrong test data will be produced. However, this technique can be used to speculatively generate test data. As a result, the search can find the solution where other techniques fail. This approach is more expensive and thus typically applied only after existing cheaper methods fail to find the required test data. If the transformation fails, then nothing additional is lost, so the method need only improve test data generation in some cases in order to be valuable [27].

The goal of the transformation is to produce a program that contains only the statements responsible for the computation of the fitness function. The major advantage of the transformed program is that it is easy to execute any statement that affects the fitness function. As a result, the transformed program allows efficient exploration of different paths in order to identify paths that lead to the target value of the fitness function. The technique has five steps. First a data-dependence subgraph is built. This is then used to generate the transformed program. In the next step, paths in the data-dependence subgraph are selected for exploration. For each selected path test data is generated using the transformed program to identify *promising* paths (i.e., paths that lead to the target value of the fitness function). Finally, *promising* paths are used to guide the search for test data using the original program. A good data-flow analysis tool is only well suited to handle the first step [27].

The technique is data-dependence based and thus stands in contrast with existing techniques that are strongly tied to program control flow [26]. To motivate this choice, the authors note that finding test data can frequently require executing parts of the program that are (from the control flow perspective) unrelated. Data dependence analysis, however, ties these regions together as it captures the situation in which one statement assigns a value to a variable that another statement uses. For example, in the function of Figure 7 there exists a data dependence between Statements 13 and 20 because Statement 13 assigns a value to variable top, Statement 20 uses variable top, and there exists a the control path (13, 14, 15, 19, 23, 6, 7, 8, 9, 15, 19, 20) from 13 to 20 along which variable top is not modified.

The technique's first step builds a data dependence graph and then extracts the subgraph for a particular statement. In a data dependence graph nodes represent statements from the program, and directed arcs represent data dependencies [17]. For a chosen node, the extracted data-dependence subgraph includes all the nodes for which there exists a path to the selected node. These represent the statements that may influence the chosen statement. For example, Figure 8 shows the data dependence subgraph for the node corresponding to Statement 20 from Figure 7.

This statement is referred to as a *problem* statement because Statement 21 is difficult for other test-data generation techniques to generate test data for (its execution requires Statement 13 to be executed 101 times before reaching Statement 20). The next step uses the subgraph extracted for a problem statement to guide the construction of the transformed program. Each statement that belongs to the subgraph is included in the transformed program as the case of a switch-statement. This program includes the statements whose nodes appear in the extracted subgraph (e.g., see Figure 9).

```
1   void F(int A[], int C[])
    {
     int AR[100];
     int a, i, j, cmd, top, f_exit;
2    i=1;
3    j = 1;
4    top = 0;
5    f_exit=0;
6    while (f_exit==0)
     {
7      cmd = C[j];
8      j = j + 1;
9      if (cmd == 1)
       {
10       a = A[i];
11       i = i + 1;
12       if (a > 0)
         {
13         top++;
14         AR[top] = a;
         }
       }
15     else if (cmd == 2)
       {
16       if (top>0)
         {
17         write(AR[top]);
18         top--;
         }
       }
19     else if (cmd==3)
       {
20       if (top>100)
21         write(1);
22       else write(0);
       }
23     else if (cmd>=5)
24       f_exit=1;
     }
25  }
```

Fig. 7. A sample C function

In addition, to the input parameters from the original program, the transformed program includes two new input parameters, S and R. The array S represents *data dependence paths* from the extracted subgraph. Only paths that begin with a node that has no incoming arcs and end at the problem node are considered. For example, 4, 13, 18, 20 is a data dependence path in the subgraph shown in Figure 8. Array S indicates the sequence of statements from the data dependence path that are to be executed. The transformed program contains a while-loop with a switch-statement inside it. These combine to execute the statements as indicated by S.

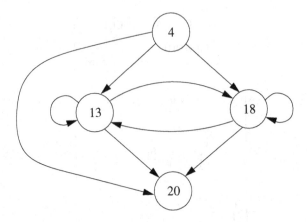

Fig. 8. Data Dependence Subgraph

Some nodes in the data dependence subgraph have self-loops (statements such as i++ within a loop depened on themselves). In order to explore the influence of such data dependences on the fitness function, the corresponding nodes need to be repeatedly executed. This is the purpose of the input array, R; thus, $S[i]$ indicates the particular statement to be executed and $R[i]$ indicates a number

```
1    float transformed(int S[], int R[])
     {
       int i, j, top;
2      i=1;
3      while (i <= length(S))
       {
4        switch (S[i])
         {
5          case 4: top = 0;
6                  break;
7          case 13: top++;
8                   for (j=1; j<R[i]; j++)
                    top++;
9                   break;
10         case 18: top--;
11                  for (j=1; j<R[i]; j++)
                    top--;
12                  break;
13       }
14       i++;
15     }
16     return 100-top;
     }
```

Fig. 9. Transformed version of the code from Figure 7 for the data dependence subgraph of Figure 8. The result value is the fitness function for Statement 20 of Figure 7.

of repetitions of this statement. In essence, the transformation has produced a function from the inputs S and R to the value of the fitness function for the problem node.

For example, a transformed version of the function from Figure 7 for problem Statement 20 is shown in Figure 9. The transformed function contains the statements that are part of the data dependence subgraph from Figure 8 (statements 4, 13, and 18). The end point is omitted because it does not modify the state. These statements affect the computation of the fitness function associated with problem Statement 20. For statements 13 and 18, for- loops are included because these statements have self-looping data dependences in the data dependence subgraph.

After transformation, a search generates different data dependence paths for exploration. A path is represented by S. For each S, the goal is to find values for R such that the fitness function evaluates to the target value. The search uses the existing test generation techniques [16,32,44] to find an input on which the fitness function evaluates to the target value in the transformed function. If the target value is achieved, the path is considered a promising path. Otherwise, the path is considered to be unpromising and it is rejected. Finally, promising paths in the transformed program are used to guide the search in the untransformed program.

For example, the transformed program for problem Statement 20 from Figure 7, shown in Figure 9, captures the five acyclic paths in the data dependence subgraph of Figure 8. The following table shows these paths and their corresponding inputs

path	corresponding input
P_1: 4, 20	$S[1] = 4$
P_2: 4, 18, 20	$S[1] = 4, S[2] = 18$
P_3: 4, 13, 20	$S[1] = 4, S[2] = 13$
P_4: 4, 13, 18, 20	$S[1] = 4, S[2] = 13, S[3] = 18$
P_5: 4, 18, 13, 20	$S[1] = 4, S[2] = 18, S[3] = 13$

For each path, the goal is to find values for array R such that the value of the fitness function returned by the transformed function is negative. The search fails for paths P_1 and P_2 and these paths are rejected. When path P_3 is explored, the search finds the values $R[1] = 1; R[2] = 101$ for which the fitness function evaluates to the negative value in the transformed function. Therefore, path P_3 with 101 repetitions of Statement 13 is considered as a promising path. When this path is used to guide the search of the function of Figure 7, an input is easily identified for which target Statement 21 is executed. Using the transformed function of Figure 9, it is possible to find a solution although only five data dependence paths need be considered as opposed to over one hundred path explorations when the transformed function is not used.

5   A Road Map for Future Work on Testability Transformation

This chapter has surveyed the current state-of-the-art of testability transformation. There remain many open problems. This section sets out a road map for future work on TeTra.

1. **Algorithms**
   Currently there are several algorithms for test-data generation using testability transformation. These tackle a variety of problems such as flag variables [2], nesting [31], and unstructured control flow [21]. The existence of these algorithms demonstrates the potential and wide applicability of testability transformation. However, there remain many open problems in test data generation for which algorithms have yet to be developed. For example, the problems of internal state [29], continuous input [3], and the loop problem for symbolic execution [11].

2. **Semantics**
   As shown in Section 2 the ideas behind testability transformation require a new notion of semantic correctness since the transformations are neither more abstract nor more concrete than the standard semantics. There are a number of open problems in testability transformation work, relating to the semantic foundations of the approach. Initial work has explored the proof obligations for testability transformation [21]. This work considers a transformation that reduces multi-exit loops to single exits loops and illustrates the need for different kinds of proof obligation in reasoning about testability transformation. Specifically, the proof obligations are not that the transformations preserve the behaviour of the program, rather that any test suite that provides 100% branch coverage for the transformed program is guaranteed to provide 100% coverage for the original program. However, no semantic investigation of correctness has yet been performed for other testability transformation algorithms. Such a proof would be relatively uncomplicated for the work on flag removal reported in Section 4.1 (because this algorithm aims to preserve standard semantics). However, for the other two algorithms, described in Sections 4.2 and 4.3, the proof obligations require the formulation of an alternate semantics. This result is a more challenging and enticing problem as both transformations preserve only *aspects* of the semantics.

3. **Raising the Abstraction Level**
   Existing work in testability transformation has considered the problem of applying standard and non-standard code level transformation rules and tactics to improve testability at the source code level of abstraction. However, there is a general movement in testing and design away from the code level to the model level, and so there may be a case for the application of testability transformation at higher levels of abstraction, such as the design and specification level. There is a particularly strong current interest in model driven development, with a consequent interest in development of approaches for testing at the model level. It is likely that there will be many problems for

test data generation at the model level and this suggests the possibility of applying testability transformation at the model level of abstraction.

There has also been much work on development of techniques for testing from formal specifications. Here too, it may be possible to use testability transformation to transform specifications into a format more amenable to testing.

4. Other Kinds of Testability Transformation

The focus of this chapter has been upon testability transformations that transform programs (and possibly the adequacy criterion). However, it is not hard to imagine scenarios in which the criterion is transformed while the program remains unchanged. For example, one could imagine a testability transformation, that takes a program, p, and a test adequacy criterion, c, and returns the test adequacy criterion, c' that is the 'lowest' possible criterion below c in the subsumes relationship for which all adequate test sets are identical to those for p and c. This would make it possible to capture the way in which certain programs are constructed in such a way that weaker test data generation methods will suffice for achieving stronger testing results. Such an approach complements cost reduction techniques considered in the existing literature such as test-set minimization [18].

For example, consider the program fragment

```
if (E) x=1; else x=2;
```

In this simple example, covering all statements will also cover all branches of E. However, in general this is not the case. The problem is to compute the weakest adequacy criterion (in the subsumes lattice [47]) that is sufficient to meet a given adequacy criterion c for a given program p. This general problem is more challenging and can be formulated as a testability transformation. Such a formulation would have useful practical ramifications. Where, for example, it can be determined that a weaker test data generation technique can be used, then it is possible to employ a test data generation tool with performance advantages that accrue from its attempt to satisfy only the weaker criterion. This is particularly advantageous when the original, more demanding adequacy criteria, has no tool capable of generating test data.

5. Other Testing Oriented Transformation

The definition of Testability transformation (in Section 2) is couched in terms of a "Testing Oriented Transformation." This is a transformation that takes and returns a pair containing the program under test and the adequacy criterion under consideration. It may be that there are other forms of testing-oriented transformation that may turn out to be useful. There may also be other interesting relations on programs, test data, and test adequacy criteria that remain to be explored.

6   Related Work

Testability transformation is a novel application of program transformation that does not require the preservation of functional equivalence. This is a departure from most work on program transformation, but it is not the first instance of non-traditional meaning-preserving transformation. Previous examples include Weiser's slicing [46] and the "evolution transforms" of Dershowitz and Manna [14] and Feather [15]. However, both slices and evolution transforms do preserve some *projection* of traditional meaning. Testability transformation as introduced here does not. Rather it preserves an entirely new form of meaning, derived from the need to improve test data generation rather than the need to improved the program itself.

There has only been non-transformation based previous work on the first of the three application areas considered in Section 4. For the other two applications of testability transformation (to the nested predicate problem and the chaining method), testability transformation is currently the only method to have been applied. The first application, to the problem of evolutionary testing in the presence of flags, has been considered in three previous papers [7,4,20]. Bottaci [7] introduces an approach which aims to correct the instrumentation of the fitness function. Baresel and Sthamer [4] used a similar approach to Bottaci [7]. Whereas Bottaci's approach is to store the values of fitness as the flag is assigned, Baresel and Sthamer use static data flow analysis to locate the assignments in the code that have an influence on the flag condition at the point of use.

The paper that introduced testability transformation by Harman et al. [20] presented a testability transformation approach to the flag problem, based upon substituting a flag variable with its computation. The approach could not handle loop-assigned flags. Work since then, summarised in this chapter, has improved the technique in terms of its generality, applicability, and effectiveness.

7   Conclusion

Testability transformation is a new application for program transformation. It concerns the application to aid testing rather than the more familiar application areas of optimization, comprehension, re-engineering, or program development through refinement. However, testability transformation is more than merely a novel application area of a long-standing area of research and practice; the fundamental nature of the transformations takes a different form than conventional transformation.

Testability transformations are applied in order to improve testing. The equivalence that needs to be preserved is not functional equivalence (as with almost all prior work on transformation). Rather, it is the set of adequate test sets. This has been shown to be neither more abstract nor more concrete than normal transformation, with the result that testability transformation is not simply an instance of abstract interpretation [10]. Rather, it includes novel transformation rules and algorithms and suggests the need for novel formulations of programming language semantics in order to reason about testability transformations.

Furthermore, testability transformation is a means to an end and not an end result in itself. This has important practical ramifications, such as a reduced importance for correctness of transformations and a lower psychological barrier to acceptance of transformation. If a transformation rule is incorrect, the consequence is not an errant program, it is merely the (possible) failure to find desired test data. This is both a less critical consequence and it is also an easily computable outcome. That is, should a conventional transformation be incorrect, the problem of determining whether there has been an impact upon the transformed program is undecidable, whereas the problem of determining whether test adequacy has been satisfied is usually trivial as it simply requires running the program. With the continued need for extensive unit testing and the growing available of 'spare' processor cycles, techniques such as testability transformation should continue to see increased interest and application.

Acknowledgments

The work summarized in this chapter has been largely conducted as a result of the UK EPSRC funded project TeTra – Testability Transformation (GR/R98938) and by the project's collaborators. David Binkley is funded, in part by US National Science Foundation grant CCR0305330. More details concerning the TeTra project are available on the TeTra website at

http://www.dcs.kcl.ac.uk/staff/linhu/TeTra

References

1. Altman, D.G.: Practical Statistics for Medical Research. Chapman and Hall, Boca Raton (1997)
2. Baresel, A., Binkley, D., Harman, M., Korel, B.: Evolutionary testing in the presence of loop-assigned flags: A testability transformation approach. In: Proceedings of the International Symposium on Software Testing and Analysis (ISSTA 2004), Boston, Massachusetts, USA, pp. 43–52. ACM, New York (2004)
3. Baresel, A., Pohlheim, H., Sadeghipour, S.: Structural and functional sequence test of dynamic and state-based software with evolutionary algorithms. In: Cantú-Paz, E., Foster, J.A., Deb, K., Davis, L., Roy, R., O'Reilly, U.-M., Beyer, H.-G., Kendall, G., Wilson, S.W., Harman, M., Wegener, J., Dasgupta, D., Potter, M.A., Schultz, A., Dowsland, K.A., Jonoska, N., Miller, J., Standish, R.K. (eds.) GECCO 2003. LNCS, vol. 2724, pp. 2428–2441. Springer, Heidelberg (2003)
4. Baresel, A., Sthamer, H.: Evolutionary testing of flag conditions. In: Cantú-Paz, E., Foster, J.A., Deb, K., Davis, L., Roy, R., O'Reilly, U.-M., Beyer, H.-G., Kendall, G., Wilson, S.W., Harman, M., Wegener, J., Dasgupta, D., Potter, M.A., Schultz, A., Dowsland, K.A., Jonoska, N., Miller, J., Standish, R.K. (eds.) GECCO 2003. LNCS, vol. 2724, pp. 2442–2454. Springer, Heidelberg (2003)
5. Baresel, A., Sthamer, H., Schmidt, M., 2002, J.: Fitness function design to improve evolutionary structural testing. In: GECCO 2002: Proceedings of the Genetic and Evolutionary Computation Conference, San Francisco, CA, July 9–13, 2002, pp. 1329–1336. Morgan Kaufmann Publishers, San Francisco (2002)
6. Binkley, D.W., Gallagher, K.B.: Program slicing. In: Zelkowitz, M. (ed.) Advances in Computing, 43th edn., pp. 1–50. Academic Press, London (1996)

7. Bottaci, L.: Instrumenting programs with flag variables for test data search by genetic algorithms. In: GECCO 2002: Proceedings of the Genetic and Evolutionary Computation Conference, New York, July 9–13, 2002, pp. 1337–1342. Morgan Kaufmann, San Francisco (2002)

8. British Standards Institute. BS 7925-1 vocabulary of terms in software testing (1998)

9. Clarke, L.A.: A system to generate test data and symbolically execute programs. IEEE Transactions on Software Engineering 2(3), 215–222 (1976)

10. Cousot, P., Cousot, R.: Abstract interpretation frameworks. Journal of Logic and Computation 2(4), 511–547 (1992)

11. Coward, P.D.: Symbolic execution systems – a review. Software Engineering Journal 3(6), 229–239 (1988)

12. Darlington, J., Burstall, R.M.: A tranformation system for developing recursive programs. Journal of the ACM 24(1), 44–67 (1977)

13. Richard A DeMillo and A.J. Offutt. Experimental results from an automatic test generator. *ACM Transactions of Software Engineering and Methodology*, 2(2):109–127, March 1993.

14. Dershowitz, N., Manna, Z.: The evolution of programs: A system for automatic program modification. In: Conference Record of the Fourth Annual Symposium on Principles of Programming Languages. ACM SIGACT and SIGPLAN, pp. 144–154. ACM Press, New York (1977)

15. Feather, M.S.: A system for assisting program transformation. ACM Transactions on Programming Languages and Systems 4(1), 1–20 (1982)

16. Ferguson, R., KorelThe, B.: The chaining approach for software test data generation. ACM Transactions on Software Engineering and Methodology 5(1), 63–86 (1996)

17. Ferrante, J., Ottenstein, K.J., Warren, J.D.: The program dependence graph and its use in optimization. ACM Transactions on Programming Languages and Systems 9(3), 319–349 (1987)

18. Graves, T., Harrold, M.J., Kim, J.-M., Porter, A., Rothermel, G.: An empirical study of regression test selection techniques. In: Proceedings of the 20th International Conference on Software Engineering, April 1998, pp. 188–197. IEEE Computer Society Press, Los Alamitos (1998)

19. Harman, M., Hu, L., Hierons, R., Baresel, A., Sthamer, H.: Improving evolutionary testing by flag removal ('best at GECCO' award winner). In: GECCO 2002: Proceedings of the Genetic and Evolutionary Computation Conference, July 9–13, 2002, pp. 1359–1366. Kaufmann Publishers, San Francisco (2002)

20. Harman, M., Hu, L., Hierons, R.M., Wegener, J., Sthamer, H., Baresel, A., Roper, M.: Testability transformation. IEEE Transactions on Software Engineering 30(1), 3–16 (2004)

21. Hierons, R., Harman, M., Fox, C.: Branch-coverage testability transformation for unstructured programs. The Computer Journal 48(4), 421–436 (2005)

22. Jones, B.F., Sthamer, H.-H., Eyres, D.E.: Automatic structural testing using genetic algorithms. The Software Engineering Journal 11, 299–306 (1996)

23. King, J.C.: Symbolic execution and program testing. Communications of the ACM 19(7), 385–394 (1976)

24. King, K.N., Offutt, A.J.: A FORTRAN language system for mutation-based software testing. Software Practice and Experience 21, 686–718 (1991)

25. Korel, B.: Automated software test data generation. IEEE Transactions on Software Engineering 16(8), 870–879 (1990)

26. Korel, B., Chung, S., Apirukvorapinit, P.: Data dependence analysis in automated test generation. In: Proceedings: 7th IASTED International Conference on Software Engineering and Applications, pp. 476–481 (2003)
27. Korel, B., Harman, M., Chung, S., Apirukvorapinit, P., Gupta, R.: Data dependence based testability transformation in automated test generation. In: 16th International Symposium on Software Reliability Engineering (ISSRE 2005), Chicago, Illinios, USA, pp. 245–254, November 2005 (2005)
28. McMinn, P.: Search-based software test data generation: A survey. Software Testing, Verification and Reliability 14(2), 105–156 (2004)
29. McMinn, P., Holcombe, M.: The state problem for evolutionary testing. In: Cantú-Paz, E., Foster, J.A., Deb, K., Davis, L., Roy, R., O'Reilly, U.-M., Beyer, H.-G., Kendall, G., Wilson, S.W., Harman, M., Wegener, J., Dasgupta, D., Potter, M.A., Schultz, A., Dowsland, K.A., Jonoska, N., Miller, J., Standish, R.K. (eds.) GECCO 2003. LNCS, vol. 2724, pp. 2488–2497. Springer, Heidelberg (2003)
30. McMinn, P., Holcombe, M.: Evolutionary testing of state-based programs. In: Proceedings of the Genetic and Evolutionary Computation Conference (GECCO 2005), Washington DC, USA, pp. 1013–1020. ACM Press, New York (2005)
31. McMinn, P., Binkley, D., Harman, M.: Testability transformation for efficient automated test data search in the presence of nesting. In: UK Software Testing Workshop (UK Test 2005), Sheffield, UK (September 2005)
32. Michael, C.C., McGraw, G., Schatz, M.A.: Generating software test data by evolution. IEEE Transactions on Software Engineering 12, 1085–1110 (2001)
33. Mueller, F., Wegener, J.: A comparison of static analysis and evolutionary testing for the verification of timing constraints. In: 4th IEEE Real-Time Technology and Applications Symposium RTAS 1998, Washington, Brussels, Tokyo, June 1998, pp. 144–154. IEEE, Los Alamitos (1998)
34. Offutt, A.J.: An integrated system for automatically generating test data. In: Raymond, T.N., Peter, A., Ramamoorthy, C.V., Seifert, L.C., Yeh (eds.) Proceedings of the First International Conference on Systems Integration, Morristown, NJ, April 1990, pp. 694–701. IEEE Computer Society Press, Los Alamitos (1990)
35. Pargas, R.P., Harrold, M.J., Peck, R.R.: Test-data generation using genetic algorithms. The Journal of Software Testing, Verification and Reliability 9, 263–282 (1999)
36. Partsch, H.A.: The Specification and Transformation of Programs: A Formal Approach to Software Development. Springer, Heidelberg (1990)
37. Pohlheim, H., Wegener, J.: Testing the temporal behavior of real-time software modules using extended evolutionary algorithms. In: Banzhaf, W., Daida, J., Eiben, A.E., Garzon, M.H., Honavar, V., Jakiela, M., Smith, R.E. (eds.) Proceedings of the Genetic and Evolutionary Computation Conference, July 13–17, 1999, vol. 2, p. 1795. Morgan Kaufmann, San Francisco (1999)
38. Puschner, P., Nossal, R.: Testing the results of static worst–case execution-time analysis. In: 19th IEEE Real-Time Systems Symposium (RTSS 1998), pp. 134–143. IEEE Computer Society Press, Los Alamitos (1998)
39. Radio Technical Commission for Aeronautics. RTCA DO178-B Software considerations in airborne systems and equipment certification (1992)
40. Schultz, A., Grefenstette, J., Jong, K.: Test and evaluation by genetic algorithms. IEEE Expert 8(5), 9–14 (1993)
41. Tracey, N., Clark, J., Mander, K.: Automated program flaw finding using simulated annealing. In: International Symposium on Software Testing and Analysis, March 1998, pp. 73–81. ACM/SIGSOFT, New York (1998)

42. Tracey, N., Clark, J., Mander, K.: The way forward for unifying dynamic test-case generation: The optimisation-based approach. In: International Workshop on Dependable Computing and Its Applications (DCIA), IFIP, January 1998, pp. 169–180 (1998)
43. Ward, M.: Reverse engineering through formal transformation. The Computer Journal 37(5) (1994)
44. Wegener, J., Baresel, A., Sthamer, H.: Evolutionary test environment for automatic structural testing. Information and Software Technology Special Issue on Software Engineering using Metaheuristic Innovative Algorithms 43(14), 841–854 (2001)
45. Wegener, J., Mueller, F.: A comparison of static analysis and evolutionary testing for the verification of timing constraints. Real-Time Systems 21(3), 241–268 (2001)
46. Weiser, M.: Program slices: Formal, psychological, and practical investigations of an automatic program abstraction method. PhD thesis, University of Michigan, Ann Arbor, MI (1979)
47. Zhu, H.: A formal analysis of the subsume relation between software test adequacy criteria. IEEE Transactions on Software Engineering 22(4), 248–255 (1996)

Modelling the Effects of Combining Diverse Software Fault Detection Techniques

Bev Littlewood[1], Peter Popov[1], Lorenzo Strigini[1], and Nick Shryane[2,*]

[1] Centre for Software Reliability, City University,
Northampton Square, London EC1V 0HB, UK
{b.littlewood,ptp,strigini}@csr.city.ac.uk
http://www.csr.city.ac.uk
[2] School of Psychological Sciences,
University of Manchester, Manchester M13 9PL, UK
N.Shryane@manchester.ac.uk

Abstract. The software engineering literature contains many studies of the efficacy of fault finding techniques. Few of these, however, consider what happens when several different techniques are used together. We show that the effectiveness of such multi-technique approaches depends upon quite subtle interplay between their individual efficacies and *dependence* between them. The modelling tool we use to study this problem is closely related to earlier work on software *design diversity*. The earliest of these results showed that, under quite plausible assumptions, it would be unreasonable even to expect software versions that were developed 'truly independently' to fail independently of one another. The key idea here was a 'difficulty function' over the input space. Later work extended these ideas to introduce a notion of 'forced' diversity, in which it became possible to obtain system failure behaviour better even than could be expected if the versions failed independently. In this paper we show that many of these results for *design* diversity have counterparts in diverse *fault detection* in a single software version. We define measures of fault finding effectiveness, and of diversity, and show how these might be used to give guidance for the optimal application of different fault finding procedures to a particular program. We show that the effects upon reliability of repeated applications of a particular fault finding procedure are not statistically independent – in fact such an incorrect assumption of independence will always give results that are too optimistic. For *diverse* fault finding procedures, on the other hand, things are different: here it is possible for effectiveness to be even greater than it would be under an assumption of statistical independence. We show that diversity of fault finding procedures is, in a precisely defined way, 'a good thing', and should be applied as widely as possible. The new model and its results are illustrated using some data from an experimental investigation into diverse fault finding on a railway signalling application.

1 Introduction

Diversity is ubiquitous in human activity. In quite mundane contexts it is common to use diversity to improve confidence: for example, I might ask a colleague to check my

---

* Work performed while this author was at the Department of Psychology, University of Hull, Hull HU6 7RX, UK.

R.M. Hierons et al. (Eds.): Formal Methods and Testing, LNCS 4949, pp. 345–366, 2008.

arithmetic in a complex calculation. The informal idea is that the mistakes he might make will differ from those that I might make, and our arriving at the same answer suggests that neither of us has made a mistake, thus increasing my confidence that the answer is correct.

The key to the approach is, of course, the presence of intellectual differences in the two procedures. Note that this notion of diversity differs fundamentally from that of *redundancy* in which there is simply *replication* (e.g. of a component to increase hardware reliability) of exactly similar items: I would have less trust in my own exact replication of the calculation than in the different calculation of my colleague.

In software, *design diversity* has been proposed as a means of achieving higher reliability than could be achieved (for the same outlay of effort) from a single version. Such design diverse software architectures have seen fairly widespread industrial use [1]. In the early days, it seems that the motivation for the approach owed a great deal to the hardware redundancy metaphor, to the extent that independence of failures of the versions was seen as the goal (albeit recognised as difficult to achieve). Later, several experiments [2, 3] showed that such a goal was probably unrealistic: version failures tended to be highly dependent. Thus, whilst considerable improvement in reliability could be expected from a multi-version architecture compared with the reliabilities of the single versions, this nevertheless fell far short of what would have been achieved if these versions failed independently.

An insight into the nature of the dependence came from a probabilistic model developed by Eckhardt and Lee (EL) [4], and later generalised by Littlewood and Miller (LM) [5]. The basic idea here is that different inputs have different 'difficulty' – roughly, the difficulty (and thus proneness to failure) faced by the designer of the software in providing a correct way of processing them. As an example, consider an aircraft flight control system: we might think of the set of inputs corresponding to landing in turbulent wind-shear as 'more difficult' than those corresponding to straight and level flight in calm conditions. It is shown in EL that this variation of difficulty induces dependence upon the version failures, even though these might fail *conditionally* independently. The intuition here is simple. If there are two versions, A and B, and for a particular input we see that A has failed, we infer that the input was 'probably difficult', and *that B is therefore more likely to fail*. This is true even though, for every input, the versions fail (conditionally) independently – and it is this *conditional* independence that is the difficult goal to which the systems designers aspire.[1]

The LM model generalises EL by introducing the possibility that the procedures used by the A and B teams may be different ('forced diversity'), and thus that what the A team finds difficult may be different from what the B team finds difficult. It introduces the possibility that diversity can be forced so that the versions will fail in

---

[1] In more precise mathematical terms, we say that A and B fail *conditionally* independently if, for every possible input, x, $P(A \text{ and } B \text{ both fail} \mid x) = P(A \text{ fails} \mid x)P(B \text{ fails} \mid x)$. They fail *unconditionally* independently, on the other hand, if for a randomly chosen (i.e. unknown) input $P(A \text{ and } B \text{ both fail}) = P(A \text{ fails})P(B \text{ fails})$. The point is that, in general, conditional independence does not imply unconditional independence.

negatively correlated ways – thus giving better system reliability even than from independence. It has to be admitted, however, that such an outcome may be unlikely in practice.

A major conclusion to be drawn from these models is that there are traps for the unwary in simple reliability models of multi-version software. In particular, assumptions of conditional independence generally do not carry through to justify claims of unconditional independence.

Although the models are quite subtle, their intuitive underpinnings are quite simple. What is surprising is their very wide applicability. In this paper we shall show that similar results apply to diversity in the fault detection processes that are applied to a *single* software version. Once again, the benefits that we get from the application of diverse fault detection procedures may sometimes be less than we could expect under naïve assumptions of independence. However, the possibility of obtaining real benefits from forced diversity, and *predicting* the extent of these benefits, seems more plausible here than it does in the case of design diversity.

2   A Model of Diverse Fault Detection

Consider a single program that is going to be subjected to two different ('diverse') fault detection procedures, *A* and *B*. For simplicity we shall assume that the program is demand-based (e.g. a nuclear reactor protection system). As an example, one of the fault detection procedures might be testing, in which the program is subjected to a particular number of demands; another might be some form of static analysis, for which a certain amount of staff effort is allocated.

The practical intuition here is that each fault detection procedure varies in its efficacy from one fault to another, and that the different procedures may target *different* faults most effectively. That is, procedure *A* may be stronger on those faults for which *B* is weaker. This is a kind of forced diversity – applied to fault detection – similar to the forced diversity of design and development methods in the LM model. The difference here is that the diverse fault detection is being applied to a single program. We shall try to keep the notation here as close as possible to that of LM, so that readers familiar with this model can see the similarities.

We shall assume that there is at most one fault associated with each input. One way of thinking of a fault in a program is as the set of all inputs that change from being 'faulty' (i.e. cause a failure when executed) to 'non-faulty' (i.e. do not cause a failure when executed) when the program is changed 'in order to remove a fault' [6].

It is now possible to imagine all possible faults that *might* be in a program. We shall label these with the natural numbers: $\{i: i=1,2,3,...\}$. Clearly, some of these faults will be more likely to be present in a particular program than others. Let

$$p_i = P(\text{fault } i \text{ is present in a randomly selected program}) \tag{1}$$

This notion of randomly selected program is exactly the same as that used in EL and LM. There is a set of all programs that *could* be written, and the act of writing a program is modelled as an act of selection, via some probability distribution over this set of all programs. Thus, the single program that we are dealing with can be regarded as having been randomly selected from this set of possible programs.

Of particular interest is the *probability distribution* $\{p_i{}^*\}$ where

$$p_i^* = \frac{p_i}{\sum\limits_i p_i} = P(\text{randomly selected fault is fault } i) \qquad (2)$$

For any particular fault, i, we define $\theta_A(i)$ to be the probability that a (randomly chosen) application of the fault detection procedure A fails to find this fault. The key idea, as in EL, is that this function varies from one fault to another. For a particular fault it can be thought of as the 'difficulty' of finding that fault using procedure A, similar to the 'difficulty' of inputs in the EL and LM models.

If, as an example, we think of A as being the execution of n operational test cases – i.e. chosen at random using the operational profile over the input space – then clearly each such 'test' will either reveal the fault i or it will not. If we were to repeat this procedure many times, generating many sequences, each of n inputs, from the operational profile, $\theta_A(i)$ can be thought of as the proportion in which the procedure fails to detect the fault i.

The difficulty functions determine the efficacy of the fault detection procedures. For example, we can define a measure of A's fault-detection efficacy as the chance that an 'average' or 'typical' fault is found in a (randomly chosen) application of A. In order to keep our notation in step with that of the EL and LM models we shall generally express the results here in terms of *ineffectiveness* (cf. unreliability in the earlier models) of the fault detection procedure A:

$$P(\text{A fails to detect a randomly chosen fault})$$
$$= \sum_i p_i^* \theta_A(i) = E_{p^*}(\theta_A(i)) \qquad (3)$$

where the notation E_{p^*} indicates a mean obtained with respect to the probability distribution p^*. We have the following:

Result 1

$$E(\text{number of faults in program undetected after the application of A})$$
$$= E_{p^*}(\theta_A(i))E(\text{number of faults in program } before \text{ the application of A}) \qquad (4)$$

and

$$E(\text{number of faults detected by the application of A})$$
$$= (1 - E_{p^*}(\theta_A(i)))E(\text{number of faults present in program}) \qquad (5)$$

Proof

E(number of faults in program undetected after the application of A)

$= \sum_i P$(fault i present and is not detected by the application of A)

$$= \sum_i p_i \theta_A(i) = \left(\sum_i p_i \right) \left(\sum_i p_i^* \theta_A(i) \right)$$

$= E_{p^*}(\theta_A(i)) E$(number of faults in program *before* the application of A)

The second part of the result follows trivially.

QED

We shall define the *effectiveness* of A to be

$$1 - \text{ineffectiveness}\left(1 - E_{p^*}(\theta_A(i))\right)$$

which is simply the probability that A successfully detects a randomly chosen fault.

For a different fault removal procedure, B, we could define similarly $\theta_B(i)$ and $E_{p^*}(\theta_B(i))$. If $E_{p^*}(\theta_A(i))$ were greater than $E_{p^*}(\theta_B(i))$ we would say that A is less effective at finding faults than B, in the sense that it would be expected to detect fewer faults.

We shall now show that, corresponding to the EL result in design diversity, we have here a lack of independence in the effects of successive applications of the same fault detection procedure, and that this implies a *law of diminishing returns*. Consider again, as an example, the situation where A is operational testing. An interesting question is how the effectiveness of this kind of testing changes as we apply more randomly chosen operational inputs. Consider the case where we carry out *two* such fault detection procedures, independently, A_1 and A_2. Each comprises n independently randomly chosen inputs, and the two sequences of n inputs are independent of one another. In general, in such a case of a double application of a procedure we have:

Result 2

$P(A_1$ and A_2 fail to detect a randomly chosen fault$)$
$\geq P(A_1$ fails to detect a randomly chosen fault$) \times$ (6)
$\qquad\qquad P(A_2$ fails to detect a randomly chosen fault$)$

or, *equivalently*,

$P(A_2$ fails to detect a randomly chosen fault $|\ A_1$ failed$)$
$\geq P(A_2$ fails to detect a randomly chosen fault$)$.   (7)

Proof
Clearly, for each fault i

$$P(A_1 \text{ and } A_2 \text{ fail to detect a fault } i) = \theta_A^2(i)$$

i.e. failures of the two applications of the fault detection procedure are conditionally *independent*, for every fault.

For a randomly selected fault, on the other hand

$$P(A_1 \text{ and } A_2 \text{ fail to detect a randomly chosen fault}) =$$

$$= \sum_i p_i^* \theta_A^2(i) = E_{p^*}\left(\theta_A^2(i)\right) \geq \left[E_{p^*}(\theta_A(i))\right]^2 \qquad (8)$$

since $E_{p^*}\left(\theta_A^2(i)\right) - \left[E_{p^*}(\theta_A(i))\right]^2 = Var(\theta_A(i)) \geq 0$ *(Var(X)* stands for the variance of the random variable *X)*.

QED

It is easy to show *(cf.* the EL and LM models) that there is equality in these expressions *if and only if* $\theta_A(i) = \theta$ identically for all faults. Clearly, it seems certain that no real fault finding procedures have the property of completely constant difficulty with respect to all faults.

Another way to think of these expressions is in terms of the number of faults you would expect to detect in a program by applying a particular fault finding procedure. Clearly, if you apply the procedure twice you would not expect to find twice as many faults as applying it just once – informally, there is a chance that some of the faults that could have been found in the second application would already have been found in the first application. This would be true even if there were complete independence in the two applications (i.e., in the terminology of the model, $\theta_A(i) = \theta$ identically for all faults). What the result above says is that things are even worse than this independence case when there is variation of difficulty: i.e. you would expect to find even fewer faults with two applications than you would if you could assume independence.

These results depend on the fact that, even though the two applications of the fault detection procedure are conditionally independent for all faults, they are not unconditionally independent. Informally, the failure of the first application of *A* to find the fault suggests that it is a 'difficult' fault for *A*, and thus that a second application of *A* will also be likely to fail to find it. If the first application of operational testing has revealed only a few faults, for example, we should tend to lose confidence in the likely effectiveness of a second application of the procedure.

This result corresponds to our intuition. Most people would not persevere with putting all their fault detection effort into a single procedure, such as, for example, inspection or operational testing. Rather they would tend to expect there to be a law of diminishing returns operating, whereby most of the faults that *can* easily be detected by a procedure, *are* eventually detected. At some point, therefore, it would seem sensible to cease one fault detection activity and switch to another, which it is hoped will target a different class of faults. We now examine this case of *diverse* fault removal: the reader familiar with the earlier models of design diversity will see that the following is similar to the LM model, as the former was similar to EL.

Consider now, therefore, two different fault detection procedures *A* and *B*:

Result 3

$$P(\text{A and B fail to detect a randomly selected fault})$$
$$> P(\text{A fails})P(\text{B fails}) \tag{9}$$

and

$$P(\text{B fails to detect a randomly selected fault} \mid \text{A failed})$$
$$> P(\text{B fails to detect a randomly selected fault}) \tag{10}$$

if and only if

$$Cov_{p^*}(\theta_A(i), \theta_B(i)) > 0 \tag{11}$$

where $Cov(X)$ stands for the covariance of the random variable X.

Proof
We assume conditional independence in the following obvious way:

$$P(\text{A and B fail to detect fault } i \mid i \text{ present}) = \theta_A(i)\theta_B(i) \tag{12}$$

for every fault i.
 For a randomly selected fault, on the other hand:

$$P(\text{A and B fail to detect a randomly selected fault}) \tag{13}$$
$$= \sum_i p_i^* \theta_A(i)\theta_B(i) = E_{p^*}(\theta_A(i)\theta_B(i))$$

which, in general

$$> E_{p^*}(\theta_A(i))E_{p^*}(\theta_B(i)) = P(\text{A fails to remove a randomly selected fault}) \times$$
$$P(\text{B fails to remove a randomly selected fault})$$
if and only if $Cov_{p^*}(\theta_A(i), \theta_B(i)) > 0$

QED

In other words, you would expect to find fewer faults by applying A and B when $Cov_{p^*}(\theta_A(i), \theta_B(i)) > 0$ than you would if you could assume independence (and, of course, this latter expected number will be smaller[2] than the sum of the numbers you would expect from a single application of A and a single application of B).

There is an intriguing possibility of *better than independent* behaviour of the two procedures if the covariance is negative. Such negative covariance would be possible whenever the different fault detection procedures targeted different types of faults, i.e. whenever the 'difficult' faults for one procedure are the 'easy' ones for the other, and vice versa.

---

[2] Strictly 'less than or equal to'. There can be equality here if there is a kind of 'complete disjointness' in the difficulty functions of the two procedures, i.e. if for every fault i one of the difficulty functions takes the value 1 - for every fault one of the procedures is completely ineffective. Such a case does not seem to have any practical relevance.

An expectation of something like negative covariance does seem to lie behind the intuition of those people involved in software verification and validation, for whom an eclectic mix of different fault finding procedures is preferred to the extensive application of a single one. What is novel in the work reported here is that we introduce the possibility of *measures* that characterise this desirable diversity between different procedures. Interestingly, the measures seem more amenable to statistical estimation than the corresponding ones in design diversity, as we shall see in a preliminary example in Section 6.

3 Effects on Reliability

The results of the previous section concern the efficacy of different procedures at finding faults. Of course, knowing that a procedure is good at finding faults is not the same as knowing that it is good at improving *reliability* (when the faults that are detected are removed). It is well-known that in real programs different faults can have very different impacts on a program's unreliability [7]: a fault-finding procedure that was very efficient at finding 'small' faults could be very inefficient at finding 'large' ones, and thus at improving reliability. A 'good' fault finding (and removal) procedure is one that tends to improve reliability most efficiently [6]. We now show that similar results to those above also apply to the efficacy of fault finding procedures in improving reliability. Throughout this section we shall assume that when a fault is detected it is removed with certainty.

Let

$$\pi_i = P(\text{fault } i \text{ is activated by a randomly selected} \atop \text{input and is detected and fixed}) \tag{14}$$

The unreliability of the program is then

$$P(\text{program fails on randomly selected input}) = \sum_i \pi_i \tag{15}$$

and

$$\pi_i^* = \frac{\pi_i}{\sum_i \pi_i} = P(\text{randomly selected failure caused by fault } i) \tag{16}$$

Consider now the effect of applying the fault removal procedure A on the program unreliability, i.e. on the probability that it fails on a randomly selected input.

Result 4

$$P(\text{program fails on a randomly selected input following application of A}) \tag{17}$$
$$= E_{\pi^*}(\theta_A(i))P(\text{program fails on a randomly selected input } \textit{before} \text{ applying A})$$

Proof

P(program fails on a randomly selected input following application of A)

$= \sum_i P($fault i activated following application of A)

$= \sum_i P($A has not removed fault i *and* it is activated$)$

$= \sum_i \pi_i \theta_A(i) = \left(\sum_i \pi_i\right)\left(\sum_i \pi_i^* \theta_A(i)\right)$

$= E_{\pi^*}(\theta_A(i)) P($program fails on randomly selected input *before* applying A$)$

QED

Thus, the factor $E_{\pi^*}(\theta_A(i))$ can be seen as a measure of the *ineffectiveness* of procedure A in improving reliability: the smaller this is, the better. Similarly, its complement can be thought of as the *effectiveness*.

Consider now the application of fault removal procedure A twice, A_1, A_2. We have a result similar to Result 2:

Result 5

The ineffectiveness of A_1 and A_2 together is greater than or equal to the product of the ineffectiveness of A_1 and the ineffectiveness of A_2.

Proof

P(program fails on a random input following application of A_1 and A_2)

$= \sum_i P($fault i activated following application of A_1 and A_2)

$= \sum_i P($A_1$ and A_2 have not removed fault i *and* it is activated$)$

$= \sum_i \pi_i \theta_A^2(i) = \sum_i \pi_i \sum_i \pi_i^* \theta_A^2(i)$

$= E_{\pi^*}(\theta_A^2(i)) P($program fails on a random input before applying A_1 and A_2)

$\geq (E_{\pi^*}(\theta_A(i)))^2 P($program fails on a random input before applying A_1 and A_2)

QED

As before, there will be equality here if and only if $\theta_A(i) \equiv \theta$ for some constant θ, identically for all faults.

The effectiveness of applying A_1 and A_2 together in reducing the probability of failure of the program on a randomly selected input is always less than the result we would expect under independence, since $E_{\pi^*}(\theta_A^2(i))$ is always less than $E_{\pi^*}(\theta_A(i))^2$. This is, again, the analogue of the EL result.

If, on the other hand, we apply *diverse* fault removal procedures, *A* and *B*, we find, as before, that we can do better than this:

Result 6

The ineffectiveness of applying *A* and *B* together is greater than the product of the ineffectiveness of *A* and the ineffectiveness of *B* if and only if $Cov_{\pi^*}(\theta_A(i), \theta_B(i)) > 0$.

Proof

P(program fails on a random input following application of A and B)

$= \displaystyle\sum_i P$(fault *i* activated following application of A and B)

$= \displaystyle\sum_i P$(A and B have not removed fault *i* *and* it is activated)

$= \displaystyle\sum_i \pi_i \theta_A(i)\theta_B(i) = \left(\sum_i \pi_i\right)\left(\sum_i \pi_i \, {}^*\theta_A(i)\theta_B(i)\right)$

$= E_{\pi^*}(\theta_A(i)\theta_B(i))P$(program fails on a random input *before* applying A and B)

$> E_{\pi^*}(\theta_A(i))E_{\pi^*}(\theta_B(i))P$(program fails on a random input *before* applying A and B)

if and only if $Cov_{\pi^*}(\theta_A(i), \theta_B(i)) = E_{\pi^*}(\theta_A(i)\theta_B(i)) - E_{\pi^*}(\theta_A(i))E_{\pi^*}(\theta_B(i)) > 0$

QED

Thus the factor $E_{\pi^*}(\theta_A(i)\theta_B(i))$, which determines the reduction in unreliability (improvement in reliability) coming from the successive applications of *A* and *B*, can be either smaller or larger than the equivalent expression that assumes independence, $E_{\pi^*}(\theta_A(i))E_{\pi^*}(\theta_B(i))$, according to whether the covariance $Cov_{\pi^*}(\theta_A(i), \theta_B(i))$ is positive or negative. We would like it to be smaller, i.e. the covariance to be negative.

4 Optimal Allocation of Fault Detection Procedures

The results of the previous two sections show that, in a limited sense, negative correlation between the difficulty functions of two fault finding procedures is 'a good thing'. In practice, of course, this does not tell us how to deploy *A* and *B* when we have a fixed amount of effort available. There will be a trade-off between the efficacies of the individual fault finding procedures and their dependence, and it may be that it will be most effective to use only *A* (or only *B*). In this section we provide some tentative advice for optimal allocation of procedures, by showing that, *when we believe that there is nothing to choose between the different procedures in terms of their individual efficacies, their most diverse application is always best.*

Consider the case where we have two fault finding procedures, *A* and *B*. For example, let *A*, as before, be operational testing; let *B* be a form of static analysis. Assume that we are *indifferent* between a randomly chosen application of *A* (i.e. a randomly chosen set of operational inputs), and a randomly chosen application of B (i.e. a particular application of the static analysis procedure). That is, if we were to apply only one of these procedures to our program we would have no preference between them. Then we can show that it is always better to apply A once and B once rather than either of them twice; more precisely:

Result 7

If $E_{\pi*}\left(\theta_A^{\ 2}(i)\right)= E_{\pi*}\left(\theta_B^{\ 2}(i)\right)$ then

    P(program fails on a random input following application of A and B)

    $< P$(program fails on a random input following application of A_1 and A_2)

and

    P(program fails on a random input following application of A and B)

    $< P$(program fails on a random input following application of B_1 and B_2)

Proof

By the Cauchy-Schwarz inequality

$$E_{\pi*}\left(\theta_A(i)\theta_B(i)\right)< \left(E_{\pi*}\left(\theta_A^{\ 2}(i)\right)\right)^{\frac{1}{2}}\left(E_{\pi*}\left(\theta_B^{\ 2}(i)\right)\right)^{\frac{1}{2}} = E_{\pi*}\left(\theta_A^{\ 2}(i)\right)= E_{\pi*}\left(\theta_B^{\ 2}(i)\right)$$

so

    P(program fails on a random input following application of A and B)

    $= E_{\pi*}\left(\theta_A(i)\theta_B(i)\right)P$(program fails on a random input before fault finding)

    $< E_{\pi*}\left(\theta_A^{\ 2}(i)\right)P$(program fails on a random input before fault finding)

    $= P$(program fails on a random input following application of A_1 and A_2)

and similarly for B_1 and B_2.

QED

A similar result holds for efficacy defined in terms of the expected numbers of faults removed: we would expect more faults to be removed by an application of A and B than by two applications of A or two of B (subject to a similar indifference assumption[3]). The similarity of this result to that just proved is a generalisation of the parallelism that we have seen between the results involving efficacy of fault removal (results 1-3) and those involving improvement in reliability (results 4-6). The proof follows simply and will not be given here: similar comments apply to all the results of this section.

    This result can be generalised to more than two fault finding procedures. Thus for three procedures A, B and C, we have a choice between the following applications (in an obvious notation): AAA, BBB, CCC, AAB, AAC, ABB, . . . , BCC, ABC. If we are indifferent between all the single fault finding procedures

$$E_{\pi*}\left(\theta_A^{\ 3}(i)\right)= E_{\pi*}\left(\theta_B^{\ 3}(i)\right)= E_{\pi*}\left(\theta_C^{\ 3}(i)\right) \tag{18}$$

and between all those using two procedures

---

[3] Note, however, that indifference with respect to fault finding ability does not generally imply indifference with respect to reliability improvement, nor *vice versa*.

$$E_{\pi^*}\left(\theta_A^{\ 2}(i)\theta_B(i)\right) = E_{\pi^*}\left(\theta_A^{\ 2}(i)\theta_C(i)\right) = E_{\pi^*}\left(\theta_A(i)\theta_B^{\ 2}(i)\right) \tag{19}$$

it can be shown that $E_{\pi^*}\left(\theta_A(i)\theta_B(i)\theta_C(i)\right)$ is smaller than all these other inefficiency factors, and so the greatest improvement in reliability will come by applying ABC.

More generally, when k different fault finding procedures are available, subject to certain indifference assumptions between them, it is best to use all of them and to spread their use as evenly as possible. Thus, for example, if we are prepared to apply 5 randomly chosen fault finding procedures, but only have 3 different types, then $AABCC$ is better than $AAABC$, etc. This can be expressed in general as:

Result 8

Let $(n_1, n_2, ... n_k)$ represent the allocation of n_i randomly chosen applications of fault finding procedure i $(i=1,2,...k)$,

$$\sum_{i=1}^{k} n_i = n.$$

Assuming indifference between allocations that merely involve permutations of procedures, the best allocations (there will generally be more than one) are those for which

$$\left[\frac{n}{k}\right] \le n_i \le \left[\frac{n}{k}\right] + 1, \quad 1 \le i \le k \tag{20}$$

where $[x]$ denotes the greatest integer not greater than x.

Proof

See [5].

The importance of this result lies in its potential for optimally allocating a given amount of effort among several fault finding procedures. The key to its practical application lies in the notion of 'indifference': we need to define a unit of fault finding effort which is meaningful for all the different types and which is such that there is indifference in the terms required by the result. The simplest way that this could be done would be for indifference between a single application of A and B to imply indifference between double applications, between triple applications, etc. In such a case, defining the initial 'unit' of each kind of fault finding effort is sufficient to ensure that the conditions of the result apply, and the best allocation(s) are those that 'spread effort as equally as possible' among different procedures.

If A were, as before, operational testing, and B were a type of static analysis, we would need to select a number of test cases for the 'unit' of operational testing, and an 'amount' of static analysis (e.g. the time for an analyst of a particular competence) so that we would be indifferent between (randomly chosen) single applications of each of the two[4]. It seems likely that in practice there is usually some appropriate 'cost' variable that will allow us to define units of different fault finding procedures that we

---

[4] Notice that indifference does not mean that we believe the effects will be the same. On the contrary, we know that the effects of the testing and analysis will be different in their fault finding - they will target different types of faults differently. The point is that we do not prefer one to another in their ability to *improve reliability*.

think are equivalent in their likely impact upon reliability. This result can be seen as a formalisation of the kind of informal allocation between different procedures that is carried out on a day-to-day basis during real system verification and validation.

5 Degrees of Diversity

It seems intuitively plausible that, if diversity is 'a good thing', then *more* diversity is better than *less*. In this section we present a measure of diversity between pairs of fault finding procedures that gives meaning to the notion of 'more diverse'.

Consider the two procedures A and B. Since a procedure is completely character-ised by its difficulty function over faults, θ, we can define a distance between the two procedures in this function space:

$$\|\theta_A - \theta_B\|^2 = E_{\pi^*}\left((\theta_A(i) - \theta_B(i))^2\right) \tag{21}$$

Clearly, $\|\theta_A - \theta_B\|^2 > 0$ unless $\theta_A(i) \equiv \theta_B(i)$. It follows trivially that

$$E_{\pi^*}(\theta_A(i)\theta_B(i)) < E_{\pi^*}\left(\theta_A^2(i)\right) = E_{\pi^*}\left(\theta_B^2(i)\right)$$

if we assume indifference between the procedures when applied singly. This is pre-cisely Result 7, which says that the improvement in reliability by applying A and B is better than that obtained by applying either twice.

Consider now the case where three procedures are available, A, B and C, but it is only feasible (e.g. on cost grounds) to apply two of them. Suppose further that we believe that A and B are more diverse, in the sense of (21), than are A and C, or B and C. This is shown schematically in Figure 1:

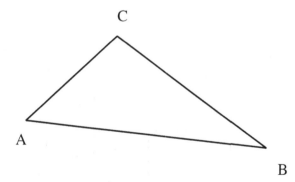

Fig. 1.

Result 9

If A and B are more diverse than B and C, i.e.

$$\|\theta_A - \theta_B\| > \|\theta_B - \theta_C\|,$$

and we are indifferent between two-fold applications of each of the three procedures, i.e.

$$E_{\pi*}\left(\theta_A{}^2(i)\right) = E_{\pi*}\left(\theta_B{}^2(i)\right) = E_{\pi*}\left(\theta_C{}^2(i)\right),$$

then

$$E_{\pi*}(\theta_A(i)\theta_B(i)) < E_{\pi*}(\theta_B(i)\theta_C(i))$$

[The proof is trivial]

In other words, if we have a choice of two procedures that are more diverse than another pair, we should prefer the former, all things being equal.

6 Example

Data to illustrate parts of the new model were obtained from a study into the verification of safety-critical computer programs used in railway signalling systems: this experiment pre-dated the development of the model described here.

Observational fieldwork conducted on-site at a number of railway signalling contractors had revealed qualitative differences between faults typically found by diverse verification methods, in this case static code checking and functional testing. However, variability in the complexity of work and personnel expertise found at different contractors' sites, and most importantly the lack of independence between the fault-finding methods as practised *in situ*, could have been confounding this result.

Computer-aided simulations of the checking and testing tasks were therefore developed to allow controlled laboratory experiments to be conducted and 88 university computer science students were recruited for these experiments. After a period of 'core' instruction in railway signalling principles common to all participants, half were then given specific training for the code checking task and half were trained for the testing task.

Table 1. Proportions of testers and checkers unsuccessful in finding each of eight seeded faults in two programs

Program 1			Program 2		
Fault id	Proportion in checking	Proportion in testing	Fault id	Proportion in checking	Proportion in testing
F11	.7778	.4168	F21	.2222	.0833
F12	.0000	.1389	F22	.8148	.2778
F13	.2593	.5556	F23	.5926	.5000
F14	.4815	.4722	F24	.1481	.9444
F15	.7778	.1944	F25	.4444	.2778
F16	.3704	.7222	F26	.2963	.7778
F17	.1852	.3611	F27	.2222	.8056
F18	.4444	.9167	F28	.7778	.2778

Participants were then required to verify two simulated railway signalling programs, either by code checking or functional testing as appropriate. Each program was seeded with eight faults (taken from those found during the fieldwork), each of the faults being potentially detectable with either verification method. The dependent variable was thus the proportion of the total faults detected by each participant, the independent variable being whether the participant was a checker or a tester. For reasons that are beyond the scope of the present paper, some participants were excluded from the experiment, leaving a total of twenty-seven checkers and thirty-six testers (Further information on this issue, and on the experimental task in general, can be found in [8, 9]; for more information on the railway signalling task on which it is based, see [10]).

The raw data are shown in Table 1. Here the entries in the table are, for each fault, the proportion of the individuals in that part of the experiment who were unsuccessful in finding the fault: for fault i and procedure A we take this to be an estimate of $\theta_A(i)$ in the notation of the model. If we treat each program separately, we have $p_i^* = 1/8$ for each of the eight faults in each program. If we let A represent checking and B represent testing, it is then easy to show that for Program 1 (estimates of) the relevant parameters of the model are:

$$E_{p*}(\theta_A(i)) = 0.412, \ E_{p*}(\theta_B(i)) = 0.472$$
$$E_{p*}(\theta_A^2(i)) = 0.235, \ E_{p*}(\theta_B^2(i)) = 0.282 \tag{22}$$
$$E_{p*}(\theta_A(i)\theta_B(i)) = 0.199, \ E_{p*}(\theta_A(i))E_{p*}(\theta_B(i)) = 0.194$$
$$Cov_{p*}(\theta_A(i), \theta_B(i)) = 0.0040$$

and for Program 2:

$$E_{p*}(\theta_A(i)) = 0.440, \ E_{p*}(\theta_B(i)) = 0.493$$
$$E_{p*}(\theta_A^2(i)) = 0.253, \ E_{p*}(\theta_B^2(i)) = 0.329 \tag{23}$$
$$E_{p*}(\theta_A(i)\theta_B(i)) = 0.179, \ E_{p*}(\theta_A(i))E_{p*}(\theta_B(i)) = 0.217$$
$$Cov_{p*}(\theta_A(i), \theta_B(i)) = -0.0381$$

Notice that the efficacies of A and B are roughly similar between the two programs, but that B seems to be consistently worse than A. Also, there seems to be 'more diversity' between A and B in their application to Program 2 than to Program 1: there is negative correlation between the difficulty functions in the case of Program 2, but small positive correlation for Program 1.

After two applications of A to Program 2, we would expect 25.3%[5] of faults to be undetected; after two applications of B, 32.9% of faults to be undetected; but after an application of each of A and B, we would expect only 17.9% of faults to be undetected. Thus, in this case we would expect the application of A and B to be more

---

[5] A word of warning about the number of significant figures here and in later expressions. Essentially, we are computing finite-sample estimates of parameters, which can be regarded as exact, and then truncating the decimal expressions for convenience. If we regard these as estimates of infinite populations, of course, the number of significant figures here may be too optimistic. This observation does not affect the general reasoning of the paper.

effective than a double application of A or of B. This is so even though we are not indifferent between A and B here: in fact A seems significantly better than B (and AA than BB). Here the naïve 'independence' argument would seriously underestimate the efficacy of AB, suggesting that it would leave 21.7% of faults undetected, rather than the correct figure of 17.9%.

For Program 1, the corresponding figures are: after two applications of A, we expect 23.5% of the faults to be undetected; after two applications of B, 28.2%; and after one application of A and one of B, 19.9%. Once again, the diverse application of AB is better than either AA or BB, even though the difficulty functions show slight positive correlation – but this superiority is less dramatic than in Program 2, where the procedures have negatively correlated difficulty functions. In this case the naïve 'independence' assumption would slightly *overestimate* the efficacy of AB, suggesting it would leave 19.4% of faults undetected rather than the correct figure of 19.9%.

The differences in the examples above, (22) and (23), suggest how we might use this model in practice. If we believe that the effectiveness of successive applications of particular diverse fault finding procedures will vary from one class of problem to another (e.g. real-time versus non-real-time), but are constant within each problem class, then we should strive to estimate the parameters of the model for each problem class. Thus if we had two sets of data, like those for Programs 1 and 2, corresponding to two different types of program, we could estimate the parameters relating to their different behaviours.

If, on the other hand, we have no reason to believe that there are such differences, we should regard data from all programs as being evidence to be used for obtaining a single set of parameter estimates for the model. If we aggregate the above data in this way, treating each program as having been sampled with constant probability from a population of programs, we find that the model parameters are estimated as follows:

$$E_{p*}(\theta_A(i)) = 0.426, \ E_{p*}(\theta_B(i)) = 0.483$$
$$E_{p*}(\theta_A^2(i)) = 0.244, \ E_{p*}(\theta_B^2(i)) = 0.306 \tag{24}$$
$$E_{p*}(\theta_A(i)\theta_B(i)) = 0.189, \ E_{p*}(\theta_A(i))E_{p*}(\theta_B(i)) = 0.206$$
$$Cov_{p*}(\theta_A(i), \theta_B(i)) = -0.0168$$

Now, after a double application of A we would expect 24.4% of faults to be undetected; after a double application of B, 30.6%; and after application of a single A and a single B, 18.9%. Once again, rather informally, the strong diversity of the procedures, indicated by their negative correlation, means that an application of each of A and B is best, even though A is clearly superior to B (and AA to BB). Once again, because of the negative correlation of the difficulty functions, the naïve independence estimate gives an underestimate of the efficacy of AB: it suggests that this will leave behind 20.6% of faults undetected whereas the true figure is 18.9%.

These results illustrate the quite subtle interplay that there can be between the efficacies of the individual procedures and their 'degree of diverseness': in general we need to know all first and second moments of the (random variable) difficulty functions before we can determine the most effective mix of procedures. We have been able to show earlier that by imposing certain indifference constraints it is possible to know that AB will be better than AA or BB whenever there is negative correlation.

When we cannot make such assumptions, however, mere diverseness, as represented by negative correlation between the difficulty functions, is not sufficient to ensure that it will be best to apply both procedures. It is easy to show that when there is negative correlation *AB* will always be better than the *worst* of *AA* and *BB*, but it could be either better or worse than the *better* of these. Equally, negative correlation is not *necessary* for *AB* to be superior to *AA* and *BB*: there can be benefit in diversity even when the procedures are positively correlated, as in the case of Program 1.

These comments notwithstanding, the results of Section 3 (and similarly those of Section 4) do seem like a promising way of giving designers advice about the best fault finding approach when, as is sometimes the case, we are in a position to balance the efficacies of different procedures by applying one of them 'more' or 'less' extensively. Thus, in the example here we might require the testers to spend more time – examining more test cases – so as to make $E_{p*}(\theta_B(i)) = E_{p*}(\theta_A(i))$ in (24). Whenever we can do this, we shall have a *guarantee* that *AB* will be superior to *AA* or *BB*, even when we do not have the detailed extra information about the parameters of the model that we have from this controlled experiment.

So far, the model described here has been predictive – e.g. predicting the best fault finding combination of procedures for a novel program – only if we can assume that the program about which we wish to make a prediction is 'similar' to the ones used for the estimation of the model parameters. Clearly it would be desirable to lift this restriction, and in some cases this may be possible. The idea here is to deal with *classes* of faults, rather than with the faults themselves, and it can be illustrated again by the railway data example.

The psychologists who devised this experiment were interested in investigating differences in diverse fault finding between different types of fault; details can be found in [8-10]), but the following is a brief account. As part of the signalling system design task, engineers must translate information contained in track layout plans, regarding permitted directions of movement of trains over track sections, into a machine-readable label. Configurations of track sections are variable, and so a rule is used to specify the mapping between the label and the route of the train. Engineers made mistakes when generating the labels, and more importantly when performing an independent check of others' work, a vital part of the rigorous verification and validation process to which safety critical systems must be subjected. Faults in Programs 1 and 2 varied as to whether the code involved the use of such train subroutes (S) or not (N). There were thus two classes of fault, S and N: in Table 1, faults F11, F15, F22, F25 were of type S and the remaining 12 faults were of type N.

We can now easily compute a table similar to Table 1, but involving *classes of faults* rather than the individual faults themselves:

Table 2. Estimates of the probabilities that a randomly chosen fault of type S (N) will fail to be detected by an application of procedure A (B), obtained from the data of Table 1 aggregated over the two programs

Fault class id	Probability in checking (A)	Probability in testing (B)
S	.704	.292
N	.333	.546

In an obvious notation, the entries of Table 2 can be thought of as estimates of $\theta_A(s)$, etc. We can now perform calculations similar to those carried out earlier, using $p_S{}^* = 0.25$, $p_N{}^* = 0.75$, to obtain:

$$E_{p^*_{classes}}(\theta_A(i)) = 0.426, \quad E_{p^*_{classes}}(\theta_B(i)) = 0.483$$

$$E_{p^*_{classes}}(\theta_A{}^2(i)) = 0.207, \quad E_{p^*_{classes}}(\theta_B{}^2(i)) = 0.245 \tag{25}$$

$$E_{p^*_{classes}}(\theta_A(i)\theta_B(i)) = 0.188, \quad E_{p^*_{classes}}(\theta_A(i))E_{p^*_{classes}}(\theta_B(i)) = 0.206$$

$$Cov_{p^*_{classes}}(\theta_A(i), \theta_B(i)) = -0.0178$$

Clearly, the estimates of the efficacy of multiple procedures obtained from this class-based treatment will generally be in error compared with the 'correct' results obtained in (24) from the full fault-based data. It is therefore interesting to compare the results of (24) and (25). The first moments, representing the single application efficacies, are completely identical, as is to be expected. The ineffectiveness estimates for AA and BB, on the other hand, are significantly underestimated in (25) in comparison with (24). The reason, of course, is that values in (25) ignore the variation in the difficulty functions of A and B *within* each class of faults (see the appropriate entries in Table 1): essentially they assume that all faults within a class have the same value of the difficulty function for a particular fault finding procedure (in Table 2 such a value has been computed as the average, over the different faults in the class, of the *actual* difficulty functions from Table 1). Thus, for example (in an obvious notation), the ineffectiveness of AA based on the full fault data can be expressed as:

$$E_p(\theta_A^2(i)) = p_S^* E_{i\in S}(\theta_A^2(i)) + p_N^* E_{i\in N}(\theta_A^2(i))$$

$$= p_S^*\left((E_{i\in S}(\theta_A(i)))^2 + Var_{i\in S}(\theta_A(i))\right) + p_N^*\left((E_{i\in N}(\theta_A(i)))^2 + Var_{i\in N}(\theta_A(i))\right) \tag{26}$$

$$= E_{between\ classes}\left(E_{within\ classes}(\theta_A(i))\right)^2 + E_{between\ classes}\left(Var_{within\ classes}(\theta_A(i))\right)$$

and similarly for B.

That is, the first term – which we have called $E_{p^*_{classes}}(\theta_A{}^2(i))$ in the condensed notation of (25), and which takes the value 0.207 – underestimates the true value by an amount $E_{between\ classes}\left(Var_{within\ classes}(\theta_A(i))\right) = 0.037$. This agrees with (24), since $0.244 = 0.207 + 0.037$.

What is interesting and surprising, though, is the closeness between the ineffectiveness estimates of AB in (24) and (25). We would expect these to differ since the expression in (24) can be expressed:

$$E_p(\theta_A(i)\theta_B(i)) = p_S^* E_{i\in S}(\theta_A(i).\theta_B(i)) + p_N^* E_{i\in N}(\theta_A(i).\theta_B(i))$$

$$= p_S^* E_{i\in S}(\theta_A(i))E_{i\in S}(\theta_B(i)) + Cov_{i\in S}(\theta_A(i), \theta_B(i))$$

$$+ p_N^* E_{i\in N}(\theta_A(i))E_{i\in N}(\theta_B(i)) + Cov_{i\in N}(\theta_A(i), \theta_B(i)) \tag{27}$$

$$= E_{between\ classes}\left(E_{within\ classes}(\theta_A(i))E_{within\ classes}(\theta_B(i))\right)$$

$$+ E_{between\ classes}\left(Cov_{within\ classes}(\theta_A(i), \theta_B(i))\right)$$

The first term here is the approximation using aggregated fault class data from (25), which in the condensed notation used there is $E_{p^*_{classes}}(\theta_A(i)\theta_B(i)) = 0.188$. The second term is the weighted average, using $p_S^* = 0.25$ and $p_N^* = 0.75$ respectively, of the covariances of the A and B difficulty functions for the different fault classes, which take the values 0.000 and 0.001 respectively (to 3 decimal places). The smallness of these is the reason for the closeness of the estimate of AB effectiveness based on the aggregated fault class data to the correct figure based on the full fault data.

The surprise here is that the devisors of the experiment have managed to arrive at fault classes, S and N, for each of which the difficulty functions of A and B are almost independent. It would be worth investigating whether this can be done in other circumstances: if it can, we shall be able to obtain accurate estimates of AB ineffectiveness even from aggregated fault class data.

The practical advantage of the treatment via classes of faults, rather than the individual faults themselves, is as follows. Individual faults are likely to be 'sparse'. If we collect our data from only a few real programs, we are likely to see each fault in no more than one program, in contrast to the artificially seeded programs, which are used repeatedly in the experiment. There will thus be no opportunity to estimate the probabilities p_i^*. If, on the other hand, we can identify meaningful and interesting fault classes the associated probabilities may be estimable. Most importantly, we would be able to predict the efficacy of diverse fault finding, as in (25), for *an entirely novel program* if we can estimate the $p^*_{classes}$ values for this new program.

An especially desirable situation would be achieved if the fault classes identified had the special property that was fortuitously obtained in this experiment, i.e., that the difficulty functions for different fault detection methods have zero covariance over the different fault classes. Then, estimating the *mean* of the θ functions for each {fault class, fault detection method} combination – which is much simpler than estimating complete distributions – would be sufficient to allow useful predictions in many cases. As can be seen from (26), the predictions would be exact for combinations of diverse methods, and optimistic for repeated applications of one method: when the methods are 'diverse' enough, these estimates would provide sufficient conditions for a project manager to decide in favour of combining two diverse methods.

Essentially this approach reuses the hard-won data such as that of Table 2, gained from past experience of other projects or from experiments, by applying it to prediction in a new context. Whilst this does require that we know, or are prepared to estimate, the new $p^*_{classes}$ values, this is a feasible task in contrast to attempting to do so for the set of all faults. As an example, if we believe that for the new program $p_S^* = 0.50$, $p_N^* = 0.50$, we obtain:

$$E_{p^*_{classes}}(\theta_A(i)) = 0.519, \ E_{p^*_{classes}}(\theta_B(i)) = 0.419$$
$$E_{p^*_{classes}}(\theta_A^2(i)) = 0.303, \ E_{p^*_{classes}}(\theta_B^2(i)) = 0.192 \tag{28}$$
$$E_{p^*_{classes}}(\theta_A(i)\theta_B(i)) = 0.194, \ E_{p^*_{classes}}(\theta_A(i))E_{p^*_{classes}}(\theta_B(i)) = 0.217$$
$$Cov_{p^*_{classes}}(\theta_A(i), \theta_B(i)) = -0.0235$$

For a new program with these $p*_{classes}$, B is superior to A, and BB to AA. More interestingly, BB is now slightly better than AB, even though there is negative correlation between the difficulty functions.

7 Discussion and Conclusions

Most work in the software engineering literature on the efficacy of fault finding procedures has concentrated upon assessing and comparing their individual efficacies. Whilst this is important, the reality is that in practice several of these techniques will be employed together. There are some well-known intuitions about how such combinations of procedures will work: we all know, for example, that it is best to use fault finding procedures that are effective in some general way; but we equally know that any single such procedure may miss a whole class of faults even when applied most extensively. Many experimental comparisons for alternative fault-finding methods have been reported, e.g. [11-16]. Those experimenters that looked at the effectiveness of the methods on individual faults (e.g. [15]) corroborated the intuitive belief that different methods were most effective at discovering different faults. Thus, even when we know that procedure A is better at fault finding than B, we would be wary of using *only* A because it may have little chance of finding certain faults that B may find quite easily. The work described here is an attempt to formalise intuitions of this kind. The ultimate aim is to provide advice to practitioners on the best way of combining different approaches to fault finding on a single program.

An example of these arguments about fault finding efficacy has long raged in the testing community between advocates of operational testing, and those of other testing practices [6]. It is known that operational testing has the useful property that its chances of finding faults (for a given outlay of effort) are in direct proportion to the impact of these faults on the unreliability of the software – the greater the occurrence rate of a fault, the greater its chance of being discovered in an operational test. However, this is not the same as saying that operational testing is more efficient at finding faults than other testing procedures, and advocates of these alternatives often claim that it is very inefficient. Essentially they argue that it takes no account of any knowledge that the software designer may have about the possible location of faults. With such knowledge it may be possible to find certain faults more effectively by actively seeking them, than by allowing them to occur purely randomly. In our terminology, the two testing procedures have different 'difficulty' functions over the set of faults: the optimal allocation of testing to the two types would depend upon the diversity between them as well as upon their individual efficacies.

The model presented here shows that the key to understanding how best to apply different fault finding procedures lies in understanding the interplay between, on the one hand, the efficacies of the individual procedures (in single and multiple applications), and on the other the dependence between their 'difficulty functions'. Probably the most important results are those of Sections 3 and 4. There we show that the effects upon reliability of repeated applications of a particular procedure are not statistically independent – in fact such an incorrect assumption of independence will always give results that are too optimistic. When we have *diverse* fault finding procedures, however, things are different: here it is possible for effectiveness to be even greater than it would be under an assumption of statistical independence. We show in Result 8 that diversity of fault finding procedures is 'a good thing', and should be applied as widely as possible. However, this result relies upon assumptions of indifference between the different procedures. As we have seen in the example of Section 6, it is likely in practice that such an assumption of indifference would be unreasonable unless it had been deliberately contrived. We believe that for some procedures it may be possible to contrive it: in our own example it may be possible to increase the *amount* of testing to make the checking and testing equally effective (in both single and double applications).

When we compare this model with its mathematically similar equivalent in software design diversity, it is striking how much easier it is to obtain estimates of the key model parameters here. Thus in the example of Section 6, although the experiment pre-dates the model, we were able to find estimates of the parameters representing procedure effectiveness and diversity. When we look at *classes* of faults, the estimation problem becomes a tractable one even for real life applications where the experimental replications of our experiment are infeasible. What is needed now is a systematic investigation of these parameters for different fault-finding procedures - and different classes of software application domains – in industrially realistic situations.

Intuitive notions of diversity in fault finding have been around for a long time, and are used informally quite extensively, but they have lacked a rigorous formal basis. In particular, it has not been clear what were the important factors to *measure*. The work reported here is the start of such a formal measurement-based understanding. We hope that it will lead to a theory of fault detection – and removal – that allocates different fault finding procedures optimally to each problem, taking account of the likely distribution of fault types for that problem.

Finally, we are grateful to a reviewer for pointing out that these results might have application to hardware as well as software. Whilst we have not had the opportunity to analyse any hardware data, we agree that the models are formulated in a very general way and could find use outside software engineering.

Acknowledgements

This work was supported partially by Scottish Nuclear under the DISPO project, by EPSRC under the DISCS project and by the ESPRIT Long Term Research Project 20072, 'Design for Validation' (DeVa).

References

1. Rouquet, J.C., Traverse, P.J.: Safe and reliable computing on board of Airbus and ATR aircraft. In: 5th International Workshop on Safety of Computer Control Systems (SAFECOMP 1986), Sarlat, France, pp. 93–97. Pergamon Press, Oxford (1986)
2. Eckhardt, D.E., Caglayan, A.K., et al.: An experimental evaluation of software redundancy as a strategy for improving reliability. IEEE Transactions on Software Engineering 17(7), 692–702 (1991)
3. Knight, J.C., Leveson, N.G.: An experimental evaluation of the assumption of independence in multi-version programming. IEEE Transactions on Software Engineering SE-12(1), 96–109 (1986)

4. Eckhardt, D.E., Lee, L.D.: A theoretical basis for the analysis of multiversion software subject to coincident errors. IEEE Transactions on Software Engineering SE-11(12), 1511–1517 (1985)
5. Littlewood, B., Miller, D.R.: Conceptual modelling of coincident failures in multi-version software. IEEE Transactions on Software Engineering SE-15(12), 1596–1614 (1989)
6. Frankl, P., Hamlet, D., et al.: Choosing a testing method to deliver reliability. In: 19th International Conference on Software Engineering (ICSE 1997), pp. 68–78 (1997)
7. Adams, E.N.: Optimizing preventive service of software products. IBM Journal of Research and Development 28(1), 2–14 (1984)
8. Westermann, S.J., Shryane, N.M., et al.: Engineering Cognitive Diversity. In: Redmill, F., Anderson, T. (eds.) Safer Systems: Proceedings of the Fifth Safety-critical Systems Symposium, p. 111. Springer, Heidelberg (1997)
9. Westerman, S.J., Shryane, N.M., et al.: Cognitive diversity: A structured approach to trapping human error. In: SAFECOMP 1995: 14th International Conference on Computer Safety, Reliability and Security, Belgirate, Italy, pp. 142–155. Springer, Heidelberg (1995)
10. Shryane, N.M., Westerman, S.J., et al.: Task analysis for the investigation of human error in safety-critical software design: a convergent methods approach. Ergonomics 41(11), 1719–1736 (1998)
11. Basili, V., Green, S.: Software process evolution at the SEL. IEEE Software 11(4), 58–66 (1994)
12. Basili, V.R., Selby, R.: Comparing the effectiveness of software testing strategies. IEEE Transactions on Software Engineering 13(12), 1278–1296 (1987)
13. Frankl, P.G., Weiss, S.N.: An experimental comparison of the effectiveness of branch testing and data flow testing. IEEE Transactions on Software Engineering 19(8), 774–787 (1993)
14. Grady, R.B.: Practical Software Metrics for Project Management and Process Improvement, p. 282. Prentice-Hall, Englewood Cliffs (1992)
15. Shimeall, T.J., Leveson, N.G.: An empirical comparison of software fault tolerance and fault elimination. IEEE Transactions on Software Engineering 17, 173–182 (1991)
16. So, S.S., Cha, S.D., et al.: An empirical evaluation of six methods to detect faults in software. Software Testing, Verification & Reliability 12(3), 155–171 (2002)

Author Index

Lecture Notes in Computer Science

Sublibrary 2: Programming and Software Engineering

For information about Vols. 1– 4294
please contact your bookseller or Springer

Vol. 4609: E. Ernst (Ed.), ECOOP 2007 – Object-Oriented Programming. XIII, 625 pages. 2007.

Vol. 4608: H.W. Schmidt, I. Crnković, G.T. Heineman, J.A. Stafford (Eds.), Component-Based Software Engineering. XII, 283 pages. 2007.

Vol. 4591: J. Davies, J. Gibbons (Eds.), Integrated Formal Methods. IX, 660 pages. 2007.

Vol. 4589: J. Münch, P. Abrahamsson (Eds.), Product-Focused Software Process Improvement. XII, 414 pages. 2007.

Vol. 4574: J. Derrick, J. Vain (Eds.), Formal Techniques for Networked and Distributed Systems – FORTE 2007. XI, 375 pages. 2007.

Vol. 4556: C. Stephanidis (Ed.), Universal Access in Human-Computer Interaction, Part III. XXII, 1020 pages. 2007.

Vol. 4555: C. Stephanidis (Ed.), Universal Access in Human-Computer Interaction, Part II. XXII, 1066 pages. 2007.

Vol. 4554: C. Stephanidis (Ed.), Universal Acess in Human Computer Interaction, Part I. XXII, 1054 pages. 2007.

Vol. 4553: J.A. Jacko (Ed.), Human-Computer Interaction, Part IV. XXIV, 1225 pages. 2007.

Vol. 4552: J.A. Jacko (Ed.), Human-Computer Interaction, Part III. XXI, 1038 pages. 2007.

Vol. 4551: J.A. Jacko (Ed.), Human-Computer Interaction, Part II. XXIII, 1253 pages. 2007.

Vol. 4550: J.A. Jacko (Ed.), Human-Computer Interaction, Part I. XXIII, 1240 pages. 2007.

Vol. 4542: P. Sawyer, B. Paech, P. Heymans (Eds.), Requirements Engineering: Foundation for Software Quality. IX, 384 pages. 2007.

Vol. 4536: G. Concas, E. Damiani, M. Scotto, G. Succi (Eds.), Agile Processes in Software Engineering and Extreme Programming. XV, 276 pages. 2007.

Vol. 4530: D.H. Akehurst, R. Vogel, R.F. Paige (Eds.), Model Driven Architecture - Foundations and Applications. X, 219 pages. 2007.

Vol. 4523: Y.-H. Lee, H.-N. Kim, J. Kim, Y.W. Park, L.T. Yang, S.W. Kim (Eds.), Embedded Software and Systems. XIX, 829 pages. 2007.

Vol. 4498: N. Abdennahder, F. Kordon (Eds.), Reliable Software Technologies - Ada-Europe 2007. XII, 247 pages. 2007.

Vol. 4486: M. Bernardo, J. Hillston (Eds.), Formal Methods for Performance Evaluation. VII, 469 pages. 2007.

Vol. 4470: Q. Wang, D. Pfahl, D.M. Raffo (Eds.), Software Process Dynamics and Agility. XI, 346 pages. 2007.

Vol. 4468: M.M. Bonsangue, E.B. Johnsen (Eds.), Formal Methods for Open Object-Based Distributed Systems. X, 317 pages. 2007.

Vol. 4467: A.L. Murphy, J. Vitek (Eds.), Coordination Models and Languages. X, 325 pages. 2007.

Vol. 4454: Y. Gurevich, B. Meyer (Eds.), Tests and Proofs. IX, 217 pages. 2007.

Vol. 4444: T. Reps, M. Sagiv, J. Bauer (Eds.), Program Analysis and Compilation, Theory and Practice. X, 361 pages. 2007.

Vol. 4440: B. Liblit, Cooperative Bug Isolation. XV, 101 pages. 2007.

Vol. 4408: R. Choren, A. Garcia, H. Giese, H.-f. Leung, C. Lucena, A. Romanovsky (Eds.), Software Engineering for Multi-Agent Systems V. XII, 233 pages. 2007.

Vol. 4406: W. De Meuter (Ed.), Advances in Smalltalk. VII, 157 pages. 2007.

Vol. 4405: L. Padgham, F. Zambonelli (Eds.), Agent-Oriented Software Engineering VII. XII, 225 pages. 2007.

Vol. 4401: N. Guelfi, D. Buchs (Eds.), Rapid Integration of Software Engineering Techniques. IX, 177 pages. 2007.

Vol. 4385: K. Coninx, K. Luyten, K.A. Schneider (Eds.), Task Models and Diagrams for Users Interface Design. XI, 355 pages. 2007.

Vol. 4383: E. Bin, A. Ziv, S. Ur (Eds.), Hardware and Software, Verification and Testing. XII, 235 pages. 2007.

Vol. 4379: M. Südholt, C. Consel (Eds.), Object-Oriented Technology. VIII, 157 pages. 2007.

Vol. 4364: T. Kühne (Ed.), Models in Software Engineering. XI, 332 pages. 2007.

Vol. 4355: J. Julliand, O. Kouchnarenko (Eds.), B 2007: Formal Specification and Development in B. XIII, 293 pages. 2006.

Vol. 4354: M. Hanus (Ed.), Practical Aspects of Declarative Languages. X, 335 pages. 2006.

Vol. 4350: M. Clavel, F. Durán, S. Eker, P. Lincoln, N. Martí-Oliet, J. Meseguer, C. Talcott, All About Maude - A High-Performance Logical Framework. XXII, 797 pages. 2007.

Vol. 4348: S. Tucker Taft, R.A. Duff, R.L. Brukardt, E. Plödereder, P. Leroy, Ada 2005 Reference Manual. XXII, 765 pages. 2006.

Vol. 4346: L. Brim, B.R. Haverkort, M. Leucker, J. van de Pol (Eds.), Formal Methods: Applications and Technology. X, 363 pages. 2007.

Vol. 4344: V. Gruhn, F. Oquendo (Eds.), Software Architecture. X, 245 pages. 2006.

Vol. 4340: R. Prodan, T. Fahringer, Grid Computing. XXIII, 317 pages. 2007.

Vol. 4336: V.R. Basili, H.D. Rombach, K. Schneider, B. Kitchenham, D. Pfahl, R.W. Selby (Eds.), Empirical Software Engineering Issues. XVII, 193 pages. 2007.

Vol. 4326: S. Göbel, R. Malkewitz, I. Iurgel (Eds.), Technologies for Interactive Digital Storytelling and Entertainment. X, 384 pages. 2006.

Vol. 4323: G. Doherty, A. Blandford (Eds.), Interactive Systems. XI, 269 pages. 2007.

Vol. 4322: F. Kordon, J. Sztipanovits (Eds.), Reliable Systems on Unreliable Networked Platforms. XIV, 317 pages. 2007.

Vol. 4309: P. Inverardi, M. Jazayeri (Eds.), Software Engineering Education in the Modern Age. VIII, 207 pages. 2006.